Infrastructures and Social Complexity

Contemporary forms of infrastructural development herald alternative futures through their incorporation of digital technologies, mobile capital, international politics, and the promises and fears of enhanced connectivity. In tandem with increasing concerns about climate change and the anthropocene, there is further an urgency around contemporary infrastructural provision: a concern about its fragility and an awareness that these connective, relational systems significantly shape both local and planetary futures in ways that we need to understand more clearly. Offering a rich set of empirically detailed and conceptually sophisticated studies of infrastructural systems and experiments, present and past, contributors to this volume address both the transformative potential of infrastructural systems and their stasis. Covering infrastructural figures – their ontologies, epistemologies, classifications and politics – and spanning development, urban, energy, environmental and information infrastructures, the chapters explore both the promises and failures of infrastructure. Tracing the experimental histories of a wide range of infrastructures and documenting their variable outcomes, the volume offers a unique set of analytical perspectives on contemporary *infrastructural complications*. These studies bring a systematic empirical and analytical attention to human worlds as they intersect with more-than-human worlds, whether technological or biological.

Penny Harvey is Professor of Social Anthropology at the University of Manchester, UK.

Casper Bruun Jensen is Associate Professor/Senior Researcher at Osaka University, Japan.

Atsuro Morita is Associate Professor in the Department of Anthropology, School of Human Sciences, Osaka University, Japan.

Culture, Economy and the Social
A new series from CRESC – the ESRC Centre for Research on Socio-Cultural Change

Professor Tony Bennett, Social and Cultural Theory, University of Western Sydney; Professor Penny Harvey, Anthropology, Manchester University; Professor Kevin Hetherington, Geography, Open University

The *Culture, Economy and the Social* series is committed to innovative contemporary, comparative and historical work on the relations between social, cultural and economic change. It publishes empirically based research that is theoretically informed, that critically examines the ways in which social, cultural and economic change is framed and made visible, and that is attentive to perspectives that tend to be ignored or side ined by grand theorizing or epochal accounts of social change. The series addresses the diverse manifestations of contemporary capitalism, and considers the various ways in which the 'social', 'the cultural' and 'the economic' are apprehended as tangible sites of value and practice. It is explicitly comparative, publishing books that work across disciplinary perspectives, cross-culturally, or across different historical periods.

For more info please see: www.routledge.com/CRESC/book-series/CRESC

Recent series titles include:

Cultural Pedagogies and Human Conduct
Edited by Megan Watkins, Greg Noble and Catherine Driscoll

Culture as a Vocation
Sociology of career choices in cultural management
By Vincent Dubois

Topologies of power
By John Allen

Distinctions of the Flesh
Social class and the embodiment of inequality
By Dieter Vandebroeck

Infrastructures and Social Complexity
A companion
Edited by Penny Harvey, Casper Bruun Jensen and Atsuro Morita

Film Criticism as a Cultural Institution
Crisis and continuity from the 20th to the 21st century
By Huw Walmsley-Evans

Infrastructures and Social Complexity
A companion

Edited by
Penny Harvey, Casper Bruun Jensen and
Atsuro Morita

LONDON AND NEW YORK

First published 2017
by Routledge
2 Park Square, Milton Park, Abingdon, Oxon OX14 4RN

and by Routledge
711 Third Avenue, New York, NY 10017

Routledge is an imprint of the Taylor & Francis Group, an informa business

© 2017 Penny Harvey, Casper Bruun Jensen, Atsuro Morita

The right of the editors to be identified as the authors of the editorial material, and of the authors for their individual chapters, has been asserted in accordance with sections 77 and 78 of the Copyright, Designs and Patents Act 1988.

All rights reserved. No part of this book may be reprinted or reproduced or utilised in any form or by any electronic, mechanical, or other means, now known or hereafter invented, including photocopying and recording, or in any information storage or retrieval system, without permission in writing from the publishers.

Trademark notice: Product or corporate names may be trademarks or registered trademarks, and are used only for identification and explanation without intent to infringe.

British Library Cataloguing in Publication Data
A catalogue record for this book is available from the British Library

Library of Congress Cataloging in Publication Data
Names: Harvey, Penelope, 1956- editor. | Jensen, Casper Bruun, editor. | Morita, Atsuro, editor.
Title: Infrastructures and social complexity : a companion / edited by Penny Harvey, Casper Bruun Jensen, Atsuro Morita.
Description: Abingdon, Oxon ; New York, NY : Routledge, 2016. |
Identifiers: LCCN 2016013854| ISBN 9781138654945 (hardback) | ISBN 9781315622880 (ebook)
Subjects: LCSH: Infrastructure (Economics)–Social aspects. | Economic development–Social aspects. | Technological complexity–Social aspects. | Social systems.
Classification: LCC HC79.C3 I5247 2016 | DDC 306.3–dc23
LC record available at https://lccn.loc.gov/2016013854

ISBN: 978-1-138-65494-5 (hbk)
ISBN: 978-1-315-62288-0 (ebk)

Typeset in Times New Roman
by Taylor & Francis Books

Contents

List of figures	ix
List of contributors	x
Acknowledgment	xvii

1 Introduction: Infrastructural complications   1
PENNY HARVEY, CASPER BRUUN JENSEN AND ATSURO MORITA

PART I
Development infrastructures   23

2 Keyword: infrastructure: How a humble French engineering term shaped the modern world   27
ASHLEY CARSE

3 Surveying the future perfect: Anthropology, development and the promise of infrastructure   40
KREGG HETHERINGTON

4 Containment and disruption: The illicit economies of infrastructural investment   51
PENNY HARVEY

5 Infrastructure reform in Indigenous Australia: From mud to mining to military empires   64
TESS LEA

6 Becoming a city: Infrastructural fetishism and scattered urbanization in Vientiane, Laos   76
MIKI NAMBA

PART II
Urban infrastructures 87

7 On pressure and the politics of water infrastructure 91
NIKHIL ANAND

8 Infrastructuring new urban common worlds?: On material
politics, civic attachments, and partially existing wind turbines 102
ANDERS BLOK

9 Remediating infrastructure: Tokyo's commuter train network and
the new autonomy 115
MICHAEL FISCH

10 The generic city: Examples from Jakarta, Indonesia, and
Maputo, Mozambique 128
MORTEN NIELSEN AND ABDOUMALIQ SIMONE

11 Ecologies in beta: The city as infrastructure of apprenticeships 141
ALBERTO CORSÍN JIMÉNEZ AND ADOLFO ESTALELLA

PART III
Energy infrastructures 157

12 Living with the earth: More-than-human arrangements in
seismic landscapes 161
JAMES MAGUIRE AND BRIT ROSS WINTHEREIK

13 Revolutionary infrastructure 174
DOMINIC BOYER

14 Infrastructure and the earth 187
ANDREW BARRY

15 Off the grid: Infrastructure and energy beyond the mains 198
JAMIE CROSS

PART IV
Environmental infrastructures 211

16 River basin: The development of the scientific concept and
infrastructures in the Chao Phraya Delta, Thailand 215
ATSURO MORITA

17 Multinatural infrastructure: Phnom Penh sewage 227
CASPER BRUUN JENSEN

18	Burial and resurrection in the Anthropocene: Infrastructures of waste MYRA J. HIRD	242
19	Evidence, infrastructure and worth SANDRA CALKINS AND RICHARD ROTTENBURG	253

PART V
Infrastructural figures 267

20	When infrastructures fail: An ethnographic note in the middle of an Aegean crisis SARAH GREEN	271
21	Infrastructure as gesture GISA WESZKALNYS	284
22	The black list: On infrastructural indeterminacy and its reverberations MADELEINE REEVES	296
23	Infrastructural inversion and reflexivity: A "postcolonial" biodiversity databasing project in India MOE NAKAZORA	309
24	Survivals as infrastructure: Twenty-first-century struggles with household and family in formal computations JANE I. GUYER	323

PART VI
Digital infrastructures 335

25	Downscaling: From global to local in the climate knowledge infrastructure PAUL N. EDWARDS	339
26	The problem of action: Infrastructure, planning and the informational environment HANNAH KNOX	352
27	Machinic operations: Data structuring, healthcare and governmentality ANDREW GOFFEY	366

28 Infrastructures in name only?: Identifying effects of depth and scale 379
ADRIAN MACKENZIE

29 How knowledge infrastructures learn 391
GEOFFREY C. BOWKER

Index 404

List of figures

8.1 Kids decorating the blade of a wind turbine in Copenhagen's town hall square   103
8.2 Counter-visualization of wind turbines from concerned public group   108
9.1 A section from a *daiya* representing two hours of train traffic on one train line   118
9.2 Diagram comparing the former centralized system with the contemporary decentralized system   121
11.1 *Congealed affects*   142
11.2 *(a) and (b)* Two views of *The Urban Parliament* by Zuloark   143
11.3 *Atlas* table map   144
11.4 *Pictogramas* by Iconoclasistas, a portfolio of creative commons licenced ideograms used to facilitate community storytelling and cartographies   148
11.5 *Inteligencia colectiva*, a public domain self-archival project on do-it-yourself, grassroots, retrofitted architectural designs   150
12.1 Wellhead and geologist on the day of the awakening   161
13.1 Map of major natural gas and oil pipelines in the United States   179
17.1 Entering the Phnom Penh sewer system   229
17.2 Inside the sewage pipe   230
17.3 Rebuilding a sedimentation chamber   231
17.4 Entering the pumping channel   238
17.5 Underneath the pumping station at Phnom Penh riverside   239
17.6 Cockroach colony living inside flooding infrastructure   239
20.1 Aylan Kurdi's body being carried by Mehmet Ciplak, the Turkish police officer   273
20.2 Antonis Deligiorgis saving Wegasi Nebiat on 20 April 2015   273
26.1 Screen shot of image from Covenant of Mayors website   353
26.2 Aims and objectives of the Green Digital Project   357
26.3 Overview of action fields for Green Digital Charter (GDC) implementation   361
28.1 The most popular repositories on Github in 2014   383
29.1 Diagram of infrastructural dimensions   392

Contributors

Nikhil Anand is Assistant Professor of Anthropology at the University of Pennsylvania. His research focuses on the political ecology of urban infrastructures and the social and material relations that they entail. Through ethnographic research, he examines how natures, technologies, and specific gatherings of experts and publics are mobilized to effect environmental projects and relations of difference in postcolonial cities. His first book, *Hydraulic City* (Duke University Press, 2017), explores how cities and citizens are made through the everyday maintenance of water infrastructures in Mumbai. His work has been published in *Public Culture, Cultural Anthropology, Antipode,* and *Ethnography.*

Andrew Barry is Chair of Human Geography at University College London. His most recent books are *Material Politics: Disputes along the Pipeline* (2013) and *Interdisciplinarity: Reconfigurations of the Social and Natural Sciences* (2013). He is currently interested in the geography of chemicals.

Anders Blok is Associate Professor in Sociology at the University of Copenhagen, Denmark. His current research inquires into the knowledge politics of urban environmental change in Europe and East Asia. He has published widely within science and technology studies (STS), urban studies, environmental sociology and social theory, and he is co-author (with Torben E. Jensen) of *Bruno Latour: Hybrid Thoughts in a Hybrid World* (Routledge, 2011).

Geoffrey C. Bowker is Professor at the School of Information and Computer Science, University of California at Irvine, where he directs the Evoke Laboratory, which explores new forms of knowledge expression. Together with Susan Leigh Star he wrote *Sorting Things Out: Classification and its Consequences*; his most recent books are *Memory Practices in the Sciences* and (with Stefan Timmermans, Adele Clarke, and Ellen Balka) the edited collection: *Boundary Objects and Beyond: Working with Leigh Star.* He is currently working on big data policy and on scientific cyberinfrastructure; as well as completing a book on social readings of data and databases. He is a founding member of the Council for Big Data, Ethics and Society.

List of contributors　xi

Dominic Boyer is Professor of Anthropology at Rice University and Founding Director of the Center for Energy and Environmental Research in the Human Sciences (CENHS, culturesofenergy.org). He is part of the editorial collective of the journal *Cultural Anthropology* (2015–2018) and edits the *Expertise: Cultures and Technologies of Knowledge* book series for Cornell University Press. His most recent monograph is *The Life Informatic: Newsmaking in the Digital Era* (Cornell University Press, 2013). With James Faubion and George Marcus, he has recently edited *Theory can be more than it used to be* (Cornell University Press, 2015) and with Imre Szeman has developed *The Energy Humanities Reader* for Johns Hopkins University Press. His next book, *Energopolitics*, with Cymene Howe, will explore the complexities of wind power development in southern Mexico.

Sandra Calkins holds a PhD in Anthropology from the University of Leipzig. She is a research fellow at the Max Planck Institute for Social Anthropology and a member of the Law, Organization, Science and Technology Group at the University of Halle. Her previous research explored connections between indeterminacy, reflexivity, and ordering (*Who Knows Tomorrow? Uncertainty in Northeastern Sudan*, Berghahn, 2016). Her current project examines modalities of evidence production about biofortification, an agricultural public health strategy to ameliorate micronutrient deficiencies.

Ashley Carse, an anthropologist, is Assistant Professor of Human and Organizational Development at Vanderbilt University. He is the author of *Beyond the Big Ditch: Politics, Ecology, and Infrastructure at the Panama Canal* (MIT Press, 2014).

Alberto Corsín Jiménez is Reader in Social Anthropology in the Department of the History of Science at the Spanish National Research Council in Madrid. He has an interest in the organization of ethnography and anthropological knowledge as descriptive and theoretical forms. He recently finished a book, *A Trompe L'oeil Anthropology for a Common World* (Berghahn, 2013). He is the editor of *Prototyping Cultures: Art, Science and Politics in Beta* (Routledge, 2016), *Culture and Well-Being: Anthropological Approaches to Freedom and Political Ethics* (Pluto, 2008), and *The Anthropology of Organisations* (Ashgate, 2007). His current work examines the rise of an urban commons movement and the development of open-source urban hardware projects by architects, artists, and engineers.

Jamie Cross is Senior Lecturer in Social Anthropology and Director of the Global Development Academy at the University of Edinburgh. He is the author of *Dream Zones: Anticipating Capitalism and Development in India* (2014, Pluto Press).

Paul N. Edwards is Professor of Information and History at the University of Michigan. He writes and teaches on the history and politics of knowledge and information infrastructures. Edwards is the author of *A Vast Machine:*

Computer Models, Climate Data, and the Politics of Global Warming (MIT Press, 2010) and *The Closed World: Computers and the Politics of Discourse in Cold War America* (MIT Press, 1996), and co-editor of *Changing the Atmosphere: Expert Knowledge and Environmental Governance* (MIT Press, 2001), as well as numerous articles.

Adolfo Estalella is an anthropologist and postdoctoral researcher at the Spanish National Research Council (CSIC). His research dialogues with the Anthropology of knowledge and Science and Technology Studies (STS). Grassroots urbanism and digital cultures are the two main topics of inquiry he have carried out in the last years by investigating the Indignados/15M movement (the Spanish Occupy movement) and a diversity of civic projects of urban intervention in Madrid (Spain).

Michael Fisch is an Assistant Professor in the Department of Anthropology at the University of Chicago. His work is situated at the intersection of sociocultural anthropology and science and technology studies and looks at the dynamic between changing conceptualizations of nature, culture, and technological innovation. He is currently finishing an ethnography of Tokyo's train infrastructure entitled *An Anthropology of the Machine: Tokyo's Commuter Train Network*. In addition, he is conducting new research around the development of and opposition to disaster infrastructure in northeast Japan.

Andrew Goffey is an Associate Professor and Director of the Centre for Critical Theory at the University of Nottingham. He is the author (with Matthew Fuller) of *Evil Media*, the editor (with Eric Alliez) of *The Guattari Effect* and (with Roland Faber) of *The Allure of Things*. He is currently writing books on the politics of software and the work of Félix Guattari and is doing research on institutional analysis and the materiality of information. He is also the translator of numerous works in the fields of philosophy and critical theory, including *In Catastrophic Times* and *Capitalist Sorcery* (by Isabelle Stengers) and *Schizoanalytic Cartographies* and *Lines of Flight* by Félix Guattari.

Sarah Green is Professor of Social and Cultural Anthropology at the University of Helsinki. She is interested in the dynamics of location, particularly questions of establishing where people are as opposed to who they are. In earlier years this focused around questions of the politics of gender and sexuality; later, on the introduction of digital technologies to people's spatial lives. For many years since then she has been studying the logic of borders in the Balkan and European regions more widely and the relative locations involved (*Notes from the Balkans*, 2005). More recently, she has shifted her attention to the Aegean and is studying how locations overlap and the relations and separations between locations.

List of contributors xiii

Jane I. Guyer retired in 2015 from her position as George Armstrong Kelly Professor in the Department of Anthropology, Johns Hopkins University, and moved to membership in the Academy at Hopkins. Trained at undergraduate level at the London School of Economics, and at graduate level at the University of Rochester, her full-time academic career moved from Harvard, to Boston University, to the Directorship of the Program of African Studies at Northwestern University, and finally to Johns Hopkins University. Her research and publications have focused on livelihoods and money, from an empirical focus on West and Central Africa (Nigeria and Cameroon). She was elected to the National Academy of Sciences in 2008.

Penny Harvey is Professor of Social Anthropology at the University of Manchester. She co-directed the ESRC Centre for Research on Socio-Cultural Change. She has done ethnographic fieldwork in Peru, Spain, and the UK and published widely on language and communication, technology, engineering practice, and material politics. Recent publications include *Roads: An Anthropology of Infrastructure and Expertise* (with Hannah Knox), (Cornell University Press, 2015); *Objects and Materials: A Routledge Companion* (edited with Hannah Knox and CRESC colleagues) (Routledge, 2013); *Roads and Anthropology: Ethnography, Infrastructures, (Im)mobility* (edited with Dimitris Dalakoglou) (Routledge, 2014). She is co-writing a book with Deborah Poole on decentralization in Peru entitled *Experimental States*.

Kregg Hetherington is Professor of Anthropology at Concordia University in Montreal. His research focuses on environment, infrastructure, bureaucracy, and rural social movements. His most recent book is *Guerrilla Auditors: The Politics of Transparency in Neoliberal Paraguay* and he has recent articles in *American Ethnologist*, *Cultural Anthropology*, *Economy and Society*, among others. He is currently editing a book on *Infrastructure, Environment and Life in the Anthropocene* and is leading new research on energy transitions and sovereignty in Quebec.

Myra J. Hird is Professor, Queen's National Scholar and FRSC in the School of Environmental Studies, Queen's University, Canada (www.myrahird. com). She is Director of *Canada's Waste Flow*, an interdisciplinary research project focused on waste as a global scientific-technical and socio-ethical issue (www.wasteflow.ca), and Director of the *genera Research Group* (gRG), an interdisciplinary research network of collaborating natural, social, and humanities scholars focused on the topic of waste. Hird has published eight books and over sixty articles and book chapters on a diversity of topics relating to science studies.

Casper Bruun Jensen is Senior Researcher at Osaka University and Honorary Lecturer at Leicester University. He is the author of *Ontologies for Developing Things* (Sense, 2010) and *Monitoring Movements in Development Aid* (with Brit Ross Winthereik) (MIT, 2013) and the editor of *Deleuzian*

xiv List of contributors

Intersections: Science, Technology, Anthropology with Kjetil Rödje (Berghahn, 2009). His present work focuses on delta ontologies and environmental infrastructures in Southeast Asia.

Hannah Knox is a Lecturer in Anthropology at University College London. Her research looks at the interplay between technology, materiality, and social change and she has conducted fieldwork in the UK and Peru. Her publications include two books: *Objects and Materials: A Routledge Companion* and *Roads: An Anthropology of Infrastructure and Expertise*. Her current work is exploring the cultural politics of climate change mitigation.

Tess Lea is an anthropologist at the University of Sydney, specializing in the anthropology of policy and the ethnography of infrastructure. She is the author of *Bureaucrats and Bleeding Hearts* (UNSW, 2008) and *Darwin* (New South, 2014). Her fundamental interest is with issues of (dys)function: how it occurs and to what, whom, and how it is ascribed. Looking at social housing, infrastructure, schools, and efforts to create culturally congruent forms of employment, home indebtedness, and enterprise from the respective points of view of policy formulators, service delivery organizations, contractors, and Indigenous families, her work asks why the path to realizing seemingly shared ambitions is so densely obstacled.

Adrian Mackenzie (Professor in Technological Cultures, Department of Sociology, Lancaster University) has published work on technology: *Transductions: Bodies and Machines at Speed*, (2002/6); *Cutting Code: Software and Sociality* (2006); and *Wirelessness: Radical Empiricism in Network Cultures* (2010). He is currently working on an archaeology of machine learning and its associated transformations. He co-directs the Centre for Science Studies, Lancaster University, UK.

James Maguire is a PhD Fellow at the IT University of Copenhagen, where he is part of a broader research collective called Alien Energy. James is currently writing up his PhD dissertation after conducting ten months of fieldwork in a volcanic zone in the south-west of Iceland. His work mainly focuses on geothermal energy as a specific configuration of human–earth relations in the anthropocene.

Atsuro Morita teaches anthropology at Osaka University. He has done ethnographic research on technology development in Thailand, focusing on how ideas, artifacts, and people travel in and out of Thailand. He is recently co-convening a Japan–Denmark collaborative project titled Environmental Infrastructures funded by the Japan Society for Promotion of Science. In this project he studies the co-existence of heterogeneous components – including cosmological scientific and multispecies ones – of the water management infrastructure in the Chao Phraya Delta.

Moe Nakazora is currently a postdoctoral research fellow of the Japan Society for Promotion of Science (JSPS) and an affiliate of the Institute for

Research in the Humanities at Kyoto University. Her main fields of interest are the anthropology of science, technology, and medicine; critical legal studies; and South Asian area studies. Her research contributes to the understanding of 'biodiversity' as a site of encounter between modern science and indigenous knowledge as well as postcolonial engagements with intellectual property. In two years of field research in India she has pursued these themes by examining Indian state actors' attempts to database traditional medical knowledge related to biodiversity.

Miki Namba is a doctoral candidate in anthropology at Hitotsubashi University and a research fellow of the Japan Society for the Promotion of Science (JSPS). Her research focuses on complex relation between infrastructural development, urban formation, and modernity in Laos. Her work is forthcoming in *Transnational Frontiers of Asia and Latin America from 1800,* eds J. Moneiro Tejada and B. Tatar (Routledge).

Morten Nielsen is an Associate Professor in the Department of Anthropology at Aarhus University and coordinator of the interdisciplinary research network Urban Orders (URO). Based on his fieldwork in Brazil, Mozambique, and, most recently, Scotland, he has published on issues such as urban citizenship, time and temporality, urban aesthetics, materiality, infrastructure, and political cosmologies. Recent publications include articles in the *Journal of the Royal Anthropological Institute, HAU: Journal of Ethnographic Theory, Social Analysis,* and *Social Anthropology.*

Madeleine Reeves is Senior Lecturer in Social Anthropology at the University of Manchester and a member of the ESRC Centre for Research on Socio-Cultural Change. Her interests lie in the anthropology of politics, space, and (im)mobility. She is the author of *Border Work: Spatial Lives of the State in Rural Central Asia* (Cornell, 2014), and the co-editor, most recently, of *Affective States: Entanglements, Suspensions, Suspicions* (Social Analysis, 2015), with Mateusz Laszczkowski.

Richard Rottenburg holds a chair in anthropology at the University of Halle, where he directs a research group focusing on the anthropology of 'Law, Organization, Science and Technology' (LOST). Inspired by STS and renditions of pragmatist social theory, the emergence of material-semiotic orderings and their institutionalizations are at the heart of his current work. These inquiries center stage evidentiary practices (experiments, tests, measurements) and multilayered infrastructures, which solidify and circulate evidence, and ask how it is mobilized to design and critique specific futures.

AbdouMaliq Simone is an urbanist and currently Research Professor at the Max Planck Institute for the Study of Religious and Ethnic Diversity and a Visiting Professor at Goldsmiths College and the African Centre for Cities, University of Cape Town. His work concerns the relationship between emerging forms of urban collective life and political institutions.

Gisa Weszkalnys is Assistant Professor in anthropology at the London School of Economics. She is author of *Berlin, Alexanderplatz: Transforming Place in a Unified Germany* (2010) and co-editor of *Elusive Promises: Planning in the Contemporary World* (2013). Her current research deals with speculation, potentiality, and absence in the context of an emerging West African oil economy.

Brit Ross Winthereik is Associate Professor at the IT University of Copenhagen in the Technologies in Practice faculty group and the author of *Monitoring Movements in Development Aid* with Casper Bruun Jensen (MIT, 2013). She is lead investigator of *Marine Renewable Energy as Alien: Social Studies of an Emerging Industry* with Laura Watts and Head of the ETHOS Lab – an experimental space for ethnography of/through the digital. She has published on ethnographic methods, accountability, information infrastructures, ontology, and critique.

Acknowledgment

Our collaboration began with a visit by Casper Bruun Jensen and Atsuro Morita to the University of Manchester to participate in a workshop that Penny Harvey was running on 'Infrastructures of Social Change.' That meeting and our subsequent discussions on putting together a joint publication were possible thanks to the networks of funding and of collaboration that had supported our individual research trajectories. Our key sources of funding have been the UK Economic and Social Research Council (CRESC), which funded the ESRC Centre for Research on Socio-Cultural Change, and the Japan Society for Promotion of Science (JSPS), which funded the Environmental Infrastructures project (KAKENHI-24251017). We are also grateful to the Institute for Research in Humanities, Kyoto University, whose funding enabled us to work intensively together in Japan on the collection in the summer of 2015.

Beyond these general funding possibilities we have, as ever, many intellectual debts. Penny Harvey would like in particular to thank her colleagues from CRESC. Here our research group, which went by the name of Theme 4, was formally configured to study "Politics of Cultural Change", then "Topologies of Cultural Change" and most recently "Infrastructures of Social Change". Theme 4 continues to be a wonderful space for dialogue and exploration. Some of the key figures from that group are in this publication: Hannah Knox, Madeleine Reeves, Adolfo Estalella, and Sarah Green. Others whose influence is strong and much appreciated are Eleanor Casella, Damian O'Doherty, Gillian Evans, Christine McLean, Elizabeth Silva, Nick Thoburn, and Kath Woodward. We are already taking our infrastructural work forward into new conversations on mega-projects.

CRESC also had a research group known as SLOM or the Social Life of Methods. Evelyn Ruppert was a key member of that group and in collaboration with Hannah Knox she initiated a project on 'Socializing Big Data' that experimented with new methods of collaborative research, staging conversations with genomic scientists, national statisticians, and waste management practitioners, opening new horizons for thinking about digital infrastructures. Key collaborators on that project were Adrian Mackenzie, Ruth McNally, Celia Lury, Stephanie Barker, Camilla Lewis, and Yannis Kallianos.

As infrastructures began to take off as a topic of anthropological interest, Penny has also had the chance to work closely with other colleagues who have opened the field up in wonderful ways. Nikhil Anand, Hannah Appel, and Akhil Gupta convened a SAR seminar on the 'Promise of Infrastructure' that allowed us a generous five days to live, think, and talk infrastructure in the company of Brian Larkin, Antina von Schnitzler, Christina Schwenkel, Cassie Fennell, Geof Bowker, and Dominic Boyer. The support for these seminars from the School for Advanced Research is invaluable, and shows that you can learn a great deal while having fun!

Atsuro Morita and Casper Bruun Jensen would like in particular to thank the colleagues in the 'Environmental Infrastructures' project, Brit Ross Winthereik, Anders Blok, Keiichi Omura, Miho Ishii, Shuhei Kimura, Osamu Nakagawa, Keiichiro Matsumura, and Moe Nakazora. Some of these names are found in this publication. Our view of infrastructure has dramatically expanded through discussions with many stimulating scholars who joined the project's workshops. Among them, Atsuro and Casper particularly thank Eduardo Viveiros de Castro, Natasha Myers, Mei Zhan, Marilyn Strathern, Geof Bowker, Andrew Pickering, Hugh Raffles, Marisol de la Cadena, Kregg Hetherington, Shiho Satsuka, Rebecca Empson, Jakkrit Sangkhamanee, Arjen Zegwaard, Mohacsi Gergely, Wakana Suzuki, Liv Nyland Krause, Miki Namba, and Fukachi Furukawa. Atsuro and Casper's thanks also go to the professors and the secretaries of the Department of Anthropology and administrators of the School of Human Sciences, Osaka University, whose generous support made all these international workshops and the collaboration for this publication possible.

Last but not least we are grateful to Gerhard Boomgaarden for his ongoing support of the CRESC series at Routledge, to Tony Bennett for his collegial support, and to Alyson Claffey for her wonderful attention to detail.

1 Introduction

Infrastructural complications

Penny Harvey, Casper Bruun Jensen and Atsuro Morita

Over the past decade, infrastructures have emerged as compelling sites for qualitative social research. This occurs in a general situation where the race for infrastructural investment has become quite frenzied as world superpowers compete for the most effective means to circulate energy, goods, and money. At the same time, millions of people disenfranchised by trade corridors, securitized production sites, and privatized service provision seek to establish their own possibilities that intersect, disrupt, or otherwise engage the high-level investments that now routinely reconfigure their worlds. The projects of the powerful and the engagements of the poor are thus thoroughly entangled in this contemporary drive to "leverage the future."[1]

The study of infrastructure can lead researchers in multiple directions. Some take an interest in embedded power relations or their symbolic or spectacular dimensions. Others focus on the effects of categorization and standardizations and the modes of support and connectivity enabled by infrastructural systems, including the reconfigurations of the lives and subjectivities of those who live in and around them. Yet others emphasize their scale-making capacities, their recursive, or loopy, relations with social formations, and their role in the emergence of new ontologies. This volume offers a compendium of approaches to this increasingly populated field of social research.

For obvious reasons, the selection is far from comprehensive. This introductory essay discusses a range of issues that we have been particularly interested in, and engaged by. At the end, we set out the principles that have guided the selection of contributions, some of which are written by established figures, many others by new voices. Our hope is that others will find inspiration and their own sense of possibility for engaging what can appear as vast, uncontainable networks that may be resistant to established social methods. The aim is to exhibit a range of ways to examine the textures, social complexities, and complications of infrastructure.

The volume grew out of overlaps that appeared between two research groups, one affiliated with the Centre for Research on Socio-Cultural Change (CRESC) based at the University of Manchester and the Open University in the UK and one centered at Osaka University in Japan, in collaboration with Danish researchers at the IT University of Copenhagen and the University of

Copenhagen. Our shared interests coalesced at a time when each project was beginning to work on edited collections. Rather than joining our projects, we joined our networks; yet much of the impetus of the original projects remains visible within the collection.

At CRESC, Penny Harvey and her colleagues were exploring how infrastructures such as roads, airports, or digital information systems draw together political and economic forces in complicated ways and often with unexpected effects. This focus had developed from previous interests in the role that objects and materials play in the shaping of social worlds and the dynamic configuration of social relations (Harvey et al. 2013). Following diverse practices of standardization, engineering, gridding, contractual negotiation, resource allocation, and scientific investigation, the research group had tracked the ways in which infrastructural practices were implicated in broader dynamics of social change.[2]

Based at Osaka University, Atsuro Morita, and Casper Bruun Jensen, formerly at the IT University in Copenhagen, were developing a focus on infrastructure to think about the challenges of environmental transformation. The original impetus for this project was the observation that "infrastructure" and "nature" both often operate as unseen backgrounds for the study of social relations and practices. As it unfolded, the project gradually came to zoom in on infrastructure as a double means to know and control environments.

Environmental infrastructures turned out to be about the making and remaking of worlds at once material and semiotic and inhabited not only by people but also by a multiplicity of nonhumans. Focusing on these under-the-radar entanglements allowed project members to explore the involvement of a wide range of entities – from bacteria and landforms to rice and spirits – in infrastructural projects, while also paying attention to the involvement of infrastructures in multiple world-shaping, or ontological, projects (see Jensen and Morita 2015). Similarly, the CRESC research group was finding that entities such as soil, concrete, fake passports, airport lounges, cats, ghosts, digital data, and earth beings were integral to infrastructural systems and to the worlds that these systems brought into being.

What coincided across these projects was thus an interest in several aspects of infrastructural formations that resonate with multiple conceptual concerns of contemporary anthropologists, sociologists, historians, cultural geographers, STS scholars, artists and others. These aspects relate to the experimental, uncertain, affective, temporal, and political dimensions of infrastructures, seen as relational worlds. Thus, we shared an orientation to the interfaces between infrastructure and social formations, as exemplified by projects and designs of the engineering sciences, currently being implemented and planned at an unprecedented rate on a planetary scale. Our interests also converged around conceptual and empirical questions of how to get the social complexities and other complications of such projects adequately into view.

In spite of our projects' aspirations to novelty, they are in many ways indebted to existing scholarship as well as to recent research taking part in the unfolding "turn" to infrastructure in the social sciences and humanities.[3] In the following sections we spell out what we see as particularly exciting about the way in which this infrastructural turn turns.

Turning to infrastructure: some inversions

In the mid-1990s, a time at which infrastructures generated less excitement than presently, Geoffrey C. Bowker (1995) developed the idea of infrastructural inversion. Infrastructural inversion aimed to address the tendency of infrastructures to remain as invisible backdrops to social action, their characteristics instead seen as explainable by the social forces, interests, or ideologies that went into making them. Crudely put, American automobile culture might be said to *reflect* individualism, while the reliance of the Japanese on jam-packed trains would *mirror* their group orientation. According to such views, infrastructures were surfaces from which social, cultural, or political motives could be decoded.

Compared with these kinds of approaches, infrastructural inversion entailed a figure-ground reversal. The insistence that our analytical attentiveness to infrastructures must be inverted was grounded in the realization that, short of breakdown, infrastructures tend to remain invisible at the level of use and experience. Rather than assuming cultural, political, or knowledge-based explanations *of* infrastructures, Bowker thus suggested an analytical entry-point via a focus on materiality. He noted, for example, that while it used to be thought that advances in life expectancy in the nineteenth century were due to improved scientific knowledge, the major causes actually related to changing systems of food production and consumption, and to improved sewage systems (1995: 235). Bringing the infrastructural "ground" up front in this way facilitated understanding of how complex chains of material relations reconfigure bodies, societies, and *also* knowledge and discourse in ways often unnoticed.[4]

Inversion thus drew attention to the silent, unnoticed work done by infrastructures. Indeed, in Susan Leigh Star and Karen Ruhleder's (1996) classic definition, this invisibility is central to the *infra*-structural quality of a system. Their focus on the "when" rather than the "what" of infrastructure highlighted that seamless flow was a fragile achievement. In contexts where such flows have been achieved, inversion emerged as the key methodological and conceptual move by which *analysts* were able bring to light the hidden relations on which smooth circulation depended. This also meant, though, that infrastructural inversion seemed particularly relevant in contexts where infrastructures *did* work quite well. In many situations, however, infrastructures do not generate anything resembling smooth flows.

A significant impetus behind the current vogue for infrastructural analysis is the increasingly obvious fragility of many infrastructures. Where breakdown is regular (Harvey 2005; Campbell 2012), or where infrastructures have collapsed (Simone 2004; Harvey 2015; Jensen 2016), patterns of visibility are quite different from those where connectivity can be routinely assumed.

In a much cited review article, Brian Larkin (2013) highlighted that infrastructures are in fact often *not unnoticed*. Instead, he argued, they inhabit a whole spectrum of visibilities, from opacity to spectacle. Larkin pointed to diverse cases, like Indonesian satellites (Barker 2005), Mongolian electricity (Sneath 2009), or the urban development of Congo's Kinshasa (de Boeck 2011), in which infrastructures, far from being invisible, were designed to elicit awe and admiration. If premised on the idea of an initial invisibility that must be foregrounded by the analysis, the notion of infrastructural inversion would have no purchase in these situations. Its use would be delimited to a subset of infrastructures falling on the low-end of the scale of visibility.

Arguably, however, the significance of infrastructural inversion is not obviated by these spectacular examples. For whereas Larkin's use of visibility centers on infrastructure as public displays, the invisibility to which Bowker attends refers to mundane operational processes. These are not immediately comparable forms of visibility, since the regular operations of infrastructures may remain opaque or unknown, even as the infrastructure is publically exhibited. At the very least, these entry points for the study of infrastructure tend to configure them as quite different kinds of objects. This observation encourages further questions about the specific relational forms or collectives that constitute various infrastructural systems, including the patterns of visibility and invisibility to which they give rise.

Thus, even if television shows and advertisement posters represent infrastructural development as testimony to national innovation and achievement, or to the prowess and foresight of a particular politician, we need to also understand how exactly satellite images enter Indonesian homes. We also need to attend to the specific material relations, ideas and expectations that accompany the arrival of electricity (Boyer 2015), the appearance of a road (Harvey and Knox 2015), or a database (Jensen and Winthereik 2013). As Tess Lea and Paul Pholeros (2010) have shown in the context of aboriginal housing, the public exhibit of material artifacts, like pipes, is no guarantee of a *functioning* infrastructure.

To our minds, however, infrastructural inversion poses a different kind of difficulty, relating to the relatively sharp distinction it assumes between the conceptual-analytic and the empirical-ethnographic (cf. Jensen 2014). In the original formulation, as noted, it is the *analyst* that brings to light infrastructural invisibilities. In situations where infrastructural problems or breakdowns are at once ubiquitous and highly visible, however, we come across some *different kinds of inversion*.

For one thing, some situations elicit *naturally occurring inversions* in which various exigencies make infrastructural operations abundantly visible to some people (Blok this volume; Fennell 2011; Nakazora this volume), or that induce new forms of practical engagement, tinkering, or sabotage (Anand 2012; Howe 2014; von Schnitzler 2008). In these situations, where the relations that working infrastructures depend on are revealed through disruption, disturbance, or absence, inversion is an empirical condition *before* becoming an analytical tool. Second, naturally occurring inversions may induce among the users of infrastructure and analysts alike radically new ideas of what infrastructure *is*. Atsuro Morita (2016) has thus documented how changing relations between delta infrastructures and rice farming gradually led engineers and hydrologists to see rice not as an end product supported by an external hydraulic infrastructural system but rather as infrastructural in its own right. As these examples suggest, it is not so much that the importance of inversion has been obviated by the recognition of new forms of infrastructural visibility, but rather that the forms of inversion have multiplied in a way that blurs the distinction between the conceptual and the empirical.

But what is infrastructure? A minimal point of entry

Indicating an unstable relation between the conceptual and the empirical situations of naturally occurring inversion obliges us to address a question, confounding in its seeming simplicity: what, actually, do we mean by an infrastructure?

Even when we have quite a good grasp of the questions *addressed to us by* infrastructures, it is far more difficult to define them in general. The significantly variable perspectives discussed above exemplify this difficulty. Provisionally, and minimally, we might say that we are dealing with technologically mediated, dynamic forms that continuously produce and transform sociotechnical relations. That is, infrastructures are extended material assemblages that generate effects and structure social relations, either through engineered (i.e. planned and purposefully crafted) or non-engineered (i.e. unplanned and emergent) activities. Seen thus, infrastructures are doubly relational due to their simultaneous internal multiplicity and their connective capacities *outwards* (Harvey 2017). If infrastructures fail, this can accordingly be due either to internal disruption or because of a breakdown in the relations between the infrastructure and the domain of activity it is expected to sustain. The tension between the engineered and the non-engineered system is important here. It also introduces new complexities because an engineered system might break down, or fail to deliver as intended, yet continue to give rise to emergent effects. Dysfunctional or collapsed sewage systems, for example, continue to generate health hazards across urban space (Jensen this volume).

In spite of our provisional clarifications, a *definitive definition* of infrastructure remains elusive. Yet, given the ongoing transformation and emergence of sites taken *by other actors* to be infrastructural, the aspiration to unequivocal specification can be seen as itself conceptually and empirically counter-productive. Though minimal, the characterization offered above allows us to begin inquiry with firm focus on the "infra" qualities of these systems, on their temporal and spatial reach, and, crucially, on the complexities and complications attending their open-ended relational capacities (Carse this volume). It does not, however, allow us to predict how people will apprehend and identify infrastructures as relevant in their lives, or even what *they* will see as infrastructural. Nor does it allow us to know just where or how radically new forms of infrastructure might emerge as significant forces.

We thus embrace the diverse possibilities that a focus on infrastructure affords in the broadest sense – looking for those underlying configurations that are *not necessarily* the site of active reflection on the part of those whose lives they shape, while also attending to the ways in which people *do* sometimes reflect on the socio-material conditions that shape their life worlds. In this way, we think, a focus on infrastructure can cut across the tensions between surface and depth that mark social theory. Once we approach infrastructures as dynamic and emergent forms, it is clear that we cannot specify their contours in advance. The question "what is infrastructure" must therefore be addressed, and experimented with, in registers at once conceptual and empirical.

The insistence on experimentation is undergirded by the observation that infrastructure seems presently to be bursting at the seams. This is empirically the case as we watch news about oil and renewable energy, droughts and floods, pipelines and transnational politics, river basin management, surveillance and privacy, cyber security and drone warfare, and many other things, all conceptualized in some or other quarters *as infrastructural issues.* But it is also the case analytically, as the rubric of infrastructure is put into conversation with, collapsed into, or bounced off against, a multitude of ideas and theories, from Foucault's biopolitics and Marxist updates, to actor-network theory and a broad swathe of ecological thought, and on to multi-species anthropology and Deleuzian rhizomes and affects. As this incomplete list suggests, consistency and agreement about infrastructure are to be found neither empirically nor analytically, while ongoing conceptual and practical work on and with infrastructures routinely traverse or threaten the conceptual–empirical divide.

It seems clear that infrastructure amongst the engineers of the Suez canal, in the Chao Phraya delta, or among anthropologists or STS scholars at conference panels has no definite, common measure, responding as it does to entirely different concerns and problems depending on the setting. As we see it, however, this conceptual–empirical proliferation and divergence is just what makes infrastructure so exciting at the present moment.

The fact that infrastructure is a divergent phenomenon does not need to lead to mutual indifference among differently invested actors. To the contrary, as we see it, one of the most exciting things about the current STS and anthropological interest in infrastructure is that it *draws into* unfolding conversations an increasingly varied array of infrastructural actors materials, offering an ever-expanding range of resources for thinking and acting. In our estimation, these lateral movements are crucial for coming to terms with infrastructure as concept and practice in continuous variation.

Even so, some argue that infrastructure entails more specific stakes. At the 2015 Manchester Group for Debate in Anthropological Theory (GDAT), for example, Laura Bear defended the motion that "Attention to infrastructure offers a welcome reconfiguration of anthropological approaches to the political." In the ensuing discussion, where many participants objected to the ambiguous and vague nature of the infrastructure concept, Bear affirmed that anything can indeed be called into being as an infrastructure. She further insisted, however, that to call something infrastructure has implications in and for the formation of sites of governance. From this perspective, to call an infrastructure into being is also necessarily to draw attention to the complications of other-than-human dimensions of the political relations that join and divide us.

Complexity, complication, experimentation

Initiatives involving engineered infrastructural systems are tightly bound to modernist notions of progress and development. The trope of linearity and singularity remains fundamental to popular histories of technical and political change (Hetherington this volume). Over time, we can read, stone, bronze, or iron gave way to oil, steel, and microelectronics. Or, we used to live in feudal systems, now we live in representative democracies. Such stories of progressive development are presently weakened, if not supplanted, from a variety of angles. Who are the "we" telling stories of progress at the level of humanity in general? Are the forms of political and technological transformation not more diverse, and uneven, than assumed by the voice of universality?

Histories of the emergence of infrastructural systems tend to carry a similar narrative of increasing complexity. Thus, we encounter arguments to the effect that infrastructures such as ancient roads and canals *used to be* relatively localized and technologically simple, but extended networks – like those of railways and electricity grids – *gradually evolved*, which later morphed into systems of amazing complexity, typically exemplified by *ubiquitous* information and communication technologies. The threads of the latter now permeate all dimensions of life, from pervasive surveillance of public space and workplaces, to the most intimate aspects of personal life (Edwards this volume).

In some cases, however, the assumption of a linear move from simplicity to complexity ignores key features of prior infrastructural forms. Inka roads provide a good example (Hyslop 1984). These roads were simple structures by comparison with the connectivity afforded by the Internet. Yet in Inka times they did not simply connect dispersed geographical sites. They also traced geometries of power across a landscape that was *sentient* rather than *natural*. These infrastructures held the Inka world together through complex alignments of geological, astrological, and social forces. The Inka capacity to mobilize the people and the materials to create the structures through which we apprehend their social organization today allows us to glimpse a former world characterized by extreme infrastructural complexity.

In an analysis of the construction of social order, Shirley Strum and Bruno Latour (1987) made a number of provocative observations that help us reorient the linear story of increasing complexity. Deploying a contrast between "order" as made by primates and humans, they suggested that it was the former, rather than the latter, who were overwhelmed by complexity. The lives of baboons, argued Strum and Latour, are inherently complex, because the hierarchy and relations of the troop are subject to continuous social negotiation. At no point does the exhausted baboon have the opportunity to leave social interaction behind. It can never just go home and lock the door. In contrast, for many (though certainly not all) people, objects like locks and doors operate as devices that can be manipulated to temporarily simplify interactions.

Now, Strum and Latour did not, of course, argue that technologies *in general* make human lives simpler rather than more complex. Instead, they evoked a distinction between the complex and the *complicated*. Whereas complex relations, like those of baboons, are intrinsically unsettled, the complications of technologically mediated relations pivot on their potential extendibility and the ways in which they *fold together* heterogeneous entities in networks, allowing for temporary simplification of certain kinds of relations. Yet, although networks and their components can be interconnected, their alignments are never exact. Infrastructural formations always to some degree remain out of synch with each other – they may also run in parallel or even work against one other.

The implication is that different networks embed varied conceptions of progress and diverse answers to the question of who should be provided with services, why, and through what means. For example, we can begin to see fights over environmental futures as instances of networked infrastructural politics. By way of illustration, tourism in the European Alps is increasingly dependent on the management of technical snow as the extensive and expensive infrastructures of ski resorts can only be supported as long as the snow cover is reliable. Technical snow is thus made to replace the receding glaciers and to mitigate the effects of climate change. In this story, snow has to be folded into the existing structures of roads, hotels, ski lifts, and rescue services, requiring the building of reservoirs and an ever-deeper investment in just those carbon energy expenditures that created the problem in the first place.[5] In this complicated sequence, the notion that infrastructural development is generically progressive evaporates alongside the melting glaciers.

The fact that, whether we turn to the scholarly literature, the news, blogs, or artistic practice, we are presently met with stories of infrastructural crisis also speaks to the issue of infrastructural complication. Cities flood, or black out (if they indeed had electricity in the first place). And digital infrastructures, not too long ago seen to herald a new age of open information and enlightened citizenship, have brought about forms of insecurity, terror, and surveillance on scales previously unimagined. The decoupling of infrastructure development and the notion of progress has indeed become increasingly evident.

Signs of crisis, then, are increasingly common to many infrastructures, whether obviously material, as with sewage pipes and waterworks, or supposedly virtual, as with the Internet. Rather than unmitigated *public* goods, different infrastructures turn out only to be good for some people, some of the time. Even infrastructures that are generally perceived to be benign, like water provisioning and waste treatment, face numerous problems (Harvey this volume). Not only do such infrastructures extend their benefits unevenly, they are also very expensive to maintain. In contexts of fiscal constraint and austerity characterizing much of the world today, these costs prove prohibitive. Thus, many places are having increasing trouble keeping their infrastructures in good condition, not to mention upgrading their capacities.

One consequence is what Graham and Marvin (2001) refer to as the splintering effects of infrastructural systems in contemporary urban settings. Such splintering is a consequence of the fact that many systems that were once shaped and held together by elected public authorities deploying funds from taxation are now distributed amongst many different owners and property regimes, deploying funds that derive from diverse charges to users. Civic infrastructural systems are increasingly managed by public authorities in partnership with private capital and shaped by a politics of decentralization that encourages the monetization of component networks in line with neoliberal agendas focusing on the out-sourcing of service provision. The consequences of such decentralization processes are not only less accountable forms of provision but also an increased differentiation of access to services within any particular infrastructural formation. This splintering effect, too, is indicative of a flourishing set of complications that are not significantly attenuated by patchy efforts at regulation, monitoring, and control.[6]

Increasingly liable to fragment under regimes of neoliberal governance, infrastructures disconnect from one another and from particular people, populations, or areas (e.g. Anand this volume; Lea this volume). Yet, splintering is also generative of new relations. AbdouMaliq Simone (2004), Julya Elyachar (2010) and Brenda Chalfin (2016), for example, have documented how particular social relations gain infrastructural properties vis-à-vis wider collectives in consequence of the inability of technical infrastructures to provide the material underpinnings for urban living.

In other contexts, by contrast, established environmental relations are assumed to lack an inherent infrastructural capacity and are increasingly made subject to engineered modifications (Blok, Nakazora and Winthereik 2016). What used to be seen as autonomous rivers, deltas, or watersheds are subsumed within wider infrastructural orbits. Thus, while "nature" itself is technologically modified, it is also rendered infrastructural (Jensen 2015). Such cases have been documented by scholars like Helen Verran (2011), Atsuro Morita (2016), and Ashley Carse (2012), all of who depict situations where "nature" is presently enrolled to do jobs previously assigned to infrastructures. As environments now have to be supported in order to continue to meet the demands people make on them, engineered and non-engineered systems are increasingly folded into one another. The result is complicated, emergent patterns in which the line between the natural and the engineered becomes progressively harder to draw.

The splintering of infrastructures of transportation, health, or communication has multiple implications for peoples' lives. Accordingly, it is not surprising that scholars from STS, anthropology, or cultural geography often bring a political sensitivity to the study of infrastructural crises. Often, including in descriptions offered above, notions of splintering and collapse are related to neoliberal policies. Yet, while these diagnoses are undoubtedly significant, they may overestimate the extent to which those in power are themselves able to foresee, not to say control, infrastructural transformations. The unpredictable relation between political intent and infrastructural outcomes is another consequence of complication.

This observation invites a careful rethinking of the politics of infrastructure. If it is assumed that infrastructural development follows a linear, progressive, and rational path defined by government or corporations, responsibility for the outcome is also placed squarely in the hands of these actors. Thus it makes sense to *center* political critique on the flawed motives or poor execution of infrastructure development. Yet, from a vantage point that has given up on the belief in progressive history, it would be odd to think that anyone, even government or corporate managers and experts, hold the power to enforce linear development.

From the point of view of *complication*, infrastructures are shaped by multiple agents with competing interests and capacities, engaged in an indefinite set of distributed interactions over extended periods of time. The characteristics of infrastructure emerge out of these interactions, making it exceedingly unlikely that they will function according to the plans of *anyone* in particular (cf. Latour 1996). As we further discuss below, this infrastructural emergence is important because it indexes the experimental character of infrastructure development (Jensen and Morita 2015).

Emergence nevertheless introduces a troubling political issue, since responsibility for infrastructural effects can no longer be straightforwardly attributed to the autonomous choices of individuals or even organizations. With reference to Hannah Arendt's (1963) analysis of the banality of evil, Susan Leigh Star discussed the difficulty of assigning responsibility for catastrophes in technological contexts characterized by a very complex division of labor. In the case of the Challenger space shuttle launch decision (see Vaughan 1996), which led to the death of seven people, for example, Star (1995: 114) remarks that one form of "engineering ethics" might view each person involved as "one millionth responsible." As she goes on to comment, "such statements make no sense," but they do point to the difficulty of figuring responsibility within massively complex and distributed projects.

Even so, in our age of cranked-up extraction, financialization, and the ambition to control global flows, many affected individuals and communities *expect* or *demand* those who garner the greatest profits to take responsibility for non-linear infrastructural effects. Corporate and state agents are at times clearly the joint agents of displacement and often also sources of biopolitical neglect, marked by the absence or paucity of infrastructures (de la Cadena 2015, Lea this volume, Reeves this volume). However, where lines of causality become too complicated to disentangle, a different ethic of care and/or concern is required. Haraway's call for response-ability (1997; see also Maguire and Winthereik this volume) challenges us to think about the importance of acknowledging the suffering of others (other humans, other species) and of recognizing that some ways of life *depend on* such suffering. What Annemarie Mol (2008) has called an ethic of care thus offers an important counterpoint to the prevailing ethics of choice, within extended, technologically mediated, arrays of humans and nonhumans.

As we have highlighted, infrastructures can be seen as emergent and often unstable constellations of heterogeneous entities. Even so, due to their scale and scope, they are often depicted as barely changeable behemoths. In his conversations with Bruno Latour, Michel Serres (1995) offers an arresting possibility for thinking differently about the relation between scale and power. Encouraging the reader to contemplate an old vase, Serres notes that while it takes skill, patience, and effort to make it, all that is required to destroy it is a push. Transposed to the realm of infrastructure, this image is analytically consequential. Rather than monolithic blocks, it makes it possible to think of large-scale infrastructures as achievements *that remain fragile* (e.g. Edwards 2010).

From this starting point, we would no longer need to be surprised by the apparently unending series of mishaps, dysfunctions, and inefficiencies of complicated large-scale infrastructures. Nor would it be surprising that critics always find it easy to point to the failures and breakdowns of infrastructure. But if such occurrences are *to be expected*, the task of pointing to them becomes less interesting. It follows that the conceptual and empirical task of picking apart infrastructures, must be complemented with analyses, images, and visions that help us understand what makes (some) infrastructures function *against the odds*. It also encourages contemplation of what it would mean for infrastructures to take more viable forms.

Orders and interstices: on the politics of infrastructure

In *Sorting Things Out*, Geoffrey C. Bowker and Susan Leigh Star (1999) analyzed multiple dimensions of classifications and their consequences. Their interest in practices of social categorization was not radically new, as exemplified by earlier work by scholars as diverse as Mary Douglas (1966) and Julia Kristeva (1984). What was novel, however, was their attentiveness to the technologically mediated processes through which classifications become standards, invisibly embedded in the spines of infrastructure (see also Lampland and Star 2009). Their novel contribution was to invite us to enter the machine rooms in which the standards by which people live are made.

Others have pointed to what we can call the *recursive* relation between the making of infrastructure and the shaping of society. While engineers and builders made railways, paving the way for the "information revolution" (Beniger 1986), for example, trains generated new forms of perception (Schivelbusch 1977) and action (Fisch 2013), which, in turn, become input for further infrastructural development. Having learned to think of their work in terms of networking, NGOs created new, networked activities and organizational forms (Riles 2000). Again, being committed to the idea of mutual accountability and partnership in development, aid organizations busy themselves developing infrastructures that embed these commitments and thus change the form of development aid itself (Jensen and Wintherik 2013). Yet again, global oil infrastructures co-emerged with particular political formations, forms of democracy and warfare, and modern lifestyles that in turn made oil seem indispensable (Mitchell 2013). In all of these instances, we are witness to a recursive movement in which forms of infrastructure generate effects that loop back upon society, organizations, and people, *re*-shaping them in turn.

The image of a looping relation between society and infrastructure offers an alternative to conventional views of infrastructure as a distinct technological domain *external* to other bounded spheres, such as the social, the economical, or the political. Assuming a categorical separation between these domains leads to an image in which infrastructure is *passive* – "influenced" or "determined" – by politics or economics. In contrast, the recursive shaping of infrastructure, society, economics, and politics offers an image of relations that are *a priori* underdetermined and thus subject to experimentation. As previously noted, we are unable to say what infrastructure, politics and the relations between them will turn out to be in any concrete instance, since this will be the result of an unfolding experimental process.

No one could know in advance, for example, that oil extraction in the Middle East would end up being a (or the) main factor in twentieth-century politics, creating wars and zones of incredible richness and poverty and leading to ecological catastrophe (Mitchell 2013). Often taken as self-explanatory by critics, the politics and economics of oil *co-emerged* with oil infrastructures in a contingent process.

At the same time, of course, oil offers a vivid demonstration of the fact that infrastructures can have massive ordering effects across multiple scales. Its infrastructures have shaped individual subjectivities (including the ability or aspiration to live "modern lives"), local communities, cities, vast corporate structures, nation states, international relations, and global environments. And yet, no matter how extended, no infrastructure encompasses everything. Following Michel Serres (1991), we might even surmise that they are constitutively *unable* to do so, since any order always generates its own correlative disorder.

Knowledge of the simultaneous generation of orders and their others has been advanced by the STS scholars Marc Berg and Stefan Timmermans (2000) who showed, in the context of medical standards, that the very act of creating zones of visibility and intervention also generated areas of opaqueness. The same insight is implicitly part of Star and Bowker's studies of the consequences of classifications. In a famous example, Star (1991) thus described how her allergy to onions caused consistent problems when she ordered a meal at McDonalds. Because the standard operating procedures did not include any guidance on how to make onion-free burgers, responsibility for avoiding onions was invariably delegated back to herself. Allergy to onion thereby provided Star with insight into the gaps, or interstices, of the organization of fast food meals. Anthropologists like Paul Kockelman (2010) and Richard Rottenburg (2009) have made broadly similar observations about the gaps and interstices produced by *any* infrastructure.

The upshot is a view of infrastructure quite different from the idealized notion of seamlessly integrated systems that facilitate smooth flows of people, goods, or services if not for some *unusual* obstruction. Rather than assuming flow as the "natural" outcome of well-functioning infrastructures, what comes into view are complicated pleated arrangements, in which every new connection also creates new gaps. It is not, however, that such arrangements are chaotic rather than orderly. Instead the order is fractal, since relations and gaps multiply simultaneously rather than canceling each other out (Strathern 1991; Jensen 2007).

These internal disruptions do not necessarily disable infrastructural systems. And they certainly do not preclude powerful infrastructural effects. They do, however, direct our attention to how infrastructures work *through* their own internal inconsistencies. Stalled by gaps of their own making, infrastructures are not least propelled by the energy put into solving the problems posed by these tensions or gaps; interventions that in turn produce new connections and disconnections. Paraphrasing Deleuze and Guattari (1983: 151),[7] say that infrastructures work only by breaking down. However, rather than taking this point as established by philosophical fiat, it can be used to sharpen attention on the empirically variable ways in which gaps and breakdowns sometimes, but not necessarily always, become constitutive of infrastructural innovation. As an image to keep us curious, Deleuze and Guattari's machines that work by breaking down turn us toward careful examination of infrastructural qualities and relational forms.

In these spaces of dynamic connection and disconnection it is little wonder that infrastructures often look less "rational" than one might have imagined. Indeed, as Atsuro Morita (2014) has written, a significant number of infrastructures can be likened to Rube Goldberg machines, extraordinarily complicated devices for accomplishing what appear as relatively straightforward tasks.[8]

In our view, the characterization of the complicated trajectories through which infrastructural patterns of relations and gaps are made, and of their proliferating effects, is crucial for contemporary social studies of infrastructure. Rather than assuming flow as the basic infrastructural fact, with the consequence that breaks in the flow appear deviant, and thus in need of special explanation, the question can be reversed. Infrastructural studies might *begin* with gaps, interstices, and zones of opacity as infrastructural facts, which raise questions concerning the kinds of ordering these apparent "flow-stoppers" participate in and how they do so. Meanwhile, as we have already noticed, the proliferation of ambiguity and the distribution of responsibility through infrastructures pose important questions concerning politics and justice.

As we also have insisted, however, these are fundamentally *compositional* questions, concerning the processes whereby certain actors, materials, standards, ideas, and images get *folded into* infrastructures, whereas others get designated as its invisible, irrelevant, or denigrated "others."

Infrastructural visions

As noted, linear history assumes that infrastructures improve over time, as they become progressively better at solving the issues they are meant to deal with. Since this evolution of infrastructural capacity requires taking into account more and more actors, the result is increasing technical complexity. Because of this complexity, the technical dimensions of infrastructure in turn become impenetrable to most people, grasped only by swarms of experts and managers (Hughes 1983; Winner 1986).

Yet, even as it is beyond the reach of most users to gain any *comprehensive* understanding of their infrastructures this does not necessarily entail powerlessness. Rather, the inconsistencies and gaps of infrastructure, due to relational complications, makes it possible for users to navigate and manipulate infrastructures in various ways, without for that matter having any more than localized knowledge of certain of its features (Von Schnitzler 2008; Jensen and Winthereik 2013).

Moreover, if infrastructural orders constantly produce new "others," new gaps and zones of opacity, uncertainty and incomprehensibility extend beyond end-users and mundane consumers to also encompass designers and experts. The observation of infrastructural opaqueness encourages reconsideration of some images of control prevalent in contemporary discussions about digital infrastructures.

Famously brought to light by Edward Snowden, the constant expansion of the ambitions and abilities of governments and multinational corporations to know ever more about the movements and desires of individuals leaves one with the impression that digital infrastructures are almost all seeing. Metaphorically, they seem to resemble the eye of Tolkien's Sauron, capable of zooming in *anywhere*, penetrating to the depths of human, elf and hobbit souls. Of course, the *horror* attending the experience of being gazed upon by Sauron's evil eye is not matched by most contemporary experiences with surveillance. To the contrary, the tablets, smart phones and laptops that make up our digital environments are generally perceived as friendly and benign. While surveillance researchers find analytical resources for thinking through this situation in George Orwell's *1984* and Foucault's (1991) work on the Panopticon, apologists of market-based surveillance tend to highlight the possibilities for enhanced connectivity and social visibility offered by Facebook and other platforms.

At least, these dichotomous perspectives suggest the difficulties of balancing concerns between the right to privacy and the need for security. There are complicated trade-offs between safety and control, visibility, and opacity. Even as Facebook stresses integration and connectivity rather than control, enabling users to choose what they display to whom, it also makes their every move traceable. Here, as elsewhere, consumer data creates information on populations that is routinely tracked and analyzed in order to influence future actions.

In *Seeing Like a State*, James Scott (1998) emphasized that the standardizing gaze of states was unable to handle mess and complexity. *What* a state or business can see depends on the standards and classifications embedded in its infrastructures. As in the old adage, "garbage in, garbage out," the quality of state vision is no better than the quality of the standards it uses as prostheses for seeing. Yet, though Scott recognized the general weakness of state vision, and while emphasizing the importance of practices of everyday resistance, his argument centered on the power of states to make and remake citizens and landscapes in its own simplified image. His analysis thus took *smooth flow* as fact rather than problem, rendering *gaps and interstices* as residual problems rather than predominant facts.

Yet, once we begin with the indeterminacy of the gap, the understanding of infrastructural vision and its power transmutes. Rather than all seeing and effective, what comes into view is a state with significant sight impediments, supported by some rather strange infrastructural prostheses.

This is the kind of analysis offered by Bruno Latour and Emile Hermant's *Paris: Invisible City*.[9] Explicitly contrasting their image of surveillance with Foucault's Panopticon, Latour and Hermant characterize infrastructural vision as *oligoptic*. Whereas everything can in principle be seen from the Panoptic tower (though it is not certain things are actually seen), the oligopticon is capable of gaining very fine-grained views but only of very specific things. It remains constitutively unable to produce an overview (Gad and Lauritsen 2009).

Instead of focusing on the grand sweep of state surveying, Latour and Hermant's Parisian "photo-montage" thus documents the *infrastructural trails* (see also Jensen 2016), consisting of monitoring and measuring devices distributed across urban space, which enable city planners to know very much but only about very particular things. The infrastructural vision is comparable to the analysis offered by Patrick Carroll (2006) who analyzes the "political arithmetic" experimentally deployed by William Petty for the colonial governance of Ireland.

The Oligopticon draws attention to contingent arrangements of the social and the technical that make particular types of visions possible (Haraway 1989). Even in the age of "big data," filtering algorithms and advertisements tailored on Google searches, it remains central to understand the particular infrastructural trails whereby vision is generated. Moreover, even in global contexts of massive data collection practices, infrastructural indeterminacies quickly appear, upon closer inspection, as exemplified by misidentified terror suspects held back in airports across the globe or by the irrelevance of most product recommendations popping up on your Google browser. Even in the age of big data, information is never exact and overviews never total.

Relying upon massive data reservoirs – that in turn depend on a highly skilled labor force of programmers and data analysts – the use and manipulation of big data requires enduring work, vigilant monitoring and huge investments of time and money. The complicated relations that make up these systems generate internal disorders, gaps, and indeterminacies. They also attract the attention of committed and resourceful hackers and tinkerers, who aim either to exploit the weaknesses of existing databases (as in the *Ashley Madison* hack)[10] or to support those targeted by big data by providing new forms of encryption and protection. Surveillance infrastructure, too, it seems, is a machine that works only by continuously breaking down.

This discussion has focused on advanced technologies, but in our view it has much broader infrastructural purchase. Inasmuch as there are margins of indeterminacy and gaps for maneuvering (Fisch 2013) even within sophisticated global surveillance infrastructures, it seems safe to assume that such margins are even more prevalent elsewhere.

Certainly, states and corporations may deploy infrastructural vision with a view to repression (Reeves this volume). From the unwanted "attention" gained if one ends up on a poorly constructed list of potential terrorists, to threats of imprisonment or violence directed at political and environmental activists, the question of whether and how people want to be "seen" and what kinds of infrastructural safeguards might help keep them unseen remains central. Since pockets of invisibility and crevices of indeterminacy are strewn across infrastructural landscapes, the question of relative visibility is crucial for the understanding of infrastructures and their consequences. It is also crucial for the possibility of formulating different, collective projects of making and sharing knowledge (Bowker this volume, Nakazora this volume).

Data is never fully controlled from a single source, any more than responsibility can be traced to a single subject. In a world of distributed knowledge, standards themselves are vulnerable. Big data rests on infrastructural systems that can produce far more comprehensive and up-to-date information than the sample survey or the statistical methods that policymakers depended on in the past. Yet whereas earlier knowledge infrastructures carried institutionalized certainties, standards of analysis, controls and protocols that were ultimately deployed by National Offices of Statistics to inform governments and enable rational policy decision-making, big data infrastructures are more opaque (Ruppert et al. 2015). Data is generated and owned by private companies such as Google, and released partially while key algorithms and parameters remain secret. Moreover, as described by Peter Galison (2005), very large quantities of data are deliberately *removed* from public scrutiny in the name of national security.

Questions concerning how infrastructures configure the accessibility of the information they hold are therefore central to studies of infrastructure. It also links up with issues concerning the *scale* of infrastructure. Indeed, as outlined in this introduction, it is not so much that infrastructures *have* a scale, but rather that scales are generated through the work of configuring, extending, maintaining, or disrupting infrastructures (Jensen 2007, Harvey this volume). In these processes, infrastructures come to produce some settings, situations, or systems *as large* and others *as small*, but always with the potential for further transformation or reversal.

One implication is that, rather than being developed and disseminated from centers to peripheries, infrastructures are part of *making these geographies* (Callon and Latour 1981; Harvey 2012; Jensen 2007; Tsing 2005). As previously mentioned, for example, Timothy Mitchell has depicted the complicated trajectories through which oil infrastructures came to shape the scales of modern politics, democracy, lifestyles, and global climate change. In quite a different vein, Tess Lea (2014 and this volume) has studied scale-changes relating to Darwin, the capital of Australia's Northern territory. Whereas, from the point of view of Sydney or Melbourne, Darwin often appears as a rural backwater, due to its strategic location this "local place" has become a central node in the Pacific "theater" imagined and operated by the American military. Consequently, the Territory is flooded with money distributed for particular tactical or strategic purposes, along very specific infrastructural channels, with typically uneven consequences. These consequences, however, are also *scale-changing*, for whereas Darwin is "small" in Australia, it has become "large" in the Pacific region. Rather than *a* margin responding to *the* center, we are confronted with a fractal image, in which a multiplication of margins and centers proliferate alongside infrastructural developments.

The structure of the collection

We have gathered the chapters that follow into six thematic sections each of which initiates a conversation around a general topic: development, urban, energy, environmental, and digital infrastructures, and a section on what we call infrastructural figures. These topics are not self-contained. Our section introductions give short summaries of the key arguments and point towards other connections that could be drawn across these sections. The index (or the Kindle edition) should also help allow the chapters to take on something of the shape of the digital knowledge infrastructures presented by Bowker in Chapter 29.

As stated at the beginning of this introductory essay, our collection is far from exhaustive. We do not, for example, cover either media infrastructures or financial infrastructures in any depth – although both topics do appear at various points in the collection. What we have attempted is to bring into view questions about relative visibility, connectivity and gaps, governance or control, and the possibilities of alternative configurations. Throughout we are interested in the sense of experimentation and ambiguity that a focus on infrastructures can bring to our empirical investigations and a commitment to the tension between the fragility and the obduracy of the infrastructural foundations on and through which such worlds are built.

Notes

1 This felicitous phrase was deployed by AbdouMaliq Simone at the 2015 Manchester Group for Debate in Anthropological Theory (GDAT), which focused on the question of whether or not "Attention to infrastructure offers a welcome reconfiguration of anthropological approaches to the political."
2 For further detail see our website at www.cresc.ac.uk/our-research/infrastructures-of-social-change/.
3 For a discussion of "turns" see Boellstorff (2016).
4 This approach is exemplified by Richie Nimmo's (2010) socio-material analysis of the British milk industry in the late nineteenth and early twentieth centuries.
5 This draws on Herta Nöbauer's insights on technical snow presented to the workshop on "Infrastructure in the Arctic (and elsewhere) as a social and ecological challenge," Vienna, January 2016.
6 Edward Simpson's comparative project on the roads of South Asia looks in detail at the non-coherence of regulatory systems and their disruptive effects on what might otherwise appear as continuous infrastructural spaces (www.soas.ac.uk/anthropology/research/roads/).
7 "The social machine's limit is not attrition, but rather its misfirings; it can operate only by fits and starts, by grinding and breaking down, in spasms of minor explosions. The dysfunctions are an essential element of its very ability to function" (Deleuze and Guattari 1983: 151).
8 The suggestion was originally made by Christopher Gad (pers. comm.).
9 Available at: www.bruno-latour.fr/virtual/EN/index.html.
10 *Ashley Madison* is a dating website catering to married people wanting to have an affair. In July 2015, it was hacked by "The Impact Team," which eventually released the personal information of thousands of profiles.

References

Anand, Nikhil (2012) "Municipal Disconnect: On Abject Water and Its Urban Infrastructures," *Ethnography* 13(4): 487–509.
Arendt, Hannah (1963) *Eichmann in Jerusalem: A Report on the Banality of Evil*. New York: Viking Press.
Barker, Joshua (2005) "Engineers and Political Dreams: Indonesia in the Satellite Age," *Current Anthropology* 46(5): 703–727.
Beniger, James R. (1986) *The Control Revolution: Technological and Economic Origins of Information Society*. Cambridge, MA and London: Harvard University Press.
Berg, Marc and Stefan Timmermans (2000) "Order and Their Others: On the Constitution of Universalities in Medical Work," *Configurations* 8(1): 31–61.
Blok, Anders, Moe Nakazora and Brit Ross Winthereik (2016) "Introduction: Infrastructuring Environments," *Science as Culture* 25(1): 1–22.
Boellstorff, Tom (2016) "For Whom the Ontology Turns: Theorizing the Digital Divide," *Current Anthropology*. Online First: DOI: 10.1086/687362.
Bowker, Geoffrey C. (1995) "Second Nature Once Removed: Time, Space and Representations," *Time and Society* 4(1): 47–66.
Bowker, Geoffrey C. and Susan Leigh Star (1999) *Sorting Things Out: Classification and Its Consequences*. Cambridge, MA and London: MIT Press.
Boyer, Dominic (2015) "Anthropology Electric," *Cultural Anthropology* 30(4): 531–539.
Callon, Michel and Bruno Latour (1981) "Unscrewing the Big Leviathan: How Actors Macrostructure Reality and How Sociologists Help Them do So," in K. Knorr-Cetina

and A. Cicourel (eds) *Advances in Social Theory and Methodology: Toward an Integration of Micro and Macro Sociologies*. London: Routledge & Kegan Paul, pp. 277–303.
Campbell, Jeremy M. (2012) "Between the Material and the Figural Road: The Incompleteness of Colonial Geographies in Amazonia," *Mobilities* 7(4): 481–500.
Carroll, Patrick (2006) *Science, Culture and Modern State Formation*. Berkeley, CA: University of California Press.
Carse, Ashley (2012) "Nature as Infrastructure: Making and Managing the Panama Watershed," *Social Studies of Science* 42(4): 539–563.
Chalfin, Brenda (2016) "'Wastelandia': Infrastructure and the Commonwealth of Waste in Urban Ghana," *Ethnos*. Online First: http://dx.doi.org/10.1080/00141844. 2015.1119174.
de Boeck, Filip (2011) "Inhabiting Ocular Ground: Kinshasa's Future in the Light of Congo's Spectral Urban Politics," *Cultural Anthropology* 26(2): 263–286.
de la Cadena, Marisol (2015) *Earth Beings: Ecologies of Practice Across Andean Worlds*. Durham, NC: Duke University Press,
Deleuze, Gilles and Felix Guattari (1983) *Anti-Oedipus: Capitalism and Schizophrenia*. London: Athlone.
Douglas, Mary (1966) *Purity and Danger: An Analysis of the Concepts of Pollution and Taboo*. London and New York: Routledge.
Edwards, Paul (2010) *A Vast Machine: Computer Models, Climate Data, and the Politics of Global Warming*. Cambridge, MA and London: MIT Press.
Elyachar, Julia (2010) "Phatic Labor, Infrastructure, and the Question of Empowerment in Cairo," *American Ethnologist* 37(3): 452–464.
Fennell, Catherine (2011) "'Project Heat' and Sensory Politics in Redeveloping Chicago Public Housing," *Ethnography* 12(1): 40–64.
Fisch, Michael (2013) "Tokyo's Commuter Train Suicides and the Society of Emergence," *Cultural Anthropology* 28(2): 320–343.
Foucault, Michel (1991) *Discipline and Punish: Birth of the Prison*. London: Penguin.
Gad, Christopher and Peter Lauritsen (2009) "Situated Surveillance: An Ethnographic Study of Fisheries Inspection in Denmark," *Surveillance and Society* 7(1): 49–57.
Galison, Peter (2005) "Removing Knowledge," in Bruno Latour and Peter Weibel (eds) *Making Things Public: Atmospheres of Democracy*. Cambridge, MA and London: MIT Press, pp. 590–602.
Graham, Stephen and Simon Marvin (2001) *Splintering Urbanism: Networked Infrastructures, Technological Mobilities and the Urban Condition*. London and New York: Routledge.
Haraway, Donna (1989) *Primate Visions: Gender, Race and Nature in the World of Modern Science*. New York and London: Routledge.
Haraway, Donna (1997) *Modest_Witness@Second_Millennium. Femaleman©_Meets_ Oncomouse^{TM}: Feminism and Technoscience*. New York: Routledge.
Harvey, Penny (2005) "The Materiality of State Effects: An Ethnography of a Road in the Peruvian Andes," in C. Krohn-Hansen and K. Nustad (eds) *State Formation: Anthropological Perspectives*. London: Pluto Press, pp. 216–247.
Harvey, Penny (2012) "The Topological Quality of Infrastructural Relations; An Ethnographic Approach," *Theory, Culture and Society* 29(4/5): 76–92.
Harvey, Penny (2016) "Waste Futures: Infrastructures and Political Experimentation in Southern Peru," *Ethnos* [OnlineFirst]. http://dx.doi.org/10.1080/00141844.2015. 1108351.

Harvey, Penny (2017) "Infrastructures In and Out of Time: The Promise of Roads in Contemporary Peru," in Nikhil Anand, Hannah Appel, and Akhil Gupta (eds) *The Promise of Infrastructure*. Durham, NC and London: Duke University Press.

Harvey, Penny and Hannah Knox (2015) *Roads: An Anthropology of Infrastructure and Expertise*. Ithaca, NY: Cornell University Press.

Harvey, Penny, Eleanor Conlin Casella, Gillian Evans, Christine McLean, Elizabeth Silva, Nicholas Thoburn and Kath Woodward (eds) (2013) *Objects and Materials: A Routledge Companion*. London: Routledge.

Howe, Cymene (2014) "Anthropocenic Ecoauthority: The Winds of Oaxaca," *Anthropological Quarterly* 87(2): 381–404.

Hughes, Thomas P. (1983) *Networks of Power: Electric Supply Systems in the US, England and Germany, 1880–1930*. Baltimore, MD: Johns Hopkins University Press.

Hyslop, John (1984) *Inka Road System*. New York: Academic Press.

Jensen, Casper Bruun (2007) "Infrastructural Fractals: Revisiting the Micro-Macro Distinction in Social Theory," *Environment and Planning D: Society and Space* 25(5): 832–850.

Jensen, Casper Bruun (2014) "Continuous Variations: The Conceptual and the Empirical in STS," *Science, Technology and Human Values* 39(2): 192–213.

Jensen, Casper Bruun (2015) "Experimenting with Political Materials: Environmental Infrastructures and Ontological Transformations," *Distinktion: Scandinavian Journal of Social Theory* 16(1): 17–30.

Jensen, Casper Bruun (2016) "Pipe Dreams: Sewage Infrastructures and Activity Trails in Phnom Penh," *Ethnos*. Online First: http://dx.doi.org/10.1080/00141844.2015.1107608.

Jensen, Casper Bruun and Atsuro Morita (2015) "Infrastructures as Ontological Experiments," *Engaging Science, Technology and Society* 1: 81–87.

Jensen, Casper Bruun and Brit Ross Winthereik (2013) *Monitoring Movements in Development Aid: Recursive Partnerships and Infrastructures*. Cambridge, MA and London: MIT Press.

Kockelman, Paul (2010) "Enemies, Parasites, and Noise: How to Take up Residence in a System without Becoming a Term in It," *Journal of Linguistic Anthropology* 20(2): 406–421.

Kristeva, Julia (1984) *Powers of Horror*. New York: Columbia University Press.

Lampland, Martha and Susan Leigh Star (eds) (2009) *Standards and Their Stories: How Quantifying, Classifying, and Formalizing Practices Shape Everyday Life*. Ithaca, NY and London: Cornell University Press.

Larkin, Brian (2013) "The Politics and Poetics of Infrastructure," *Annual Review of Anthropology* 42: 327–343.

Latour, Bruno (1996) *Aramis, or the Love of Technology*. Cambridge, MA: Harvard University Press.

Lea, Tess (2014) *Darwin*. Sydney: NewSouth.

Lea, Tess and Paul Pholeros (2010) "This Is Not a Pipe: The Treacheries of Indigenous Housing," *Public Culture* 22(1): 187–209.

Mitchell, Timothy (2013) *Carbon Democracy: Political Power in the Age of Oil*. New York: Verso.

Mol, Annemarie (2008) *The Logic of Care: Health and the Problem of Patient Choice*. New York and London: Routledge.

Morita, Atsuro (2014) "The Ethnographic Machine: Experimenting with Context and Comparison in Strathernian Ethnography," *Science, Technology and Human Values* 39(2): 214–235.
Morita, Atsuro (2016) "Multispecies Infrastructure: Infrastructural Inversion and Involutionary Entanglements in the Chao Phraya Delta, Thailand," *Ethnos*. Online First: http://dx.doi.org/10.1080/00141844.2015.1119175.
Nimmo, Richie (2010) *Milk, Modernity and the Making of the Human: Purifying the Social*. London: Routledge.
Riles, Annelise (2000) *The Network Inside Out*. Ann Arbor, MI: University of Michigan Press.
Rottenburg, Richard (2009) *Far-Fetched Facts: A Parable of Development Aid*. Cambridge, MA and London: MIT Press.
Ruppert, Evelyn, Penny Harvey, Celia Lury, Adrian Mackenzie, Ruth McNally, Stephanie Alice Baker, Yannis Kallianos and Camilla Lewis (2015) "Socialising Big Data: From Concept to Practice," CRESC Working Paper no. 138. Available at: www.cresc.ac.uk/medialibrary/workingpapers/wp138.pdf.
Schivelbusch, Wolfgang (1977) *The Railway Journey: The Industrialization of Time and Space in the 19th Century*. Berkeley and Los Angeles: University of California Press.
Scott, James C. (1998) *Seeing Like a State: How Certain Schemes to Improve the Human Condition Have Failed*. New Haven, CT: Yale University Press.
Serres, Michel (1991) *Rome: The Book of Foundations*. Stanford, CA: Stanford University Press.
Serres, Michel and Bruno Latour (1995) *Conversations on Science, Culture, and Time*. Ann Arbor, MI: University of Michigan Press.
Simone, AbdouMaliq (2004) "People as Infrastructure: Intersecting Fragments in Johannesburg," *Public Culture* 16(3): 407–429.
Sneath, David (2009) "Reading the Signs by Lenin's Light: Development, Divination and Metonymic Fields in Mongolia," *Ethnos* 74(1): 72–90.
Star, Susan Leigh (1991) "Power, Technology and the Phenomenology of Conventions – on Being Allergic to Onions," in John Law (ed.) *A Sociology of Monster: Essays on Power, Technology and Domination*, London: Routledge, pp. 26–56.
Star, Susan Leigh (1995) "The Politics of Formal Representation: Wizards, Gurus, and Organizational Complexity," in Susan Leigh Star (ed.) *Ecologies of Knowledge: Work and Politics in Science and Technology*. Albany, NY: State University of New York Press, pp. 88–119.
Star, Susan Leigh and Karen Ruhleder (1996) "Steps Towards an Ecology of Infrastructure: Design and Access for Large Information Spaces," *Information Systems Research* 7(1): 111–134.
Strathern, Marilyn (1991) *Partial Connections*. Lanham, MD: Rowman & Littlefield.
Strum, Shirley and Bruno Latour (1987) "Redefining the Social Link: From Baboons to Humans," *Social Science Information* 26(4): 783–802.
Tsing, Anna L. (2005) *Friction: An Ethnography of Global Connection*. Princeton, NJ: Princeton University Press.
Vaughan, Diana (1996) *The Challenger Launch Decision: Risky Technology, Culture, and Deviance at Nasa*. Chicago, IL: University of Chicago Press.
Verran, Helen (2011) "Imagining Nature Politics in the Era of Australia's Emerging Markets in Environmental Services Interventions," *The Sociological Review* 59(3): 411–431.

von Schnitzler, Antina (2008) "Citizenship Prepaid: Water, Calculability, and Technopolitics in South Africa," *Journal of Southern African Studies* 34(4): 899–917.
Winner, Langdon (1986) *The Whale and the Reactor: A Search for Limits in an Age of High Technology*. Chicago, IL: University of Chicago Press.

Part I
Development infrastructures

This section on "development infrastructures" starts from the entanglements of infrastructure, development and modernization. Ashley Carse's "keyword" analysis of "development infrastructures" tracks the diverse ways in which the infrastructure concept has been associated with technological, social and economic development. The term, variously dubbed as "promiscuous," "plastic," or even as "meaningless" and "obscure officialese" carries considerable historical baggage.

Such baggage was what made such words interesting to Raymond Williams (1976) in his research into the "vocabulary of culture and society." Infrastructure was not among his original selection but it meets his criteria: commonly used, polysemous, categorical, contested and clustered with other words. Carse's analysis of the English-speaking context shows how "infrastructure" clusters with "development," "system," "network," "modern," "capital," and "investment." This clustering is visible in the other chapters but, as we might expect, each chapter, and each setting (Paraguay, Peru, Australia, and Laos) produces further baggage and modes of extension that exceed any categorical or national framing. Yet this baggage is not random, since "development" qualifies the infrastructural and in all cases directs analysis to issues of temporality, of power, of inter-dependence and of disruption.

All the chapters in this section have something to say about the temporality of infrastructural investment, the transformational intent, the promise of improvement, and the complications that arise as technical design is disrupted by other forces, as systems interact, and as partial connections disrupt dreams of effortless flow. Thus we approach development infrastructures as sites of investment that bring together states, capital and particular modes of expectation. The infrastructural investments that the chapters in this section discuss are investments that point or gesture (see Weszkalnys this volume) towards a future in the making and at the same time reveal the gaps between expectations and the compromised or unexpected outcomes of these potent socio-material reconfigurations.

Kregg Hetherington approaches the question of temporality directly in his examination of the future perfect as the tense of infrastructure. Drawing from his research on this history of land reform in Paraguay, the chapter examines how the linear aesthetic that marked the surveyor's transformation of land in the marking of boundaries was echoed by a linear temporality positing a move away from the anachronous and unwanted peasant past to a desired, more civilized, future. The future perfect of infrastructural development implies regimes of differential visibility. What would the future look like? What should be seen and what should disappear? The future perfect thus exhibits infrastructures in an ethical mode that designates a future in which some relations will flourish and others disappear. In the Paraguayan case, peasant farmers have long occupied the space of those who preceded the new future and a time that had to be overcome. Indigenous peoples were long since erased from this national topos, no longer visible on the timeline of national emergence. The arrival of soybean mega-farms brought new surveying techniques, GPS systems that displaced the previous survey methods that had required engagement between the land, the surveyor, and peasant farmers. The peasant farmers now fear that they, like the indigenous peoples before them, no longer have a place in the unfolding history of Paraguay. In response they have begun to block the very surveying processes, which, until now, offered hope that straight lines and demarcated landholdings would route them towards an improved future. Now they hold out for the right to exist apart rather than be swallowed up. These are relations of life and death that are also addressed centrally in Tess Lea's chapter.

Lea's study looks at road development on Groote Eylandt off the coast of Arnhem Land, in the Northern Territory of Australia. These roads are built in the places were aboriginal people have been dispossessed, their land taken for the mining of rich resources, and for military purposes. The infrastructures reveal shady connections, visible but indirect, between global trade, the military protection of that trade, and the extractive mining on which both the trade and the military depend.

Manganese is what they take from Groote Eylandt. This material makes steel pliable and is deemed a basic material, designated of strategic importance to the US economy. The roads that aboriginal communities are given in return for the destruction of their land have less resilient material qualities. They quickly become "past tense" entities, their surfaces rapidly degrading and contributing to the list of fatalities that they initially promised to preclude. Indigenous labor in Australia, as in Paraguay (and many other parts of the world) becomes increasingly irrelevant to the key sites of accumulation – financial markets and multinational extraction industries. In these circumstances the infrastructural return – the possibilities for some kind of civic integration – also becomes less "necessary." Thus Lea, like Hetherington, points to a new infrastructural topography where a remote region of Australia is "at once at the margins of development and at the epicenter of contemporary capital."

The state has a central role in the provisioning and the legitimation of where and how infrastructural provisioning occurs. However, state agency is entangled with other interests. Lea looks particularly at supra-state and military interests, Hetherington at the ways in which agri-business can shape a national territory. Penny Harvey's chapter by contrast introduces discussion of infrastructural provision in times of state decentralization, where conflicting scales of autonomy and integration come to the fore. The ambiguous rescaling capacities of infrastructural systems are discussed in an ethnographic account of a sanitation system that fails to materialize in the southern Peruvian Andes. What does appear, in and through the efforts to finance the flows of water and sewage, are administrative structures that integrate but in ways that effectively erode local autonomy. Thus new connections and disconnections appear simultaneously, from within a project that seemed to promise something else entirely. The study shows how instruments of transparent planning deployed to support the emergence of coherent systems in response to public need, proceed by a deliberate down-playing (obfuscation and transcendence) of all that does not fit, the unresolved, and often unresolvable material and social differences of which all such systems are ultimately composed. Corruption emerges as the idiom most commonly deployed to express why it is that the promise of infrastructural provision so often fails to materialize. In spite of "failure," however, a new ecology of connections also appeared, and people were beginning to work out how to live with what it offered.

Miki Namba expands on this in her chapter. A development expert from the Ministry of Public Works and Transport told her that there is no such thing as failure in any infrastructure construction project. There are, after all, no finished projects. Projects (the linear projection of a path towards a more or a less specified future) are always ongoing. The tense of infrastructures is thus not only the future perfect, or the past tense of abandonment, but also the present continuous, the ongoing unfolding of possibilities. Namba looks at infrastructural fetishism in Vientiane, Laos. Her chapter describes the attempts by city authorities to create an infrastructural effect, a surface or a stage on which they could perform their role as hosts to the Tenth ASEAN summit, the annual meeting of the members of the Associations of Southeast Asian Nations. The hosting of this meeting was intended to consolidate membership in the growing economies of SE Asia and to build diplomatic status and credibility with trade partners and potential inward investors. The infrastructural initiative was a push for "contemporaneous modernity," assumed as a process of temporal alignment or catch-up and taking the form of new buildings, areas of recreation, and roads. These initiatives, though they often did not operate as intended, were both full of symbols and politics *and* generative of what Namba calls scattered urbanization. Vientiane has not quite become a modern city, but it continues a dramatic process of urban transformation set in motion by infrastructure.

Carse's keyword essay focuses on the productive ambiguity of the term infrastructure and points to one specific tension that is particularly pertinent to our discussion of development infrastructures. "Infrastructure," he notes, entered popular usage from French as an engineering term. However, it also arrived from France by another route, carried along by social theory. Throughout this volume we are concerned with the ways in which empirical and conceptual understandings of infrastructure are folded together and separated out. Carse alerts us to the double movement of infrastructure, which appears both as a collective term (mirroring the modernist inclination to singularize) and as inherently heterogeneous (mirrored in the ethnographic move to pluralize). The tension between singularity and multiplicity is central to all the chapters in this section, reminding us that this relational tension is less of a limit point and more a point of departure.

Reference

Williams, Raymond (1976) *Keywords: A Vocabulary of Culture and Society*. London: Croom Helm.

2 Keyword: Infrastructure

How a humble French engineering term shaped the modern world

Ashley Carse

In common usage, the keyword infrastructure and its non-English variants (infraestructura, infrastruktura, infrastruktur, imprastraktura, infrastruttura) refer to the vast, complex, and changing systems that support modern societies and economies. The *Oxford English Dictionary*'s (2015) definition begins broadly – "a collective term for the subordinate parts of an undertaking; substructure, foundation" – and then becomes specific, referring to "the permanent installations forming a basis for military operations, as airfields, naval bases, training establishments, etc." The definition points to two important dimensions of the word. First, it is a collective term: a singular noun that, like system and network, denotes a plurality of integrated parts. Second, those collective parts are understood to support some higher-order project. As the prefix *infra* – meaning beneath, below, or within – suggests, infrastructure diverges from system and network by suggesting relationships of depth or hierarchy. Here, we see the legacy of the word's origins in nineteenth-century French civil engineering. When it was adopted in English in the early twentieth century, infrastructure referred primarily to the organizational work required before railroad tracks could be laid: either establishing a roadbed of substrate material (literally beneath the tracks) or other work functionally prior to laying tracks like building bridges, embankments, and tunnels. In the post-war era, the word was adopted in new projects of spatial integration, particularly supranational military coordination and international development. By the late twentieth century, the word was in common use.

In this chapter, I examine the changing use of the word infrastructure in English, particularly as it relates to international development theory and practice. This is no easy task because the word development is also complex. Nevertheless, its etymology and conceptual role in concerted programs of social, economic, and technological change has been explored elsewhere (Cooper 2010; Rist 2014). There is, to my knowledge, no analogous study of the infrastructure concept that is thorough and recent (cf. Batt 1984). The scope of this chapter prohibits a comprehensive study. Thus, my more modest goal is to provide a broad historical overview and analysis of the word's changing usage. By tracking this keyword, we will see connections, overlaps, and divergences among fields like engineering, military coordination, economics, logistics, and social theory that reshaped the human condition in the twentieth century and reverberate in the present.

Historian Rosalind Williams (2012) has described infrastructure as a promiscuous term that has taken on new meanings shaped by the very historical phenomena it describes. Since it was adopted in English in the early twentieth century, the usage of the word infrastructure has gradually expanded and its meanings have multiplied. In the twenty-first century, the collective noun refers to the subordinate parts of many projects, from the built systems that move water, sewage, people, and power to components assembled under the rubrics of security, information, health, finance, political mobilization, and environmental management. What should we make of infrastructure's ascent? Infrastructure might be characterized as a plastic word (Poerksen 1995) that has been stripped of its former specialized meaning and can now fit nearly any circumstance. Seen in this way, the term's vagueness is not a weakness, but central to its utility in a wide variety of projects (Jensen and Winthereik 2013: 13). The word infrastructure has long been the subject of scorn for the same reason. "By the middle of the century," lexicographer John Ayto writes, "it had already acquired its bad reputation as a jargon word" (2006: 67). In light of infrastructure's widespread usage in recent decades, this undercurrent of anxiety makes its etymology even more interesting, because negative labels like "jargon" and "meaningless" fail to explain the historical conjunctures in which the word became useful and contested.

We might understand the emergence of the infrastructure concept as an event in thought (Collier and Lakoff 2015: 20; Foucault 2005: 9). Its ascent indexes a form of calculative reason (Mitchell 2002) that, from specialized origins, has come to organize social expectations, everyday experiences, and public discourses about the proper relationships among economy, development, governance, and technology. Infrastructural reason informs the organization of planetary transportation, communication, and logistics networks that are modular in form and organized around managerial and technical standards (Barry 2006; Cowen 2014; Easterling 2014). It also flags the modernist desire to render social and environmental heterogeneity manageable and amenable to standardized solutions.

Infrastructure as a keyword

What is a keyword? For Raymond Williams, a keyword essay is a "record of an inquiry into a vocabulary" (1983: 15) that encourages reflection on the historical baggage carried by our language, particularly the multiple and contested meanings of common, socially significant words. Keyword essays often use *Oxford English Dictionary* definitions as a point of departure, but, unlike dictionary entries, they emphasize discontinuity and conflict rather than universal meanings, mapping "fissures and fault lines" over time (Burgett and Hendler 2014: 2). Following Williams and his successors, we might say that keywords have five salient dimensions.[1] First, they are *currently and commonly used*, typically with both technical and popular usages. Second, they are *polysemous*: their meanings change over time and across space. Third, they are *categorical*, designating cultural concepts and practices; so they tend to be abstract rather than concrete. Fourth, keywords are *contested* and deployed in public discussions and debates. Fifth, they emerge with – and are defined in relation to – *clusters of interrelated words*. As we will see, infrastructure meets these criteria and clusters with development, system, network, modern, capital, and investment.

Why write a keyword entry for infrastructure? The histories of keywords index social shifts. In the introduction to *Keywords*, Raymond Williams explains why he began working on the project. He served in the Second World War between 1941 and 1945. Returning to England, he found a "new and strange world." New words were in use and the meanings of old words had changed. Williams seized on the word culture, which was suddenly being used to refer to a "particular *way of life*" (1983: 12). The word was moving from the specialized terminology of academic anthropology to the broad and variable usage of a popular vocabulary (1983: 14). Something similar has happened with infrastructure over the past few decades, a shift that can be seen through the increasingly unbounded use of the word as well as the criticism and resistance that its ambiguity has provoked.

The meanings of keywords multiply as they move from specialized communities of practice where usage is technical into broader domains. They begin as neologisms, their instability suggested by quotation marks and trailing definitions. If and when those shackles are removed, their meanings broaden and, in many cases, become contested. The keyword infrastructure underwent precisely such a transformation in the twentieth century as it transitioned from a technical engineering term to a generic term used by bureaucrats pursuing projects of spatial integration to a word describing a wide range of projects.

A specialist term: infrastructure emerges in the early twentieth century

The *Oxford English Dictionary* tells us that the word infrastructure came to English from French in 1927, citing an early reference in *Chambers's Journal* to a French railroad project: "The tunnels, bridges, culverts, and 'infrastructure' work generally of the Ax to Bourg-Madame line have been completed." Although 1927 is often cited as the first use in English, the word actually appears in late-nineteenth-century English-language writing about railroad projects in French- and Spanish-speaking countries (Castro 1893: 25–27; Holt 1888: 342; *Railway Engineer* 1889: 39; *Railway Times* 1879: 168).[2] Regardless of when the word was adopted, the passage above underlines a key point: infrastructure was initially an organizational and accounting term used to distinguish the construction work that was literally conducted *beneath* unlaid tracks (roadbeds) or was otherwise organizationally *prior* to them (surveys, plans, bridges, tunnels, embankments) from the *superstructure* of roads, train stations, and workshops that was situated *above* or constructed *after* the tracks.

30   Ashley Carse

English-speakers borrowed the word infrastructure from French around the same time as a group of transportation-related nouns that also included garage (1902), limousine (1902), metro (1904), marque (a make of car, 1906), and couchette (railroad car with sleeper berths, 1920) (Schultz 2012: 169–170). The technological changes of the period, including aviation and automobiles, required a new vocabulary and terms were adopted from French, France being a leader in science and technology (Ayto 2013). However, the community who used the new word infrastructure in English – unlike some of the other words adopted at the time – was composed mainly of professional engineers and those writing about engineering. It is not surprising, then, that the word does not appear in general English-language dictionaries of the period.[3] Moreover, its use was limited even within the engineering community in the early twentieth century. It primarily circulated in transnational conversations concerning transportation projects – particularly railroads, but also navigation and aviation projects – across English, French, and, to a lesser degree, Spanish. During this period, governments worldwide aimed to develop urban, industrial societies through the construction and management of roads, waterworks, and power grids associated with social progress and the modernist impulse to universalize, systematize, and standardize. At that time, however, such large engineering projects were not categorized as infrastructure but described as systems, networks, or internal improvements.

The word system had been used in English since the seventeenth century, often with reference to a set of things or parts that are somehow arranged, connected, or organized to form a complex whole. In its varied usages, the constituent parts of a system could be immaterial (ideas, doctrines, principles) or material (biological, geological, technological).[4] For example, one might speak of a railroad system made up of connected branches. The word network was used in the same way, but also referenced a specific form (netlike, made up of wires, threads, or lines) – a type of "complex system" that, in the nineteenth century, included transportation lines such as canals, rivers, and railroads.[5] Thus, when infrastructure was adopted in English, what it shared with the more expansive words system and network was its general emphasis on the integration of parts and a specific connection to railroads. A third, more specific term, internal improvements, was also used in the United States in the nineteenth century to refer to national integration through the construction of projects like roads, turnpikes, and canals (Larson 2001).

As used in engineering, the word infrastructure, unlike system or network, suggested a relationship of depth or hierarchy, a form of calculative reason that was (and remains) useful for institutions seeking to demarcate responsibility and investment. For example, in French railroad projects dating to the mid-nineteenth century, the infrastructure portion of a project (below/before) was built by the state and the superstructure (above/after) constructed by private contractors.[6] The above/below distinction was "a useful compromise by its simplicity," as one report put it (International Congress of Navigation 1931). After the Second World War, the allocation of investment and responsibility across institutions would involve organization and coordination at more extensive spatial scales.

A generic term: infrastructure's rise in the post-war years

In the post-war era, infrastructure was both an ascendant term and an increasingly abstract concept. Moving beyond engineering, it took on new meanings through the intertwined projects of supranational military coordination and international economic development. Infrastructure was more than a word. It was world-making. Military projects and economic theories were enacted through the coordination of physical installations shaped by specific visions and theories of political and socioeconomic organization.

NATO inaugurated its Common Infrastructure Programme in 1949. Lord Ismay, NATO's Secretary General at the time, noted that the word had been borrowed from engineering and suggested that its vague meaning was advantageous. He wrote:

> It has been adopted by NATO as a generic term to denote all those fixed installations which are necessary for the effective deployment and operations of modern armed forces, for example airfields, signal communications, military headquarters, fuel tanks and pipelines, radar warning and navigation aid stations, port installations, and so forth.
>
> (Ismay 1954)

The "common" military platform was to be funded through contributions by NATO member countries. As Ismay's framing ("all those fixed installations which are necessary") suggests, the word infrastructure's generic nature made it an inclusive category amenable to a variety of open-ended projects in which the subordinate parts to be integrated were defined incrementally.

As soon as the word infrastructure appeared on the global stage, the criticism began. Politicians and pundits in the English-speaking world characterized it as a bureaucratic neologism of suspicious European origin. In 1951, the *New York Times* published two columns on new government jargon – "gobbledygook" – linking infrastructure to the creation of NATO (Krock 1951). US secretary of state Dean Acheson called the word's appearance "baffling." "One thing I can't explain," he wrote, "is how these facilities [roads, communications, buildings that accompany the construction of military facilities] came to be called by the name 'infrastructure'" (*New York Times* 1952). Around the same time, Winston Churchill denounced "the usual jargon about 'the infrastructure of supra-national authority'" within the context of a debate about creating a pan-European authority for steel and coal production. (This economic integration plan would precipitate the creation of the European Economic Community in 1958 and European Union in 1993.) "The original authorship," he continued, "is obscure, but it may well be that these words 'infra' and 'supra' have been introduced into our current political parlance by the band of intellectual highbrows anxious to impress British labour ..." (Churchill 1950; Langworth 2008: 53–54). By 1953, the *Dictionary of New Words in English* included a seemingly derogatory entry for infrastructure: "n. *Officialese*. The understructure or substructure" (Berg 1953). Making explicit reference to the Churchill quotation above, this early dictionary entry's categorization of the new word as "officialese" – a vague, convoluted, and pretentious type of bureaucratic jargon – anticipated the gradual but uneasy acceptance of infrastructure in the language.

Although infrastructure's status as a bureaucratic neologism was the focus of initial confusion and scorn, its generic character was precisely what made it useful for military and economic integration. Many of the installations built through the NATO program – bridges, tunnels, warehouses, air fields, and pipelines – would have been familiar to engineers of the previous generation as physical artifacts, but what made post-war "infrastructure" different was the supranational orientation of its conception, design, and coordination. Organized around relationships of depth or levels of organization, this usage extended the concept's history as a heuristic for coordinating projects to new areas.

The modern international development era arguably began after the Second World War, even though it echoed colonial civilizing missions and earlier twentieth-century programs (Cooper 2010). European colonists claimed a moral obligation to help peoples in Africa, Asia, and the Americas and often saw science and technology as a measure of and catalyst for social progress (Adas 1989). The institutional groundwork for development as a concerted form of intervention was laid in 1944 and 1945 with the founding of the United Nations, International Monetary Fund, and International Bank for Reconstruction and Development, the precursor to the World Bank. In his 1949 inauguration speech, US president Harry Truman famously called for a program to bring about "the improvement and growth of underdeveloped areas," emphasizing the potential of US scientific and technical expertise to raise standards of living overseas. This was, notably, the same year that NATO inaugurated its Common Infrastructure Programme. Rather than simply renaming an existing condition – poverty – the development imaginary was a new way of seeing that defined most of the world's peoples by what they supposedly lacked: development (Escobar 1995). Infrastructure would be central to defining development.

Development economics, the professional field associated with post-war development, was dominated by modernization theory, a standardized approach to national development modeled on an idealized version of US history (Gilman 2003). Development institutions emphasized investment in big infrastructure projects like highways, irrigation systems, and electrical networks – rather than education, health, or social sectors – to accelerate the modernization process and create the conditions for economic "take-off" (Rostow 1960). As a material substrate for and symbolic manifestation of that vision, the installations called infrastructure or social overhead capital were supposed to precipitate industrialization and growth. More than 60 % of World Bank loans went to such projects in the 1950s and 1960s (Stein 2008: 10–14). During the

1960s – known as the "development decade" – large dams, a concrete icon of modernization and state power, were built at the rate of more than one per day worldwide (McNeil 2000: 159). The focus on infrastructure investment dovetailed with the methodological nationalism of the Bretton Woods system, which assumed that all countries needed the same types of large projects to catalyze growth and that they could be conceived and implemented from afar.

Infrastructure was Cold War politics by other means. Under modernization theory, the geography of infrastructure investment often reflected the priorities (e.g. export-led growth) of the orthodox economic development model: roads, rails, and pipelines often linked sites of resource extraction directly to cities and ports (Ferguson 2006; Mitchell 2011). Infrastructure projects were considered steps along the path to a modern national economy engaged in international trade. This idea – that infrastructure enacted social and economic theories – was, of course, not isolated to capitalist development (Scott 1998). Under state socialism, a rival form of modernism, the Soviet Union built infrastructures at home and abroad that concretized its priorities and values (Collier 2012; Humphrey 2005; Schwenkel 2015). Across the so-called Third World, infrastructures became the "sinew of development" (Sneddon 2012), material manifestations of Cold War geopolitical struggle.

A plastic word: infrastructure enters the mainstream

In the 1960s, infrastructure appeared for the first time in general English dictionaries. One early entry defined it as "*n:* foundation, groundwork; *esp.:* the permanent installations required for military purposes" (*Webster's Seventh New Collegiate Dictionary* 1963) and others followed suit, also focusing on military installations (*Random House Dictionary* 1967, 1969). Over time, it was less frequently placed between quotation marks, preceded by phrases like "what experts call" or defined in text. By the 1970s, dictionaries defined the word more broadly as "basic" or "essential" facilities for a community, state, system, structure, organization, or undertaking (*Webster's Collegiate Dictionary* 1973; *Supplement to the Oxford English Dictionary* 1976). In the dictionaries of the period, military coordination was dropped entirely or became secondary to the more expansive definition.

Infrastructure also appeared in economics dictionaries of the 1960s and 1970s, where it was treated as a synonym of social overhead capital, meaning capital goods like roads, schools, hospitals, and public parks that are broadly available to the public and typically provided by the government. One early entry defined infrastructure as "The foundation underlying a nation's economy (transportation and communication systems, power facilities, and other public services) upon which the degree of economic activity (industry, trade, etc.) depends" (*McGraw-Hill Dictionary of Modern Economics* 1965). In development economics, infrastructure was associated with national-level development and its construction was presented as a state responsibility, rather than site of private investment, due to high initial cost and long payoff period (ibid.). This language echoed debates around the division of institutional responsibility and investment in railroad engineering projects decades before.

In the 1960s and 1970s, modernization theory came under fire. Critics argued that, despite massive infrastructure investments, most underdeveloped countries never "took off." Radical theorists pushed the critique further, arguing that infrastructure built to facilitate industrial, capitalist, export-led growth was part of the problem, not the solution, because it facilitated extraction and dependency (Frank 1969). In the wake of these critiques, development economists began to define infrastructure as more than capital embedded in technical projects; it referred to "intangible assets" like health, education, social attitudes, industrial skills, and administrative experience (Gilpin 1973; Bannock, Baxter, and Rees 1977). This paralleled a paradigm shift in development practice, which moved away from the grandiose infrastructure projects of modernization theory to focus on poverty alleviation and meeting basic needs (e.g. Dag Hammarskjöld Foundation 1975).

Even as the word infrastructure seemed to outgrow its military roots, that legacy bubbled beneath the surface of emerging infrastructural forms of economic organization. The 1960s marked the beginning of the logistics revolution and an attendant shift in the organization of economic space (Cowen 2014). Logistics, like infrastructure, is a testament to the intertwined histories of military coordination and economic development. It began as a military science for moving soldiers, food, and fuel to the front (ibid.: 24–31). Business logistics was infrastructural in its logic, insomuch as it sought to add value through the integration of supply chains by conceptualizing production and distribution as a single system (ibid.: 34–35). The logistics revolution reworked global economic geographies and made the infrastructures of transnational corporate supply chains important spatial forms of development and military security (ibid.: 53–90). The logistics revolution also had implications for how infrastructure was conceptualized in development practice. For example, the World Bank prioritized investment in infrastructure designed to increase countries' capabilities to meet the needs of production and logistics companies (rather than domestic industry) and ranked countries in terms of their logistics systems (ibid.: 56–61).

As the word infrastructure entered common usage, commentators worried about its promiscuity. Was it "losing its conceptual rigor" (Batt 1984: 3) as it was extended from transportation, communication, and other physical installations to health, education, and social organization? Had it become meaningless? Indeed, by 1982, the term was sufficiently common that President Ronald Reagan described his foreign policy objective as fostering "the infrastructure of democracy, the system of a free press, unions, political parties, universities, which allows a people to choose their own way ..." (quoted in Batt 1984: 5).

Conclusion: infrastructure in social theory

What are we talking about when we talk about infrastructure? Given the word's ubiquity in public and scholarly discourse, I have argued that understanding its genealogy is important because, as Raymond Williams wrote of keywords generally (1983, 15), historical problems of meaning are bound up with the contemporary problems we use them to discuss. This is a useful point for those thinking about infrastructure and social complexity to keep in mind.

Even as infrastructure – once a humble French engineering term – began to appear in general English-language dictionaries in the 1960s, it re-entered English via another Francophone tributary: social theory. The post-war decades were a high-water mark for "structure" – and, by extension, infrastructure – in the social sciences and humanities. Like the arrival of French transportation terms in the early twentieth century, the use of infrastructure in Anglophone social theory highlights the influence of Francophone scholarship. The approaches gathered under the banner of structuralism varied greatly, but shared the philosophical assumption that variation observable in the phenomenal world could be analyzed in terms of *deep* and abiding structures, whether linguistic (Saussure 1959), cognitive (Levi-Strauss 1966), or economic. In late-twentieth-century Marxism, infrastructure was generally synonymous with the base (the means and relations of production), as opposed to a superstructure of law, politics, ideology, and culture. For Louis Althusser (1971), the infrastructure was the "edifice" that, in the last instance, determines what happens in the "upper 'floors'" of the superstructure. The 1980s saw the wave of structuralism break on the shores of post-structuralist critique and a turn to agency and practice theory. As popular usage expanded, infrastructure receded in social theory.

Several decades later, infrastructure is back, but in a different way. Moving away from theories of deep structure, social scientists and humanists analyze the mix of materials, practices, and meanings that comprise what we call infrastructures. In anthropology, the key analytical move has been to open up the black box of infrastructure to analyze social relations (Elyachar 2010; Simone 2004), political forms (Anand 2011; Harvey 2005) and environmental concerns (Carse 2014; Morita 2016). We have learned that infrastructures ideally operate in the experiential background of modern life (Edwards 2003), though not in practice across much of the world (Donovan 2015; Furlong 2014). Conceptualized in relational terms (Star and Ruhleder 1996), infrastructures are woven into the fabric of society: they are situated, heterogeneous, and quotidian. But this important corrective to previous modes of analysis – let's call it flattening infrastructure – comes with its own potential analytical opportunity costs. It can lead us to neglect the *infra* in infrastructure: the logics of depth and hierarchy that manifest in design, management, and maintenance.

In conclusion, I argue, building on Bill Maurer's (2005) call for a lateral anthropology, that we study infrastructures as both abstractions and material assemblages. What made this keyword so useful in post-war military and economic coordination was arguably both its conceptual plasticity and the undeniable materiality of its common referents like roads, pipes, rails, and cables. As a form of calculative reason, infrastructure promises to collect a heterogeneous, changing group of elements "beneath" some higher-order goal. Following Madeline Akrich's (1992) call for the de-scription of technological objects, it makes analytic sense to tack back and forth between the "insides" and "outsides" of infrastructures – between the realities projected by their organizers and the social worlds in which materials are assembled. Infrastructure studies might locate this double movement – the modernist move to standardize and the anthropological move to pluralize – in the same analytical frame, focusing ethnographic and historical attention on sites of tension and mismatch.

Acknowledgments

Many thanks to Kevin Donovan and Christopher Jones for their smart and constructive comments on earlier versions of this chapter. Research and writing were supported by a National Science Foundation Postdoctoral Fellowship (Award #1257333).

Notes

1 The following characteristics come from the website for the Keywords project based at the University of Pittsburgh, see http://keywords.pitt.edu/whatis.html. Accessed 13 May 2015.
2 At that time, the word was relatively new in French, as well (Ayto 1999: 147). French accountants and engineers seem to have begun using it in the 1850s and 1860s with reference to railroad construction expenditures incurred before the tracks were laid (Hofmann 2014: 255).
3 This claim is based on a review of the *Century Dictionary*, Funk and Wagnall's *New Standard Dictionary*, Murray's *Oxford English Dictionary*, Richardson's *New Dictionary*, *A Thesaurus Dictionary of the English Language*, *Webster's Collegiate Dictionary*, and *Webster's New International Dictionary*.
4 See definitions of "system" in *Concise Oxford Dictionary of Current English* 1935: 1242; *Shorter Oxford English Dictionary* 1936: 2115–2116) and its etymology as discussed in Barnhart 1995: 790.
5 See, for example, the definition of "network" in the *Shorter Oxford English Dictionary* 1936: 1322).
6 For example: "[t]he infrastructure which comprises earthworks and bridges should be carried out by the French Colonial Government…the remainder of the work should be given to a Company who would contract" (Holt 1888). During the construction of the Paris metro, the city planned to construct the infrastructure, with the superstructure to be built by a private company (*Scientific American* (Supplement) 1899).

References

Adas, Michael (1989) *Machines as the Measure of Men: Science, Technology, and Ideologies of Western Dominance*. Ithaca, NY: Cornell University Press.
Akrich, Madeleine (1992) "The De-Scription of Technical Objects," in Weibe E. Bijker and John Law (eds) *Shaping Technology/Building Society: Studies in Sociotechnical Change*. Cambridge, MA: MIT Press, pp. 205–224.

Althusser, Louis (1971) "Ideology and Ideological State Apparatuses," in *Lenin and Philosophy and Other Essays.* New York: Monthly Review Press.
Anand, Nikhil (2011) "Pressure: The Politechnics of Water Supply in Mumbai." *Cultural Anthropology* 26(4): 542–564.
Ayto, John (1999) *Twentieth Century Words.* Oxford: Oxford University Press.
Ayto, John (2006) *Movers and Shakers: A Chronology of Words That Shaped Our Age.* Oxford: Oxford University Press.
Ayto, John (2013) "Twentieth Century English: An Overview," in *Oxford English Dictionary.* http://public.oed.com/aspects-of-english/english-in-time/twentieth-century-english-an-overview/.
Bannock, Graham, R. E. Baxter, and Ray Rees (eds) (1977) "Infrastructure," in *Penguin Dictionary of Economics.* London and New York: Allen Lane/Viking Press.
Barnhart, Robert K. (ed.) (1995) "System," in *Barnhart Concise Dictionary of Etymology.* New York: Harper Collins.
Barry, Andrew (2006) "Technological Zones." *European Journal of Social Theory* 9(2): 239–253.
Batt, William H. (1984) "Infrastructure: Etymology and Import." *Journal of Professional Issues in Engineering* 110(1): 1–6.
Berg, Paul C. (1953) *A Dictionary of New Words in English.* London: George Allen & Unwin Ltd.
Burgett, Bruce, and Glenn Hendler (2014) *Keywords for American Cultural Studies.* New York: New York University Press.
Carse, Ashley (2014) *Beyond the Big Ditch: Politics, Ecology, and Infrastructure at the Panama Canal.* Cambridge, MA: MIT Press.
Castro, Juan José (1893) *Treatise on the South American Railways and the Great International Lines.* Montevideo: La Nación Steam Printing Office.
Churchill, Winston (1950) "No Title," in *Hansard Commons* CDLXXVI: 2145.
Collier, Stephen J. (2012) *Post-Soviet Social: Neoliberalism, Social Modernity, Biopolitics.* Princeton, NJ: Princeton University Press.
Collier, Stephen J., and Andrew Lakoff (2015) "Vital Systems Security: Reflexive Biopolitics and the Government of Emergency." *Theory, Culture & Society* 32(2): 19–51.
Concise Oxford Dictionary of Current English (1935) "Infrastructure." Oxford: Oxford University Press.
Cooper, Frederick (2010) "Writing the History of Development." *Journal of Modern European History* 8(1): 5–23.
Cowen, Deborah (2014) *The Deadly Life of Logistics.* Minneapolis: University of Minnesota Press.
Dag Hammarskjöld Foundation (1975) *What Now? Another Development.* Uppsala: Dag Hammarskjöld Foundation.
Donovan, Kevin P. (2015) "Infrastructuring Aid: Materializing Humanitarianism in Northern Kenya." *Environment and Planning D: Society and Space* 33(4): 732–748.
Easterling, Keller (2014) *Extrastatecraft: The Power of Infrastructure Space.* London and New York: Verso.
Edwards, Paul N. (2003) "Infrastructure and Modernity: Force, Time, and Social Organization in the History of Sociotechnical Systems," in Thomas J. Misa, Philip Brey, and Andrew Feenberg (eds) *Modernity and Technology.* Cambridge, MA: MIT Press, pp. 185–226.
Elyachar, Julia (2010) "Phatic Labor, Infrastructure, and the Question of Empowerment in Cairo." *American Ethnologist* 37(3): 452–464.

Escobar, Arturo (1995) *Encountering Development: The Making and Unmaking of the Third World*. Princeton, NJ: Princeton University Press.

Ferguson, James (2006) *Expectations of Modernity: Myths and Meanings of Urban Life on the Zambian Copperbelt*. Berkeley: University of California Press.

Foucault, Michel (2005) *Hermeneutics of the Subject: Lectures at the College de France, 1981–1982*. New York: Palgrave Macmillan.

Frank, Andre Gunder (1969) *Capitalism and Underdevelopment in Latin America*. New York: Monthly Review Press.

Furlong, Kathryn (2014) "STS Beyond the 'Modern Infrastructure Ideal': Extending Theory by Engaging with Infrastructure Challenges in the South." *Technology in Society* 38: 139–147.

Gilman, Nils (2003) *Mandarins of the Future: Modernization Theory in Cold War America*. Baltimore, MD and London: Johns Hopkins Press.

Gilpin, Alan (ed.) (1973) "Infrastructure," in *Dictionary of Economic Terms*. London: Butterworths.

Harvey, Penny (2005) "The Materiality of State Effect: An Ethnography of a Road in the Peruvian Andes," in Christian Krohn-Hansen and Knut G. Nustad (eds) *State Formation: Anthropological Perspectives*. London: Pluto, pp. 216–247.

Holt, Hallett S. (1888) "France and England in Eastern Asia." *Asiatic Quarterly Review* 5 (April): 336–361.

Hofmann, Klaus Markus (2015) "Connecting People – An Evolutionary Perspective on Infraculture," in Arnold Picot, Massimo Florio, Nico Grove and Johann Kranz (eds) *The Economics of Infrastructure Provisioning: The Changing Role of the State*. Cambridge, MA: MIT Press, pp. 237–264.

Humphrey, Caroline (2005) "Ideology in Infrastructure: Architecture and Soviet Imagination." *Journal of the Royal Anthropological Institute* 11(1): 39–58.

International Congress of Navigation (ICoN) (1931) Report of Proceedings of the XVth Congress, Venice. Brussels: Office of the ICoN.

Ismay, Hastings Lionel (1954) "NATO: The First Five Years 1949–1954." www.nato.int/archives/1st5years/index.htm.

Jensen, Casper Bruun, and Brit Ross Winthereik (2013) *Monitoring Movements in Development Aid: Recursive Partnerships and Infrastructures*. Cambridge, MA: MIT Press.

Krock, Arthur (1951) "In the Nation: Bringing the Political Lexicon up to Date." *New York Times*, October 12.

Langworth, Richard (2008) *Churchill by Himself: The Definitive Collection of Quotations*. London: Ebury Press.

Larson, John Lauritz (2001) *Internal Improvement: National Public Works and the Promise of Popular Government in the Early United States*. Chapel Hill, NC and London: University of North Carolina Press.

Levi-Strauss, Claude (1966) *The Savage Mind*. Chicago, IL: University of Chicago Press.

Maurer, Bill (2005) *Mutual Life, Limited: Islamic Banking, Alternative Currencies, Lateral Reason*. Princeton, NJ and Oxford: Princeton University Press.

McGraw-Hill Dictionary of Modern Economics (1965) "Infrastructure (Social Overhead Capital)." New York: McGraw-Hill Book Company.

McNeil, J. R. (2000) *Something New Under the Sun: An Environmental History of the Twentieth-Century World*. New York: W.W. Norton and Company.

Mitchell, Timothy (2002) *Rule of Experts: Egypt, Techno-Politics, and Modernity*. Berkeley: University of California Press.

Mitchell, Timothy (2011) *Carbon Democracy: Political Power in the Age of Oil.* London and New York: Verso.
Morita, Atsuro (2016) "Multispecies Infrastructure: Infrastructural Inversion and Involutionary Entanglements in the Chao Phraya Delta, Thailand." *Ethnos* 81: 1–20.
New York Times (1952) "Use of 'Infrastructure' is Baffling to Acheson." *New York Times,* March 1.
Oxford English Dictionary (2015) "Infrastructure." Oxford: Oxford University Press.
Poerksen, Uwe (1995) *Plastic Words: The Tyranny of Modular Language.* University Park: Pennsylvania State University Press.
Railway Engineer. 1889) "The Progress of French Railways During 1888." February: 39–40.
Railway Times (1879) "Spain." February 22.
Random House Dictionary (1967) "Infrastructure." New York: Random House.
Random House Dictionary (1969) "Infrastructure." New York: Random House.
Rist, G. (2014) *The History of Development: From Western Origins to Global Faith.* London and New York: Zed Books.
Rostow, Walter W. (1960) *The Stages of Economic Growth.* Cambridge: Cambridge University Press.
Saussure, Ferdinand de (1959) *Course in General Linguistics.* New York: Philosophical Library.
Schultz, Julia (2012) *Twentieth Century Borrowings from French to English: Their Reception and Development.* Newcastle upon Tyne: Cambridge Scholars Publishing.
Schwenkel, Christina (2015) "Spectacular Infrastructure and Its Breakdown in Socialist Vietnam." *American Ethnologist* 42(3): 520–534.
Scientific American (supplement). 1899) "Metropolitan Underground Railway in Paris." 48(1226): 19654–19655.
Scott, James C. (1998) *Seeing Like a State: How Certain Schemes to Improve the Human Condition Have Failed.* New Haven: Yale University Press.
Shorter Oxford English Dictionary (1936. Oxford: Oxford University Press.
Simone, AbdouMaliq (2004) "People as Infrastructure: Intersecting Fragments in Johannesburg." *Public Culture* 16(3): 407–429.
Sneddon, Chris (2012) "The 'Sinew of Development': Cold War Geopolitics, Technical Expertise, and Water Resource Development in Southeast Asia, 1954–1975." *Social Studies of Science* 42(4): 564–590.
Star, Susan L. and Karen Ruhleder (1996) "Steps Toward an Ecology of Infrastructure: Design and Access for Large Information Spaces." *Information Systems Research* 7(1): 111–134.
Stein, Howard (2008) *Beyond the World Bank Agenda: An Institutional Approach to Development.* Chicago, IL: University of Chicago Press.
Supplement to the Oxford English Dictionary (1976) "Infrastructure." Oxford: Oxford University Press.
Webster's Collegiate Dictionary (1973) "Infrastructure." Springfield, MA: G. & C. Merriam Company.
Webster's Seventh New Collegiate Dictionary. 1963) "Infrastructure." Springfield, MA: G. & C. Merriam Company.
Williams, Raymond (1983) *Keywords: A Vocabulary of Culture and Society.* New York: Oxford University Press.
Williams, Rosalind (2012) "Keynote Lecture: Infrastructure as Lived Experience." Landscape Infrastructure Conference, 23–24 March, Harvard University Graduate School of Design.

3 Surveying the future perfect

Anthropology, development and the promise of infrastructure

Kregg Hetherington

Infrastructure has always been a central part of development thinking because both concepts share a similar progressive temporality. Infrastructure is, of course, that part of an assemblage which fades into the background and which enables the foregrounding of other parts. But it is also, by extension, that which comes before something else, that which lays the conditions for the emergence of another order. The tense of infrastructure, like any development project, is therefore the future perfect, an anticipatory state around which different subjects gather their promises and aspirations. Yet any given infrastructural intervention does this differently, and the materiality of infrastructure enables the gathering of pasts and futures in novel ways. I argue here for an anthropology of development that pays more attention to the specific ways that infrastructures organize these progress narratives. And I do so in part because I recognize how often the ethnography of development falls into an evaluative mode and ends up uncritically reproducing the promissory time of infrastructure.[1]

I encountered this problem while trying to make sense of the history of land reform in Paraguay, where the infrastructure of rural property, and the technical practices meant to secure it, has played a crucial role in rural development aspirations since the Cold War (Hetherington 2011). Since the 1960s, when the dictatorship of General Stroessner was at its height and national development projects seemed capable of reaching the entire country, surveyors played the role of emissaries of progress. Their arrival in government trucks and the authoritative aesthetic of straight lines carved through forests and villages were often the most explicit state promise that campesinos would soon enjoy the benefits of a new, more egalitarian, social structure. The actualization of these futures was often beside the point. The main effect of infrastructural promises was the production of a linear temporality that arranged aspects of the landscape into a natural past and a civilized future. On this landscape campesinos lived in the future perfect, that suspended tense that will someday have been the past of a better future (Koselleck 2004; Mrázek 2002).

In the last two decades, the infrastructure that supports property markets in much of the world has changed, and with the introduction of title insurance, new policies governing land transactions and digital cadastres and registries, land reform in the twenty-first century has also shifted. Today, these policies are less about redistribution than they are about overhauling the technical practices that secure property ownership. In the international development literature this is usually seen as progress, a move from inadequate forms of record-keeping and inefficient bureaucracy to more technologically advanced ways of governing rural economies. According to proponents of these reforms, advances in land-market infrastructures will secure everyone's assets against legal uncertainty and finally unleash the productive power of the market, particularly to the benefit of the rural poor.[2] And yet such promises do not exhaust the effects of infrastructural changes. New surveying techniques, registration systems and legal frameworks change the performance of development promises themselves. To put it differently, new infrastructures make their promises in different ways to different people.

In Paraguay, the most visible of these changes was the shift in surveying technology used to divide rural holdings for the purpose of titling. An older system involving painstaking measurements with a theodolite, and maps hand-drawn by state functionaries, has recently given way to short visits by officials with GPS units and ephemeral computer-generated polygons. Although clearly more efficient, the new techniques also signal a shift in the locus of the future perfect, from land reform colonies that used to gather around the performance of the survey to the new mechanized mega-farms owned by migrants and speculators.

Of course, this shift is not accomplished solely by a shift in surveying technology; it also has to do with changes in agricultural economies and a larger abandonment of redistributive policies in development thinking. Many social scientists criticize this shift (e.g. Li 2014; Borras et al. 2012; Wolford et al. 2013), arguing that previous land systems were more likely to produce egalitarian outcomes than current ones. I don't dispute this claim. But in this paper I show that the critique itself (and often the larger critique of the neoliberalization of development, of which it is a part) relies on its own kind of infrastructural promise, building its own version of the future perfect and implicitly privileging which subjects ought to inhabit it. By following a material semiotic history of infrastructural promises, I argue here that such a critical take overlooks the way the future perfect moves around the development landscape. Ultimately I argue for an ethnography that slows down this reasoning to be more fully attuned to the operations of infrastructural promises in the present rather than competing to produce other futures perfect.

Infrastructural time

Since Bowker and Star (2000) first popularized the idea, it has become commonplace in anthropology to think of infrastructure as the invisible component in an ecology of material relations (e.g. Anand 2011; Larkin 2013). In these studies, infrastructure's invisibility becomes an analytic problem to be addressed through "infrastructural inversions" that aim to make visible the material relations undergirding a given phenomenon that have disappeared from view as they've become routinized (Star 1999; Bowker 1994). But as Paul Edwards has pointed out, the "notion of infrastructure as an invisible, smooth-functioning background 'works'" only in certain places and times (Edwards 2003: 188). Infrastructural invisibility corresponds to an ideal which is only ever tenuously achieved. In those places where infrastructure seems always in need of repair, or where it is unfinished or disappointing, infrastructural invisibility is an elusive goal.

The correlation between the visibility of infrastructure and its location in geography of uneven development is not incidental, but necessarily part of what we are talking about when we evoke the term (Hetherington 2014; Harvey 2010; Sneath et al. 2009; Simone 2004; Barker et al. 2005; Larkin 2008). Infrastructures are precisely those structures that are *supposed to become* invisible, to provide the stability necessary for the emergence of processes of a different order – alternately imagined as development, civilization, or simply progress – and progress itself is experienced as a comparison between places and times. Infrastructures can be promises about the future, as in Walt Rostow's "take-off" model of development (1960), or historical origin narratives, as in path-dependence models of change (Martin and Sunley 2006), or responses to risk, as in the increasing role of "critical infrastructure" in disaster planning (Lakoff and Collier 2008). It is not invisibility that links these examples but priority in a narrative of progress which sees shifts in and out of visibility in normative terms.

Infrastructural time is more than merely chronological: it is progressive in the sense that it gathers past and future into meaningful narratives (Koselleck 2004) and turns the present into an unfolding anticipation. To behold something as infrastructure is to suspend that thing's present as the future's necessary past, the tense we call the "future perfect." As Povinelli notes, the future perfect is also an ethical mode, by which "the ethical nature of present action is interpreted from the point of view of a reflexive future horizon" (2011: 3). This turns infrastructural thinking into a temporal trap for certain subjects (such as indigenous people) who are condemned to disappearance in an emerging order (ibid.; Stengers 2015). But the future perfect is also an aspirational mode for other subjects, the condition within which most self-styled pioneers live: not in hope of remaining as they are, but in hope that their current hardship will have been the necessary precursor to future prosperity. The point is that the future perfect produces different kinds of subjects, including those who very much wish to inhabit it.

Development proposals, which justify current investments in anything from roads to archival restructuring, each invent a future for which a donor, taxpayer or other public can imagine themselves to be the precursor (Rottenburg 2009). Public rituals such as ground-breaking and inaugurations serve as validating closures for politicians (Harvey and Knox 2015), but they also scaffold a narrative future around which its anterior subjects can gather.

Surveying, especially when carried out with an audience in mind, serves much the same function in land reform.

The future perfect of land reform

The Paraguayan land reform was one of many in the region that built on the idea that *latifundios* (massive landholdings run as private fiefdoms) were "unproductive" and "inefficient" and therefore a drag on the rural economy (Latham 2000). This dynamic was particularly acute in Paraguay, where most latifundios were forested tracts owned by absentee landlords who promoted little formal economic activity (Kleinpenning 1987). The land reform was supposed to change this through modest redistribution, accomplished through expropriation and minimal infrastructural intervention: road-building, agricultural extension, surveying and distribution of property titles. The project began in earnest in 1963 with the creation of the Institute for Rural Welfare (IBR) that for 40 years thereafter created pioneer *colonias* that were intended to grow into thriving communities of titled smallholders or *campesinos*.

The law that created the land reform addressed the "injustice" of Paraguay's highly unequal land distribution. But its primary rationale looked beyond redistribution to future national development. Halley Mora, one of the ideological architects of the reform, described it this way: "Agrarian Reform" should be seen "not as an end, but as a stage to achieve a higher goal, Rural Welfare" (1976: 3). "Rural welfare" was never adequately defined in the scores of government manifestos about the reform. Instead, land reform focused on describing the inadequacies of the physical landscape and the subjects who inhabited it, so that both could be superseded.[3]

Using longstanding colonial language, Paraguayan territory was said to be a "desert," inhabited only by "natural" indigenous peoples and the slovenly elites who would soon be part of the past. Onto this empty land, the land reform agency would inscribe a network that would carry goods, vehicles, electricity, police, and a metrological consistency that would enable the emergence of a new national order. Even this, however, is to overstate the amount of actual state investment that occurred. Almost none of the resettlement was planned or coordinated in advance. The main activity of the IBR was to recognize land that squatters had settled "spontaneously," making their own roads, schools and churches. In a process that sometimes took decades, the IBR would expropriate the land squatters were living on, and send in a surveyor to divide the land into lots, issue occupancy permits and eventually land titles (Sánchez González 1997).

The arrival of a surveyor in an isolated squatter community was a crucial moment in this process, a moment of encounter which validated the entire trajectory of the pioneer narrative. The survey first rendered the territory as desert by representing it as a geometric abstraction on a blank piece of paper with the help of a theodolite, which measures angles between lines of sight. To do this, the surveyor needed to literally cut lines through whatever obstacles might lie in the way, such as trees, fences and houses, until an adequately detailed polygon could be drawn and become the blank slate of development.

The performance of blankness was more than a little violent, particularly to indigenous people living in the forests, who would explicitly be erased by campesino colonies. Indeed, addressing campesinos as subjects of modernization meant reinforcing the distinction between them and indigenous people, who were at that moment being subjected to genocide (Arens 1976). The survey performed this separation by constantly reminding campesinos that whatever lines they themselves made on the landscape needed to be corrected, and that the labor they put into pioneering was only one step away from the very decadent indigeneity that they were trying to overcome. But this was just the point: as indigenous people were swept into the past, campesinos would inhabit the future perfect, not a fully desirable subjectivity but one that would serve as the precursor for future modernity.

In other words, the Paraguayan state's primary infrastructural intervention was a performance of temporal disruption,[4] the division of past from future through the application of technical knowledge from the city. Given how crucial this moment was to establishing the progress narrative, it makes sense that campesinos would hold a certain reverence for the surveyors they encountered. Decades later, most campesinos could remember the names of the surveyors who had measured their colonies and could recount the events in detail. And even in 2005 and 2006, when I was living in rural Paraguay, many local squatter organizations considered it a major achievement to have a surveyor measure one's community.

I was able to accompany one of these surveyors, a man I'll call Peña, on a two-day trip to measure the colony of Yvymoroti.[5] Like many communities in the area, Yvymoroti figured in land reform jargon as "spontaneous" and "precarious" (i.e. illegal) but had been laid out by squatters *as though* it were an officially recognized colony, with straight roads spaced 1,000 meters apart. Squatters had already internalized the infrastructural mode of the land reform and used it as a marker of the seriousness of their aspirations. It occupied land with a layered legal history that made it hard to expropriate, so IBR agents couldn't easily legalize the colony. However, one thing that the agency *could* do was to carry out a survey, a performance that would reinforce the claim of residents with the promise of *eventual* legal title. It hardly mattered that most of those present assumed it was unlikely that titling would ever happen, much less that it would significantly improve their lives. The promise of the survey held open a space that allowed people to go on living as they had for decades.[6]

The survey itself had almost no discernible effects either on the landscape beyond shaving lines of sight. As I've said, the colony had already been built on a straight-line model, following the fence of an adjoining estate, and all the surveyor did was to correct the inevitably approximate geometry of the original settlers. But it turned out that this too was a critical part of the performance. For instance, in the ten years since the lines had originally been cut, there had been many property divisions, most of which were carried out with a meter stick from the local school. Thus, even if Peña was at times grudgingly impressed by the straightness of the road, he could still mock the units of distance used to space the houses out. Men from the community accompanied him for all of the physical work, including carrying his tools. They shaved lines through thick grasses along the road, and even removed a few trees to mark where the road or property divisions *ought* to go. Then they began counting off the lots and shaving more lines back from the road, cutting directly into gardens of cassava and sugar cane. In one place, the property line hit the middle of a house, leading to uncomfortable joking about what the neighbors would do about it. Surely they could work out an agreement, they said. Nonetheless, Peña planted his post right in front of the house as a reminder that campesinos rarely get things quite right.

For Peña, there was a clear relationship between campesinos' inability to keep property lines straight and their inability to overcome their own poverty. The lines he made with polygon and the lines that locals made with a meter stick performed the very distinction that structured the development promise. Knowing this, Peña was pompous and unpleasant, and spent much of the day finding ways to denigrate his male hosts from the local organization. Even before we arrived, on the way to the community in his jeep, he pointed dismissively to the first bedraggled campesino huts. "We call the campesinos around here *capi'atĩ*," he said, referring to an invasive burr. "You know what I mean, right? Those plants that the more you whack at them with your machete, the more they stick to your clothes and your face." He saw his work as being on the losing end of the development game – of the great project to elevate the frontier from unwanted vegetation to civilization.

It would be easy to be cynical about this process and to see campesinos as dupes. It was clear that politicians could use visits from surveyors to hold more radical politics at bay while acquiring short-term political capital. But to stop there would be to miss the point that most campesinos were deeply critical of this process. That political promises were by and large empty was no more news to them than it is to anybody. And yet they continued to request surveys because they knew that the promises were not *completely* empty and that the invocation of infrastructure was not *only* deceptive or conniving. Even if official recognition of places like Yvymoroti was rare, the very performance of the theodolite's promise had its own kind of value in keeping infrastructural time alive. Whether or not standardized land measurement was the necessary precondition for rural development, campesinos and functionaries could assemble under that premise. Surveying was quintessentially infrastructural because its practice enacted the future perfect, and interpellated campesinos as its suspended subjects. As a form of inclusion there's much to dislike here, but it *is* a form of inclusion all the same, far preferable, for campesinos, than the displacement to the past perfect suffered by indigenous people, who don't even figure as an important precursor to the desirable future.

Infrastructural past

Or rather, it *was* a form of inclusion. The story I've just told happened before the closing of the Paraguayan frontier under a wave of land acquisitions by large-scale soy farmers, before the political collapse of the land reform, and before the arrival of GPS-based surveying techniques. That winter, Peña was one of the last remaining men doing surveys with a theodolite for the IBR. He told me this on the ride back home, and when he began complaining about GPS, I almost felt sorry for him. His life's work, what he properly considered a refined craft, was quickly being replaced by young whippersnappers who'd never looked through a lens in their lives and whose computer-assisted drawings were mere approximations of land they'd never had to slash with a machete. It was clear that back at the office, Peña's job as the bringer of civilization was at risk. It turned out that his own disappointment with vegetating campesinos was over-determined by his nostalgia for a moment when his work was still genuinely promising.

Everywhere else in the IBR GPS held all the promise, linked to an almost unimaginably high-tech infrastructure of satellites, international computing grids and a new, not-yet-built but endlessly promising land information system (Hetherington 2012). "Efficiency" was key to this new narrative, just as it had been during the land reform. But now it was not the infrastructure of the survey that would make farmers more efficient but rather the GPS technology that would make surveyors more efficient. The failure of an earlier form of development had led to development projects to develop developers and promises to improve the nature of promising, so that agriculture could boom with better-allocated resources, less corruption, and prosperity for all. ("Rural welfare" had completely disappeared from the future.) Just as the promise of the theodolite was a creature of Cold War populism, the GPS is a creature of neoliberal "good governance," whose development temporalities are built of complex meta-promises about properly-framed market behavior.[7]

But the GPS is not merely a better version of the theodolite. The instrument changes the entire performance of the infrastructural promise. For all of the technological impressiveness of small electronic devices connected to webs of satellites, the great advantage of surveying with a GPS unit over the theodolite is that it is bureaucratically fast and cheap.[8] Imagine the contrast then. In 2005, the arrival of the surveyor to a campesino colony meant the arrival of an authoritative man with impressive equipment to the community, often for days or weeks at a time. The survey was an event, a costly and careful activity undertaken with the collective help of groups of young men holding stakes and measuring tapes and occasionally steeling glances through the lens, imagining a better road, a better electrical wire, a better ditch. The GPS did no such thing. These new men (and now occasionally women) only showed up in their communities for a few hours at a time, waved a GPS unit around in the air, and claimed that their work was done. No performance of disdain, no shared physical labor, and no apparent relationship. If for men like Peña the rural masculine sociality of surveying was part of the job, for the new functionaries it wasn't clear that their job had much to do with campesinos at all. Campesinos were no longer a site of investment and the project of the campesino colony was no longer taken seriously – they were no longer the necessary past of a desirable future but vegetative remains to be cleared for new infrastructure.

So to whom was the promise of the GPS addressed?[9] In the capital city it clearly appealed to the young professional managerial crowd taking over the bureaucracy from old-guard party appointees like Peña. In the countryside, the arrival of GPS began happening just as colonies like Yvymoroti were no longer considered the forefront of development. Instead, a wave of soybean mega-farms was rolling across the landscape from Brazil, destroying campesino colonies the same way that they had once destroyed indigenous colonies. The GPS brought an end to those meticulously-drawn surveying lines, and the future that they were supposed to have preceded, as whole communities were rolled into soybean fields with few visible boundaries. Most conspicuously, GPS units were mounted in the cabs of tractors, remotely guiding the very machinery that undid campesino existence. Everyone in this new configuration, from the campesinos being displaced to the soy farmers going into debt, and the cynical IBR representatives doing their quick GPS surveys of colonies that would soon disappear, recognized that the soy pioneers were working extraordinarily hard, and many of them suffered severe hardship and isolation. But this was all worth it because the future perfect now belonged to them, and the GPS, among a host of other infrastructural practices (new roads, silos, airplane hangars, digital platforms, international logistics corporations and ports appearing every year) continuously reaffirmed this.

By 2006, under pressure from the soy boom, certain groups of campesinos refused IBR surveyors in their communities. More radically, they began to refuse land titles altogether, and on a couple of occasions considered blocking other projects, such as paved roads, for which they had fought for decades. Planners in Asuncion and in the Inter-American Development Bank who oversaw a lot of these changes found these attitudes impossible to fathom. To them, these technological advances were merely the newer, better version of the same infrastructure campesinos had always desired. Largely unaware of the infrastructural inversions which they themselves were performing, they saw these changes as part of a larger but similarly unilinear developmental narrative, in which one technique simply led to another. Any refusal could only be interpreted as a step backward.

Anthropology without infrastructure

Much of the social science literature describing the end of land reform sees these processes as the retreat of the welfare state (e.g. Li 2014; Wolford et al. 2013). There's a nostalgic tone to this critique that echoes Peña and the men of Yvymoroti's pining for a Cold War promise of state inclusion. None of these authors would claim they wanted to hang onto the racist, patriarchal qualities of these colonies, or to the destruction they meted out with chainsaws and fire, or the violence that attended the shift of indigenous people into the past perfect. But they would like to return to a moment when infrastructure seemed to be set for improving these conditions. And on many days I sympathize with this lament. The soy boom is devastating, turning a flawed pastoral landscape into a chemical wasteland. I'd love to believe that this could be stopped by some kind of statist intervention that promised the emergence of a more just, more environmental form of campesino colony. But that desire is already trapped by the terms of the infrastructural promise that make it sound quaint even as I write it.

The infrastructural mode is easy to fall into in part because social scientists were the ones who invented it for development theorists. The early thinkers who created the model of progress on which development policy operates drew on a rich history of critical theory, from Marx to Durkheim and Foucault. All of these authors carried out what Bowker (1994) called "infrastructural inversions," drawing attention to some social formation – class relations, kinship categories or enlightenment reason – as the past infrastructures that gave rise to present conditions or that promised future ones. Particularly in its normative mode, social science often reaffirms the promissory structure of development discourse. In the argument outlined above, for instance, all the authors acknowledge problems with the welfare state but argue that it will surely produce a better future than the free market in land. These are worthwhile arguments to make. But any anthropology of development that doesn't also take up the question of how promise itself is operating in its own analysis risks being merely evaluative – did X infrastructure actually have Y promised effect? Or does it have some other nefarious effect that we can illuminate by appealing to another kind of infrastructure – say economic inequalities, gender relations or ecological conditions – and through them tweak our expectations and derive a new set of promises? In its evaluative mode, anthropology remains at the service of developmental time. What the story of the GPS unit in Yvymoroti suggests is that in addition to this important work, we also need ethnographies of the semiotic materiality of development infrastructures that account for the lives of those living in the future perfect without analytically reproducing the temporality that placed them there in the first place.

Notes

1 Such a project is closely allied with Stengers' (2010) call to "slow down reasoning" to avoid the analytic seductions of progress.
2 See de Soto 2000; World Bank 2008; Li 2014; Hetherington 2012.
3 This section is based on a reading of IBR reports between 1963 and 1985, as well as collections of essays and speeches by Halley Mora and IBR president Juan Manuel Frutos.
4 Compare with Mrázek (2002).

5 Yvymoroti is also a pseudonym. For more on this encounter see Hetherington 2014.
6 See Nielsen 2011 for a comparable example of anticipatory time in Mozambique.
7 This is the central claim of de Soto's influential book, *The Mystery of Capital* (2000) which was cited to me by almost every land reform expert I spoke to in Paraguay about these new systems.
8 Indeed, in other respects, the GPS unit is not a very good tool for surveying – it can locate a person in space and generate a map from this, but it cannot trace the measurements on the land with much accuracy.
9 On the addressees of technological development aid, see Jensen and Winthereik (2013: Chapter 3).

References

Anand, Nikhil (2011) "Pressure: The PoliTechnics of Water Supply in Mumbai." *Cultural Anthropology* 26(4): 542–564.
Arens, Richard (1976) *Genocide in Paraguay*. Philadelphia, PA: Temple University Press.
Barker, Joshua, Webb Keane, Peter Redfield, Gustavo Lins Ribeiro, Margaret Wiener and Joshua Barker (2005) "Engineers and Political Dreams: Indonesia in the Satellite Age 1." *Current Anthropology* 46(5): 703–727.
Borras Jr., Saturnino, M., Cristóbal Kay, Sergio Gómez and John Wilkinson (2012) "Land Grabbing and Global Capitalist Accumulation: Key Features in Latin America." *Canadian Journal of Development Studies* 33(4): 402–416.
Bowker, Geoffrey C. (1994) "Information Mythology and Infrastructure," in Lisa Bud-Frierman (ed.) *Information Acumen: The Understanding and Use of Knowledge in Modern Business*. Cambridge, MA: MIT Press, pp. 231–247.
Bowker, Geoffrey C. and Susan Leigh Star (2000) *Sorting Things Out: Classification and its Consequences*. Cambridge, MA: MIT Press.
de Soto, Hernando (2000) *The Mystery of Capital: Why Capitalism Triumphs in the West and Fails Everywhere Else*. New York: Basic Books.
Edwards, Paul N. (2003) "Infrastructure and Modernity: Force, Time and Social Organization in the History of Sociotechnical Systems," in T. J. Misa, P. Brey and A. Feenberg (eds) *Modernity and Technology*. Cambridge, MA: MIT Press, pp. 185–225.
Halley Mora, Mario (1976) "Prólogo," in J. M. Frutos, *De La Reforma Agraria Al Bienestar Rural Y Otros Documentos Concernientes a La Marcha De La Reforma Agraria*. Asunción: Instituto de Bienestar Rural.
Harvey, Penelope (2010) "Cementing Relations: The Materiality of Roads and Public Spaces in Provincial Peru." *Social Analysis* 54(2): 28–46.
Harvey, Penelope and Hannah Knox (2015) *Roads: An Anthropology of Infrastructure and Expertise*. Ithaca, NY: Cornell University Press.
Hetherington, Kregg (2011) *Guerrilla Auditors: The Politics of Transparency in Neoliberal Paraguay*. Durham, NC: Duke University Press.
Hetherington, Kregg (2012) "Promising Information: Democracy, Development, and the Remapping of Latin America." *Economy and Society* 41(1); 127–150.
Hetherington, Kregg (2014) "Waiting for the Surveyor: Development Promises and the Temporality of Infrastructure." *Journal of Latin American and Caribbean Anthropology* 19(2): 195–211.
Jensen, Casper Bruun and Brit Ross Winthereik (2013) *Monitoring Movements in Development Aid: Recursive Partnerships and Infrastructures*. Cambridge, MA: MIT Press.

Kleinpenning, J. M. G. (1987) *Man and Land In Paraguay.* Amsterdam: CEDLA.
Koselleck, Reinhart (2004) *Futures Past: On the Semantics of Historical Time.* New York: Columbia University Press.
Laclau, Ernesto (2005) *On Populist Reason.* London and New York: Verso.
Lakoff, Andrew and Stephen J. Collier (2008) *Biosecurity Interventions: Global Health & Security in Question.* New York: Columbia University Press.
Larkin, Brian (2008) *Signal and Noise Media, Infrastructure, and Urban Culture in Nigeria.* Durham, NC: Duke University Press.
Larkin, Brian (2013) "The Politics and Poetics of Infrastructure." *Annual Review of Anthropology* 42(1): 327–343.
Latham, Michael E. (2000) *Modernization as Ideology: American Social Science and "Nation Building" in the Kennedy Era.* Chapel Hill, NC: University of North Carolina Press.
Li, Tania (2014) "What is Land? Assembling a Resource for Global Investment." *Transactions of the Institute of British Geographers* 39(4): 589–602.
Martin, Ron and Peter Sunley (2006) "Path Dependence and Regional Economic Evolution." *Journal of Economic Geography* 6(4): 395–437.
Mrázek, Rudolf (2002) *Engineers of Happy Land: Technology and Nationalism in a Colony.* Princeton, NJ: Princeton University Press.
Nielsen, Morten (2011) "Futures Within: Reversible Time and House-Building in Maputo, Mozambique." *Anthropological Theory* 11(4): 397–423.
Povinelli, Elizabeth A. (2011) *Economies of Abandonment: Social Belonging and Endurance in Late Liberalism.* Durham, NC: Duke University Press.
Rostow, Walter W. (1960) *The Stages of Economic Growth: A Non-Communist Manifesto.* Cambridge: Cambridge University Press.
Rottenburg, Richard (2009) *Far-Fetched Facts: A Parable of Development Aid.* Cambridge, MA: MIT Press.
Sánchez González, Bartolomé (1997) *Políticas Agrarias Y Desarrollo, Paraguay: 1954–1994.* Asunción: Amambay Ediciones.
Simone, AbdouMaliq (2004) "People as Infrastructure: Intersecting Fragments in Johannesburg." *Public Culture* 16(3): 407–429.
Sneath, David, Martin Holbraad and Morten Axel Pedersen (2009) "Technologies of the Imagination: An Introduction." *Ethnos* 74(1): 5–30.
Star, Susan Leigh (1999) "The Ethnography of Infrastructure." *American Behavioral Scientist* 43(3): 377–391.
Stengers, Isabelle (2010) "Including Nonhumans in Political Theory: Opening Pandora's Box?" in Sarah Whatmore and Bruce Braun (eds) *Political Matter: Technoscience, Democracy, and Public Life.* Minneapolis: University of Minnesota Press, pp. 3–34.
Stengers, Isabelle (2015) "Accepting the Reality of Gaia," in Clive Hamilton, Francois Gemenne and Christophe Bonneuil (eds) *The Anthropocene and the Global Environmental Crisis: Rethinking Modernity in a New Epoch.* London: Routledge, pp. 134–144.
Wolford, Wendy, Saturnino M. Borras, Ruth Hall, Ian Scoones and Ben White (2013) "Governing Global Land Deals: The Role of the State in the Rush for Land." *Development and Change* 44(2): 189–210.
World Bank (2008) *World Development Report: Agriculture for Development.* Washington, DC: The World Bank.

4 Containment and disruption
The illicit economies of infrastructural investment

Penny Harvey

The common articulation of economic growth and infrastructural investment is an expression of a basic and normative understanding of how value accrues through the unimpeded flows of persons, products, resources, information and money. Investments in public infrastructures are routinely justified as public goods in these same terms, and contemporary state-sponsored infrastructural projects (such as roads, water, sanitation and refuse disposal systems) are supported for their potential to generate both social welfare and economic growth. Development infrastructures in particular carry a moral charge in the promise of an improved future. This promise rests on the assumption that infrastructures provide what Butler (2014: 2) has referred to as 'inhabitable ground', the basic material conditions on and through which specific life worlds are built.

This sense of inhabitable ground also underpins contemporary anxieties over threats to infrastructural capacity whether from climate change, financial instability or hostile attacks. 'Critical infrastructures' are now routinely identified by governments as the assets, systems and networks that underpin economic and political stability. Public health, energy provision, finance, transport and information infrastructures have become integral to a sense of national security, and in turn become key sites of securitization.[1]

This fear that infrastructures might fail finds a refracted echo in those parts of the world where the promised foundations for productive futures are endlessly deferred.[2] In Peru, for example, people articulate their desire for roads as a longing (anhelo).[3] Longing is a particular mode of expectation (Schweizer 2008). Devoid of urgency it suggests a long-term, open-ended waiting, expressive of a deeply embodied desire for something that is palpably absent, and that in turn generates a particular kind of demand, the meaning and force of which 'derives precisely from that lack' (Butler 2014: 2).

But what exactly is lacking? What is the longing for? And why does anybody really think that the infrastructures that might feasibly appear in such situations might have the capacity to address the deep social divisions that generate and sustain this sense of longing? In this chapter I suggest that there are fundamental disconnections between the longing for inhabitable ground and the lived realities of infrastructural projects. My argument is that these disconnections are manifest in the widely held assumption that infrastructural projects are steeped in corruption. These assumptions in turn are rooted in the procedures through which infrastructural projects are formulated, funded and delivered in the name of the public good.

Development projects are formulated around specific interventions and outcomes that require the articulation of a clearly specifiable lack, or gap, and a calculable outcome. Thus, a road or a bridge can be built to address a sense of physical isolation or a lack of connectivity; a dam can promise a reliable and manageable flow of water, or a source of energy; a sanitation system can be aligned to metrics of child mortality or other measures of public health. However, the specificity of the engineered solution (the material provision) in each of these cases aligns only vaguely with the wider social effects and expectations. The instigators of large-scale infrastructure projects are of course aware of this limit to the linear topos of development planning, hence the ubiquitous risk assessments, environmental impact studies and expert consultations. However, there is little such instruments can do to confront the non-alignment between engineered solution and social expectation. The problem is amplified in large projects where the interests of the capital investors are not necessarily connected in any way at all to agendas of public service provision,[4] leaving it to politicians to suture the gaps between public and private interests. Even relatively modest projects that appear to have general support struggle to hold together competing and often quite divergent hopes and expectations. And while these might cohere momentarily in a general and under-specified notion of the public good, once a project begins to materialize and take a specific form, the tensions will re-emerge.[5] Public infrastructures in practice thus tend to comprise a deeply ambiguous 'public good', an ambiguity that creates the ground in which suspicions of corruption thrive.

In this chapter, I set out to explore the ways in which public infrastructure projects foster the symbiotic relationship between corruption fears and transparency measures and offer sites of thriving sensibility to all that cannot be seen, all that is not available to public scrutiny.[6] I explore these issues ethnographically, drawing on a study of an attempt to create a new water and sanitation system in the Vilcanota Valley, in the Cusco region of Southern Peru. This sanitation project was one strand of a wider ethnographic exploration of decentralization processes in contemporary Peru.[7] The history of decentralization in Peru has been a complex process specific to the political conditions of that particular nation state with its strong regionalisms and its colonial legacies of entrenched racialized inequality.[8] The process is also consonant with the more general turn to neoliberalism and the reconfiguration of state functions, promoted by global institutions such as the World Bank, and the Inter-American Development Bank.[9] Decentralized government is never a straightforward re-distribution of power. Autonomies are partial and the terms of such autonomy are subject to constant renegotiation. In Peru, fiscal and legislative power remain firmly in the hands of the central government, and the distribution of competencies articulate limitations as much as possibilities. Politics in such settings becomes technical, and successful politicians have to be well versed in the law in order to know where the ambiguities and possibilities for manoeuvre lie. Infrastructural projects loom large in such settings because their capacity to rescale relations carries an inherent ambiguity. Thus, while the law might stipulate what kind of infrastructure is appropriate to a particular instance of the state – such as a local road or a regional highway, a national or an international project – the value of infrastructural initiatives lies in their generative capacity and their ability to connect across scales. It is the potential to rescale the local through the facilitation of flows of money, materials and information, and at the same time to localize capital flows through emplacement in the specific sites from which value can be accrued, that allows infrastructural projects to draw together otherwise divergent interests and expectations, even as they enact separation and disconnection.

Such capacities threaten the coherence of controlled and regulated decentralization because this rescaling potential is difficult to anticipate and contain. In Peru, the central Ministry of Finance attempts to enact overarching control through an armature of instruments and prescriptions to ensure appropriate decision-making at the local level. One such instrument is the SNIP,[10] the national system for public investment, devised to ensure that public investments are both transparent and rational and to curb what are seen as the politically motivated and inappropriate expenditures of local populist politicians. The instrument requires that costs and benefits are stipulated and that a linear causal narrative articulates a specified problem with a designated solution. Such instruments carry their own infrastructural force. They are integral to the financialization of public services and are one of the means by which public services are repackaged for privatization. The SNIP is designed to ensure that reasoned choice underpins capital investment and supports the public good rather than private interest.

Calling a new infrastructure into being

In October 2011, I joined the members of three rural communities, Huarán, Arín and Sillacancha, who had been summoned to a public meeting by the provincial mayor. He had come in person to proudly announce that he had found a way to provide an integrated sanitation system that would bring drinking water and sewage disposal facilities to their individual houses. The project was the latest of a whole list of public works that this man had delivered, as part of a political bargain that had been struck when they had voted for him. He stressed that these projects were testimony to the fact that he looked after them. Their water system was going to be better than the systems in neighbouring provinces. He had found ways to make these projects possible. He had lobbied the regional government and had found a way to draw down the funds. It had not been easy. But he wanted them to know that he had made the effort to secure the flow of money because he cared about them. He knew the importance of water. The project was his expression of gratitude for their support. He was a poor man, like them. He piled on the rhetoric and built to a passionate crescendo as the town councillors and engineers leapt to their feet to embrace him. The assembled public also dutifully applauded until somebody burst the bubble by shouting out: 'Thank you, Mr Mayor – from now on we will think of you every time we go to the toilet! We will always remember you!'

Everybody laughed and the mayor handed the microphone to his chief of public works, who began to explain the project in more detail. Then things began to look more complicated. He informed us that the funds that the provincial authorities had drawn down from the regional government were tied to a technical norm of public investment that required the money to be spent on the installation of an integrated water/sewage system to provision an urban settlement with a minimum of 2,000 residents. We were told that they had met these conditions by aggregating the populations of Arín, Huarán and Sillacancha, none of them large enough to qualify for such a system in their own right. However, this aggregation had implications for how the project would be implemented, and how it would be administered in the future. 'This area is no longer a community,' he declared, 'It is now an urban area.'

The task of this physical and administrative transformation fell to the more junior resident engineer, who was the last to speak. He began by drawing attention to the benefits of the project. He wanted everybody to be involved. He unfolded the plans to show how this project would bring water from five kilometres away, from four different water sources. He stressed that there would be jobs for local people and that they would also need to organize traditional collective work parties (faenas) to move rocks and facilitate the main construction process. He then touched on the more thorny issue of private property. The water pipes would have to pass through people's land and they would have to agree to the 'widening' of streets and identify an exact location for the sewage treatment plant. He called for collaboration from the community.

Despite the obvious challenges, the audience did not pay much attention to the issue of how to transform these rural settlements into an urban area. They were more concerned about whether the engineers could be trusted. The mayor assured them that the quality of all the materials would be guaranteed. But histories of trust and mistrust hung in the air. The resident engineer tried to reassure them. He also pointed out that this project was subject to the regulatory framework of the SNIP. He found the SNIP number and read it out to them, stressing that everything about this project was public. It had a code. In the planning of this work, and following the requirements of the SNIP, the project had been deemed viable in the participatory budgeting process in which local people themselves had formally suggested and approved their public spending priorities.[11]

However, it was precisely in the conditions of the SNIP that this project was both open and obscure. The requirement for a minimum of 2,000 residents would have been explicitly addressed in the documentation that the mayor and his colleagues needed to secure the funding. However, it was clear that the mayor took the conditions of the SNIP as a bureaucratic hurdle that should not be allowed to thwart the project. From his perspective what a project such as this required was political will, including the will to creatively address the regulatory conditions of the SNIP. People were not unduly perturbed by this attitude, and there was no expectation that these instruments of transparency would serve local interests in any straightforward way. Indeed, as Coronil (1997) noted in his study of the Venezuelan state, people were habituated to the idea of the state as a vector of disorganization rather than as the staunch defender of the public good. Distrusting the instruments of transparency the mayor's project to bring money by whatever means was not a problem in and of itself.

The resident engineer was more hesitant about the mayor's methods. Without wanting to undermine his boss, he gently reminded people that political will was not sufficient to ensure public benefit. The clarity of technical procedures was what mattered.

Either way, people by now had captured the sense that this project was far from straightforward. The issue of the sewage treatment plant was worrying. Was land going to be forcibly expropriated? Whose land? The mayor assured them that nobody's land was going to be taken, but he had nothing to say about where the plant would eventually be located. Others were concerned that projects such as these never emerge according to plan. There were murmurings about transparency and corruption, the mismatch between what was accounted for and what was built, missing figures, or paperwork but no actual construction work. There were concerns over how money was spent, but less concern over how money was made to appear. Arguments surfaced about previous problems, ongoing fights over materials and disputes, and over the beneficiaries of projects. The resident engineer asked people not to fight about these things today when they were here to celebrate the project. The mayor pulled out a final rhetorical flourish to close the meeting on a high note. Taking the microphone he stressed that 'This is a public work – it is for you.'

This short meeting demonstrates the intrinsic ambiguity surrounding the 'public' dimension of a public work. In one sense, the mayor's act of address convened the assembled crowd as a public (Warner 2002). But this public was required to attend (those who did not were fined) and the public meeting was thus also coercively constituted. Some demonstrated their reluctance in expressions of boredom and distraction, others in their gestures of ironic support. The mayor also spoke as a public figure, performing his public duty of care. In his terms this entailed the provision of a sanitation system both as a basic infrastructure of citizenship, and as his delivery of a bargain struck in the voting process. Finally there was the instrument of transparency that ensured the visibility or publicization of the technical procedures. However, this act of disclosure in which the normative possibilities for the project were specified, also offered a space for manipulation[12] – specifically the possibility to reconfigure three rural settlements as an urban area through an aggregation process that produced a single number, 2,000, as an indicator of viability.

Underpinning the increasingly murky sense of the public work was also the labour required to bring this system into being. The mayor stressed that he had come to them to ask for their participation – they had to work together to create a new common ground. Working together however was going to be very difficult. The proposed system was to connect three communities whose relationships were entrenched in decades of mistrust and suspicion, a history that centred furthermore on the very issues of land and water that the project assumed as neutral components of the new sanitation infrastructure.

The disruptive force of prior relations

Until the Land Reform Act of 1969 this area of the Vilcanota Valley had been controlled by the owners of the Huarán hacienda, an estate of some 6,000 hectares that stretched from the fertile valley floor to the high pasturelands above. These extensive landholdings had been consolidated over time, at the expense of two adjacent indigenous communities, Arín and Sillacancha (Mayer 2009: 63), each with quite divergent attitudes to the landowners. Arín was hostile, a position exacerbated by the landowners' systematic refusal to grant them access to any of the hacienda's water sources. With very little productive land of their own the people of Arín were obliged to work for the hacienda. They also stole what they could and sought alternative employment as migrant workers in the fertile adjoining lowland province of La Convención. It was here in La Convención that the political movement for Land Reform was taking root, and the community of Arín spearheaded the expropriation of hacienda lands in the wake of the Agrarian Reform. The residents of Sillacancha had had a more accommodating relationship with the hacienda and were in general less politicized. This history continued to play out in the subsequent formation of state-sponsored co-operatives.

In the 1970s, membership in the co-operative was initially shaped by a government reform process that favoured the residents of Arín over those from Sillacancha. The overall effect exacerbated the divisive relations of the hacienda period and created a situation in which many members of both communities had no stake in the co-operative at all. By 1980, the co-operatives were in decline and a law was passed that allowed for their dissolution. Animosity between Sillacancha and Arín again structured the process:

> Those from Sillacancha, now mouthing socialist principles, were for equal proportions of land for each member (regardless of how much each one had in his own community), whereas the once collectivist cadres from Arín argued that land should be distributed according to the amount of work done for the cooperative. In the end the latter faction won. Thus the originally landless, hostile, less disciplined, politicized Arín members who had dominated the cooperative since its inception ended up with larger shares of land than the others.
>
> (Mayer 2009: 67)

Today the co-operative continues in diminished form. Membership is still distributed across several local communities, and co-operative land still offers one possibility for the location of collective community resources. However, relationships between the communities and the co-operative are poor. Between the generations, and even within communities there are accusations of corruption and ineptitude. There is secrecy and resentment about co-operative funds and while those families who can, seek to retain membership, there is little trust, and little positive memory of what were at the time heroic struggles for collective resources.

It is thus not surprising that the young engineer ran into difficulties in his attempts to get people to work together. Even a simple system of pipes, pumps and water sources quickly came to involve conflicting dimensions of public actions and dynamic and changing configurations of public and private investment.

Political will or technical solution

A year on from the celebratory announcement of the project there was still no agreement as to where the sewage treatment plant would be located. We found the resident engineer anxious and in confessional mood. He admitted that the original design had been based on poor information. For a start there had been an assumption that this 'community' had communal land. The error suggests that whoever had written the original plan had never visited the area. The tensions between the three communities and the crosscutting complications of the Huarán co-operative are hard to miss. The measurements were also wrong. The suggested siting for the sewage treatment plant involved a drop of about 30 metres. He wondered wryly if somebody had imagined that Sillacancha might market a waterfall of sewage as a new tourist attraction!

He was also critical of local people and complained about their inability to think in the right time frame. He explained that engineers and planners think in the medium to long term, always concerned with what systems might be needed down the line. Here he had come up against the intransigence of local people who refused to release their land or to reconfigure the streets of their community. He was critical of what he saw as a lack of sensibility for the 'common good' and an inability to transcend individual, local and immediate interests.

Then there was the additional problem of a totally inadequate budget. It was one thing to demonstrate the viability of this project on paper, but quite another to make it happen. The SNIP had not generated greater control or transparency but simply helped to sustain the new market niche for the production of 'studies' and technical profiles that make projects appear viable. The fact that the regional government had signed off the project suggested agreements and deals that were far from transparent. There was no provision for the cost of linking up dispersed rural dwellings. In consequence less than half of the residents would actually be connected to the sewage system. And yet the ongoing financial sustainability of the system depended on contributions from all residents. He glumly concluded that in the end it was in nobody's interest to install the system. There was nobody in the community prepared to offer the land for the treatment plant. The landowners had even turned violent and the engineer's workers and his machinery had been attacked with stones. Yet the politicians working to the shorter time frame of electoral cycles wanted something to show for their efforts and he was under huge pressure from the mayor to deliver this project.

There was no technical solution to the problem that the proposed sanitation system had brought to light. The documentation of the SNIP had configured the infrastructural need in terms of a community who lacked a modern sanitation system, who desired such a system, and who were thus willing and determined to make it happen. With no such community, with only a diffuse sense of lack around this particular provision and with inadequate funds to provide sufficient incentive, the infrastructural project had emerged as an unwelcome intrusion rather than a longed for possibility. The mayor nevertheless continued to show political will. His achievement had been to make the money flow from the provincial government to local communities who would otherwise fall outside of the provincial government's area of responsibility. His agile manipulation of the conditions of the SNIP engaged an 'economy of appearances' (Tsing 2000) that required the figures and the plan to appear reasonable. This was achieved by obfuscating all the incommensurabilities and the uncertainties that stood in the way of aggregating three rural settlements into a single urban area.

The young engineer thus found himself caught between the 'character' of the mayor who was determined to have the legacy of this work secured for his political portfolio and the recalcitrance of a community who refused, in practice, to be reconfigured as an urban zone. From this position he felt that he had to document everything to protect himself from accusations of corruption that could come at any time from either direction.

As we have seen, the funding for the sanitation system had required only the appearance of coherence. However, the drawing down of the funds from the regional government had also activated a new administrative requirement, which could not easily be sidestepped. Now bureaucratically established as an urban entity, our three communities were obliged, by law, to abandon their existing (non-standard) administrative systems and operate as a single, more standardized unit. The exact shape of the new administrative entity remained opaque, beyond the stipulation that the local sanitation committee (the JASS) had to be replaced by a single service provider located in the offices of the Municipality of Calca.[13]

At the very least, the new system implied a rationalization of existing local solutions. In the new model, the residents of Arín, Huáran and Sillacancha would become administratively equivalent. The new pipes and meters proposed for the sanitation project would be assumed to provide water for all those who were actually connected, under the same terms and conditions and at standardized rates. This rationalization implied a potentially more radical change than the provision of the integrated water and sewage system.

In 1996, as Peru was confronting the devastation of the war years, a Swiss-funded NGO, Sanbasur, had begun to work in the Valley in an attempt to improve sanitation infrastructures. Sanbasur had introduced a community-based model that encouraged local communities to activate their local water committees for which provision is made in municipal law. Supported by Sanbasur's team of lawyers, engineers, educationalists and health workers, the community of Arín was particularly successful in putting pressure on the municipal government to assume their legal obligations for the provision and monitoring of sanitation services, in exchange for funds (from Sanbasur) and labour (from local communities). Sanbasur's model was interesting, and articulated an understanding of the complications inherent in infrastructural provision. The funding came with strings attached, strings that connected pipes, water and pumps to local regimes of regulation, maintenance and administration at both the community and the district level.

The project was radical because it did not simply require the provincial authorities to activate existing regulatory structures. Instead, Sanbasur sought to enact integration in a new way, which by-passed the impasse of the antagonistic nesting structure of state agencies by inverting the hierarchy of partial decentralization. Energized from below, communities could demand the support, stipulated in law, and through their own efforts maintain a viable infrastructural system. Key to the model was that not all localities had to be alike. The local water committees of Arín and Huarán/Sillacancha worked quite differently and responded to their own local conditions. The JASS of Arín had instigated a novel method of payment that embedded the JASS deep into the structures of the community. Water was charged in relation to levels of community participation, rather than metered usage. Controlled by the community assemblies, this method avoided the high levels of non-payment that habitually disrupted the possibilities of running sanitation services in rural communities. They also had close control of the fluctuating ability to pay within the community. These principles directly echoed the ways in which hacienda land was distributed and co-operative membership granted after the agrarian reform, i.e. in favour of those who had worked the land as serfs.

The new administrative conditions of service provision returned to the nested structure of incorporation that by-passed community involvement. Meters would be introduced to replace the interpersonal grounding of the community model that was deemed too susceptible to corruption and manipulation. Anger at the unfairness of differentiated payments on social grounds was already causing problems in the JASS of Huarán. There are a greater number of outsiders living in Huarán, foreigners and city people who have bought land and built houses in the relatively flat areas that used to be the heartland of the hacienda property. Community integrity was harder to achieve than in Arín. They also operated a regime of differential payments that worked through a 'collective' agreement on ability to pay, penalizing those who did not participate in community meetings and general work parties. However, in Huarán the system had given rise to intense resentment within the powerful, outsider population who were in some cases paying over a thousand times more for their water than some of their neighbours.

The illicit economies of infrastructural investment

John and Jean Comaroff (1999) have described the visceral and violent reactions to the unfulfilled promises of modernity in southern Africa, where those who remain entrenched in poverty feel cheated by what they apprehend as a toxic mix of crime and magic. In these communities, anger and fear, expressed as rumours and expectations of corruption, course through the spaces of everyday life. The ethnography on which this chapter draws suggests that contemporary public infrastructure projects in the southern Peruvian Andes also provoke rumours and expectation of corruption. However, in this case the moral threat of corruption is not simply responding to visible inequalities but is also provoked by the very transparency measures designed to counteract mistrust, for these measures are themselves opaque and subject to manipulation.

Decentralization under neoliberalism makes visible conflicting scales of control and of responsibility. Public infrastructural projects are routinely overwhelmed by the intrinsic differences (material and social) that mitigate against their intended (or stated) outcomes. The tensions internal to conflicting notions of the public good foster and reproduce the sense of endemic corruption.[14] Thus it can appear that corruption is a term most commonly deployed to indicate the limit point of flow, and more specifically the diversion of funds from their rightful (linear) course. However, the example discussed here shows that the funds were not diverted. On the contrary it was the arrival of an infrastructure project in this particular context that made evident a prior and layered fragmentation that could not be bridged by pipes alone.

The funds were not sufficient, but when we were conducting the research there was no suggestion that they had been stolen. What emerged were mutual accusations of malpractice, reinforced by the disjunctive temporalities that the combined processes of decentralization and financialization so often produce around infrastructural development projects (Bear 2014). Promise was tempered by delay, cynicism and hope surrounded the uncertain rhythms of investment and return, the short time frame that fuelled the mayor's political will, clashed with the medium-term horizon of the technical solution and the long-term histories of community tension that mitigated against their integration.

Nevertheless, the possibility of an infrastructural investment continued to hold resonance even as the system seemed to be marred by failure. In this case the administrative systems imposed from above as infrastructures of integration and of disenfranchisement produced new political ecologies in which local actors had to find new footings and assume new vulnerabilities. Decentralization is exhibited as a process of 'disconnection' and 'reconnection' in which sites of risk and vulnerability are systematically shifted, and in which the rescaling capacities of infrastructural promise play a key role. Regardless of whether or not the pipes connect water sources to people's houses, the water, the pipes, the reservoirs, the houses and the water users *are* connected in their re-articulation as objects of administration and governance. Thus we find the consolidation of specific modes of centralized administrative power alongside the decentralization of responsibility for the actual delivery of services to the point where the administrative change takes place even when there is no sign of new material configurations.

However, these new modes of integration can in turn produce unexpected consequences. As water users are incorporated into new administrative systems, the ambiguous 'public' dimension of the works continues to exercise some force. Compliance or disruption becomes integral to the ecology of the new system, suggesting internal limit points to flows that require collaborative engagement. Approaching infrastructures as ecologies that emplace persons and capital, just as they enable flow and circulation, allows us to see the mutual entanglements of the included and the excluded, the powerful and the powerless. The limit points no longer appear as disruptions to the linear narratives of progress and corruption, but rather as indicative of more uncertain dynamics. The awareness of a shared ecology, as and when it emerges, can thus act as an analytical break on linear development promises, and raise sensibilities of distributed effects.

To promise an infrastructural connection also forcefully and routinely puts the legitimacy of centralized power in question. The ironic quip 'we will remember you every time we go to the toilet' might be taken as more of a threat than a compliment. Every time a tap runs dry, or the lack of sanitation systems comes to mind we will remember that you did not deliver, that you undid our autonomy. We will continue to hold you responsible.

Notes

1 Collier and Lakoff (2008).
2 See Abram and Weszkalnys (2013), Harvey and Knox (2015) and Weszkalnys (this volume).
3 For more detail see Harvey and Knox (2012, 2015).
4 Discussion of infrastructures as asset classes is not within the scope of the chapter (e.g. Hildyard 2012).
5 See Harvey and Knox (2012, 2015) and Thévenot (2002).
6 See for example Strathern (2000), Nuttall and Mbembe (2015), Harvey and Knox (2015).
7 This research project, entitled 'Experimental States', was funded by the NSF-AHRC, the ACLS, the Wenner Grenn Foundation and the ESRC, and conducted together with Deborah Poole, Annabel Pinker, Jimena Lynch Cisneros and Teresa Tupayachi Mar.
8 The brutal war between state forces and Shining Path (*Sendero Luminoso*) that devastated peasant communities for over a decade in the 1980s and 1990s has loomed large in attempts by the Peruvian state to rebuild the macro-economy.

Racialized discrimination shaped both the war and subsequent attempts to rebuild the social fabric.
9 See Remy (2005).
10 El Sistema Nacional de Inversión Pública. For more detailed discussion of this instrument see Harvey, Reeves and Ruppert (2013) and Harvey (2016).
11 See Hordijk (2009) and Vincent (2010).
12 See Nuttall and Mbembe (2015).
13 This location added a further layer of administrative uncertainty as Calca is both the District and the provincial municipality – a status that had allowed the Mayor to bend the rules of the SNIP as he aggregated the communities and passed the project up to the region for funding.
14 See Taguchi (2015).

References

Abram, Simone and Gisa Weszkalnys (eds) (2013) *Elusive Promises: Planning in the Contemporary World*. Oxford: Berghahn.
Bear, Laura (ed.) (2014) "Doubt, Conflict and Mediation: An Anthropology of Modern Time", *Journal of the Royal Anthropological Institute* (Special Issue) 20(S1): 3–30.
Butler, Judith (2014) "Rethinking Vulnerability and Resistance". Lecture delivered at the Instituto Franklin, Madrid, June. www.institutofranklin.net/sites/default/files/files/Rethinking%20Vulnerability%20and%20Resistance%20Judith%20Butler.pdf.
Collier, Stephen and Andrew Lakoff (2008) "The Vulnerability of Vital Systems: How "Critical Infrastructure" Became a Security Problem", in Myriam Dunn and Kristian Soby Kristensen (eds) *The Politics of Securing the Homeland: Critical Infrastructure, Risk and Securitisation*. London: Routledge.
Comaroff, Jean and John Comaroff (1999) "Occult Economies and the Violence of Abstraction: Notes from the South African Postcolony", *American Ethnologist* 26(2): 279–303.
Coronil, Fernando (1997) *The Magical State: Nature, Money and Modernity in Venezuela*. Chicago, IL: University of Chicago Press.
Harvey, P. (2016) "Waste Futures: Infrastructure and Political Experimentation in Southern Peru", *Ethnos*. www.tandfonline.com/doi/full/10.1080/00141844.2015.
Harvey, P. and H. Knox (2012) "The Enchantments of Infrastructure", *Mobilities* 7(4): 521–536.
Harvey, P. and H. Knox (2015) *Roads: An Anthropology of Infrastructure and Expertise*. Ithaca, NY: Cornell University Press.
Harvey, P., M. Reeves and E. Ruppert (2013) "Anticipating Failure: Transparency Devices and Their Effects", *Journal of Cultural Economy* 6(3): 294–312.
Hildyard, Nicholas (2012) "More than Bricks and Mortar. Infrastructure as Asset Class: A Critical Look at Private Equity Infrastructure Funds", *The Corner House*. www.thecornerhouse.org.uk.
Hordijk, M. A. (2009) "Peru's Participatory Budgeting: Configurations of Power, Opportunities for Change", *Open Urban Studies Journal* 2: 43–55.
Mayer, Enrique (2009) *Ugly Stories of the Peruvian Agrarian Reform*. Durham, NC: Duke University Press.
Nuttall, Sarah and Achille Mbembe (2015) "Secrecy's Softwares", *Current Anthropology* 56(S12): 317–324.

Remy, M. I. (2005) *Los múltiples campos de la participación ciudadana en el Perú: Un reconocimiento del terreno y algunas reflexiones*. Lima: Instituto de Estudios Peruanos.

Schweizer, Harold (2008) *On Waiting*. London: Routledge.

Strathern, Marilyn (2000) "The Tyranny of Transparency", *British Educational Research Journal* 26(3): 309–321.

Taguchi, Yoko (2015) "The Quest for Integrity: Middle-class Values and Corruption in Mumbai". Presented at the 'Theorizing the New Middle Class' panel at the 28th Annual Conference of the Japanese Association for South Asian Studies, Tokyo University, September 27.

Thévenot, Laurent (2002) "Which Road to Follow? The Moral Complexity of an 'Equipped' Humanity", in J. Law and A. Mol (eds) *Complexities: Social Studies of Knowledge Practices*. Durham, NC: Duke University Press, pp. 53–87.

Tsing, Anna (2000) "Inside the Economy of Appearances", *Public Culture* 12(1): 115–144.

Vincent, S. (2010) "Participatory Budgeting in Peru: Democratization, State Control, or Community Autonomy?" *Focaal: Journal of Global and Historical Anthropology* 56: 65–77.

Warner, Michael (2002) *Publics and Counterpublics*. Brooklyn, NY: Zone Books.

5 Infrastructure reform in Indigenous Australia

From mud to mining to military empires

Tess Lea

In his recent overview of the anthropology of infrastructure, Brian Larkin calls attention to the cultural work enacted by infrastructure, such as how it impels a modernist orientation to a perfectible future via the promise of movement and progress (Larkin 2013). Present ills will be solved when techno-science and engineering delivers desired transformations. For this teleological viewpoint to have traction, Larkin points out, it is not enough for infrastructures to simply exist as technologies or conveyors of function. They must also operate semiotically, aesthetically, affectively, changing bodily and psychic expectations through their operations. Yes, a road that replaces dust and dirt with sealed surfaces, that transforms the softness of a pre-colonized world to the hardness of a colonial order, 'cultivates citizens' technical skills and knowledge as a condition of [their] operation in the modern world' (Larkin 2013: 337). But, Larkin says, there's more. The whole enterprise also operates along visceral and aesthetic registers: 'the hardness of the road, the intensity of its blackness, its smooth finish – produces sensorial and political experiences':

> Infrastructures operate at the level of surface, what Buck-Morss (1992) refers to as the *terminae* of the outside of the body – skin, nose, eye, ear – rather than the mind inside. Softness, hardness, the noise of a city, its brightness, the feeling of being hot or cold are all sensorial experiences regulated by infrastructures.
>
> (Ibid.)

This chapter takes up Larkin's invitation to subvert the developmentalist claims made by projects of infrastructural improvement. But while it attends to the sensory impacts of infrastructure and the vibrancy of matter (Bennett 2010), it also turns its back on detailed poetics, to reconnoitre infrastructure's hidden structural interests, the better to engage the 'infra' below the surface of structures. Looking at a road development on Groote Eylandt off the east coast of Arnhem Land in the Northern Territory of Australia, enacted precisely to replace the soft dust and mud of an existing track with the hard allure of a bitumen road, I explore how mining activities – an industry at the heart of most forms of civic infrastructure[1] – sit within contemporary forms of Indigenous dispossession, affectively and materially, ineluctably and inevitably. Mining is not only at the heart of Indigenous dispossession, it paradoxically also supplies the material means for surviving in reduced and displaced circumstances. Resources dragged raw from Aboriginal lands are returned as construction materials, road sealing aggregates, in the bodies and engines of the freight trucks delivering infrastructural materials, or in the form of the word processor an ethnographer might use to capture field data, bringing minerals, oils and their rich synthetic products through elaborate and unseeable circuits that connect dispossession to the tips of her agile fingers.

The scales are at once microbial and monumental. The drivers of infrastructure may very well be to do with the greater governance of Indigenous bodies through sensory enticements as well as regulatory mechanisms; but they are also part of a complicated web in which the interests of militarily protected global trade are in play (Cowen 2014). For their part, Aboriginal people have to give in to mining to receive infrastructural services, just as they have to cede to pathological portraits of their population for health and education programmes (Kowal 2015). The sensual and physical properties of the material events which conjoin these interests – such as the sealing of a lethal dirt road – remind us that infrastructures are not simply material, an insight reinforced by a growing literature disturbing the divisions of human and other, subject and object, sociocultural and techno-material (Haraway 1997; Escobar 2005; Kirksey and Helmreich 2010). At the same time, if resources are not simply there, inert, waiting to be found and used, but are lively natural-social-technological attainments, they are also part of trade agreements and military strategy.

It is difficult to trace the weavings suturing financial and undeclared military-industrial interests to the desire for and supply of infrastructure, and the sketchiness of what follows is only partly to do with space constraints. Because Indigenous issues, like the promise of modernising infrastructure, are treated either in the teleological terms of settlement history, in which massacres are concretised as the past acts of bad colonialism before today's more enlightened development approach (cf. Wolfe 2007) or as pathologies that need assorted carrot and stick policy remedies in the present, it is difficult to link the reproduction of Indigenous disadvantage to the reproduction of militarily defended liberal settler capitalism. It is not as if, say, manganese from Groote Eylandt ends up in a drone which ends up shooting Australian Aboriginal citizens from a distance (although, as we will learn, manganese is of particular strategic interest to the American military). The points of interconnection are more elusive and dispersed, operating as a complex relaying of forces which do not quite have a causal relation in the strict sense but nevertheless accumulate and shape conditions of infrastructural and thus lifeworld possibility for Indigenous people. As an illustrative adjacency, Australia's stock markets are heavily weighted to two sectors – the finance sector and resources – which have differentiated interests in (former and current Indigenous) land as (non-sentient) divisible property; for, among other things, Australian middle-class lifestyles survive on the affordances of the country's resource extraction and property development industries. Increasingly, it is the last remnants of the world's frontier spaces that have most left to yield to these co-dependent interests in the pursuits of economic growth (Klare 2012).

To sense the scale of the bulk-handling and export infrastructures behind mining operations and why they tie into defended trade routes (while also materially scaffolding the same), just imagine standing at the bottom of a five-kilometre-wide pit, 500 metres deep into the earth. The mammoth reinforced steel carriers that ply iron ore across the waters to China, Japan, India and Korea are of such a size they daunt the surveyors meant to inspect them for signs of corrosion and fatigue,[2] while the major ports needed to manage their loading and unloading are limited to a few key countries, given the dazzling expense of the militarily protected navigation routes and multimodal integration systems needed to guide their passage, let alone the capital needed for the swarming technologies at harbourage (Mezzadra and Neilson 2015). The infrastructure needed for steel manufacture is similarly extensive and expensive, involving railways, highways, docks, storage areas for the iron ore and smelting fuels for the blast furnaces, all the way to factories and accommodation for workers (Cowen 2014). At the risk of radical oversimplification, the global supply chain that brings us just about everything we own, use or consume is a vast, largely unseen, logistical network, all fed by extractive mining, as part of what used to be called military-industrial capitalism.

In Australia and elsewhere, the principal country where this mining takes place is occupied by remnant Indigenous populations – those who, having survived settler colonial dispossessions by being on land of such low commercial interest it was eventually reserved for Aboriginal use, now find themselves at the heart of the 'race for what is left' (Klare 2012).[3] As Richardson and Weszkalnys note (2014: 5), 'the contradictions and violence of [resource industry] endeavors are most apparent in state-sanctioned encroachment of multinational companies on indigenous and other rural lands'. Aboriginal people and their country are often at the coal face of extraction industry escalation and the Warnindilyakwan people of Groote Eylandt are no different, hosting what BHP Billiton boast as being the largest sea-borne manganese operation in the world.[4]

Where mud-fed mines meet mud-filled roads

In the watery world of Groote Eylandt, where the annual monsoon reliably deteriorates poorly maintained gravel roads and culverts, the creation of a sealed road, a vital piece of infrastructure in the modern socio-economic realm, sealing the 50-kilometre dirt road stretching from the original settlement of Umbakumba to the mission town of Angurugu was an urgent matter. Poorly signposted and barricaded even when dry, the Umbakumba–Angurugu road had bad sight distances (drivers could not see over the humps and abrupt turns) and with the annual flood runoff, deep gouges would destroy the road altogether. Sudden patches of heavy corrugation, treacherous sand dips and dangerous, fast flowing drainage culverts regularly pulled travellers to injury, disability and death. Infrastructures press into bodies, as Casper Bruun Jensen notes, changing 'forms of physicality and modes of living' (Jensen 2015). On Groote, this shaping would manifest as the gross disfigurement or decomposition of maimed or lifeless bodies. An Internet search around the coronial catchwords of motor vehicle accident, road fatality or unsealed roads in Australian remote localities will call up great Warnindilyakwan surnames of Groote: Bara, Lalara, Amagula, Wunungmurra.

It is from this island that the highest quality of manganese ore currently available on the planet is daily ripped and shipped by BHP Billiton's subsidiary Groote Eylandt Mining Company (GEMCO). GEMCO's Groote operation accounts for more than 15 per cent of the world's high-grade manganese ore production, a market currently driven by China, India, Japan and Europe, but also nominated as a 'strategic mineral' for US military operations – meaning an element that is needed to supply the military, industrial, agricultural and civilian needs of the United States during a national emergency but which is not found or produced in the US in sufficient quantities to meet this need.[5] An essential ingredient for making steel pliable, the USA does not produce manganese of a quality to do much more than colour house bricks red.[6]

That lethal dirt road, the main route for cross-island travel, only became sealed as it drew near to a T-junction, at the point of meeting a well-maintained and carefully sealed two-lane road, the Rowell Highway, linking GEMCO's open-cut strip mine to their private shipping port. Despite decades of yielding to the mining industry, with its ongoing promise of positive investment in Indigenous development, the dirt road would have remained dirt and lethal subsidence in perpetuity. It would have remained dirt until the Anindilyakwa Land Council (ALC) entered a Regional Partnership Agreement with the Australian and Territory governments, the regional arm of local government known as the East Arnhem Shire Council, and GEMCO. It is important to note that the Anindilyakwa Land Council is not a mendicant group but a complex organisation with in-house policy officers, a lawyer, geologist, anthropologists, linguists, art centre managers and a fully serviced managerial executive. It includes a separate corporate venture known as GEBIE (Groote Eylandt and Bickerton Island Enterprises) which invests across a diverse portfolio, from real estate off-island to business ventures on island, spanning everything from fish farms to a civic and civil building company. The Land Council has this capacity precisely because it was formed to manage the royalties arising from the compulsory manganese mine visited on Groote Eylandt in the missionary past.[7]

The project budget for making the road an eight-metre-wide, two-lane, flood-immune sealed road, capable of being driven on at a specified 80-kilometre speed limit, was estimated at AUD$20M, of which AUD$9.5M was to come from the Australian Government's Aboriginal Benefits Account (ABA), itself largely composed of royalty culls from mining on Aboriginal land; with a further $5M from GEBIE, the Land Council's investment arm (a mechanism for reinvesting mining compensation); and $5.5M from the Northern Territory government. Here further precision halts, for the NT government keeps the sources of the money it allots for Indigenous programmes under the guard of information opacity. Such confusing cannibalising intricacies are nonetheless important to plot, for this flimsy data trace is one of the few available ways to show how Indigenous people must effectively pay for their own services, through monies meant to compensate for land gouges; a circumstance arising at least in part because of the state's underinvestment in Indigenous infrastructure over the many years that it has been simultaneously smoothing the path for mining (Levitus 2009).[8]

What of that road? Responding to the call for road construction tenders, a New Zealand family-owned company, Fulton Hogan Construction Pty Ltd, bringing their extensive experience in surfacing roads and pavements in new urban subdivisions, bid well below the estimated cost and won the job. Five project managers later, the road was eventually sealed, at a far greater final cost.[9] The road eventually became a past tense entity, although as we know from works on the liveliness of infrastructure, such a steady state is all but impossible. Almost immediately, parts of the road started to subside, eaten by water and poor construction techniques, and the road shone where it shouldn't, revealing a non-mathematical attention to the spread rates for bitumen and asphalt under the unforgiving glare of a tropical sun. The road is a liquid form in dynamic intra-action with its other watery kin, humans included (Lea 2015), and as new potholes appear, attention has shifted to managing speed-related fatalities and tightening the prosecution of unregistered vehicles, project management minutiae long forgotten.

In military parlance, the burgeoning ineptitude surrounding the road construction might be called collateral damage. In policy analyses, if such mundane technicalities are mentioned at all, it attracts the term 'unintended policy consequence', implying a truer original intentionality, a greater initial logic. Like infrastructure projects, policy programmes are also conceptualised as if they are linear and entirely human-centric processes leading to an end point, a resolution, in which a bundle of services or goods or people are made available to address a problem, when in fact policy ideas become tangible within bio-cultural worlds. House bearings corrode with rust, roads subside, and infrastructure is expensive to maintain because of the way materials are in dynamic interplay with their environments. Interacting with organic worlds, by definition what policy is addressing through infrastructure schemes, cannot be treated as if it is purely technical. It is wilder.

Important as this is to understanding why infrastructure projects so often decompose, this is to draw only one part of the interconnections webbing Indigenous circumstances to more complex global forms. Some of the more fiercely human entanglements are as invisible as the water seepages which begin to pull new roads apart even as they are being laid. As this final section will argue, the coincidence of mining, the supply of essential services and the ongoing forfeit of survival rights is obscured by demands that Aboriginal people be assisted by whatever means necessary to reach their full potential (which means to be socialised as a wealth-accumulating, debt-servicing individual through school-based education and other mechanisms of cultural tutelage, including tightly defined forms of employment). With serial domestic and community policy intrusions demanding front stage attention, further diminishment of rights to negotiate access to the subsurface resources of large parts of traditional territories can take place without this ever needing to be fully articulated as the underbelly of the (humanitarian) policy common sense on offer. Like the question of funding, the trace has to be captured through chance examples, here supplied by the most recent Indigenous infrastructure policy: that of complete withholding.

'I have no choice'

In March 2015, as yet another searing summer was breaking climate records in Australia, Prime Minister Tony Abbott declared his full support of a campaign to shut down over half the remote Aboriginal communities of Western Australia (WA), stating that taxpayers should not be expected to finance Indigenous people's 'lifestyle choices' (Griffiths 2015). The WA Premier, Colin Barnett, had made it clear approximately 150 Aboriginal communities – precise locations deliberately unspecified – were no longer viable.

'I have no choice', said Premier Barnett:

> It will cause great distress to Aboriginal people ... [and] in regional towns as Aboriginal people move into them. But high rates of suicide, poor education, poor health, no jobs ... They [communities] are not viable and the social outcomes, the abuse and neglect of young children, is [sic] a disgrace ... .
>
> (Vidot 2014)

Notably, Barnett's humanitarian appeal which here makes forced relocations seem so reasonable – radical poverty, poor health, lack of employment, substandard education, at-risk youth – is the exact rationale posed at other times for increased state expenditure on service provision. The most notorious recent instance of marshalling resources toward intervention (promptly nicknamed 'the Intervention') was the *Northern Territory National Emergency Response Act 2007*, a legislative mandate to 'stabilise', 'normalise' and then 'exit' 73 prescribed communities in the Northern Territory, justified as a response to widespread allegations of sexual abuse (Altman and Hinkson 2007). Many large-scale expenditure programmes were introduced as part of the Intervention, including the Strategic Indigenous Housing and

Infrastructure Program, out of which the Groote Eylandt road project was an eventual legacy.[10]

The convenience of Aboriginal pathology, in issuing both the licence to act and action's refusal, reveals what development rhetorics otherwise disguise: there are always other interests at stake. Provision and denial are just two different ways of justifying capital accumulation through dispossession (cf. Harvey 2005); two sides of the fast-spinning coin of arbitrary Indigenous policy-making under settler colonialism, now that Indigenous labour is marginal to both financial markets and multinational extraction industries, Australia's major sources of profit.[11] For the state, the difference between insisting upon (the structured chaos of poorly conceptualised and technically negligent) service and infrastructure provision, versus selectively withdrawing (or never faithfully providing) government support, seems to depend upon an old-fashioned definition of political–economic interests. If the construction industry is languishing in the metropolitan regions, remote area infrastructure is promoted. When infrastructural booms from extraction industry or military expansions, municipal rail works, tunnels, bridges and tollways or when other such profitable and large-scale enterprises are afoot, remote area infrastructure languishes.

Mining, Aboriginal lands and militarisation

In this swift account of how Indigenous conditions of infrastructural possibility are shaped by the gougings of extractive capital and the anarchic entailments of local policy, I have hinted at the military interests also operating as the policing arm of shipping routes and trade agreements. To move beyond these side glances, let me conclude with a brief consideration of American global primacy and Australia's role in serving as an instrument for the achievement of military and trade ends, using Aboriginal lands.

In April 2016, as the annual monsoonal rains subsided and communities across the north of Australia looked forward to leaving the bitumen roads behind for ceremonies and hunting trips, the deployment of US marines through Darwin entered its fifth iteration, bringing the total to 1250, heading toward a minimal target of 2500 marines by 2016/17 on permanent rotation. When complete, the marine deployment will constitute a fully equipped Marine Air Ground Task Force (MAGTF), one of only four deployed in the Asia-Pacific region, joining those in Guam, Hawaii and Okinawa. This is no innocent quartet. Its purpose is to respond rapidly to low- and high-end contingencies by combining command, maritime, ground, air, logistics and lift capabilities that can deploy together. The Darwin MAGTF is thus a key node in America's much vaunted 'pivot to Asia', through which the US seeks to maintain its global military dominance in the face of a rising China, among other things by being able to choke China's trade and energy corridors through the Straits of Malacca – the skinny stretch of water between Singapore, Malaysia and Indonesia (Lea and Rollo 2016).

However, it is not the geostrategic reasons for Darwin's new role as a 'lily pad'[12] that concerns me here so much as how it is that large swathes of real estate are available to make the Northern Territory such a useful foreign policy asset in the first place. For Darwin is not only near the Indonesian archipelago, Timor Leste, Papua New Guinea, Malaysia and the South China Sea; it also has a hinterland uncluttered by the kinds of civilian infrastructure that might attract controversy if yielded to a foreign power in more densely settled regions. A key part of the package of offerings Australia has gifted the US military (including new barracks, sealed roads, airport facilities and other infrastructure) is access to Bradshaw Field Training Area, some 800,000 hectares of defence-owned property on a former cattle station in the notorious Victoria River Downs district, historic home to some of the worst frontier massacres and enslavements (Rose 1991). The lack of infrastructure on Indigenous estates is testimony to the underinvestment in Aboriginal people in regional and remote Australia more generally. It is a backgrounded, structurally enabled impoverishment, which also helps explain why country the size of Cyprus is available for warfare simulations in one place, and for extraction in another. Mining and military training are exemplary reminders that what we are considering in regional and remote Australia is at once at the margins of development and at the epicentre of contemporary capital. Perhaps well-worn colonialist figures of margins and epicentres could be displaced by a new infrastructural topography which accounts for simultaneities, enmeshments and layers.

This visible marginality and opaque centrality also connect the sealing of a road between two small settlements on an island to the north-east of Australia to the declaration that up to 150 remote communities must be shut down over in the west. Moves to access what lies 18 inches below the topsoil, and state licence to remediate the more disruptive and visible damages of these renewed dispossessions under the rubric of necessary development, can as easily take place as infrastructure provision or denial. Infrastructure is thus a portal not only into the poetics of human desires and non-human agencies, but into the very heart of state, supra-state and military interests, united by the (ostensibly humanitarian) task of governing differentially displaceable Indigenous peoples.

Notes

1 This point is at once basic and complicated. Mining provides the raw ingredients for the bolts and beams of structural forms, and are the source for the methods of extraction, production, logistics, transport and cargo that distribute mining outputs into and across global networks. Bulky built forms are not the only destination. Platinum group minerals sit within jet engines, catalytic convertors and exquisitely exact time keepers; columbite-tantalite in nuclear reactors and mobile phones; lithium in unmanned mining vehicles and laptop batteries. As Michael Klare reminds us, while such substances might be deeply unfamiliar to the general public, they are nonetheless indispensable to contemporary civic

existence, and the hunt for them takes front line extractors – the profiteers we would like to blame over our own metropolitan dependencies – into new and old frontiers (see Klare 2012, especially Chapter 6, 'Rare Earths and Other Critical Minerals).

2 A key reason why the tankers breach at sea, especially those loaded with heavy iron ore, is that checking so much steelwork (bulkheads, storage tanks, brackets, rivets and underwater surfaces) for signs of corrosion and fatigue is not only expensive (requiring loss of shipping operations, specialist staging and lighting equipment to try to discern what may be tiny yet lethal infractions), it tests the stamina of those assigned the task: searching for metal fatigue in turn fatigues their eyes. For information about bulk carriers and their regulation see the International Maritime Organization website www.imo.org/ and the engineering reports assembled by Lloyd's Register, a charitable foundation dedicated to research and safety compliance concerning critical infrastructure – principally maritime but also oil and gas, rail, nuclear and process industries – see www.lr.org/en/ (consulted 21 January 2015).

3 Land repossession under land rights and native title laws 'has by and large been limited to unalienated Crown land in an inverse relationship to the colonial settlement pattern' (Altman 2009: 27). Land reclamation legislation differs from state to state in Australia but uniformly denies Aboriginal people mineral or other resource rights (ibid.: 17). The most generous act was the first: the *Aboriginal Land Rights (Northern Territory) Act 1976 (Cwlth) (ALRA)*, which at least requires prior informed consent for mining (albeit, a right that can be repealed 'in the national interest'). Subsequent state legislations have been progressively weaker, with each round heavily contested by the extractive industries. The national *Native Title Act 1993 (Cwlth) (NTA)* only requires that Aboriginal people be consulted about proposed mining, within a tight six-month window, after which mining can proceed apace, with any recompense assessed against a meagre set rate rather than the market value of the extracted items.

4 www.bhpbilliton.com/home/investors/news/Pages/Articles/BHP-Billiton-Celebrates-50-Years-of-Mining-on-Groote-Eylandt.aspx (accessed 2 April 2015).

5 www.usgs.gov/blogs/features/usgs_top_story/going-critical-being-strategic-with-our-mineral-resources/.

6 United States Department of Defense (2009). 'Reconfiguration of the National Defense Stockpile Report to Congress', Appendix F-6, available at www.acq.osd.mil/mibp/docs/nds_reconfiguration_report_to_congress.pdf.

7 The first load was shipped out in 1966, when the Groote archipelago was still under the combined administration of the Anglican Church Missionary Society (CMS) and the Northern Territory administration's welfare branch. More broadly, Australia's small number of Aboriginal land councils, the legal representative bodies for negotiating mining access or veto and the sole organisations left with the political and economic power to push for consultations over development issues, are also dependent on mining for their funding. That is, their existence as representative bodies depends on a levy that is taken out of royalty payments.

8 Complicating the entanglements even further, the mining industry is repeatedly pushed as a source of employment in 'school to work' (or now, 'womb to work' (Forrest 2014)) policies for Indigenous people, despite the industry's equal determination to automate all labour-intensive roles.

9 This last is no surprise: budget overruns are commonplace. But under the terms of the 'partnership' contract, the cost variations were met by Groote Eylandters, investing the compensation money ('royalties') that come to the Land Council from having Warnindilyakwan songlines dug up, somewhat akin to Malagasy taxpayers paying for the infrastructure (roads, bridges, plantations) that their French colonisers insisted Madagascar needed to be self-sufficient (Graeber 2011: 5).

10 To be specific, not that it helps with clarity, the Regional Partnership Agreement (RPA) which included the road as an action item (Anindilyakwa Land Council, Commonwealth of Australia et al. 2009) was part of the *Closing the Gap* campaign and its predecessor, the *Northern Territory Emergency Response* (aka 'the Intervention') or what is now called a Local Implementation Plan, which is part of a new Indigenous strategy called *Stronger Futures in the Northern Territory*, which apparently is not 'the Intervention' despite the doppelganger content and moralities. The RPAs also share kinship with Shared Responsibility Agreements (SRAs) which were part of a former policy experiment concerning conditional welfare provision called *Mutual Obligation* which preceded the Intervention (Collard et al. 2005). These bewildering shape-shifting policy formulations are of course part of their conjoined disempowering and bureaucracy-spreading effects (cf. Graeber 2015).

11 The processes alluded to here are historically dense and deeply entangled. Anthropologist Gerald Sider (2014: 179) provides a searing account of analogous 'epidemics of collective self-destruction which make people into the authors of their own and each other's misery' among Canada's Innu and Inuit peoples, together with the forced resettlements and cruelly pathetic service offerings that aid and abet this process in the name of modernisation and development (see also Mignolo and Escobar 2010). Sider argues that Innu and Inuit moved from being exploitable peoples (labour that could be used ruthlessly) to being disposable peoples (unneeded for capital) and, accordingly, are now under pressure to either assimilate fully and disappear into the neoliberal economy, or suffer the remedial humiliations dealt to those who resist by insisting on living even 'harder lives in harder places' (2014: 182). This, in a nutshell, is the predicament of Indigenous people within the Australian settler colony (see also Dombrowski 2010).

12 An American euphemism for their new style of technologically agile military positioning worldwide (Vine 2013).

References

Altman, J. (2009) "Indigenous communities, miners and the state in Australia", in J. Altman and D. Martin, *Power, Culture, Economy: Indigenous Australians and Mining*. Canberra: ANU e-Press, pp. 17–49.

Altman, J. and M. Hinkson, eds (2007) *Coercive Reconciliation: Normalise, Stabilise, Exit Aboriginal Australia*. Melbourne: Arena Publications.

Anindilyakwa Land Council, Commonwealth of Australia, et al. (2009) "Groote Eylandt Regional Partnership Agreement (RPA) (Stage 2)". Available from www.atns.net.au/agreement.asp?EntityID=4993.

Bennett, J. (2010) *Vibrant Matter: A Political Ecology of Things*. Durham, NC and London: Duke University Press.

Collard, K. S., H. D'Antoine, D. Eggington, B. R. Henry, C. Martin and G. Mooney (2005) ""Mutual" obligation in Indigenous health: can shared responsibility agreements be truly mutual?", *Medical Journal of Australia* 182(10): 502–504.

Cowen, D. (2014) *The Deadly Life of Logistics: Mapping the Violence of Global Trade*. Minneapolis and London: University of Minnesota Press.

Dombrowski, K. (2010) "The white hand of capitalism and the end of indigenism as we know it", *Australian Journal of Anthropology* 21(1): 129–140.

Escobar, A. (2005) "Imagining a post-development era", in M. Edelman and A. Haugerud, *The Anthropology of Development and Globalization: From Classical*

Political Economy to Contemporary Neo-Liberalism. Malden, MA: Blackwell Publishing, pp. 341–351.

Forrest, A. (2014) *The Forrest Review: Creating Parity*. Canberra: Commonwealth of Australia.

Graeber, D. (2011) *Debt: The First Five Thousand Years*. New York: Melville House Publishing.

Graeber, D. (2015) *The Utopia of Rules: On Technology, Stupidity and the Secret Joys of Bureaucracy*. Brooklyn, NY and London: Melville House Publishing.

Griffiths, E. (2015) "Indigenous advisers slam Tony Abbott's "lifestyle choice" comments as "hopeless, disrespectful"", *ABC Premium News*. Australian Broadcasting Corporation, Sydney. Available at: www.abc.net.au/news/2015-03-11/abbott-defends-indigenous-communities-lifestyle-choice/6300218.

Haraway, D. (1997) *Modest_Witness@Second_Millennium .FemaleMan_Meets_Onco Mouse: Feminism and Technoscience*. New York: Routledge.

Harvey, D. (2005) *The New Imperialism*. Oxford and New York: Oxford University Press.

Jensen, C. B. (2015) "Pipe dreams: Sewage infrastructure and activity trails in Phnom Penh", *Ethnos: Journal of Anthropology*, http://dx.doi.org/10.1080/00141844.2015.1107608.

Kirksey, E. and S. Helmreich (2010) "The emergence of multispecies ethnography", Special Issue, *Cultural Anthropology* 25(4): 545–576.

Klare, M. T. (2012) *The Race for What's Left: The Global Scramble for the World's Last Resources*. New York: Metropolitan Books.

Kowal, E. (2015) *Trapped in the Gap: Doing Good in Indigenous Australia*. New York and Oxford: Berghahn.

Larkin, B. (2013) "The politics and poetics of infrastructure", *Annual Review of Anthropology* 42: 327–343.

Lea, T. (2015). "What's water got to do with it? Indigenous public housing and Australian settler colonial relations", *Settler Colonial Studies* 5(4): 375–386.

Lea, T. and S. Rollo (2016) "A servant is not greater than his master: American primacy in Australian security", in *Hearts and Minds: US Cultural Management in 21st Century Foreign Relations*, M. Chambers. Bern: Peter Lang.

Levitus, R. (2009) "Aboriginal organisations and development: The structural context", in J. Altman and D. Martin, *Power, Culture, Economy: Indigenous Australians and Mining*. Canberra: ANU ePress, pp. 73–97.

Mezzadra, S. and B. Neilson (2015) "Operations of capital", *South Atlantic Quarterly* 114(1): 1–9.

Mignolo, W. D. and A. Escobar, eds (2010) *Globalization and the Decolonial Option*. London and New York: Routledge.

Richardson, T. and G. Weszkalnys (2014) "Introduction: Resource materialities", *Anthropological Quarterly* 87(1): 5–30.

Rose, D. B. (1991) *Hidden Histories: Black Stories from Victoria River Downs, Humbert River and Wave Hill Stations*. Melbourne: Cambridge University Press.

Sider, G. (2014) *Skin for Skin: Death and Life for Innuit and Innu*. Durham, NC and London: Duke University Press.

Vidot, A. (2014) "Colin Barnett: closing WA's remote Aboriginal communities will cause "great distress" but he has no choice", The World Today, *ABC News*. Available at: www.abc.net.au/worldtoday/content/2014/s4127560.htm.

Vine, D. (2013) "The lily-pad strategy: How the Pentagon is quietly transforming its overseas base empire and creating a dangerous new way of war", *TomDispatch*. Available at: www.tomdispatch.com/blog/175568/.

Wolfe, P. (2007) "Settler colonialism and the elimination of the native", *Journal of Genocidal Research* 8(4): 387–409.

6 Becoming a city

Infrastructural fetishism and scattered urbanization in Vientiane, Laos

Miki Namba

Already in 1975, when Pathet Lao, the predecessor of LPRP (Lao People's Revolutionary Party), took over Vientiane, the intention was to impose a revolutionary transformation on the city. However, the urban forms typically associated with the capitals of socialist states – densely packed high-rise buildings rationally organized in homogeneous blocks—never emerged. Indeed, in the early 1990s, the view of Laos as an isolated and inherently *laid-back* country was still widely held by foreigners who saw Vientiane as nothing more than a "big village." What brought changes to the urban formation of Vientiane was not Pathet Lao but rather an unprecedented amount of foreign aid and funds for development, which began flooding the city in the late 1990s. During this period many infrastructural projects were initiated and it became increasingly obvious that things were changing. Researchers, anthropologists included, have responded with mixed feelings to these transformations (e.g. Evans 1998; Reihbein 2007). Moreover, foreign development consultants and engineers hired by aid agencies and businessmen have also been concerned with the ways in which infrastructural development unfolded in Laos. Central to this paper, new infrastructures are often seen as nothing more than temporary makeshift solutions, *feigned* rather than real development.

Focusing on several high-profile infrastructure projects – a series of urban developmental projects carried out in preparation for the Tenth ASEAN Summit and two competing riverbank protection works in Vientiane – this chapter examines these projects from the point of view of infrastructural fetishism. This emphasis does not imply that I consider only the symbolic dimensions of Vientiane's development, for, as I show, infrastructural fetishes also give rise to material effects. In Vientiane, one of these effects is what I refer to as a *scattering* of urban space.

A ticket to 'The World Society'

In 2004, Vientiane held the Tenth ASEAN Summit. This was Laos' first international conference, and 25 meetings were to take place at newly built hotels and convention centers. During the preparations, the appearance of the city center altered drastically. The transformation was brought about by several new infrastructural facilities, most of which were built with foreign support: ITECC (Lao International Trade Exhibition and Convention Center), the first international conference hall in Laos, several hotels in the city center, including the state guesthouse compound for foreign leaders, the 14-storey Don Chan Palace Hotel, and six main roads.

These new facilities were not alone in changing the façade of Vientiane. People living along the six main roads, or owning restaurants or shops there, were requested by the local authorities to remove corrugated iron roofs and large umbrellas in front of their houses and shops. Such 'voluntary' activities were cheerfully referred to as a "facelift." *Vientiane Times* duly reported that people "were happy with the advice from the state officials (…) to make Vientiane a city of beauty" (*Vientiane Times*, 18/11/2004).[1]

While these improvements were happening, VUDAA (Vientiane Urban Development and Administration Authority) stopped repairing minor roads. Khampiene Inthaluxa, deputy director of the authority explained that "[w]e want to ensure that the 300m stretch from Patuxay [the Victory Gate] to Sibounheuang [the village next to the major road] has a *good surface* for the ASEAN summit" (*Vientiane Times*, 6/10/2004, my emphasis). Somewhat surprisingly, Khampiene added that the major roads actually had only been temporarily repaired for the summit. They would "undergo complete reconstruction at a later date." (*Vientiane Times*, 15/10/2004). Just behind the modernized ASEAN front-stage, people continued to live in traditional raised-floor houses along narrow unpaved dirt roads.

One day I asked Khone,[2] the owner of the apartment in Phonsaart village in Vientiane where I stayed during fieldwork, how things had changed in 2004. "Not much changed," he said, with an embarrassed smile, "because this village is behind [the main roads]." Though Phonsaart is not located smack in the center of Vientiane, the village is only five kilometers from the city center. However, what mattered was not this geographical proximity but rather the fact that the village was situated two streets behind one of the major roads. Khone's answer emphasized this peripheral position.

At the time of my stay in the village between 2012 and 2014, people were still growing vegetables and catching frogs along a small stream at the edge of the unpaved street. Meanwhile, Khone had hired two young men to dig a drainage channel along our street on his own initiative. From his perspective, the infrastructural changes around the 2004 event seemed like the construction of a distant stage. Giving a metaphorical spin to the literally intended description of deputy director Khampiene, we might thus say that the preparation had indeed created a *good surface* for the summit, but nothing more.

And indeed, it sometimes appeared as if almost everyone agreed that Vientiane's change was purely cosmetic; a facelift, precisely, rather than a substantial transformation. The fact that only the surface (the area next to the main roads) of the central area of Vientiane was developed while residential areas behind were ignored led to regular complaints among the locals (partly because the behind-ness directly affected land values) but also among those who participated in the development projects. Based on the understandable assumption that the primary or perhaps *only real* role of an infrastructure is to achieve its functional aim, the newly developed infrastructures in Vientiane appeared to foreign commentators and experts as a *faux* modernity, mere spectacle.[3]

Given this broadly shared sentiment, it is remarkable that when people think of the time when Laos entered world society, they almost always have the year 2004 in mind. Foreign businessmen, experts, and anthropologists who knew Vientiane prior to 2004, refer to the year as a turning point. In an interview, for example, the eminent anthropologist of Laos, Grant Evans (see e.g. Evans 1990), recalls that 2004 was "when Laos was truly, fully recognized as a modern nation state by the others, and in a sense by the Lao government itself. All the insecurity and vague sense of illegitimacy that had been there beforehand disappeared" (Reihbein 2011: 105–106). In contrast with the repeated argument that the new infrastructures were a matter of poor mimicry, Evans' description suggested that they also achieved a non-technical objective: They functioned as tickets to world society (Ferguson 2002). And indeed, after 2004 the flow of foreign funds and development aid accelerated. The country currently receives assistance from the Asian Development Bank, the United Nations Development Programme, the World Bank, and bilateral development aid from Japan, Korea, Australia and other countries, including Laos' remaining ideological allies China and Vietnam.

As preparations for the summit got underway, headlines like "Laos into world scene" (26/11/2004) or "Global recognition for Laos" (25/11/2004) began sprinkling the English *Vientiane Times*. The newspaper referred to the Japanese ambassador to Laos, who ventured that the event "would enhance Laos' role in the eyes of the world and would give more confidence to the country" (*Vientiane Times* 25/11/2004). Similarly, the newspaper quoted a Lao student: "[t]he ASEAN Summit will allow our country to *show off* our potential to foreigners especially members in ASEAN countries" (*Vientiane Times* 21/10/2004, my emphasis).

Infrastructure fetishism and fetishes as infrastructure

Infrastructures are conventionally understood as material, technological systems that allow for the interconnection and movement of people, things, and ideas (Mattelart 2000; Edwards 2003). Thus, it is not surprising that dominant paradigms of development have viewed infrastructure as prerequisite to attaining modernity.[4] Thus, as Brian Larkin notes:

> [m]any infrastructural projects are copies, funded and constructed so that cities or nations can take part in a contemporaneous modernity by repeating infrastructural projects from elsewhere to participate in a common visual and conceptual paradigm of what it means to be modern
> (2013: 10)

In such settings, however, infrastructures also held rich potential for turning into fantastic objects, or fetishized spectacles. For one thing, infrastructures often came to symbolize colonial superiority or even instantiate what it meant to be modern (Mrázek 2002).

In a recent review, Brian Larkin (2013) argues that anthropology is particularly attentive to the symbolic processes attending infrastructures. Among these studies, a subset has focused specifically on infrastructure as *spectacle* and *fetish* (e.g. Dalakoglou 2010; Khan 2006). For example, Dimitris Dalakoglou writes about an Albanian motorway which was to be constructed "within a framework of socialist modernism and infrastructure fetishism" (2010: 132) even as private car ownership was not allowed, and Naveeda Khan (2006) focused on the first "American-style" motorway in Pakistan, which failed to attract popularity due to modern features such as vehicle speed and the massive protection walls that blocked drivers from seeing the surrounding landscape. Far from responding to "rational" or "functional" requirements, these infrastructures were constructed to represent state power and thus to symbolize modernity. In this sense they can be seen as infrastructural fetishes.

The historical emergence of the fetish has been traced to fifteenth-century West Africa (Pietz 1985; 1987), where the notion came to be used by early merchants, sailors, and maritime adventurers. The notion of the fetish conventionally refers to the mistaken ascription of various immaterial powers to material objects. This primary connation of illusionary efficacy inspired many later studies. In contrast, William Pietz's discussion centered on the fact that the fetish emerged during a period of upheaval, at a time when new contact zones and modes of exchange were formed. Thus, Pietz saw the emergence of the fetish as a creative social attempt to come to terms with, and in some sense commensurating, radically different value systems. In the remaining part of this chapter I take this observation as an entry point for studying infrastructure. In this context, however, the fetish gets a somewhat different inflection.

To see the relation between fetishism and infrastructure, we can return to two previous observations. First, infrastructures are crucial *symbols* of modernity. Second, they also emerge in *contact zones* where development experts and locals intermingle. Thus, as I have indicated, infrastructural development in Vientiane has begun to link Laos not only to the broader world, considered in the abstract, but also to concrete flows of money and projects. Infrastructure is all about systemic connectivity or its lack, and this is one important sense in which it differs from notions like technology or artifact.

Conventionally, as noted, infrastructural connections are seen as technical and material. Thus, a properly functioning infrastructure is one that provides material support for the flow of people and things (cf. Larkin 2013, Lea and Pholeros 2010). Yet, aside from their proper, intended functions, infrastructures are generative also of other modes of relationality (Anwar 2015). Akin to Miho Ishii's insistence "that people acting in the world with fetishes as mediators means, in turn that people are mediums for the fetishes to act in the world" (2014: 61), infrastructural fetishes create conduits between value systems and forms of understanding. Socially creative in their own right, these are forms of relationality to which the experts who complain about fake infrastructures rarely pay attention.[5]

To recognize infrastructures as spectacles, however, is not necessarily to see them as fake. For just like the technical and material qualities of infrastructures do not prevent them from having symbolic efficacy, the symbolic efficacy of non-functioning infrastructures does not mean that they stop being material. For example, while the projects initiated in connection with ASEAN 2004 turned out to be both spectacular and functionally inadequate, these technical deficiencies did not mean that they had no material consequences. For one thing they *did* function as generators of development futures (cf. Jensen 2010). For another, as I will discuss below, they left a lasting material imprint on the urban settings of Vientiane. One of its outcomes was the creation of new kinds of spatiality and temporality, and a different distribution of the rhythms of urban life.

To understand the operations of infrastructural spectacle in Vientiane, I argue, therefore requires recognition of the complex *relations between* the spectacular dimensions of infrastructure, their modernizing impetus, and their materialities (Lea and Pholeros 2010; Jensen 2015). Pursuance of these relations makes it possible to engage a question not often explored in the literature on the politics and poetics of infrastructure: What do infrastructural fetishes achieve in material terms?

"A box comes first, the contents come later"

In 2009, due to concerns with erosion along the Mekong, the Lao government began envisioning a riverbank management project. The eventual solution focused on building a 12-km concrete embankment, a paved road leading to the Don Chan Palace Hotel, and a park between the river and the busiest area in the city center. Critical observers have insisted that this was mainly a matter of showing off to the Thais on the other side of the river and to the outside world more generally. In an interview, Tanaka, a development expert who works as a planning advisor in the Ministry of Public Works and Transport, had the following to say about the issue:

> Recently, Laos has been keen to work on riverbank protection. The biggest project was the embankment built on the Vientiane riverfront. It is the first full-scale, real embankment in Laos. But there is a problem ... There is no master plan! Normally, riverbank works need to estimate the return-period of flood. Then, a master plan is made of the whole river basin, followed by building flood-control facilities like dams or embankments. In Vientiane, the entire process was skipped. Yes, it looks good. But if a flood happens, the embankment will only protect 12 km along

the center of Vientiane, whereas the lower area and the opposite side of the river [Thailand] can be flooded... This embankment is not acceptable. It is too selfish.

(Interview on 3/7/2014)

Tanaka insisted that the project ought to have begun with preparing a master plan, one that relied on careful hydrological analysis and took into account the Mekong basin as a whole. Failure to do so marked the project as improper, a fetish with no material efficacy. Other foreign development experts and engineers concurred.

Meanwhile, some of these experts were involved in competing infrastructural schemes. The Japan International Cooperation Agency (JICA) Project on Riverbank Protection Works Phase I (2005–2007), for example, was based on technology transfer of traditional Japanese river engineering techniques, including the use of riprap groynes and fascine mattresses[6] to protect the riverbed and riverbank. It was designed to allow for willow trees to grow on the groynes and for each groyne to have an open space for vegetation. In contrast with the concrete embankment, the benefit of this approach was said to be its low cost and "friendliness" to nature (Kobayashi 2007; Matsuki 2013).

As the concrete embankment project was taking form in 2009, it became obvious that the construction site partly overlapped with the location of JICA's three fascine mattresses. Two of the three mattresses thus had to be moved from the city center. Though kicked out of the city center, where the modernizing forces concentrate, the project quietly continues in the suburbs.

Here we have two competing models. On the one hand, a 'traditional' Japanese solution that offered little by way of infrastructural spectacle. Quite the opposite, one might even say, for it was in the nature of the Japanese solution that it would become increasingly invisible, and eventually disappear from the scene entirely as plants grew and mingled with the river bank. Yet whereas this solution supposedly functioned well in protecting the riverbank basin and while it had no negative downstream effects, it was entirely lacking in modernizing force. As the Lao government saw it, the solution thus did little to assist Vientiane in gaining modernity. In contrast, the concrete embankment offered very visible testimony to just such progress.

Before the concrete embankment was built, the waterfront of central Vientiane was still a semi-natural landscape, where local restaurants and food stalls sat along the unpaved riverbank. Now this landscape has given way to a tourist night market built on an asphalt foundation. While the *nouveau riche* jog and do aerobics by the riverside, villagers grow vegetables and fish by the relocated fascine mattresses.

"'A box comes first, the contents follow later.' This is not how it should be, right?" These words were uttered, rather ironically, with reference to recent changes in the center of Vientiane, by a Japanese urban planner who works in development consultancy. The irony stems from the fact that Japanese public policies of the 1980s and 1990s had focused on constructing as many public works as possible. An inordinate amount of convention halls, IT centers, and other buildings sprung up all over Japan. They came to be known as *hakomono* ("box things"), a term that implies a lack of utility and, as the urban planner indicates, missing content.

Critiques of *hakomono* occurred at home, but also in the context of development aid. About the Laotian context, for example, the development expert Noriyuki Mori wrote that while there are numerous projects to be done, care should be taken to spend well the limited budget of the Lao government. For Mori, taking care meant that project proposals should be prioritized based on scientific and technological estimates (Mori 2013: 141–171). From the perspective of this chapter, the affinity between the *hakomono* metaphor and the critique of infrastructures as mere spectacle is noticeable. Both start from the critical observation that some infrastructural projects produce only a surface effect. Behind the façade, the box remains empty.

But is the box really empty? The anthropological literature as well as my discussion of riverside development in Vientiane both suggest a more complex situation. For one thing, if one looks inside the *hakomono*, one finds it to be chock-full of symbols and politics. So in this sense it is hardly void of content. Moreover, if one traces the *effects* of supposedly "empty" infrastructures, one finds that they attract investment and interest, and even appear to propel Laos into modernity. Finally, even though notions like spectacle, mimicry, and fetish emphasize symbolic dimensions, infrastructures also take physical form and have material consequences.

When a *hakomono* is built in the middle of Vientiane, or along the river, these effects show in many, often unintended and unpredicted, ways. New roads, for example, even if badly built, change the flow of traffic between parts of the city. Similarly, new centers and hotels create different possibilities for people to mix or segregate. If many such "boxes" are built rapidly, and without master plan, as has happened in Laos, the aggregate effect is a change in the overall landscape of the city. Thus, even apparently dysfunctional infrastructural fetishes are involved in dynamic and material processes of urban transformation.

Infrastructural loop: scattering effects and future promises

The infrastructural projects discussed in this chapter are indicative of a recurrent pattern. Whenever official Laos is confronted with the question of their position in relation to the international community, Vientiane is called upon to offer proof of its modernity. In response infrastructural fetishes are built.

If we stick to their material details, the forms of modernity thus produced seem quite brittle. For example, whereas some hotels and roads have been built, they remain irrelevant to most people in the city. Furthermore, the roads are made of cheap materials with a propensity to crack.[7] During my fieldwork in Vientiane (2012–2014), one of the major roads leading to Lao

ITECC was heavily potholed again, causing heavy traffic, accidents, and – for drivers – a general feeling of unease.

Given this situation, it is little surprise that experts routinely characterize Lao infrastructure development as fake. Emphasizing that proponents of infrastructure impute to these infrastructures functions and qualities they do not really possess, the characterizations made by these experts resemble the view of fetishes as objects with illusory powers. In contrast, following Pietz's emphasis on the fetish as a creative social response to new situations, I have shown that Vientiane's infrastructural fetishes are far from ineffectual. However, many of their noteworthy effects are non-technical. For example, even in the form of 'good surfaces,' or '*hakomono*,' Vientiane infrastructures operate as 'tickets to the world society,' supporting the Vientianese dream of becoming a city.

But to understand the efficacy of infrastructural fetishes it is necessary to add one more dimension to this story. This addition centers on the observation that while Vientiane's infrastructure projects are *effective* fetishes (symbolically and politically speaking) they are also materially effective. Almost as a *side effect* they generate real forms of urban transformation.

What is at stake is thus something akin to a reversal of the critical diagnoses offered by foreign technical experts. These experts, as we have seen, view the infrastructures of Vientiane as failures, even while recognizing that they project a sense of Lao achievements to the broader world. In contrast to this view, which sees material function as primary and symbolic efficacy as secondary, I have suggested that the primary task of these infrastructures is in fact to operate as effective fetishes. Moreover, they are quite successful at this job. Conversely, the issue of material transformation and functionality, which is seen by the experts as primary, is only of secondary importance.

Since material functionality is in a sense secondary, it is no surprise that projects often unfold with no master plan, or that buildings and roads are routinely made with cheap materials. Yet, the fact that the issue of material transformation is secondary does not mean that these infrastructures have no material effects: it simply means that these effects are often unintended and usually unanticipated. From the point of view of the technical experts this is of course just what makes them unsatisfactory in the first place. In turn, their feelings of dissatisfaction lead to the characterizations of Vientiane's infrastructures as fake and failed with which I began this chapter.

Observing different parts of the city, one may presently have a sense of inhabiting different zones and temporalities. Central Vientiane presents itself as a 'modern city,' whereas the surrounding areas are more like rural areas. Whereas the new river promenade is a site for exercise and entertainment for the wealthy, only a mile from the embankment people eat and drink along unpaved roads by the river.

Even as the new (potholed) major roads are not physically connected to village lives, this very lack of connection has concrete effects. Decoupling the fast and modern center from the slow life 'behind,' the roads generate different urban times and spaces. One side effect of Vientiane's fondness for infrastructural fetishism is thus a set of redistributions of the rhythms of urban life. The consequence is a *scattering effect*. Assorted infrastructural facilities, undeveloped sites, and 'infrastructures of legitimization' grow in the center, while the backstreets remain unchanged.

Urban scattering is not the same as infrastructural failure. This point was vividly brought home to me during an interview with Tanaka:

MN: What happens if certain finished project is evaluated as a failure?
TANAKA: Basically, there is no such thing [failure] in any infrastructure construction project. I mean, basically, there are no *finished* projects. Like riverbank projects, they usually go on for several decades or a century. Roads also take thirty to forty years. So, most of the projects are always *ongoing*.

Vientiane infrastructures, Tanaka says, cannot fail because they do not finish. They unfurl in a process, which, even as it changes this or that surface feature of the city, remains perennially incomplete.[8]

Even as they continuously interfere with urban space in multiple ways, in a certain sense it is thus as if infrastructures remain suspended in time. I would suggest that this sense of temporal suspension plays an important role in allowing people to continuously re-orient infrastructures to new future possibilities just getting visible on the horizon.

In this chapter, I have argued that infrastructural fetishes in Vientiane not only create bridges to the 'modern' world, but also generate urban scattering. Rather than a dichotomous choice between symbolic and technical efficacy, the picture I have offered suggests something like a continuous *loop* between spectacle and materiality. The proliferating projects that currently reshape Vientiane in profound ways – without, for all that, *really* turning the town into a modern city – testifies to the simultaneous dynamism and stasis of this loop.

Acknowledgment

This work was supported by Grant-in-Aid for JSPS Fellows. I am particularly grateful for the comments and support given by Casper Bruun Jensen.

Notes

1 During the summit, most regular people did not actually access the 'facelifted' Vientiane. The Prime Minister's Office put in place several regulations on the use of the major roads, while public bus services were suspended and companies and schools were closed.
2 All the names of informants in this chapter are pseudonyms.
3 Foreign experts are key figures in this chapter. The term experts, phu sīaw sán in Lao, is used to refer to foreigners who are dispatched from aid agencies or employed by development consultancies, which are contracted by the agencies for

particular development projects. They comprise engineers, people with specialized knowledge, ministry officials and researchers. Many of them have worked on development projects in other countries. They occasionally refer to such other projects (whether they have participated or not). As I will compare later, they also compare these projects with one another (see also Morita 2013).

4   The English word "infrastructure" has proliferated through development discourses via the work of influential economists like Albert O. Hirschman (1958), who argued that the provision of core infrastructure such as electricity, roads and transport was the state's responsibility (Anwar 2015: 5).

5   Not all experts were deeply concerned with the question of fake infrastructures, certainly not all the time. What particularly captures my attention is the difference between their modes of accounting, while experts often do recognize the symbolic efficacy of infrastructure, when arguing for the advantages of their own projects or when criticizing other projects they invariably take the perspective of rational functionalism.

6   Groynes are hydraulic structures meant to prevent erosion. They can be constructed of concrete, stone, or, as in Vientiane, riprap. Fascine mattresses are bundles of wood submerged in the river to protect the riverbed. They were introduced to Japan by Dutch engineers in the nineteenth century and further developed there.

7   Mostly so-called double bituminous surface treatment (DBST).

8   In this sense, it is doubtful that making a master plan would be the effective solution for a 'real' development.

References

Anwar, Nausheen (2015) *Infrastructure Redux: Brisis, Progress in Industrial Pakistan & Beyond*. Basingstoke: Palgrave Macmillan.

Dalakoglou, Dimitris (2010) "The Road: An Ethnography of the Albanian–Greek Cross-Border Motorway." *American Ethnologist* 37(1): 132–149.

Edwards, Paul N. (2003) "Infrastructure and Modernity: Force, Time, and Social Organization in the History of Soiotechnical Systems," in T. J. Misa and P. Brey (eds) *Modernity and Technology*. Cambridge, MA: MIT Press, pp. 185–225.

Evans, Grant (1990) *Lao Peasants under Socialism*. New Haven, CT: Yale University Press.

Evans, Grant (1998) *The Politics of Ritual and Remembrance: Laos since 1975*. Honolulu: University of Hawai'i Press.

Ferguson, James (2002) "Of Mimicry and Membership: Africans and the 'New World Society.'" *Cultural Anthropology* 17(4): 551–569.

Hirschman, Albert O. (1958) *The Strategy of Economic Development*. New Haven, CT: Yale University Press.

Ishii, Miho (2014) "Jubutsu no genwaku to genwaku (The Enchantment and Dazzlement of Fetish)." In *Ekkyousuru mono* (Border-crossing Things). Kyoto: Kyoto University Press, pp. 41–68.

Jensen, Casper Bruun (2010) *Ontologies for Developing Things: Making Health Care Futures through Technology*. Rotterdam: Sense.

Jensen, Casper Bruun (2015) "Pipe dreams: Sewage infrastructure and activity trails in Phnom Penh", *Ethnos: Journal of Anthropology*, http://dx.doi.org/10.1080/00141844.2015.1107608.

Khan, Naveeda (2006) "Flaws in the Flow: Roads and their Modernity in Pakistan." *Social Text* 24(4): 87–113.

Kobayashi, Rokuro (2007) "Mekon no kagan wo midori ni: raosu-koku e no soda-chinshoukouhou no ishoku (Turning Mekong Riverbank to Green: Transplanting Fascine Mattresses to Laos)." *Civil Engineering Consultants* 235): 24–25.

Larkin, Brian (2013) "The Politic and Poetics of Infrastructure." *Annual Review of Anthropology* 42: 327–343.

Lea, Tess and Pholeros, Paul (2010) "This Is Not a Pipe: The Treacheries of Indigenous Housing." *Public Culture* 22(1): 187–209.

Matsuki, Hirotada (2013) "Groyne to Prevent Riverbank Erosion on Mekong River." *Dobokugakkai Kasengijutsu Ronbunshu* 19: 1–6.

Mattelart, Armand (2000) *Networking the World 1794–2000*. Minnesota: University of Minnesota Press.

Mori, Noriyuki (2013) "Raosu no infura-seibi (Infrastructural development in Laos)," in M. Suzuki (ed.) *Henbousuru raosu no shakai to keizai: genjou to tenbou* (Society and Economy of Laos in Transition: Recent Condition and Prospect). Vientiane, Laos: JICA Laos, pp. 141–171.

Morita, Atsuro (2013) "Traveling Engineers, Machines, and Comparisons: Intersecting Imaginations and Journeys in the Thai Local Engineering Industry." *East Asian Science, Technology and Society: An International Journal* 7(2): 221–241.

Mrázek, Rudolf (2002) *Engineers of Happy Land: Technology and Nationalism in a Colony*. Princeton, NJ: Princeton University Press.

Pietz, William (1985) "The Problem of the Fetish I." *RES: Journal of Anthropology and Aesthetics* 9: 5–17.

Pietz, William (1987) "The Problem of the Fetish II: The Origin of the Fetish." *RES: Journal of Anthropology and Aesthetics* 13: 23–45.

Reihbein, Boike (2007) *Globalization, Culture and Society in Laos*. London: Routledge.

Reihbein, Boike (2011) "Interview with Grant Evans." *Journal of Lao Studies* 1(2): 97–107.

Newspaper articles

Vientiane Times. 6/10/2004. "Vientiane's roads pave the way for ASEAN summit."
Vientiane Times. 15/10/2004. "Facelift to finish well ahead of summit."
Vientiane Times. 21/10/2004. "A view of the summit: Are we ready for the 10th ASEAN Summit?"
Vientiane Times. 18/11/2004. "Roofs to come down for summit."
Vientiane Times. 25/11/2004. "Japan urges global recognition for Laos."
Vientiane Times. 26/11/2004. "Pre-summit thrusts Laos into world scene."

Part II

Urban infrastructures

Since the heyday of the Chicago school of sociology, the question of urbanism has revolved around the relationship between configurations of urban infrastructure and particular forms of life. Important dimensions of urban forms of life include consumerism, a dense and disorderly space, tendencies towards unpredictable and sometimes rapid change, and the formation of new publics. Whereas each of these dimensions, and, of course, many others, have been extensively documented by social science, infrastructure has conventionally played a much more muted role, as a background upon which the dramas of urban forms of life unfold.

The ecological model affiliated with the Chicago school offers an illustration of this tendency. In the 1920s, Robert E. Park and his colleagues explored the emergent complexity of urban life in Chicago. Their notion of "concentric zones," and others such as "competition" and "adaptation" borrowed from contemporary ecology, were deployed to grasp this complexity (Park, McKenzie and Burgess 1925). In putting the ecological model to use, however, the material and technical aspects of the city – namely urban infrastructures – were simply treated as a canvas upon which social and cultural processes took place; these processes being the primary or indeed almost exclusive concern of the research.

The later history of urban studies can be seen as a continued effort to go beyond this limitation. Scholars, such as Henri Lefebvre, David Harvey or Manuel Castells, have repeatedly criticized the socio-cultural view of the Chicago school. For them, the resources with which to overcome the limitation were compiled from the toolbox of Marxist materialism, and centered on to the production and structuring of space. Here, one can locate as well an interesting intersection with yet another tradition. As Jeanne Haffner (2013) argued, research initiated by Durkheim and Mauss on "social morphology," which preceded that of the Marxist scholars, was also keenly attentive to the social organization of space. Social morphology deals with the configuration of houses, buildings, roads and ports that collectively provide the material basis of a society (Mauss 2005). Mauss and Beuchat's (1979) *Seasonal Variation of the Eskimo* is a well-known example, but the scope of social morphological studies go far beyond Eskimo societies, encompassing the material bases of industrial society in general. Because Mauss (2006) explicitly developed the idea of social morphology in relation to the study of technology, one might view it as an early, and largely forgotten, attempt to develop an anthropology of infrastructures.

Even so, we find one persistent, and limiting, feature in these varied efforts to link the social and the material in urban studies. From Durkheim to David Harvey, these studies have tended to see the two as separate realms and thus focus on their "interaction" or "articulation." In contrast, one important merit of recent studies of urban infrastructure is that they explore the intermingling of the social and the material in the development, maintenance and, sometimes, collapse of infrastructures. Moreover, a strong current in these studies is to emphasize the political consequences of this infrastructural entanglement. As Graham and Marvin (2001) indicate, for example, the ongoing privatization of urban infrastructure has turned maintenance and restructuring into a new form of politics. Similarly, Nikhil Anand shows that political life in Mumbai has become inseparable from the technicalities of waterworks, with wide-ranging consequences for citizenship, urban governance, and communities. Yet, in contrast with Graham and Marvin who described infrastructural governance as a neoliberal strategy, Anand foregrounds infrastructural gaps, exhibited for example in insufficient water pressure, as an integral part of Mumbai's political life.

Infrastructural gaps can also be seen as a meeting point between strategies of infrastructural innovation, organizations, and individual subjects. Thus, as described by Michael Fisch, JR East, the operator of the largest train network in Tokyo, turned the gap between the maximum capacity of the railway system and the excessive flow of commuters into an opportunity for developing a new train operation system. By designing a largely automated process flow of trains and redefining the autonomy of commuters, this distributed system experimented with the infrastructural gap, thereby simultaneously changing trains and people.

The study of infrastructural gaps holds potential for changing the morphology of long-standing questions in urban studies. For one thing, as noted, it facilitates examination of the simultaneous reorganization of the technicality of urban infrastructure and forms of individual and collective agency. While their approaches differ significantly, Anand and Fisch both show that infrastructural gaps generate certain types of subjectivities that are nevertheless not over-determined by infrastructural configurations. In spite of their margins of indeterminacy, however, both authors also show that urban infrastructures nevertheless tend to reproduce and maintain certain political and economic forms.

Considering the infrastructural and political changes brought about by social movements, Alberto Corsín Jiménez and Adolfo Estalella trace a somewhat different analytical path. While the Tokyo commuter train network and the Mumbai waterworks both create and depend upon particular kinds of user subjects, Madrid's urban activists try to invent an urban open source ontology that mediates new infrastructures and communities. What is a stake is the realization that open source infrastructures require not only new technologies, forms of communication, and legal procedures but also forms of learning and engagement that enable communities to accept open source invitations. Here, too, technologies and people are inseparable, but the politics of their mutual constitution is not fixed, and can evolve in many different directions.

The foregrounding of infrastructure makes it possible to address yet another venerable urban question. As Morten Nielsen and AbdouMaliq Simone suggest, modern urbanism puts individual subjectivities and urban infrastructures in a seemingly contradictory relation. On the one hand, urban life promises the emancipation from traditional life, "starting from scratch" within new, modern-built environments. On the other hand, the constant rearrangement or decay of urban infrastructures often leads to disorder or chaos, which betrays the promise of newness. Characterizing this contradictory process as the "twinning" of cities, Nielsen and Simone depict the constant bifurcation between visions of the generic city and the chaotic infrastructural effects generated in the process of trying to achieve it.

This bifurcation furthermore links to the tension between approaching infrastructure as a spectacular object and as an invisible assemblage sunk into the background of urban life. Nielsen and Simone illuminate the political effect of infrastructural twinning, or bifurcation, by insisting that visions of new urban districts in Maputo, Mozambique also give new meaning to existing and decaying infrastructures in the city center. One can presently observe a similar effect in Copenhagen, Denmark, though it relates to different kinds of infrastructural entanglement and their embedded values. As described by Anders Blok, at one point, new wind turbines in the city seemed spectacular objects that gestured towards a future energy infrastructure. However, detached from the infrastructure and relocated as stand-alone objects in the landscape they lost their political aura. Here, the imagined and planned urban landscape of turbines encountered another urban value, characterized by Blok as attachments to material ecologies and particular sensory qualities.

Collectively, the chapters in this section exhibit the divergent ways in which urban infrastructures are simultaneously generative of urban life, entangled with it, and challenged by it. A crosscutting theme is attentiveness to the tensions and implications of infrastructural gaps. *Material* gaps, such as insufficient water pressure or the extraordinary congestion of Tokyo's trains are integral *parts* of social and technical assemblages. They yield varied political effects and bodily affects. Meanwhile gaps in *vision* generate other kinds of effects, affects and tensions between them. These infrastructural processes are crucial for understanding urban life, its vicissitudes, and its transformations.

As Nielsen and Simone note, the tension between the generic future and chaotic present plays an important role not only in urban infrastructural projects but also in relation to the urban question more broadly. Just like the twinning of the city in infrastructural projects, the generic urban sense of novelty, and the specific and chaotic circumstances of the present mutually highlight one another. In this sense, the bifurcation between the generic and the specific also moves laterally between empirical and the conceptual.

We might venture that the study of urban infrastructure requires a particular attunement not only to the recursive relations between the material and the social and between the technical and the subjective but also between empirical reality and social scientific re-descriptions.

References

Graham, Stephen and Simon Marvin (2001) *Splintering Urbanism: Networked Infrastructures, Technological Mobilities and the Urban Condition.* London and New York: Routledge.

Haffner, Jeanne (2013) *The View from Above: The Science of Social Space.* Cambridge, MA and London: MIT Press.

Mauss, Marcel (2005) *The Nature of Sociology: Two Essays.* New York and Oxford: Durkheim Press/Berghahn.

Mauss, Marcel (2006) *Techniques, Technology, and Civilisation.* New York: Durkheim Press/Berghahn Books.

Mauss, Marcel and Henri Beuchat (1979) *Seasonal Variations of the Eskimo: A Study in Social Morphology.* London and Boston, MA: Routledge & Kegan Paul.

Park, Robert E., R. D. McKenzie and Ernest Burgess (1925) *The City: Suggestions for the Study of Human Nature in the Urban Environment.* Chicago, IL: University of Chicago Press.

7 On pressure and the politics of water infrastructure

Nikhil Anand

Introduction

> Now there is a [state] policy regulation for water that we are bound by. Those structures prior to 1/1/1995 are eligible for basic amenities. We are allowed ... supposed to give water to them. Those [who have unauthorized structures built] after that date also get water. They make arrangements to take connections, forge ration cards and do such things to get them ... . In slums our policy is to give water connections to federations of 15 employees. We bring the connection to them, and their secretary is responsible for bill collection maintenance, bill payment etc. If the population is at higher elevations, then we provide them with a suction pump and infrastructure at the bottom, and make them responsible for its operation and maintenance. The total revenue of the department is Rs. 1480 crores, of which Rs. 800 crore is the profit.[1] It is the only public utility with such performance. The slum dwellers are good paymasters. The government is not.

Early in my fieldwork, I was talking with Patkar, a senior hydraulic engineer at the headquarters of Mumbai's water supply department. I asked him to tell me about the city's water system, particularly as it pertains to slum dwellers. Experienced in talking with reporters and researchers about the city's water supply, Patkar began telling me about the city's system, its lakes, pipes, scarcities and topographies. As he spoke about the ways in which the settlers[2] of Mumbai's *bastis* access water, however, his narrative shifted to a language of incomplete entitlements and differentiated state policies. This slippage, enacted in the gap between what state technocrats are 'supposed' and 'allowed' to do, reveals the flexibility and contingency that informalized settlers are subject to when accessing water in the city. Even though city water rules only allow certain settlers to formally access the system, Patkar is aware that nearly all settlers access some municipal water. Patkar takes care to point out that the circumscribed legitimacy of settlers in accessing water was not based on their inability to pay water bills in Mumbai, or due to the lack of funds or expertise of the city water utility. The ability of settlers (currently comprising 60 % of Mumbai's population) to access water could also not be explained with reference to the (il)legality of housing. Instead, settlers' access to water is differentiated by politically mediated "cutoff dates" and by materially mediated topographies.

Based on three years of ethnographic fieldwork between a settlement in northern Mumbai and the field offices of the city water department, the paper draws together literatures in political ecology, citizenship and state formation to theorize how cities are made livable, inhabited and claimed. In this revision of a previous article (Anand 2011), I highlight the ways in which city councilors, plumbers, and water engineers respond to claims for water supply in an uncertain legal and infrastructural terrain figured by fungible political relations of formality and informality, by states and markets, and by pipes and city councilors. As water pipes connect homes to the rationalities and technopolitical operations of the city's municipal state, Mumbai's water infrastructure is productive not only of human bodies and political relations. The city's water infrastructure also urges an extension of the political to an accreted material terrain of pipes, valves, and machines.

In this chapter I suggest that 'pressure' is a useful analytic to understand how the human bodies that inhabit the city are formed and sustained. Thus, I take pressure seriously as both a social and natural force. In Mumbai, settlers mobilize the fungible pressures of politics, pumps, and pipes to get water. Through manipulations of pressure, water is made available to diverse social groups. These practices not only enable settlers to live in the city, they also effect what I call hydraulic citizenship: forms of belonging to the city enabled by claims made to the city's water infrastructure.[3] Produced in a field that is social *and* physical, hydraulic citizenship is borne out of diverse articulations between the histories technologies of politics and the politics of technology. It depends on the fickle and changing flows of water, the social relations through which everyday political claims are recognized, and the materials that enable urban residents to connect to, and receive, reliable water from the urban system. As settlers and other residents respond to the dynamic flow of water in the city, these connections elucidate and differentiate how settlers are able to claim and live in the city.

Drawing attention to the ways in which hydraulic citizenship is made through personal, political and material claims on the city infrastructure, I show that the public realm is saturated with diverse social and political claims that exceed the frameworks of liberal citizenship. Mobilizing electoral politics, settlers pressure state bureaucracies and make them respond to their needs. They modify pipes and pumps, sometimes with the support of city officers and sometimes despite their sanctions, to make resilient and powerful settlements in the city (Sundaram 2010, Benjamin 2005). Drawing on Scott's (1990) articulation of "infrapolitics," I suggest that these practices are not merely pre-political coping strategies. They critically compromise and compose the authority of city engineers and other technocrats to control the system. As such, they are central to understanding the contemporary urban hydraulic system in cities like Mumbai.

By attending to the work of making pressure, I further show that water is made by the punctuated efforts of diverse authorities working in (and on) an uncertain infrastructural terrain. The often, but not always, materialized relations of the city's water infrastructure, made by subaltern groups, compromise the designs and plans of government and produce uncertainties that structure the system. Previously joined pipes continue to matter to the water network long after they have been abandoned by the city. The city's leaky water connections are thus both constitutive of and constituted by political relations made not only by humans but also with non-humans, including steel, plastic, and water. Taking shape over the last one hundred and fifty years, the politics of pipes and pressures are not easily encompassed by humanist framings of agency. The dynamic forms of water infrastructure and the regimes of pressure they require exceed conventional modes of politics and the political (Jensen, this volume). They also continue to introduce into governmental distribution regimes a significant degree of uncertainty.

Political technologies

On a wet July afternoon in 2008, I arrived at the house of Rané, a leader of one of the more prominent women's groups in a settlement that was approximately twenty-five years old. Rané's house was clean and neat, painted in pink, with floor tiles. The room was well lit and ventilated. I was introduced to her three-year-old, who peered at a television flanked by a fish tank, and a cluster of blond, blue-eyed dolls. Her husband worked as a clerk in a municipal (BMC) office, a reliable job that guaranteed a degree of financial stability. For many years Rané had led a women's group affiliated with the women's wing of the Shiv Sena.[4] Like other groups in the area, it seemed like the group had been more active in times past. Now it was activated twice a year, primarily when it collected donations to host the Ganpati festival in the settlement and also when it distributed school books given to them by the Shiv Sena at the beginning of the school year.

Rané began her narrative about the settlement's history in a way similar to many other settlers. She told me of water difficulties in the early 1980s, when no councilors would pay them any attention. They would get water from the well. Soon after, they began going to the nearby cemetery to buy municipal water from the caretaker at 10p a *handa* (vessel). As the price of water rose to Re. 1, they decided to petition a political leader for help:

> A Congress MLA helped us … . He provided a two-inch line at first, but soon after, the pressure wasn't there. People began making holes in the ground (*gaddha*) for water when the public standpost no longer gave enough water. Then later, Tendulkar came [to power in the Municipal council]. He put in a nine-inch line, which also was good for a while before it no longer gave pressure … . The morning line was brought by Tendulkar [a Sena councilor], and some people have formed groups to get water from there. Others are hesitant; because after paying, and waking up at seven at least there should be water there. Oftentimes there is no

water in the morning line. People have paid plumbers to put T's on that line as well, and take water without paying, without a meter.

I was impressed by Rané's technopolitical knowledge of the water system. From buying water by the *handa* to getting municipal water from a line installed by the politician, Rané's story describes the process by which the state has extended itself into the settlement over the last two decades. Like many others, she focused on the vagaries of water "pressure" (using the English word) as her main problem. When there is little pressure in municipal pipes, Rané suggested, settlers survived by drawing water from markets, wells, ditches and plumbers, and by exerting pressure on politicians. It is telling that Rané identified the pipes with the political leader responsible for their installation. Infrastructure development is indeed often a personal and political project. In recent years, city and state representatives have spent a significant proportion of their local area funds on extending the city's water system into the settlements, making sure that their names are attached to a water line, a road, or a community center. As city councilors have become personally involved in the administration of water in the settlement, many areas now have better access to water than before.

The work of councilors stands in marked contrast to the work of the municipal administration, whose projects are frequently less known or invisible, particularly in the settlements. Nevertheless, as Rané indicates, access to water remains precarious and taps frequently stop working. Votes, evidently, aren't in and of themselves sufficient to guarantee hydraulic citizenship in Mumbai. Hydraulic citizenship, realized by the receipt of pressured water from municipal pipes, also depends on the legal histories of the settlement, the city's water network, and the practices of its engineers.

Rané's vulnerability to the vagaries of water pressure draws on longer histories of exclusion and marginalization. As Rané and her colleagues pressured the city councilor to extend water services (yet again), the ability of the councilor to respond to their claim through routine channels indicates how, in Mumbai, *most* settlers that inhabit the city's settlements are eligible for legal water services. Settlers living in unrecognized settlements who can document their presence prior to the "cutoff date" (1995) are now permitted to apply for standpost water connections. Settlers share these connections with approximately six to eight other households and are responsible for the bills. That many (and yet not all) settlers now have legal access to water, however, does not necessarily mean they are actually able to access it. Nevertheless, the legal accommodation stands in marked contrast (and is yet continuous) with the exclusions embedded and produced through prior, colonial regimes of water governance.

Mumbai's water supply department was founded in 1860, when the colonial government responded to a debilitating drought by designing and constructing dams. From its earliest days, the water supply system was inadequate to serve all residents (Dossal 1991). Colonial officials and the elite municipal council only extended the water networks to a limited population – typically the wealthier classes and British subjects.[5] This approach of "salutary neglect" left large populations out of biopolitical systems of government, and in the sovereign control of "customary leaders" in many settlements, whose primary function was to ensure that their populations kept quiet (Chandavarkar 2007). Working beyond the regimes of liberal government since the colonial era, *dadas* (big men) managed these areas as patrons, disciplining them with discretionary resources and violence (Hansen and Verkaaik 2009).

The expansion of national political citizenship in the postcolonial period, exercised by settlers by voting in elections, has steadily reconfigured relationships between *dadas* and their local populations. Because settlers are now critical to electoral success, the city's dominant political outfits have worked to bring the services of the state (water, electricity, hospitals, schools) to settlements in a highly visible manner. Nevertheless, while they have been made more inclusive over the years, the city continues to restrict the ways in which settlers can legitimately claim water.

Today, *certain* settlers can form a group and apply for 'standpost' connections as per the city's water rules. If their applications are approved, settlers can hire licensed plumbers to make connections from their homes to the nearest service main *at their own cost*. As per city water rules, settlers are only sanctioned thin pipes – ranging from half an inch to an inch in diameter. Because service mains are often located at some distance from settler homes, these pipes often travel great distances to the 'common washing place' of settlers. Running above ground, they are vulnerable to breakage, leakage, or getting blocked every few years. Further, not *all* settlers are able to apply for standpost connections. Only settlers who can prove that they occupied their settlements before January 1995 can apply for water services.[6] To do so, they need to distinguish themselves from others by providing an extraordinary set of documents. These are:

a   An application form for a new connection.
b   A resolution/memorandum issued by settlers declaring a new (water) society, with a secretary in charge of collecting and paying dues.
c   A list of 'members' with their ration card numbers in one column and their electoral ID numbers in another.
d   Supporting documentation that includes copies of every member's [food] ration card, and a copy of the 1995 electoral roll, with each of their names highlighted. Each page must be certified as a true copy by the junior engineer.
e   A list of members 'verified' as per the junior engineer.
f   A receipt that Rs. 200 has been paid to the BMC for 'scrutinizing' the application.
g   A certification nominating a licensed plumber to do the pipe laying works.

While the revised water rules provide a means for millions of settlers to formally apply for water connections, the complexity of the process renders it almost impossible for settlers to apply for connections directly. For instance, it is not easy to find the 1995 voter list required by the procedure. Further, the unofficial norms of water applications are such that every application tacitly requires a letter of support from the politician, 'requesting' the engineer to approve the application. Thus, despite changes in the water rules, it remains difficult to get a water connection approved in a timely manner without the support of a councilor or legislator.

In the introduction to a special issue on *Urban Charisma,* Thomas Blom Hansen and Oskar Verkaaik directed attention to charismatic figures, urban specialists who, "by virtue of their reputation skills and imputed connections provide services, connectivity and knowledge to ordinary dwellers in slums and popular neighborhoods" (Hansen and Verkaaik 2009: 16). Settlements are filled with such specialists offering their services as 'brokers' who navigate settlers to access different state services. However, the laws, rules and policies of municipal government are themselves critical to the authority of urban specialists (Gupta and Sharma 2006). The various application requirements are designed to turn people away from directly accessing water as generalized citizens, directing them instead to seek the support of the system's experts – specific councilors and their plumbers. The practice of applying for an official water connection thus produces the discretionary power of councilors and other charismatic leaders in the settlement. Straddling the boundaries of the in/formal and il/legal, councilors are able to re-inscribe their power in their settlement by mediating and facilitating access to the procedures of government (Gupta 1995).

A former Shiv Sena councillor, Surve, made this clear to me early in 2008. Retired from politics, Surve now worked in a public bank. When I visited his offices, he took time to explain the system to me. I had asked why settlers and their plumbers didn't go to the water authority directly. Why did they first stop by the party office? He replied:

> Here the plumbers know that in the final instance you need a councilor's letter. The procedure has been *made* in the BMC (procedure BMC *mein bana diya*). The BMC can sanction water connections without the councilor or the Shakha Pramukh [the Shiv Sena's branch office head]. But if they give it, then they won't get any *maal* (stuff, colloq. for money) in the middle. So they have made a "system" [English usage] ... . You tell the councilor or political party member [you want a water connection]. That way, the local councilor is respected, he will get *maal*. [Otherwise he will object, saying] if you give it direct, what will my position be here [in the settlement]? ... So people say instead of [having to come] eventually to the councilor, let's do it first.

Following 'recognition' of their homes, settlers are expected to connect to the water system without councilors calling in favors. But as Surve argues, this is not how the public system works. It continues to require personal networks of legitimation and endorsement to move application documents through the bureaucracy (Hull 2003). Even after urban residents achieve state recognition after years of delicate clientelism, popular voting, and social mobilization, their relations *dadas* and their political parties continue to play a significant role around matters of water supply. Because councilors need to be seen as useful to settlers to get elected, they make themselves necessary to the hydraulic system. They 'help' both recognized and unrecognized settlers. If settlers can claim tenancy prior to the cutoff date, they write letters of support on their behalf. If settlers do not have the necessary documents, they organize forged copies, to send along with letters for a price. Thus, while the legality of settlers matters, as does their ability to pay for connections, their relationship with councilors and other charismatic leaders in the settlement remains crucial for enabling them to connect to the system.

For settlers, councilors are thus a critical locus of authority in the municipal water system. Mediating demands, they do precious screening work for the overworked engineers of the water department. In turn, they need engineers to validate their requests. Councilors frequently spoke to me about the skills and techniques required to "take work out of the BMC." Yet engineers do not only respond to councilors out of goodwill. They also depend on councilors to approve their requests, applications and tenders for a range of works on water pipelines, roads, sewage networks, etc. Accordingly, engineers need to ensure that they do not upset councilors, or deny their requests on the basis of rules. To ensure that the councilors' concerns are duly addressed, each city engineer is delegated to 'take care' of designated councilors, even outside the scope of municipal law.

Engineers are only too aware of how councilors manipulate documentation. A former chief engineer told me that the Water Department had been compelled by politicians and administrators "not to go into depth of every application." As long as engineers can maintain ignorance about an application's illegitimacy, they cannot be accused of violating the law. Knowing not to know the violations thus allows the city's rules to remain unchallenged, even as it permits engineers to remain open to allowing profitable, political, and sympathetic systems of access for the urban poor.[7]

City engineers, however, are not in a position to accede to every councilor's demands. Receiving only a limited quantity of water to distribute in their wards, they are unable to give every ward more water with more pressure. If a councilor or his constituency pressures engineers to deliver more water, the engineer can only do so if he reallocates the water from a different neighborhood.[8] Unable to respond to the demands of all councilors, engineers are constantly subject to verbal abuse by councilors who demand responses to their mutually incompatible requests. Simultaneously obliged to satiate the councilors' relentless demands for more water and manage the department's limited water allocation, field engineers have the unenviable task of balancing the different pressures of the hydraulic system. In their effort to cope with these demands, they often reallocate water from areas of low political pressure to areas of higher pressure.

I have focused here on the most common way of mobilizing pressure: through councilors. However, pressure can also be mobilized in other ways – through significant protest at the offices of the water department or by words written in an official complaint. The different repertoires through which pressure can be exerted are very familiar to settlers. To get water, settlers like Rané depend on the recommendations of councilors, and the social workers and city engineers they know, to recognize the legitimacy of their claims. The ensuing technopolitical arrangements are indicative of the dynamic ways in which residents assert claims of belonging to the city.

Conclusion

In this paper, I have urged attention to the quotidian practices of settlers and engineers in Mumbai as they make and respond to water pressure. By drawing attention to the ways in which settlers make pressure through differentiated rights and material technologies, I do not seek to reify the material powers of water with the clever use of a metaphor.[9] Rather, the metaphor and social practice of making water pressure helps apprehend the simultaneity of the social, political, and physical cities of Mumbai, as they matter to those who live there. Attending to the ways in which settlers are able to mobilize pressure with the politics and materials of Mumbai's water system is to recognize the compromised, punctuated, and graduated ways in which they have been able to establish themselves in the city.

As citizen-clients of leaders they elect, settlers mobilize diverse kinds of relations to access water. Made necessary by the city's formal water rules, these informal relations – located at the blurred boundaries of legality and illegality, state and society – trouble attempts to theorize politics through normative regimes of civil society (or political society), the state and the market, or even the analytics of informality (Chatterjee 2004, Gupta 1995). To draw water from the public system requires settlers to mobilize their votes as political citizens, relations of patronage, *and* their own money. Though legal categories, rules, and policies matter, neither legality nor formality can fully explain either how water is accessed or how populations are differentiated through its regimes. Neither is informality or illegality a prerogative of poor and marginal groups. As recent articles have revealed, wealthy residents, industries, and businesses also make discreet connections to the water network. Thus, I urge attention to be given to how pressure is generated on the system by differently positioned social actors in conjunction with city representatives, engineers, pipes, pumps, and plumbers. In an environment of uncertainty, attention to these relations reveals that city councilors and social workers have become a critical means through which settlers are able to make water connections. By making connections in this way, settlers' practices transcend simple distinctions between politics and the material world on one hand and civil and political society on the other.

Nevertheless, the entitlements of hydraulic citizenship are temporary and precarious. As engineers continue to reorder the diverse demands and pressures on the water system, settlers like Rané often find that their pipes slowly dry over time. Thus they continuously need to reiterate claims and re-establish relations to re-pressure their pipes. For this reason, hydraulic citizenship is not experienced as a one-way extension of the bio-political state. Rather, it is an iterative process that needs repetition, renewal and revalidation. As settlers and councilors continuously connect to pipes with constantly waning water levels, they constitute an infrastructure whose control is frequently beyond control, and often even unknown to the engineers of the municipal water department. The hydraulic state this brings into being is therefore not one of "total power" (cf. Wittfogel 1957). Nor is it encompassed and regulated by formal policies alone. Instead, as unknown pipes are connected to the water mains, they constitute a fickle, partial, political formation exceeding the control of engineers, councilors and governmental institutions that seek to control water.

For some time, leaking, creaking infrastructures have been seen as the provenance of cities of the "not-quite"-modern, developing world (Graham 2010). However, I do not think the fickleness and partiality of Mumbai's infrastructure is unique to the cities of the Global South. Instead, I suggest that non/human ways of making water pressure through fitful social/material relations has broader purchase (see also Harvey and Knox 2015). Engineers and residents everywhere struggle with managing the political effects of unstable assemblages that frequently exceed their designs. Infrastructure in this account emerges therefore not just as a base upon which modern urban life unfolds. Instead, infrastructure is always in an uneasy *process* of becoming, one whose very viability depends on continuous forms of always already inadequate social labor. In Mumbai, pressure is not only critical force in mobilizing and making water infrastructures perform. As a situated intervention on an infrastructure that is always in formation, discrete pressures are also generative of instabilities in an infrastructure that has long been on the verge of teetering out of control.

Notes

1 In 2008, when I spoke with Mr. Patkar, Rs. 5 crore was roughly $1 million. Thus the amounts that Patkar spoke of correspond roughly to $298 million and $160 million respectively.
2 Uncomfortable with the words 'slum' and slum dweller, I use the terms 'settlement' and 'settler.' In part, this is a better translation of the Hindi word 'basti' which is frequently used to describe settlements in Mumbai.
3 The hydraulic system that emerges here is not a centralized formation of power and knowledge as imagined half a century ago by Karl Wittfogel (1957). Instead, I describe a hydraulic regime, which is durable, yet has diverse locations of control, authority, and leakage.
4 The Shiv Sena is a parochial, nativist Hindu right-wing party particularly powerful in Mumbai, which has run its civic administration for a number of years (Hansen 2001).

5 As Zérah (2008) points out, colonial cities have thus been "splintered" from their very inception. See also McFarlane (2008).
6 This provides further evidence of the ways in which citizenship is tied to claims of property in the city (see Joyce 2003). In the time since conducting this research, the cutoff date has been extended to 2000. First established in the 1970s, as a means to permit *some* settlements the benefits of municipal infrastructural improvement, the cutoff date has been consistently extended over the last four decades (see Weinstein 2014, Doshi 2012).
7 Recent works on ignorance and the public secret has drawn attention to the ways in which "active not-knowing" is critical to the power and authority of states (Taussig 1999: 7, Mathews 2008, Harvey and Knox 2015, Anand 2015). By knowing not to know about illegal connections, engineers produce and occupy an "ambiguous moral space" (Harvey and Knox 2015), in which unlawful connections, necessary to the lives of certain settlers, are connected to and become the city's water infrastructure.
8 Unlike Coelho's (2006) experiences in Chennai, all the engineers I met in Mumbai's water department were men.
9 In a remarkable paper, Stefan Helmreich (2010) urges us to think with water, but cautions against fetishizing its materiality. Instead, he urges us to examine how theory can emerge with and "athwart" the dynamic ways in which water is made to flow. Athwart Helmreich, I focus on pressure not to reify water's materiality but rather to locate the materiality of water amidst the political processes that govern its flow.

References

Anand, Nikhil (2011) "Pressure: The PoliTechnics of Water Supply in Mumbai". *Cultural Anthropology* 26(4): 542–564.

Anand, Nikhil (2015) "Leaky States: Water Audits, Ignorance and the Politics of Infrastructure". *Public Culture* 27(2): 305–330.

Benjamin, Solly (2005) "Touts, Pirates and Ghosts," in *Bare Acts*, Sarai Reader 05. Williamsberg, NY: Autonomedia.

Chandavarkar, Rajnarayan (2007) "Customs of Governance: Colonialism and Democracy in Twentieth Century India". *Modern Asian Studies* 41(3): 441–470.

Chatterjee, Partha (2004) *The Politics of the Governed: Reflections on Popular Politics in Most of the World*. New York: Columbia University Press.

Coelho, Karen (2006) "Tapping In: Leaky Sovereignties and Engineered Dis(Order) in an Urban Water System," in *Turbulence*, Sarai Reader 06. Williamsberg, NY: Autonomedia.

Doshi, Sapana (2012) "The Politics of the Evicted: Redevelopment, Subjectivity, and Difference in Mumbai's Slum Frontier". *Antipode* 45(4): 844–865.

Dossal, Mariam (1991) *Imperial Designs and Indian Realities: The Planning of Bombay City, 1845–1875*. Bombay: Oxford University Press.

Graham, Stephen (2010) "When Infrastructures Fail," in S. Graham (ed.) *Disrupted Cities: When Infrastructure Fails*. New York: Routledge.

Gupta, Akhil (1995) "Blurred Boundaries: The Discourse of Corruption, the Culture of Politics, and the Imagined State". *American Ethnologist* 22(2): 375–402.

Gupta, Akhil, and Aradhana Sharma (2006) "Globalization and Postcolonial States". *Current Anthropology* 47(2): 277–307.

Hansen, Thomas B. (2001) *Violence in Urban India*. New Delhi: Permanent Black.

Hansen, Thomas B., and Oskar Verkaaik (2009) "Introduction – Urban Charisma: On Everyday Mythologies in the City". *Critique of Anthropology* 29(1): 5–26.

Harvey, Penelope, and Hannah Knox (2015) *Roads: An Anthropology of Infrastructure and Expertise*. Ithaca, NY and London: Cornell University Press.

Helmreich, Stefan (2010) "Nature, Culture, Seawater". Paper presented at the Meeting of the Society of Cultural Anthropology, Santa Fe, May 7.

Hull, Matthew (2003) "The File: Agency, Authority, and Autography in an Islamabad Bureaucracy". *Language & Communication* 23(3/4): 287–314.

Jensen, Casper Bruun (2016) "Pipe dreams: Sewage infrastructure and activity trails in Phnom Penh", *Ethnos: Journal of Anthropology*. Online First: http://dx.doi.org/10.1080/00141844.2015.1107608.

Joyce, Patrick (2003) *The Rule of Freedom: Liberalism and the Modern City*. New York: Verso.

Mathews, Andrew (2008) "State Making, Knowledge, and Ignorance: Translation and Concealment in Mexican Forestry Institutions". *American Anthropologist* 110(4): 484–494.

McFarlane, Colin (2008) "Governing the Contaminated City: Infrastructure and Sanitation in Colonial and Post-Colonial Bombay". *International Journal of Urban and Regional Research* 32(2): 415–435.

Mehta, Lyla (2005) *The Politics and Poetics of Water: Naturalising Scarcity in Western India*. New Delhi: Orient Longman.

Scott, James (1990) *Domination and the Arts of Resistance: Hidden Transcripts*. New Haven, CT: Yale University Press.

Sundaram, Ravi (2010) *Pirate Modernity: Delhi's Media Urbanism*. New York: Routledge.

Taussig, Michael T. (1999) *Defacement: Public Secrecy and the Labor of the Negative*. Stanford, CA: Stanford University Press.

Weinstein, Liza (2014) *The Durable Slum: Dharavi and the Right to Stay Put in Globalizing Mumbai*. Minneapolis: University of Minnesota Press.

Wittfogel, Karl August (1957) *Oriental Despotism: A Comparative Study of Total Power*. New Haven, CT: Yale University Press.

Zérah, Marie (2008) "Splintering Urbanism in Mumbai: Contrasting Trends in a Multilayered Society". *Geoforum* 39(6): 1922–1932.

8 Infrastructuring new urban common worlds?

On material politics, civic attachments, and partially existing wind turbines

Anders Blok

> You now have all this fancy technology, and you are still unable to represent any controversy about projects, about windmills and so on, which is now the normal state of affairs for technology.
> (Bruno Latour, interview in Blok and Jensen 2011: 153)

Introduction: the publicization of infrastructures?

On September 18, 2009, the blade of a giant wind turbine descended on the town hall square in Copenhagen. Using paint made available by the Environmental Office of the municipal administration, local kids were invited to literally "lend a hand" to the city's green energy transition by imprinting their fingers onto this future-laden technology (Figure 8.1). Symbolically, this gesture would serve to publicly endorse a new municipal Climate Action Plan, in which 100 wind turbines were to be installed on the city's territory, marking at once an infrastructural and eco-political ambition. As such, the event bore all the insignia of techno-political spectacle as a familiar format of modern power (Larkin 2013), carefully staged this time in front of the concrete architectural form of the urban collective, the town hall. Speeches of local politicians made clear that, from now on, wind turbines were to be the *res publica*, the public thing, of Copenhagen life – a visible and celebrated marker of the city's dedication to "the climate fight."

A little less than two years later, however, the fate of four 140-meter-tall wind turbines, forming part of the action plan, came to a much less spectacular end. Projected by architects and engineers to be build off the tip of a 350-hectare peninsula undergoing urban renewal, known as *Nordhavn* (North Harbor), the national parliament decided to pass legislation that banned wind turbines from this otherwise 'green' and 'sustainable' urban planning project. Acting on the direct initiative of the Ministry of Transport, the wind turbines were sacrificed as part of a wider national infrastructural settlement, meant to authorize the construction of a new container ship terminal on the site. Journalists and others were quick to note a backdrop of civic anti-wind turbine protest (see Blok and Meilvang 2015). Whatever the trigger, the resultant

Figure 8.1 Kids decorating the blade of a wind turbine in Copenhagen's town hall square
(Photo by Ilan Brender, copyright Polfoto)

show of legal sovereignty met with much dismay among Copenhagen planners and politicians, who saw little justification for such heavy-handed interference in what was, presumably, a shared ambition of infrastructural redesign in the face of global challenges.

In this chapter I leverage the Copenhagen wind turbine story – part of wider and ongoing fieldwork[1] – in order to pose questions about the material politics of urban infrastructures, including the place of public contestation and civic attachments in its enactment. If, as anthropologist Alberto Corsín-Jiménez argues (2014: 342), "cities worldwide are witnessing today a transformation of their infrastructural and material landscapes," such transformation is effected in no small part in the name of how planetary ecological threats become tangible and urgent in cities. Concern with climate change, in particular, animates a range of urban infrastructural interventions to achieve (so-called) low-carbon and resilient cities. As I will argue here, however, analyses of this urban situation have so far failed to take sufficiently note of the ways in which material infrastructural objects, like the Copenhagen wind turbines, come to be embroiled in public and democratic politics in the city.

Conversely, the present chapter suggests that, understood as specific settings of material politics, eco-urban planning interventions in the wake of climate change pose important analytical challenges to work on infrastructures in science and technology studies (STS), anthropology, sociology, and beyond. In these fields, infrastructures have often been described as the sunk, unnoticed, and indeed invisible backdrops to socio-cultural life, requiring for their study the figure-ground reversal that Geoffrey Bowker famously dubbed infrastructural inversion (e.g. Bowker 1994). In urban-ecological settings, however, infrastructures are inverted, so to speak, almost by default: here, multiple and conflicting actors engage in an explicit material politics of urban redesign, in which relations among urban life, technologies, and nature(s) are turned into contested matters of public concern. These settings, in short, enact a certain publicization of infrastructures (Rubio and Fogué 2013).

Wind turbines are good candidates for inquiring into such dynamics – in part because they are, in a banal sense, highly *visible* infrastructural objects (the theme of in/visibility, as we shall see, comes with more complications). More importantly, what the not-yet-stabilized energy infrastructural transition signaled by the Copenhagen wind turbines entails is a situation in which the social and the material is, as it were, held in mutual suspension (see Corsín-Jiménez 2014). Whereas technology may indeed be "society made durable," in Bruno Latour's (1991) famous phrase, the ethical-political ground on which new infrastructures are to stabilize is here as unsettled as the technologies. The work of socio-technical redesign thus becomes a site of forging and stabilizing – that is, of infrastructuring, or "infra-commoning" (Amin 2014) – a set of new urban habits and habitats.

Rephrased in these terms, the question elicited by the Copenhagen wind turbines is the following: under what conditions do socio-material urban worlds acquire qualities that we may call *infrastructural*, in the sense of ordering heterogeneous technical and ethical-political forces in converging, layered, and relatively stabilized ways? In what follows, I pursue this question by way of engaging certain intersections of STS and political theory, specifically of a pragmatist bent. In particular, I hope to show that Noortje Marres' work on material publics (2007) in conjunction with the French neo-pragmatists Bruno Latour and Laurent Thévenot prove helpful in rethinking the politics of civic contestation and attachments to material ecologies at stake in the redesign of urban infrastructures. In complementary fashion, I argue, concepts from each of these analysts prove helpful in staying sensitive to the very *shifts* in meanings and material practices of infrastructural politics. The Copenhagen wind turbines provide a suitable test site for the argument.

Urban infrastructure transitions in question

Over the past few years I have conducted multi-sited ethnographic work in an attempt to trace the way supposedly global climate risks come to be differently mediated in and through the built environments of cities, including Surat in India, Kyoto in Japan, and Copenhagen. These otherwise disparate cities are tied together by certain investments on the part of planners, politicians, architects, and civic groups in the promise of new eco-adjusted infrastructures to mediate a range of local and global concerns (Blok 2014). Indeed, while a recent phenomenon, the idea that cities around the world are undergoing 'low-carbon transition,' accompanied by a more specific 'energy transition,' is fast becoming something of a truism within urban studies, as well as amongst wider industry, urban policy, planning and activist circles (see, e.g. Broto and Bulkeley 2013). In niche-like and 'experimental' fashion, such actors turn city spaces into open-ended field trials for infrastructural innovation.

While there is, in general, little doubt in the real-world significance of this welter of urban activity, the *analytics* of urban infrastructural transition, as this has arisen mainly in urban governance studies, arguably leaves something to be desired. One recurring trope of this literature is the figure of the gap: across geographical sites, some authors report, for example, "a large gap between the symbolic representation of a low carbon future and their material manifestations in low carbon technologies and infrastructure in particular places" (Hodson, Marvin and Bulkeley 2013: 1403). Low-carbon transition, in short, is depicted as a matter of 'closing the gap' between symbolic gesturing and material realities. I suggest, however, that what is missing here is rather the *reality* of material infrastructural politics, something to which this literature pays scant attention.[2]

One way of cultivating such attention is to return to what is arguably *the* canonical STS statement on infrastructures. As Susan Leigh Star (1999: 380) notes, the image of infrastructure as an invisible substratum – railroad lines, pipes, wires, electrical power plants – is immediately complicated once we begin to investigate large-scale technical systems *in the making*. Here, the fundamentally relational nature of infrastructure becomes visible: to the wind turbine planner, renewable energy systems are not background but foreground; "one person's infrastructure is another's topic, or difficulty" (ibid.). Whereas Larkin (2013: 336) is thus right to critique the somewhat repetitive emphasis on Star's claim that infrastructures are "by definition invisible" and only "become visible on breakdown" – including as these points are made in relation to networked urban energy infrastructures (e.g. Graham and Marvin 2001) – his own corrective to some extent rehearses well-worn STS points.

The more obvious trouble with Star's assertion, it seems to me, is one of changing political settings: having studied contexts of information infrastructure that were, in her memorable words, widely taken as "singularly unexciting," it is not clear how this bears on settings, such as those of urban low-carbon transition, which a whole array of powerful actors find endlessly exciting. To some extent this parallels the argument made by Noortje Marres and Javier Lezaun (2011) on the territory of material politics: classical STS studies, they argue – including Winner's study of highway bridges (1980) – inscribed technologies into a politics of ordering that was always silent, implicit, invisible, or at least under-articulated.[3] By contrast, analyzing the materials and devices of public engagement allows one to see how material things, technologies, and infrastructures become invested with more or less *explicit* political and moral capacities. This point, as noted, has clear traction for wind turbines.

Expanding further, Marres (2013: 2) notes how the idea that non-human objects and technologies, such as urban infrastructures, participate actively in socio-cultural and political life is fast becoming increasingly obvious and widespread, in part due precisely to the proliferation of sustainability initiatives in policy, business, science, and culture. Such proliferation, she argues, entails a need to retool STS analytics, towards seeing the politics of material objects as itself an 'experimental' effect of specific empirical settings. In other words, rather than simply positing objects *as* political, "we must investigate how they become *invested* with specific normative powers through the deployment of particular settings and devices" (ibid.: 3). Among other things, I argue, this means asking how infrastructural objects like wind turbines come to be deployed as part of the public settings of urban democratic politics.

This debate on the explicitness or otherwise of material infrastructures and their attendant forms of public politics also already has its urban version. In an interesting article, Rubio and Fogué (2013) thus show how, far from given, urban infrastructures *became* invisible as part of modernist urban planning initiatives from the mid-nineteenth century onwards. What such plans enacted was a strong and materialized border between, on the one hand, the above-surface human world of socio-cultural and political relations and, on the other, the below-surface 'sub-political' world of black-boxed technological flows, governed by expert knowledge. Nowadays, however, Rubio and Fogué suggest, this border is coming undone once again, in a process of infrastructural publicization. The example they give is a set of energy system design interventions, undertaken by architectural consultants and including solar panels as a key technological presence, to be embedded in a public square in Madrid.

While this neat historical narrative of the 'in/visibilizing' of urban infrastructures is surely in danger of redoing Euro-centrism (cf. Larkin 2013), to highlight how urban infrastructures increasingly come into public view, and to insist on the emplaced nature of this process, seems highly pertinent to discussions on urban low-carbon transition. Indeed, to my mind, it seems hardly coincidental that Rubio and Fogué should point to *renewable* energy technologies as the material mediator of this publicization process. If one thinks of the histories of wind and solar power since the 1970s, for instance, it might be credibly claimed that these 'environmental' infrastructures are central to the way energy issues have become politicized across a variety of settings for public engagement and contestation. I return now to Copenhagen, as a recent instantiation of this material politics in action.

The shifting settings of urban infrastructural politics

At first sight, the story of wind turbines in Copenhagen is rather mundane, as far as technological politics goes. Conflict has attended the spread of wind turbines over Danish (and other) rural landscapes since the 1970s (see Krauss 2010) – and there is nothing surprising in the fact that wind turbines should be contested objects in an urban setting as well. From their early days as products of a technology-oriented social movement (Hess 2005), wind turbines have since become the business of multinational companies, growing progressively larger and more visually intrusive in the process. The attending controversies over landscapes and aesthetic codes are well documented in many parts of the world (e.g. Rygg 2012). Yet, this relative ordinariness feeds my purpose, because it facilitates a focus more specifically on the settings and devices of urban politics, whereby "partially existing" (Jensen 2010) wind turbines become matters of public concern in Copenhagen.

The techno-political spectacle of the town hall square and the national parliamentary judicial machinery, with which this chapter opened, might be considered two such settings, in which wind turbines come to be invested with specific and indeed conflicting moral–political capacities. In the first setting, the town hall square, wind turbines mediate the risks of climate change in engaging, tactile, responsible, and future-oriented ways. In the second setting, the parliamentary law-making committee, wind turbines have been radically rescaled and repositioned, now sacrificed as part of an infrastructural entanglement considered of national rather than only city-wide importance. In between these two events, the partially existing wind turbines have traveled through the urban fabric, acquiring and losing moral–political capacities for mediating public concerns with infrastructures – including some less environmentally benign ones, like visual pollution, noise, and the killing of birds.

Whereas material wind turbines are clearly visible, partially existing wind turbines are not so – until, that is, they *become* visible in and through the devices and settings of urban planning, participation. and civic activism. Such devices, broadly speaking, take the shape of visual inscriptions, making for a contested politics of sensible cityscapes in-the-making (cf. Blok and Meilvang 2015). They include the urban planning aerial map, with future wind turbines dotted onto them; the architectural model, where wind turbines form part of a techno-utopian green aesthetic; and the civic activist photograph, visually manipulated to project the technical object into situated contexts and perspectives. Each of these different visual inscriptions, and the way they circulate in documents and on the web, allow for their own set of attendant possibilities for public engagement and articulation of concern.

Tracing such shifts and turns in the fate of wind turbines, in short, provides an "issue-oriented" (Marres 2007) approach to a distinctly *urban* material politics of infrastructuring. Importantly, this issue trajectory activates a range of legal–political devices of urban planning, such as the hearing and the environmental impact assessment, which serve as settings for the articulation of public concern. A full empirical rendering is beyond the scope of this chapter. One important tension, however, is the way in which wind turbines respectively gain and lose infrastructural qualities, understood as their networked and distributed character, as they move across shifting settings. Hence, for instance, whereas these qualities are clearly present in the way the municipal Climate Action Plan envisages the 100 new wind turbines, they are less so when attention shifts to the specific setting of future *Nordhavn* architectural designs. Here, the four projected wind turbines look more like isolated technical objects. In this sense, the material politics of urban

108 Anders Blok

infrastructures in-the-making traces a complicated and uneven path of shifting in/visibilities, inversions, and scales of socio-technical change.

At their most explicit, the Copenhagen Climate Action Plan and its set of aligned visual inscriptions serves to articulate what Bruno Latour (2007) might call a new "cosmogram," an urban planning diagram that renders publicly visible a set of strived-for relations between the city, material infrastructures and natures, both proximate and more distant. However, as I have hinted, this urban planning cosmogram meets with public contestation, turning the wind turbine story into a case of urban 'cosmopolitics' – the politics, as Latour notes (ibid.), of sorting out conflicting cosmograms as part of searching for a common world of human and non-human cohabitation (Blok and Farías 2016). Notably, as often observed around wind turbine issues, such tensions tend to arise at the point of transition from infrastructural plans to concrete technical objects, the projection of which spark civic groups into being through their shared concern with specific place-based attachments (cf. Marres 2007).

In one case of civic concern, which I have studied quite intensely, opposition comes from an ad hoc group of upper-middle-class residents residing along the north coast of Copenhagen, alarmed by the prospect of having their seaside views and historical townscape adversely impacted by the *Nordhavn* urban redevelopment plans, in general, and its four projected wind turbines, in particular (Blok and Meilvang 2015). Through various acts of counter-visualization and counter-mobilization (see Figure 8.2), enacted via new assemblies of concerned citizens and local politicians, this group eventually succeeded in forging alliances that reached well into the halls of national power – more specifically, the Ministry of Transport. This work of civic activism thus formed part of the background when, as noted, the Ministry in 2011 decided

Figure 8.2 Counter-visualization of wind turbines from concerned public group (Copyright: Grundejerforeningen Hellerup og Maglegaard and FOGUS)

to enact its own set of infrastructural and material-political entanglements, by way of mobilizing the law-making machinery of the national parliament.

Quite predictably, the resulting law, which authorized the construction of the country's largest container ship terminal, set in motion a new set of public environmental contestation. Meanwhile, to the Copenhagen planners, the law shifted the terrain for their material politics of wind turbine expansion. Hence, the municipality had to initiate a new search, undertaken together with consultants, for other sites in which to house their low-carbon ambitions. Until now, this search has proven largely in vain, stranded in various legal complications. Six years after the techno-political spectacle on the town hall square, just three wind turbines have come to material fruition in the city.

Which pragmatist material politics of urban infrastructuring?

With this brief recounting of the Copenhagen wind turbine story, I hope to have shown that, far from being confined to one well-defined setting or device, the material politics of this emerging infrastructural object is one in which the object itself – and the issues and scales attached to it – is constantly moving, attaining and losing moral-political qualities, and becoming embroiled in a shifting terrain of conflicts. To subsume all of this activity under the figure of a generalized political 'gap' between symbolic visions and material realities is clearly untenable. This is where the STS encounter with pragmatist philosophy, as instantiated in the material politics of Noortje Marres (2007, 2013) in particular, offers a much more promising route for an empirically sensitive approach to infrastructural techno-politics.

Yet, while enjoying the distinct advantage of highlighting the normative *variability* of technical objects across settings and devices, I also believe that Marres' (2013) "experimental" political ontology runs the risk of abstracting such settings from what we might call their 'political infrastructures' – that is, from the procedures and protocols, such as those of urban planning and activism, whereby the material politics of wind turbines and other energy infrastructures is shaped and articulated.[4] This, I suggest, is the juncture at which the analysis of infrastructures and infrastructuring in STS, anthropology, urban studies, and beyond requires not just new imaginations of what infrastructures might be, but also, crucially, of how to conceptualize and trace their complex fate as political objects. In the remainder of this chapter, I want to suggest two such neo-pragmatist possibilities.

First, alongside the general notion of cosmopolitics (borrowed from Isabelle Stengers), Bruno Latour (2007) has also attempted, in more differentiated terms, to outline a pragmatist theory of the *trajectories* traced by techno-political issues. Put simply, this model hinges on paying attention to the variable meanings of the very term 'politics' as it is articulated via shifting settings that each allow socio-material relations to be contested in specific ways. Latour detects five such movements and moments in material politics: STS renders new socio-material associations and cosmograms visible; Dewey and pragmatism pays attention to publics and their concerns; Carl Schmitt theorized the conditions of sovereignty; Habermas articulated the conditions of deliberative forums; and Foucault paved the way for seeing the machineries of bureaucratic techniques and rationalities as a paradoxical form of non-political politics. Not everything is 'political' in the same way.

So, to paraphrase the wind turbine story in this Latourian language, we might say that it started out with the articulation of a new urban cosmogram, coordinated into (partial) existence via the offices of municipal planners, architects, and engineering consultants. At this point, the infrastructural qualities of wind turbines were relatively explicit. From here, the wind turbines spilled over and became a problem of the public, as witnessed in the emergence of new concerned civic activist groups, who took visual inscriptions of what were by now isolated technical objects as their point of contention. Finally, in a dramatic twist of events, the wind turbines and their associated issues became part of the machinery of national sovereignty, terminating in a show of legal force which enacted its own set of techno-political entanglements vis-à-vis new large-scale shipping and trade infrastructures.

While thus helpful in articulating the empirical trajectory of wind turbine politics, this Latourian specification also leaves at least two questions pending. First, how exactly are we to account for the very *shifts* in the ontological-political state of infrastructural objects? It is one thing to offer a suitable descriptive language, but this is still not quite an account of the politics involved. Second, how seriously are we to take the claim – also enacted to some extent in my story – that the five senses of material politics recognized by Latour should constitute a well-ordered sequence of contestation and stabilization, replicated across infrastructural contexts? New infrastructural forms, this approach seems to suggest, will stabilize in the city by the time they become a matter of governmentality, that is, of routine bureaucratic disciplining of spaces, relations, and bodies.[5] While this is an interesting proposition, Latour's cosmopolitics is perhaps better treated as an open-ended set of modalities for different socio-material worlds than as a process with a pre-defined infrastructural outcome.

Which brings me, finally, to the second neo-pragmatist option for reimagining the politics of infrastructural objects, this time coming from Laurent Thévenot's recent notion of "commonality in the plural" (Thévenot 2014). While space prevents me from fully engaging this elaborate conceptual scheme, the central point is that Thévenot attempts to rethink the very conditions under which technological (and other) differences may be 'composed' in the political community. In doing so, he draws attention to certain distinctive *formats* of material politics that are hard to capture in the vocabularies of either Marres or Latour, in terms of how a shared socio-material world may be differently constructed and ordered in the first place (see Blok 2015). To readers of Thévenot, the best-known format is that of plural orders of worth, the very backdrop to the sociology of critique and justification developed with Luc Boltanski. However, Thévenot (2014) now adds two other formats: the format of choosing between options in a liberal public; and the format of personal affinities to common-places.

Whenever urban planning enacts officially scripted forms of public engagement with urban techno-politics, I have argued elsewhere (Blok and Meilvang 2015), it relies heavily on the format of choice in a liberal public. This is a format in which a set of well-delineated options (or 'stakes') is made publicly available to facilitate the expression of interests amongst 'stakeholders.' By contrast, civic activists tend to enact their critiques in ways that intricately combine all of the three techno-political formats. In the case of concerned anti-wind turbine publics, this includes acts of valuing the cityscape as such according to a compromise of 'green' and 'domestic' forms of public worth, while also investing specific material common-places, such as a historical harbor front, with shared attachments expressed in vernacular memories. As such, the work of urban techno-political activism articulates a version of what Thévenot calls the 'art of composition,' in which different formats of commonality must be coordinated around specific intermediary objects of concern, such as that of partially existing wind turbines.

Standard analyses and critiques of 'NIMBY-ism' ('not-in-my-back-yard'), arguably alive and well in expert worlds of infrastructure planning (e.g. Schick and Winthereik 2013), fails entirely to take into account this art of composition, in which civic attachments are rendered at least potentially sharable with others in ways that reach beyond the immediate material setting. For this reason, Thévenot's conceptual scheme opens up a different dimension of material politics, one attuned to the *variety* of ways in which socio-material worlds are rendered common and sharable. As such, it also assists in specifying the place of civic attachments to specific material ecologies and their embodied sensory qualities, in ways that neither totalizes their importance nor excludes them prematurely from public relevance (Blok 2015). As I have tried to show in this chapter, attention to the politics of civic attachments is only becoming more timely, as renewable energy infrastructures and related drives for urban low-carbon transitions turn infrastructures into visible and explicit forms of material politics.

Conclusion: the political unruliness of infrastructures?

To briefly recapitulate, this chapter has attempted to (re-)claim the situation of urban low-carbon transitions as fertile analytical territory for the (re-)turn to infrastructures in science and technology studies (STS), anthropology, sociology, and beyond. It has done so by elaborating an approach to the material politics of urban infrastructures in-the-making, taking recent controversies over wind turbines in Copenhagen as testing ground. Apart from the work of Noortje Marres (2007, 2013), whose reading of Dewey's political theory informs my understanding of the devices and settings of urban publics, I invoked the related but distinct neo-pragmatisms of Bruno Latour and Laurent Thévenot in order to rethink the techno-political trajectories by which infrastructures emerge and, possibly but not always, stabilize. Overall, I have taken these conceptual repertoires as complementary resources for undoing the less than productive way in which studies of urban low-carbon transition has postulated a general political 'gap' between symbolic visions and their (lack of) materialization.

In this sense, my chapter responds to the way in which the ongoing publicization of infrastructures in settings of low-carbon transition – where infrastructures are, so to speak, inverted by default – also requires, as Corsin-Jiménez notes (2014: 358), "a reconsideration of the very techno-material nature of that thing called 'public' or 'commons' in the city." The pragmatist-inspired notion of material politics, I argue, is well suited to undertake this reconsideration in empirically sensitive and normatively open-ended ways. Pursuing this agenda, however, will involve also a careful (re-)consideration of the conceptual tools needed to trace the *shifting* fates of infrastructures as contested urban political issues. Here, my exploration of wind turbines is meant to join related calls for experimenting with different resources for bringing the multiplicity of political materials into view (Jensen 2015), in ways that remain attentive to the specific devices and settings of urban (cosmo-)politics.

In engaging this line of inquiry, one is also ultimately forced, I believe, to agree with Larkin (2013: 329) in noting that "infrastructures are conceptually unruly." Within contemporary settings of urban material politics in action, it is no longer obvious, to paraphrase Star (1999), what parts of the socio-material landscape form the 'infrastructure,' as opposed to the 'difficulty,' of our shared co-existence. Such shifts, I have suggested, become particularly obvious in the case of wind turbines, as these are translated back-and-forth between an infrastructural state of political being and the emplacement as contested technical objects in the landscape. More generally, orienting urban planning towards low-carbon transition arguably means holding the social and the material in mutual suspension (Corsin-Jiménez 2014), with uncertainty and critical tensions accruing on all sides of the contested search for novel ways of 'infra-commoning' our socio-material worlds.

Such, I would argue, is the sense in which the infrastructural, in its technological and ethical-political senses, becomes newly problematic in the face of global ecological *unsettlements*, as mediated not least through urban settings around the world. If responding to these challenges require of us to reinvent, tooth and nail, the ingredients of our urban socio-technical worlds, then we clearly need more experiments on the moral–political capacities of infrastructures, in research and in practice.

Notes

1 I draw in this chapter on a combination of empirical materials, including fieldwork at public hearings, interviews with experts and civic activists, media reports, official planning documents, and architectural visualizations. For lack of space, I allow

myself to background methodological choices and tribulations. See Blok and Meilvang (2015) for a fuller account.
2 A similar critique is echoed in more recent work on urban energy transitions, where calls are now made for attending more closely to the materiality and politics of energy (Rutherford and Coutard 2014: 1369).
3 For these reasons, Marres and Lezaun (2011) speak of "sub-politics" (in a sense different from Ulrich Beck) when describing this approach. In ways reminiscent of the very distinction between infra- and superstructures, then, their argument arguably amounts to an infrastructural inversion of the politics of things.
4 For an analysis of national parliaments as political infrastructures for taking nature issues into account, see Asdal and Hobæk 2016.
5 In my view, Latour's intervention casts interesting light on much Foucault-inspired work on the disciplinary effects of already-established infrastructures (cf. Larkin 2013), where authors tend to conflate a sense of politics as governmentality with the quite different Dewey-inspired claim around concerned publics.

References

Amin, Ash (2014) "Lively Infrastructure," *Theory, Culture & Society* 31(7/8): 137–161.
Asdal, Kristin and Hobæk, Bård (2016) "Assembling the whale: parliaments in the politics of nature," *Science as Culture* 25(1): 96–116.
Blok, Anders (2014) "Worlding cities through their climate projects?" *CITY* 18(3): 269–286.
Blok, Anders (2015) "Attachments to the common-place: pragmatic sociology and the aesthetic cosmopolitics of eco-housing design in Kyoto, Japan," *European Journal of Cultural and Political Sociology* 2(2): 122–145.
Blok, Anders and Jensen, Torben Elgaard (2011) *Bruno Latour: Hybrid Thoughts in a Hybrid World*. London: Routledge.
Blok, Anders and Farías, Ignacio (eds) (2016) *Urban Cosmopolitics: Agencements, Assemblies, Atmospheres*. London: Routledge.
Blok, Anders and Meilvang, Marie L. (2015) "Picturing urban green attachments: civic activists moving between familiar and public engagements in the city," *Sociology* 49(1): 19–37.
Bowker, Geoffrey C. (1994) *Science on the Run: Information Management and Industrial Geophysics at Schlumberger, 1920–1940*. Cambridge, MA: MIT Press.
Broto, Vanesa C. and Bulkeley, Harriet (2013) "A survey of urban climate change experiments in 100 cities," *Global Environmental Change* 23(1): 92–102.
Corsín-Jiménez, Alberto (2014) "The right to infrastructure: a prototype for open source urbanism," *Environment and Planning D* 32(2): 342–362.
Graham, Stephen and Marvin, Simon (2001) *Splintering Urbanism*. London: Routledge.
Hess, David J. (2005) "Technology- and product-oriented movements: approximating social movement studies and science and technology studies," *Science, Technology & Human Values* 30(4): 515–535.
Hodson, Mike, Marvin, Simon and Bulkeley, Harriet (2013) "The intermediary organisation of low carbon cities: a comparative analysis of transitions in Greater London and Greater Manchester," *Urban Studies* 50(7): 1403–1422.
Jensen, Casper Bruun (2010) *Ontologies for Developing Things: Making Health Care Futures Through Technology*. Rotterdam: Sense Publishers.

Jensen, Casper Bruun (2015) "Experimenting with political materials: environmental infrastructures and ontological transformations," *Distinktion: Scandinavian Journal of Social Theory* 16(1): 17–30.

Krauss, Werner (2010) "The 'Dingpolitik' of wind energy in Northern German landscapes: an ethnographic case study," *Landscape Research* 35(2): 195–208.

Larkin, Brian (2013) "The politics and poetics of Infrastructure," *Annual Review of Anthropology* 42(1): 327–343.

Latour, Bruno (1991) "Technology is society made durable," in J. Law (ed.) *A Sociology of Monsters: Essays on Power, Technology and Domination.* London: Routledge, pp. 103–132.

Latour, Bruno (2007) "Turning around politics," *Social Studies of Science* 37(5): 811–820.

Marres, Noortje (2007) "The issues deserve more credit: pragmatist contributions to the study of public involvement in controversy," *Social Studies of Science* 37(5): 759–780.

Marres, Noortje (2013) "Why political ontology must be experimentalized: on eco-show homes as devices of participation," *Social Studies of Science* 43(3): 417–443.

Marres, Noortje and Lezaun, Javier (2011) "Materials and devices of the public: an introduction," *Economy and Society* 40(4): 489–509.

Rubio, Fernando Domínguez and Fogué, Uriel (2013) "Technifying public spaces and publicizing infrastructures: exploring new urban political ecologies through the square of General Vara del Rey," *International Journal of Urban and Regional Research* 37(3): 1035–1052.

Rutherford, Jonathan and Coutard, Olivier (2014) "Urban energy transitions: places, processes and politics of socio-technical change," *Urban Studies* 51(7): 1353–1377.

Rygg, Bente Johnsen (2012) "Wind power: an assault on local landscapes or an opportunity for modernization?" *Energy Policy* 48: 167–175.

Schick, Lea and Winthereik, Brit Ross (2013): "Innovating relations: or why smart grid is not too complex for the public," *Science & Technology Studies* 26(3): 82–102.

Star, Susan Leigh (1999) "The ethnography of Infrastructure," *American Behavioral Scientist* 43(3): 377–391.

Thévenot, Laurent (2014) "Voicing concern and difference: from public spaces to common-places," *European Journal of Cultural and Political Sociology* 1(1): 7–34.

Winner, Langdon (1980): "Do artifacts have politics?" *Daedalus* 109(1): 121–136.

9 Remediating infrastructure

Tokyo's commuter train network and the new autonomy

Michael Fisch

In urban centers throughout the world the integration of computer technology into existing crucial urban infrastructures (transportation, water, power) is being welcomed by governments, city planners, and corporations alike as key to the realization of an ecologically and economically sustainable and resilient platform for future society. The urban form emerging from these projects – often glossed as the "smart city" – has for some time captured the attention of scholars in architecture and urban design, media studies, geography, and sociology. However, as the sociocultural anthropologist Brian Larkin suggests, anthropology has only just begun to explore its significance (Larkin 2013). A central challenge for anthropology, I want to suggest in this regard, is to explore the ontologies of this emerging form. What I mean by ontologies draws on an understanding of the term developed in science and technology studies as the "worlds" constituted vis-à-vis the situated and analytical practices and materialities of a given environment (Gad, Jensen, and Winthereik 2015). But it refers more specifically to the kind of thinking that is elicited within that given environment.[1] In placing an emphasis on the relation between ontology and thinking, I share an intellectual and methodological concern with the geographer Nigel Thrift, who asks how the advent of smart infrastructure produces a fluid "movement-space" that lends itself to new limits and possibilities of thinking (Thrift 2004). In other words, the question is not what such spaces mean but how they compel us to think and to become. At the same time, my approach departs from Thrift's central assumption in an important way.

As with many analyses of smart infrastructure, Thrift underscores the way in which smart infrastructure transforms built environments from fixed structures into dynamic fields able to respond to changes in the environment.[2] As another thinker concerned with the dynamic quality of smart infrastructure puts it, the analytical emphasis falls on the way in which urban space becomes "interactive" rather than "delineated" (Steiner 2011). Whereas interactive space is defined as networked and reflexive, delineated space is treated as confining, determined, static, and imposing. As such, the smart city seems in many ways to fulfill the desire of early cyberneticians for the displacement of modernity's "logic of compartmentalization" with a (postmodern) "logic of connection" (Martin 1998). It is Gilles Deleuze who then takes up the question of the ontological significance of this new computer-driven networked world, parsing the transition in terms of a move from institutional enclosures of disciplinary society (á la Michel Foucault) to modulating networks of "societies of control" (Deleuze 1992).

Deleuze's argument seems wonderfully prophetic in many ways. But the issue of control that Deleuze raises quickly leads to a dilemma, or rather paralysis, for thinking about autonomy if we understand the term as referring to individual independence as manifest in the ability to act free of external influences. What Deleuze offers, it would seem in this regard, is a cynical vision in which the moment we break free from the institutional enclosures of disciplinary society and are on the cusp of realizing autonomy is also the moment when we find ourselves even more deeply entrapped in a far more nefarious system of control. Consequently, we find ourselves longing as well for a return to disciplinary society as a time when autonomy seemed at least more of a possibility. At least then we were able to nurse the illusion that there was hope outside enclosure or, better yet, in revolution.

In the following argument, I want to propose that approaching enclosure and modulation, compartmentalization and connection as entangled rather than antithetical modalities of infrastructural control guides us to thinking autonomy not only in different terms but also in a different conceptual register. To do so, I turn to Tokyo's commuter train network. Beginning in the late 1990s, Tokyo's largest commuter train operator, JR East, began upgrading its train lines with an advanced information technology system. Designated an Autonomous Decentralized Transport Operation System (ATOS), the new technology works to transform JR East's train network into a dynamic decentralized smart system that optimizes the flows of trains and passengers through the city. Yet Tokyo's century-old phenomenon of packed trains remains the network's defining feature and a modular space par excellence. As such, the system straddles infrastructural modalities that are typically differentiated as twentieth-century mechanical and twenty-first-century informational. In situating myself between these modalities, I hope to elaborate this different conceptual register of autonomy, or what I am calling the new autonomy of smart systems.

Revisiting enclosures

Nothing embodies enclosure in modern Tokyo quite like the packed commuter train. Every weekday millions of commuters throughout the Greater Metropolitan Area of Tokyo converge on the region's dense web of train stations to board trains in which they must stand compressed together so tightly that they can barely breathe. As one commuter described it for me, "you feel as if your organs are going to be crushed."[3] But Tokyo's commuter trains are not simply crowded – they operate beyond capacity. On average, during the morning rush hours train lines carry between 175 to 230 % beyond capacity

(Mizoguchi 2007). In tangible terms, this means that a train car designed for a maximum of 162 riders will actually accommodate between 300 to 400 commuters.[4] It also means that train companies must stream one train after another to stations with an absolute minimal gap between them in order to accommodate platform crowds. A delay of any kind introduces a vicious cycle, leading to intense platform crowding and more delay, which spreads quickly throughout the network to other train lines. Insofar as trains do not remain congested throughout the day, operation beyond capacity is the central defining characteristic of train operation.

How, then, does operation beyond capacity and the packed train ask us to think about autonomy? At first glance Tokyo's packed train figures as nothing less than a literal instantiation of Max Weber's "Iron Cage" (Weber 1976). It is a spectacular expression of capitalism's rationalizing logic whereby human beings are objectified as mere cargo conveyed in accordance with capitalism's merciless imperatives of mass production. To be a commuter, according to this thinking, is to submit to mechanistic conditioning, to be "trained," as it were, to comply with the operational imperatives of the apparatus. The more rationalized the system, the more intense the training and the less leeway there is for play between its parts."[5] The end result is an increasing loss of commuter autonomy, with commuters becoming mere automatons performing as disciplined cogs in the machine. If we stick to this story, smart technology then enters the picture as effecting a paradigm shift. Specifically, its schema of decentralization, self-organization, and network flexibility are seen as liberating commuters from the rigid dictates of the machine and restoring individual autonomy.[6] Indeed, as we will see at a later point, this is one way in which the introduction of smart systems in Tokyo's commuter train network was embraced.

What if there was another way to tell this story in which the move to smart infrastructure did not constitute a radical break from a rigid system to flexible network but rather a transition with continuity? How might this approach change how we think autonomy? The Japanese economist and railroad historian, Yuko Mito, offers an initial avenue toward a different approach when she explains that the system realizes its high degree of punctuality and capacity through its ability to be both precise and imprecise (Mito 2005). This quality, Mito shows, is the consequence of a social and technological evolution whose emergence can be traced back to periods when train companies faced the challenge of drastically increasing capacity without the benefit of additional infrastructure.[7] The formative period was around World War I when an economic boom spurred an increase in demand for rail transport. As one might expect, train companies devoted significant effort to rationalizing operations so as to increase the number of trains per hour and capacity per train. But rationalization is not the whole story. More importantly, train operators learned to finesse the system. That is, they realized that rather than strive for absolute precision, which would demand that commuters and train operators comply with an increasingly rigid schedule, they could surpass

118 *Michael Fisch*

the systems' threshold by increasing its resilience to imprecision. This realization took shape in an informal strategy of organized imprecision that allowed for regular divergence from the schedule (to accommodate platform crowds) followed by the quick recovery of lost time. The strategy was then refined and optimized in subsequent periods of rapid urbanization.

With the strategy of finessing the system the focus of train operators shifted from maintaining the schedule to maintaining the gap between schedule and divergence. We can see this clearly in the use of the train traffic diagram or, *ressha daiya* – hereafter just *daiya* (see Figure 9.1). As I have explained elsewhere (Fisch 2013), a train traffic diagram is a universal technology for planning and managing a train schedule. Each train line has its own *daiya*, and each line of the diagram represents a single train, with the angle of the line indicating the specified speed of the train on sections of track – the more vertical the line, the faster the speed; and the more horizontal the line, the slower the speed (Tomii 2005). Importantly, the *daiya* is composed of two parts: a planned (ideal) diagram that is developed in accordance with data collected on transport demand, and an operational diagram that reflects the lived

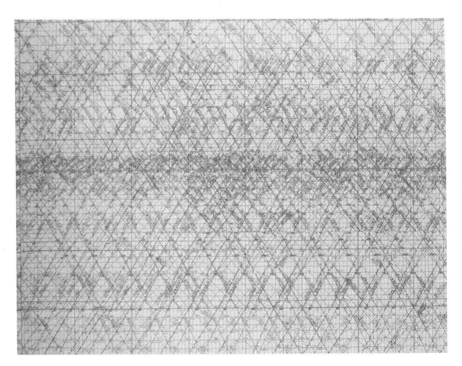

Figure 9.1 A section from a *daiya* representing two hours of train traffic on one train line
(Tomii 2005)

tempo of the network and is produced in conjunction with the system's actual performance. What railroad operators strive to maintain is the gap between these different *daiya*.

Such attention to the gap recalls what the French philosopher of techne, Gilbert Simondon, explains as the "margin of indeterminacy" of a technological ensemble. Put simply, a technical ensemble's margin of indeterminacy denotes the degree to which its functioning remains open to changes and contingencies within its environment of operation. It is the viable parameter of divergence in the pattern of interaction among heterogeneous elements constituting a machine or technological ensemble, designating a zone of undetermination that is opened in the functioning of a technology. The media theorist Adrian Mackenzie aptly paraphrases the significance of this undetermination in a work that mobilizes Simondon toward a reassessment of technology when he writes, "A fully determined mechanism would no longer be technological; it would be an inert object, or junk" (Mackenzie 2006, 53). As Mackenzie suggests, the margin of indeterminacy is what allows the technological ensemble to "suspend its final determination" such that it remains flexible to environmental changes. Moreover, the more an ensemble is able to "suspend its final determination," the more optimized it performs, allowing it, for example, to operate beyond capacity. Such thinking overturns the logic dictating that the more optimized the commuter train network performs for operation beyond capacity, the more intense its automatizing effect. Instead it suggests that the more the system operates beyond capacity, the more skill and flexibility is elicited from commuters in accommodating the intensification of intensities within the packed train – the extreme pressure of compressed bodies in various stages of fatigue, decay, health, and sickness, the utter silence, the mix of noxious odors from half-digested breakfasts, the smell of stale coffee and cigarette smoke, and the flowery fragrance of shampoos and body soaps.

Importantly, Simondon's conceptualization of the margin of indeterminacy takes us beyond a mere discussion of machine functionality. It presents a philosophical intervention into questions of human autonomy, particularly in regard to the relationship between humans and machines. Specifically, the margin of indeterminacy is the space in which human beings and technical ensembles interact and in-form each other, which is to say human and machine ensemble emerge through a process of co-production whereby the form that each takes is a product of the interaction between the disparate human and machine materialities.[8] Accordingly, the margin of indeterminacy constitutes a space of collective, where "collective" is understood in heteropoietic terms as encompassing the agentive work of both human and machine. The critical corollary here is one that Bruno Latour has worked hard to show us throughout his work, which is that there is no autonomy that precedes collective just as there is no human that precedes a relation with the non-human.[9] But such apparent irreverence for the purity of a human autonomy is of course just a radicalization of Immanuel Kant's insistence on the indivisibility of the public and the private or the tenet espoused by such foundational thinkers of anthropology as Emile Durkheim and Marcel Mauss that there is no individual without the social.

In sum, in contrast to the vision I offered earlier of the packed train as an objectifying medium that turns commuters into automatons, thinking from gap urges us to understand that to commute is never simply to submit to a determined technological order. Instead, it involves an active dialogue between commuter and technological apparatus in which commuters remain aggressively attuned to the system's modulating ambience, even if at an unconscious embodied level. At the same time, as the operational *daiya* suggests, the technological apparatus never simply operates according to a given pattern. It must be constantly reconfigured in relation to the shifting pattern of commuter behavior. It is into this configuration of relations that ATOS is introduced as a means of bringing autonomy, not just agency, to the machine ensemble.

Distributed autonomy

JR East began research and development for its new Autonomous Decentralized Transport Operation Control System (a.k.a. ATOS) soon after the company was formed in 1987 from the privatization and breakup of the once massive national railroad company, Japanese National Railways. The technology was introduced initially in December 1996 on Tokyo's Chūō Line (the most crowded and traffic congested train lines). Since then JR East has deployed ATOS throughout its entire Kanto commuter network. The Tokyo Metro System also began adopting ATOS in the mid-2000s. In general, ATOS replaces a Centralized Traffic Control (CTC) system that was introduced widely in Japan beginning in the late 1950s and is still the main traffic control technology used by many train companies.[10] As with the centralized system, ATOS is concerned with managing the gap between the planned and operational *daiya* in accordance with the stress of operation beyond capacity. How it does that and the results, however, are very different.

Under the centralized system, the gap is administered top-down according to a conventional command and control paradigm whereby a human controller located in a Central Command Center monitors the progress of traffic on a large schematic of the system and issues orders to trains and stations. Insofar as the centralized system was adequate to a certain degree, it was also vulnerable to collapse as a result of sudden surges in commuter demand, which would overwhelm the controller's ability to maintain the gap between the *daiya*. ATOS resolves this vulnerability to a great extent through an engineering principle of Autonomous Decentralized Systems (ADS) called "distributed autonomy" (*jiritsu bunsan*) in which "the functional order of the entire system is generated by the cooperative interactions among its subsystems, each of which has the autonomy to control a part of the system" (Ito 1993, 130). Practically speaking, this means that computers in each station manage the flow of traffic in their vicinity. Each station's system then produces an operational *daiya* that it shares with surrounding stations in an information pool called the "data field." See Figure 9.2.

In distributing command and control, distributed autonomy disperses the system's center of gravity away from the central command center and into its shared space of communication (the data field), thus increasing system resilience.

In other places I have traced the emergence of the principle of distributed autonomy as a response to the specific problem of how to treat irregularity as part of the regular operational order of complex urban infrastructure (Fisch 2013). My argument showed how the conceptual innovation for the principle derived from thinking of the body and immune system of complex living organisms as decentralized systems whose capacity for self-organization allows for enfolding irregularity into a generative metastable order. My concern in that discussion was with how the principle of distributed autonomy realized through ATOS remediates the disorder produced by commuter train suicides and how it then asks us (and commuters) to think about the body on the tracks. By contrast, I want to focus here on how distributed autonomy

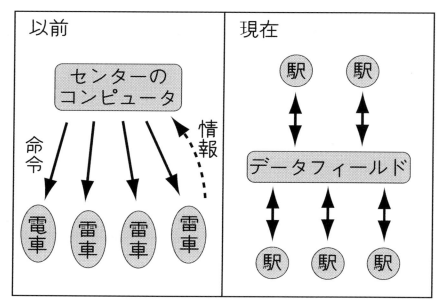

Figure 9.2 Diagram comparing the former centralized system (left) with the contemporary decentralized system (right). The diagram of the centralized system specifies commands flowing unidirectionally from a central computer with a dotted line and arrow indicating tentative information feedback. The diagram of the decentralized system shows information flowing bidirectionally between stations mediated by the data field
(Yamamoto 2003)

urges us to think autonomy. In so doing, I turn briefly to the concept itself before exploring its ontological ramifications.

Self-control versus control of oneself

"Distributed autonomy" is a complicated term in Japanese, in part because autonomy, *jiritsu,* can be written using two different character combinations. Each of these combinations refers to a different notion of autonomy. One way combines the characters for "oneself" (*ji*) and "stand" (*ritstu, tatsu*) to mean "independence." Another combination uses the character for "oneself" (*ji*) with the character for "rhythm, law, regulation, control" to mean something like "self-control." As such, this second combination aligns with the philosophical and anthropological notion of autonomy noted earlier that underscores the self as not only always embedded in but also subsequent to a relational framework involving other actors and forces. Autonomy, in this sense, is about a relational dependence, not independence. Accordingly, "self-control" is not the capacity to act on one's own. It is the capacity, rather, to act through interaction – through communication and in moderation and accordance with others who constitute the field of one's possibility for action.

The different character combinations make the term prone to typographical error when composing on a computer. I was reminded of this when I mistakenly used the combination for "independence" when first corresponding via email with Mori Kinji, the Japanese information scientist and engineer who developed the distributed autonomy system. Mori was quick to correct my error. But as it turned out, my mistake was more enlightening than embarrassing as it brought to my attention contrasting conceptualizations of autonomy that have been set in motion with the introduction of the ATOS network. Specifically, there is on the one hand a notion of autonomy that fetishizes individualism and needs to disavow its collective origin in the packed train. And on the other hand there is a notion of autonomy that maintains the enclosure of the packed train as its condition of possibility. This latter notion of autonomy corresponds with the idea of self-control. What is truly innovative about it is that it affords the technological apparatus not just agency but autonomy; it becomes capable of self-control, which is to say interacting through communication and in moderation and accordance with other "autonomous" components of the system, including commuters. Before I look at this instantiation of autonomy as self-control, I turn briefly to the articulation of autonomy as independence.

From commuter to consumer/individual

Over the course of the last decade JR East has been busy rebuilding and remodeling its network of train stations throughout the Greater Metropolitan Area of Tokyo. As a result of this work, the spaces and passageways between ticket gates and platforms have been transformed from zones of optimized commuter flow into frictionless spaces of festive consumption replete with a wide variety of bakeries, bookstores, cafes, clothing stores, and delicatessens. The impetus behind this immense project is a perceived immediate need to refashion the commuter network into an environment adequate to Japan's twenty-first information (Egami 2003) and commensurate with an autonomous decentralized transportation infrastructure able "to satisfy the variable demands of each passenger ... [and] offer the variable kinds and the variable quantity of transportation, as there are various passengers' needs" (Kawakami 1993). The notion of autonomy that this environment invokes is not the self-control of distributed autonomy but rather a bare-boned and philosophically impoverished understanding of autonomy as owned and absolute in which the commuter figures as consumer/individual – not worker or student – with specific lifestyle needs and tastes. Such a conceptualization of autonomy seeks nothing less than to extract the mass from mass transportation as it transforms the commuter train network into a system responsive to the spontaneous consumer whims of each commuter.

Key to enabling this realization of autonomy is an autonomous decentralized system integrated with ATOS called the "Super Urban Intelligent Card," otherwise known as SUICA. The technology replaces the conventional paper train ticket and commuter pass with an integrated circuit chip embedded in a SUICA card, credit card, or Smartphone. SUICA also serves as a type of electronic wallet that can be used for purchases inside the system and increasingly throughout the city. SUICA relieves one of the burden of purchasing a ticket with the appropriate fare for a desired destination. One simply enters and exits the system wherever one pleases with the wave of the SUICA-enabled device or card over a sensor on the electronic wicket, leaving the complex fare calculation to a distributed network of computers. On a basic level SUICA is about convenience. But on another level it is about the promises of a frictionless space in which no course need be determined at the outset so at to leave one open to the seemingly endless possibilities of the city and its limitless points of consumption. Nothing conveys this better than the television and train commercials for SUICA that debuted early in the rollout of the new system.[11] The commercials follow the daily adventures of an attractive and fashionably dressed woman in her mid-twenties and her cute penguin companion. The penguin is the official SUICA mascot, chosen for the metaphoric correspondence between its ability to swim smoothly (*sui sui*) and SUICA's promise of frictionless mobility through urban system space. The penguin is presumably the woman's sole companion. The two live together and enjoy a seemingly carefree life of fun and adventure in and around Tokyo's commuter train network. We see them in various commercials riding the train together, taking walks in quaint neighborhoods, shopping for quirky items, sightseeing in rural locals, and so on. Each outing involves some kind of purchase, which the young woman handles effortlessly with a touch of her SUICA card at a sensor. The commercials always end with the woman declaring, "I live with SUICA," (*watashi wa suica to kurashite imasu*). The phrase carries plain double meaning, referring to the fact that the woman actually lives with SUICA the penguin mascot, and that SUICA provides the means for her to pursue her carefree, self-satisfying lifestyle. As such, the commercials promote an image of the commuter train network as a medium for the realization of one's customized lifestyle through frictionless mobility, spontaneity, and impulse consumption. Conspicuously absent in these scenes is any reference to commuting, namely packed commuter trains and crowded stations. The emphasis falls instead on the systems as a medium of leisure, play, and adventure while the reality of operation beyond capacity is expelled.

A new autonomy

What if distributed autonomy had nothing to do with the emancipation of the commuter as individual? What if it were only the persistence of human conceit exacerbated by the tactical and affective elicitations of consumer capitalism that leads us to believe every technological development should translate into some kind of net material and/or emotional gain for humans as individuals? What if distributed autonomy was instead about an emerging machine autonomy? Indeed, is this not what the term actually implies? In realizing a technological system with a level of self-control commensurate with the working of the body, distributed autonomy allows the technological apparatus to act autonomously. This is not to say that machines become individuals like human individuals, as this would simply be an inversion of the individualistic interpretation of autonomy discussed above. Rather, machines realize a certain "autonomy of will" (as Kant would say) in their capacity for self-control – to act through interaction, through communication and in moderation and accordance with a field of autonomous actors. In transforming the agency of the technological apparatus into autonomy, distributed autonomy gives the technological apparatus a capacity to act in relation *with* commuters. As such, it takes us beyond what Andrew Pickering calls the "dance of agency" marked by a "dialectic of resistance and accommodation" with the technological apparatus in that the machine becomes an attuned and willful (not just a reactive) partner (Pickering 1995). Just as commuters engage in a dialogue with the system whereby they cultivate a heightened attentiveness to the system's modulating ambience, under distributed autonomy the system returns this attentive engagement.

How might we understand such machine autonomy in more tangible terms? The information science scholar, Masahito Yamamoto offers some insight into its quality when he explains ATOS' capacity to handle sudden surges in commuter demand via an analogy that compares the old centralized train traffic system to a conventional sit-down sushi restaurant and ATOS to a "conveyor belt sushi restaurant" (*kaiten zushi*). He writes:

> In a conveyor belt sushi restaurant the sushi chefs prepare the sushi and place it on the conveyor belt, from which customers choose the pieces

they want to eat. The sushi chefs thus do not take orders from each customer and the customers do not place orders. Rather, the sushi chefs determine what kind of sushi to prepare by looking at the conveyor belt and seeing what is being eaten. The conveyor belt is analogous with the system's data field. Because the conveyor belt (data field) is a place where the customer and sushi chef (subsystem) can share information, it makes cooperative data processing possible ... . In this sense, we can think of the old centralized system as a conventional sushi restaurant in which the chefs start preparing sushi only after they have received the orders from the customers. That is to say, the customers compel (*kyoseiteki ni*) the sushi chefs to work. With this system, if many orders come in at once the sushi chefs become overwhelmed and the system encounters delays. But in the instance of the *kaiten zushi* paradigm, because the sushi chefs make the sushi according to their own will (*ishi*), there is no peak and they can continue to make sushi (Yamamoto).

The conveyor belt, in this analogy is the ATOS data field, while the sushi chefs are the system. We can think of the customers as either train stations or actual commuters since the sudden surge of demand for trains at stations corresponds with the flow of commuters into train stations. Although the analogy is far from perfect, it distills the novel quality of distributed autonomy as endowing the apparatus with the capacity to participate in the shared space of interaction with other actors in the field of operation. What is important to emphasize is first that the problem of packed trains (operation beyond capacity) is at the center of this analogy as the problematic that autonomy as self-control handles, not that which it expels. Second, there is no spoken communication between the sushi chefs and the customers. Rather, interaction takes place through the deep attentiveness of all actors to the condition of the conveyor belt, which is the shared space of interaction (the data field). Moreover, the sushi chefs (i.e. the technological apparatus) participate in this shared space of interaction according to their own "will," their own judgment, not simply as a reactive force. As cumbersome as this analogy may be, it gets to the core of the way in which distributed autonomy elicits thinking the technological apparatus on the threshold of a kind of sentience. This is not about machines on the path to taking over the world as imagined in many dystopic science fictions. Indeed, distributed autonomy does not render human train drivers and platform attendants obsolete. Rather, those human actors now operate *with* the machine as partners in a novel heteropoietic matrix.

Conclusion

Are commuters aware of their relation with this new autonomy? I have found that most are surprised to hear about the distributed autonomy of Tokyo's commuter train network. The noise of media promoting the system as a novel means of individual consumption seems to drown out alternative ontologies.

And yet commuters who remember the pre-ATOS days do sense that the system has become a more social partner. Yamamoto conveys such sentiments when he recalls how in instances of disorder prior to ATOS commuters were informed merely that rescheduling was in process (*chōsei chū*) whereas now they receive detailed information of changes underway (Yamamoto 2003). What commuters perhaps do not recognize is that this deepened sense of dialogue reflects the degree to which they have been enfolded into the constitutive space of the heteropoietic matrix and given the possibility of realizing their distributed autonomy.

Notes

1 In specifying the character of practical ontology Gad et al. (Gad, Jensen, and Winthereik 2015) emphasize its departure from the epistemological style of ethnographic engagement that aims to represent the discrete worlds constituted through different cultural practices. Practical ontology shifts the emphasis from a representational to performative mode of engagement whereby the ethnographer is enfolded into the generative processes – not structures – of contextualized practices and materialities.
2 See for example the essays in the edited volume, (Shepard 2011) as well as the work by one of the central advocates of smart infrastructure, William J. Mitchell (Mitchell 1995, 2003).
3 Ethnographic field notes, April 2, 2006.
4 This example is drawn from Tokyo's Chūō Line.
5 See Wolfgang Schivelbusch's explication of the significance of "play" in Franz Reuleaux's theory of machine development (Schivelbusch 1986: 19).
6 My argument here extrapolates celebratory approaches to smart technology as developed by such thinkers as William J. Mitchell. See (Mitchell 1995, 2003). But we could also include here Michael Hardt and Antonio Negri's argument in *Multitude: War and Democracy in the Age of Empire* (Hardt and Negri 2004).
7 New rolling stock was extremely limited since Japan had not yet developed a robust manufacturing industry of its own at the time and imports from the United States and Europe were curtailed by the international conflict. See (Mito 2005: 76–78).
8 Mackenzie highlights this aspect of Simondon's theory in his explication of information in Simondon as that which in parts form or "in-forms" the machine (Mackenzie 2006: 26).
9 This is a theme that traverses much of Latour's work. See Latour 1993, 2005.
10 I qualify this, as "in general" since some of the less congested train lines had not been converted to full CTC control by the time ATOS was introduced.
11 Train commercials are soundless commercials that play on screens within commuter trains.

Bibliography

Deleuze, Gilles (1992) "Postscript on the Societies of Control." *October* 59 (Winter): 3–7.
Egami, Setsuko (2003) "Idō to seikatsu ni okeru aratana kachi no kōzō wo mezashite – kachi kaiteki kukan no kōzō." *JR East Technical Review* 4.
Fisch, Michael (2013) "Tokyo's Commuter Train Suicides and the Society of Emergence." *Cultural Anthropology* 28(2): 320–343.

Gad, Christopher, C. B. Jensen, and Brit Ross Winthereik (2015) "Practical Ontology: Worlds in STS and Anthropology." *NatureCulture* 3: 67–86.
Hardt, Michael and Antonio Negri (2004) *Multitude: War and Democracy in the Age of Empire*. London: Penguin.
Ito, Masami and Yuasa Hideo (1993) "Autonomous Decentralized System with Self-organizing Function and Its Application to Generation of Locomotive Patterns." Paper delivered at the International Symposium on Autonomous Decentralized Systems (ISADS), Kawasaki, Japan, March 30–April 1.
Kawakami, Takashi (1993) "Concept of Friendly Autonomous Decentralized System for Next Generation Train Traffic Control." Paper delivered at the International Symposium on Autonomous Decentralized Systems (ISADS), Kawasaki, Japan, March 30–April 1.
Larkin, Brian (2013) "The Politics and Poetics of Infrastructure." *Annual Review of Anthropology* 42: 327–343.
Latour, Bruno (1993) *We Have Never Been Modern*. New York: Harvester Wheatsheaf.
Latour, Bruno (2005) *Reassembling the Social: An Introduction to Actor-Network Theory*. Oxford and New York: Oxford University Press.
Mackenzie, Adrian (2006) *Transductions: Bodies and Machines at Speed*. London and New York: Continuum.
Martin, Reinhold (1998) "The Organizational Complex: Cybernetics, Space, Discourse." *Assemblage* 37: 102–127.
Mitchell, William J. (1995) *City of Bits: Space, Place, and the Infobahn*. Cambridge, MA: MIT Press.
Mitchell, William J. (2003) *ME++: The Cyborg Self and the Networked City*. Cambridge, MA: MIT Press.
Mito, Yuko (2005) Teikoku hassha: nihon no tetsudôwa naze sekai de mottomo seikaku nanoka. Shinchōsha.
Mizoguchi, Masahito (2007) "Nihon no tetsudō shyaryō kōgyō ni tsuite." Japan Association of Rolling Stock Industries. Available at: www.tetsushako.or.jp/pdf/sharyo-kogyo.pdf.
Pickering, Andrew (1995) *The Mangle of Practice: Time, Agency, and Science*. Chicago, IL: University of Chicago Press.
Schivelbusch, Wolfgang (1986) *The Railway Journey: The Industrialization of Time and Space in the 19th Century*. Berkeley, CA: University of California Press.
Shepard, Mark (ed.) (2011) *Sentient City: Ubiquitous Computing, Architecture, and the Future of Urban Space*. New York and Cambridge, MA: Architectural League of New York/MIT Press.
Steiner, Hadas (2011) "Systems, Objectified," in *Sentient City: Ubiquitous Computing, Architecture, and the Future of Urban Space*, edited by Mark Shepard, 36–45. New York and Cambridge, MA: Architectural League of New York/MIT Press.
Thrift, Nigel (2004) "Movement-space: The Changing Domain of Thinking Resulting from the Development of New Kinds of Spatial Awareness." *Economy and Society* 33(4): 582–604.
Tomii, Norio (2005) *Resshya daiya no himitsu: teiji unkō no shikumi*. Tokyo: Seizandō.
Weber, Max (1976) *The Protestant Ethic and the Spirit of Capitalism*. New York: Scribner.
Yamamoto, Masahito (2003) "Sekai ni hirogaru jiritsu bunsan." *Landfall* 48: 1–5.

10 The generic city

Examples from Jakarta, Indonesia, and Maputo, Mozambique

Morten Nielsen and AbdouMaliq Simone

Introduction

Urbanity as a form of redemption, of starting anew, has long been at work in cities nearly everywhere. Through the dissolution of existing urban forms and technologies and the replacement by carefully planned environments, the emergence of cities that offer citizens full access to ideal futures based on a near-perfect constellation of the corporeal, material, and technological elements of urban life is envisaged. Crucially, such utopic urban models necessarily operate on the basis of a paradoxical doubling or "twinning": as a system of reason, utopian urbanity is incapable of realizing its own promises (Grosz 2001). The fulfillment of a projected future essentially dissolves urbanity's utopic systematicity and thus puts an end to its own problem-solving capacities. Hence, in order to preserve its capacity to reboot the city, urbanity needs to constantly double itself as an exterior and always deferred stranger. Attempts to simultaneously escape history and realize the purportedly deep-seated capacities of a nation or city are particularly evident in contemporary Africa and Asia.

Based on ethnographic data from Maputo, Mozambique, and Jakarta, Indonesia, this chapter explores recent processes of urban gestation where infrastructural configurations, some old and some new, seem to develop though the internal twinning of the existing city. Across sub-Saharan Africa and Southeast Asia, the spatial layouts of urban environments are currently being reshaped through the construction of entirely new "parallel cities" from scratch rather than rehabilitating the existing built environment.[1] Often initiated by private real-estate developers and large-scale construction consortia, these spatial reconfigurations, if successfully implemented, aim at serving the interests of a cosmopolitan property-holding elite while completely bypassing long-honed, if often messy, practices of urban management on the ground of sub-Saharan African and Asian cities today. Alternatively, they constitute bets for young lower-middle-class households demonstrating faith that they will eventually be at the core of the "real city."

In the first instance, Mozambique's worn-out capital, Maputo, will serve as an apt example of this recent process. We chart how infrastructural potentialities associated with recently projected parallel cities affect the configuration and dynamics of already existing urban spaces. Often located at the physical limits of established urban spaces, parallel cities are essentially designed as secluded islands with independent systems of security, social services, and high-quality infrastructure (e.g. road net, electricity, and sanitation). Given the lack of human and financial resources, the Maputo municipality has de facto surrendered entire sections of inner city neighborhoods to foreign entrepreneurial developers seeking to profit on the increasingly lucrative real-estate market. Hence, as we will claim in this chapter, these recent and relatively inconspicuous processes of urban take-over crystallize (and are rendered possible through) a peculiar "twinning" of the conspicuous infrastructures of emerging parallel cities. We argue that the gestation of new infrastructural configurations articulates a symmetrical "twinning" of seemingly opposing principles. As a paradoxical kind of urban "fetus-in-fetu," as it were, the twinned symmetrical relation is constituted through the enveloping of the city's overall layout and aesthetics by its more recent and potentially detrimental anti-twin.

At the same time, in looking at Jakarta, one of the world's fastest growing urban regions, the massive carving up of the existing landscape prompts the proliferation of unsteady interfaces everywhere, which make more visible the frictions between different settlement and city-making practices and also temporalities. The "familial" form at work is less a twinning process than a reference to a "people" (*rakyat*) that is somehow expected to subsume all of the vast changes taking place – many of them with highly uncertain consequences and replete with injustice. Nevertheless, the concerted and monumental effort to homogenize Jakarta through highly standardized built environments confronts the intricate and plural singularities of efforts undertaken to ensure a capacity on the part of lower-, working-, and lower-middle-class residents to adapt and transform the city according to their own terms. They know they cannot sit still and so have to continuously redescribe their aspirations and capacities into new formats, which also unsettle the status quo, so that there are different kinds of unsettling at work – only provisionally stabilized, and then through the invocation of the "people." For what is at work is not the variation of a self-modulating whole but a re-invention of the modes of connection through which different actors construct and cohabit specific spaces of operation. Whether incremental, impetuous, or disjunctive, the initiatives undertaken by these residents iterate new potentialities informed yet at the same time detached from what the social constellation of efforts was capable of before. *Rakyat* becomes a *generic* infrastructure detached from any particular evidence; the notion never has to be proved empirically. A wide range of details might be invoked to demonstrate its failure or diminished existence, but, in the end, this demonstration doesn't seem to matter. Such a situation also seems to point out inversely that the "details" – for example, private ownership, collective tenure – are free to associate with whatever conceptual infrastructure or mode of existence available to make use of them.

The *generic*, adopted from the work of François Laruelle (1999, 2011), refers both to the condition of being "anything whatsoever" and the condition of being "nothing beyond what one is." As such, no matter how the details of city experience and components might be explained, it will be insufficient to indicate what these details might be and how they might act. It doesn't mean that anything we might identify as an entity or actor has a capacity or being on its own, separate from other things, or that it is impermeable to being affected and connected into all kinds of arrangements and structuring. Rather, Laruelle is suggesting that we might view infrastructural arrangements, which are usually seen as combining, rearticulating, representing, and enjoining, as also a process of subtracting and *detaching*, so that a more maximally definitional term is converted into a more minimally definitional one.[2] Instead of seeing such detachment as exclusion or segregation, we might also see it as grounds for viewing urban spaces in new ways, of keeping things out of analytical connections, and to think of the potentials of the supposedly useless, marginal, or anachronistic in different ways (Galloway 2014).

So while various multilateral institutions assemble intricate data sets to document the massive infrastructural deficits of cities as evidence of their progressive dissipation, the city may persist as a detached, ineluctable gathering up of details from which nothing can really be abstracted. It is as if urban inhabitation takes place in the gap, others might say trap, between systems of time–space distancing with uninterrupted communicative interaction and systems of logical distancing, where things remain close to each other but no longer communicate.

In this chapter, then, we trace genericity across two otherwise disparate urban domains. In Maputo, a generic form of the city asserts itself as an unmarked twinning of an ideal that might never be realized, whereas in Jakarta, the force of a minimally defined "people" metastasizes across a fractured urban landscape. In both instances, the generic has an a priori function for a given domain or set of elements without imposing a universal (transcendent) dominance. As a form of "limited universalism," if you like, it intervenes in unknown territories that are thereby transformed but not fully subjected to the force of the generic.

Detaching the city (Jakarta, Indonesia)

Jakarta is one of the world's most restless cities. Restless in the massive transformations of its built environment, the profusion of small initiatives undertaken for the endurance of popular neighborhoods, and the speeded-up circulation of both residents and capital across the highly differentiated districts of this urban region of nearly thirty million people. Embodying heighted accumulation, consumption, dispossession, inventiveness, and brute force, trajectories of urban development on various scales and circuits intersect in multiple ways, producing dispositions in the built and social environment not easily subsumed under a single overarching logic or mode.

Infrastructure is not simply the roads, the buildings, the pipes, or the wires; it is also a particular formatting of stability, a means of coagulating liquid relationships among materials and objects with apparent solidity and definition. While infrastructural products may be replete with technical specifications, the enactment of infrastructure entails a complex process of assembling sentiment, authorization, finance, and labor. It has to disrupt and implant, anticipating as much as possible the ramifying implications of this duality.

In Indonesia, the generic notion of the people, the *rakyat*, provides an increasingly vague but nevertheless enduring sense of the egalitarian that does not exist as a concept but more a formatting of feeling, a sense of commonality repeatedly rehearsed but also something that has to be repeatedly denied and fought against. But as this generic form does not sum up, does not stabilize for "sure" or for "good"; it focuses attention on the details of the volatile grounds on which urban transformation takes place and provides an occasion for continuous redescription of those details into different kinds of narratives about what *might* be taking place.

Rakyat is something referred to as residents diversify the use of the small landholdings, collaborate in neighborhood improvement projects, invest in entire floors of cheap apartment buildings, and try to explain their contradictory behavior as they circulate through different roles in different political, ethnic, religious, or commercial associations. It is particularly evident in how they refer to the ultimate value of land: land in the last instance is the property of the *rakyat*, no matter how much it is bought and sold and grabbed and ruined.

Consider the details of plots that sit side by side throughout the city and think what can be made of them. What kind of overarching rubric could be available to sum them all up? The inadequacy of overarching explanations doesn't mean that nothing changes about these details or that land is not consolidated into massive undertakings driven by the maximization of ground rent. It simply means that infrastructural projects also entail complicated twists and turns that attempt to momentarily hold all of these details in place so that particular spatial imprints can ensue. While neoliberal development may appear to run roughshod over Jakarta's landscape, the prolific range of details remain formatted with this elusive, generic sense of the "people" that informs the ways in which people of all class and residential backgrounds both actively do something and, often, do nothing as a means of shaping their living conditions.

Some acquire land that hibernates for years in parcels too small to fall under legal injunctions to immediately develop it and too large to immediately do something affordable. Some land has been subdivided so many times that the original family owners have lost track of which members are responsible for what and have long lost the paper trail. Some land retains the same occupants, function, or commercial operation for decades, with only minimal repair or renovation, and their appearance is that of relics that will crumble to dust before the land is sold or used for something else. Some land witnesses a constant turnover of unrealistic plans and bad debts, of disputes and financial miscalculation. Some land witnesses cautious, incremental yet determined additions, the emplacement of a steady accrual of "facts on the ground" (such as buildings put up without permits or in violation of zoning regulations) and enhanced capacity.

Some bits of land are like pieces in games of political chess, acquired in bulk through various complicities and favors and dispensed for political loyalty, seats on company boards, or to shore up a faction in the police or military. Some land represents the long-term savings of entire districts, which, faced with various problems of flooding or rapidly escalating costs, have acquired something that enables them to continue to reside together. Some land is simply the perfect vehicle to clean corrupt money. Some land was agglomerated in large land banks decades ago and subsequently developed at various different rhythms according to intricate calculations about construction and labor costs, bond rates, consumer markets, and anticipated outlays of bulk infrastructure. Some land has been acquired because of a prevailing sense of exigency, the owners simply wanting a stake in the market regardless of likely profitability. Some land seems haunted, lush and overgrown, sitting in prime locations like a void in some aspiration. Some land is preoccupied with games of hide and seek – factories pretend to be boarding houses, boarding houses pretend to be factories, offices pretend to be single family homes, single family homes pretend to be offices. The varying mixtures of use rights, de facto ownership, adherence to or blatant disregard for legality, speculative acquisition, or the withdrawal of land from markets altogether presents an ambiguous complexion of both fortitude and vulnerability.

So the generic is an infrastructure outside the incessant need to divide things, outside the fundamental epistemological maneuvers that cut the world into specific existent conditions and then bring in the analytical tools needed to account for them. Concept, cause, and case are equilibrated on a plane where each, in the last instance, exerts equal weight. Even as Brenner and Schmid (2014) rightly claim that the city is not the embodiment of urbanization and that urbanization has now achieved a planetary scale in terms of the intensity and extension of urbanization processes (the urban as a force in itself), might the details of specific city lives and materials also simply act in ways that have nothing to do with such overarching processes of urbanization?

After all, the *details* of what residents do with each other belongs to them, not just as a reflection of what takes place when they act but as components for their arriving at their own conclusions about what is possible or not. Government agencies and other large institutions may have the capacity to aggregate these details – provided they are paying attention – into specific overall patterns, which then inform planning and budgetary decisions. Yet, both formal and informal mechanisms of working with these details within localities are critical aspects of governance. Sometimes these interstices of detachment, between the abstractions of governance and the details of everyday management, generate infrastructural voids, where nothing seems to be happening but, within the apparent opacities, much experimentation takes place.

For example, the diffused markets of Kali Baru, close to one of the most important historical railway stations in Jakarta (which in past decades used to be the point of arrival for the bulk of new migrants to Jakarta but is now ensconced in an overcrowded, volatile series of districts under intense threat of mega redevelopment), has spread like wildfire along tracks, thoroughfares, lanes, and creeks. It has become the center of a thriving printing business and is estimated to handle almost 50 % of whatever is printed in Indonesia.

The whole gamut of printing is available in almost any medium and almost any kind of production mode. Interspersed with this business is the possibility of buying almost anything in any quantity. In some ways, in a city that has some 137 shopping malls, areas like Kali Baru seem like an anachronism. Many other "traditional" markets and commercial zones in Jakarta are gone or are in rapid decline. They all had their singular characteristics and lures and these particularities enabled them to endure for years past their prime. But the onslaught of development has been too extensive, particularly as medium-scale enterprises, such as banks, automobile dealerships, restaurant chains, and supermarkets extend outward, escalating land prices and drawing commercially based revenues into municipal coffers.

When we asked different people about what has enabled Kali Baru to attain its edge and vitality, the common response was that this is a place "now big enough to take what we have and make something happen in ways we could never expect before" *and* "that leaves us alone to see what we do" *and* "that gives all kind of new people to work with." It is a place that doesn't "forget who we are" but still gives us the opportunity to "forget everything we did in the past." What is evident in these sentiments is that Kali Baru generically *redescribes* the singularities of other markets across the city into a new modality of operation – one which does not mirror each former or fading market in their entirety and collect them like some bricolage.

Rather, the driving features of the others are resituated in a distinctive structure of finance, distribution, production, and exchange. These pasts become components that enable an elaboration of multi-scalar and multi-perspectival economic transactions, where big business coincides with variously scaled and managed networks that are not subsumed by the "big bosses" in exclusive subcontracting arrangements. Instead, a plurality of ways of inputting goods, soliciting customers, filling orders, and configuring services remain detached from each other, enabling the particularities of other ways of doing things in other places to retain a certain autonomy, even if they persist only through various ways being folded into something that exceeds themselves.

Twinning the city (Maputo, Mozambique)

If a city can be withdrawn from the urges to actualize its provisional figuration, what are the moments in the operation of acquiring its genericity? How does the city that is held in abeyance manifest itself across the fractured landscapes and dysfunctional infrastructures from which it was once detracted? Since the generic city is also inaccessible to those who imagine it, it makes itself felt as an acute sensation that something is missing: the "people," the "centre," the "vibe," etc. Indeed, while moving along vectors that are no longer fully known, the generic city seems to have lost its relational intensities. Affects, spaces, and materialities can be discerned and still their visibility works through a sequencing of detachment and distance. Almost like Indra's net, the generic city is structured as an intricate configuration of contracted absences that hold together thin threads of urban desires. Looked at closely, however, the lines that give to the city's absences and voids a certain aesthetic immediacy and presence are themselves made up of singular dots and disconnected fragments between which flow an endless stream of incomputable materials and patternless data.

The city operates on itself, then, not merely through a process of retheorization based on the amassing of intricate data sets (*pace* Brenner and Schmid 2015) but also by attempting to conjure and manipulate a proliferation of things that are not determinable, what was in Jakarta manifest as *rakyat* – "the people." According to Laruelle, the generic is never in a relationship with anything else (1999) and so it cannot affix itself to the urban through immediate forms of causality, reciprocity, and exchange. Between the generic and the specific there are no connectors or "sutures of the materialism type" (Laruelle 2011: 258). Hence, while the generic is relatively unproblematic as it is always-already-given, the question is how it becomes possible to move between immanent genericity and the particulars of urban life.

The generic is a determining condition; it is, as Srnick tells us, "a type of determination which is itself indifferent to what it determines, while maintaining its radical immanence to what it determines" (2011: 170). Consequently, if the generic city does not assert itself as a transcendent force, it can only be approached by attempting to configure the specificities of the urban as if they were determined as such. In so doing, things and dispositions are experimentally aligned in order to momentarily suspend imposed limitations on the specific and thereby attain an urban aesthetic that is in accordance with the generic city. As we suggested in the introduction to this chapter, this can also be considered as an act of *twinning* the urban, where a dual entity is produced through an identical copy. Still, the twinning of the urban does not result in a relationship of similarity. By reconfiguring the specificities of the urban so as to be in accordance with the generic city, a copy is produced that is now a stranger to its twin. While being completely identical to its double, the twin (or "clone," as Laruelle calls it) emerges as an instantiation of the foreclosure of the generic city to the urban. It arises from the materials, urgencies, and calculations of the urban but operates in accordance with its own mode of being, which is precisely the hypothesis of the generic city. Indeed, it is in this regard that the generic is a form of "limited universalism," which intervenes and transforms another domain as a weak a priori force.

For why is it that certain urban operations and movements cause a constant oscillation between twinned-out spaces and positions? When is it, we might ask, that the urban produces an identical but dissimilar twin? If national capitals are paired with mercantile cities in their vicinity, it is often to allow extranational trading centers to operate unhindered by the cumbersome regulations of government. Although often cast as shadowy sister cities that cede power and official jurisdiction, they are, in fact, more like independent city-states engineered as "islands of immunity and exemption" (Easterling 2007: 10). Across such twinned-out spaces, the city emerges as a topography of affects, economic deliberations, and political sensibilities that never manage to fully stabilize. Marked by contrasting but mutually dependent urban desires, the urban doubles shadow each other in a never-ending battle for influence, power, and resources. Indeed, while the twinned-out city is less than two, it is certainly more than one.

But do the inadequacies that come to feed the parallel growth of the urban arise merely from the mutual mirroring of desires? If they do, the expansion of a twinned-out city would have at its core a lack that could only be expressed through the medium of a fractured and partially shared vocabulary. Could it not be that the insufficiencies and absences that keep the urban doubles orbiting around each other are, in fact, the very cause of their existence? Rather than the twinning of the urban generating a lack, which is then eternally reproduced, the urban is twinned-out in order for its *genericity* to assert itself. Considered as such, the city needs the absences, the inadequacies, the lack, and therefore it bifurcates as two-in-one.

Take, for example, the twinning of Maputo, Mozambique's hard-tried capital. Here, the projected (but still unrealized) building of a parallel city serves a double purpose. While offering the national political elite an appropriate scenery for staging widely held fantasies of urban extravagance and global outreach, the parallel city actualizes new potentialities in the existing politico-material infrastructure of the national capital. To municipal officials, foreign investors and local real-estate agents, the parallel city is a mirage, which is already reconfiguring what the existing capital might be. Municipal architects working at the barely functioning Department for Urban Planning are increasingly referring to the planned parallel city as a modular form, which ought to be used also to structure and upgrade existing neighborhoods in the old "cement city" (*cidade de cimento*). As a generic "twin" of the building physical project that is still manifest only as a shielded lot on the outskirts of the city, the projected parallel city thus generates new and potent insufficiencies at the heart of the urban fabric: rather than charting what the existing city already is, it indicates what it might never become.

In many ways, the twinning of Maputo reflects a form of "surgical" development that is rapidly spreading across the sub-Saharan continent (cf. Bergesen 2008). With little or no economic benefit to the wider society, financial investments are concentrated in secured enclaves that are ring-fenced against the expected inefficiencies of the local economy. In contrast to earlier "socially thick" economic models focusing on the national development state, these enclave investments (e.g. oil extraction and logging) are particularly noteworthy for their ability to bypass the frame of the nation-state altogether. As Ferguson argues:

(C)apital "hops" over "unusable Africa," alighting only in mineral-rich enclaves that are starkly disconnected from their national societies. The result is not the formation of standardized national grids, but the emergence of huge areas of the continent that are effectively "off the grid."

(2005: 380)

This economic rationality, based on the dissection and "enclaving" of national territories, is guiding also urban deliberations and strategies. In seeking to fast-forward into a future unhindered by the past, city builders have become enthralled by the idea of creating self-sufficient island-like enclosures on the outside of existing sub-Saharan African cities. Urban planning has always been deeply affected by utopian dramas staging the death of traditional cities and their replacement by pulsating and planned spaces where urbanites would live unencumbered by the entrenched legacies of already collapsed futures (Soja 2000). What seems to drive the making of a growing number of "city doubles" (Murray 2013) in sub-Saharan Africa, however, is not merely the utopian aspiration for a perfectly designed environment, but an urgent desire to create entire cities from scratch.

In the KaTembe Peninsula across the Maputo Bay, a Chinese construction consortium has won the contract of building an entirely new capital for the barely surviving Mozambican nation-state. According to urban planners working in KaTembe, the projected "China Town," as they aptly call it, will comprise more than 2,000 housing units intended primarily for the growing middle-class, as well as a number of official buildings and public plazas, including a "Heroes' Square" (*Praça dos Heróes*) designed by Chinese architects. Having previously been cut off from the city centre by the Maputo Bay, access to the Katembe Peninsula will soon be considerably improved. In September 2012, the Chinese Roads and Bridges Corporation commenced building what will be the most important infrastructure project in Mozambique since the country's independence in 1975. A 680-meter suspension bridge will connect the peninsula to the city center and thus allow thousands of wealthy urbanites easy access to the master-planned enclave city from whence they will be able to gaze upon the old and rapidly deteriorating city center that no longer constitutes a proper site for creating a viable urban future.

From their damp and dimly lit offices in the heart of the dilapidated capital, municipal cadres are struggling to re-imagine the city on the basis of a bifurcated urban infrastructure. Although the capital's new utopia is located on its outside, the old city centre has not yet been switched off. Like so many other cities across the continent, Maputo has opened up its urban infrastructure networks to private sector participation and many sectors have already replaced state monopoly with market-driven management (cf. Graham and Marvin 2001). Urban development has never been a political priority for the country's political elite, which is why the recent upsurge of private investments in urban infrastructure cannot be considered as a corollary of the retreat of public authorities from the management of their cities. In a very practical sense, they were never really there. Hence, if urban infrastructure management never constituted a void to be filled, why do foreign investors invade this field with increasing pace and intensity? Could it be, we speculate, that the reason is to be found in the twinning of the urban? Without a doubt, when urban planners move between the projected "parallel city" in KaTembe and the derelict city center, generic imageries of the city travel with them.

In Maxaquene B, a densely populated neighborhood located near the bustling city center, a group of entrepreneurial Pakistani investors are buying up derelict high-rise buildings, which they upgrade before selling individual apartments to newcomers in need of relatively cheap housing. For more than a decade, these buildings have been abandoned by public authorities, which acted only to remove "problematic" individuals when the fragile social infrastructure was considered fundamentally threatened. According to municipal planners, they have de facto surrendered the entire block of high-rise buildings to the Pakistani investors. Without sufficient human and financial resources, the Maputo Municipality has been almost completely incapable of controlling the pirate-like seizure of the area.

Crucially, municipal officials are not opposing the presence of foreign investors. Although the infrastructure systems of the high-rise buildings are barely working, the sense is that the Pakistani investors have produced an operational urban machinery that functions in and by itself and, crucially, in a manner that derives its utopic drive from the generic form of the still unrealized "parallel city" in KaTembe. Water, electricity, Internet cabling, and sanitation are taken care of by the foreign investors. In addition, a team of security guards was recently contracted by the Pakistani developers, who do not accept disorderly behavior in their privately run public spaces.

Through a process of dissimilar copying, Maputo has twinned itself without the "twin-parent" and the "twin-child" establishing a relationship with each other. Returning again to Laruelle, we might say that the "twin-child" is a "duality, which is an identity but an identity which is not a synthesis" (1999: 143). Between the projected building of a "China-town" in the KaTembe Peninsula and the recent surrendering of an entire block of high-rise buildings to a group of entrepreneurial Pakistani investors, an awkward and twinned-out symmetrical relationship has emerged, which seems to figure the latter as a vague and malleable clone of the former. Hence, while the projected parallel city will be sealed off from the surrounding urban landscape and operate on the basis of a master-planned and independent infrastructural system, the high-rise buildings are located in the old city center where they are constantly affected by the contractions and relaxations of the surrounding environment. But it is precisely the flexible and only partial actualization of the enclave as "ideal form" in the old city center that reveals its tactical force. Again: the generic as a weak a priori force. Having sloughed off the conspicuous aesthetics of the parallel city, it can inconspicuously delineate new and hypothetical imageries of the urban without having to operate through the brute materiality of the "twin-parent." No longer the deformed clone of a fortress-like "privatopia" (MacKenzie 1994), the constantly mutating "twin-child" is the modular form by which the city expands. The hypothesis of the generic city.

Conclusion

In *City of Quartz: Excavating the Future in Los Angeles,* Mike Davis (1992: 232) describes how "(t)he city is engaged in a merciless struggle to make public facilities and spaces as 'unliveable' as possible for the homeless and the poor." Urban surfaces are consciously "hardened" (ibid.) against "bad citizens" who are aimlessly roaming the streets while "good citizens" are enclaved in high-security urban environments. As Harvey poignantly argues, the result of this exaggerated emphasis on separation is that the urban realm is being divided into a "patchwork quilt of islands of relative affluence struggling to secure themselves in a sea of spreading decay" (2000: 152). Still, while taking seriously Harvey's dystopic description of the urban condition, could it not be that the biggest challenge to the making of liveable and democratic cities lies not so much in the building of fenced-off enclaves as the release – or *liberation* – of an urban topography of absolute detachment? It is, in other words, at the precise moment when a social-cum-physical infrastructure asserts itself as a constantly mutating generic formula for engineering urban life that it becomes a "diagram of a mechanism of power reduced to its ideal form" (Foucault 1975: 205). A move from the specificities of the urban to the hypothetical realm of the generic city.

As a weak a priori force – a "limited universalism" – the generic city is something that always seems to "take care of itself," regardless of the incessant conformities of imagination or spatial and infrastructural recalibrations that it prompts and ignores. Whatever urbanization appropriates from the detailed singularities of particular ways of living as part and parcel of imposing itself as a force in its own right, as that which constantly refigures what has value, the genealogies of cities need not adhere to specific inheritances or "familial obligations." Indeed, if the city is an intensive formation in that it is capable of generating "strange syntheses," where exchanges are freed from producing something recognizably useful, we may have to recognize it in another way: we may need to detach ourselves from the familiar images and vernaculars and let the details speak another language, which, we propose, is that of the *generic*.

Notes

1 In both sub-Saharan Africa and Southeast Asia, the number of "satellite cities" is growing explosively. In sub-Saharan Africa, exemplars include Tatu City, Nairobi; Malabo II, Equatorial Guinea; Eko-Atlantic, Lagos; Luanda Sul, Angola; Bagatelle City, Mauritius; New Cairo City, Cairo; La Cité du Fleuve, Kinshasa, Congo; and

Waterfall City, Pretoria, South Africa. In Southeast Asia, examples are Ciputra Hanoi Vietnam, BSD Jakarta, Grand Phnom Penh International City, and Muang Thong Thani (Bangkok).
2 In his lucid analysis of Laruellian non-philosophy, Galloway explains how the logic of subtraction might fruitfully be considered as a form of withdrawal: "(P)eople of color subtracted from structures of alterity; or the working class subtracted from alienated labor" (2014: 204). In both instances, the former is a more maximally definitional term than the latter.

Reference

Bergesen, A. (2008) "The New Surgical Colonialism: China, Africa, and Oil." Paper presented at the American Sociological Association Annual Meeting, Boston, July 31.

Brenner, N. and C. Schmid (2014) "The 'Urban Age' in Question." *International Journal of Urban and Regional Research* 38(3): 731–755.

Brenner, Neil and C. Schmid (2015) "Towards a New Epistemology of the Urban?" *CITY* 19(3): 151–182.

Davis, M. (1992) *City of Quartz: Excavating the Future in Los Angeles*. New York: Vintage Books.

Easterling, K. (2007) "Extrastatecraft." *Perspecta* 39: 4–16.

Ferguson, J. (2005) "Seeing Like an Oil Company: Space, Security, and Global Capital in Neoliberal Africa." *American Anthropologist* 107(3): 377–382.

Foucault, M. (1975) *Discipline and Punish: The Birth of the Prison*. New York: Vintage Books.

Galloway, Alexander R. (2014) *Laruelle: Against the Digital*. Minneapolis: University of Minnesota Press.

Graham, S. and S. Marvin (2001) *Splintering Urbanism: Networked Infrastructures, Technological Mobilities and the Urban Condition*. London: Routledge.

Grosz, E. (2001) *Architecture from the Outside. Essays on Virtual and Real Space*. Cambridge, MA: Massachusetts Institute of Technology.

Harvey, D. (2000) *Spaces of Hope*. Edinburgh: Edinburgh University Press.

Laruelle, F. (1999) "A Summary of Non-Philosophy." *Pli* 8: 138–148.

Laruelle, F. (2011) The Generic as Predicate and Constant: Non-Philosophy and Materialism," in L. Bryant, N. Srnicek and G. Harman (eds) *The Speculative Turn: Continental Materialism and Realism*. Melbourne: re.press, pp. 237–260.

Lash, S. (2013) "Experience, Time, and the Religious: From Classical Subject to Technological System." *New Formations* 79: 104–124.

MacKenzie, E. (1994) *Privatopia: Homeowner Associations and the Rise of Residential Private Government*. New Haven, CT: Yale University Press.

Murray, M. J. (2013) "'City Doubles': Re-Urbanism in Africa." Paper presented at ECAS 2013, Fifth European Conference on African Studies: Multi-polar Urban Spaces in Africa: Everyday Dynamics, Creativity and Change. Lisbon, July 27–29.

Parisi, L. (2012) "Digital Design and Topological Control." *Theory, Culture and Society* 29: 165–192.

Parisi, L. (2013) *Contagious Architecture: Computation, Aesthetics and Space*. Cambridge, MA and London: MIT Press.

Soja, E. (2000) *Postmetropolis: Critical Studies of Cities and Regions*. Oxford: Blackwell.

Srnicek, N. (2011) Capitalism and the Inhuman: Conjectures on Capitalism and Organic Necrocracy," in L. Bryant, N. Srnicek and G. Harman (eds) *The Speculative Turn: Continental Materialism and* Realism. Melbourne: re.press, pp. 164–181.

Totaro, P. and D. Ninno (2014) "The Concept of Algorithm as the Key to Modern Rationality." *Theory, Culture and Society* 31: 29–49.

11 Ecologies in beta

The city as infrastructure of apprenticeships

Alberto Corsín Jiménez and Adolfo Estalella

Early in February 2014 we received an email inviting us to join a project that went by the name of *Atlas*, the purpose and contents of which remained mysteriously concealed from us. The message included a document that 'defined Atlas' and was structured into six headings or chapters: Map-Territory, Pause-Sequence, Myth-Ritual, Public-Private Space, Critical Object-Accumulation, and Ephemeral-Unfinished. The document resembled, perhaps, the catalogue of an exhibition-to-be.

Some forty people were copied into the original email, most of them belonging to a young cohort of artists, architects and cultural mediators that have over the last ten years coalesced around a project for 'free culture' activism in Madrid. These included architectural collectives Basurama and Zuloark with whom we had ourselves been carrying out fieldwork in the city over the past three years.

As it turned out, *Atlas* was the graduate research project of Madrid-based scenographer, Jacobo García. Despite his youth, García was already well known in various activist circles in Madrid for his creative re-appropriation of a number of occupied spaces in the city by using the language and resources of theatre. This proved to be a novelty in a city whose tradition of occupation had long been dominated by the discourses of political economy and autonomism. In this context, the symbolic and material resources of theatre offered a somewhat different repertoire of analytical forms with which to explore notions of public, private and common spaces; engagement, movement and participation; or affect, embodiment and care.

Over the following months, those who remained interested in the project were asked to produce a 'box' for one of the chapter headings in the *Atlas* document. These boxes would eventually be used to produce an installation performance for Jacobo's graduation viva at Madrid's School of Drama Studies. The call to put 'inside' a box some of the sources that characterized the work of well-known 'outdoors' activists was a provocation of sorts. However, as it evolved over time, *Atlas*'s explicit convocation of an urban-wide apparatus of free culture activism took issue with the very notion of the city as a 'source' for common life. The many collaborators that *Atlas* strategically mobilized had long been struggling and working in 'open-sourcing' their own architectural or artistic practice in the city. For these collectives, the toolkits of open-source and free culture activism offered a stock of technical and legal, conceptual and political resources with which to refurnish the infrastructural and political capacities of the city (Corsín Jiménez 2014).

Yet what *Atlas* managed to accomplish rather spectacularly was to *theatricalize* the alleged symmetry of all such projects as sources of urban openness. For example, one participant created small sculptures of 'congealed affects' produced by melting wax over objects and mementos of significance to her, generating a form that was then emptied-out of the material that supported it (see Figure 11.1). These affects were meant to crystallize and make visible the emotional turbulence and topological intensity of specific urban relations. The architectural collective Zuloark, for its part, was challenged to build a 'street parliament' that would serve as 'democratic furniture' for people assembling to discuss matters publicly in the open air (see Figure 11.2a, b). Each intervention thus captured different 'sources' of the idea of the city as an 'open source', and triggered unsettling relations of symmetry between them. The form of theatre – the material, spatial and temporal resources through which the illusions of spectatorship, engagement or performance are designed in a theatrical production – functioned in this context to hold fleetingly and fragilely together the idea of the city as a radical and symmetrical form of openness.

Atlas drew on the dramaturgical resources of theatrical productions to design what we might refer to as an 'ecology of open sources' for the city. It literally laid out an ecological, scenographic and cartographic artefact that

Figure 11.1 Congealed affects
Photograph: Atlas Project

Ecologies in beta 143

Figure 11.2 (a) Two views of *The Urban Parliament* by Zuloark
Photograph: Adolfo Estalella

Figure 11.2 (b)
Photograph: Atlas Project

was itself sourced on the radical praxis of well-known free culture activists in Madrid (see Figure 11.3). In this sense, we may think of *Atlas* as a pluriverse: a world invested with a commitment towards radical and emergent openness. Yet such a pluriverse was short-lived. It was a product of artistic design, a theatrical experiment.

In this chapter we want to explore some of the issues raised by the production of *Atlas*, in particular the political and infrastructural imagination of the city as an 'ecology of open sources' – or as we shall refer to it hereafter, an *ecology in beta*. Such an ecology, we shall argue, challenges some of the descriptive and conceptual conventions of recent social and urban theory. On the one hand, the work of free culture activists helps cast new light on how and where politics is sourced and re-sourced in the city. This notion of 're-sourcing'

Figure 11.3 *Atlas* table map
Photograph: Atlas Project

will play an important part in our argument. Re-sourcing points to the materiality that subtends all political work, at the same time as it interrogates the nature of its sourcing – its foundations and support structures but also its springs and openings.[1] Re-sourcing offers an alternative location from where to describe what the city is made up of and how we get to know it. As the example of *Atlas* already illustrates, whatever the political might turn out to be, it is hardly just a space of representation, reclamation or participation. The political is also re-sourced on affective, choreographic and infrastructural dimensions that contribute to its holding in place (see also Corsín Jiménez, Estalella and the Zoohaus Collective 2014).

On the other hand, the notion of an ecology in beta calls also for re-examining social theory's own 're-sourcing' as a methodological and critical design for social life. It helps us articulate a question about the sources and resources that we use in the making of theory, as well as about theory more amply as an open-source endeavour. We may want to ask, for example, what it would take to open-source the methods and infrastructures of theory-making in the social sciences (and anthropology in particular).

Finally, the question of re-sourcing helps us make visible what we believe is an important distinction about the ontologies subtending political life. Thus, the scenography of experiment that *Atlas* set on stage exemplifies contemporary interest in the emergent dynamics of affect and material vitalism that traverse systems thinking today. *Atlas* presents in this light a view of cityness as an ontology that sources the open.

Yet there is an alternative take on the idea of ontological openness that is afforded by a focus on re-sourcing. We will describe a project carried out hand in hand with guerrilla architectural collectives and various community organizations in Madrid when we came to realize that the move from 'sources' to 're-sourcing' demanded our collective designing of an infrastructure of apprenticeships. Re-sourcing apprenticeships, the city emerged not just as an ontology that sources the open but as an open-source ontology.

The city liberated

The global free culture movement saw the light in the 1990s in response to widespread corporate efforts to extend patent protection and copyright control over cultural works (Lessig 2004). Inspired by the copyleft licences of free and open-source (F/OS) software, it quickly spilled over the technical domain of software development to encompass tangible and intangible cultural forms. When we first met Basurama and Zuloark in February 2012 we had already been carrying out ethnographic work among free culture activists for three years in a variety of sites in Madrid, including a social squat center, a media lab and a number of Occupy assemblies. Despite the obvious urban dimension of some of these movements, the relation between free culture and the city remained unclear: what specific qualities did parlance of 'freedom' inflect the architectural imagination of urban public space with? What made a plaza, an urban community garden or a social squat center 'free'? In the wake of the Occupy movement these became guiding concerns for Basurama and Zuloark. Both collectives had a long tradition of social and urban activism in Spain and Latin America yet in the aftermath of the economic crisis turned their attention to the specific forms of autonomy and sustainability that free culture seemed to open up for urbanism. In part this was provoked by the culture of creativity and collaboration on which open-source projects are sustained, and the promises they seemed to offer against the legacy of ruination brought about by the politics of austerity. But it was also partly a response to the heightened attention paid by liberal governmentality to new trends in sentient and smart urbanism. So let us briefly look at some of these developments before returning to Basurama and Zuloark's experiments with open-source urbanism.

As the editors of the volume have noted, the rise to prominence of the concept of 'infrastructure' has coincided with both the empirical proliferation of new interfaces, media and digital sensor networks and a recent analytical sensibility that attends to the complex, adaptive and emergent processes lending epistemic continuity and/or sustainability to social and biotic systems. Thus, there seems to be growing consensus that the functional and ontological dimensions of self-organized systems are assembled together as relational epistemic ecologies (Morton 2012; Connolly 2013).

Critical geography was perhaps pioneering in its embracing of an ecological framework for approaching the study of urban systems, even though this was at the time framed in terms of the metabolic flows dis/abled by the circulation of capital (Heynen, Kaika and Swyngedouw 2006). Infrastructures stood here as both skeletal support-systems for capital flows and capital-intensive lattices in their own right. Recent years, however, have seen scholars turning their attention away from the political ecology of capital flows and towards the medial and processual affordances of infrastructural work. That is, an interest not only in how infrastructures stand, how they stand out or what they stand for but also in their deportment as *stances* – platforms or stations, but also orientations – through which people hold their worlds together. Thus, there is an awareness today that these stances are mediated, orientated and shaped by a multifarious array of 'sentient' and 'ambient intelligences' (Crang and Graham 2007), from data sensors and 'smart' micro-computational devices to surveillance systems. Nigel Thrift sums it up nicely when he says that:

> [c]ities are more than collections of flows channelled by their various infrastructures: they are not just a set of assembled entities ... . Rather, cities are means of revealing new things, means of fostering and animating ramifications which are centrifugal in nature.
>
> (Thrift 2014: 7)

These centrifugal forces build up into waves of anticipation and expectation, westerly winds of data-streams that, in the atmospheric idioms favoured by urban theorists today, sway and whirl our bodies into larger 'informatic weather systems' (Shepard 2011: 18) and infrastructures of 'network weather' (Greenfield 2009). In other words, cities open up as emergent semiotic life-worlds and forms of 'urban wilderness' (Hinchliffe et al. 2005): luxuriant forests and intensive pressure fields of signals and 'outstincts', as Thrift calls them (2014), that stretch and dilate the terms through which we are urged to rethink the *polis* as a dynamic cosmos.

This casts an exciting and promising scenario for urban theory. Yet we would like at this juncture to return to our account of Basurama and Zuloark's open-source urban projects to offer a gentle ethnographic displacement to this narrative about emergent forms of urban ontological pluralism.

Open-source infrastructures

Open-source architecture poses challenges of a rather different nature to the digital projects that have become flagships for theories of sentient and smart urbanism, or indeed very different, too, from the F/OS software projects that have become widely iconic of social innovation and citizen engagement in the age of the Internet.

For example, open-source architecture is different from F/OS software in that the work of design is different from the final output. Design and output do not coincide in the same object. Thus, unlike software, where writing code is at once a form of self-grounding design *and* deploying infrastructure (Kelty 2008), in the case of architecture one can make designs freely accessible (architectural drawings, 3D renders) yet the actual process of building the infrastructure may still be carried out behind closed doors. In other words, whereas for some digital projects opening access is tantamount to opening the sources, in the case of hardware projects, opening access and opening sources are in fact different operations.

The question of the 'sources' of the urban condition is therefore at the heart of how open-source architecture projects carry out their work. For when guerrilla architectural collectives speak of open-sourcing their practice they don't just mean granting access to their designs. What they mean, rather, is that every stage in the process of designing and building an architectural project should be open. This certainly involves refunctioning the technical, legal and material resources with which they equip their practice: using creative commons or free hardware licences; employing recycled materials; making all designs publicly and freely available, etc. But it also goes beyond such resourceful solutions. Taking seriously the question of how to open the sources of the urban condition demands on the part of these collectives an exhaustive inquiry into and mobilization of the *re-sources* that draw the city together today as a vibrant, emergent and dynamic field. It is the nature of *sourcing* that is at the heart of how the city is assembled as a vital system. There are some examples below:

- The work of sourcing calls for an imaginative exploration of the *visual and iconographic systems* through which objects and interfaces becomes intelligible and usable, not least by those who have never seen or worked with architectural designs before. These novel diagrammatic or 'logo-graphic' systems (Thrift 2009), mobilize and re-arrange media surfaces, digital iconologies, even traditional ideographic resources into intuitive but also radically counter-political informational interfaces (see Figure 11.4).
- It further involves coming up with imaginative solutions to the technical and legal systems, and perhaps most importantly, the *expert and authorial regimes* that underwrite the governance of urban projects. Thus, open-source architectural collectives have come up with novel contractual models that re-articulate architects' responsibilities over the signing-off of construction work. These contractual forms maintain the authority of the architect as the certificatory agent (holding him or her accountable for public liability insurance – in the Spanish context it would be a violation of law to do otherwise) yet they define ways, too, in which local communities re-absorb part of that responsibility in exchange for much longer-term commitments on the part of the architects. Contractual obligations are therefore recast along lines that redefine the temporal expectations and outputs of traditional regimes of commercial liability.
- At the very heart of the work that open-source architectural collectives engage in is also the head-on investigation of *openness as an ontology* – that is, of the material, infrastructural and social capacities that 'source'

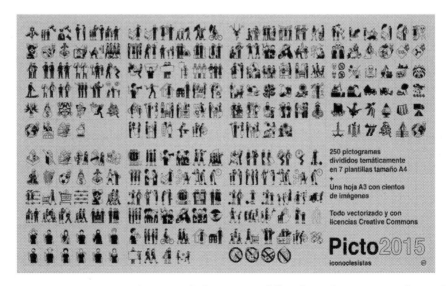

Figure 11.4 Pictogramas by Iconoclasistas, a portfolio of creative commons licenced ideograms used to facilitate community storytelling and cartographies
Source: www.iconoclasistas.net/post/picto-2015/

the nature of openness. For example, it is common for guerrilla architects to enlist communities into designing, developing and maintaining the very infrastructures of collaboration that will support future community work (e.g. email lists, websites, archives, auto-construction toolkits) (see Figure 11.5). Thus, for architects, as far as infrastructural installations go, the distinction between human/social and non-human/material dimensions is meaningless and counterproductive. What is at stake is not the ontological status of urban resources but their *re-sourcing*: how does an infrastructure/architectural work become a 'source' of community concerns? How are these various interests and agendas negotiated, mediated and 'mattered' into a project management programme: resources, materials, skills, competences, capacities, tools, availabilities, deadlines, etc.?

- The work of open-source architectural collectives further tests the limits of the city as an administrative unit, confronting numerous *bureaucratic and institutional trials* over legal permits, public liability insurance, tenure rights over public landholdings, access to electricity and water, waste disposal, etc. In facing up to these challenges, guerrilla architectural collectives have taken upon themselves the task of opening up and designing new spaces and forums of political interlocution, enabling local administrations and communities to meet each other outside established frameworks of political bargaining.
- Last, these projects face chronic *funding and financial challenges*, due for the most part to their disruptive and uncertain status, but also because of the ambiguity of their accounting practices (for example, how to account for cooperative and community work). Over the years guerrilla architectural collectives have learned to exploit unsuspected financial openings and opportunities, such as crowdfunding, local patronage or community sponsorship, or quite simply tapping into and recircuiting local communities' basic material, recycling or waste management systems.

Ecologies in beta

To recap, opening the sources of an architectural project requires both making its designs available *and* re-sourcing its social and infrastructural capacities. Such an orientation to the urban unsettles the material, legal, technical and socio-political conceptions of how we have traditionally come to think of the city as an infrastructural system. Guerrilla architectural collectives struggle to think and open anew what and where the sources of a project might lie while simultaneously standardizing its technical and documentary legacies – as well as devising pedagogies about its technical design systems, legal form, collaborative dynamics, governance mechanisms, materials and resources, and social and political capacities. In such an ecology of open sources there is little time for conventional notions of knowledge, description, epistemology or ontology. Sources constantly re-source themselves, now as materials, now as media, or iconographies, code, language,

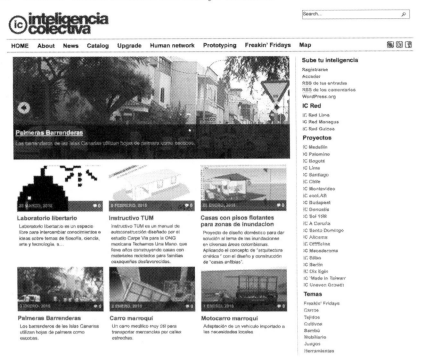

Figure 11.5 Inteligencia colectiva, a public domain self-archival project on do-it-yourself, grassroots, retrofitted architectural designs.
Source: www.inteligenciascolectivas.org/

infrastructures, public spaces, archives, persons, collectives, etc. The ecology is therefore always and everywhere a 'beta' version of itself.

The view of the city as an ecology in beta is exhilarating but can also at times be distressing. There are personal, economic and cultural factors to the sources of distress, not least in a climate of crisis and uncertainty. However, over the course of our work with Basurama and Zuloark we slowly came to realize that the sources of distress were also, in part, conceptual: the view of the city as an infrastructural system is itself stressed by the notion of a complexity in beta. Thus, to circumvent the sources of distress an ecology in beta demands a different ontology of infrastructure. Let us explain.

The revelation that an ecology in beta demands a different ontology of infrastructure came to us at one such moment of distress. Despite their best efforts at developing open-source grassroots projects, throughout 2011–2013 Basurama and Zuloark garnered ever more attention as proponents of a novel regime of urban governance. If at one level theirs was a challenge to the governance of experts, at another it seemed as if they were becoming the new experts. The situation was physically and emotionally stressful because it demanded from the collectives material and affective resources which surpassed their own capacities. It soon became obvious to us that this was partly the result of open-source urbanism not having an infrastructural counterpart to the recursive infrastructures of F/OS software projects. As noted above, in software, code works simultaneously as both infrastructure and design. Design and output coincide in the same object. But the urban condition has no pre-given infrastructure wherein open-source designs can self-ground themselves. There is no standardized F/OS infrastructure holding the city together as a larger ontological and epistemic space. In the idiom used earlier, open-source infrastructures stand alone but they have no widespread purchase as urban stances.

It occurred to us then that one way to develop such a stance would be to design open-source infrastructures such that they became immediately part of a wider learnable infrastructure. In other words, where every infrastructural project contributed to enriching, eliciting and widening an ever-growing infrastructure of apprenticeships. What would the city look like, we asked ourselves, as an open-source urban pedagogical project?

In 2013 we sat down with Basurama and Zuloark to design such an infrastructure of apprenticeships. We pondered over the grassroots skills, tools and resources that were proving useful for community projects across the city: did these capacities overlap in places (physical or conceptual), did they mobilize similar or analogous resources, and could they be systematized or built upon? Moreover, could we mobilize the communities themselves in opening all such capacities as pedagogical projects, to have them lay out the sources of their own learning? Using Open Badges technology[2] we designed and developed a digital platform that enabled community projects to warrant visibility to the multifarious ecology of practices they mobilized and deployed in pursuing their own infrastructural projects. We invited them to design their own badges – to have them 'source' their own technical, legal, pedagogical, associative and political needs – and gave our common infrastructure for urban apprenticeships the name *Ciudad Escuela* (http://ciudad-escuela.org/).

The challenge was straightforward: could such a platform help communities carry out their work better? Could it play a role in legitimizing their practices vis-à-vis local authorities or neighbouring communities? Could it provide a means for communities to learn about their own practices, thereby becoming more robust and sustainable? Take the example of urban community gardens: would it make sense for Madrid's Network of Urban Community Gardens to design one or various badges about different aspects of their practice – for instance, the skills or resources assiduously employed or mobilized at a garden site? And if it would, what design and pedagogical routes should they take in explicitating and standardizing all such tacit urban knowledge? In the case of Madrid's Network of Community Gardens, the Network convened a series of workshops to better understand the diversity of material, media and social relations shaping gardening experiences across the city. An outcome of such a process has been the production of documentary materials on the registers, formats and resources shaping the cultural experiences and material pedagogies of community gardening, which led over time to the development of *Ciudad Huerto* (http://ciudad-huerto.org/), an open-source fork of the original *Ciudad Escuela* platform turned now into an infrastructure of urban apprenticeships for community gardening.

We return thus to the point with which we started: why an ecology in beta demands a different ontology of infrastructure. This is an ontology whose sources – its 'natures' – are opened up, expanded to include a capacity for self-learning, indeed, that make of such a capacity for pedagogical exfoliation their 'nature'. Here the nature of infrastructures is displaced from the techno-material to the poetic and social (Larkin 2013). However, this is a social vector that places a premium not in its sources but in its re-sourcing, in its being taken up, learned and reproduced by third parties; in its functioning as an infrastructure of apprenticeships. It is in this fashion that we therefore speak of a shift in the ontological signature of infrastructures: from ontologies that source the open (that source material affordances or capacities, human and non-human assemblages and relations) to open-source ontologies – ontologies that *re-source* the open.

Infrastructures of experiment and infrastructures of apprenticeship

In a recent essay that attempts to sound out a political ontology alternative to capitalism, Philippe Pignarre and Isabelle Stengers employ the idiom 'getting a hold on' to capture the analytical stance that in their view is required of our times (Pignarre and Stengers 2011). 'Getting a hold,' they write, 'designates here struggle situations, when the question is coming to grips with capitalism, but it is also *what allows one to learn*' (Pignarre and Stengers 2011: 19; emphasis added). For Pignarre and Stengers, getting a hold sets in motion a particular type of experimental moment, one that 'suspends all evidence-based argument and demands that we accept the need for experimentation, that is, that we risk being interested by concrete situations in which the precarious beginning of *trajectories of apprenticeship* may be discerned' (Pignarre and Stengers 2011: 22; emphasis added).

The notion of experimentation has recently gained currency among scholars intent in exploring novel and emerging scenarios for political praxis (Jensen and Morita 2015). Much of this work concerns, too, the role that social scientists themselves play in enabling or designing such experimental arrangements. Thus, for example, Helen Verran and Michael Christie have described their partnership with Australian Aborigines in a project that uses digital technologies to curate and assemble Aboriginal natural knowledge traditions (Verran and Christie 2014). This form of 'postcolonial databasing', as they call it, has been carefully designed so as to remain faithful to and accommodate the ontic difference that Aboriginal understandings bring to the very notion of a digital object. This required on the part of Verran and Christie to engage in 'collaborative ontic work' (Verran and Christie 2014: 63), where some of the prevalent Euro-American assumptions about digital archiving, such as the classificatory and ontological distinction between data and metadata, were suspended and reworked. In their words, this entailed:

> assuming the existence of a third translating domain. This move involves an ontology that is both and neither Aboriginal nor scientific. But this is not a meta-ontology. It is not an ontic domain that supervenes and contains the other two. On the contrary, it is an infra-ontology, an inside connection ... effecting among other things a separation of the ontic and the epistemic. Learning how to do this in on-the-ground situations is not easy because it involves working with contradictions in disciplined ways ... . The work in this infra-ontological space is essential empirical work centering on metaphysics.
> (Verran and Christie 2014: 66–67)

The work of the infra-ontological, then, opens up a space that Verran and Christie describe as an 'experimental metaphysics':

> a framing of issues of difference that takes elements of both metaphysical systems to develop what we might call an ad hoc hybrid translation borderland. It can provide a way to imagine how we might connect in partial, strategic, and opportunistic ways.
> (Verran and Christie 2014: 75)

The notion that there are formats of encounter that are conducive to the framing of issues as experimental metaphysics resonates, too, with recent work in social studies of science and technology, where 'experimental ontologies' have been strategically counterposed to 'empirical ontologies'. According to Steve Woolgar and Javier Lezaun, whereas:

> empirical ontology draws attention to the practices that determine 'what there is' and to how the norms embedded in those practices then grant the world a particular political valence, an experimentalization of ontology opens up (rather than answers) the question of how particular objects come to be invested with normative and political capacities.
> (Woolgar and Lezaun 2013: 327)

In this vein, Noortje Marres has offered for example an account of the 'experimentalization' 'by design' of political ontology in an ecoshow home, where the spatial layout, interactive dynamics and material affordances of technologies and interfaces are deliberately invested with specific environmental and political significations (Marres 2013: 423). The ecoshow home functions as an experiment insofar as it enacts a particular 'distribution' of human and non-human force fields (Marres 2013: 428). There is ontological aperture because there is an experimental (socio-infrastructural) distribution.

Let us bring our argument to a close by offering some remarks on this recent coupling of experimentation and political ontology. As outlined in Marres' and Verran and Christie's arguments, the work of experimentation is here fundamentally conceived as an *enabling* technology: an ecology and arrangement of infrastructures that bodies forward new onto-political capacities. The experiment frames and incites possible new worlds into existence. There is a sense, then, in which in these accounts the space and infrastructures of experiment are themselves enabling of political work. It would seem that the relational force field that weaves together human and non-human energies becomes, in its very conjuring as an experimental infrastructure, a driver of enablement.

Yet closer inspection shows us that the liberation of the ontological affordances that these experiments presume often demands the discernment, too, of what Pignarre and Stengers call 'trajectories of apprenticeship' (Pignarre and Stengers 2011: 78 and *passim*). In the quote cited above on the affordances of the infra-ontological, Verran and Christie similarly point out how '[l]earning how to [get the infra-ontological to work] in on-the-ground situations is not easy' (Verran and Christie 2014: 67). It would appear, then, that the work of experimentation sets in fact two simultaneous operations of enablement in motion. First, an ontological aperture, such that a partially novel arrangement and distribution of agencies is born into the world. This is the experimental moment, where a strategically framed distribution is generative of political ontological work. But there is a second form of enablement, which underpins and accompanies the first. We shall call this second moment, a moment of apprenticeship, where it is in fact the opening of a pedagogical process that procures and subtends the form of enablement.

Thus, to go back to our opening vignette, we may read the scenography of *Atlas* as an infra-ontological and collaborative experiment, one that lays out the city's sources of openness. Yet this was an experimental arrangement that was not designed as a space of apprenticeship. As noted, *Atlas* staged a 'theatrical experiment' where the city's sources of radical openness were rendered symmetrical vis-à-vis each other. Like Marres' ecoshow homes, *Atlas* performed its experimental function as a demonstrational device; and like Verran and Christie's postcolonial databasing, it cast itself as a cartography of the city, one that could be read as an 'ad hoc hybrid translation borderland' (Verran and Christie 2014: 75).

We wish to suggest, however, that there might be room for a complementary understanding of how the work of political ontology and liberation gets done. This would entail approaching the field of distribution of human and non-human agencies not just as onto-experimental devices, but as infrastructures for the liberation of apprenticeships. The case of *Ciudad Escuela* offers one such example. Here the work of collaboration looks out for and cares for tending, not only ontologies that source the open, but open-source ontologies too.

Notes

1 We play here with the etymology of the word 'resource', from the French *ressourse, ressourdre*: to rise up again, to spring up again; to recover or recuperate, from the Latin, *resurgere*, to re-surge.
2 The Mozilla Foundation's Open Badges project (http://openbadges.org). Open Badges use free software and open technical standards to enable people to get recognition for learning that happens anywhere, online or offline. Anyone can issue a badge, from traditional higher educational institutions to community organizations or online projects, and it is up to the issuer to decide the achievements that the badge recognizes. In this sense, Open Badges have been praised for the double liberation they bring to pedagogy: first, the liberation or open-sourcing they bring to the very technology that underwrites certificatory standards; but also for the fact that they enable all kinds of learning programmes, on all kinds of topics, to claim recognition.

References

Connolly, William E. (2013) *The Fragility of Things: Self-Organizing Processes, Neoliberal Fantasies, and Democratic Activism*. Durham, NC and London: Duke University Press.
Corsín Jiménez, Alberto (2014) "The right to infrastructure: A prototype for open-source urbanism". *Environment and Planning D: Society and Space* 32(2).
Corsín Jiménez, Alberto, Adolfo Estalella and the Zoohaus Collective (2014) "The interior design of [free] knowledge". *Journal of Cultural Economy* 7(4): 493–515.
Crang, Mike and Stephen Graham (2007) "Sentient cities: Ambient intelligence and the politics of urban space". *Information, Communication & Society* 10(6): 789–817.
Greenfield, Adam (2009) "*The City Is Here*: Table of contents", *Speedbird*. Available at: http://speedbird.wordpress.com/2009/02/14/the-city-is-here-table-of-contents/.
Heynen, Nikolas C., Maria Kaika and Erik Swyngedouw (2006) *In the Nature of Cities: Urban Political Ecology and the Politics of Urban Metabolism*. Oxford and New York: Routledge.
Hinchliffe, Steve, Matthew B. Kearnes, Monica Degen and Sarah Whatmore (2005) "Urban wild things: A cosmopolitical experiment". *Environment and Planning D: Society and Space* 23(5): 643–658.
Jensen, Casper Bruun and Atsuro Morita (2015) "Infrastructures as ontological experiments". *Engaging Science, Technology, and Society* 1(0): 81–87.
Kelty, Christopher M. (2008) *Two Bits: The Cultural Significance of Free Software*. Durham, NC and London: Duke University Press.
Larkin, Brian (2013) "The politics and poetics of infrastructure". *Annual Review of Anthropology* 42: 327–343.
Lessig, Lawrence (2004) *Free Culture: The Nature and Future of Creativity*. New York: Penguin.
Marres, Noortje (2013) "Why political ontology must be experimentalized: On eco-show homes as devices of participation". *Social Studies of Science* 43(3): 417–443.
Morton, Timothy (2012) *The Ecological Thought*. Cambridge, MA: Harvard University Press.
Pignarre, Phillipe and Isabelle Stengers (2011) *Capitalist Sorcery: Breaking the Spell*. Basingstoke: Palgrave Macmillan.

Shepard, Mark (2011) "Toward the sentient city". in Mark Shepard (ed.) *Sentient City: Ubiquitous Computing, Architecture, and the Future of Urban Space*. Cambridge, MA and London: MIT Press, pp. 16–37.

Thrift, Nigel (2009) "Different atmospheres: Of Sloterdijk, China, and site". *Environment and Planning D: Society and Space* 27(1): 119–138.

Thrift, Nigel (2014) "The "sentient" city and what it may portend". *Big Data & Society* 1(1): 1–21.

Verran, Helen and Michael Christie (2014) "Post-colonial databasing? Subverting old appropriations, developing new associations". in James Leach and Lee Wilson (eds) *Subversion, Conversion, Development: Cross-Cultural Knowledge Exchange and the Politics of Design*. Cambridge, MA: MIT Press, pp. 57–78.

Woolgar, Steve and Javier Lezaun (2013) "The wrong bin bag: A turn to ontology in science and technology studies?" *Social Studies of Science* 43(3): 321–340.

Part III
Energy infrastructures

In 1943, the anthropologist Leslie White argued for a correlation between energy and "the evolution of culture." Cultural evolution, he suggested, varies directly with the expenditure of energy and with the efficiency of the technologies used to put it to work. White's energy determinism was quickly sidelined as Boasian cultural anthropology took center stage. However, in the present moment of climate change driven by oil-based capitalism, it has gained a new lease on life. Thus, across the social sciences we are currently witness to a surge of interest in energy and its infrastructures. Vividly illustrating this tendency, Dominic Boyer's (2014) revamping of Foucault's biopolitics as energopolitics locates the question of sustainable energy systems at the forefront of social scientific concerns.

Updating earlier arguments, including Langdon Winner's (1986: 32) suggestion that complex technological systems, like nuclear power plants, are "strongly compatible" with authoritarian forms of politics, the renewed interest in energy also raises questions of democracy and citizen involvement in our age of energy transition. There is little question that energy must move to the center of social scientific concerns.

The contributions to this section evince such concerns. Yet, while they all grapple with the importance of energy for people, societies, economies, or cultures, they do not reach the determinist conclusion that energy is the final arbiter of social transformation. Instead, they experiment with analyses of energy infrastructures that simultaneously keep energy's effects and peoples' activities and perceptions in view.

One of the most striking features of energy infrastructures is undoubtedly their size. Images of endless oil pipelines crossing natural and national boundaries or the electricity pylons dotting cities and countryside conjure a sense of immutable fixity, seemingly vindicating Bruno Latour's (1991) claim that technology is indeed society made durable. In contexts where durability is wanted this may be cause for applause, but in a situation where what is most needed may be the *undoing* of such systems, the effect, as Dominic Boyer suggests may be numbing anxiety.

Even so, the papers in this section all show *openings* towards alternative energy futures. As Andrew Barry emphasizes, pipes and cables corrode and crack so the functioning of these infrastructures requires constant monitoring and maintenance. Left to their own devices, energy infrastructure, in spite of their vaunted durability, quickly begin deteriorating.

Infrastructures are thus also surprisingly fragile achievements. Directing our attention to the elements out of which it is achieved, the contributors to this section highlight *the force of things*. This is not only a matter of reiterating that society and technology are mutually shaped, for the elements at stake are not simply technological. Rather, the papers encourage engagement with the very different forces of water, earth, oil, uranium, coal, sunlight, and wind.

The distinctiveness of this approach, deployed in different forms by Barry and Maguire and Winthereik, becomes clear in comparison with analysis of energy in the Boasian tradition. Such studies insist that the energy challenges facing us today are "fundamentally cultural and political" (Strauss et al. 2013: 10) and that the issue for anthropologists is to understand how people "construct socially meaningful worlds" (11). Contrasting with the emphasis on politics, culture, and the construction of meaning, contributors to this section emphasize that the differential powers of water, sun, or uranium fundamentally inflect not only the temporalities and spatialities of the energy infrastructures with which we live but also the kinds of subjects we may be able to become.

The times and spaces of earthquakes or storms, for example, cannot easily be predicted. Yet in the Fukushima catastrophe in Japan these forces combined to disrupt the nuclear power plant, energy systems more broadly, and the ecologies, livelihoods – indeed, the "socially meaningful worlds" – of a huge number of people. That the still undetermined scale of the event also encompassed Japanese politics and economics together with animal life in the Pacific cannot be disentangled from the conjunction of forces that generated it: earthquake, tsunami – and uranium. While the relative stability or instability of energy infrastructures, depends on peoples' perspectives and motivations, it also depends on many other things. This exuberance of elements in turn helps to generate infrastructural spaces of experimentation. Indeed, Dominic Boyer *urges* such experimentation, with a view to undoing the oil–climate change death spiral and producing alternative energy systems.

Offering a comparative ethnographic perspective, Jamie Cross examines the differential possibilities, aspirations and challenges of "off the grid" electricity in Scotland, India, and Papua New Guinea. Meanwhile, Maguire and Winthereik explore what they call the constitutive "alterity" at the heart of Icelandic energy infrastructures. Whereas Boyer deploys a contrast between the present and the future and Cross finds difference by moving across geographical locations, Maguire and Winthereik locate difference *within* the system. Doing so, they use the notion of the "otherwise" of energy infrastructures to characterize the *internally generated* room for maneuver that emerges where designed infrastructures *meet the various elements of energy.*

Recognition of contextual variability, room for maneuver, and the internal or external instability of infrastructures is crucial in order to go beyond the numbing anxiety described by Boyer. It creates openings that in turn encourage, or indeed oblige, social scientists, and societies as a whole, to learn to become responsible to, and for, the events set in motion by their modes of energy consumption. The unavoidable next step is to develop modes of infrastructured living less environmentally harmful and self-destructive.

When it comes to energy infrastructures, neither stability nor instability is a cause for celebration as such. Stable patterns of energy consumption may lead to future instabilities, "deathward", as Boyer writes. Thus he advocates finding the potentials within such infrastructures for blowing current social arrangements "sky high." As Cross reminds us, however, from the point of view of off-grid Papua New Guinean villages, a bit more infrastructural stability would be preferable.

As this makes clear, the revolutionary potentials of infrastructure are different, and must be evaluated differently, depending on just *which* arrangements are blown up or transformed, and what comes to replace them. Boyer's focus on revolutionary infrastructure revolves around the need to "disable the anthropocenic trajectory," replacing it with decentralized and renewable energy forms, an argument inspired by the visionary German politician Hermann Scheer. Such transformations, Boyer estimates, will also invariably lead to the formation of new subjects. In contrast, geophysical scenes from Turkey and Georgia (Barry), off-the-grid locations in Scotland, India, or Papua New Guinea (Cross), and thermal landscapes in Iceland (Maguire and Winthereik) relativize and complicate the notion of a single trajectory.

Here we can point to the emergence of a key tension, which relates to the question of the singularity or multiplicity of energy infrastructure(s). The question can be condensed like this: is it still important to emphasize variable contexts, in a situation where energy use in the aggregate may threaten the world as a whole? For Barry and for Maguire and Winthereik, who emphasize the variable composition of *elements*, the heterogeneity of infrastructures clearly remains central. So, too, for Cross, who examines the incongruence between what it means to be off-grid in affluent Scotland and deprived Papua New Guinea. For these contributors the question of response, and response-ability, remains fundamentally relative. Boyer, however, takes a different route. At this moment of impending climate collapse, he asks whether it is not time to let go of the urge to particularize. For some purposes, in order to ward off anxiety and regain an optimism of the spirit, it might be preferable to speak of a "singular" anthropogenic trajectory, even if this goes against one's relativist sensibilities ... .

It seems, then, that there are not only questions to be raised concerning the infrastructural politics of energy decentralization, but *also* about whether such politics can and should unfold in a decentralized and context-relative manner, or must rather be centralized by a singular narrative. Contrary to the insistence on ethnographic heterogeneity, Boyer emphasizes that climate change has created a process of convergence, generating something like a *hyper-object* that operates, virtually and actually, at scales and locations across the whole earth.

The papers in this section indicate that to understand this convergence and to find ways of responding, disrupting, or dismantling it, social scientists need to look carefully not only at energy infrastructures seen as technical systems but also at the operations of the energy elements themselves.

References

Boyer, Dominic (2014) "Energopower: An Introduction," *Anthropological Quarterly* 87(2): 309–334.

Latour, Bruno (1991) "Technology is Society Made Durable," in John Law (ed.) *A Sociology of Monsters: Essays on Power, Technology and Domination*. London: Routledge, pp. 103–132.

Strauss, Sarah, Stephanie Rupp and Thomas Love (2013) "Powerlines: Cultures of Energy in the Twenty-first Century," in Sarah Strauss, Stephanie Rupp and Thomas Love (eds) *Cultures of Energy*. Walnut Creek, CA: Left Coast Press, pp. 10–41.

White, Leslie (1943) "Energy and the Evolution of Culture," *American Anthropologist* 45(3): 335–356.

Winner, Langdon (1986) *The Whale and the Reactor: A Search for Limits in an Age of High Technology*. Chicago, IL: Chicago University Press.

12 Living with the earth

More-than-human arrangements in seismic landscapes

James Maguire and Brit Ross Winthereik

An awakening

The wellhead sits like a small silver igloo atop the blackened lava encrusted earth (Figure 12.1). Its pipes are thick and rusted and they pulsate and screech as Bjarni and his team attempt to coax up 300 degree fluid. Compressed air at 60 bars is delivered down into the directionally drilled well in an attempt to pressurize the fluids and boil them up through the wellhead – or 'awaken' the well, as Bjarni puts it.[1] Being up here on the Hengill lava plains is visually striking, staggering even, but for the geologists at Reykjavik Energy

Figure 12.1 Wellhead and geologist on the day of the awakening
(Photograph by Maguire)

being attentive to how the well is responding is what matters. Bjarni turns my attention to geothermal metabolic processes; captured rainfall meanders through permeable subterranean rock, all the while reacting with magmatic heat and fluctuating pressure to phase transition between water and steam as explosions drive these fluids to the surface. This particular well, drilled in 2013, had formerly been a reinjection well but had recently been converted to a production well. I ask why we are trying to awaken it today. 'Well, there have been many earthquakes here over the last while, both natural and from reinjection,' says Bjarni. 'All sorts of things are changing down there, and while we're not really sure how, we think there'll be some sort of response.' The radical uncertainty of the intensive forces of the earth are constantly altering the seismic landscape, and converting, and subsequently awakening a well is one way the energy company can respond.[2] Bjarni instructs me to pull my ear mufflers down as the screeching noise intensifies. The entire arrangement of well, igloo and pipes shakes and roars, intermittently yet violently, as dense, thick steam billows out from the earth.

As I learn on this day,[3] it takes a little encouragement to awaken a converted well and trigger the first series of explosive events that possibly lead to a productive geothermal well. Wondering how the geothermal field[4] has responded to recent seismic activity, both 'natural' and otherwise, Bjarni and his team initiate one of a range of possible interventions into the seismic landscape, an intervention they refer to as an awakening. In such a zone of seismic instability entities are constantly responding to one another. Geothermal metabolics respond to earthquakes, as fracturing rock increases permeability and hence subterranean fluid flow. Geologists respond to the earth as they try to order, or arrange, its liveliness, knowing that the earth can, in turn, respond to geological interventions in its own particular way. While these sets of interactions between geologists and earth are dynamic and emerging, they are also the result of infrastructural arrangements that are usually considered more stable. What we want to suggest in this paper is that infrastructural arrangements unfold among and between different kinds of actors as they respond to each other in seismic landscapes. Acknowledging how response-ability can be distributed across human and non-human entities has the advantage of bringing into view the binding quality of more-than-human engagements.

Infrastructures and non-humans

Infrastructure has long played a role in anthropological thinking as an empirical site for social and political change, although the focus of attention seems to have leaned heavily towards clear infrastructural projects that talk to, amongst other things, issues of state power and spatial organization (Appel et al. 2015). In recent years, as certain branches of anthropology have intersected with specific work from within Science and Technology Studies (STS), the concept has gained in analytical traction (Edwards et al. 2009;

Carse 2012; Harvey and Knox 2012; Jensen and Winthereik 2013, Morita and Jensen 2015). What still remains residual in infrastructure thinking, however, is the idea that infrastructure (or overlapping infrastructures – this pluralization is of itself an important move) is what distributes, circulates, or moves people, objects, ideas, and relations, and that it does so in rather stable and durable ways. While Geoff Bowker and Susan Leigh Star coined the term, 'infrastructure as second nature' (Bowker 1995; Bowker and Star 1999), it is Ashley Carse's work that breaks with the notion of infrastructure as nature plus cultural additives, demonstrating 'nature as infrastructure' in the provision of essential ecological systems services (2012). Yet even Carse's interesting work still leaves a sense of a nature-object that is, to a significant extent, a provisioning demarcated entity.

This paper treats Bowker, Star and Carse's work as an invitation to further extend our thinking about infrastructure as nature and nature as infrastructure. In trying to account for the ways in which actors respond to the seismic instability that occurs in the Hengill volcanic zone, we contemplate a series of analytically interconnected questions through the ethnographic moment of awakening a well. Although a pervasive concern with infrastructures is the manner in which they distribute or circulate objects, ideas and entities through their stability, we analyze instability as a thriving part of infrastructural arrangements. In doing so, we make two further related points. First, we argue that non-human actors generatively participate in infrastructuring processes. In suggesting this we are exploring the role of non-humans in our world, and particularly how infrastructural relations bring this role to bear. While infrastructures have conventionally been conceived as technical or sociotechnical systems, ideas of multispecies Morita (this volume) or multinatural (Jensen this volume) relations have now productively entered the discussion. This chapter sits in conversation with such infrastructure work as well as those theorizing the role of non-human actors in other settings (Serres 1995; Haraway 2008; Barad 2010; Yusoff 2013; Povinelli 2014). Second, we argue that infrastructures are premised on recursive sets of responses between and within humans and non-humans and on the binding nature of actors' mode of engaging with one another – their response-ability. To help us with this, we draw upon the insights from those thinkers that conceptualize infrastructures as ontologically generative (Rheinberger 1994; Morita and Jensen 2015; Jensen 2015).

Seismic instability

The Hengill volcanic zone in the south-west of Iceland is a lively place. Located at a triple point junction, an intersection zone of three broader geological phenomena, the area amply affords the conditions for the extraction of geothermal energy (water and steam) from the earth's crust.[5] While geothermal energy has been used to provide energy for cooking, washing and spatial heating for the majority of Icelandic homes for the best part of a century, it is only in the very recent past that it has become a real option for industrial production, mostly aluminium. After a brief flirtation with finance capital led to an International Monetary Fund intervention in 2008, the Icelandic government and business community have been busily refocusing their efforts on natural resources (fish and energy) as a way to resuscitate the economy. But as fish stocks continue to decline, the potential of extracting heat from the earth's crust is becoming increasingly attractive. Landsvirkun (Iceland's national power company) as well as Reykjavik Energy and a handful of smaller subsidiary players are continually on the lookout for new projects in order to live up to the energy supply contracts they entered into with the aluminium industry during the previous decade of unperturbed financial expansion. The Hengill volcanic zone has become a site of particular energetic interest for Reykjavik Energy (RE) over the last decade, hosting the Hellisheiði geothermal power plant as well as several other prospective areas of interest.[6] Ramping up geothermal production to meet the needs of aluminium smelters has taken a surprising toll on the seismic landscape, and both geologists and environmentalists, including concerned residents of Hveragerði, a small town on the outskirts of the volcanic zone, are currently trying to figure out how best to respond. The dominant critique of the power plant is that the scale and tempo of extraction is occurring at a pace that is not affording the seismic landscape enough time to recuperate. Recuperation, in this sense, is indexed by drops in pressure, the cooling of specific mountains within the volcanic zone, and the particular issue that this chapter will address: induced seismicity, or the triggering of man-made earthquakes.

As an active volcanic site, Hengill is a bubbling, hissing, deforming set of intensive forces. Eruptive magma can emerge from swelling chambers only a couple of kilometres beneath, producing fissures that appear as gaping, elongated incisions in the surface. The friction that holds faults together in tensile balance can be overcome, triggering earthquakes and producing a more fractured, and at times, permeable rock matrix. These forces bring about the interplay of elements (rock and fluid) at varying phases (magma–rock and water–steam) through varying intensities (heat, pressure). But extracting the effects of these intensities requires other sets of forces, as technologies, knowledge practices and capital co-mingle in just as intensive a fashion. One could say that geothermal extraction is a process of responding to the eruptive, intensive forces of the earth; it is an attempt at arranging the liveliness of the earth directed towards a particular arrangement of living together. But in seeking to order liveliness, other forces are triggered, creating disorder at the same time.

In the vignette above, Bjarni and his colleagues from RE were attempting to awaken a well, unsuccessfully as it turned out. The reason for the awakening, as they articulated it to me, was in response to a series of earthquakes that had recently occurred. The magnitude of such earthquakes can vary considerably, as can the ways in which they affect the geothermal field. However, it is not the case that RE responds to all seismic activity by awakening a well; this is unfeasible in terms of both cost and time. Instead, they have a series of strategically positioned wells (strategic in the sense that they are in close proximity to areas known for seismic activity) that have been drilled but yet not activated. In addition they have the option of converting a reinjection well into a production well, as was the case on this particular day with the geologists from RE. Reinjection wells are those that pump processed geothermal brine back into the geothermal field.[7] Doing so not only avoids lava pollution and ground water contamination, it also recharges the pressure of the field. The rate of extraction necessary to satisfy aluminium production (1,400 kilos of water per second) is depleting the water level in the rock matrix, and although there is a natural recharge mechanism it is not substantial enough to compensate. Reinjecting water back into the fracture system recharges the field, keeping the water pressure at a rate sufficient enough to drive water, and steam, upwards and into the wells – the mechanism that the whole operation pivots upon. So in many ways reinjection is an environmental response to geothermal activity; not only a way of dealing with wastewater but also a process of stabilizing the seismic terrain at the right levels of pressure and hence sustaining the area into the future. However, reinjection triggers a further series of effects. As the water is reinjected at pressure, and at a colder temperature, it causes contractions and pressure flux in the rock matrix, which at times overcomes the tensile balance that holds faults and fractures in place. RE refers to this as induced seismicity; both my geology friends and others also refer to it as man-made earthquakes. While RE publicly acknowledges responsibility for the triggering of man-made earthquakes[8] and while there are multiple initiatives underway to mitigate their production and consequences, they still occur on a regular basis.

Infrastructuring the otherwise

In the opening vignette Bjarni and his team were in the process of trying to awaken a well after its conversion from reinjection to production. The reinjection process, had, a couple of years prior, been switched from the Gráuhnúkar area, in the southern part of the volcanic zone, to the Húsmuli area in the north-west. However, this section of the volcanic zone is part of what is called the South Iceland Seismic Zone (SISZ), a micro tectonic plate that releases built up stress in the rock matrix (earthquakes) at intervals of approximately a hundred years. The hundred-year release cycle began in 2000 with an earthquake of 5.5 on the Richter scale; there was another in 2008 at 6.5. Geologists, estimating that about 50 per cent of the stress has been released to date, believe that there will be several more incidents over the coming years. The geologists at RE are pretty clear that constant reinjection of pressurized and cooler water into a fault system already under stress is lubricating, contracting and prematurely releasing that stress, inducing seismic responses. While the story of why reinjection was switched to this area is too detailed to enter into here, one prominent explanation is that its proximity to a more actively faulting area is a more effective way of redistributing reinjection water. What was an effort to stabilize the water level in the geothermal field has begun to trigger far more instability than anyone had anticipated. It was never imagined, according to Bjarni, that their intervention into this volcanic zone could be significant enough to affect the area's seismicity. However, that said, a knock-on effect of induced seismicity is the ongoing fracturing of rock, generating a more permeable rock matrix and potentially activating a greater flow of extractable water and steam. While this particular well at Húsmuli was formerly a reinjection site, the response to increased seismicity was to convert and awaken the well in an attempt to capitalize on potentially more bountiful fluidity. Responses to and from the earth at Hengill are arranged infrastructurally.

The word 'earth', however, is an over-simplification. There is no such thing as an earth, a singular entity. By using the shorthand placeholder word 'earth' we are invoking a whole series of differentiating turbulent forces, which play out as pressure, magmatic heat, rock and phase-transitioning fluids boil and explode water and steam out of the ground into wells, through pipes, into turbines, and into electricity pylons. Moreover, once such infrastructural interactions between these eruptive forces and geologists get underway within seismic landscapes, they are extraordinary difficult to unwind. Attempts to halt production, change pressure levels or change reinjection temperatures invariably induce additional seismic responses. As the geologists are at pains to point out, it is not that they have not made serious efforts; every time they attempt one of the above remedial measures, seismic activity increases.[9] While public pressure to do something about this is also on the rise, the potentially productive benefits of consistently inducing seismic responses should not be underestimated. While we do not intend this to be a critical statement – that is, we are not suggesting that the energy company is intentionally triggering earthquakes for their own benefit – it does talk to the manner in which instability plays a crucial part in this particular infrastructural arrangement. In trying to arrange the liveliness of tectonic landscapes, other forces are triggered, but such forces are also, at times, generative.[10] As the opening vignette points towards, Bjarni and his colleagues were responding to seismic activity that had the potential to change the geothermal metabolic system. But this tectonic activity was itself partially man-made. That is, the tectonic response that the geologists were responding to was itself a partial response to geological work. Through this series of infrastructural practices and responses an infrastructural recursion, or loop, emerges.

While a lot of infrastructure thinking leans on the idea of stability as a key component of its setup and functioning, what we are seeing here is that a certain degree of instability thrives as a generative force of infrastructural arrangements. While stabilizing the seismic landscape is absolutely necessary, in fact a huge degree of work goes into doing just that, it is never the full story. Stabilizing processes (reinjection) are themselves productive of moments of instability (induced seismicity) that, in turn, enhance the metabolics of the geothermal field. While Brian Larkin suggests that infrastructures are 'matter that enable the movement of other matter' or 'objects that create the grounds on which other objects operate' (2013: 2–3), the implication, as we read it, is that such grounds need to be stable enough to allow those other objects to operate. Yet what we are seeing in the Hengill volcanic zone is that stability is only ever partial and that instability is a thriving, at times generative, component of infrastructural arrangements. As geologists arrange the eruptive capacities of the earth they provoke turbulent counter forces, and these forces in turn become part of a continually emerging seismic infrastructure. In his book *Genesis*, Michel Serres (1995) suggests that our metaphysical systems have become beholden to the metaphorics of the solid. As such we seem to have developed a binary classification system of solids (ordered states) on the one hand, and fluids (disordered states) on the other. As a partial antidote Serres hints at 'thinking with turbulence'. Describing the disorderly motion of heat molecules, he depicts a world of agitation and disruption, one in which turbulent forces produce mixtures tensed between order and disorder, or that are order and disorder at the same time. Turbulence, Serres suggests, directs our thinking towards processes of arranging and distributing that produce such mixtures, mixtures in which order and chaos co-exist, and through which both the one (unitary) and the multiple can emerge. 'The turbulent state mixes or associates the one and the multiple, systemic gathering together and distribution. System appears there in the distribution, and disappears there, distribution appears there in the system and disappears here' (Serres 1995: 109).

For Serres, then, order and disorder co-exist within the same system. Elizabeth Povinelli adopts a similar, yet slightly modified set of terms. For Povinelli the forces of the world are ongoing processes of arranging, which install their own possible derangements and rearrangements. As such, what she refers to as the 'otherwise' is built into all arrangements of existence (2014), and exploring this otherwise is a political and ethical concern. Thinking with these ideas from Serres and Povinelli, we are suggesting that geothermal extraction is a process of *infrastructurally arranging* the eruptive, turbulent forces of the earth; it is an arrangement of liveliness ordered towards a particular arrangement of living together. However, such processes of arranging come with their own generative *derangements*, their own *otherwise*, as stabilizing efforts trigger even more seismic instabilities, which in turn are then productively re-arranged. The intensive, eruptive capacities of the earth become generative participants in recursively emerging infrastructures as these capacities trigger a binding relationship with humans.

More-than-human de-(ar-)rangements

In suggesting that the capacities of the earth are generative participants in emerging infrastructures, we zoom in on both the role of non-humans in infrastructural arrangements and some specific characteristics of the relations between humans and non-humans. As we mentioned earlier, both multinatural and multispecies thinking are now entering infrastructure discussions. Both Morita (this volume) and Jensen's (this volume) work disrupts and pushes our thinking on the role of nature within infrastructures. The former does so by making visible the role of multispecies (rice and farmer) relations within infrastructures, and the latter by demonstrating that nature–culture configurations can go through many figure-ground reversals depending upon which entity's perspective one takes. This work is pushing Ashley Carse's notion of 'nature as infrastructure' in interesting ways by bringing other non-human species into play.

In contrast, what we are trying to grapple with is what would traditionally be conceived of as inorganic, or inanimate, forces. While authors such as Katherine Yusoff and Nigel Clark refer to such forces as 'inhuman natures' (Clark 2011, Yusoff 2013), we find this characterization problematic on several fronts. Not only does it reintroduce the concept of nature, a term the thrust of which emerging infrastructures militates against, but it does so by invoking the affectively loaded term, inhuman, which is, we feel, too difficult to rehabilitate. While we will invoke the term non-human to designate other than human forces and processes, we will thus deploy the term more-than-human arrangements to encompass the sets of infrastructural practices and responses that occur in the Hengill volcanic zone.

Andrew Barry (this volume) contemplates similar issues, namely, how to conceive the earth as part of infrastructural setups. He argues that although infrastructure is usually considered to sit upon an 'installed base' of some kind, there continues to be many infrastructural forms, such as tracks, tunnels and pipes, whose installed base is the earth – that is, such components are built on and into the earth. However, the earth itself is an entity in motion and in need of infrastructuring (in his case the seismic monitoring of earthquake prone areas). In this way, Barry skilfully characterizes the moving earth as both a resource for infrastructures and as something in need of infrastructuring. Following Connolly and Born, he suggests the idea of 'distinct but interacting force-fields' that 'periodically encounter each other as outside forces' as a way to conceive of the relationships between the earth, its seismic monitoring and a small urban town in Turkey With a view to pushing the logic of force-fields further, in the following we consider how the earth, as a set of eruptive capacities, generatively participates in its own on-going infrastructuring. For us, this is an analytical response to a set of ethnographic questions about the ways in which actors respond to seismic instability in the Hengill volcanic zone. What we are arguing is that these responses, while recursive, are arranged, deranged and rearranged infrastructurally – that is, the capacity of actors to respond, their response-ability, is enacted through sets of more-than-human infrastructuring de-(ar-)rangements.

While the notion of responsibility arises in copious volumes of social scientific literature, we would like to take as our point of departure the work of Donna Haraway. In her work on companion species, Haraway (2008: 77) both praises and takes to task Jacques Derrida for his approach to relations with non-humans, specifically an incident concerning his cat:

Living with the earth 169

For Derrida, only the Human can respond; Animals react. The animal is forever positioned on the other side of an unbridgeable gap, a gap that reassures the Human of his excellence by the very ontological impoverishment of a life world that cannot be its own end or know its own condition.

In essence, response-ability for Haraway is the capacity to respond, which she critiques Derrida for limiting to the human. For her, response-ability is a relationship crafted in intra-action through which entities, subjects and objects come into being (Hathaway 2008: 71). However, although her work opens up the space of possibility for non-human animals to exercise such a capacity, it delimits the conversation to animals. Driving in a similar direction, yet more fruitful for our purposes is some parts of Karen Barad's work. For Barad (2010), the very nature of matter entails an exposure to the Other. For her, response-ability is neither an obligation that a subject chooses nor a calculation to be performed; it is instead a relation, *an enabling of responsiveness.*

In a similar vein Kathryn Yusoff, drawing on the work of Jean Luc Nancy, suggests that the etymology of the word response comes from 'a given guarantee, a promise, an engagement, hence an engaged responsibility'. For Nancy, engagement is about exposure in a crowded world and as such 'a mere rock "responds" just as much as a man named Peter' (Nancy cited in Yusoff 2013: 208). For these authors, response precedes the intentional calculating subject, who may or may not choose to act; it opens up the possibility that, for example, rocks respond, or can be responsive, a sentiment that the RE geologists would be only too eager to endorse. However, while some of the vocabulary of both Barad and Yusoff may be couched in what is, for them, unusually phenomenological language (subject – intentionality), their drive, it seems to us, still remains entirely performative. Such performativity is evidenced by their ambition to hold open a space of possibility for the potential agency of inorganic forces and entities. Such a move, however, is not without its risks. Rendering such entities or forces in a performative mode while at the same time not stabilizing them in advance is a complex task.[11]

While the earth has always been unruly in Iceland, the attempt to live – or be-in-the-world-together – with it, beyond relations of asymmetry (the earth destroys) or dominance (we utilize the earth at will), requires a responsive mode of engagement. Such engagement is about understanding the earth in its plurality of forces and powers. Moreover, such understanding has to translate into a way of practicably relating to the earth by allowing for responses and counter-responses. On the Hengill lava plains, such response-ability is arranged infrastructurally. As geologists operating in an industrial setting, Bjarni and his colleagues are working within the structure of a municipal company. As such they are trying to balance the desire to utilize geothermal as efficiently and effectively for the citizens of Reykjavik under the conditions of late industrial capitalism, while at the same time being concerned for the recuperative capacities of the seismic landscape. They do not always get the balance right, as they will readily admit. More-than-human arrangements are complex, as responses and counter-responses generate derangements, and require rearrangements. Converting and awakening a well is but one response to one of many eruptive occasions that occur on the Hengill lava plains, as the intensive capacities of the earth continue to preform a generative role in the ongoing infrastructural lives of those in the vicinity.

Conclusion

We began by suggesting that we wanted to treat Bowker, Star and Carse's work as an invitation to further extend our thinking about nature as infrastructure. While Barry, Morita and Jensen push the envelope, each in their own way, in interesting directions, we used an ethnographic moment of a well awakening as a way to arrange our own analytic response. We opened our chapter with a vignette from a day on the Hengill lava plains with Bjarni and his geologist colleagues. On that day these geologists were attempting to awaken a well – one of a range of possible interventions into the seismic landscape – in response to recent seismic activity, both natural and otherwise. We have argued that this otherwise is a derangement, or disturbance, and that such derangements are participants in a set of recursive responses between and within the eruptive, intensive capacities of the earth and geologists. When derangements are responded to infrastructurally – that is, when they are rearranged through infrastructural means – they can be generative.

In this chapter we have not dwelt upon how seismic derangements are responded to by the local town in the vicinity of the volcanic zone. Nor have we focused too much on the *natural* part of the seismic responses that we characterized above as 'natural and otherwise'. By selectively focusing on the concept 'otherwise', it has not been our intention to be remiss about the forces that the otherwise is other to. Rather, the trajectory of this chapter suggests that in Hengill, what is natural and what is not is no longer discernable. Such recursive responses are not between the earth's capacities and geologists, they are among and within 'arrangements of existence' (Povinelli 2012) that the concept infrastructure helps to elucidate. These infrastructural arrangements encompass eruptive turbulent forces, technologies, knowledge practices, capital, sets of ideas and values on the proper use of seismic landscapes and so on. They install the possibility of derangements and rearrangements – that is, their own otherwise and its ongoing modification. As such one could call such arrangements ontologically transformative (Jensen and Morita 2015), sites where human and non-humans act in response to one another, with one another, and through one another.

In a country that has had difficult, at times deadly, relations with the forces and powers around them, developing a mode of engagement that is responsive to the seismic terrain becomes critical. In a talk at Halifax a few years ago, Isabelle Stengers (2012) struck a similar note. In this talk she argued for

Living with the earth 171

a way of moving beyond the conservation–utilization dichotomy, suggesting that in the new world, identified by the trope of Gaia, we are past the time where it is possible to think that the earth is either in need of our protection or ripe for our sole use.[12] This sentiment resonates very strongly with geologists working in the Hengill volcanic zone. For them response-ability is a method of composition, a way of arranging the forces and intensities of the earth towards an arrangement of living together under the constraining conditions of late industrial capitalism. As analysts, operating under analogous constraints, we are also concerned about our own analytical response-ability, our own methods of composition. The constant sense of the otherwise in Iceland is palpable, and we hope to have elucidated the generativity of such an otherwise, not in any romanticized sense, but as one possible analytical response in a process of continuous variation in an ever-emerging seismic, and academic, landscape.

Notes

1 Each drilling platform contains four wellheads. While the igloo shape of the wellhead protrudes out of the ground, the rest of the well structure extends downwards through the earth to a distance of between two to three kilometres, dependant on the site. Recent improvements in drilling technology allow for what is called directional drilling. The first 800 metres of the subterranean drill hole are vertical. Over the next two kilometres the well begins to move in a more horizontal direction targeting specific faults and fractures.
2 As we will go on to explain, reinjection wells are those through which processed geothermal brine is sent back into the subterranean geothermal field. Converting a well from reinjection back into production is a multi-phase operation. After halting the process of reinjection a period of rest, or dormancy, is required to allow the fracture system to adjust to the change. After this period of dormancy, the well needs to be reactivated, or awoken, to encourage the upward flow of water and steam. Reykjavik Energy awoke this particular well in response to what it perceived as a possible change in the underground flow of steam and water after increasing seismic activity, something they felt necessary in a situation where production levels have been continuously falling.
3 This chapter is based on the first author's fieldwork as part of his PhD dissertation. The PhD is part of a broader collective project called Alien Energy.
4 Sometimes it is referred to as the geothermal reservoir, although this designation tends to generate an image of a large open expanse of water. This is why the term field is more commonly used by geologists who describe the subterranean system as a matrix of porous and permeable fractured rock within and through which water runs, rather than an open expanse of water in which rocks are situated.
5 The Hengill triple point junction in the south-west of Iceland is an area where two rifting sections of the mid-Atlantic ridge, pulling in opposite directions, intersect with a lateral transform fault. In essence it is the meeting point of the Reykjanes Peninsula oblique rift, the western rift zone of Iceland, and the south Iceland transform. The three plates meeting at this junction are the North American plate, the Eurasian plate, and the Hreppar micro plate located between the overlapping western and eastern riff zones in southern Iceland (Sigmundsson et al. 1997).
6 Reykjavik Energy is a municipally owned utilities company providing hot and cold water, electricity, sewerage, and Internet connectivity to the greater Reykjavik area.

Not unlike many privately owned companies, the municipality underwent a broad programme of debt-leveraged expansion in the 2000s. Hellisheiði geothermal power plant is the result of such investments and became fully operational in 2011. It provides 130 megawatts of hot water to the residents of Reykjavik and 303 megawatts of electrical power to Nordural, an aluminium company in the west of Iceland. Hellisheiði is the first geothermal power plant to provide power on an industrial scale and the consequences of such an expansion are still being felt, in terms both of the financial arrangements and the impact of such extraction on the volcanic zone.

7 Reinjection wells were originally mandated by the national planning authority's environmental impact assessment. It was only later that they became a production strategy for the plant. The original environmental concern was that releasing extracted geothermal brine back into the volcanic landscape would be too damaging (eroding lava formations, killing off particular species of moss, damaging recreational walking pathways) as well as running the risk that the toxic fluids would seep back into the freshwater supply.

8 The burden of proof question, that is, the question of how one can prove that RE are triggering these earthquakes is, surprisingly, not one that the company raises as a form of defence. While space does not permit a more extensive discussion of this point here, Maguire does address this issue in full in a chapter of his upcoming PhD thesis.

9 The counter story that my geologist friends consistently repeated was from an enhanced geothermal project in Basel, Switzerland. After multiple seismic tests concluded that the project was leading to an unacceptable level of risk to a nearby town, the project was shut down. It was only after the shutdown that the biggest and most damaging series of earthquakes hit. Starting injecting processes disturbed the area, but stopping them elevated the disturbances.

10 We are not using generative in any normative sense. While derangements (disturbances) in and of the seismic landscape can be geothermally generative for Reykjavik Energy, when responded to infrastructurally, that is, rearranged through infrastructural means, they can and do remain deranged for the residents of Hveragerði. While the responses of the residents of the town cannot be gone into here, they will be addressed in a chapter of Maguire's upcoming PhD thesis.

11 This seems to be the problematic that speculative realists and object-oriented ontologists struggle with.

12 The full quotation was: 'Gaia is the figure of the many figured earth, not in need of our love or protection, but the kind of attention to be paid to a powerful being. Our time as being the only actors in history is over, as is our freely discussing if the earth is available for our use or in need of our protection, we have to learn to compose, even with a devastating power.' The talk is available at: www.situsci.ca/event/isabelle-stengers-cosmopolitics-learning-think-sciences-peoples-and-natures.

References

Appel, H., Nikhil A. and A. Gupta (2015) "The infrastructure toolbox". Theorizing the Contemporary, *Cultural Anthropology* [Online], 24 September. http://culanth.org/fieldsights/725-the-infrastructure-toolbox.

Barad, K. (2010) "Quantum entanglements and hauntological relations of inheritance: Dis/continuities, spacetime enfoldings, and justice-to-come". *Derrida Today* 3(2): 240–268.

Bowker, G. C. (1995) "Second nature once removed: Time, space and representations". *Time & Society* 4(1): 47–66.

Bowker, G. C. and S. L. Star (1999) *Sorting Things Out: Classification and its Consequences.* Cambridge, MA: MIT Press.

Carse, A. (2012) "Nature as infrastructure: Making and managing the Panama Canal watershed". *Social Studies of Science* 42(4): 539–563.

Clark, N. (2011) *Inhuman Nature: Sociable Life on a Dynamic Planet.* London: Sage.

Edwards, P. N., G. C. Bowker, S. J. Jackson and R. Williams (2009) "Introduction: An agenda for infrastructure studies". *Journal of the Association for Information Systems* 10(5): 364–374.

Haraway, D. J. (2008) *When Species Meet.* Minneapolis: University of Minnesota Press.

Harvey, P. and H. Knox (2012) "The enchantments of infrastructure". *Mobilities* 7(4): 521–536.

Jensen, C. B. (2015) "Experimenting with political materials: Environmental infrastructures and ontological transformations". *Distinktion: Scandinavian Journal of Social Theory.* DOI: 10.1080/1600910X.2015.1019533.

Jensen, C. B. and B. Winthereik (2013) *Monitoring Movements in Development Aid: Recursive Partnerships and Infrastructures.* Cambridge, MA: MIT Press.

Jensen, C. B. and A. Morita (2016) "Infrastructures as ontological experiments: From cultures(s) to infrastructure(s)". *Ethnos: Journal of Anthropology*, Special Issue. Online First: DOI: 10.1080/00141844.2015.1107607.

Larkin, B. (2013) "The politics and poetics of infrastructure". *Annual Review of Anthropology* 42: 327–343.

Morita, A. and C. Jensen (forthcoming) "Delta ontologies: Infrastructural transformations in Southeast Asia". *Social Analysis*, Special Issue: Multiple Nature-Cultures, Diverse Anthropologies.

Povinelli, E. (2012) "The will to be otherwise/the effort of endurance". *South Atlantic Quarterly* 111(3): 453–457.

Povinelli, E. (2014) "Geontologies of the otherwise". *Cultural Anthropology*, http://culanth.org/fieldsights/465-geontologies-of-the-otherwise.

Rheinberger, H.-J. (1994) "Experimental systems: Historiality, narration, and deconstruction". *Science in Context* 7(1): 65–81.

Serres, M. (1995) *Genesis.* Ann Arbor: University of Michigan Press.

Sigmundsson, F., P. Einarson, S. Rögnvaldsson, G.R. Foulger, K.M. Hodgkinson and G. Thorbergsson (1997) "The 1994–1995 seismicity and deformation at the Hengill triple junction, Iceland: Triggering of earthquakes by minor magma injection in a zone of horizontal shear stress". *Journal of Geophysical Research* 102(B7): 15151–15161.

Stengers, I. (2012) "Cosmopolitics: Learning to think with sciences, peoples and natures", paper presented at the 'To See Where It Takes Us' conversation series, Scotiabank Theatre, Sobey Building, Saint Mary's University, 903 Robie St, 5 March. www.situsci.ca/event/isabelle-stengers-cosmopolitics-learning-think-sciences-peoples-and-natures.

Yusoff, K. (2013) "Insensible worlds: Postrelational ethics, indeterminacy and the (k)nots of relating". *Environment and Planning D: Society and Space* 31(2): 208–226.

13 Revolutionary infrastructure

Dominic Boyer

Normally, one associates the term "infrastructure" with massive, durable works of material artifice: bridges, dams, highways, grids, to name a few. Even when such works are multiple or invisible (e.g. pipes, wiring), even when the term is used metaphorically, it still conjures images of material systems that are either singularly massive or near ubiquitous in their distributed networks (Barry 2013, Edwards 2013, Harvey and Knox 2015, Star and Ruhleder 1996). Infrastructures are apparatuses that allow things to happen; and their scale and ubiquity suggest a temporality of perdurance. Infrastructures enable, persistently, at scales greater than their elements.

Following this line of thinking – a relatively common one, I would argue – leaves us with an intuitive understanding of infrastructure as almost necessarily a source of friction or impasse from the point of view of rapid social transformation. And yet we are also living in an era in which modernity's many infrastructures are increasingly exposing their planetary scale of impact and their capacity to enable dangerous and undesirable processes such as global warming, oceanic acidification, and massive species extinction. A shudder is passing through the image of infrastructural persistence; for, under contemporary conditions, that persistence points deathward. "Infrastructure" (in its general, categorical form) has unsurprisingly become a site of renewed political attention and expert speculation in the past decade: we wonder whether existing infrastructure can be retrofit in time to avert catastrophe, whether it will be necessary or possible to generate entirely new infrastructure, or whether the inertial force of infrastructure will condemn all efforts at remediation to failure. Temporality and scale seem to be against us. How can we coordinate action to generate "sustainable" modern infrastructure at a planetary level in the dwindling time horizon within which earth and climate scientists are urging us to act? It is little wonder that numb anxiety rather than fervent activity continues to be the affect of the day. Taking both the urgent necessity of intervention and the condition of impasse seriously, I will argue in this chapter that we need to cultivate "revolutionary infrastructure," particularly in domains that are catastrophogenic such as fuel (my main focus here).

My discussion explores the relationship between infrastructure, potential energy, and revolution in three parts. The first section builds upon metabolic reinterpretations of Marxian theory, reimagining infrastructure as a form of stored or potential energy. The second section explores some less examined (epistemic) dimensions of infrastructure that retard its revolutionary potentiality. The third section of the paper asks where else we might look for blueprints for the revolutionary infrastructure needed to disable the present anthropocenic trajectory.

As a final point, I put forward the idea that we humans – as the second species to decisively transform the lifeworld of all species (the cyanobacteria who oxygenated the earth's atmosphere 2.3 billion years ago being the first) – need to practice becoming revolutionary infrastructure ourselves.

Infrastructure as potential energy

In his influential review essay, Brian Larkin (2013) describes infrastructures as "built networks that facilitate the flow of goods, people, or ideas and allow for their exchange over space" (328). He also notes that the "peculiar ontology" of infrastructures "lies in the facts that they are things and also the relation between things" (329; cf. Jensen and Morita 2015; Strathern 1995).

Characterizing infrastructure in terms of mediation makes good conceptual sense given not only what material infrastructures typically do (e.g. providing conduits for the transit of energy, bodies, and resources) but also in terms of the general conceptual emphasis on flow and friction in analytics of the post-Cold War era of globalization (Appadurai 1996; Tsing 2005). Likewise, emphasizing that infrastructure is always relation as well as thing importantly underscores the fact that an infrastructure can never exist outside of a deictic (e.g. *infra* "below") relationship to something else. In other words, whatever else it might be an infrastructure must always serve as the foundation that enables something else to happen (and, as Larkin rightly points out, be enabled to enable in this way). Here, I linger on infrastructure's capacity for enablement and I argue that this enablement deserves to be viewed as a problem of energy. Nothing enables or is enabled without storage and expenditure of energy.

I will begin with an enabling relationship that is already well known: labor and capital in the classic Marxian formulation. Capital for Marx was a dimension of the objectification of human labor power – specifically, a result of how the division of labor severed labor's capacity to channel human will in the development of the self. Instead of an ideal dialectical process of self-realization, capital congealed labor power in a way that could circulate beyond the self, be appropriated and commanded by others, and thus transformed into new social and material forms. Capital was in this way a means of remote enablement (yet one always enabled *de infra* by labor power). And, once it was set into motion on a mass scale and stabilized by institutions such money and wage labor, quantifiable appropriated labor-time became the logic of social value in modern society. As Marx wrote in the first chapter of *Das Kapital*, "As values, all commodities are only definite masses of congealed labor-time."

Here there is an interesting twist to the story we all know. "Congelation," from the Latin verb *congelare*, "to freeze together" is actually a slightly misleading translation of the actual noun Marx uses, *Gallert*, which refers to a gelatinization process in which different animal substances with the potential to yield glue (e.g. meat, bone, connective tissue) are boiled and then cooled to produce a "semisolid, tremulous mass … a concentrated glue solution" (Sutherland 2008). Rather than a freezing together of independent parts, *Gallert* indicates an ontological transformation through adding and then subtracting thermal energy: a recipe of different fleshy forms rendered through heating and cooling into a single sticky material: human labor-in-the-abstract binding commodities, people, machines, and "nature" together with its glue. Indeed, one might go a step farther and say that this glue potential was unlocked by the thermal rendering process itself.

Burkett and Foster (2006) argue that this is more than just metaphor. Their view is that there is a powerful energo-metabolic substrate to Marx's theories of labor power, alienation, and value extraction. On the topic of surplus value, they write, "this value (energy) surplus is not really created out of nothing. Rather, it represents capitalism's appropriation of portions of the *potential* work embodied in labor power recouped from metabolic regeneration largely during non-worktime" (127). In this context, capital becomes an appropriation quite literally of fleshy power, a sapping and storage of the regenerative potential of being. The authors go on to conclude more generally that Marx and Engels generated "a theory of the capitalist labor, production, and accumulation process that was not only consistent with the main conclusions of thermodynamics originating in their time, but also extraordinarily amenable to ecological laws" (144).

This surfacing of energic substrata of thought belongs to the method of "energopolitical" analysis I have advocated elsewhere (Boyer 2014). Porting this analytic strategy over to the *Grundrisse* and the second volume of *Kapital* where Marx describes an ineluctable evolution of circulating capital toward fixed capital and of fixed capital toward automated machinery, we come to glimpse infrastructure as potential energy storage system, as a means of gathering and holding productive powers in technological suspension.

In Marx's vision, capital strives across its historical development to make itself independent of labor, to be able to absorb the productive powers of labor into itself. As one might expect of the logic of bourgeois economy, capital seeks its liberty. The development of fixed capital (the part of the production process which retains its use-form over a period of time rather than being wholly consumed in a production process – that is, a machine, or even cattle pulling a plough, but not the coal burned to produce steam) is the first stage of this process. Marx emphasizes that durability is crucial: fixed capital must *durably* stand in for direct human labor. But the more decisive phase is the movement from fixed capital toward automated machinery, a productive apparatus that operates mechanically according to human design and in which "the human being comes to relate more as watchman and regulator to the production process ... instead of being its chief actor" (Marx 1974 [1861]: Notebook VII).

Automation not only advances capital's desire to durably emancipate itself from labor but also precipitates the final paradox between exchange value and use value that Marx believed would necessitate the eventual collapse of the capitalist mode of production:

> On the one side, then, [capital] calls to life all the powers of science and of nature, as of social combination and of social intercourse, in order to make the creation of wealth independent (relatively) of the labor time employed on it. On the other side, it wants to use labor time as the measuring rod for the giant social forces thereby created, and to confine them within the limits required to maintain the already created value as value. Forces of production and social relations – two different sides of the development of the social individual – appear to capital as mere means, and are merely means for it to produce on its limited foundation. *In fact, however, they are the material conditions to blow this foundation sky-high.*
> (Ibid., emphasis added)

In Marx's model, what we would call "infrastructure" begins as the outer skin of capital like the steel casing of a pipeline that allows precious liquid to flow through its center. But over time, the labor power invested into the technological development of automated machinery hardens into a solid form that is both persistent and near-autonomously productive of useful things. This apparatus is not, as it were, a perpetuum mobile, generating productivity from nothing. Its productivity depends wholly on the gelatinized combination of expertise, activity, materials, and forces that have filled the mold of its infrastructural design. In other words, infrastructure stores the productive energies of labor (mental, material, natural, to use Marx's categories) in such a way that they can be released later in magnitudes that appear to transcend nominal inputs. Technology, as productive infrastructure, thus appears to be capable of generating and distributing usevalues with limited need for direct (human) labor power.

Even without an extensive Marxian detour, I believe that it makes sense to view infrastructure as "stored" or "potential" energy in that it is no secret that a great variety and density of distinct forms of activity go into the production and maintenance of the sort of mediation systems normally conceived as infrastructure (e.g. roads, pipelines, grids, networks), designed to facilitate flows and to enable other things to happen. We need not and indeed should not be limited by a Marxian focus on commodity production in this respect. Neither a pipeline nor an electrical grid directly produces a commodity, but without their mediational apparatuses, what flows through them could scarcely be commoditized, even less could their energic vitalities be brought to the making of so many other useful things. Pipelines and grids are also *Gallerte* in their own right. The ingredients of a medium or high voltage grid, for example, include not only expertise in electrical engineering, and expert construction labor, but also the legacies of centuries of materials science and manufacture (Hughes 1983) that have provided serviceable steel, concrete, aluminum, copper, reinforced plastics, ceramics, tempered glass, silicone rubber, and carbon and glass fiber for the making of pylons, power cables, transformers, and insulation.

But the detour is also not without purpose. The reason I think a Marxian path to rethinking infrastructure is critically relevant to the Anthropocene is that it allows for the possibility that infrastructure can not only enable a certain arrangement of other things to happen but that its potential energy can also blow the very same arrangement "sky high." Infrastructure, in other words, can be revolutionary as well as reproductive, a lesson not lost on Lenin who famously proclaimed to the Moscow conference of the Russian Communist Party in 1920 that "Communism is Soviet power plus the electrification of the whole country."

In the Anthropocene, we desperately need to consider and where possible to enable this revolutionary potential of infrastructure. A decades-long incremental transition away from fossil fuel sources and infrastructures is simply not a luxury we can afford. We thus need to discover "revolutionary infrastructure." But we also need to consider that whatever revolutionary infrastructure may be, it may not resemble familiar infrastructures with which we in the human sciences are coming to concern ourselves. And it may not coexist easily with the gridded, pipelined, roaded modernity that currently encompasses and enables us.

Infrastructure, carbon epistemics, revolution

It takes just a 30-minute boat ride down what is perhaps the densest corridor of fossil fuel infrastructure in the world, the Houston Ship Channel, to witness the massive supertankers loading liquid natural gas for sale abroad, the petroleum refineries the size of small towns, the sprawling plastics industries, even the spectacular hills of recycled materials and wind turbines from Denmark being unloaded to be shipped to West Texas, to gain an appreciation for the colossal energic apparatus that would need to be un-made or re-made to make a serious effort at returning to the Holocene. It is an awesome and dispiriting journey, not a little sublime. Below (Figure 13.1) is an image I like to call "BodyWorld United States," its plastinated blue veins and red arteries (natural gas and oil pipelines) made visible, all leading back to the beating heart of carbon energopower in Louisiana, Oklahoma, and Texas. Never has the coastal United States – with all its supposed loci of financial, cultural, and governmental power – seemed more peripheral to national political infrastructure.

This image corresponds well with Timothy Mitchell's brilliant analysis of "carbon democracy" (2011), which argues persuasively that political institutions, ideas and imaginaries have been decisively shaped, in aptly

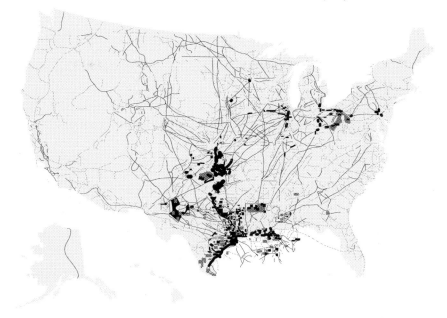

Figure 13.1 Map of major natural gas and oil pipelines in the United States (*ProPublica*, Groeger 2012)

subterranean ways, by the material politics of fossil fuels. In particular, Mitchell shows that the Keynesian model of governance, with its characteristic belief that high levels of economic growth could be maintained through the medium of public investment and moderate welfarism, was only made possible by post-WWII Anglo-American imperial control over the Middle East's oil resources. This control guaranteed more or less free energy, free power, to the Western world, reigniting the fantasies of endless industrial growth and prosperity that had echoed throughout the eras of coal, steampower and atomic power before it. Oil was the enabling infrastructure of every aspect of the "American Century" (Huber 2013; LeMenager 2014). Yet, only a few decades later, with the formation of OPEC and the oil shocks of the 1970s, the geopolitics of carbon energy changed dramatically. Since the 1970s, despite whatever neo-Keynesian or neoclassical policy package has been thrown at it, high levels of economic growth have not been restored to the West. Mitchell argues that this model of "economic growth" and its attendant developmentalism was always premised upon oil as an infinite, inexpensive resource in the first place. The many subsequent wars waged or instigated by the West across the Middle East have all desperately sought to recapture growth's oily infrastructure, even as rising winds and waters induced by fossil fuel use begin to wreak serious havoc across the world.

Mitchell's analysis of the breadth and depth of what we might term "carbon epistemics" helps us understand the substantial public deafness to increasingly shrill warnings from climate and earth scientists that what amounts to revolutionary action is needed to prevent the acceleration of global warming and the ecological catastrophes that warming is predicted to entail. The scientists do not always use the explicit language of revolution, but they might as well. And, some, like Kevin Anderson of Manchester University, are willing to speak bluntly, "After two decades of bluff and lies, the remaining 2°C budget demands revolutionary change to the political and economic hegemony."[1]

We human scientists understand – even if we perhaps underestimate the deep phenomenological roots of the problem – the extent to which this revolution is impeded by the convenience, pleasure and luxury of an energy-intensive modernity that has been enabled by fossil fuels since its beginning. But we are also less obviously hampered by the fact that even our political models of revolution (at least since the mid-nineteenth century) have been closely aligned with the harnessing of still more massive magnitudes of energy and industrial productivity in order to catalyze a breakthrough in the fabric of the bourgeois capitalist order. It is true that Marx's critique of capital was more sensitive to energo-metabolic questions than is often recognized but his vision for post-capitalist society contains no consideration of the possibility of human action permanently changing or damaging natural order, let alone rumination upon specific anthropocenic processes such as greenhouse gas emission, ocean acidification and species extinction. Not unlike the bourgeois political economists he otherwise roundly condemned, Marx appeared to think that industrialization was an intrinsically historically progressive development in its creation of a technological basis for the automated production of commodities, an abundance of useful things that could unite and benefit the entire (human) species after (for Marx) the negation of capital. In this respect Marx stands on the side of many contemporary apologists for fossil fuels as an optimist regarding the development of praxiological and technological solutions to the problems generated by energy-intensive industry.

Given this, it is not surprising that massive energo-infrastructural growth was central to the Leninist-Bolshevist revolutionary state as well. Indeed, the 1920s rural electrification campaign served as a prototype for the Stalinist five-year plan of organized economy. It is worth hearing a little more from Lenin's speech to the Moscow conference of the Russian Communist Party to understand why electrification was such a priority:

> Communism is Soviet power plus the electrification of the whole country, since industry cannot be developed without electrification. ... Without [the] reconstruction of all industry on lines of large-scale machine production, socialist construction will obviously remain only a set of decrees, a political link between the working class and the peasantry ... ; it will remain an example to all powers of the world, but it will not have its own

basis. ... Economic success ... can be assured only when the Russian proletarian state effectively controls a huge industrial machine built on up-to-day technology; that means electrification. For this, we must know the basic conditions of the application of electricity, and accordingly understand both industry and agriculture.

(Lenin 1965[1920])

Without electrification enabling the constitution of a massive industrial apparatus, communism is unthinkable. And not only communism. The making of a huge electrified "industrial machine" was surely the work of the twentieth century that has spilled over into the twenty-first century, always expanding on a global basis under the banner of "development" (see Gupta 2015). All the dominant economic and political philosophies of the past century have made their contributions to expanding and intensifying this apparatus: liberalism, socialism, Keynesianism. Even neoliberalism can claim the expansion of information, telecommunication, and fossil energy infrastructures as signature contributions. None, interestingly, seems to have doubted that an expanded industrial apparatus would give their philosophy political-economic leverage over the others. It may be the sole issue they all agreed upon.

Throughout governmental bureaucracies, we meanwhile find cultures of expertise whose epistemic norms attune to an imagined security and necessity of fossil fuel infrastructure. When my partner, Cymene Howe, and I spoke with engineers at Mexico's para-statal power utility, CFE, for example, we encountered widespread ambivalence regarding the merits of renewable energy sources because of their perceived lack of constancy. Although there was general agreement that Mexico had wonderful wind and solar resources that ought to be utilized in some way, our interlocutors expressed concern that the nature of these energy forms did not correspond well to the needs and logic of grid. "From the perspective of the administration of energy, there's a type of energy we call 'baseload' [*energía base*]," Francisco Diaz, a department director from CFE explained to us:

> Above all this is thermoelectric energy where you supply it with combustible fuel and it works, just like a motor. It's *muy constante* [very constant]. Geothermal is that way too. But with all other sources, even hydroelectrics, output will depend on the rains of the previous year. So in a dry year you might not have enough supply to meet demand. It is the same way with *las eólicas* [the turbines]. You might have a peak supply and an average supply. But those are just numbers. In reality the supply is constantly fluctuating between highs and lows. And for that reason in most cases of wind energy you need to build extra thermoelectric support installations just to guarantee the supply of energy.

Perversely then, the engineers felt that investments in wind and solar power necessitated still further investment in fossil fuel plants, just to guarantee that "average supply" could be maintained on windless days and at night. To be clear, CFE officials also expressed pride in Mexico's participation in the Kyoto Protocol and understood the environmental disadvantages of the intensification of fossil fuel use. They simply felt, as "administrators of energy," that renewable energy was a threat to the stability and reliability of energy provision. As Diaz put it, the grid needed a ceaseless "motor" to keep it running.

So we return to the problem of an impasse in what might be called "epistemic infrastructure." Whether one is looking at familiar paradigms of revolutionary action or the "baseload" expertise of electrical engineers, one finds little hope for remediating anthropocenic conditions swiftly and broadly. Countless op/ed pieces published in mainstream news media counsel patience with energy transition, deferring fossil-free futures to 2050 or beyond, declaring any faster transition to be hopelessly utopian. Even in the deepening shadow of the Anthropocene, carbon epistemics continue to flourish, negating post-carbon lines of imagination.

Antidotes and prototypes

There are, however, effective antidotes to the paralytic agents of carbon epistemics. And also prototypes for revolutionary trajectories that are not predicated on the growth and motor ideologies of the fossil fuel era. Let us begin with Hermann Scheer's call for a decentralized "solar economy" (2004). Scheer was an interesting figure, for 30 years a parliamentarian in Germany's Social-Democratic Party, a revolutionary thinker in a party that had long lost its thirst for radical politics. He was one of the chief political architects of Germany's *Energiewende* (renewable energy transition) and co-wrote Germany's famous feed-in tariff law that forced utilities to guarantee long-term above-market-price electricity purchase agreements for renewable energy to create stability and incentives for small solar and wind power producers. In 2015, over 35% of gross electricity production in Germany came from renewable resources, in large part thanks to Scheer's feed-in tariffs. And, in the past 15 years, versions of the German legislation have been adopted by many other countries. The feed-in tariff has proved to be the single most effective policy instrument for accelerating renewable energy production despite facing concerted resistance from electricity utilities and the fossil fuel industry.

Scheer himself ruminated at great length about the reasons for resistance and argued it was more than simply a desire to maintain a profitable industry. Scheer pointed to the adaptation of global and national economies to the "long supply chain" infrastructures characteristic of fossil and nuclear fuel resources. Like Mitchell, Scheer viewed twentieth- and twenty-first-century globalization as largely driven by the extraction and control of these fuels. Scheer observed that long energy supply chains are, in their very nature, inefficient and thus demand allied infrastructures of translocal domination to guarantee unimpeded flows of critical resources. This domination imperative has been masked by nationalist discourses of security and wellbeing, by post/neo/colonial missions of civilization and development and most recently by the utopian logic of a self-regulating "market."

Solar energy, whether in its direct form of insolation or indirectly in the forms of wind and biomass, has the physical advantages, Scheer argued, of ubiquity and superabundance, thus allowing for more efficient and decentralized short supply chains that are also more susceptible to democratic political control: "shorter renewable energy supply chains will make it impossible to dominate entire economies. Renewable energy will liberate society from fossil fuel dependency" (ibid.: 89).

Recognizing that reliance upon fossil and nuclear fuels is driving the world to anthropocenic ruin, Scheer challenges the notion that we need to maintain large-scale power grids and pipeline systems at all. He calculates that even energy-intensive modernity can be maintained purely on the basis of small-scale solar resources given contemporary technologies. The problem is that grids and pipeline systems – products of early twentieth-century political and industrial concentration enabled in turn by the burning of fossil fuels – have become a chief instrument in the monopolization of political authority, an energopolitical apparatus mutually reinforcing the inertia of a particular organization of fuel and a particular organization of political power. Their convergence constitutes an energo-material path dependency while also casting a dark shadow of improbability over any imagined alternative to the long-chained fossil status quo. Grids and pipelines are allowed to hide their inefficiencies through inflated "black boxed" pricing and unwarranted public subsidies, which amount to vassalage fees paid by the population to the masters of fossil fuels and centralized authority. Although Scheer is sympathetic to Marxian revolution in certain respects, he argues that a solar energy revolution will act to dissolve centralized energopower into distributed systems:

> Comprehensive use of renewable energy would take the wind from the sails of an economic globalization and industrial concentration process driven by the scarcity of fossil fuel reserves. This alone would spark a process of de-concentration, de-monopolization and the re-regionalization of economic structures.
>
> (Ibid.: 86)

The broad strokes of Scheer's economic philosophy are neo-physiocratic, an argument for re-establishing the "primary economy" of agriculture and forestry over industry and services as the center of economic life. But, like Marx and Lenin, he seeks not a retreat backwards into pre-industrial conditions but rather a revolutionary leap forward into a new form of sociality, one that is energy intensive and technologically enabled but resolutely local, sustainable, and diverse.

In this respect Scheer's model of solar economy resonates strongly with recent social movements organized in opposition to climate change and large-scale society and industry, for example the "degrowth" movement, the "cooperative economy" movement and perhaps especially "transition culture."[2] His emphasis on the disablement of grid modernity also echoes with recent and potentially revolutionary prototypes like the Tesla Powerwall and other advances in electrical storage that provide their own response to accusations of renewable "intermittency" and "unreliability." Scheer's insistence on locally sourced, owned, and managed electricity likewise echoes in a surge of community-owned renewable energy projects worldwide. Elsewhere in our Mexico research, for example, we encountered the Yansa Ixtepec partnership, an unprecedented proposal by a rural farming cooperative and a NGO to create the first community-owned wind park in Latin America. Contrary to the corporately owned, transnationally managed wind parks that are the norm in Mexico, and which pay approximately 1.5–2.5 % of their net profits back to landowners in the form of rents, the Yansa Ixtepec park would return 50 % of its net profits to the Ixtepecan *comuna* as a whole in order to fund ambitious social development projects in health and retirement care and new opportunities for women and youth (Howe and Boyer 2016).

The abundance of technomaterial prototypes for revolutionary infrastructure is certainly encouraging. But to await revolutionary infrastructure simply in technomaterial forms also reinforces the myth, if we may now call it that, of necessary infrastructural persistence and retardation of rapid social transformation. It summons again the sublime spectacle of the Houston Ship Channel, the "hyperobjective" (Morton 2013) infrastructural abyss that paralyzes and negates the formation of alternative futures. Not to mention that awaiting technomaterial salvation seems no great improvement over accepting technomaterial damnation.

It is important to remember that the hyperobjects that most concern us today have largely been brought into being by the "hypersubjective" disposition of certain kinds of human beings – typically but not exclusively white, male, northern humans – who have built a global apparatus of resource control, industry, trade, and war to guarantee their convenience and dominion. If we agree that these hypersubjects have finally created conditions that are beyond their ability to fully understand and control – and, more to the point, conditions that now obviously threaten the survival of all other species on the planet – then it may be time to think through what it would mean to become human again as "hyposubjects." This is not the optimal place to summarize our reflections on hyposubjectivity (see instead Boyer and Morton 2016). For present purposes, suffice it to say that revolutionary infrastructure and hyposubjectivity share in a common project of ethical reorientation and rebecoming. Whatever revolutionary infrastructure is, it will have to be ecological and transhuman in its ethical orientation but also hold blissful extinction fantasies at bay. It will necessarily be feminist, colorful, and queer in its relationship to the androleukoheteropetromodernity that both epitomizes and reinforces the apex species behavior that has made catastrophe our everyday companion.

I strongly suspect that to contemporary optics and epistemics, revolutionary infrastructure will not exist. That is to say, it will be less the Marxian seizure of global infrastructure by a mass revolutionary movement, than a kind of ubiquitous creative squatting in, and repurposing of, a gridworld that will find itself incrementally disabled by a redistribution of its materials and energies. As Scheer believed, proliferating decentralized small-scale action is our revolutionary path forward. Urban spaces and municipal politics – blending as they do relatively small spaces with relatively dense humanity – will thus become especially critical zones of experiment, engagement, and transformation. In these spaces, designs and prototypes for revolutionary infrastructure are already well underway. As human scientists we need to offer critical contextual analysis of the promise of those designs and their effects. Above all, as small vulnerable creatures living on a damaged planet, we need to practice becoming infrastructure; that is, we need to enable ourselves to enable the ending of the Anthropocene.

Notes

1 http://kevinanderson.info/blog/why-carbon-prices-cant-deliver-the-2c-target/.
2 See, e.g. the Greek Festival for Solidarity and Cooperative Economy (www.festival4sce.org), the Biannual International Conference on Degrowth since 2008, and www.transitionnetwork.org.

References

Appadurai, Arjun (1996) *Modernity at Large: Cultural Dimensions of Globalization*. Minneapolis: University of Minnesota Press.
Barry, Andrew (2013) *Material Politics: Disputes Along the Pipeline*. Hoboken, NJ: John Wiley & Sons.
Bennett, Jane (2010) *Vibrant Matter: A Political Ecology of Things*. Durham, NC: Duke University Press.
Boyer, Dominic (2014) "Energopower: An Introduction". *Anthropological Quarterly* 87(2): 309–333.
Boyer, Dominic and Timothy Morton (2016) "Hyposubjects". Theorizing the Contemporary, *Cultural Anthropology* [Online], January 21. Available at www.culanth.org/fieldsights/798-hyposubjects (Accessed on June 6, 2015).
Jensen, Casper Bruun and Atsuro Morita (2015) "Infrastructures as Ontological Experiments". *Engaging Science, Technology, and Society* 1: 81–87.
Burkett, Paul and John Bellamy Foster (2006) "Metabolism, Energy and Entropy in Marx's Critique of Political Economy: Beyond the Podolinsky Myth". *Theory and Society* 35: 109–156.
Edwards, Paul N., Steven J. Jackson, Melissa K. Chalmers, and Scout Calvert (2013) *Knowledge Infrastructures: Intellectual Frameworks and Research Challenges*. Ann Arbor, MI: Deep Blue.
Groeger, Lena (2012) "Pipelines Explained: How Safe are America's 2.5 Million Miles of Pipelines? *ProPublica.org*. Accessed at www.propublica.org/article/pipelines-explained-how-safe-are-americas-2.5-million-miles-of-pipelines on February 6, 2015.
Gupta, Akhil (2015) "An Anthropology of Electricity from the Global South". *Cultural Anthropology* 30(4): 555–568.

Harvey, Penny and Hannah Knox (2015) *Roads: An Anthropology of Infrastructure*. Ithaca, NY: Cornell University Press.
Howe, Cymene and Dominic Boyer (2015) "Aeolian Politics". *Disktintion* 16(1): 31–48.
Howe, Cymene and Dominic Boyer (2016) "Aeolian Extractivism and Community Wind in Southern Mexico". *Public Culture* forthcoming.
Huber, Matthew T. (2013) *Lifeblood: Oil, Freedom, and the Forces of Capital*. Minneapolis: University of Minnesota Press.
Hughes, Thomas P. (1983) *Networks of Power: Electrification in Western Society, 1880–1930*. Baltimore, MD: Johns Hopkins University Press.
Larkin, Brian (2013) "The Politics and Poetics of Infrastructure". *Annual Review of Anthropology* 42: 327–343.
LeMenager, Stephanie (2014) *Living Oil: Petroleum Culture in the American Century*. Oxford: Oxford University Press.
Lenin, Vladimir Ilich (1965[1920]. Our Foreign and Domestic Position and Party Tasks". Accessed at www.marxists.org/archive/lenin/works/1920/nov/21.htm on May 21, 2015.
Marx, Karl (1974[1861]) *Grundrisse der Kritik der Politischen Ökonomie*. Berlin: Dietz Verlag.
Mitchell, Timothy (2011) *Carbon Democracy: Political Power in the Age of Oil*. New York: Verso.
Morton, Timothy (2013) *Hyperobjects: Philosophy and Ecology after the End of the World*. Minneapolis: University of Minnesota Press.
Scheer, Hermann (2004) *The Solar Economy: Renewable Energy for a Sustainable Global Future*. London: Earthscan.
Star, Susan Leigh and Karen Ruhleder (1996) "Steps Toward an Ecology of Infrastructure: Borderlands of Design and Access for Large Information Spaces. *Information Systems Research* 7(1): 111–134.
Strathern, Marilyn (1995) *The Relation: Issues in Complexity and Scale*. Cambridge: Prickly Pear Press.
Sutherland, Keston (2008) "Marx in Jargon". *World Picture* 1(Spring). Accessed at http://worldpicturejournal.com/WP_1.1/KSutherland.html on February 6, 2015.
Tsing, Anna (2005) *Friction: An Ethnography of Global Connection*. Princeton, NJ: Princeton University Press.

14 Infrastructure and the earth

Andrew Barry

It is sometimes thought that infrastructures are the static and solid base through which things such as people, money and resources can flow. Indeed, for much of the time the existence of infrastructures, such as electricity and telecommunication networks, may be taken for granted. But in practice infrastructures are never as static as they might seem. Infrastructures corrode and crack and shift all the time. Their stability cannot be assumed but needs to be maintained. A working infrastructure needs to be monitored for faults and kept in good repair. It is perhaps not surprising that infrastructures such as railways, pipes, satellites, lights, roads and cables often co-exist with a second order of infrastructure of information production that keeps their movement and transformation within working limits. In this way, infrastructures generate the need for monitoring devices, engineering consultants and security guards who keep more or less close watch on their condition. No wonder that a well-maintained infrastructure is sometimes taken to be an index of good government. When cracks in the infrastructure are noticed, this is a sign that the state or economy itself is not in order (Humphrey 2003). The state of the infrastructure has to be kept visible if it is to endure over time (Barry 2010), while the everyday users of infrastructure need to be alert to the moments and places in which infrastructures may break down.

In this chapter, however, I focus on a further aspect of infrastructure. According to Susan Leigh Star and Karen Ruhleder's influential formulation, infrastructures are often built on an 'installed base' (Star and Ruhleder 1996). In their account, computer networks, for example, are built on the installed base of the existing telecommunications network. In practice, however, many infrastructures, such as tracks, tunnels and pipes, are built not on an installed base but literally on and into the earth. In this chapter I argue that we need to see the earth, its rocks, soil and water, as integral to the ongoing existence of infrastructure. Infrastructures such as pipes, roads and cables should not be considered a solid and static base in part because they rest on, or are built into, a further base. At the same time, the earth in which infrastructures are embedded is itself neither static nor stable. The earth thus becomes a further source of instability for infrastructures, as well as the infrastructure on which infrastructures are constructed. In broad terms, the stability of infrastructure depends on the relation and interference between two different infrastructural assemblages: the infrastructure and the more-than-human infrastructure of the earth in and on which the infrastructure is assembled (cf. Jensen, this volume).

As I have suggested, the existence of infrastructure is likely to be bound up with the operation of an additional infrastructure of inspection and monitoring. The state of an infrastructure may or may not be routinely inspected, and the failure of monitoring regimes may have catastrophic effects (Barry 2002). But the importance of the relation between infrastructures and the earth introduces a further complexity; for the movements of the earth are often the objects of a further infrastructure of measurement and monitoring by, amongst others, geo- and environmental scientists and engineers. In the context of this layering of infrastructure upon infrastructure, all of them mobile and subject to transformation, I argue that a focus on the relation between infrastructure and earth can contribute to a wider analysis of both the complexity of infrastructure and its politics. In the chapter, I focus on two issues.

First, the relation between earth and infrastructure exhibits a series of complex temporalities. It is well known that the timing of earthquakes, tsunamis and volcanoes, for example, cannot be predicted precisely, although seismologists and volcanologists may estimate the probability of major events. And it is also widely recognised that volcanoes, fault lines and landslide systems may lie dormant for long periods. In this way, the earth's activity adds a further complexity to the complexity of infrastructure, catalysing events that may or may not be anticipated, and at timescales that do not correspond to the human timescales of political and economic life. In turn such geophysical events may provoke social and political crises that cannot always be contained. In thinking about the relation between the temporality of socio-technical infrastructures and the geophysics and geochemistry of the earth I draw on the work of William Connolly and Georgina Born, who direct us to consider multiple force fields or systems, each 'periodically encountering others as outside forces' (Connolly 2011: 7, Born 2015). Infrastructure and earth can be understood, in Connolly's terms, as distinct but interacting force fields.

But, second, the relation between earth and infrastructure also has its own spatiality. This corresponds neither to the political space of territory nor to the networks associated with the flows of capital and persons or, indeed, the zones formed through the development of technological and regulatory standards (Barry 2006). Seismic faults, for example, may cut across major roads, cables and pipelines. They do not necessarily respect the topology of regions and networks that are the typical product of human activity. Earthquakes shake the foundations of infrastructures, generating catastrophic ruptures at particular sites, not everywhere. The relation between earth and infrastructure is distinctly uneven. It interferes at particular times and places or over extended regions or periods; in this way, it may generate new spaces and sites of politics.

In order to give these arguments empirical substance, I want to consider the importance of a series of disciplines and practices, including geophysics, seismology and hydrogeology. My focus is on Turkey and the South Caucasus and I discuss, in particular, work carried out by the Nodia Institute for Geophysics in Tbilisi and the Kandilli Earthquake Observatory at Boğaziçi University, Istanbul. In this way, the chapter dwells on the relation between earth and infrastructure and the infrastructure of the earth sciences that monitor this relation. As I discuss, the work of the geophysical institutes of Tbilisi and Istanbul both explicitly addresses the stability and environmental sustainability of infrastructures, including bridges, pipes and tunnels, and contributes to their government and politics. I first focus on the work of the relation between the North Anatolian fault, the city of Istanbul and the Kandilli Observatory, before turning to consider the relation between the work of the Nodia Institute of Geophysics in Tbilisi, the mountains of the Lesser Caucasus and the structure of the Baku-Tbilisi-Ceyhan oil and South Caucasus gas pipelines.

Seismology: Istanbul

The Kandilli Observatory for Earthquake Monitoring is situated in a leafy campus, high on the hill on the Asian side of the Bosphurus on the opposite shore to the main campus of Boğaziçi University. The observatory was originally established as a metereological station during the Ottoman empire; earthquake observations only began in 1939 following an earthquake that devastated the city of Erzincan in north-east Anatolia, leading to as many as 30,000–40,000 deaths. However, in the early years it was difficult for the observatory to obtain seismological data from across Anatolia. Indeed, a seismic research station was established at Belbasi near Ankara in 1951, but at that time its work was devoted to monitoring Soviet nuclear tests and the data were not made publicly available. It was not until 2000, following the end of the Cold War, that data from Belbasi Nuclear Monitoring Center were routinely sent to the Kandilli Observatory. In recent decades, however, the Kandilli Observatory has acquired an established regional and international role in seismological monitoring, generating data on seismic activity from a vast array of monitoring stations from across Anatolia, the eastern Aegean and beyond, as well as feeding its analyses to other seismic observatories worldwide. In short, it has become a critical node in a transnational metrological zone (cf. Barry 2006) while also operating a permanent infrastructure of seismic monitoring stations (MARNET) across the Marmara Sea, in the vicinity of Istanbul itself (Gülen et al. 2002: 233).

The contemporary importance of the observatory has doubtless been made possible by the growing capacities of computer networks, digital monitoring instruments and satellite communication in the geosciences (Edwards 2010). But the significance of Kandilli is also a function of the movements of the earth and of the potential proximity of seismic activity to the city of Istanbul. Over the course of the life of the observatory, the North Anatolian seismic fault has progressively slipped, generating a series of major earthquakes that have lurched westwards across northern Turkey from Erzincan in the north-east in

1939 to the Mudurnu Valley in 1967 to the Marmara Earthquake near the city of Izmit in 1999, only 80 km to the east of Istanbul (Gülen et al. 2002: 231). The Marmara earthquake resulted in 20,000 deaths and is said to have caused billions of dollars of damage (Angell 2014: 668).

As the anthropologist Elizabeth Angell (2014) has argued, the Marmara earthquake is of particular significance to anyone concerned with the politics of infrastructure and housing in Istanbul. In her account, the earthquake has to be understood as the product of 'heterogeneous agencies', which include the material force of the earthquake itself but much else besides. In this she follows the approach suggested by theorists of 'urban assemblages', including Ignacio Farías and Colin McFarlane, who argue that 'urban politics ... is not about subjects, subjectivities or discourses, but about things, complex entangled objects, socio-material interminglings' (Farías 2011: 371 cited in Angell 2014: 668; see also McFarlane 2011).

Angell's analysis highlights three aspects of the assemblage of which the earthquake formed a part. First, in the latter half of the twentieth century, the city's population had expanded tenfold, and 'the resulting transformation of its built environment produced an unprecedented level of vulnerability to earthquake disasters' (Angell 2014: 668). Second, much of the public concern that followed the Marmara earthquake focused on the state of the city's houses. In these circumstances, 'visible traces of past earthquakes – such as cracks on the walls – were the subject of anxious scrutiny' (ibid.: 669–70). Indeed the apparently poor state of the built environment to withstand the shock of earthquake was taken, by some, to be an index of the 'fragility of the Turkish state'. Drawing on Deville et al.'s (2014) contention that the materiality of concrete has come to shape the relation between population and the state more broadly, Angell argues that:

> the failure of the governance mechanisms that were supposed to ensure safe buildings [in Istanbul] was part of a ... kind of concrete governmentality, one that functioned to serve other ends: the provision of inexpensive housing to a booming population, the manipulation of elections through retroactive authorization of squatter-built settlements (*gecekondu*) in exchange for votes, the supplementation of civil servants' salaries with bribes and the reliable profitability of the construction sector. It took the failure of the buildings on ... a massive scale to make these earlier failures apparent ... .
>
> (2014: 671–72)

The third issue that Angell asks us to consider is the question of whether the earthquake is a 'natural' disaster or not. Her answer is that 'to call the earthquake a natural event is also to stake out a position in this debate; one that is not universally accepted' (ibid.: 673). Indeed, in diverse ways, local commentators and urban dwellers recognise that the earthquake is distinctly unnatural. Some assume that it must have been caused by an external force, such as the 'Israelis and the Americans' (ibid.: 673); others viewed the earthquake as an act of 'retribution for the secularism of the Turkish state'; while yet others blamed corruption, policy failures, or even the national character. Angell convincingly argues that the Marmara earthquake not only had devastating consequences but highlighted 'the kaleidoscope quality of [urban] assemblages as political matter' (ibid.: 673).

Finally, Angell shows how the aftermath of the earthquake had further infrastructural consequences. While seismic risk assessment existed prior to 1999, it acquired a remarkable political and economic significance after the quake. In the context of widespread concern about the risks of future earthquakes, and six months after further devastating earthquakes in the eastern Anatolian city of Van in 2012, the Turkish parliament passed a 'Transformation of Areas under Disaster Risk Law' which facilitated the demolition of housing in *riskli alan* or risk zones. In this way, Istanbul's housing came to be mapped and classified through the further development of the infrastructure of seismic engineering and risk assessment. In turn, the disaster risk zone policy was criticised by academics, activists and community groups, who argued that 'the government is using earthquake risk to bypass legal obstacles against previous urban renewal projects (such as those in Sulukule and Tarlabaşı) and create profit opportunity for the construction sector' (Angell 2014: 675). Amongst other things, critics pointed to the lack of transparency in the determination of risk zones and in the implementation of the new law. Thus, through the mediation of seismic risk assessment and the 'disaster risk' law, the disputes over the causes and significance of the Marmara earthquake became one aspect of the politicisation of urban transformation in Istanbul in the 2010s (Karaman 2014; Yıldırım and Navaro-Yashin 2013).

I have dwelt on Angell's analysis at some length because it gives us a rich sense of the complexity of earthquake politics in Istanbul since 1999. As she makes clear, there is no one response to the Marmara earthquake. It generated a series of governmental, technical and affective responses, including the production of administrative maps of seismic risk. In this way, earthquakes came to form part of both a governmental project and one aspect of a growing range of disputes about the wider political economy and cultural politics of housing and infrastructure development across Istanbul. There was not one controversy about the Marmara earthquake and its causes and effects but a series of controversies: what I have termed, a 'political situation' (Barry 2013: 9–11, 16–17).

However, although Angell provides us with an compelling analysis of the place of the Marmara earthquake in urban politics, she is not primarily concerned with the seismology of the earthquake, nor with the progressive motion of the North Anatolian fault that generated it. While she highlights the remarkable significance of the infrastructure of seismic risk assessment in urban political life, as well as the proliferation of speculation about the (un)natural causes of the disaster, she does not dwell on the movements that constituted the earthquake itself.

In this light, Angell's account of the dynamics of an urban political situation, and the political and governmental significance of seismic risk assessment, can be productively supplemented by an account of the dynamics of the earth, and the political and governmental significance of seismology. Here I draw on the work of William Connolly, whose metaphysics centers on the idea of open systems and drawing explicitly on the notion of complexity. For Connolly, the world can be understood as a series of heterogeneous open systems, which encompass not only socio-material systems (such as urban infrastructures) but also the kinds of open systems described by bio-, geo- and physical scientists. In Georgina Born's interpretation, Connolly's account directs us to take into consideration both the distinction between diverse sociomaterial human and nonhuman systems and their contingent intersection and interference:

> Among these heterogeneous open systems he makes room for the dynamic long-term trajectories wrought not only by political economy—the temporalities animated, for example, by global capital flows, changing legal and policy regimes—but by biological evolution, physical 'force-fields',[1] climate change and the 'soupy earth'. Each temporal system is therefore 'marked by pluri-potentiality as it forms intersections with others', engendering through their mutual interferences emergent causalities.
>
> (Born 2015: 367–68)

To understand the politics and complexity of infrastructure, I suggest, we need to understand the interference between infrastructural assemblages and the earth: in this case, between the infrastructures of the city and seismic risk assessment, the geophysical infrastructure of the earth and the infrastructure of seismic monitoring. In considering this relation, the work of the Kandilli Observatory is of critical significance in two ways. First, as I've suggested, the development of the infrastructure of seismological research across Turkey highlights the contingency of the interference between the shifting geological 'force field' of the North Anatolian fault and movements in Istanbul's urban politics, which have increasingly focused on the politics of urban redevelopment. The North Anatolian fault is oblivious to the rapid urban development of Istanbul, the conservatism and neo-liberal policies of the AKP government, and the occupation of Gezi Park that came to oppose these policies. Yet at the same time, the dynamics of the fault and the dynamics of urban politics interfere in unexpected ways. The work of the Kandilli Observatory mediates between these two open systems or force fields.

Second, the Observatory's seismologists consistently emphasise the unpredictability of the location and timing of any future earthquake in the Marmara Sea or the surrounding region. While speculative predictions and anticipations of future earthquake activity have become part of the politics of urban development, as Angell makes clear, the observatory's seismologists are necessarily uncertain about whether any future earthquake will occur in the vicinity of the city or not. It is not possible to predict the timing and location of earthquakes in general; but one of the difficulties in making predictions about the location of future earthquakes in this region is that whereas the North Anatolian fault is well defined in the vicinity of the Mudurnu Valley, further east it 'splays out into three branches in the Marmara region', in the vicinity of Istanbul itself (Gülen et al. 2002). In short, the interference between infrastructure and earth is both unpredictable and generates unanticipated emergent and site-specific effects. The possibility of a future earthquake in the Marmara Sea has evident immediate consequences in Istanbul, generating an anticipatory politics. But this anticipatory politics is both connected and distinct from the movements of the North Anatolian fault; whether the next major earthquake in the region will have a direct impact on the urban fabric of Istanbul or not is unknown.

Hydrogeology: Tbilisi

If the relation between the North Anatolian fault and Istanbul is dispersed and includes an array of seismic monitoring devices, distributed across the Marmara Sea and beyond, in the second part of this chapter I consider the work of a more specific and localised relation between earth and infrastructure, one that has been the object of research by hydrogeologists and seismologists at the Nodia Institute of Geophysics in Tbilisi, Georgia. This case highlights the interference between the earth and the infrastructures of multinational capital and 'geopolitical assemblages' (Dittmer 2013).

The Nodia Institute is currently housed in two low-rise Soviet-era buildings in central Tbilisi. One, the former atmospheric physics laboratory, is an extraordinary space-age circular construction with vast curved windows, formed around a huge cylinder, designed to generate clouds and fogs. However, the two buildings are now situated in the middle of a patchwork of apartment blocks, which are mushrooming across a city that lacks any planning regulation. Situated in the middle of the property boom in Tbilisi, both buildings are crumbling, and the institute's infrastructure is in a poor state. The institute has only one seismological monitoring station with up-to-date technical equipment, situated just outside Tbilisi. Moreover, its staff are poorly paid, even by Georgian standards. At the same time, the institute, which is the major institution for seismological research in Georgia, is marginalised. Unlike in Istanbul, there is no systematic seismic risk assessment of housing in Tbilisi, even though a lot of the housing stock is also in a poor state of repair and a magnitude-7 earthquake in the vicinity of the city is possible and, if it occurred, could cause widespread damage and loss of life.[2]

However, while the infrastructure of geophysical research in Georgia is underdeveloped due to lack of investment and political interest, the Nodia Institute has carried out significant research on the geoscientific risks associated with the development of energy infrastructures. In one NATO-funded project, institute researchers identified a number of locations where there was a risk that seismic activity would lead to significant damage either to the Baku-Tbilisi-Ceyhan (BTC) oil pipeline or to the South Caucasus gas pipelines. They noted that neither of these pipelines 'had been evaluated comprehensively … for their seismic safety and risk [and neither] … has any seismic monitoring system' (Tsereteli et al. 2012: 98). Earlier, one of the institute's hydrogeologists, George Melikadze, had argued that a leak from the BTC pipeline in the mountains of south-west Georgia could potentially lead to the contamination of the major source of mineral water in Georgia: the spa town of Borjomi in the Lesser Caucasus.

Melikadze's research project was concerned with the production and circulation of water in the Borjomi-Bakuriani region. It addressed what we might call the hydrogeological assemblage of the Lesser Caucasus and its interaction with the infrastructural assemblage of the BTC and South Caucasus pipelines. The possibility of an interaction between hydrogeological systems and energy infrastructure arose in the years prior to Melikadze's study for quite contingent reasons. On the one hand, according to Western geopolitical strategists, Georgia provided a means of exporting oil from the Caspian Sea to the West along a route that bypassed Russia, Armenia and Iran. Georgia was seen as an 'energy corridor' in the post-Soviet political order. On the other hand, the pipeline was constructed through the Borjomi region in particular in order, in part, to bypass the presence of Armenian minorities and a Russian military base in southern Georgia, even though a more southerly route was considered to be environmentally preferable to the Borjomi route.

In these circumstances, the pipelines were thought to have a critical geopolitical function; tying Georgia into the Western sphere of influence while enabling exports of Caspian oil and gas to the West. Yet at the same, its projected and actual construction in the vicinity of Borjomi and Bakuriani generated an unexpected hydrogeochemical source of instability. Indeed, as early as 2002, the possibility of a leak from the BTC pipeline had already been considered an environmental threat to Borjomi mineral water, provoking a highly public dispute during the last year of the Shevardnadze government (Barry 2013: 44). While Shevardnadze's critics accused the government of betraying Borjomi, the speaker of the Georgian parliament viewed the pipeline system as an essential guarantee of 'our future security' (ibid.: 46). While the pipeline was subsequently constructed near Borjomi, the question of its potential environmental threat remained contested.

During the development of the pipeline, a hydrogeological model, which had been used to assess the risk of a pipeline leak, suggested that water was 'naturally discharged in the Borjomula, Gujareti and Tsemula river-beds and its outflows are on the slopes of river gorges' (Melikadze 2010: 14). On the basis of this model, a leak in the pipeline, whether caused by earthquakes, landslides, sabotage or corrosion, would enter the mineral water supply in Borjomi through surface water run-off. In order to prevent this from happening, containment facilities had been constructed by the BTC company in the 'riverbeds near to the Tskhratskaro-Kodiana section of the pipelines, as well as regular monitoring and incident reporting' (BTC/PMDI 2006: 12, quoted in Barry 2013: 49).

Melikadze, however, contested the analysis that informed the company's decision. His methodology was based on an analysis of how the isotopic composition of water varied over time and space. By drawing on the existing infrastructure of hydrochemical measurement in Europe, including support from a series of Austrian, Polish and Slovakian laboratories as well as funding from the International Atomic Energy Agency, he was able to map the concentration of both heavy hydrogen (deuterium and tritium) and heavy oxygen ($\delta\ ^{18}O$) isotopes in water across the Borjomi region (Melikadze 2010: 16–19). From these measurements he demonstrated that the Borjomi water took a long time to reach the town Borjomi from the mountains: 'it means that the pathway of water from recharge area to spring discharge area is longer (by 30–40 days) than the pathway to the river' (Melikadze 2010: 22). The implication was clear that the water had travelled to Borjomi through an underground aquifer rather than run off the surface as the earlier model had assumed. The spatial and temporal variation of both the mineral content and isotopic composition of water could be a subtle indicator of its origins and history. On the basis of his mapping of water composition, he came to the following critical conclusion, which directly contradicted the conclusions of the earlier study. In the event of a leak from the BTC pipeline, the existing containment facilities would not be ineffective and, as a result, 'it is necessary to take effective measures for protection of water source areas' (Melikadze 2010: 22).

Prior to its construction the possibility that there might be an interaction between the pipeline infrastructure and its geophysical environment had generated intense criticism of the Shevardnadze government. The BTC company's construction of containment facilities was intended to keep the infrastructural system and the 'force field' of the physical environment separate. But if Melikadze's analysis is correct, existing containment measures, which are designed to prevent surface water run-off, are insufficient. The implication is that if an oil leak from the BTC pipeline were to occur, the interaction between the pipeline infrastructure and hydrogeology of the Lesser Caucasus could still have complex and emergent effects. While the work of the Kandilli Observatory directs us towards the contingent interference between the North Anatolian fault and Istanbul's urban politics, the research of the Nodia Institute highlights the contingent relation between the earth, the dynamics of 'geopolitical assemblages' and the infrastructure of the hydrocarbon economy.

Conclusions

One of the commonest representations of infrastructure is a map of a network. In this image, an infrastructure is a set of connections and nodes that makes the movement of people, information and materials possible. It is the base through which things flow. In recent years, however, anthropologists and geographers have been increasingly, and rightly, concerned with not only the networked space of infrastructure but also the temporality of infrastructure. Infrastructures corrode, rust and crack (Barry 2013); they are sabotaged and destroyed, they break down (Graham et al. 2013) and they acquire accretions (Anand 2015). Infrastructures require monitoring, repair and periodic updating. Infrastructures not only extend spatially, but they are also enduring, as well as shifting and mutating over time.

This chapter is a contribution to an understanding of both the spatiality and temporality of infrastructure. My contention is that if we are understand the spatiality and temporality of infrastructure we must attend to the relation between infrastructural assemblages and the infrastructure of the earth, or what Connolly might term the 'force fields' of the geophysical. This interaction is complex in the sense that it entails a relation between heterogeneous elements, which generate unexpected and emergent effects (Born 2015; Connolly 2011; DeLanda 2006; Dittmer 2013). But I have also insisted that the significance of the work of seismologists and hydrogeologists is under-acknowledged; it both mediates between earth and infrastructure and traces their contingent interaction.

Notes

1 According to Connolly (2011: 5), a force field is 'any energized pattern in slow or rapid motion periodically displaying a capacity to morph, such as a climate system, biological evolution, a political economy, or human thinking' (cited in Born 2015).
2 Fieldwork notes, Tbilisi, March 2015.

References

Anand, N. (2015) "Accretion". Theorizing the Contemporary, *Cultural Anthropology* [Online], 24 September. Available at www.culanth.org/fieldsights/715-accretion.
Angell, E. (2014) "Assembling disaster: earthquakes and urban politics in Istanbul", *City* 18(6): 667–678.
Barry, A. (2002) "The anti-political economy", *Economy and Society* 31(2): 268–284.
Barry, A. (2006) "Technological zones", *European Journal of Social Theory* 9(2): 239–253.
Barry, A. (2010) "Visible invisibility', *New Geographies* 3: 67–74.
Barry, A. (2013) *Material Politics: Disputes along the Pipeline.* Chichester: Wiley-Blackwell.
Born, G. (2015) "Making time: temporality, history, and the cultural object", *New Literary History* 46(3): 361–386.
Connolly, W. (2011) *A World of Becoming.* Durham, NC: Duke University Press.
DeLanda, M. (2006) *A New Philosophy of Society: Assemblage Theory and Social Complexity.* London: Continuum
Deville, J., M. Guggenheim and Z. Hrdličková (2014) "Concrete Governmentality: Shelters and the Transformations of Preparedness", in M. Tironi, I. Rodriguez-Giralt and M. Guggenheim (eds) *Disasters and Politics: Materials, Experiments, Preparedness.* Chichester: Wiley-Blackwell, pp. 183–210.

Dittmer, J. (2013) "Geopolitical assemblages and complexity", *Progress in Human Geography* 38(3): 385–401.
Edwards, P. (2010) *A Vast Machine*. Cambridge, MA: MIT Press.
Farías, I. (2011) "The politics of urban assemblages", *City* 51(3/4): 365–374.
Farías, I. (2014) "Misrecognizing Tsunamis: Ontological Politics and Cosmopolitical Challenges in Early Warning Systems", in M. Tironi, I. Rodriguez-Giralt and M. Guggenheim (eds) *Disasters and Politics: Materials, Experiments, Preparedness*. Chichester: Wiley-Blackwell, pp. 38–60.
Graham, S., R. Desai and C. MacFarlane (2013) "Water Wars in Mumbai", in S. Graham and C. MacFarlane (eds) *Infrastructural Lives: Urban Infrastructures in Context*. London: Routledge, pp. 61–85.
Gülen, L., A. Pinar, D. Kalafat, N. Özel, G. Horozan, M. Yılmazer and A. Işıkara (2002) "Surface fault breaks, aftershock distribution, and rupture process of the 17 August 1999 of the İzmit, Turkey, earthquake', *Bulletin of the Seismological Society of America* 92(1): 230–244.
Humphrey, C. (2003) "Rethinking Infrastructure: Siberian Cities and the Great Freeze of January, 2001", in J. Shneider and I. Susser (eds) *Wounded Cities: Construction and the Reconstruction in a Globalized World*. Oxford: Berg, pp. 91–107.
Karaman, O. (2014) "Resisting urban renewal in Istanbul", *Urban Geography* 35(2): 290–310.
McFarlane, C. (2011) "Assemblage and critical urbanism", *City* 15(2): 204–224.
Melikadze, G. (2010) "Assessment of the Pollution Probability in the Borjomi-Bakuriani area by Application of Hydrochemical and Stable Isotope Methods", in A. Weller, G. Melikadze and N. Kapanadze (eds) *Exploration and Exploitation of Groundwater and Thermal Water Systems in Georgia*. Tbilisi: Ilia State University/TU Clausthal, pp. 13–23.
Star, S.L. and K. Ruhleder (1996) "Steps towards an ecology of infrastructure: design and access for large information spaces", *Information Systems Research* 7(1): 111–134.
Tironi, M., I. Rodriguez-Giralt and M. Guggenheim (eds) (2014) *Disasters and Politics: Materials, Experiments, Preparedness*. Chichester: Wiley-Blackwell.
Tsereteli, N., G. Tanircan, E. Safak, O. Varanzanashvili, T. Chelidze, A. Gvencadze and N. Goguadze (2012) "Seismic Hazard Assessment for Southern Caucasus – Eastern Turkey Energy Corridors: The Example of Geogia", in D. L. Barry (ed.) *Correlation between Human Factors and the Prevention of Disasters*. Amsterdam: IOS Press, pp. 96–111.
Yıldırım, U. and Y. Navaro-Yashin (2013) "An impromptu uprising: ethnographic reflections on the Gezi Park protests in Turkey", Hot Spots, *Cultural Anthropology* [Online], 31 October. Available at www.culanth.org/fieldsights/391-an-impromptu-uprising-ethnographic-reflections-on-the-gezi-park-protests-in-turkey.

15 Off the grid

Infrastructure and energy beyond the mains

Jamie Cross

In January 2013 my partner and I returned to Wakaisor, a tiny Girawa-speaking hamlet in the Begasin Hills on the north coast of Papua New Guinea. A pig had been killed to mark our arrival and, as we waited for the meat to be distributed between each of the hamlet's nineteen households and their seventy inhabitants, the sun went down.

Like most of rural Papua New Guinea, the Wakaisor hamlet has never been electrified. The nearest electricity grid ends fifty kilometres away, at the edge of Madang town. A line of high voltage transmission cables carries electricity to the town from the Yonki hydro-electric dam in the Papua New Guinea highlands, the pylons following the route of a national highway. At night, from a Begasin hilltop, you can see light from the town on the skyline. The bush is dark.

In the dusk we sat on a tree trunk around an open fire. When the time came for us to eat, we sat cross-legged beside the home of our hosts Benok and Mary. As the food was dished out, battery-powered LED lanterns were produced to illuminate the feast, one of them placed carefully on a workbench, another held aloft. Until recently most people had sought to meet their desires for modern, artificial sources of illumination by burning kerosene. Now almost every household had a Chinese-manufactured battery-powered LED lamp and travellers to town frequently returned with a carton of D-size Panasonic batteries, the country's best-selling brand, to use, sell or give away as gifts.

Forty minutes walk down river from the Wakaisor hamlet, the Manipur health center has had the capacity to generate electricity for at least thirty years. There have been solar-powered lighting systems in the outpatients building, the ward and the homes of resident health workers since 1982, when they were installed by the Lutheran Development Service. In 1992, when a local Madang-based businessman and politician was serving as the national health minister, the health center was fitted with a solar-powered shortwave radio system, paid for by the Australian government's aid and international development agency, and a solar-powered vaccine refrigerator, paid for by the Japanese government's international development agency. In 2013, however, these four solar-powered systems – lighting, radio, refrigeration and water pump – existed in various stages of disrepair. The radio could receive signals but not send them out. The vaccine refrigerator could be switched on but its temperature could not be monitored or adjusted. Some of the lights had blown and none of the systems had received any checks or maintenance in at least three years.

Life off the grid here is a historic condition and a future predicament.

Infrastructure off the grid

Thinking about life off the grid is to be reminded that the grid is an important keyword and conceptual tool for thinking about infrastructure. The electricity grid is more than a physical network for the distribution of electricity. As Cymene Howe (2017, forthcoming) has put it, the grid is 'the working relationship between humanity and the electron'. Yet globally, one-seventh of humanity, somewhere between 1.3 and 1.6 billion people according to the statistics published by the World Bank and the International Energy Agency, continue to live without any connection to planned, centralised networks for the transmission or distribution of electricity. What, we might ask, are the infrastructural arrangements and emergent infrastructures that constitute working relationships to the electron for people who live off the grid? What kinds of infrastructural investments animate people off the grid? And, what does the ethnography of life off the grid bring to an anthropology of energy and infrastructure?

In this chapter I gather together reflections on these questions that have emerged through a collaborative research project on infrastructures for energy and health in places that have never been connected to national or regional electricity grids (www.lifeoffthegrid.net). Since 2012, myself and Alice Street at the University of Edinburgh have worked to bring ethnographic fieldwork in the Begasin Hills, Papua New Guinea, into conversation with ethnographic fieldwork in rural Koraput, India, and the Highlands of Scotland. Across these field sites we have sought to understand the social and material arrangements through which people meet their energy needs in the absence of a connection to the grid. Drawing from this comparative project, I propose a number of ways in which thinking about energy off the grid allows us to extend the 'relational mix' (Harvey and Knox 2015) through which we apprehend and interrogate infrastructure.

First, thinking about life off the grid compels us to expand our analysis of the 'biopolitics or energo-politics' (Boyer 2014) of massive, centralised electricity systems and to focus critical attention on the proliferation of decentralised, small-scale or micro infrastructures that are divorced from national or regional electricity grids or any project of grid extension.

Second, life off the grid reminds us that grids are good to think with. Even off the grid, grids remain vital infrastructural objects. Life lived off the electricity grid is always life lived in relationship to other grids – physical, literal, virtual and metaphorical. Thinking through off the grid infrastructures allows us to engage with different orientations to these grids, with global politics of connection and disconnection, with struggles for recognition, rights and entitlements.

Finally, I set out to emphasise the role of off-grid energy infrastructures as living laboratories. Unlike the grid-based infrastructures that have faded from view or become normalised and taken for granted, off-grid infrastructures retain important experimental or demonstrator qualities.

What anthropologists today refer to as infrastructure describes specific configurations of 'material forms, expertise, social priorities, cultural expectations, aesthetics and economic investments' that sustain the conditions for life (Howe et al. 2016). Life off the grid might describe a world beyond mains electricity, but it does not, or very rarely, describe life without energy infrastructures. On the contrary, across global contexts of poverty and wealth, demands for electrically powered lighting, heating, refrigeration, information and communications bring people into relationships with what we might call off-grid infrastructural assemblages.

The off-grid infrastructural assemblages described here include technologies of generation, distribution and storage: from computer-managed hydro-electric turbines and silicon photovoltaic panels that convert wind, wave and solar energy, to lead acid or lithium iron batteries that store electrochemical energy. They also include the expertise to keep these technologies functioning and operational: from the formalised and standardised checks dictated by technical manuals or service providers to the acquired practical knowledge of components that allow people to carry out everyday repairs and maintenance. And they include the social networks and everyday exchanges through which people secure access: from the contracts that link community energy providers and customers, to pyramid selling schemes that extend markets, to the everyday forms of reciprocal sociality through which skills and goods are redistributed.

Decentralised infrastructures

At the very same historic moment that global patterns of energy consumption are called into question by climate change and ecological collapse, electricity has become an unquestionable public good. Yet, at the same time, the connection of people to grids of wires, cables and pylons, to planned, centralised networks for the distribution of electricity, is no longer seen as the only sustainable or achievable model for securing sustainable access to energy. There is nothing new about attempts to build decentralised energy systems that are capable of generating and distributing electricity without a connection to the grid. But in the past decade the promise of producing power beyond the mains has gained political and moral impetus. Against the backdrop of concerns with climate change, energy security and justice, the possibility of sustaining electric life off the grid has become immensely influential: mobilising people, shaping politics and driving policies.

Today, across contexts of wealth, economic growth and chronic poverty we can find renewed interest in the promise of decentralised energy and the proliferation of infrastructural assemblages that enable the generation and consumption of electricity beyond the mains. To the extent that these are infrastructures that are capable of operating with a minimal of materials and that articulate a minimal bio-politics, they might be described as minimalist (e.g. Redfield 2016; Cross and Street 2009; Street 2015).

Thinking about energy off the grid compels us to examine the social and material politics of a decentralised infrastructure, the shape infrastructure takes when it is not part of nationwide networks or point-to-point grids, and the vocabularies we use to add people and their social networks into infrastructural assemblages. Decentralised energy infrastructures share much with large-scale electricity infrastructures. Indeed, if we understand infrastructure as an 'architecture of circulation' (Larkin 2013), then distributed or decentralised energy technologies have much in common with large-scale grid-like networks of power. Whether in Papua New Guinea, India or Scotland, hydroelectric turbines, household-level solar photovoltaic systems and electrochemical batteries are all 'things that make other things relatable' (ibid.), putting electrons into relationships with people and creating the ground upon which electrically powered things can work.

As Fran Tonkiss (2015) reminds us, in making materials, resources, capital, information and people 'relatable', all infrastructures involve diverse economies of investment, exchange, ownership and use. As scholars in STS and geography have emphasised, grid-based network infrastructures mediate the circulation, movement or exchange of things over great distances (Larkin 2013; Graham and Marvin 2001). By contrast, decentralised energy infrastructures keep these distance short, reducing the time and space between points at which electricity is generated and consumed. Thinking across three comparative global contexts has challenged us to engage with the economies of this decentralised infrastructure and the different modes of market and non-market exchange that facilitate the transmission, distribution and storage of electricity off the grid.

If there is an energy around off-grid energy in the global north and south it can frequently be found in attempts to create the infrastructural architecture for decentralised solar electricity. At the beginning of the twenty-first century the unique affordances of the silicon-based solar photovoltaic cell – which converts sunlight into direct current, allowing electricity to be generated and distributed at the point of demand without the need for large-scale, grid-like networks of power – has put solar-powered things at the center of off-grid infrastructural assemblages. More than any other off-grid energy technology, the solar-powered lantern – a portable, plastic device that connects a photovoltaic panel to a rechargeable battery and a light-emitting diode – has become a quintessential, micro-technical 'infrastructure in a box', lauded as a vanguard technology at the cutting edge of sustainable design and innovation (Cross 2013).

Places like the un-electrified highlands of Odisha, in India, for example, have become frontiers for off-grid solar energy, as a consequence of entrepreneurial efforts to expand access to energy at the bottom of the economic pyramid. Nestled amid the high plateaus of southern Odisha in the shadow of one of the country's largest bauxite mines, lies the tiny, un-electrified hamlet of Jholaguda. The inhabitants of Jholaguda are Porajas, an Adivasi or indigenous community which rank amongst India's poorest and most marginalised. Here life 'off the grid' is no longer simply a condition of chronic poverty but a market opportunity for the sale of basic infrastructural goods, and solar lanterns are now central to a basket of consumer durables designed and marketed to people living without access to electricity.

In January 2011, one of India's largest non-governmental organisations established a solar lighting project in Jholaguda as part of a nationwide energy access programme. They mounted a bank of solar panels outside the home of Trinath and converted one room into a recharging station, capable of charging the batteries of sixty small portable lanterns each day. Trinath was given a stapled collection of photocopied papers that contained Oriya language instructions on how to be an entrepreneur. The booklet described how Trinath was to charge his fellow villages two rupees (equivalent to $US0.02) per night to rent out a lantern, with the income deposited in a bank account where it could be saved for essential repair and maintenance in the future.

Over the next three years, however, Trinath neither asked for nor received any money for charging the lanterns. In the absence of any long-term relationship to the NGO that had installed the charging station and with a lack of clarity about who precisely had paid for it, the people of Jholaguda saw no reason to pay. By 2014, however, few of the lanterns were capable of producing light at night. The rechargeable batteries could no longer store their charge and the lanterns could only be used during the daytime when the panels could convert sunlight to electricity.

Eighteen-year-old Limkudi wanted to throw his family's lantern away. But his mother kept it, using it to illuminate their windowless, un-electrified home during daylight hours. One day he watched a storekeeper in the nearby market town show a customer how to connect a 120-rupee AC/DC convertor to a solar panel in order to charge mobile phones. He bought one for himself and brought it home. He cut the plug off the charger, releasing two wires, and connected these directly to the positive and negative cables hanging off his solar panel, twisting the wires together and tying them closed with strips torn from an old plastic bag. The system worked and he played around a little bit further, eventually discovering that he could connect both the LED lantern and the mobile phone charger to the solar panel simultaneously, twisting the wires together and tying them tight with strips of plastic. Over the following months he helped young men from other households in the hamlet reconnect their solar panels to mobile phone chargers, teaching them what he had done. 'If I had to show people from another village I might take some money from them,' he said. 'But here, in my village, I do these things for nothing.'

While off-grid infrastructures may involve transactions between users and far off entities – government departments, non-government organisations or social entrepreneurs – keeping these infrastructures operational involves everyday, face-to-face interactions and transactions. The movement, circulation and maintenance of infrastructural things in off-grid locations – from India to Papua New Guinea – brings the economy of decentralised infrastructure and its diverse transactional logics into focus. To think ethnographically about these technologies and people's relationships to them is to open up novel points of departure for regional scholarship, providing fresh perspectives on questions of exchange, modernity and personhood that have long preoccupied the anthropology of South Asia and Melanesia (Cross, n.d.). At the time, same thinking about life here as life lived off the grid is also to open up new space for an anthropology of energy and infrastructure.

In Papua New Guinea, batteries were carried into the Begasin Hills from urban trade stores to be sold in bush markets or from the porch of people's homes. But they were also gifted and given as expressions of mutuality, 'co-operation' or mutual aid and as expressions of delayed 'reciprocity' across extended social networks. Here in the tropics, micro-electronic goods mass-manufactured in mainland China are fragile things. Bulbs and switches fall out of their fittings. Plastic casings crack or break. Battery acid leaks and corrodes the internal circuitry. The soldering comes away and wires work themselves free of assembly boards. This fragility has given rise to new kinds of village specialist, people adroit at fixing or mending things. Rebuilt technologies often combine components acquired through exchanges with an array of different people, so that a repaired lantern reveals the fixer's ability to elicit goods through exchange.

Whether in India or in Papua New Guinea, decentralised energy systems are woven around everyday obligations and exchanges that animate relationships between neighbours and friends, as well as those connected by caste and kinship. We might describe the language habits and practices that establish and maintain lines of communication as phatic infrastructures (Elyachar 2010), or extrapolate from these forms of economic collaboration to characterise 'people as infrastructure' (Simone 2004). However, we might also elaborate the infra-transactional arrangements and practices – modes of exchange marked by mutuality, reciprocity or equivalence, and hierarchy (Graeber 2010) – through which working relationships to the electron are established, maintained and distributed.

On/off the grid

For electrical engineers, the managers of utility companies, energy policymakers and some sociologists, the phrase 'off the grid' is a precise, technical expression. The earliest use of the term 'grid' in reference to a network of transmission lines is also the moment at which the possibility of being off the grid emerges. In post-colonial South Asia and Melanesia, as in post-war

Europe, the creation and expansion of physical networks for the transmission of electricity, pylons and wires, substations and transformers played an important role in the imagination of national communities. Yet just as these twentieth-century projects of electrification connected communities and markets, they also created populations who came to know themselves as excluded or unconnected. Always and everywhere, it seems, the electricity grid simultaneously established connectedness and disconnectedness: 'on' and 'off'.

This binary offers a useful analytic for an anthropology of energy and infrastructure. Grids are not synonymous with infrastructure. But perhaps all infrastructures involve or accommodate some kind of grid. Whether in Papua New Guinea, India or Scotland, off-grid energy infrastructures remain dependent upon or reimagine grids for transportation, information, communication and governance. Visitors to an off-grid community in Knoydart, for example, a remote peninsular on the north-west coast of Scotland where electricity is generated by a small-scale hydro-electric system, frequently imagine a technologically sparse environment, free from digital things and practices. Yet here life off the grid has increasingly involved investment in digital data. Over the past five years, as the community's hydro-electric system has been upgraded, new digital components have been introduced to help manage supply and demand. These technologies, information systems and logics (Walford and Knox 2016) are reshaping the conditions of possibility with which people encounter electricity, making it possible for off-grid energy consumers to see their electricity not just as something that can be on or off, but something that can be more or less.

What we mean by the grid, of course, indexes both networks of things and networks of power and knowledge, the lattice-work through which states govern and markets are made. These infrastructural overlaps are vital for the movement of the materials, components and parts that allow decentralised energy infrastructures to be assembled, just as they are vital for the movement of information about prices, credit and debt that allow energy markets to perform. Experiences of grid connection and disconnection are also the outcome of uneven processes of development, neoliberal state policies and political initiatives. In Papua New Guinea and India, one enduring legacy of structural adjustment was the abandonment or reconfiguration of universal programmes of rural electrification. In their wake, private electricity suppliers focused on the needs of economically important populations and places, giving rise to highly energised enclave spaces or economic zones.

Electricity grids often appear to exemplify the capacity of infrastructural forms to make things relatable in unequal ways. Thinking more deeply about life off the grid in Papua New Guinea and India from spaces of relative global wealth and privilege in Scotland is to be constantly reminded of the distributive politics of energy and the stark contrasts in resources as well as infrastructural imaginaries. In Scotland, for example, low-carbon energy policies are producing off-grid populations and places as spaces of infrastructural speculation and investment. Here a proliferation of decentralised infrastructures is being driven by government policies, legislative arrangements, and public financing initiatives that make it possible for communities to manage and take ownership of local energy systems.

Such political histories and legacies mean that off-grid worlds are not a smooth space into which the energy solutions championed by 'transnational green capitalists' or 'eco-liberals' can effortlessly slide. Instead this is a rough terrain, a space of encounter where decentralised energy systems meet the materially and symbolically dense politics of infrastructure that shape lives lived off the grid. Off the grid, grids do not disappear into the background but become the object of heightened attention. In places that are not connected to the electricity grid and have little prospect of future connection, large-scale electricity infrastructures can become more rather than less prominent. In rural Papua New Guinea and India, for example, life off the grid is not just life without access to a networked infrastructure for electricity distribution but also life lived in proximity to or in the shadow of bigger grids, centralised systems for the distribution of public goods, rights and entitlements.

Like the relationships between urban slum dwellers and water systems in Mumbai (Anand 2011), villagers living without access to energy in the highlands of Orissa dream of electric citizenship, and the wires, transformers and pylons that connect homes to the electricity grid are the infrastructure through which rural people imagine they can claim recognition, resources and entitlements from the state. For the Poraja Adivasis of Jholaguda, the electricity grid registers expectations of modernity and government and citizenship even as it maps experiences of abandonment and invisibility. In this valley a material connection to the network of transformers, pylons and wires that carry electricity from regional power stations into other people's homes and villages holds out the promise of recognising claims, rights and entitlements as equal members of the nation state, of establishing or realising citizenship. Little surprise, perhaps, that companies selling solar energy technologies here have begun to market their products as 'grid-like'.

'Durable, modern, human,' runs the tagline for one of the world's leading manufacturers of distributed, solar energy systems, that markets its products to people living without access to mains electricity across India. The company's off-grid solar technologies – from simple lighting and mobile phone-charging systems to 'solar power systems' that claim to offer a 'personal grid' for homes and businesses – simultaneously map the boundaries and limits of grid-based infrastructures, producing state infrastructures as obsolete, inefficient and ineffective.

Living labs

Thinking off the grid reminds us that the same kinds of energy infrastructures can accommodate diverse values and futures. Off-grid infrastructures can fuse ecological and market logics. They can be 'morally encoded by the mandate of sustainability and the rhetoric of collectivity' (Hulme 2009) even as they are motivated by profit margins and private gain. Like all infrastructural assemblages, the material technologies, technical expertise and devices that energise lives off the grid are threaded with ideology and a global comparative approach throws these material politics into sharp relief.

On the north-west coast of Scotland, for example, off-grid energy infrastructures are often underpinned by autonomist, ecological and libertarian commitments. Here, environmental and ecological activists cohabit and collaborate with climate change sceptics. A community-owned green energy supplier manages a hydro-electric turbine which supplies electricity to around 120 homes. For those involved in the day-to-day management of the hydro-electric system, the sale of green energy is an opportunity to change the behaviour of their consumers, encouraging reflexive energy consumption and feelings of collective ownership with a renewable resource.

Small-scale, off-grid energy systems, like those on the Isle of Eigg and the Knoydart peninsular, have become such high-profile models of community-owned and managed infrastructure that they have become beacons for journalists, activists and academics. By contrast with rural Papua New Guinea or India, where life off the grid is a condition of chronic poverty and socio-economic exclusion, in the Scottish Highlands a life lived off the grid is often an attempt to live at some degree of 'remove' from infrastructural complexity (Vannini and Taggart 2013, 2014). Such attempts are frequently contradictory, less an escape from infrastructure than new or renewed commitments to alternative infrastructural forms.

In Papua New Guinea and India the fragility or absence of grid-based energy has opened up new arenas for the intervention of state and non-actors. Here the proliferation of off-grid energy systems is underpinned by what we might call an 'electric humanitarianism' (Delbourgo 2006) that marries electricity to projects of governance, development and social reform. Under the auspices of the UN's Sustainable Energy for All initiative, for example, governments and non-government organisations worldwide have been revising their measurements and indices of poverty to accommodate the view that modern, efficient forms of electricity are essential for human health and wellbeing. Today, technologies and systems built and designed for people living off the grid in the global south are inscribed with a set of ideas about the capacity of electricity to transform users into economically productive, rational moral subjects. Here, we can find solar-powered lanterns, solar home systems and decentralised solar micro-grids championed as a technical solution to problems of child literacy, global health and poor livelihoods. And, we can find the manufacturers and distributors of off-grid energy infrastructures deploying experimental research methodologies like the randomised controlled trial to test the impact of their technologies on human subjects.

Over the past thirty years, remote or rural locations that had never been electrified in Papua New Guinea, to India and Scotland have repeatedly acted as test or demonstration sites for off-grid energy systems. Across these diverse global contexts we can trace past projects aimed at demonstrating the ecological promise and everyday functionality of off-grid energy systems. A micro-hydro-electric system was first built on the Knoydart estate in the Scottish Highlands, for example, in 1978. As detailed above, the first solar-powered lighting systems were installed in Papua New Guinea's Begasin Hills in 1982. And the Government of India first installed solar-powered street lights in villages and railway stations across the highlands of Odisha in 1984. Each of these pilot installations established that micro-energy infrastructures could be successfully installed, operated and maintained in these locations and could meet minimal requirements for electric lighting and telecommunications.

Amidst the ruins of modernist projects and a deep cynicism with infrastructural projects, off-grid energy infrastructures continue to be imbued with hope. Even in places like Begasin, Papua New Guinea, where attempts to sustain life off the grid remain deeply unassured, the promise of a radical alternative energy future is yet to completely fall apart. Despite the unmet promises of modernist projects and infrastructures, off-grid infrastructures continue to embody hope, so that we rarely find accounts of lives lived amidst the ruins of off-grid energy projects (e.g. Alexander and Reno 2014). More, when coupled to the promise of an alternative, clean green energy future, off-grid energy infrastructures around the world appear as an emergent (even insurgent) infrastructural form. In the 1990s, for example, South Asia and the Pacific emerged as a testing ground for market-oriented, neoliberal models of solar technology transfer and diffusion. In the 1990s the World Bank helped solar entrepreneurs in India to set up small solar businesses in the expectation that they would have a demonstration effect, revealing a market to future businesses and larger competitors.

At the beginning of the twenty-first century, off-grid infrastructures remain sites of testing and experimentation, even as their 'demonstrator qualities' have been reoriented around their economic capacities. They are living laboratories. Like other kinds of experiments with green living (Marres 2008) and renewable energy systems (Reno 2010), off-grid infrastructures incorporate their end users in a phenomenological way, through sensory engagements with new material things, and call upon wider publics to testify to outcomes or verify results. And they also stimulate public engagement with debates about energy and fuel in the context of national and international responses to climate change.

Today, across diverse global locations, we can find a combination of non-government organisations, corporations, social enterprises and community groups working to demonstrate the role of renewable energy technologies in creating new markets for eco-tourism, agricultural commodities and consumer appliances at the same time as generating value for investors. In the global south, the prospect and challenge of increasing access to electricity off the grid is animating new coalitions of governments, corporations and charities, bringing politicians, philanthro-capitalists and humanitarians into new alignments. Here, infrastructural things like the silicon solar panel have a political vitality, connecting circuits of business, government, finance and social activism in new ways, generating effects not just by successfully allying different groups of people but by electrifying the network. Just as sunlight on a silicon solar module has a photovoltaic effect – animating, exciting and energising electrons – so too the proliferation of solar technology has had a photovoltaic effect on social reformers and social entrepreneurs, moving people to action, charging them with purpose.

* * *

Around the world, investments in off-grid energy infrastructures are frequently accompanied by claims that they are more progressive, efficient and democratic than 'grid-based' alternatives. Thinking across comparative global contexts allows us to tease out the tensions and ambiguities in these claims. To paraphrase Susan Leigh Star's (1999) classic manifesto for an ethnography of infrastructure, the politics of the un-electrified world are profoundly impacted by the energy infrastructures that sustain life off the grid.

Study a rural community in India, Papua New Guinea or Scotland and neglect how its residents meet their demands for electrical energy and you miss essential aspects of distributive justice and power. Study their hydroelectric systems, solar home systems, battery-powered devices or generators but neglect their settings, standards or component parts and you miss the play of power in their design and aesthetics. Study the contexts in which these technologies are used and neglect the transactions through which people acquire, share and maintain them and you overlook how exchange mediates the distribution of electricity as a resource.

Acknowledgements

The research on which this essay is based was funded by the Economic and Social Research Council and the Leverhulme Trust. The ethnographic material presented here emerges out of a long-term collaboration with Alice Street, who made substantive comments on the final draft.

References

Alexander, C. and Reno, J. O. (2014) From biopower to energopolitics in England's modern waste technology". *Anthropological Quarterly* 87(2): 335–358.

Anand, N. (2011) Pressure: the politechnics of water supply in Mumbai". *Cultural Anthropology* 26(4): 542–564.

Bijker, W. E. (2009) How is technology made? That is the question! *Cambridge Journal of Economics* 34(1): 63–76.

Boyer, D. (2014) Energopower: an introduction". *Anthropological Quarterly* 87(2): 309–333.

Cross, J. (2013) The 100th object: solar lighting technology and humanitarian goods". *Journal of Material Culture* 18(4): 367–387.

Cross, J. (n.d.). After kerosene: energy and exchange through Melanesian anthropology.
Cross, J. and Street, A. (2009) Anthropology at the bottom of the pyramid". *Anthropology Today* 25(4): 4–9.
Delbourgo, J. (2006) *A Most Amazing Scene of Wonders: Electricity and Enlightenment in Early America*. Cambridge, MA: Harvard University Press.
Elyachar, J. (2010) Phatic labor, infrastructure, and the question of empowerment in Cairo". *American Ethnologist* 37(3): 452–464.
Graeber, D. (2010) *Debt: The First 5,000 Years*. New York: Melville House Publishing.
Graham, S. and Marvin, S. (2001) *Splintering Urbanism: Networked Infrastructures, Technological Mobilities and the Urban Condition*. Hove: Psychology Press.
Harvey, P. and Knox, H. (2015) *Roads: An Anthropology of Infrastructure and Expertise*. Ithaca, NY: Cornell University Press.
Howe, C. (2017, forthcoming). "Grids", in Jennifer Wenzel, Imre Szeman and Patricia Yaeger (eds), *Fueling Culture: Energy, History, Politics*. New York: Fordham University Press.
Howe, C. et al. (2016) Paradoxical infrastructures: ruins, retrofit, and risk". *Science, Technology & Human Values* 41(3): 547–565. DOI: 10.1177/0162243915620017.
Hulme, M. (2009) *Why We Disagree About Climate Change: Understanding Controversy, Inaction and Opportunity*. Cambridge: Cambridge University Press.
Larkin, B. (2013) The politics and poetics of infrastructure". *Annual Review of Anthropology* 42: 327–343.
Lazar, S. (2012) Disjunctive comparison: citizenship and trade unionism in Bolivia and Argentina". *Journal of the Royal Anthropological Institute* 18(2): 349–368.
Redfield, P. (2016) Fluid technologies: the Bush Pump, the LifeStraw^R and microworlds of humanitarian design". *Social Studies of Science* 46(2): 159–183.
Reno, J. (2010) Managing the experience of evidence: England's experimental waste technologies and their immodest witnesses". *Science, Technology & Human Values* 35(1): 1–22.
Simone, A. (2004) People as infrastructure: intersecting fragments in Johannesburg". *Public Culture* 16(3): 407–429.
Star, S. L. (1999) The ethnography of infrastructure". *American Behavioral Scientist* 43(3): 377–391.
Street, A. (2014) *Biomedicine in an Unstable Place: Infrastructure and Personhood in a Papua New Guinean Hospital*. Durham, NC: Duke University Press.
Street, A. (2015) Food as pharma: marketing nutraceuticals to India's rural poor". *Critical Public Health* 25(3): 361–372.
Tonkiss, F. (2015) Afterword: economies of infrastructure". *City* 19(2/3): 384–391.
Vannini, P. and Taggart, J. (2013) Voluntary simplicity, involuntary complexities, and the pull of remove: the radical ruralities of off-grid lifestyles". *Environment and Planning A* 45(2): 295–311.
Vannini, P. and Taggart, J. (2014) *Off the Grid: Re-assembling Domestic Life*. London: Routledge.
Walford, A. and Knox, H. (2016) Is there an ontology to the digital". *Cultural Anthropology*. Published online: www.culanth.org/fieldsights/818-is-there-an-ontology-to-the-digital.

Part IV

Environmental infrastructures

The relationship between infrastructure and environment is characterized by complex material and conceptual entanglements. "Environment" is broadly defined as a sum total of things in interaction, constituting the surroundings of human society or any kind of human activity. As a collection of things that surround an object in focus, the "environment" is inherently relational, akin to Susan Leigh Star's (1999) definition of infrastructure as a background in relation to an activity in focus. Forty-five years ago, Roy Wagner (1981) argued that modern Western culture usually focuses on collective aspects of human life such as social institutions and conventions as potential objects of reflection and improvement, while taking non-human living things, landscapes and so on, as given, located in the background or potential materials for human endeavors. The conventional Western dichotomy between nature and culture centers on this distinction (Strathern 1980). As Wagner notes, however, this focus is far from universal and people in other parts of the world have developed different orientations.

In this context, environment and infrastructure have a similar relationship to human activities. The fact that both infrastructures and environments are conventionally seen as backgrounds complicates the question of their relations and the question of how to bring them into view.

How can one tell infrastructure from environment if both are relational backgrounds? This is not only an analytical problem for social scientists but also a practical problem for managers of infrastructures (Morita 2016). Thus, the relationship between infrastructure and environment is centrally related to the theme of infrastructural inversion and, consequently, the unstable relation between the conceptual and the empirical as well. The chapters in this section illuminate divergent ways of exploring the dual entanglement between infrastructure and environment and between the conceptual and the empirical. Developing different approaches, they exhibit points of both tension and convergence.

The first point of divergence concerns a rather simple question concerning the way in which one conceptualizes the infrastructure–environment relation in terms of spatiality. Are infrastructures embedded *in* the environment? Or does the environmental rest *within* infrastructures? By elucidating the multifaceted entanglement of waste infrastructures and ecological and geological environments, Myra Hird focuses on the embeddedness of infrastructure in environments. Landfills, common destinations of waste, are part of extensive chains of excavation, processing, use, and waste of natural resources. At the same time, landfills are disturbances of the "natural" stratigraphic order, since they themselves form strata of waste. Hird also argues that urban infrastructure is itself creating a new geological structure, since abundant infrastructures left buried underground contain more mineral than natural deposits. In contrast, Casper Bruun Jensen looks at this entanglement from within. Taking up Phnom Penh's dilapidated sewage infrastructure, he examines its profound entanglement with a variety of nonhuman agents. The flow, leakage and stagnation of the waste water in the sewage involves, and rests on, divergent species from bacteria contributing to waste water processing, to morning glory filtering waste water, and trees intruding into sewage pipes to access nutritious waste water.

Although these two chapters exhibit contrasting orientations, they are by no means incompatible. Rather, as is clear from Hird's references to the activities of bacteria in the landfills and Jensen's corresponding descriptions of the loop of materials that connects the sewage network, residents of the city and the Bassac river, the inside and the outside of infrastructure are mutually implicated. It is precisely this mutual relation that makes infrastructures at once conceptually interesting and challenging.

The complex entwinement of environment and infrastructure, and the inside and the outside, blurs infrastructural boundaries. While social scientists may take this as an analytical challenge, engineers and managers encounter a practical conundrum. Indeed, as discussed in the Introduction, infrastructural inversion is not an exclusive feature of social analysis. In situations of breakdown and crisis, managers and users of infrastructures often perform their own infrastructural inversions, setting out to explore the operations of infrastructures. Blurred infrastructural boundaries can lead these explorations in unexpected directions.

In order to get a handle on the blurred boundaries of infrastructures, infrastructural inversion often depends on new ways of analyzing and classifying a heterogeneous array of data. The surprises of infrastructural inversion, that is, often relates to the creation of new knowledge infrastructure.

This question is thematized in different ways in the two other chapters of this section. Atsuro Morita illuminates how a particular type of infrastructure became a model for understanding the environment and how that model eventually brought about a reconceptualization of infrastructures. Central to this story is the drainage basin, a basic unit of analysis for hydrology, geomorphology, and natural resource management, continuously molded by interactions between infrastructure and science. Whereas the drainage basin was originally nested in the design of water infrastructures such as irrigation systems, it began to act back *on* urban infrastructures, which came to be seen as particular types of drainage basins. The drainage basin thus offers a case in which a large-scale technological system became a knowledge platform that connected diverse practices in environmental science, from simulation models and measurement networks to the design of urban infrastructure.

While Morita begins with the materiality of infrastructure and ends with knowledge, Calkins and Rottenburg focus on the entanglement of knowledge infrastructure and values. In relation to the construction of knowledge infrastructure, neither data nor knowledge of environments are ever neutral. Questions concerning knowledge infrastructure include not only how to gather data but also how to assess them and what kind of questions one should ask about them. Thus, infrastructures of evidence for genetically modified organisms (GMO) often become a platform for struggle and compromise between almost incommensurable interests, embodying different ways of seeing, evaluating, and enacting worlds. In contrast to the drainage basin, where the design of infrastructure became a scientific model, GMO knowledge infrastructure has served to further entangle environment and values.

As these chapters collectively illustrate, infrastructure and environment intertwine in very different ways. As we see in the chapters by Jensen and Hird, infrastructures are deeply intertwined with environments, both externally and internally. As Morita and Calkins and Rottenburg show, environmental infrastructures define an experimental space in which not only technology and "nature" but also the material and the conceptual, and values and data, become entangled.

Together, the chapters make clear that current environmental challenges bring about constant reconfigurations in which new connections between values and data and new imaginations about infrastructure and environment emerge. Such transformations are consequential, not only for those who study infrastructures but also for social scientists more generally, since the reconfigurations of environmental infrastructures often displace or redefine the roles of the social and the cultural.

References

Morita, Atsuro (2016) "Multispecies Infrastructure: Infrastructural Inversion and Involutionary Entanglements in the Chao Phraya Delta, Thailand," *Ethnos*. Online First, doi: 10.1080/00141844.2015.1119175.

Star, Susan Leigh (1999) "The Ethnography of Infrastructure," *American Behavioral Scientist* 43(3): 377–391.

Strathern, Marilyn (1980) "No Nature, No Culture: The Hagen Case," in Carol P. MacCormack and Marilyn Strathern (eds) *Nature, Culture and Gender*. Cambridge: Cambridge University Press, pp. 174–222.

Wagner, Roy (1981) *The Invention of Culture*. Chicago, IL: University of Chicago Press.

16 River basin

The development of the scientific concept and infrastructures in the Chao Phraya Delta, Thailand

Atsuro Morita

Introduction

As Casper Bruun Jensen and Myra Hird both note in their chapters for this volume, infrastructures and environments are profoundly entangled. Infrastructures are often deeply embedded in ecological and geological environments, their functioning depending on ecological processes, like the activities of microbes living within them. Whereas designers and managers of infrastructures are often aware of this entanglement, until recently the implications of this situation have rarely been examined in the social science literature.

This chapter aims to explore this entanglement from a slightly different angle to that of Jensen and Hird. By focusing on the drainage basin, which has served as a basic unit for the environmental sciences and management, it examines the recursive relation between infrastructures and scientific concepts. The formation of the scientific concept of the drainage basin is entwined with the histories of water infrastructures such as irrigation systems and waterworks. However, after having been established as the "universal unit of landform," the drainage basin in turn began reshaping understandings of infrastructure. It contributed to such reshaping by revealing hidden water flow beneath and behind the solid surface of infrastructures as well as the entwined ecologies and forms of cohabitation of humans and non-humans. In the following, I explore how infrastructures came to serve as models for understanding ecological processes and how this subsequently led to a transformed, ecological view of infrastructure.

The drainage basin is the area where water from rainfall flows into a single river. Because (a significant part of) rainfall flows on land surfaces from higher to lower areas, the runoff from a given area eventually gathers in a river that flows downstream towards the sea. Drainage basins have a long history in Europe. For example, they have long been used to demarcate regions because they are so readily identifiable. One can find caricatured drawing of watersheds – higher areas that hinder water flow across them and thus divide the drainage basins – in historical maps of Europe (Clifford 2011). The European notion of drainage basin gained *scientific* significance since the seventeenth century through successive efforts to estimate the relation between rainfall and river discharge. At this time, it was realized that the size of the drainage basin is important for predicting increases of river flows from rainfall (Clifford 2011). As new measurement and calculation methods were introduced in the nineteenth and early twentieth century, the relation between rainfall, drainage basin area, and river discharge was continuously elaborated and refined. After the 1950s, these developments laid the foundation for the development of mathematical simulation models (Singh and Woolhiser 2002).

Since the mid-twentieth century, however, the importance of the drainage basin has moved beyond the boundaries of hydrology. In the 1960s, the field of geomorphology came to recognize the fundamental importance of the drainage basin as "the universal unit of landform" (Clifford 2011). Since then, the notion has become a basic unit for hydrology, geomorphology and natural resource management. Due to the prevalence of watershed management in environment policy since the 1980s, it has even taken on moral and aesthetic value. Because the drainage basin reveals hitherto unseen relations between social and environmental processes, it has become significant for imagining sustainable forms of cohabitation of humans and non-humans (Newson 2009).

By now, the drainage basin is a central concept-object that holds various aspects of the environment together. Indeed, it would be no exaggeration to say that it has exhibited a quite extraordinary capacity to connect diverse processes from river hydrology and landform development (Chorley 1969, Clifford 2011) to fluid dynamics and computer simulation (Singh and Woolhiser 2002), to ecological processes and agriculture (Takaya 1987), and, finally, to community and aesthetics (Newson 2009).

As I show in the following, the shifting ways in which the drainage basin model has captured land–water interactions rest on, and resonate with, parallel developments between scientific concepts and water management infrastructures. Facilitating a continuous movement back and forth between science and infrastructure, the drainage basin enabled the revelation of unexpected flows beneath the solid surface of infrastructures. Indeed, it has opened up a new view of infrastructure as shared habitat between humans and non-human species. To develop this argument, I focus on a specific, and rather peculiar, location in the international network of hydrology and hydraulic engineering.

The Chao Phraya Delta in Thailand is a very interesting place to explore shifting framings of water–land interaction. While peripheral to the networks of science, it holds significance as a place where colonial hydrological technoscience and indigenous development intersected. In fact, the delta boasts one of the world's largest irrigation infrastructures, epitomizing a high modernist view of social and economic development. At the same time, however, the delta is also known for extensive canal networks built in pre-modern times. These canal networks have survived the massive transformation brought about by modern irrigation and, in the face of climate change, they are now gaining much attention as a resilient and flood-adaptive infrastructure (Thaitakoo and McGrath 2010; Morita 2016). As I discuss below, the encounter between the traditional delta infrastructure and the new field of urban ecology has resulted in a new vision of the city as a waterscape, *a sort of drainage basin*, which connects natural, social and economic processes through complex water flows.

Terrestrializing the delta: the Chao Phraya Dam

On February 7, 1957, the king of Thailand, Bhumibol Adulyadej, made a speech to celebrate the opening of the Chao Phraya Dam, a barrage on which the entire Greater Chao Phraya Irrigation Project hinged. The project was one of the largest in Asia at the time and covered the major part of the Chao Phraya Delta, an area of 11,600 square kilometers. In his speech, the king emphasized the government's continuous efforts to install irrigation since the reign of the legendary King Chulalongkorn (1853–1910), who laid the foundation of the modern Thai state. The dam itself had been planned during the reign of King Chulalongkorn but had been shelved for almost fifty years due to lack of financial resources (Brummelhuis 2005).

As originally conceived by the Dutch irrigation engineer J. Homan van der Heide in 1903, the main aim of the Chao Phraya Dam was to deliver irrigation water for rice cultivation all over the delta. However, the impact of the dam was even more significant. It fundamentally transformed water flows and, thus, the delta landscape.

Before the completion of the irrigation system, the lower part of the delta consisted of unpopulated marshland. Since the delta is extremely flat, most of it was annually flooded in the rainy season. During these times, the lower part of the delta became a gigantic water zone directly connected to the sea. Meanwhile, the parts of the delta that were not connected to the rivers became extremely arid in the dry season. In most of the delta it was therefore very difficult to get drinking water, not to mention water for agriculture. These severe hydrological conditions effectively prohibited human settlements except on natural levees along the river (Takaya 1987). In this marshy environment, the Siamese states had excavated numerous canals to facilitate water transport and store drinking water for the dry seasons. Until the mid-twentieth century, the life of people in the delta was profoundly dependent on this aquatic infrastructure (Morita 2015; Morita and Jensen 2016).

The Chao Phraya Dam profoundly transformed this marshy landscape. Irrigation made it possible to not only reclaim unused lands but also transform urban planning and social life by making Western-style buildings, factories fitted with heavy machinery, and land transportation such as trains and cars. Though not as visible as the construction of roads and buildings, the irrigation system was thus of fundamental importance. Irrigation canals created the dry land upon which these terrestrial infrastructures could later be constructed.

Homan van der Heide (1903) had already foreseen that irrigation canals would open up new terrestrial possibilities. He envisioned that the irrigation system would drain excess water from villages and adjacent areas, which meant that villagers would be able to cultivate fruit trees and raise livestock. It is clear from his terrestrial development vision that the irrigation system's capacity to function as a drainage network was no coincidence. As we shall see, it also closely related to the way in which irrigation engineers came to imagine water flow in the river basin.

Water infrastructures and the drainage basin model

Before completion of the Chao Phraya Irrigation Project, the water flow in the delta was very different from what would be assumed by now the conventional notion of the drainage basin. In this extremely flat land, where the land elevation difference between the estuary and a hundred kilometers upstream is only two meters, water was poorly drained. In rainy seasons, floodwater therefore stagnated in large areas of the delta, and it occasionally flowed backwards due to high tides. Ordering this unruly flow was crucial in order to clearly separate land and water.

Homan van der Heide's report (1903) clearly exemplifies the ambition to separate the two. He viewed the most important aspect of the Greater Chao Phraya Irrigation Project as the direction of water and the maintenance of a constant flow. In his report on delta hydrology, Homan van der Heide stated that the expansion of rice cultivation required a steady water supply. He further insisted that only "perennial irrigation" would achieve this goal. Homan van der Heide recognized an existing water management infrastructure, which he referred to simply as *klong* (canal in Thai). However, these networks were almost solely for transportation, whereas irrigation was merely circumstantial. Homan van der Heide (1903) characterized the "*klong* system" as a primitive type of "inundation irrigation."

The main difference between perennial and inundation irrigation was the nature of water flow in the channels. In perennial irrigation, water constantly flowed through the channels from higher to lower places. For this reason, it also provided a constant flow of water to the fields. However, inundation irrigation only provided a sufficient flow temporarily, during the rainy season when the river swelled and overflowed its banks. It was thus a technology that supported irrigation under circumstances of naturally occurring flooding. Furthermore, contrary to perennial irrigation, inundation irrigation allowed water to flow in any direction, even from lowland to upland.

From Homan van der Heide's point of view, the central function of the Chao Phraya Dam was to organize water flows suitable for perennial irrigation. By damming the river flow at the top of the delta, the Chao Phraya Dam raised water levels of the upstream of the Noi, Tha Chin and the newly constructed Chainat-Pasak canal so that water in these channels flowed smoothly downstream – into networks of irrigation ditches. Given the extremely flat topology of the delta – where water, as noted, easily stagnates and occasionally even flows backwards – ensuring a smooth flow made raising the water level inevitable.

Living up to Homan van der Heide's vision, the Chao Phraya Dam has profoundly transformed the water flow of the entire delta. Now the water of the Chao Phraya Rivers System *basically* flows from upstream to downstream, from north to south, throughout the year. The dam thus enacts a certain type of land–water relation. It has transformed an unruly water flow into an ordered and stable one.

Homan van der Heide's vision of perennial irrigation was widely shared with other irrigation engineers at the time. And it has embedded a strong kind of normativity in the practice of irrigation engineers up to the present date. One can see this normativity in a certain aesthetics shared by irrigation engineers and hydrologists. For one thing, water management experts from the Royal Irrigation Department in charge of development and management of irrigation in Thailand often wondered why I wanted to study the Greater Chao Phraya Irrigation Project. One stated, for example that:

> It is not a cutting edge system! There is nothing interesting here (in the Chao Phraya system). You see, farmers have to pump up water from canals here because we don't have on-farm systems. If you want to see interesting things, you should go to latest irrigation systems in, for example, the Northeast Region. These newer systems are gravitational systems. It delivers water to each field through well-arranged on-farm systems.

Indeed, I often heard about the lack of "on-farm systems," networks of terminal irrigation channels that deliver water to individual plots, in the Chao Phraya system. Technical reports, too, often emphasize international efforts to install such systems in parts of the delta. Although these efforts have partly succeeded, in most of the delta farmers still have to pump water from the canals to irrigate their field.

According to this aesthetics, gravitational irrigation is seen as a superior form of irrigation. In gravitational systems, water is delivered by the constant and uniform force of gravity, rather than by the ad hoc pumping efforts of individual farmers. Thus, it functions like a carefully built machine driven by the universal force of gravity. Moreover, this aesthetic matches well with that of hydrological models, the major tool by which Royal Irrigation Department managers estimate and predict water flows. These models have evolved through longstanding efforts to estimate the relationship between rainfall and river discharge so that one can predict the size and timing of a river flow increase. As hydrology textbooks note, the prediction of river discharge is based on the hydraulic dynamic of water flows in the drainage basin. This is calculated from basic fluid dynamic equations, in which complex interactions between gravity and friction are major forces (Brutsaert 2005). Although one can complicate these models indefinitely by adding intensive rainfall, tidal effects or inundation models, they are fundamentally based on the force of gravity that *drains* water from upland to the sea.

The correspondence between perennial irrigation design and the concept of the drainage basin is indicative of the tangled relation between science and water management infrastructures. For one thing, the development of the concept of the drainage basin was deeply embedded in water management infrastructures such as irrigation systems. It is no secret to hydrologists that the possibility of demarcating the boundaries of water flows in order to measure them within drainage basins rests on water management infrastructures (Clifford 2011). These infrastructures include networks of measuring devices such as river discharge and rain gauges. These devices are often installed with other infrastructures for the control of water flow such as sluice gates and dams. Moreover, the hydrological notion of the drainage basin was itself developed via efforts to calculate the relationship between rainfall and river discharge, which was tightly tied with engineering endeavors such as the design of sewers (Todini 2011).

Perennial water infrastructures such as irrigation systems and urban sewers, which are literally huge machines driven by gravity, played a significant role in the shaping of the scientific notion of the drainage basin. The drainage basin that emerged out of these infrastructures became a conceptual framework, which allowed hydrology to grasp complex water flows on the earth's surface. As we shall now see, this concept eventually also became an important tool for the environmental sciences in general.

The drainage basin as an ecological unit

The emergence of the newly ordered flow in the Chao Phraya Delta corresponded with the growing influence of the drainage basin *beyond* the boundaries of hydrology. Several years after the completion of the dam, the drainage basin emerged as "the universal unit of landform" (Chorley 1969).

The importance of the drainage basin rests on an understanding of the driving forces in the formation of landforms. Modern geomorphology understands various landforms such as plains, valleys, and mountains to be made by the erosion of large rocky landmasses by water, wind, and geo-chemical processes. The sediments created by erosion are transported by the runoff of rainwater to lower places and eventually gather in a river. The river then transports sediments to estuaries where the sediments settle in shallows and gradually form an alluvial plain. In this framework, the drainage basin acts as the integral unit within which not only hydrological processes but also various land-forming forces interact with each other, creating a variety of landforms, from mountain slopes to valleys and plains.

For geomorphology, in other words, the fundamental appeal of the drainage basin is its capacity to frame the physical interactions that shape landforms. It provides an explanation based on the laws of physics. Until World War II, the study of landforms was predominantly descriptive and there was no satisfying scientific explanation of their formation. In this context, the concept of the drainage basin became attractive because it offered a general framework for geomorphology. Scientists came to conceive of drainage basins as a kind of universal machine that, by combining land–water interactions such as erosion, transport, and sedimentation, could generate every known landform. This view tied hydrology and geomorphology together as partners in a scheme to develop a unified science of earth surface processes. In the 1960s, geomorphologists and hydrologists came to agree that the entire surface of the planet could in principle be divided into drainage basins (Chorley 1969).

Since its establishment as the universal unit of landform, the drainage basin has gained increasing prominence in water management and land use planning. Also, because of the centrality of water flow in the ecosystem, ecologists and environmental managers have increasingly adopted the drainage basin as a basic unit to understand ecological processes. The extended use in ecology, clearly exhibits the rather surprising capacity of the drainage basin for revealing hitherto unseen relations mediated by water flows both in and outside rivers. Interestingly, this revelation led to a critical reappraisal of water infrastructure designs that originally nurtured the development of the notion of drainage basin itself.

Due to the connection between hydrology and water management, the earlier drainage basin model tended to focus on river networks. In a sense this was inevitable because most of the reliable hydrological data was, and continues to be, collected from river discharge gauges. In these days, the drainage basin was often imagined as a water channel network, not unlike the Chao Phraya irrigation system itself. Additionally, as noted, the hydrological notion of the drainage basin, based on the calculation of the rainfall–discharge relation in particular, was also tightly connected to the design of sewers.

However, it has long been known that the entire rainfall does not flow directly into rivers. Some portion stays in the soil, some infiltrates the groundwater, some is consumed by plants and evaporates into the air, and some is used by people. In order to simulate the entire hydrological cycle, it was thus necessary to integrate different models that simulated these diverse processes. Since the 1960s, and with the development of computers, hydrologists have spent much energy to develop integrated "watershed models" that combine various sub-models to simulate the entire hydrological cycle. These models eventually became available to ecologists in various fields, and this led to the discovery of a new environmental problem stemming from the existing design of water infrastructures.

Since the 1990s, growing concerns over the environmental degradation of rivers running through urban regions has stimulated the expansion of research on the impact of urban environments on rivers, alongside increasing efforts to restore streams. Based on elaborate watershed models, scientists discovered the so-called "urban stream syndrome," designating the unfavorable influence of urban land use on river environment. These findings focus on the impact of certain land surfaces – for example, those covered by asphalt and concrete, which do not allow water to infiltrate into soil – on river ecosystems. Water flows more quickly on such impervious surfaces. Doing so, it collects chemical pollutants that otherwise remain in the soil and this leads to a higher concentration of pollutants in the river. In addition, sewage and storm water drainage collects and moves rainwater much faster than vegetated surfaces, leading to "flashy" hydrographic patterns (Walsh et al. 2005: 707). Such patterns are characterized by more frequent water-rising events that occur and recede suddenly. In urban areas, rainwater therefore flows into the river much faster, and in larger volumes, than previously. These flows cause significant disturbances to ecosystems and lead to decreases in biodiversity.

In this light, "unnatural" urban hydrological processes created by infrastructures such as sewer pipes and impervious surfaces have become central concerns for the river environment. Whereas the smooth water flow in irrigation ditches and sewers acted as a proper model for the earlier efforts to capture the mechanics of water flow in the drainage basin, the later elaboration of watershed models shed critical right on smooth flows of water through and upon infrastructures.

Urban watershed and an ecology of urban patchworks

This new concern, originally held by river ecologists, was quickly taken up by infrastructural designers. By the early 2000s, urban planners, architects and civil engineers saw the critique of traditional pipe networks as representing a fundamental shift of the logic of infrastructural design (Shannon 2013). Because the urban stream syndrome locates the major problem in the urban hydrographic pattern, the infrastructural challenge is fundamental. One can no longer imagine the solution to the urban stream syndrome to be a simple cleaning up of water. What is required is now seen to be the removal of pipes. But how is this possible?

This question has led to new collaborations between infrastructure designers and ecological scientists focusing on the sustainable future of cities. In these emergent collaborations, the watershed has been adopted as a framework for integrating ecology with the social sciences and design. The urban designer Paola Viganò (2013) notes that as the urban design principle has shifted from socio-economic function to ecological rationality, water flow has emerged as a central element in designing urban space and infrastructure. Because of water flows across the boundaries of cities, the watershed model also urges urban designers to locate the city within the larger socio-eco system of the drainage basin, connected by water flows (Thaitakoo and McGrath 2010).

At the same time, this shift introduces new temporal and spatial scales into urban design. In one sense, the demand to reduce impervious surface articulated by watershed models entails a reversal of the urbanization process. This has led urban designers to look at history and to less developed areas where modern infrastructural solutions have not been fully implemented. Aside from the history of major European cities, various forms of "indigenous water management" have become reference points for urban designers (Shannon 2013; McGrath 2013). Bangkok, which used to be known as the Venice of the

East, represents one such indigenous, non-Western model. Yet the massive modern transformation of the city, and the resulting co-existence of heterogeneous elements, has also made Bangkok illustrative of another kind of dynamic model. The intersection of Bangkok's often chaotic modernization with the river ecology and with traditional infrastructures has turned the city into an experimental site for ecological urban redesign.

Using terminology from the ecological studies of cities (Pickett et al. 2011), the Thai landscape architect Danai Thaitakoo and the New York-based urban planner Brian McGrath have characterized the extended urban area of Bangkok as exemplifying "the dynamic *liquid states* of *waterscape* urbanism" (Thaitakoo and McGrath 2010: 37, emphasis in original). Rather than focusing on the urban center, their analysis presents the entire delta area, including agricultural fringes, as a unit of waterscape dynamism. From this viewpoint, Bangkok appears as a modern terrestrial urban infrastructure "superimposed on a wet rice cultivation landscape" (McGrath and Thaitakoo 2005: 45).

This heterogeneous and patchy landscape serves as a model for new watershed urbanism in two different senses. On the one hand, traditional canal-centered townscapes found in the peripheral areas of Bangkok represent a form of indigenous town planning adaptive to changing water. In these areas, flood-adaptive houses on stilts sit along rivers, while canals with irrigated orchid or paddy fields are located behind. During floods, these houses on stilts remain on top of the water. Residents use boats to commute between the houses and nearby roads built on the dikes. These amphibious townscapes that deal with excess water without pipes have stimulated Thai, American, and Japanese architects by providing a model for flood-adaptive urban planning in the age of climate change (Thaitakoo and McGrath 2010; Morita 2015).

Meanwhile, the entire watershed, composed of an amphibious semi-agricultural periphery, terrestrial urban centers filled with high-rise buildings, industrial zones, and highway networks, serves as an experimental model for new ecological design. Ecological studies of cities conceptualize such urban ecosystems as a heterogeneous patchwork of "fine vegetation, bare soil, pavement and buildings" (Thaitakoo and McGrath 2010: 30). The central focus of this form of urban ecology is called "patch dynamics," and it centers on the interaction among such patches, mediated by water flows. To this line of thinking, Bangkok's messy patchwork of semi-agricultural townscape and urban centers represents an interesting experimental model for designing a sustainable patch dynamics. It is because of its incompleteness, as seen from a conventional urban planning viewpoint, that Bangkok and the Chao Phraya Delta can serve as experimental sites for envisioning future urban design.

The irony, of course, is that this experimental model rests on the predicament of the city, which was brought about by an earlier massive and rapid terrestrial transformation. From the 1970s it gradually became clear that the construction of terrestrial infrastructures fundamentally hindered the circulation of healthy water within Bangkok's existing canal network. Small canals were often cut or narrowed by landfill for road construction and clogged with waste collected by rainfall. These clogged canals diminished drainage capacity and turned into health hazards. Sustaining water flow in the small canals therefore became an important issue for both flood management and public health. Far from intended, the current patchy nature of the city was an unintended consequence of chaotic urban development.

Within emerging movements of urban ecological design, the drainage basin works to reframe urban space from solid and terrestrial to fluid and aquatic (Thaitakoo and McGrath 2010; Shannon 2013). Rather than a machine for collecting and draining water, the drainage basin has been repurposed as a stage for various physical, chemical, biological, and social processes. These processes interact with each other in ways that cut across scales and domains – such as the urban center and basin scales and ecology and architecture – sometimes to unforeseen effect. As many environmental experts now argue, the drainage basin offers a useful framework for foregrounding such unruly interactions (Newson 2009).

Conclusion

Since the early twentieth century, scientific concepts and water infrastructure have become ever more tightly interwoven. Exemplifying such entanglements, the drainage basin has transformed both scientific understandings of the environment and the view of infrastructures held by urban designers. Previously, perennial irrigation and other water infrastructures facilitated the development of the drainage basin as an analytical unit for hydrology, which eventually became "the universal unit of landform." This universal unit, in turn, transformed understandings of the infrastructural space of cities. Rather than huge machines, they came to be seen as patchy, heterogeneous ecosystems. For both imaginaries, however, the flow of water plays a central role in connecting various components and actors.

As the scientific concept of the drainage basin has revealed evermore water-mediated relations between a whole array of unexpected entities, this fluid relationality has begun to take on a moral value. Increasingly complex water flow made abundantly visible that human activities and infrastructures crucially affect non-human species in the river environment. What is presently at stake is not merely organizing flows smoothly and efficiently but also creating flows that are sufficiently slow, or even stagnant, to allow non-human species to thrive in the aquatic environment. Infrastructure has transformed into a space of cohabitation.

As we have seen, the constant tacking back and forth between the drainage basin and water infrastructure has reconfigured the conceptual and spatial relations between infrastructure and environment. Furthermore, it has also transformed relations between the center and periphery of technoscience. During previous times, the then emergent notion of the drainage basin was nested inside a mechanical vision of perennial irrigation. Presently, initiatives to redesign urban infrastructures are nested inside a model of the drainage basin that enables the articulation of hidden flows and unexpected connections behind their solid façades. After fifty years, that is, figure and ground have reversed. Moreover, the emergence of the urban watershed has led to what might be seen as an interesting postcolonial inversion in the Chao Phraya delta. About a hundred years ago, this was an amphibious landscape that was to be subjected to terrestrial transformation and Westernization, its fractural water flow requiring transformation into a perennial flow. At present the delta has morphed into a messy but productive experimental site for a new waterscape urbanism that may be a remedy for the problems that too smooth water flows cause in modern urban infrastructures.

This tangled history is testimony to the recursive relation between the scientific concept of the drainage basin and water infrastructure. This constant looping movement has transformed both the infrastructures and the environments co-inhabited by people and other species in Bangkok and the Chao Phraya.

Acknowledgment

This work was supported by JSPS KAKENHI Grant Number 24251017 and 15K12957 and the Institute for Research in Humanities, Kyoto University. I would like to thank Rachel Douglas-Jones, Christopher Gad, Brit Ross Winthereik, Marisa Leavitt, and members of the Technology in Practice Group at IT University of Copenhagen for their comments on the earlier version of this paper. My thanks also go to Casper Bruun Jensen for commenting on the paper and editing my English.

References

Brummelhuis, Han ten (2005) *King of the Waters: Homan van der Heide and the Origin of Modern Irrigation in Siam*. Leiden, Netherlands: KITLV Press.
Brutsaert, Wilfried (2005) *Hydrology: An Introduction*. New York: Cambridge University Press.
Chorley, Richard J. (1969) *Water, Earth and Man: A Synthesis of Hydrology, Geomorphology, and Socio-economic Geography*. London: Methuen.
Clifford, Nick (2011) "Rivers and drainage basins," in John A. Agnew and David N. Livingstone (eds) *The SAGE Handbook of Geographical Knowledge*. London: Sage.
McGrath, Brian (2013) "Slow, moderate, fast: Urban adaptation and change," in Steward T. Pickett, Mary L. Cadenasso, and Brian McGrath (eds) *Resilience in Ecology and Urban Design: Linking Theory and Practice for Sustainable Cities*. Dordrecht; London: Springer, pp. 231–252..
McGrath, Brian, and Danai Thaitakoo (2005) "Tasting the periphery: Bangkok's agri- and aquacultural fringe." *Architectural Design* 75(3): 43–51.
Morita, Atsuro (2016) "Infrastructuring the amphibious space: The interplay of aquatic and terrestrial infrastructures in the Chao Phraya delta in Thailand." *Science as Culture* 25(1): 117–140.
Morita, Atsuro, and Casper B. Jensen (forthcoming) "Delta ontologies: Infrastructural transformations in Southeast Asia." *Social Analysis*.

Newson, Malcolm David (2009) *Land, Water and Development: Sustainable and Adaptive Management of Rivers.* 3rd edn. London; New York: Routledge.

Pickett, S. T., M. L. Cadenasso, J. M. Grove, C. G. Boone, P. M. Groffman, E. Irwin, S. S. Kaushal, V. Marshall, B. P. McGrath, C. H. Nilon, R. V. Pouyat, K. Szlavecz, A. Troy, and P. Warren (2011) "Urban ecological systems: Scientific foundations and a decade of progress." *Journal of Environmental Management* 92(3): 331–362.

Pickett, Steward T., Mary L. Cadenasso, and Brian McGrath (2013) *Resilience in Ecology and Urban Design: Linking Theory and Practice for Sustainable Cities.* Dordrecht and London: Springer.

Shane, D. Grahame (2013) "Urban patch dynamics and resilience: Three London urban design ecologies," in Steward T. Pickett, Mary L. Cadenasso, and Brian McGrath (eds) *Resilience in Ecology and Urban Design: Linking Theory and Practice for Sustainable Cities.* Dordrecht; London: Springer, pp. 131–161.

Shannon, Kelly (2013) "Eco-engineering for water: From soft to hard and back," in Steward T. Pickett, Mary L. Cadenasso, and Brian McGrath (eds) *Resilience in Ecology and Urban Design: Linking Theory and Practice for Sustainable Cities.* Dordrecht; London: Springer, pp. 163–182.

Singh, Vijay P., and David A. Woolhiser (2002) "Mathematical modeling of watershed hydrology." *Journal of Hydrologic Engineering* 7(4): 270–292.

Takaya, Yoshikazu (1987) *Agricultural Development of a Tropical Delta: A Study of the Chao Phraya Delta.* Translated by Peter Hawkes. Honolulu: University of Hawaii Press.

Thaitakoo, Danai, and Brian McGrath (2010) "Bangkok liquid perception: Waterscape urbanism in the Chao Phraya river delta and implications to climate change adaptation," in Rajib Shaw and Danai Thaitakoo (eds) *Water Communities.* Bingley: Emerald Group Publishing, pp. 35–50.

Todini, E. (2011) "History and perspectives of hydrological catchment modelling." *Hydrology Research* 42(2/3): 73–85.

van der Heide, J. Homan (1903) *General Report on Irrigation and Drainage in the Lower Menam Valley.* Bangkok: Ministry of Agriculture.

Viganò, Paola (2013) "Urbanism and ecological rationality," in Steward T. Pickett, Mary L. Cadenasso, and Brian McGrath (eds) *Resilience in Ecology and Urban Design: Linking Theory and Practice for Sustainable Cities.* Dordrecht and London: Springer, pp. 407–426.

Walsh, Christopher J., Allison H. Roy, Jack W. Feminella, Peter D. Cottingham, Peter M. Groffman, and Raymond P. Morgan (2005) "The urban stream syndrome: current knowledge and the search for a cure." *Journal of the North American Benthological Society* 24(3): 706–723.

17 Multinatural infrastructure
Phnom Penh sewage

Casper Bruun Jensen

Over bar foods and beer in a Japanese *izakaya* in the Boeung Keng Kang district in Phnom Penh, I engage in leisurely conversation with Mr Inoue, a Japan International Cooperation Agency (JICA) specialist in urban infrastructure. Our discussion centers on a large project to upgrade the deteriorating sewage system of the inner city and the various problems and controversies surrounding this work. We talk of politicians, moto pathways, flooding, sewage treatment plants, the laying of pipes, and much else.

Thinking of roads, digging, and pipes, I recall having read recent news stories about Chinese cities, in which road intersections suddenly collapsed and massive, deep sinkholes opened up to the underground, right in the middle of busy cities.[1] Inoue has not heard these stories, but he is undaunted; he can imagine something of what causes them. He says that roads often follow old drained river ways, since they are natural pathways. However, underground rivers continue to run along the same paths. There may thus have been hollow cavities underneath new infrastructures. If, he says, roads are made of poor-quality materials and transport intensifies as it has done in Chinese cities, then the entire road may cave in, opening massive cracks that can swallow cars and buses. On a smaller scale he has seen this happening himself in the process of laying the new pipes in Phnom Penh.

Whereas an increasing and vigorous body of work focuses on the social and political dimensions of infrastructure (e.g. Anand 2011, Jensen and Winthereik 2013), on their symbols and imaginaries (e.g. Barker 2005, Sneath 2009, Larkin 2013), and on their organizational and technical dimensions (e.g. Bowker 1994, Pollock and Williams 2009), sinkholes indexes another kind of process, which STS scholars and anthropologists have explored to a lesser degree. These are processes that elicit what might be called the multinatural characteristics of infrastructure.

In common usage, infrastructures form the material basis for the provision of social services – as in roads and railroad tracks. Infrastructure has been viewed by conventional engineering and social science as a layer added on top of, or sunk into, nature. As 'first nature" becomes "covered over" by infrastructure, it is gradually severed from social experience. When people need water or heat, that is, they increasingly interact not with rivers or sun but with faucets and radiators. Thus, infrastructure turns into "second nature" (Bowker 1995). In the case of the sinkholes, however, it would be as valid to say that nature has become infrastructure as *vice versa*. In Inoue's rendition, roads often tend to follow dried riverbeds, and it is because of cavities underneath those beds that some roads are prone to reverting to quasi-natural states – taking the form of holes, uncannily opening up in the midst of urban space.

Alberto Corsin-Jimenez has recently developed the argument that infrastructure is neither a human "entitlement" nor simply a nonhuman object. What he refers to as the "right to infrastructure" defines a certain analytical sensibility, which facilitates an escape from "the human–nonhuman and epistemology–ontology dichotomies … by opening up the agential work of infrastructures as a source (an open source) of possibilities *in their own right*" (2014: 343).

In this chapter I suggest that such an escape demands even more than heeding the agency of *infrastructures*. It obliges the researcher to focus on the unstable, emergent interrelations between infrastructures, their human developers, and numerous other entities, such as animals and trees. One way of getting into view infrastructural capacities is by exploring how this motley multinatural array makes, sustains, and disrupts them. More decentered ethnographies and conceptualizations of infrastructure, I argue in the following, might shed light on the complex entwinement between infrastructures, the human and nonhuman worlds they produce, and their possibilities and dangers.

The present chapter experiments with such a decentered, multinatural mode of exposition. It takes the reader on a tour of Phnom Penh's sewage infrastructure in order to relativize the perspective from which infrastructure is seen or experienced – a relativization that does not refer to different groups of people but to the infrastructural work done by various kinds of nonhuman agent: trees, bacteria, sludge, water plants, and cockroaches. The result is a series of figure–ground switches, in which nature and culture not only begin to hybridize but in which their descriptive and analytical relevance quickly begins to fade.

Ultimately, like sinkholes, they collapse.

Sewage

Sinkholes occur in consequence of relations between the eroding force of water, the material qualities of gravel and earth, and the load of traffic. This imagery is one of entities external to one another. Nature and society intersect at the point of infrastructure, yet as the ground collapses the two re-emerge as wholly distinct. In the case of sewage systems, however, this image, too, collapses rather quickly.

Phnom Penh's sewage infrastructure is in a fairly acute state of disorganization. Long-term neglect due to the civil war and lack of bureaucratic organization and of funds means that only part of the city is served by the sewage system. Many pipes are leaking, clogged, or missing. The result is that waste does not flow smoothly. During regular periods of heavy rain the city

Multinatural infrastructure 229

floods. The JICA project for sewage improvement, conducted in collaboration with Phnom Penh city hall and Japanese contractors is meant to improve this state of affairs. It does so by replacing old pipes, adding to the network and building treatment plants and pumps, all of which entails complex social, political, and technical arrangements (see Jensen 2016). Yet, something is also going on *inside* the pipes.

Underneath Phnom Penh's roads, in the pipes, or sometimes next to them, in open sewer channels, flows liquid sludge. It is not particularly nice to look at and worse to smell, as I had occasion to realize, joining an "educational trip" organized by JICA experts into the sewers. Outfitted with protection helmets to match sandals and shorts, our small group passed no-entry signs and fences at one of the locations where new pipes were in the process of being connected to the existing sewage network. Descending a ramshackle staircase with loose scaffolding, this little troupe of curious outsiders, NGOs consultants, officials, trainees, and a single STS ethnographer toured underneath the city streets (Figure 17.1).

It was dark down there, though sharp white lights lit part of the interior. Khmer workers, scarves wrapped around their faces to protect against dust, dirt, and the unpleasant smell, were in the process of finalizing this particular bit of new piping (Figure 17.2). At the end of the new 50-meter section, a barrier had been erected to prevent the sewage flow entering from the side of the already functioning pipe. When the section was ready, the barrier would be removed and the liquid sludge would flow into the new pipe section.

Figure 17.1 Entering the Phnom Penh sewer system

Figure 17.2 Inside the sewage pipe

The water was still and black. Even so, the interior of the underground pipes is awash with life. Comprised of excrement, urine, rainwater, foodstuffs, offal, chemical compounds from medicine, insect repellent and cleaning stuff, motor oil, and much else, the waste is organic, at least in part, and home to thriving bacteria cultures of all sorts.

That sewage sludge is not a single thing became visually obvious as we proceeded to visit a new sediment chamber, built behind the Royal Palace, next to the riverside. The area basically consisted of an open stream of water, running a circular route towards a meshed gate where sediment would filter.

The channel had been carefully dug to prevent cutting down a magnificent old tree, growing on a small patch of land in the middle. Sewage entered the stream from different pipes. And how different it looked: one stream pitch black, another brownish, yet another almost milky white. These streams comprise mixtures of culture and nature in liquid form, their composition highly variable (see also Schneider 2011: 89, 113). One stream might constitute an environmental health hazard even as another is more or less harmless. In the sediment chamber they are combined and led on as new mixtures (Figure 17.3).

Bacteria

Sludge flows through the complicated arrangement of pipes. At least ideally. For part of the problem with the pipes of Phnom Penh is that they have never moved sewage very well. The article "Noses bent by city sewage," published

Multinatural infrastructure 231

Figure 17.3 Rebuilding a sedimentation chamber

in the *Phnom Penh Post* in 2001,[2] explained that most houses use locally built septic tanks. This was still the case in 2014. These tanks tend to overflow during the rainy season, turning the streets into a "stagnant e-coli rich bacterial soup" in which people nevertheless continue to wash, work, and play. Nobody disputes the overall tenor of this description and the prevalence of gastro-intestinal disease and other water and airborne ailments is generally recognized. It is disputed, though, whether the problem is worse in the dry or rainy season.

Mr Inoue, JICA's sewage expert, insists that the main problem is not flooding but drying. It is true, he says, that the water that inundates streets in the rainy season is dirty. But, not least due to JICA's long-term project to improve the sewage system, begun in 1999 and still continuing, at a cost of at least 450M$, flooding levels are in fact decreasing. New piping has been laid in central areas, sludge suckers have been acquired to prevent clogging, and new pumping stations have been built along the riverside and elsewhere to get rid of excess water. Even as these efforts are compromised by other initiatives, especially the draining of lakes and marshes in order to clear space for upscale residential areas and shopping malls, inundation is slowly decreasing. No, Inoue says, the real problem is the dry season, when the flow stops.

During this period, large quantities of semi-dried sewage simply get stuck in the pipes. Perhaps it lives quite a satisfying existence there. But even as it does not move as intended by engineers – southward towards the marshes of Phnom Penh – it is not quite immobile. Instead it evaporates and moves *upwards*. The stench of sewage wafts across the scorching hot city streets, engulfing shops, motos, and homes. And, so Inoue insists, it is these foul odors that are the true bringers of disease. The pumping stations built by JICA therefore also have the task of ensuring adequate movement of sewage in times of drought.

In his seminal paper "Second nature, once removed," Geof Bowker (1995) argued for the importance of analyzing interactions between first nature and second nature (infrastructure), but *also* between second nature and organizational-bureaucratic representations of it (which he called *second nature, once removed*, to emphasize that turning infrastructure into second nature required long trails of bureaucratic documentation). In this process of mediation, Bowker wrote, "we can trace in operation the convergence between nature and the bureaucratic representation of second nature in forms, flow charts, and other representational devices" (1995: 63).

Such efforts are everywhere manifest in the JICA project. It requires a broad range of plans, budgets, forms of evidence, and technical documentation to articulate links between flows of water and sludge, networks of pipes, locations of pumping stations, and projections of decrease in illness and inundation. Indeed, it would be utterly impossible to imagine the Niroth water treatment plant, which opened in 2013 with a 135,000 m^3/day treatment capacity, filtration unit and a tank capacity of 23,000 m^3, without a complex set of administrative and engineering plans.[3] Certainly bacteria live inside pipes and treatment plants, but these infrastructures in turn depend on trails of documentation.

Nevertheless, inside Niroth, there they are, the bacteria, and they are neither dominated nor fully specified by paper trails. Inside the plant, pipes lead different composites into a basin, where solids sink to the bottom while grease and other substances float. After separating these substances, the leftover liquids are treated – consumed by – populations of bacteria. And *their* leftovers are flushed.

Though pivotal to public health outcomes, these interactions between bacteria and sludge are quite peripheral to commentators and politicians, if not, of course, to specialists in sewage treatment (Schneider 2011). They rarely lead to controversy or even garner public attention (Harvey 2013; Hird this volume). Operating at a scale imperceptible to the otherwise discerning public busily scrutinizing JICA's projects, the organisms inhabiting the Niroth basin quietly solve social and environmental problems.

We might say that the bacteria are hybrid entities put to work to solve hybrid problems. After all, sewage is itself a mixture generated by changing sociocultural practices and demographic changes in conjunction with changing climates and environments. Inside Niroth's basis and tanks, bacteria work upon bacteria in order to deal with socio-natural problems. But though the main protagonists are nonhuman, the effects of their actions are felt by people.

Yet, far from everything comes together in the manner wished for by planners and bureaucrats. For far from all flows makes it to the treatment plants.

Loops of nutrition

In the context of Johannesburg's collapsing infrastructure, AbdouMaliq Simone (2004) examined how people come to take on infrastructural qualities. On the one hand, people need to find ways of providing the services that the ruined city infrastructure fails to offer. On the other hand, becoming infrastructure implies a kind of neutralization of social identities. Having become infrastructured, for example, the intense dislike Nigerians and South Africans may feel for one another "does not really stop them from doing business with each other, sharing residences, or engaging in other interpersonal relations" (2004: 419). Thus, as infrastructure, people manage to form relatively stable patterns that allow them to pursue their goals.

Though compelling, Simone's argument leaves out of the picture any discussion of the materialities that after all still crowd urban spaces, Johannesburg included. There is but a short step from recognizing infrastructure as "ruined" to not seeing it at all. Once "regular" infrastructure has been rendered invisible, the ground is clear for examining the infrastructural qualities of people. Yet even in states of ruination, material infrastructures remain, and they remain lively.

Phnom Penh's sewage system, for example, though in many ways ruined, survived not only the civil war and the Khmer Rouge period but also a subsequent, decade-long lack of attention and maintenance. It did not do its job well, according to many measures. Still, cracked and leaking pipes, full of life, continued their secret existence[4] under the city's increasingly busy streets. Only occasionally did they show their cards, bursting and flooding neighborhoods with dirty liquids. Yet, even in the days of total disrepair, not *all* sewage flooded the streets. So where did it go?

Geography speaks. Phnom Penh, Penh's Hill, named after its legendary founder, is located on a stretch of elevated land, created by the Mekong, Tonle Sap, and Bassac rivers. The most pronounced slope of Penh's hill runs south. Phnom Penh's piping system is therefore also oriented in this direction. Most of the city's sewage, estimated in 2008 to consist of a daily output of "234 tons of feces, 2,335 cubic meters of urine and 8,154 cubic meters of gray water,"[5] ends up in a series of marshy lakes, Boeung Trabek, Boeung Tumpun and Boeung Choeung Ek (infamous for Khmer Rouge mass killings in the 1970s). After filtering through these lakes, the "gray water" eventually reaches the river.

This may sound like bad news, but recent evaluations have drawn the conclusion that the lakes function rather well as bio-filters, "effectively reducing pollutant loads in Phnom Penh's wastewater before it reaches the Bassac River."[6] Operating akin to an ad hoc "natural infrastructure," the marshes deliver "critical services for human communities and economies" (Carse 2012: 540).

Officially the southern marshes are government-owned, but this has not prevented people moving in from rural areas from building squalid houses at their edges. The stench there is almost unbearable, the water dirty and dangerous but also extremely nutritious. In Boeung Tumpun and Boeung Choeung Ek, water plants, including lotus and morning glory, therefore grow easily and in abundance. Indeed, it is just these plants that absorb and naturally cleanse most of the sewage before it enters the Bassac River. The natural infrastructure for Phnom Penh sewage cleansing consists of "dense morning glory fields" gardened by squatters.[7]

It is no surprise that squatters, living, fishing, and swimming in this noxious yet oddly beautiful environment, are prone to disease. A WHO report identifies diarrhea, worms, and protozoan infections as common among the local population. From the point of view of "natural infrastructure," however, it is especially interesting to observe the *loops* through which this system works. For the "dense fields of morning glory" are not grown for personal consumption. Instead, they are harvested and transported back to Phnom Penh's markets, where they are turned into delicious-smelling street meals, sold to restaurants or for home cooking.[8]

Government reports as well as scientific articles point to the presence of e.coli and parasites in morning glory grown in the southern marshes.[9] Human waste, transported by leaking, lively pipes, is bio-filtered by plants, protecting the river but making their growers sick, and eventually ending up on Phnom Penh's dinner tables, ready to begin a new infrastructural iteration. Within this infrastructural loop, the fields of morning glory in dirty waters operate akin to Jacques Derrida's (1981) *pharmakon*, at once poison and cure.

The ambiguous qualities of this natural infrastructure are vividly exhibited by the ongoing project to turn Boeung Tumpun into landfill by 2020, presumably to be sold to private investors. On the one hand, it is hard to regret the demolition of this stinking marsh, dangerous to inhabit and growing disease-ridden produce. On the other hand, landfill will inevitably lower the bio-filtering capacity of the marshlands and this will lead to heightened levels of pollution of the Bassac River. It will also diminish the water-absorbing capacities of the land, likely increasing flood levels in southern Phnom Penh. In this way it works directly against the JICA sewage and flood protection project.

Considering people as infrastructure, Simone takes an interest in the "incomplete, truncated, or deteriorated forms and temporalities" of seemingly incompatible forms of rationality and modes of production (Simone 2004: 410). With some minor but consequential adjustments this formulation makes excellent sense in the context of Phnom Penh's sewage infrastructures. They are about incomplete, truncated, and deteriorated forms of *relationality* (rather than rationality) and modes of *co-existence* (rather than modes of production). Relations and forms of co-existence, that is, between entities that are *much else besides human*.

Trees

Sludge flows inside the pipes, a teeming mass of organic and non-organic entities, whose underground activities affect peoples' lives on the ground in different ways. When the flow is obstructed it creates health problems as toxic

Multinatural infrastructure 235

fumes engulf city quarters. When the flow is regular, sewage turns into food for morning glories, which end up in the stomachs of Phnom Penh's population. And when the flow is beyond capacity, it leads to floods that impede normal city life, though in one sense, of course, this *is* normal city life. Whatever is going on underneath is thus highly consequential for what occurs above. But though the *processes and interactions* that generate these outcomes are mostly hidden from view, except to select specialists, the negative *effects* are broadly discussed. Thus, newspaper articles regularly criticize the city hall and JICA for their inadequate efforts to improve infrastructure.

In fact, though, significant efforts go into just such improvement, and they are orchestrated not least by Mr Inoue and his colleagues. In collaboration with the Phnom Penh Water Supply Authority, JICA is engaged in a large-scale and long-term project for flood protection and drainage improvement. In 1999, when JICA began the project, the focus was on improving and constructing sluiceways, reinforcing dikes, and making pumping stations in the south-west area. The second phase turned to the north-east and built underground reservoirs, pumping stations, riverbank revetments, and an interceptor pipe along the Tonle Sap River. During the third phase, coming to an end in 2015, an old sediment chamber has been rebuilt, cleaning equipment for the pipes have been acquired (sludge suckers and high-water jet machines), and the gradual repair and extension of pipes continues.[10]

In spite of all these activities, the project is not met with unequivocal praise, and at the surface level of Phnom Penh's streets, the reason is not hard to see (Jensen 2016). Wherever one goes in the central area of the city, parts of roads, sidewalks and intersections are fenced off. Inside the fences, workers with hard hats, surrounded by heavy equipment, dig into the ground, uncovering old pipes, repairing, fixing, replacing. When I described descending into the pipes, it was underneath one of these sites, next to the Olympic stadium. This kind of work is highly visible and it frustrates people. For one thing it invariably slows traffic, for the pipes always run under roads. For another it prevents people from enjoying easy access to their homes or shops. In addition, the holes are magnets for flies and mosquitoes that enjoy the humidity.

From the point of view of JICA project workers, these tangible irritants give rise to frustrating exercises in public relation management. As they see it, temporary and minor problems visible at the surface (traffic jams, pipe replacements) cast shadows over the long-term objectives and real achievements of the project (preventing floods and disease). Whereas intrusion into the underground creates a "visible transformation of dark surroundings" (Sneath 2009: 75), this visibility also obscures. Particularly obscure to the public eye are the very real difficulties inherent in achieving infrastructural improvements *amidst* these dark surroundings.

The fact that sewage infrastructure is something like the dark and invisible underbelly of visible urban lives makes large-scale, long-term intervention in the crowded city-space a very hard sell to skeptical observers. They would prefer infrastructure to act as modern infrastructure is *supposed to*: invisibly but efficiently servicing human needs rather than very visibly invading urban space. In fact, however, one of JICA's other problems is that the sewage pipes *do* invisibly and efficiently serve *other nonhuman needs*. Those of trees, for example.

The architectural and urban outline of modern Phnom Penh owes much to the French colonial period (1867–1949). Parks, villas and boulevards were inspired by French urbanity. Known as the "Paris of the East," Phnom Penh reputedly caused a visiting Charlie Chaplin to compare its avenues to "little sisters" of the Champs Elysées.[11] It is underneath these avenues that pipes now run. Majestic trees line the French-inspired avenues. And it is the needs of these trees that are quite efficiently served by the pipes. Seeking nourishment, their roots branch downward. Finding no underwater streams, instead they touch upon sewage pipes.

Even small flowers are known to crack asphalt to get out into the open – and the material of the original Soviet pipes was never of the best quality anyway. Picture the upward movements of flowers in reverse: massive roots working downwards to get into the pipes. Clearly this is not a fair competition. Just like the morning glories of the southern swamps, Phnom Penh's beautiful trees also find nourishment in the sewage. Only they do so before it has left the pipes. And thus the sewage maintenance crew is waging a constant low-intensity battle against trees. At the ground level these skirmishes are invisible. They take place on the inside, where roots are cut and materials reinforced. And this is how it must be, for imagine the uproar if JICA was to advocate felling the trees of the city in the name of *sewage*.

In Ashley Carse's story, the landscapes surrounding the Panama Canal *become* infrastructure that delivers services to humans. "As infrastructure," he says:

> nature is irreducible to a non-human world already "out there." It must, in its proponents' terms, be built, invested in, made functional, and managed. This is an active and inherently political process. As nature *becomes* infrastructure through work, human politics and values are inscribed on the landscape, much as they are embedded in arrangements of steel and concrete.
>
> (Carse 2012: 540)

Yet, if one considers the case of Phnom Penh's trees this sequence can be rearranged. For example, as nature (food source for trees and morning glories), infrastructure is irreducible to a human world. It is not just that infrastructure must be built, invested in and so forth, but that it is inhabited, exploited and lived by nonhuman others. More than an issue of human politics shaping what gets to count as nature, this is a process in which innumerable entities invisibly transform infrastructures *and* human environments. Though human politics and values are surely embedded in infrastructures, as Carse and many others insist, once infrastructure becomes a source of nutrition for trees, the values and politics inscribed on the urban landscape cease to be wholly based on the human.

Dislodging an infrastructural worldview

> Who are they, these beings so different from us and from each other? What do they do? What worlds do they make? What do we make of them? How do we live with them?
>
> (Raffles 2011: 3)

This paper has offered a decentered perspective on Phnom Penh's sewage infrastructure. It has done so by arguing that this infrastructure is constituted not only by technology, paper trails and social interests but also by the activities of a broad range of other entities. The sewage infrastructure is made, sustained, and disrupted by this multinatural constituency.

On the one hand, this infrastructure *depends on* flows of water, sludge, and the cleansing capacities of bacteria cultures. Yet, the sludge flowing under the streets of Phnom Penh's and the trees that intrude into the piping system also have seriously *destabilizing effects*, not only on the pipes, which leak or break, but also on the health of the city's inhabitants.

Writing about people as infrastructure, AbdouMaliq Simone wrote that urban spaces are imagined as "functional destinations" (2004: 408). "There are to be few surprises, few chances for unregulated encounters, as the city is turned into an object like a language." This is a nice statement of the modernist ideal of infrastructural convergence, so appealingly analyzed by Geof Bowker (1995). But this was only ever a dream and a promise, not infrastructural reality. Dislodging this idealist view (pace Strathern 1985), this paper has elicited some of the multinatural relations that constitutes the actually operating sewage infrastructure of Phnom Penh.

Describing people as infrastructure, Simone's creative analysis highlighted the making of "social compositions across a range of singular capacities and needs" (2004: 410). In a "process of conjunction" these compositions came to operate in lieu of material infrastructure. As I have suggested, however, the agents doing infrastructural things together are much else than human. Indeed, the view of people as infrastructure can be accepted only if interpreted in terms of Amerindian perspectivism (Viveiros de Castro 2004) according to which *very many things, sludge and morning glories included, might turn out to be people.*

The point is obviously not about the insignificance of humans, either as planners or builders of infrastructure, or as actors that live with them on a daily basis. If the present chapter has refrained from taking human perspectives, it is rather due to a conviction that there is much more to learn about the workings and effects of infrastructure than what can be captured by such perspectives, no matter how varied. No matter how detailed, human-centered analyses revolving around politics (as conventionally understood), social organization, or cultural meaning-making, offer no help to what goes on inside the pipes, amongst water plants, or in bacteria colonies, and the many ways in which these activities loop back and affect life in the city (see also Jensen and Morita 2016).

The decentered approach with which I have experimented thus sharpens two interrelated arguments, which I believe are broadly relevant for the further strengthening of STS and anthropological studies of infrastructure.

First, even as people and societies are instrumental in building and maintaining infrastructures, they are also continuously shaped by them. However this shaping tends to occur *silently* and, to a significant degree, to the side of human intervention or even awareness.

Second, infrastructure is *made up of* an extremely varied set of entities. It is not simply that bacteria, sludge or morning glory are "connected" with Phnom Penh's sewage infrastructure understood as "in itself" a complex technical arrangement. Rather, water plants, trees and sludge are *integral* to the infrastructure. They are part of making and sustaining it, even as they also disrupt it. People, too, are *folded into* this multinatural infrastructure. Like other organisms, they are shaped in innumerable ways by its loops, paths, and relations.

On the final stop on the underground tour of Phnom Penh's sewage systems, our small group is taken to a pumping station by the riverside. During times of flood, massive pumps force vast quantities of rain and floodwater back into the river. In the dry season, the huge pipes are damp and smelly but quiet. It is hard to imagine them filled to capacity with wildly flowing water.

Something moves, barely, on the walls. I walk over, using my camera to get a bit of light – and step back in momentary disgust. The walls are covered by colonies of cockroaches. Hundreds, thousands of cockroaches, everywhere. They too make their lives within infrastructures. Who knows what happens to them when the flood comes?

Figure 17.4 Entering the pumping channel

Multinatural infrastructure 239

Figure 17.5 Underneath the pumping station at Phnom Penh riverside

Figure 17.6 Cockroach colony living inside flooding infrastructure

Acknowledgments

This work was supported by Japanese Society for the Promotion of Science (JSPS) KAKENHI Grant Number 24251017 and the Institute for Research in Humanities, Kyoto University. I gratefully acknowledge the constructive comments of Ashley Carse, Hugh Raffles and Stefan Helmreich, and especially of my co-editors, Penny Harvey and Atsuro Morita.

Notes

1 See e.g. Sam Webb (2014) "Carnage! Giant sinkhole opens up under Chinese parking lot and takes all the cars with it," July 9. www.dailymail.co.uk/news/article-2686237/Car-nage-Giant-sinkhole-opens-Chinese-parking-lot-takes-cars-it.html (accessed October 31, 2014).
2 Bainbridge, Bill and Bou Saroeun (2001) "Noses bent by city sewage." *The Phnom Penh Post*, March 16. www.phnompenhpost.com/national/noses-bent-city-sewage (accessed September 2, 2014).
3 See JICA press release. June 11, 2013. "Phnom Penh Water Supply Extends to 1.7M Residents – Inauguration Ceremony of Niroth Water Supply Facilities on June 4th, 2013." www.jica.go.jp/cambodia/english/office/topics/press130611.html (accessed October 31, 2014).
4 Secret existence is no exaggeration. To this day Phnom Penh city hall has no complete maps of the pipelines. Apparently they vanished with the civil war. In collaboration with JICA, city hall is now gradually trying to piece together knowledge of whether the older pipes run.
5 Otis, Daniel (2013) "Putrid Lakes Offer Sweet Relief to a City Lacking Water Treatment Plants." *Next City*, November 18. http://nextcity.org/daily/entry/putrid-lakes-offer-sweet-relief-to-a-city-lacking-water-treatment-plants/ (accessed September 2, 2014).
6 Ibid.
7 Ibid.
8 Similar cases have been reported in Mexico City (Rosas et al. 1984), and the phenomenon can likely be found elsewhere. I thank Ashley Carse for this information.
9 Irvine, Kim N., et al. (n.d.) "Spatial Patterns of E. Coli and Detergents in the Boeng Cheung Ek Treatment Wetland, Phnom Penh, Cambodia." http://geography.buffalostate.edu/sites/geography.buffalostate.edu/files/uploads/Documents/publication7.pdf (accessed October 31, 2014).
10 JICA Topics and Events. October 28, 2013. "JICA, City of Phnom Penh, and Local Residents Cooperate Together to Combat Flood in Phnom Penh – Flood Protection & Drainage Improvement in Phnom Penh (Phase 3)." www.jica.go.jp/cambodia/english/office/topics/131028.html (accessed October 31, 2014).
11 National Museum of Cambodia. n.d. "Streetscapes of Phnom Penh: A Leisurely Architectural Exploration." www.cambodiamuseum.info/en_information_visitors/streetscapes.html (accessed October 31, 2014).

References

Anand, Nikhil (2011) "PRESSURE: The PoliTechnics of water supply in Mumbai," *Cultural Anthropology* 26(4): 542–564.
Barker, Joshua (2005) "Engineers and political dreams: Indonesia in the satellite age," *Current Anthropology* 46(5): 703–727.

Bowker, Geoffrey C. (1994) *Science on the Run: Information Management and Industrial Geophysics at Schlumberger, 1920–1940*. Cambridge, MA and London: MIT Press.
Bowker, Geoffrey C. (1995) "Second nature once removed: Time, space and representations," *Time and Society* 4(1): 47–66.
Carse, Ashley (2012) "Nature as infrastructure: Making and managing the Panama watershed," *Social Studies of Science* 42(4): 539–563.
Corsin-Jimenez, Alberto (2014) "The right to infrastructure: A prototype for open source urbanism," *Environment and Planning D* 32(2): 342–362.
Derrida, Jacques (1981) *Dissemination*. London: Athlone.
Harvey, Penny (2013) "The Material Politics of Solid Waste," in Penny Harvey (ed.) *Objects and Materials*. London: Routledge, pp. 61–72.
Jensen, Casper Bruun (2015) "Experimenting with political materials: Environmental infrastructures and ontological transformations," *Distinktion: Journal of Scandinavian Social Theory* (special issue: Political Materials) 16(1): 17–30.
Jensen, Casper Bruun (2016) "Pipe dreams: Activity trails, infra-reflexivity and sewage in Phnom Penh," *Ethnos* (special issue: Infrastructures as Ontological Experiments). DOI: 10.1080/00141844.2015.1107608.
Jensen, Casper Bruun and Atsuro Morita (2016) "Infrastructures as ontological experiments," *Ethnos* (special issue: Infrastructures as Ontological Experiments). DOI: 10.1080/00141844.2015.1107607.
Jensen, Casper Bruun and Brit Ross Winthereik (2013) *Monitoring Movements in Development Aid: Recursive Partnerships and Infrastructures*. Cambridge, MA and London: MIT Press.
Larkin, Brian (2013) "The politics and poetics of infrastructure," *Annual Review of Anthropology* 42: 327–343.
Pollock, Neil and Robin Williams (2009) *Software and Organisations: The Biography of the Enterprise-Wide System or How SAP Conquered the World*. London and New York: Routledge.
Raffles, Hugh (2010) *Insectopedia*. New York: Vintage Books.
Rosas, I., A. Báez and M. Coutino (1984) "Bacteriological Quality of Crops Irrigated with Wastewater in the Xochimilco Plots, Mexico City, Mexico," *Applied and Environmental Microbiology* 47(5): 1074–1079.
Schneider, Daniel (2011) *Hybrid Nature: Sewage Treatment and the Contradictions of the Industrial Ecosystem*. Cambridge, MA and London: MIT Press.
Simone, AbduouMaliq (2004) "People as infrastructure: Intersecting fragments in Johannesburg," *Public Culture* 16(3): 407–429.
Sneath, David (2009) "Reading the signs by Lenin's light: Development, divination and metonymic fields in Mongolia," *Ethnos* 74(1): 72–90.
Strathern, Marilyn (1985) "Dislodging a world view: Challenge and counter-challenge in the relationship between feminism and anthropology," *Australian Feminist Studies* 1: 1–25.
Viveiros de Castro, Eduardo (2004) "Exchanging perspectives: The transformation of objects into subjects in Amerindian ontologies," *Common Knowledge* 10(3): 463–484.

18 Burial and resurrection in the Anthropocene
Infrastructures of waste

Myra J. Hird

Introduction

In the fifteen years since Paul Crutzen and Eugene F. Stoermer (2000) published their bid in the International Geosphere-Biosphere Programme's newsletter to officially name the Anthropocene – as epoch, as symbol, as call-to-action, as intellectual and cultural turn – it has become a veritable growth industry. As a concept, the term Anthropocene signals the end of the Holocene and the point at which human activity has intersected, in its significance and magnitude, with planetary, geophysical forces. Until now, pundits have vacillated as to where to place the proverbial if not literal spike. Some say it was the late seventeenth century's Industrial Revolution when the accelerated extraction and burning of fossil fuels began to take place. Others place it some 8,000 years earlier in the Neolithic, with the clearing of forests for agriculture. Still others suggest an even longer, deeper Anthropocene, staking a claim for the Promethean moment of harnessing fire and widespread use of landscape burning. Until recently, Crutzen had been of the opinion that the Anthropocene began with the large-scale extraction of fossil fuels, but he recently changed his mind. He now places "the real start of the Anthropocene" on July 16, 1945 – the Trinity detonation – and its fallout, radioactive waste. And even more recently, the Subcommission on Quaternary Stratigraphy Working Group has agreed: "It's a well defined spot in time – it's a big historical event," according to Jan Zalasiewicz, Chair of the Working Group (Monastersky 2015).

The piously named code for this first atomic bomb testing is most commonly attributed to J. Robert Oppenheimer, who is quoted as using the term in reference to one of John Donne's devotional poems, "Holy Sonnet XIV: Batter My Heart, Three-Personed God." Steeped in Christian legacy, the Anthropocene may be the material and symbolic mark of our species' original sin. In some sense, the Anthropocene recognizes humanity's fall from Eden as that moment at which our thirst for knowledge – eating of the proverbial forbidden fruit – transmogrified into an Enlightenment dissociation of *homo sapiens* from nature; a parting that both made possible and vindicated the Great Acceleration and its industrial, corporate, and global wake. Seeming to take this further,

Oppenheimer is recorded in the 1965 television documentary *The Decision to Drop the Bomb* quoting the Hindu script from the Bhagavad Gita "'Now I am become death, destroyer of worlds.' I suppose we all thought that one way or another" (1944). According to Judeo-Christian scripture, the fall of Man brings mortality to humanity: now the Anthropocene contemplates our extinction.

Whether it is the large-scale industrial use of fossil fuels (a form of necro-waste formed from the mainly anaerobic decomposition of buried dead organisms), the Trinity detonation or any of the subsequent nuclear detonations that deposited radioactive waste into the stratosphere, or the ubiquitous dumps and landfills that proliferate the globe archiving a time line of extraction, consumption, and disposal – a strong case can be made for waste as *the* signature of the Anthropocene: the material and symbolic mark of our original sin. This chapter will consider waste as a particular form of capitalist neoliberal burial, and more recently, resurrection. I will argue there is both a denial of consumption's fallout – waste's management encourages us to forget in order to recommit our sins – and a hopeful, if naïve, rebirthing as our buried discards are resurrected for profit.

Burial

Middens inventory our unwanted past and in many regions of the world have survived modernity in the form of open dumps; the infrastructure on which grows what Mike Davis (2007) calls our "planet of slums." In so-called developed nations, modern landfills, and to a much lesser degree incinerators (some of which are energy-from-waste facilities) have replaced open dumping. Touted by the incineration industry and some governments as a greener/cleaner solution, incinerators nevertheless produce an excess, a remainder – fly ash and some forms of bottom ash – that are inevitably buried amongst the heady mix of materials that make up the abject landfill. Mining companies consider 95 % to 99.99 % of the material they extract from the earth to be waste, and this mammoth debris is either left on the landscape or reburied. Such is the case, for instance, with Canada's Giant Mine, where approximately 237,000 tonnes of arsenic trioxide dust is set to be reburied in the mine using the frozen block method, whereby mining waste is frozen in perpetuity, with the hope that a future generation will safely resolve this ongoing waste issue (Hird 2015). This extraction and reburial resembles the logic of deep geological repositories that temporarily in perpetuity store radioactive waste as part of the material fallout of our nuclear legacy. And in some developed nations – Canada's Arctic for instance – waste remains fully present on and in the landscape, where military, industrial, and municipal waste mingles with Inuit, flora, and fauna. In these regions, waste is a symptom of a violent colonial legacy and ongoing capitalist venture in resource development (Hird and Zahara, forthcoming; Scott 2008).

Prior to the Industrial Revolution, individual cartage and disposal operators in some regions of the world began to haul our discarded objects away, introducing a new form of governance that emphasized waste's isolation from community life. As the sheer volume and diversity of waste increased, much larger companies and eventually multinational corporations usurped small operators. These publicly traded corporations invested heavily in all aspects of waste's management: indeed, they have been instrumental in defining waste as something that can and should be *managed* (as opposed to decreased). Globally, waste is big business – not only is haulage and disposal a billion-dollar industry, but the land used for landfills is so lucrative that in 2001 Bill Gates became the largest shareholder in Republic Services Inc., which owns and operates landfills across the United States. As Microsoft's profits have declined steadily in the last decade, Gates's waste business has increased by over 45 % (Bélanger 2007).

Multinational waste management corporations operating in tandem with local governments increasingly ask members of the public to accede to prescribed assessment exercises that circumscribe the parameters to, for example, discussions of "end-of-pipe" responses (i.e. disposal). Once this key parameter is set in advance, discussions are further circumscribed to decisions on a limited number of sites, technologies, consultation and discussion events, and consultation time frames (Ali 1999; Coninck et al. 1999; Dodds and Hopwood 2006; Einsiedel et al. 2001; Healy 2010; Petts 1998, 2001). These corporations specialize in all facets of waste processing, from waste technology assessment, siting, construction, operations and monitoring to closure, and aftercare. With on-site engineers and scientists, strong networks with government, and sophisticated, well-budgeted, in-house public relations management teams, these new brokers increasingly manage public discussions of WM through feasibility reports, town hall meetings, presentations, and other forms of prescribed consultation (Allen 2007; Corse 2012; Marres 2005; van de Poel 2008). Indeed, neo-liberal governance enhances industry's monopoly by embedding techniques such as public consultations and feasibility studies within industry's remit. In other words, geo-engineering and economics are the primary discourses through which modern waste management operates. Keller Easterling's description of the International Association for Standardization might just as easily describe the contemporary waste management corporation:

> It strives for universal impact, but must operate as a somewhat secretive institution with no truly public dimension ... . It is an overachiever that believes in the superior fitness of its plans, but portrays itself as inoffensive and subservient. Its rather obscure processes are largely unknown to the general public but nevertheless attract a broad consensus – a consensus for a platform that does not originate in a political dialogue.
>
> (2014: 208)

Structured through these corporate interests, waste flows through a behemoth transportation infrastructure that moves waste from region to region and continent to continent. Modern landfills are themselves complex infrastructures of siting, liners, leachate and gas capture and routing, and monitoring and aftercare. This waste infrastructure is as much economic, political, cultural, and symbolic as it is material. Waste is integral to the circuits of capital: waste management as a form of neo-capitalism emphasizes a market economy, enhanced privatization, an overall decrease in government control of the waste economy, and an enhanced entrepreneurial approach to profit maximization (see Hird et al. 2014). This is largely achieved by encouraging a form of individual responsibilization whereby individuals are incited through myriad incentives and sanctions to assume responsibility for municipal solid waste (and to a lesser degree municipal liquid waste) through almost exclusively downstream techno-scientific ameliorations, touted as "solutions" to current and future waste disposals "needs" (ibid.).

These solutions are short term and do nothing to stem the tsunami of increased consumption. Reprocessing materials, for instance, requires a great deal of energy, often using non-renewable fossil fuels that pollute soil and atmosphere. Recycling may also release hazardous wastes through by-product emissions, and produces lesser quality products that may only be used once or twice more (Centre for Sustainability 2012; MacBride 2012). Moreover, the "dirty little secret" of recycling is that constantly varying markets mean that materials the public believes are destined for diversion are in fact landfilled or incinerated (Hird et al. 2014). Moreover, evidence suggests that people actually produce more waste when they have access to recycling (Lougheed, Hird and Rowe 2016). But the major accomplishment of industry and government is to deflect attention from the far greater masses of industrial and military waste that are exponentially filling up the landscape; a deflection inadvertently reproduced by researchers who focus on individual and household waste practices because they are typically far more accessible than industry and military waste statistics and practices.

Once in the ground, the assorted material of which landfills are composed is meant to stay put, and modern landfills are engineered for stasis, to "secure the volume [as a form of] vertical geopolitics" (Elden 2013). The best engineered, maintained, and after-cared for landfills are designed to contain waste for upwards of one hundred years, less than a breath in geologic time, at which point the landfill leachate's toxicity is hoped to have neutralized sufficiently to no longer pose a threat to human health or the environment. Various uncertainties attend these diverse burials; uncertainties that are transposed into calculable risks such that culpability may then be ascribed and ultimately circumscribed when landfills leak, explode, ignite, or are otherwise compromised (Hird 2014).

Our relentlessly intensifying generation of increasingly hazardous waste is also made possible through an infrastructure of memory: indeed, landfills are ubiquitous places of forgetting. Burial renders waste out of sight and, mainly, out of mind. This forgetting is made possible through legislative decision, regulations, risk models, community accession, and engineering practice. If waste bears witness to all those things we have discarded and no longer want to be associated with, then the highly lucrative waste industry is happy to oblige our desire to remove these sins from memory. To remember our waste, to keep it in sight, we would need to "bring into memory, and thus bear witness to events which we don't want to remember, nor ... be remembered for" (van Wyck 2013). An increasingly vital part of a landfill's aftercare is its removal from memory: landfills are covered over with grass, family parks, or suburban housing or made into ski hills in an attempt to repurpose the land and increase profit, while masking the waste buried beneath. But waste, as Gordillo reminds us, has an afterlife of its own, whether or not we remember the repositories are there. When brought (back) into view, waste landscapes are inevitably the "material sedimentation of destruction" (2014: 119), with sometimes devastating consequences for present and future generations.

Resurrection

If landfilling and other waste management practices attempt to remove both our material sins and their memory, then recent entrepreneurial geo-engineering speaks to a rebirth. Now there is capitalist venture in geological resurrection. Where landfills conceptualize waste as that which should stay buried and stay put, recent explorations into excavating landfills and cities speaks to a form of revival that brings our sins back to the surface, into material being, and transformed into capitalist value. These ventures join long-established practices of large-scale mining and new speculations into hydraulic fracturing.

The reconceptualization of cities as information/digital infrastructures is made possible through a material infrastructure – cables, pipes, and materials involving metals and non-renewable fossil fuels – that forms connections within and between cities, countries, and nations. As Easterling points out, "infrastructure is now the overt point of contact and access between us all – the rules governing the space of everyday life" (2014: 11). Developed as private international enterprises rather than public works, these heavy industries nevertheless "engaged in constructing the terms of civilian life – laying the cable, providing the rolling stock, building the canal or dam ... . They often shaped legislation and determined the values that were worth defending militarily" (ibid.: 152).

This, in turn, becomes a vast waste infrastructure when technologies break down and are no longer repaired, updated or replaced. The discards of urban infrastructures – urks – join the global landfill and nuclear repository infrastructure meant to contain and disappear humanity's unwanted and abandoned objects in perpetuity – out of sight and out of mind (Hird 2015). Since so much of the materials that make up urban infrastructures are already buried underground, urks are all the more easily forgotten. If the ghost is, as Jacques Derrida (1994) argued, the permanent return of the absent, then we might ask whether the resurrection of urks testifies to "a living past or a living future" (Gordillo 2014: 246). Relative to the sustained attention devoted to the sociotechnical aspects of infrastructure, the waste, emissions, land use, and contamination effects are rarely considered (Monstadt 2009), as the latter are concerned with destruction, disassembly, disconnection – what Gordillo (2014) observes is a hierarchy of waste such that that which cannot be resurrected is an inferior form of matter (see also Graham and Thrift 2007).

We have put into use almost all of the metals in the periodic table (UNEP 2010), and industries are assessing the profitability of extracting nickel, copper, iron/steel, aluminum and other metals in this distinct form of urban mining, making use of what some industries refer to as "hibernating stocks," since the amount of specific metals such as iron and copper in the built environment meets or "exceeds the amount in known geological ores" (Johansson 2013: 1; Bergbäck and Lohm 1997; Spatari et al. 2005). Pipes and cables constitute about a fourth of the weight of a city's infrastructure and in some cases contain as much or more sought-after metal as operating mines (Wallsten 2014). Resurrecting urks is a complex process, as cables and pipes laid down on top of each other over time through successive urban space planning stages has created a vast, intricate, and difficult to access material system. Deleted files, abandoned maps, and the generally haphazard record-keeping of successive local governments and competing industries ensure that the recovery of desirable metals is both tricky and uncertain (Wallsten 2014). Often the abandoned infrastructure is only discovered in the process of repair work to an existing and still reasonably functional infrastructure. This said, as contemporary titanic mining efforts (i.e. initial extraction) extract fewer and fewer sought-after minerals and metals, the increasing interest in urk mining suggests capitalism's long vertical as well as horizontal reach. Buried under layers of infrastructure that may well be destroyed in the process of extraction, "through a decisive sleight of hand, destruction is redefined as innovative, positive, desirable" (Gordillo 2014: 80). Urks, indeed, provoke ontological questions about the very conceptualization of waste as such. If urks were to be defined as waste, then they would need to be removed and landfilled, constituting a near-impossible remediation project that would jeopardize the successive layers of infrastructure built on top of the abandoned urks. As such, urks tend to be defined as other entities – contaminated soil or resource, for instance – that skirts the pressing need to remediate since other contaminated areas (such as abandoned oil refineries or chemical plants) are typically much more likely to leak and spread contamination (Wallsten 2014). Nevertheless, this definition of convenience must remain always tentative, as certain urks may contain materials – PCBs, CFCs, lead – that may not stay put, may leak and require removal and remediation (ibid.). Moreover, there is always the danger of precipitating such a leak when urks are mined. And, of course, much of the material that will inevitably be resurrected with the sought-after metals and minerals will be redefined as waste and reburied.

Despite well-publicized efforts to recycle, the majority of products collected by waste management industries globally (which have assumed control of most of the recycling industry) end up in landfills (Kim and Owens 2010; UN-HABITAT 2010). And as Johansson notes, landfills are "bursting with metals: globally over billions of tonnes of iron and millions of tonnes of copper, and other crucial resources" (2013: 33). There are numerous challenges: municipal solid landfills and even exclusively industrial landfills tend to contain a heterogeneous mix of diverse materials in a series of vertical cells built on top of each other, and gleaning the contents of each cell is difficult without detailed record-keeping (which is uncommon). A number of waste management and mining industries are conducting exploratory studies of the viability of this "post-mining" through the use of vertical bore holes that cut through vertically arranged cells. Landfill mining is precarious work since it involves disturbing sedimented landfilled material, cutting through liner systems designed to hold leachate in place, and mixing materials, an unknown quantity of which may be toxic. It means re-introducing oxygen into the landfill system, which changes the aerobic and anaerobic bacterial metabolism of the landfill. We know little of the bacterial stimulation and proliferation that occurs in landfills, which is likely to involve bacterial adaptation and diversification (Clark and Hird 2014). Thus, insofar as landfilling is a geologic relayering of materials that have already been extracted, landfill mining constitutes a re-extraction, a further destratification and mixing of the "productions of deep, planetary time" that "defy our own [temporal and geologic] sensorium" (ibid.: 49, 50).

And somewhere in between burial and resurrection lies hydraulic fracturing. Fracking stands to significantly increase the already 57,000 million tonnes of material we are annually shifting from beneath the earth to its surface (Douglas and Lawson 2000). As we further disturb geologic strata, we are significantly adding to the biological soup that traverses and variously forms and responds to the geologic. Not only is fracking literally unearthing billions of several kinds of subterranean extremophile bacteria (able to thrive in conditions of extreme heat and so on that are catastrophic to animals), but in order to dislodge the bacterial colonies that are clogging fracking wells, companies are injecting millions of liters of biocides into the earth. The EPA has thus far approved over 28 different biocides for fracking applications (Kahrilas et al. 2015; Sager 2014). These biocides may seep between rock beds, through surface soil, and into the water table. Not only do we not understand the effects of this seepage and transfection on human health, flora and fauna, but we have little idea of the consequences of the interactions between these extremophiles and the bacterial ecosystems in the soil, lakes, and oceans on which we depend for survival. Such resurrection, as Dr Frankenstein learned at cost, may well revive, or indeed create, more than we intend.

Conclusions

The Anthropocene calls our attention to humanity's geologic signature of extracting non-renewable fossil fuels, gas, and metals. The success of this capitalist operation means that in some cases, more metals exist in cities' subterranean infrastructures than in the ground, and this is leading to new calls for the re-extraction of metals and other non-renewable resources from landfills and urks. This process of extraction, disposal, re-extraction and, inevitably, re-disposal is made possible through complex political, social, economic, and cultural apparatuses concerned with profit, sustainability, and sovereignty. It is also mediated by a geosphere, pedosphere, and microcosmos that set material constraints as well as speculative possibilities (for instance in the case of the experimental employment of microorganisms in metals extraction; see Labban 2014). If the relatively stable and docile planetary time of the Holocene made possible the very extraction and material infrastructure upon which our global society is materially built, then the Anthropocene signals infrastructural limits as primary resources deplete, melting permafrost corrupts mining waste storage, and new microcosms are liberated via landfill and urk extraction.

All of this epoch-long wasting amounts to an incessantly recurring burial and resurrection. The hundreds of thousands of dumps and landfills worldwide constitute a critical yet largely unacknowledged infrastructure wherein social and material relations intersect on a global scale. Waste's profitable resurrection as a resource now enacts complex and uncertain processes of destratification and restratification as materials are unearthed, circulated, reburied, re-extracted, and abandoned (in or on the earth). Waste brings into sharp resolution the interplay between geological processes stretching through deep time and humanity's short-run but significant activity. Municipal solid, mining, and myriad other forms of waste constitute terminal capitalism's profound fallout – its excess; our faith in geo-engineering imagines waste's inert and static afterlife for generations to come "as controllable from the present" (Gordillo 2014: 255), and this relayering suggests not only a support system for urban living but also an integral component of ongoing chemical and biological life.[1]

Through extraction, disposal, re-extraction, and redisposal we are recomposing strata, but not with its original ingredients. And with the increasing use of abandoned mines as landfills, as well as the mining of landfills for reprocessing materials, different waste forms are merging in complex and unpredictable ways. But, in contrast to climate change modeling, we have little idea of waste's bio-geological thresholds in either sheer volume terms or in terms of the heterogeneous mix of "unknown unknowns" landfilled materials that bacteria metabolize into new entities or in relation to what landslides, avalanches, earthquakes, floods, and melting permafrost might make of the highly toxic restratified mining waste.

Yet unlike climate change mitigation – the Anthropocene's signature event – where technologies are the subject of debate, where they have not yet settled, there has long been a *political sedimentation* of waste management technologies. That is, waste garners relatively little public attention or democratic dialogue: the circuits of capital – production, consumption, and waste – means there is essentially "no appeal to a citizen who is not also a consumer" (Easterling 2014: 208). Waste management technologies encourage more waste, further expansion, further de- and restratification, and further landscape transformation. And these technologies, as Melinda Cooper argues, "may [themselves] be indistinguishable from the [thing we are trying to solve] – that is to say, equally unpredictable, incalculable and turbulent in its unfolding" (2010: 184). The metabolism of the Anthropocene that creates waste, then, is a particularly creative destruction that is "noticed but affectively neutralized" (Gordillo 2014: 80; see also Stoler 2009) through negation, mitigation, indifference, forgetting, enterprise, and innovation. In our efforts to bury our sins and be born again in a sustainable and sustaining environment, we have created vast subterranean sacrifice zones whose interconnections with ecosystems we can know little and control less, and yet upon which we ultimately depend.

Note

1   I thank Penelope Harvey for her insightful comments that brought my attention to the relational ontology involving support systems for urban living and chemical life.

References

Ahuja, N. (2015) "Intimate Atmospheres: Queer Theory in a Time of Extinctions," *GLQ: A Journal of Gay and Lesbian Studies* 21(2–3): 365–385.

Ali, S. H. (1999) "The Search for a Landfill Site in the Risk Society," *Canadian Review of Sociology* 36(1): 1–19.

Allen, B. (2007) "Environmental Justice and Expert Knowledge in the Wake of a Disaster," *Social Studies of Science* 37(1): 103–110.

Bélanger, P. (2007) "Airspace," in J. Knechtel (ed.) *Trash*. Cambridge, MA: MIT Press.

Bhagavad, Gita (1944) Translation by Vivekananda-Isherwood. Ch. 11, verse 32.

Bergbäck, B. and Lohm, U. (1997) "Metals in Society," in D. Brune, D. V. Chapman, M. D. Gwynne, and J. M. Pacyna (eds) *The Global Environment: Science, Technology and Management*. Oslo: Scandinavian Science Publisher.

Center for Sustainability (2012) "Problems with current recycling methods." Available at: www.centerforsustainability.org/resources.php?category=40&root= (accessed September 20, 2012).

Chandler, A. (1977) *The Visible Hand: The Managerial Revolution in American Business*. Cambridge, MA: Harvard University Press.

Clark, N. and Hird, M. J. (2014) "Deep Shit," *O-Zone: A Journal of Object-Oriented Studies* (special issue: Objects/Ecology) 1: 44–52. http://o-zone-journal.org/issue/.

Coninck, P., Seguin, M., Chornet, E., Laramee, L., Twizeyemariya, A., Abatzoglou, N. and Racine, L. (1999) "Citizen Involvement in Waste Management: An Application of the STOPER Model via an Informed Consensus Approach," *Environmental Management* 23(1): 87–94.

Carse, A. (2012) "Nature as Infrastructure: Making and Managing the Panama Canal Watershed," *Social Studies of Science* 42(4): 539–563.

Crutzen, P. J. and Stoermer, E. F. (2000) "The Anthropocene," *Global Change Newsletter* 41 (May): 17–18.
Davis, M. (2007) *Planet of Slums*. New York: Verso.
Derrida, J. (1994) *Spectres of Marx*. London: Routledge.
Dodds, L. and Hopwood, B. (2006) "BAN Waste: Environmental Justice and Citizen Participation in Policy Setting," *Local Environment* 11(3): 269–286.
Douglas, I. and Lawson, N. (2000) "The Human Dimensions of Geomorphological Work in Britain," *Journal of Industrial Ecology* 4(2): 9–33.
Easterling, K. (2014) *Extrastatecraft: The Power of Infrastructure Space*. New York: Verso.
Einsiedel, E., Jesoe, E. and Breck, T. (2001) "Publics at the Technology Table: The Consensus Conference in Denmark, Canada, and Australia," *Public Understanding of Science* 10: 83–98.
Elden, S. (2013) "Secure the Volume: Vertical Geopolitics and the Depths of Power," *Political Geography* 34: 35–51.
Gordillo, G.R. (2014) *Rubble: The Afterlife of Destruction*. Durham, NC and London: Duke University Press.
Graham, S. and Thrift, N. (2007) "Out of Order: Understanding Repair and Maintenance," *Theory, Culture & Society* 24(3): 1–25.
Healy, S.A. (2010) "Facilitating Public Participation in Toxic WM through Engaging 'The Object of Politics,'" *East Asian Science, Technology and Society: An International Journal* 4: 585–599.
Hird, M. J. (2012) "Knowing Waste: Toward an Inhuman Epistemology," *Social Epistemology* 26(3–4): 453–469.
Hird, M. J. (2013) "Waste, Landfills, and an Environmental Ethics of Vulnerability," *Ethics and the Environment* 18(1): 105–124.
Hird, M. J. (2015) "Waste, Environmental Politics and Dis/Engaged Publics," *Theory, Culture and Society* (special issue: Geo-Social Formations).
Hird, M. J. and Zahara, A. (forthcoming) "The Arctic Wastes," in R. Grusin (ed.) *Anthropocene Feminism*. Minneapolis: University of Minnesota Press.
Hird, M. J., Lougheed, S., Rowe, K. and Kuyvenhoven, C. (2014) "Making Waste Management Public (or Falling Back to Sleep)," *Social Studies of Science* 44(3): 441–465.
Johansson, J. (2013) *Why Don't We Mine the Landfills?* Linköping: Linköping Electronic Press.
Kahrilas, G. A., Blotevogel, J., Stewart, P. S. and Borch, T. (2015) "Biocides in Hydraulic Fracturing Fluids: A Critical Review of Their Usage, Mobility, Degradation, and Toxicity," *Environmental Science and Technology* 49(1): 16–32.
Kapur, A. and Graedel, T. (2006) "Copper Mines Above and Below the Ground," *Environmental Science and Technology* 40: 3135–3141.
Kim, K. and Owens, G. (2010) "Potential for Enhanced Phytoremediation of Landfills Using Biosolids: A Review," *Journal of Environmental Management* 91(4): 791–797.
Labban, M. (2014) "Deterritorializing Extraction: Bioaccumulation and the Planetary Mine," *Annals of the Association of American Geographers* 104(3): 560–576.
Lougheed, S., Hird, M. J. and Rowe, R. K. (2016) "Governing Household Waste Management: An Empirical Analysis and Critique," *Environmental Values* 2(3): 287–308.
MacBride, S. (2012) *Recycling Reconsidered: The Present Failure and Future Promise of Environmental Action in the United States*. Cambridge, MA: MIT Press.

Marres, N. (2005) "Issues Spark a Public into Being," in B. Latour and P. Weibel (eds) *Making Things Public*. Cambridge, MA: MIT Press, pp. 208–217.

Monastersky, R. (2015) "First Atomic Blast Proposed as Start of Anthropocene," *Nature*, January 16. Available at: www.nature.com/news/first-atomic-blast-proposed-as-start-of-anthropocene-1.16739 (accessed June 8, 2015).

Monstadt, J. (2009) "Conceptualizing the Political Ecology of Urban Infrastructures: Insights from Technology and Urban Studies," *Environment and Planning A* 41(8): 1924–1942.

Nixon, R. (2011) *Slow Violence and the Environmentalism of the Poor*. Cambridge, MA: Harvard University Press.

Petts, J. (1998) "Trust and Waste Management Information: Expectation versus Observation," *Journal of Risk Research* 1(4): 307–320.

Petts, J. (2001) "Evaluating the Effectiveness of Deliberative Processes: Waste Management Case Studies," *Journal of Environmental Planning and Management* 44(2): 207–226.

Sager, J. (2014) "Fracking Floods the Earth with Biocides," *The Progressive Cynic*. Available at: http://theprogressivecynic.com/2014/05/19/fracking-floods-the-earth-with-biocides/ (accessed June 10, 2015).

Scott, H. (2008) "Colonialism, Landscape and the Subterranean," *Geography Compass* 2(6): 1853–1869.

Spatari, S., Bertram, B., Gordon, R. and Graedel, T. E. (2005) "Twentieth-century Copper Stocks and Flows in North America: A Dynamic Analysis," *Ecological Economics* 54(1): 37–51.

Stoler, Ann L. (2009) *Along the Archival Grain: Thinking through Colonial Ontologies*. Princeton, NJ and Oxford: Princeton University Press.

UNEP (United Nations Environment Programme) (2010) *Metal Stocks in Society*. International Panel for Sustainable Resource Management, Working Group on the Global Metal Flows.

UN-HABITAT (2010) *Solid Waste Mangaement in the World's Cities: Water and Sanitation in the Worlds' Cities*. London: Earthscan.

van de Poel, I. (2008) "The Bugs Eat the Waste: What Else is There to Know? Changing Professional Hegemony in the Design of Sewage Treatment Plants," *Social Studies of Science* 38(4): 605–634.

van Wyck, P. (2013) "Footbridge at Atwater: A Chorographic Inventory of Effects," in A. Neimanis, C. Chen and J. MacLeod (eds) *Thinking with Water*. Montreal: McGill-Queen's University Press.

van Wyck, P. and Hird, M. J. (in preparation) "What Was the Anthropocene?"

Wallsten, B. (2013) *Underneath Norrköping: An Urban Mine of Hibernating Infrastructure*. Linköping: Linköping Electronic Press.

Wallsten, B. (2014) "Revenge of the Urks: On Processes of Material Exclusion in Infrastructural Assemblages." Unpublished paper.

19 Evidence, infrastructure and worth

Sandra Calkins and Richard Rottenburg

This chapter focuses on the mutable infrastructures through which evidence is made, travels and is challenged. Evidence production presupposes infrastructures and simultaneously reinforces some of their dimensions. Evidence about scientific matters is to a large extent produced within *experimental infrastructures or systems* with predefined protocols, laboratory regulations, research technologies, methods, skilled staff, disciplinary convictions and other elements. In spite of such definitions, infrastructures of evidence-making are also unpredictable. Scientific controversies problematize evidence in line with different worths shifting the grounds of evidence, making other elements and infrastructures visible and reconfiguring both the infrastructure and what is being transported.

Our motivation is to contribute to ongoing engagements with *infrastructuring as material-semiotic practice* in the social sciences and the humanities. In recent years this debate has moved away from an earlier focus on infrastructure as material forms enabling the making, communication, and circulation of things and facts. Core concerns of early studies were the stability, recalcitrance, and path dependency of infrastructure. Whatever assemblage of technologies, procedures, and people (hardware, software and people) was solid enough to facilitate a set of organized practices could go by the name of infrastructure in relation to that practice (Star and Ruhleder 1996: 113; Star 1999). Early definitions of infrastructure included technologies and artifacts as well as technicians, engineers, and procedures that help to keep things running and whose politics often remains hidden (Winner 1986; Joerges 1999). Unlike presently, previous work did not always refer to such arrangements as "infrastructure." Rather, these complex sets of arrangements were often called large technical or experimental systems, or assemblage or network, if the focus was less on the enabling function for a particular practice and more on qualifying the relations of its parts (for large technical systems, see Hughes 1983; Bijker et al. 1989; Edwards 1996; for experimental systems, see Rheinberger 1992; for assemblage, see Deleuze and Guattari 1987: 399, and chapter 10 on "intensive experimentation" and "becoming"; Callon 2006: 13). Similarly, Landecker (2007) and Rottenburg (2009) wrote about the working and intersecting of knowledge infrastructures but without recourse to this specific conceptual language.

Our inquiry draws on this scholarship and critically engages with recent efforts to hone the debate around infrastructure. In both the older and the newer literature infrastructures are not clearly bounded entities out there but relational configurations that unfold from practices and interpretations (e.g. Pinch 2010). They are networks that are inscribed with theories about their usage and users and yet are often put to other uses than their designers anticipated (Akrich 1992). Where an earlier generation of scholars was captivated by the systemic character of infrastructures often in relation to particular polities and above all sought to explain their material recalcitrance (for instance, Winner 1986; Star 1999: 389), newer work tends to rather emphasize their fluidity, openness, and adaptability to different material politics and traveling technologies (e.g. Anand 2011; Jensen and Winthereik 2013; Larkin 2013; von Schnitzler 2013; for a good overview see Niewöhner 2015).

In line with turns to practice theory and pragmatism, recent ethnographic engagement with infrastructures attended more to the practice of doing infrastructure – i.e. to infrastructuring in the verbal form (Bossen and Markussen 2010), suggesting that infrastructures, analogous to institutions, are less powerful in shaping the practices they enable than was often assumed. They are rather seen as experimental material-semiotic practices interweaving social, economic, political, and legal orderings with moral reasoning and technical networks that inevitably produce new and unpredictable assemblages that reconfigure the world (Jensen and Morita 2015: 84). It is perhaps exaggerated to say that older works erroneously conceived infrastructure as stable objects (Charles Perrow's 1984 book is one of many counter examples), whereas newer works discovered a deeper truth behind this and now look at the practice of infrastructuring. Still, it might not be entirely naïve to assume that with this shift of interest new dimensions are being unearthed. Along these lines, recent work has sought to stretch the notion of infrastructuring as material-semiotic practice into new terrains to accommodate its affective and imaginative properties (for instance, Harvey and Knox 2012), or, for example, to think about human relations that come into play when infrastructures break down as "people as infrastructure" (Simone 2004), or to make the invisible properties of soil visible as "infrastructure of bios" (Puig de la Bellacasa 2013). However, this conceptual broadening implies that almost anything may be called infrastructure, ignoring some of the term's classical defining features, such as its stable materiality and the techno-scientific and political dimensions of infrastructural planning, construction and maintenance.

Our contribution to this literature is to explore a specific type of knowledge infrastructure – what we call infrastructures of evidence. We assert that evidence production is a specific form of infrastructuring that connects politics, science, technologies, and objects like genes, plants, geophysical surroundings, and human bodies and promotes different forms of ethical-political reasoning. Practices shape the material-semiotic properties of infrastructures and are at the same time guided by infrastructures that have stabilized and offer orientation for actions without determining their outcomes. When we consider evidence production as practice, particular attention needs to be paid to the ways in which heterogeneous elements, such as legal regulations, laboratory devices, scientific papers, and moral arguments are made coherent (or not) and indicate the worth of what is being assembled. Our case study examines how a GMO and a supporting infrastructure are being made and how worth is being articulated.

Inspired by discussions of techno- and ontological politics, which explore the hidden normativities and ontologies implicated in the technical content of infrastructures, we give it a different twist and try to capture an array of worths mobilized by different participants in a controversy about the uses of biotechnology. Our understanding of worth (grandeur) draws on recent pragmatist thinking that investigates the various ways in which persons, objects, and actions are evaluated in public situations. Worth is understood as a general and widely accepted value, a legitimate common good according to which entities are arranged, ranked, or treated (Boltanski and Thévenot 2006: 14). We do not assume that worths are given and shape infrastructures, nor do we take infrastructures to be given in order to inquire into the worths they produce. Rather we claim that worths can only be established through situations of testing that disclose what types of materials and ideas evidentiary practices have assembled. Thereby the condition of possibility for testing whether a particular compromise between worths and ontologies is applicable in a situation is the existence of infrastructures that allow the making and mobilization of evidence; at the same time, probing reconfigures the infrastructure.

Deployment 1: Knowledge infrastructure and evidence

Like all infrastructures, "knowledge infrastructures comprise robust networks of people, artifacts, and institutions that generate, share, and maintain specific knowledge about the human and natural worlds" (Edwards 2010: 17). Two decades ago, scholars began to study the architecture of new knowledge infrastructures and technological configurations, like computers, online data bases and content management systems, pointing out how this hinges on processes of classification and standardization and how this changed the politics of research, knowledge production, and dissemination (Star and Ruhleder 1996; Bowker 1998). Here we take another step towards charting the specific trajectories knowledge infrastructuring can take. We speak of *infrastructure of evidence* as a specific form of knowledge or information infrastructure that is concerned with specific technological settings and conceptions concerning what pieces of knowledge qualify as evidence proper in a community of scholars and beyond (cf. Bowker 1998: 87).

The distinguishing mark of material infrastructures, like power grids or the Internet, which have stable classifications and standards built into them, is their relative firmness (Star 1999: 389; Pinch 2010: 82; Collier and Kemoklidze 2014). Infrastructures of evidence presuppose the interlacing of various knowledge infrastructures, such as libraries, online databases, and research technologies, and also run on other infrastructures that support this work, i.e. the Internet, electricity, etc. (Edwards 2010: 19). Our use of the term infrastructure suggests that there is something stable to modes of evidence-making that enables practices to hinge on them. Conversely, an infrastructure of evidence can only be defined in relation to practices of knowledge or evidence production (Star and Ruhleder 1996). Hence, the classical question, "How do infrastructures impact evidence making?" (Joerges and Shinn 2001), can be turned on its head: "How does evidence-making impact the emergence of infrastructures?" Bowker (1994) refers to the possibility to shift in this way between infrastructure and the practice it enables as "infrastructural inversion," indicating a gestalt switch that foregrounds infrastructuring and backgrounds the practice it enables.

Approximately during the first three decades of the sociology of scientific knowledge (SSK and later STS) fact making – the main activity and purpose of the sciences – was shown to be a collective process of turning specific interpretations of reality into a particular form of knowledge that is able to pass as a proven fact, as truth for some time. A long-standing insight is that there is no direct and unmediated access to reality since it is impossible to probe the correspondence between statement and reality without intermediate translations, such as experiments, measurements, or testimonies. This insight prepared a shift from a representational to a performative idiom (Pickering 1995: 5–20), centered on the question of nonhuman agency and the role of technology in the routinized and disciplined practice of science conceived as a machine-like field. To assess what one might gain by deploying the concept of knowledge infrastructure and, even more specifically, infrastructure of evidence we provide a short glimpse of a possible genealogy of the concept.

Ludwig Fleck's (1980 [1935]) concept of "Denkkollektiv" (thought collective) was foundational for the emerging sociology of scientific knowledge. A thought collective generates a thought style (Denkstil), which comes with a certain definition of what is considered un/thinkable. An established thought style enables fact making but at the same time inhibits radical change. The tendency towards bureaucratic inertia in the sciences is, according to Fleck (1980: 40–53), established through a number of strategies that complicate deviations from the central doctrines of the collective. Fleck's thought collectives rely on procedures and technologies that function as their infrastructures (without being named as such). What is particularly important is Fleck's observation that the accuracy of the Wassermann syphilis test – the case he examined – as material technology and the competence of the medical experts to use this technology had first to interactively stabilize before producing helpful results.

Half a century later, Steven Shapin and Simon Schaffer (1985) examined the rise of the experiment as the leading method to arrive at scientific truth. Studying the debate between Hobbes and Boyle, they not only demonstrated how fact making in the natural sciences is inextricably intertwined with the making of the political order but also showed how the establishment of matters of fact includes experimental apparatuses as well as procedures of witnessing and communicating experimental protocols, testimonies and results. This presupposes material, literary and social technologies, which depend on each other, creating an assemblage that is capable to produce objective knowledge – objectivity here means that the knowledge was produced by a collective that voluntarily agreed on procedures.

Around the same time, in 1979, Bruno Latour and Steve Woolgar (1979: 70, 71) argued in Fleck's footsteps that papers are the most important laboratory output since experimental results mostly travel as documents. Like Fleck (1980: 53–70), their scholarship emphasized that fact making is an irreducibly collective process, meaning that findings have to connect to an established body of scientific work, must be circulated within an academic community, and their facticity ultimately has to be affirmed by references and citations (Latour 1987: 26ff). In a later article, Latour (1996: 235) explained why he desisted from deploying the notion of infrastructure – namely, to leave behind the common-sense interpretation (even if the move, according to Pickering [1995: 9–20], is inconsequential) that "[infrastructures] interconnect and form a continuous material base over which the social world of representations and signs subsequently flows." Instead he made a huge investment in "network" as alternative concept. Obviously, he could have taken the other route and redefined the meaning of the word infrastructure as the newer literature tries to do.

The concepts of infrastructure – more specifically knowledge or evidence infrastructure – do not designate anything previously unknown. STS has posited for a long time that evidence production presupposes enabling material, juridical, social, economic, and semantic structures and at the same time reinforces some of their particular dimensions. These supportive structures stabilize certain modes of knowledge and evidence production while preventing others from gaining credibility. But this does not mean that assembling observations on knowledge production under the concept of infrastructure of evidence is futile. Indeed we think it enables new and important findings. Seen from the empirical end, changes of Internet technologies and related knowledge technologies (social media, crowdsourcing, wikis, big data, open source software, open access, citizen science, MOOC, etc.) have altered the basic mechanics by which knowledge is produced and circulated, and these new forms of infrastructuring demand theoretical recalibrations (Edwards et al. 2013).

Deployment 2: Orders of worth

We claim that evidence that emerges from and is circulated by infrastructures of evidence is inseparable from worths, the latter shaping what comes to count and is mobilized as evidence. In the scientific field, evidence production is not only part of technological networks but also subject to various understandings of good scientific practice, methodological rigor, and so on. Infrastructures of evidence circulate the matters of evidence and the common criteria which allow evaluating the worth and different forms of evidence. According to Boltanski and Thévenot (2006: 14), worth (grandeur) is a general and widely accepted common good according to which entities are arranged, ranked or treated. Boltanski and Thévenot inductively established six so-called orders of worth for contemporary France that are taken to stand for any advanced capitalist democracy: a civic order that prizes equality, an order of inspiration where passion, creativeness, and grace are prioritized, a domestic order where reputation and seniority come first, fame where the main worth is renown, industrial order with the main worth of efficiency, a market order of worth where price is the ordering principle. Their aim is not to provide an exhaustive list of theoretical possibilities – in practice all orders constantly compete and enter compromises with each other – but to show through which arguments people can legitimately justify their own actions and positions, how they evaluate those of others, and which objects and devices they mobilize to do so. It is remarkable though that they do not recognize science as a separate order of worth that prizes truth and thereby eschew the problem of ontological multiplicity.

Each order of worth is based on an incommensurable and distinct principle of equivalence that evaluates what is true, beautiful, good, and just differently and with different priorities. The validity of an order of worth with its principle of equivalence that can coherently arrange entities in a particular situation can only be established by testing (épreuve). Claims, qualifications, and judgments, when put to test, have to hold up to the invested material apparatus of testing. All forms of testing imply that objects, such as protocols, data, bills, etc. are mobilized as proofs and brought to bear on the situation. Orders of worth pertain to dealings in public that have to satisfy other criteria of generality than actions in more restricted or private settings. Controversies imply that arguments have to be made explicit to convince, and have to be framed in broad and general terms to connect to some commonly held onto-epistemological and moral understanding. In this context, scientific testing and the worth it produces (truth) plays a distinct role and is often used in controversies to provide proofs that strengthen positions.

All forms of testing bring to fore the worths at stake in a controversy and both presuppose and reconfigure an infrastructure of evidence. Proofs that claim to be scientific need to follow rigid protocols and systematically aim at their own falsification, yet – following insights gained in STS – can never uphold the purity of their claim. At the same time evidentiary practices are inscribed not only with normativities relating to the controversial issue but also with technical specificities of the practices, implying that only certain types of information come to count as evidence. This means that infrastructures of evidence also reconfigure the worths at play in a situation or controversy by enabling certain types of information to circulate, while disabling other types from moving and becoming known.

The impossibility of establishing final justifications that refer to one ontology results in the need for compromises that enable living with less than final truths – this is the crux of the multiplicity of orders of worth and ontologies. This multiplicity does not give way to ambivalence and controversy only but also to attempts to reach agreement and to stabilize a compromise between partly incompatible orders of worth and their supporting infrastructures – this being a key characteristic of modernity (Boltanski and Thévenot 2006: 277ff). Achieving a compromise presupposes a diplomatic agreement on the identity of the participants and their interests, on the type of situation they find themselves in, and what going concerns bother them. This in turn presupposes at least temporal agreement on standards, procedures, and metacodes. These must be robust enough to enable coordination among the diverse parties to the compromise and flexible enough to accommodate disagreements on matters that do not touch on the cooperation and the things at hand (Rottenburg 2009, 2012). Standards, procedures, and metacodes appear as neutral, are easily taken for granted and recognized as necessary. They offer rules for coordination and frame options to act, making outcomes more predictable (Lampland and Star 2009: 10). Procedures grant, as Luhmann (1969) called it, "legitimacy through procedure" while their grounds and premises are often black-boxed. Negotiating standards, procedures, and metacodes in trading zones can be a more efficient way to address urgent problems than waiting for state regulation indexing scientific facticity. To keep their different but entangled projects going when disagreements arise, participants may be willing to subscribe to standards, procedures, and metacodes they do not fully endorse as a kind of peace agreement (Rottenburg 2014). Achieving compromises between several orders of worth and multiple ontologies reconfigures what is taken to be evident and thus also modifies the infrastructures of evidence. The process explicitly affirms distributed agency, raising fundamental questions about the accountability for the directions it takes. With Luhmann (1990) and Shapin and Schaffer (1985), we suggest that Boltanski and Thévenot overlooked that modernity established science as a distinct order of worth with its own mode of evaluation (truth), format of information (testing), elementary relation (disinterested neutrality), and human qualification (critique). Like all orders of worth a scientific order of worth has to form compromises with other orders and ontologies to circulate evidence and other materials, as our case study will show.

Case study: Biotechnology and GM controversies

The crux of GMO debates anywhere in the world is where and how to draw a line between nature and culture. For biotech advocates, defining GMOs as abominations of "nature" is misleading. For them, modern biotechnologies, enabled by the 1953 discovery of DNA structure and the invention of the recombinant DNA technique in 1973, are the extension of conventional breeding techniques and non-controversial biotechnologies like tissue culture techniques, which since Mendel have sought to transform nature (Pollack and Shaffer 2009: 35). For GM opponents the fundamental ontological and moral issue is the ability to cross evolutionary or assumed God-given boundaries and combine the DNA of different species. There are no foundational answers to this ethical-philosophical problem but some specifications are needed to uphold cooperation in the development and marketing of biotechnologies, turning this into a juridical, political, and ethical dilemma (Rottenburg 2012; for an overview see Winickoff et al. 2005; Jasanoff 2006; Pollack and Shaffer 2009; and for a case study of how pro- and anti-GM movements mobilize scientific evidence, Kinchy 2012). Thousands of studies and publications have not been able to resolve doubts: rather a schism prevails between opponents and proponents. Empirical findings are aligned with different worths as they leave the biotech labs, greenhouses and trials fields to produce forms of argumentation that can convince public fora. Scientific evidence about the risks and potential of GMOs is thus mobilized and these evidences shape and are shaped by intersecting knowledge infrastructures.

We now turn to a research project that is developing transgenic beta-carotene-enriched bananas in Uganda, where one of us did fieldwork in 2015 and early 2016. This is a collaborative research of scientists from Queensland University of Technology and scientists at the Ugandan National Agricultural Research Laboratories. For Ugandan scientists participating in foreign-funded research projects, is crucial to top up their governmental salaries. Research funding comes from the Gates Foundation's *Grand Challenges in Global Health* program, which has funded the long process of crop development since 2005. Drawing on an abundant scientific literature about GMOs in journal articles, graduate textbooks, and online databases that is being added to, rethought, rewritten, and challenged, this project specifically addresses the links between genetic modification and nutritional impacts. It seeks to contribute evidence about the efficacy of beta-carotene biofortification of bananas as a public health tool against vitamin A deficiency – which according to the Ugandan Demographic Health Survey of 2012 affected nearly 36 % of Ugandan children (UBOS and ICF International 2012).

To produce beta-carotene-biofortified bananas, a gene was isolated from a Papua New Guinean banana and first inserted into Australian and later Ugandan bananas. Laboratories were the key physical sites where the molecular operations were carried out. In many regards, Ugandan biotech labs look like labs anywhere: research technology is scattered across a number of rooms with lab benches, forming an assemblage of fridges and freezers, centrifuges, incubators, electrophoresis machines, shelves, fume hoods, and storage rooms for chemicals, and much else. Lab books are opened, test tubes and labels are arranged on small racks, papers with research protocols and lists are spread out. Yet, the ways in which the practice of molecular biology is underpinned by other supporting infrastructures is more visible in Uganda than in many other settings: the work regularly comes to a halt as power outages cut the electricity supply and stop the machines from running. One researcher noted that this did not happen once during his three years of PhD training in Australia. These power outages force lab technicians to interrupt their work for hours and sometimes days; at other times, work has to be halted and is delayed because of problems in the supply infrastructure, i.e. chemicals and other resources are out of stock.

The biotech laboratory is staffed by research assistants doing most of the manual laboratory work and researchers who mainly oversee the work, ensure that protocols are met, document problems and progress, and write papers about their findings and try to place them in prestigious journals. Indeed, doing the molecular work alone does not mean that any evidence is produced. Rather, fact making means that findings have to connect to an established body of literature, they must be circulated within an academic community, and their facticity has to be affirmed by references and citations. What constitutes an innovation is not subject to scientific definitions and publication practices only, rather intellectual property rights figure as proof of an invention. Whereas patents usually promote an economic worth that the inventor may legitimately profit from, a form of compromise was negotiated between an economic and a civic worth: the Gates Foundation determined that the technology has to serve a charitable purpose and has to be made available to poor banana farmers anywhere, while not in principle ruling out profitability in other markets.

Cooking bananas (matooke) are the preferred food staple in central Uganda, but according to nutritional assessments this diet is low in pro-vitamin A, E and iron. The idea was thus to enrich bananas with these micronutrients through genetic modification. So far, however, only beta-carotene-enriched bananas have reached the stage of field trials in Uganda. Work on vitamin E was soon dropped because it interfered too much with the chemical reaction responsible for the expression of beta-carotene; and biofortification of iron is delayed due to technical difficulties. The model for gene transfer was developed in Cavendish dessert bananas in Australia, then transferred to Uganda and adapted to matooke. Australian researchers ran feeding trials to establish the safety and efficacy of these transgenic bananas. They first tested the efficacy in rodents, then designed a nutritional study to establish its efficacy in improving vitamin A levels in humans – in this case, volunteering students at a US university. Controversies ran high in 2014 internationally and within the university's campus and the experiment was much delayed. The project's principal investigator noted over a dinner in Kampala that this was not mainly due to resistance, as opponents had claimed, but rather to the complicated logistics of the feeding trial and difficulties in shipping a perishable good like bananas from Australia to the US.

While molecular biologists in Uganda are testing the evidence-making in a number of confined field trials and are waiting for the fruits to ripen from early 2016 onwards to prove that the technology is working, the banana's political future beyond the labs and trial fields is still uncertain. Whereas the president and some members of parliament declared that passing the biosafety bill is a priority of this government, there still is no law in place that would regulate the release, farming, and marketing of this public health banana or any other GMO. Public concern about GMOs and their effects on human health persists, and some Ugandan activists oppose biotechnology and what they see as the profit-driven agendas of large agribusiness.

How evidence about the Ugandan ß-carotene-biofortified banana is accepted depends on infrastructuring and on the types of worth that this product and its development are associated with. Whereas a main argument against the uses of biotechnology has been its embeddedness in capitalist enterprises geared towards profit, this project to improve the nutritional content of crops is oriented towards a public good – public health and food security – in East African countries. The acceptance of biotechnology in different African countries not only depends on the uses to which it is put but also on how inclusive infrastructures of evidence are and whether they embrace African self-determination (see Harsh 2005 for the case of Kenya where organizations in the Global North dominated crop research and development). Clearly, scientific evidence that purports to present truth is inevitably aligned with other worths that are being put to the test in GM controversies. The stability of compromises between different orders of worth depends on infrastructuring that makes, confirms, and disseminates evidences.

Conclusions

Solving disputes in public life calls for the provision of evidence, and evidence can be called into question by raising doubts about its validity. We have sought to contribute to an analysis of the underpinnings of evidence production – what we conceived as infrastructures of evidence through which facts are made, circulated. and challenged. Disputable evidence often leads to new forms of infrastructuring as it calls for processing additional information, justifying the evidence, falsifying it, or showing that it was misused. Our concern has been to look beyond technopolitics and ontologies and towards more encompassing spheres of valuation that affect what comes to count as evidence, thereby shaping infrastructures of evidence while also being recursively shaped by them. In situations of testing, when evidence is problematized, the worths and ontologies that should apply need to be worked out. Testing to determine which particular compromise between multiple orders of worth and ontologies was made – we considered mainly a civic order of worth that prioritizes public goods, a market order of worth oriented towards profit, and science that prioritizes disinterested truth-making – presupposes the existence of infrastructures that enable evidence production and dissemination, while testing itself is part of the dynamics of infrastructuring.

In a scientific order of worth, truth is the highest good, and ideally evidence (fact) and worth (value) have to be set apart. In practice, testing inevitably produces fact-values that reconfigure the world this or that way, according to the variety of worths and ontologies at play. That science is not pure or objective as it purports to be is a point that has been repeatedly emphasized in STS. Our illustration of the biotech controversy similarly points to the ways in which evidentiary practices weld technological set-ups and socio-economic, material, political and moral worlds together in a complex assemblage. Yet, we contend that taking the entanglements of science with business, politics, and other orders of worth and multiple ontologies for granted – or even to negate that science is an independent order of worth – has led to underestimation of science with its own ontology in the making of compromises. Science, like other orders of worths, affects the process of infrastructuring. It does so through its own particular techniques (testing) and criteria of evaluation (truth) to qualify entities and through its own formats that allow evidence to travel. The mutual co-constitution of infrastructuring and testing makes matters of evidence able to connect and circulate. The emergent common criteria to assess the forms, ontologies and worths of evidence are compromises that become temporarily stabilized and rendered transposable to different settings.

References

Akrich, Madeleine (1992) "The de-scription of technical objects," in Wiebe E. Bijker and John Law (eds) *Shaping Technology/Building Society: Studies in Sociotechnical Change*. Cambridge, MA: MIT Press, pp. 205–224.

Anand, Nikhil (2011) "Pressure: The politechnics of water supply in Mumbai." *Cultural Anthropology* 26(4): 542–564.

Barry, Andrew (2013) *Material Politics: Disputes Along the Pipeline*. Oxford: Wiley-Blackwell.

Bijker, Wiebe E., Thomas P. Hughes and Trevor J. Pinch (eds) (1989) *The Social Construction of Technological Systems: New Directions in the Sociology and History of Technology*. Cambridge, MA: MIT Press.

Boltanski, Luc and Laurent Thévenot (2006 [orig. 1991]) *On Justification: Economies of Worth*. Princeton, NJ: Princeton University Press.

Bossen, Claus and Randi Markussen (2010) "Infrastructuring and ordering devices in health care: Medication plans and practices on a hospital ward". *Computer Supported Cooperative Work* 19(6): 615–637.

Bowker, Geoffrey (1994) *Science on the Run: Information Management and Industrial Geophysics at Schlumberger, 1920–1940*. Cambridge, MA: MIT Press.

Bowker, Geoffrey (1998) "The History of Information Infrastructures: The Case of the International Classification of Diseases," in Trudi Bellardo Hahn and Michael Keeble Buckland (eds) *Historical Studies in Information Science*. Medford: Information Today (for the American Society for Information Science), pp. 81–93.

Callon, Michel (2006) "What does it mean to say that economics is performative? CSI Working Paper no. 005. Centre de Sociologie de l'Innovation, Ecole des Mines de Paris.

Collier, Stephen J., and Nino Kemoklidze (2014) "Pipes and wires," in William H. Rupp, *Globalization in Practice*. Oxford: Oxford University Press, pp. 67–74.

Deleuze, Gilles and Félix Guattari (1987 [1980]) *A Thousand Plateaus: Capitalism and Schizophrenia*. Minneapolis: University of Minnesota Press.

Edwards, Paul N. (1996) *The Closed World: Computers and the Politics of Discourse in Cold War America*. Cambridge, MA: MIT Press.

Edwards, Paul N. (2010) *A Vast Machine: Computer Models, Climate Data, and the Politics of Global Warming*. Cambridge, MA: MIT Press.

Edwards, Paul N., Jackson, Stephen and Chalmers, Melissa (2013) "Knowledge infrastructures: Intellectual frameworks and research challenges." *Deep Blue*. Available at http://deepblue.lib.umich.edu/handle/2027.42/97552 (accessed 8 July 2016).

Fleck, Ludwig (1980 [1935]) *Entstehung und Entwicklung einer wissenschaftlichen Tatsache. Einführung in die Lehre vom Denkstil und Denkkollektiv*. Frankfurt am Main: Suhrkamp.

Harsh, Matthew (2005) "Formal and informal governance of agricultural biotechnology in Kenya: participation and accountability in controversy surrounding the draft biosafety bill." *Journal of International Development* 17(5): 661–677.

Harvey, Penny and Hannah Knox (2012) "The enchantments of infrastructure." *Mobilities* 7(4): 521–536.

Hughes, Thomas P. (1983) *Networks of Power: Electrification in Western Society, 1880–1930*. Baltimore, MD: Johns Hopkins University Press.

Jasanoff, Sheila (2006) "Biotechnology and empire: The global power of seeds and science." *Osiris* 21(1): 273–292.

Jensen, Casper Bruun, and Atsuro Morita (2016) "Infrastructures as ontological experiments." *Engaging Science, Technology, and Society* 1: 81–87. DOI: 10.17351/ests2015.007.

Jensen, Casper Bruun and Brit Ross Winthereik (2013) *Monitoring movements in development aid. Recursive partnerships and infrastructures*. Cambridge, MA: MIT Press.

Joerges, Bernward (1999) "Do politics have artefacts?" *Social Studies of Science* 29(3): 411–431.

Joerges, Bernward, and Terry Shinn (2001) "Research-technology in historical perspective: an attempt at reconstruction," in Bernward Joerges and Terry Shinn (eds) *Instrumentation: Between Science, State and Industry*. Dordrecht: Kluwer Academic Publishers, pp. 241–248.

Kinchy, Abby (2012) *Seeds, Science and Struggle: The Global Politics of Transgenic Crops*. Cambridge, MA: MIT Press.

Lampland, Martha and Susan Leigh Star (2009) *Standards and their Stories: How Quantifying, Classifying, and Formalizing Practices Shape Everyday Life*. Ithaca, NY: Cornell University Press.

Landecker, Hannah (2007) *Culturing Life: How Cells Became Technologies*. Cambridge, MA: Harvard University Press.

Larkin, Brian (2013) "The politics and poetics of infrastructure." *Annual Review of Anthropology* 42(1): 327–343.

Latour, Bruno (1987) *Science in Action: How to Follow Scientists and Engineers through Society*. Cambridge, MA: Harvard University Press.

Latour, Bruno (1996) "On interobjectivity." *Mind, Culture, and Activity: An International Journal* 3(4): 228–245.

Latour, Bruno, and Steve Woolgar (1979) *Laboratory Life: The Construction of Scientific Facts*. Princeton, NJ: Princeton University Press.

Luhmann, Niklas (1969) *Legitimation durch Verfahren*. Frankfurt am Main: Suhrkamp.

Luhmann, Niklas (1990) *Die Wissenschaft der Gesellschaft*. Frankfurt am Main: Suhrkamp.

Niewöhner, Jörg (2015) "Anthropology of Infrastructures of Society," in Neil J. Smelser and Paul B. Baltes (eds) *International Encyclopedia of the Social & Behavioral Sciences*, 2nd edn. Oxford: Elsevier, pp. 119–125.

Perrow, Charles (1984) *Normal Accidents: Living with High-Risk Technologies.* New York: Basic Books.
Pickering, Andrew (1995) *The Mangle of Practice: Time, Agency, and Science.* Chicago, IL: University of Chicago.
Pinch, Trevor (2010) "On making infrastructure visible: Putting the non-humans to rights." *Cambridge Journal of Economy* 34(1): 77–89.
Pollack, Mark A. and Gregory C. Shaffer (2009) *When Cooperation Fails: The International Law and Politics of Genetically Modified Foods.* Oxford: Oxford University Press.
Puig de la Bellacasa, María (2013) "Encountering bioinfrastructure: Ecological struggles and the sciences of soil." *Social Epistemology* 28(1): 26–40.
Rheinberger, Hans-Jörg (1992) *Experiment, Differenz, Schrift: zur Geschichte epistemischer Dinge.* Marburg: Basilisken.
Rottenburg, Richard (2009 [orig. 2002]) *Far-fetched Facts: A Parable of Development Aid.* Cambridge: MIT Press.
Rottenburg, Richard (2012) "On juridico-political foundations of meta-codes," in Jürgen Renn (eds) *The Globalization of Knowledge in History.* Berlin: Max Planck Research Library for the History and Development of Knowledge, pp. 483–500.
Rottenburg, Richard (2014) "Experimental engagements and metacodes." *Common Knowledge* 20(3): 540–548.
Shapin, Steven and Simon Schaffer (1985) *Leviathan and the Air-pump: Hobbes, Boyle and the Experimental Life.* Princeton, NJ: Princeton University Press.
Simone, AbdouMaliq (2004) "People as infrastructure: Intersecting fragments in Johannesburg." *Public Culture* 16(3): 407–428.
Star, Susan Leigh (1999) "The ethnography of infrastructure." *American Behavioral Scientist* 43(3): 377–391.
Star, Susan Leigh and Karen Ruhleder (1996) "Steps toward an ecology of infrastructure." *Information Systems Research* 7(1): 111–134.
Thévenot, Laurent (1984) "Rules and implements: investments in forms." *Social Science Information* 23(1): 1–45.
UBOS (Ugandan Bureau of Statistics) and ICF International (2012) *Uganda Demographic and Health Survey 2011.* Kampala, Uganda: UBOS and Calverton, MD: ICF International.
von Schnitzler, Antina (2013) "Traveling technologies: Infrastructure, ethical tegimes, and the materiality of politics in South Africa." *Cultural Anthropology* 28(4): 670–693.
Winickoff, David, Sheila Jasanoff, Lawrence Busch, Robin Grove-White and Brian Wynne (2005) "Adjudicating the GM food wars: Science, risk, and democracy in world trade law." *Yale Journal of International Law* 30: 80–123.
Winner, Langdon (1986) "Do artifacts have politics?" in Donald A. MacKenzie and Judy Wajcman (eds) *The Social Shaping of Technology.* Buckingham: Open University Press, pp. 28–40.

Part V
Infrastructural figures

Rather than focusing on a specific infrastructural arena, the contributions of this section examine infrastructural figures: a black list (Reeves), the household (Guyer), the border (Green), an indigenous database (Nakazora), and infrastructural gestures (Weszkalnys).

The notion of infrastructural figure highlights that the topics examined are neither quite ethnographically found objects, nor quite conventional concepts. The Russian black list of unwelcome Kyrgyzstani subjects, for example, is obviously a thing in the world, embedded in databases and materialized in visas or evictions. Yet at the same time it is turned into a conceptual device, deployed by Madeleine Reeves to rethink relations between infrastructure and territory. Conversely, infrastructural gesture as examined by Gisa Weszkalnys is clearly an analytical abstraction. However, it is a "found abstraction," discernible in both mundane settings and public performances of the oil infrastructures of São Tomé and Príncipe. Tacking back and forth across the empirical and the conceptual, infrastructural figures thus point to the contingency and instability of both of these terms and of their relations. Doing so, they illustrate that abstraction and conceptualization is not the prerogative of the social scientists (Maurer 2005), but rather something carried out by all actors. In turn, this raises the question of how "our" analytical pathways can, or should be, complicated or redirected by "their" infrastructural forms (databases or borders) or categories (households or immigrants).

The papers in this section share a fascination with how forms of knowledge making and infrastructure bump into one another, and what happens when they do. Each exhibits an interest in how various administrative, commercial, or scientific classifications are built into infrastructural endeavors and how they ricochet off *from* such projects, in unpredictable directions. While these figures testify to a certain indeterminacy of the ethnographic and the conceptual, they thus also evince the indeterminacy of knowledges embedded in infrastructures. There is the indeterminacy experienced and generated by those who design and maintain infrastructural classifications – exemplified by the shifting contours of the household described by Jane Guyer, the emergence of parataxonomy within the indigenous databasing project examined by

Moe Nakazora, and the changing risks and opportunities of oil extraction brought to light by Gisa Weszkalnys. However, indeterminacy is also prevalent on the side of those who experience infrastructural effects, like the Syrian refugees prevented from leaving the Greek island of Lesvos (Sarah Green) or the Kyrgyzstani people whose legal status is inexplicably revoked by Russian authorities (Madeleine Reeves).

Several of these infrastructural figures offer testimony to a continuous play of determination and emergence, legacy and transformation. For one thing, there are historical legacies to the modes of knowing built into infrastructures. Even as the aim is to decolonize knowledge, for example, Nakazora describes how the making of biodiversity databases in Uttarakhand, India, draws on long-standing epistemological divisions between the knowledges of local *vaidyas* and those of colonial botanists and state bureaucrats. Jane Guyer's detailed examination of the infrastructural life of the category of the "household" also pays explicit attention to the ordering effects of legacy. On the one hand, the household has become so deeply embedded in a bewildering set of administrative practices and infrastructures that it is hardly imaginable that it might disappear. On the other hand, the ordering effect of its legacy is compromised through the same process.

Indeed, as we know from Michel Serres (1982), and as ethnographically recapitulated in the studies of the household, borders and databases here, classifications *at once* generate order *and* disorder. This point is particularly vividly illustrated by Reeves's contribution, which describes how Kyrgyzstani people respond to finding themselves on the Russian immigration black list. As far as they are concerned, the opaque, even unknowable, black list is constitutive not of orderly state security but rather of anxiety and *disorder*.

In spite of the intentions of their designers, however, there are forms of information not captured by black lists, visas, or government categories. Thus, there are gaps in both knowledge and control, and savvy people can exploit these gaps, navigating the interstices of infrastructural classification in order to, temporarily at least, elude control.

Depending on purpose and rationale, the infrastructures exhibit variable patterns of visibility and darkness. Whereas the indigenous databasing described by Nakazora is all about *putting together* and *making available* knowledge, the intimidating effects of the Russian black list are due in large part to its *unknowability*. Contrary to the Russian list, the household as a category central to bureaucratic infrastructures, or the immigration procedures that prevent the entry of Syrian refugees in the EU are presumably not *designed for* opacity. Even so, they are certainly also not experienced as transparent by those on whose lives they impinge.

Urging consideration of how to think about infrastructures that do not work as intended by their designers, Weszkalnys notes the pervasive anthropological interest in infrastructural failure. Of course, infrastructures often do seem to fail. Yet the interest anthropologists take in failure may also be related to the way in which it paves the way for symbolic analysis, for even if malfunctioning in material terms, infrastructures can emit images of modernity and power.

Weszkalnys argues, however, some infrastructures neither fail nor succeed. They simply linger on (see also Namba's contribution to this volume). Thus, the importance of infrastructural gestures – the negotiation of a contract, the delineation of a development zone, or the exploratory drilling of a well – is to temporarily attenuate, or postpone, the sense of failure.

Here is a contrast with Sarah Green's paper, which deals with the simultaneous breakdown in the summer of 2015 of the Greek financial infrastructure (related to the banking crisis) and of the administrative infrastructure (meant to deal with massive influx of refugees). Both Weszkalnys and Green grapple with the question of infrastructural reconfigurations, yet Green deploys the very lens of failure which Weszkalnys is reconsidering. Even so, Green does not use failure as a launching pad for a conventional analysis of infrastructures as spectacles, images, or symbols. Instead, she examines how the breakdown of banking and administrative systems was compounded, or amplified, due to the mutual interweaving of these infrastructures with each other, and with many other different locations. The extent to which failure is a relevant mode of analysis may hinge, among other things, on issues of temporality and speed. While using gestures to temporarily hold at bay what does not yet quite work is a viable description of many infrastructural situations, cases of swift and dramatic collapse like the Greek case analyzed by Green calls for other concepts or "found abstractions." Green's depiction of interwoven scales, politics, and territories offers one promising avenue of inquiry.

In different ways, infrastructural figures allow us to grasp the important difference between legacy and determinism. They show us the future as infrastructurally made and remade through a continuous re-alignment between old (legacy) elements – contracts, bits of knowledge, procedure, or standards – and new additions. These new elements, whether they are added to Russian governmental databases or to databases containing *vaidya* knowledges, create order *and* disorder, and introduce indeterminate gaps or suspensions. New infrastructural aspirations and arrangements *emerge from* (rather than being inhibited by) such pauses. In cases of sudden infrastructural *implosion*, such as the one depicted by Green, it becomes yet clearer that legacy systems, far from guaranteeing stability and durability, always remain open to unpredictable horizons.

Indeterminacy thus occurs where legacies recombine with new infrastructural elements. As the figures examined in the section suggest, this is the point where determinism gives way to emergence. Even as indigenous databasing in Uttarakhand draws on colonial legacies, it has given rise to dynamic, emergent forms of indigenous and scientific knowledge (Nakazora). Integrating previously unrelated sources of data, the Russian black list, too, has emergent effects (Reeves). And both the oil infrastructures of São Tomé and Príncipe and the urban development of Berlin (Weszkalnys) continue to sustain potentiality, keeping open pathways to the future. As described by

Jane Guyer, even the household, seemingly so static, has emergent properties, generative of administrative patterns that only *seem* beyond being actively constructed and *re*-constructed. Finally, as Green's analysis of the double infrastructural breakdown on Lesvos makes painfully clear, emergence – being propelled into new territory – does not come with any guarantee of improvement.

References

Maurer, Bill (2005) *Mutual Life, Limited Islamic Banking, Alternative Currencies, Lateral Reason*. Princeton, NJ: Princeton University Press.

Serres, Michel (1982) *The Parasite*. Baltimore, MD and London: Johns Hopkins University Press.

20 When infrastructures fail
An ethnographic note in the middle of an Aegean crisis

Sarah Green

The Aegean Sea region, that part of the north Mediterranean that divides Greece from Turkey, has three distinctive characteristics. The first is that it contains a double border structure: in addition to the state boundaries between Greece and Turkey, the region also contains a European Union border.[1] The second is that the Aegean is an archipelago: the sea is covered with a scatter of islands in between the mainlands of Greece and Turkey. And the third is that all but two of those islands are part of Greece, even though many of them are physically located much closer to the Turkish mainland. There are a few islets (essentially large rocks) that belong to Turkey, but all but two of the sizable and inhabited islands belong to Greece. This has often caused disagreement between the Greek and Turkish governments about exactly where the line between the two countries is located within sea and air. Given that international law stipulates that sovereignty is established from land and extends into the sea and air in a rather complex way (Acer 2003), the fact that there are so many Greek islands located just across the coast from Turkey has caused regular diplomatic and military episodes between the two countries (Green 2015).

The summer of 2015 in the Aegean was different from the usual pattern of relatively calm tourist season occasionally disrupted by a minor dispute about territorial infringements. In 2015, the proximity of the Greek islands to the Turkish coast resulted in a different dynamic that is still going on as this article is being written, and which has been reported regularly in the world's press and social media. It concerned a very large movement of people travelling through Turkey to the western Anatolian coast in order to buy passage across the sea to one of the islands from anyone willing to sell it to them; these travellers do not possess the right visas. Once they arrived on a Greek island, often in a state of exhaustion and shock from the trip, these travellers would claim asylum in the European Union.

This particular route into EU territory has in fact been used for quite a few years – particularly since the mid-2000s, when conflicts in Iraq and later in other parts of the Arab world destabilised places to the east of Turkey, resulting every year in a steady number of people fleeing to Turkey, then some of them taking the short but often dangerous trip to the shore of one of the

Greek islands. However, the numbers taking that short sea trip were not that large, and although there were regular incidents in which drowning occurred, the clandestine transportation of people from Turkey to the Greek islands in the Aegean was mostly a concern of the EU and Greek state authorities rather than a regular global news item (Green 2010). But the summer of 2015 was different: the sheer scale of the movement of people, the sheer number of deaths in the attempts to cross, and the fact that these people became increasingly vociferous, breaking the strange silence that seems to accompany asylum seekers under most circumstances (they are spoken about, and they are spoken to, but one rarely hears them speak for themselves, except in ethnographies) transformed the situation.

On the Turkish side, and most especially in Izmir, the main city of the western Anatolian coast, there was an enormous amount of unusual activity as a result of this movement of people. Large numbers of strangers – men, women, children, often exhausted from days of walking – were moving around the city and countryside in groups, waiting on street corners and in parks, buying bright orange life vests in preparation for the short crossing to one of the Greek islands located just a few kilometres away: Kos, Chíos, Samos, Rhodes, Leros and, especially, Lesvos, the island where I have carried out several years of research on the shifting relations between Greece and Turkey (Green 2008, 2010, 2013). On the Turkish side, this was not reported as a 'crisis' but simply as an unusual phenomenon. Even when the famous image of the small Syrian boy lying drowned in the sand on the Turkish side was broadcast across the world and contributed to a major change in policy in Europe,[2] there was no sense that Turkey was experiencing a crisis. The boy was pictured being attended to by a Turkish police officer – that is, the authorities were there, coping with the situation (see Figure 20.1). That's just what governments do; they handle emergencies and unexpected events when they occur. It was rather on the side of the Greek islands that this very large movement of people, including those who drowned in the attempt to cross, was defined as a crisis. There were regular reports of authorities being 'overwhelmed' by the numbers of people arriving; pictures of locals, bare-chested, rescuing drowning people out of the sea (Figure 20.2)[3] and of overcrowded refugee camps unable to deal with the numbers that were arriving.[4]

There was more: this was Greece, whose government was in the deepest financial trouble of all the governments of the EU member states during this period of such trouble for everyone. During the summer of 2015, the government appeared to be fighting for Greece's very survival in the Eurozone. And in July 2015 the banks were closed. So it can be fairly said that the basic infrastructure of Greece was failing. In contrast, Turkish infrastructure appeared to be working in an orderly fashion, despite the massive movement of people across its territory, and even though Turkey was itself dealing with hundreds of thousands – later millions – of refugees and had set up huge camps at its northern and eastern land borders.[5] But on the small Greek

When infrastructures fail 273

Figure 20.1 Aylan Kurdi's body being carried by Mehmet Ciplak, the Turkish police officer.
© Nilüfer Demir/AP Images

Figure 20.2 Antonis Deligiorgis saving Wegasi Nebiat on 20 April 2015.
© Argiris Mantikos/AP

islands, part of a state that appeared to be going bankrupt, the infrastructure was regularly reported as buckling under the strain.

Appel, Anand and Gupta note that infrastructural failure is a fundamental and normal part of infrastructural dynamics: 'infrastructural breakdowns saturate a particular politics of the present. As such, the material and political lives of infrastructure reveal fragile relations between people, things, and the institutions (both public and private) that seek to govern them' (Appel et al. 2015). Yet there are different levels and scales of breakdown, and what was happening on the Greek islands appeared to be going beyond the normal and into the category of serious structural failure. Indeed, the infrastructural troubles that Greece has been experiencing since 2009 might take the country into the category that Marianne Ferme (1998) terms the 'normally abnormal'. Ferme was referring to countries such as Sierra Leone, in which the failure of infrastructure was a basic element of the way things work. With the apparent collapse of infrastructure in mind, rather than any change in the people, many Greeks have suggested to me that their country was rapidly descending into 'third world' status. The descent concerned the material conditions, and in particular the infrastructural conditions, that make everyday life possible.

Yet this story of infrastructural failure being a sign of state failure warrants a little more attention. One of its implications is that if a government does not have an efficient grip on its territory, then the state is not functioning properly. The key word here is 'territory', which embeds assumptions about the relationship between people, governance and land. Specifically, as powerfully argued by Stuart Elden (2013) in *The Birth of Territory,* the concept of territory as it is commonly understood in contemporary political and social imagination has a particular history that is deeply bound up with concepts of modernity. In Elden's words, 'The idea of a territory as a bounded space under the control of a group of people, usually a state, is ... historically produced' (2013: 322). This means that infrastructural control over such an entity can only be seen as a sign of state control, or its lack, once it is imagined that a territory is a coherent physical space that *ought* to be under the control of a single political and legal entity. What the media were depicting as occurring on the Greek islands, and in Greece more widely, was thus a general breakdown of what was imagined to be normal state functioning.

While a reasonable enough approach in legal terms, that particular understanding of territory draws attention away from the fact that all parts of the globe are interconnected and that states are dependent upon other states in order to exist at all. That becomes obvious in studies of territories whose boundaries wind around one another to such a degree that it is hard to know, on the ground, in which state you are standing at any one time, as wonderfully described by Madeleine Reeves for the Ferghana Valley (Reeves 2014). Reeves also notes that this particular understanding of territory co-exists with other conceptualisations of space that would not carve up the world in those terms.[6] This is particularly visible elsewhere in infrastructural terms. Gas pipelines between Russia and Germany is an obvious case in point; others are less apparent. For instance, both sides of Cyprus, despite decades of territorial dispute, share the same raw sewage network. While states do at times have control over certain aspects of their infrastructure – and while they may at times feel so hostile towards neighbours that they build parallel systems rather than use the same infrastructure – on many occasions states have no choice but to share infrastructure.

The case of the Aegean in the summer of 2015 is interesting in this respect. Both the banking crisis and the refugee crisis on Lesvos involved infrastructural failures that were as much to do with Greek relations with other places and organisations as they were to do with Greek infrastructural weaknesses. This is a rather obvious point, since transnational interests in Greece have become much more explicit in politics, economy and even discourse of Hellenism than in many other countries (Ladas 1932; Clogg 1986; Herzfeld 1986; Fleming 1999; Hirschon 2003).

In spite of its importance, the particular understanding of territory that Elden examines, one that focuses on sovereign control over a coherent patch of the earth, draws attention away from what could be called the interweaving of territories and infrastructures. While the literature on globalisation has repeatedly demonstrated transnational interdependence (albeit quite weighted in favour of some powers more than others), the way in which infrastructural failures become involved in this has not received equal attention.

In this chapter, my interest in infrastructure thus concerns the way in which it constitutes both an interface and a route between places and peoples. This topic intrigues me, as an anthropologist of border dynamics, the ways in which places are mutually interdependent, and the social and cultural implications of this interdependence has been a key focus for me (Green 2005; 2010, 2012, 2013). Originally, this chapter was going to be about Mediterranean trade routes and on how the movement of cargo could be used to trace both relations and separations between places quite different from the kinds of relations and separations traceable by considering people's identities or movements. Using the same principle, infrastructure highlights the fact that location, seen as the relative position of a physical geographical space, always matters: *where* somewhere is located relative to other places has a great deal to do with the infrastructural arrangements made. The infrastructure in itself provides a material trace of the dense network of relations and separations between locations.

Yet while many studies have examined how infrastructure connects and transforms relations between people, states and places, they have less often focused on the ways in which infrastructure can create overlapping and interweaving sovereignty over territory (though see Reeves 2016 for an excellent exception). That aspect has perhaps been most intensely debated in recent years in terms of the European Union's potential encroachment on the sovereignty of its member states (Barry 2001; Barry 2015) and in terms of globalisation (Dodd 1995; Sassen 1996; Brown 2010). Yet these debates tend to look at how states are losing their sovereignty to some other powers, either commercial or political. They thus retain the idea of a zero sum game: territory is an entity that is politically controlled (or not), rather than being something else, perhaps something like a variety of collaborations or alliances, mixed in with enmities and disconnections. This would direct attention away from territory in terms of sovereignty and towards the question of how infrastructure undergirds the 'workings' of location in practice. The rest of this paper offers an ethnographic example of this approach, taken from the summer of 2015 in the Aegean. As it makes clear, the failure of infrastructures makes acutely visible the overlaps, dependencies and separations between places.

A moment in the Aegean crisis: July 2015, Lesvos

On Sunday, 5 July 2015, I arrived for a short working visit to the island of Lesvos, less than 40 km off the western coast of Turkey. I had been carrying out ethnographic research there on and off for years, but what brought me back for this short trip was a summer school, for which I had been asked to teach a course about the anthropology of borders.[7] Coincidentally, 5 July was the date of a snap referendum called by the Greek prime minister, Alexis Tsipras, just over a week earlier on 27 June. Tsipras had been in government for five months, after his radical left coalition political party, Syriza, won the general election at the end of January 2015 on a strong 'anti-austerity' platform, replacing the right-leaning New Democracy.

It was gearing up to the height of the summer season on Lesvos, yet the beaches were relatively empty, as were the restaurants and hotels. People working in the tourist trade reported there had been scores of cancellations from tourists the previous week. Only the port in Mytilene, the capital of the island, was bustling with people that morning: the main ferry from Piraeus had just docked, and people, cars and cargo were streaming out. In addition to the tourists, there were Greeks returning to their home-town to vote in the referendum; there were also deliveries of supplies for the island. The port was also full of people who had arrived not on the ferry but from the Turkish shores, most of them picked up by the Greek coastguard as they tried to cross in small inflatable crafts, a pile of which was now gathering at the other end of the port, dumped there by the coastguard. By 5 July, between 800 and 1,000 of these people – undocumented migrants, refugees, asylum seekers: call them what you will – were arriving daily on the island of Lesvos.[8] I did not know then that the daily number of arrivals would rise quite dramatically as the summer continued, only dropping a little as the weather turned colder and stormier into autumn. The authorities could not cope even in July; they could not process all these people, let alone find them adequate housing, resources or any kind of decent conditions. Even though they had been extended and expanded earlier in the year, the refugee camps had long ago been filled to overflowing. In July there were as yet virtually no international agencies on the island. Somehow, even though the newspapers were reporting regularly on the issue, and particularly from Lesvos, there was no UNHCR,[9] no Médecins Sans Frontières, no Red Cross, and no politicians visiting daily to have their photographs taken near the packed camps. (All of these would eventually arrive, but it took several more weeks of dramatic photographs in the media; it was not until September that the image of the young Kurdish Syrian boy drowned on the shore of Bodrum appeared.) There was just the Greek coastguard and navy, the merchant ships, occasional visits from Frontex (an EU agency that helps to monitor the EU's external borders), the residents of the island and the tourists.

On this morning, like every morning, a small %age of these people were having their paperwork examined in preparation for transfer to Athens for further processing. A police bus full of applicants, with the glass of its back window missing, was waiting by the municipal swimming pool, a giant concrete dome built at the edge of the port during the 1967–74 period of military rule, right next to the town's municipal beach. That, along with some public toilets, was just about all that the town received in terms of new amenities from the military regime: Lesvos had a reputation for having been communist-leaning. Still, it meant the town was not littered with the concrete monstrosities that the military regime was so fond of building in the late 1960s and early 1970s as part of its material-imaginative expression of its relationship with infrastructure and modernity.[10]

Back at the port in July 2015, many of the applicants for transfer to Athens were on foot, crowding round the bus and the offices that were supposed to deal with their paperwork. Many blended in well with the tourists and others coming off the ship; others looked distinctly different. At that time, the majority arriving on Lesvos were Syrian citizens, having travelled through Turkey in the attempt to escape the increasingly violent and unstable political and economic conditions in post-2011 Syria. Some estimates suggested that half of the country or more was under the control of ISIS/ISIL/Daesh at that moment. Many people feared for their lives – or the quality of their lives – and wanted to get out. So here they were, some of them, waiting in the port in Mytilene.

The Syrians were not the only arrivals. There were also people from Afghanistan, Iraq, Libya, even Pakistan, and many other places. Many of those had been waiting months, perhaps years, in enormous Turkish refugee camps and elsewhere, at the edge of what used to be called 'Fortress Europe'. The policies of the European Union tried to change that reputation in the early 2000s, to encourage a more 'neighbourly' approach towards the countries just outside the EU's borders. The European Neighbourhood Policy (ENP for short) was originally drawn up in 2004 after the enlargement of the EU by ten new member states. The policy was supposed to create a 'ring of friends' around the outer edges of the EU, in which mutual agreements and partnerships would be forged among those neighbours that were not EU member states. The ENP now feels like something from a different political era.

One aim at that time, at least at the highest political level, was to try to blur the distinction between the inside and outside of the EU (Delanty and

Rumford 2005: 127). Yet for the people waiting outside the borders of EU states trying to get in, it felt as though 'Fortress Europe' was not only alive and well but had in fact been strengthened. As others have noted (Kølvraa and Ifversen 2011), particularly since 2007, after Russia attacked Georgia, the policies dealing with the EU's outer borders have steadily involved ever-greater mechanisms for surveillance and control. By July 2015, the overall border management infrastructure of the EU region – the border controls, guards, regulations, surveillance and monitoring technologies and so on – had expanded to such a degree that some have suggested that the effect (or perhaps, in part, the design) was to turn border management into a major and profitable industry (Andersson 2014; Brown 2010).

One indication is that Frontex was founded at the same time as the ENP was developed.[11] This was an EU border management agency whose purpose was to help EU member states manage the borders between EU and non-EU countries (Green 2010). Frontex had been carrying out operations in the Aegean since 2007. While there may have been special reasons why there was particular pressure on the EU's external borders in the summer of 2015 (namely, political turbulence in the Arab world), the reduction of easy legal routes to enter the EU had been implemented more than ten years previously through a mixture of infrastructural and juridical means. The consequence was that most people had little choice but to use illegal routes.

As the refugee crisis began gathering momentum, the Greek referendum held on 5 July had caused considerable annoyance to the European Commission, the European Central Bank and the International Monetary Fund (collectively known as the Eurogroup, or Troika), which were collectively trying to negotiate with the new Greek government about how to handle its public debt mountain.[12] The Eurogroup had been in talks with Prime Minister Tsipras and the then Greek finance minister, Yiannis Varoufakis, an academic economist and game theory specialist, about a new agreement with creditors to secure a third bailout package for Greece.

The talks had been going on for all five months of Tsipras's premiership without results. On 25 June, the Eurogroup presented the Greek government with a set of conditions in exchange for arranging a third tranche of funds to keep Greece from going bankrupt as a result of the country's now five-year-long financial crisis. These conditions were slightly modified on 26 June, but Tsipras walked out of the negotiations, announcing that most went directly against the policies for which he had been elected (i.e. in his view, the conditions would result in greater austerity, whereas he had promised anti-austerity policies). Tsipras then announced that he had to call a referendum to ask the Greek people's opinion on whether or not these conditions were acceptable. What particularly annoyed the Eurogroup[13] was that Tsipras and Varoufakis went home and vigorously campaigned for the Greek people to vote 'no' in the referendum.

It was not, however, entirely clear what the Greek people were being asked to vote for or against. The actual referendum question was 75 words long and referred to two official English language documents that were on the negotiating table in Brussels on 25 June, but which had not been officially translated into Greek.[14] Those conditions were in any case no longer on offer, as Tsipras had gone home. But if the question was no longer relevant, what was the referendum actually asking? The Eurogroup said the referendum was asking whether or not Greece still wanted to be part of the Eurozone, or return to the Greek drachma. Tsipras said it was about giving him, as prime minister, a stronger bargaining position in getting the best deal for Greece at the negotiating table. Nobody really knows what the voters thought was the issue.

In any case, time was running out: repayments for previous bailout loans were rapidly coming due, and without further bailout funds, the Greek government would be unable to meet the deadlines. Moreover, the Greek banks were running out of money, as customers had been withdrawing their funds in quantities amounting to billions of euros weekly for months.[15] The upper limit of what the European Central Bank was willing to lend to Greek banks to maintain their liquidity was about to be reached. In light of this, Tsipras announced that the Greek banks would be closed from 29 June until after the referendum. Customers were limited to €60 per day in withdrawals, with the exception of pensioners, who would receive a one-off €120 payment. Greek bank and credit cards ceased to work, as the banking system that processed all the exchanges were closed. Foreigners were still free to use cashpoint machines and credit cards, as they were linked to foreign banks. However, visitors to Greece were warned to take cash from abroad: businesses might be reluctant to accept cards, since their own banks were closed.

Tsipras and Varoufakis promised that on the following Tuesday, 7 July, the banks would reopen, but nobody really believed them. Actually, nobody knew what to believe anymore. The newspapers started a daily diet of photographs of people queuing at cashpoint machines in Greece; images of people lining up outside banks in the bright summer sunshine appeared globally. It became the symbol of the crisis: cash machines that no longer worked. Images of a distressed pensioner, a man, weeping on the floor of a bank, went viral.

On 30 June, the Greek government missed a deadline for a repayment to the International Monetary Fund (IMF), the first time a developed country (whatever that means) had failed to meet an IMF repayment deadline. The Greek government had asked for a delay until after the referendum, but the IMF had refused; the director, Christine Lagarde, repeated her oft-quoted statement that the IMF never extends deadlines.[16] That was also the day the existing financial bailout to Greece expired. In the absence of a new agreement, the European Central Bank (ECB) announced that it would not extend or raise the cap on its emergency liquidity for the Greek banks, as the Greek government were in breach of their conditions by failing to repay the IMF, and effectively in default. Newspapers began reporting that without the ECB's help, the banks would run out of money, perhaps within a week. Varoufakis called the Eurogroup's actions 'terrorism': by refusing to keep the banks afloat until after the referendum, they had forced Varoufakis to close the banks, thereby making people so afraid of the consequences of going against the will of the Eurogroup that they would vote 'yes' in the referendum, rather than follow his advice and that of his prime minister.

In the event, 61.3 per cent voted 'no' and 38.7 per cent voted 'yes', with the votes in Lesvos almost precisely matching the national result. This was a shock result; everybody had expected it to be much closer, including the opinion pollsters; and many believed the vote would go the other way. Angela Merkel, chancellor of Germany and one of the key members of the Eurogroup because Germany provides the lion share of credit to Greece, announced that Greece had lost her trust. The banks remained closed for more than three weeks, and capital controls are still in place as I write, in early 2016, even though they are a little more relaxed than in July 2015.

By 5 July, two key infrastructures on the island of Lesvos, the banking system and the management and processing of refugees to the island, were exhibiting fairly radical signs of failure. And it was these infrastructural failures that provided the most visible aspect of the extraordinary conditions in which Lesvos found itself on 5 July – the element that made the whole situation *feel* like a crisis. The media understood this as well as everybody else: they were obsessively taking pictures of people standing around in crowds waiting for some failing bit of infrastructure to deliver. Images of large crowds waiting in front of cash machines and of the stalled processing of immigration documents became images of systemic failure.

Conclusion

In July 2015, the people of Lesvos felt like they were in the middle of a perfect storm blowing onto their shores from elsewhere. The banking system was entirely dependent upon not only the European Central Bank but also a dense network of mutually dependent transnational banking structures. And the refugee crisis had been generated through wars that occurred elsewhere. Moreover, the crisis attending the arrival of so many undocumented people on their shores was as much to do with EU border control policies developed during the 2000s as it was to do with the island's meagre resources for coping with the overwhelming pressure.

These border control policies included the Dublin Regulation, which states that foreign nationals claiming asylum must be processed in the first EU country they enter, rather than being shared between the EU countries. That regulation had been written in a different time, when it was imagined that what needed to be controlled was the free movement of people through the Schengen area. Nobody had imagined a condition like the one on Lesvos in the summer of 2015, where the infrastructures could no longer deal with the numbers of people seeking shelter. What these ethnographic examples demonstrate is that, in the case of Greece that summer, the territory no longer matched that of a sovereign state. A great deal of what happened there, including the two infrastructural failures that made the headlines that summer (the Greek banking crisis and the refugee crisis), speaks to an interweaving of widely different locations, territories and infrastructures.

Notes

1 Although Turkey is a candidate to join the EU (and has been for longer than any other state), it is currently located immediately outside the EU.
2 www.theguardian.com/world/2015/sep/02/shocking-image-of-drowned-syrian-boy-shows-tragic-plight-of-refugees, last accessed 22.1.2016.
3 www.theguardian.com/world/2015/apr/25/migrant-boat-crisis-the-sergeant-who-did-his-duty-towards-people-struggling-for-their-lives, last accessed 22.1.2016.
4 I am deliberately not providing an example of such images.
5 www.unhcr.org/pages/49e48e0fa7f.html, last accessed 22.1.2016.
6 See also Reeves (2016), where she discusses the political effort to give territory a coherence using infrastructural projects.
7 See https://migbord2015.pns.aegean.gr/.
8 I prefer 'people', which is admittedly less informative but also less classificatory. See http://time.com/3947493/migrants-greece-lesbos-refugees-asylum/ and www.theguardian.com/world/2015/jul/08/greek-island-refugee-crisis-local-people-and-tourists-rally-round-migrants for a couple of stories on the issue.
9 UN High Commission for Refugees
10 The links between infrastructure projects and hubristic political regimes hardly needs reiterating here (Horn 1991; Bastéa 2000; Weizman 2007).
11 http://frontex.europa.eu/about-frontex/origin/. See also van Houtum (2012) for a critical analysis of Frontex's mission.
12 This was the Eurogroup, which was made up of the European Commission, European Central Bank, and the International Monetary Fund.
13 Other than the fact that Tsipras and Varoufakis walked out of the negotiations just when the rest of the Eurogroup believed a deal was within reach (see http://europa.eu/rapid/press-release_IP-15-5270_en.htm).
14 The referendum question asked of Greek citizens on 7 July was (in translation) as follows: 'Must the agreement plan submitted by the European Commission, the European Central Bank and the International Monetary Fund to the Eurogroup of 25 June, 2015, and comprised of two parts which make up their joint proposal, be accepted? The first document is titled "reforms for the completion of the current programme and beyond" and the second "Preliminary debt sustainability analysis".'
15 See www.reuters.com/article/2015/02/16/us-greece-banks-deposits-idUSKBN0LK1HC20150216.
16 www.aljazeera.com/news/2015/04/imf-rules-greek-debt-repayment-extension-150417020543933.html.

References

Acer, Yücel (2003) *The Aegean maritime disputes and international law*. Aldershot: Ashgate.
Andersson, Ruben (2014) *Illegality, inc.: clandestine migration and the business of bordering Europe*. Oakland, CA: University of California Press.
Appel, Hannah, Nikhil Anand and Akhil Gupta (2015) "Introduction: The infrastructure toolbox". *Cultural Anthropology*, www.culanth.org/fieldsights/714-introduction-the-infrastructure-toolbox.

Barry, Andrew (2001) *Political machines: governing a technological society*. London and New York: Athlone Press.
Barry, Andrew (2015) "Discussion: infrastructural times'". *Cultural Anthropology*, www.culanth.org/fieldsights/724-discussion-infrastructural-times.
Bastéa, Eleni (2000) *The creation of modern Athens: planning the myth*. Cambridge: Cambridge University Press.
Brown, Wendy (2010) *Walled states, waning sovereignty*. New York: Zone.
Clogg, Richard (1986) *A short history of modern Greece*. Cambridge and New York: Cambridge University Press.
Delanty, Gerard and Chris Rumford (2005) *Rethinking Europe: social theory and the implications of Europeanization*. London: Routledge.
Dodd, N. (1995) "Money and the nation-state: contested boundaries of monetary sovereignty in geopolitics". *International Sociology* 10(2): 139.
Fleming, K. E. (1999) *The Muslim Bonaparte: diplomacy and orientalism in Ali Pasha's Greece*. Princeton, NJ: Princeton University Press.
Green, Sarah (2005) *Notes from the Balkans: locating marginality and ambiguity on the Greek-Albanian border*. Princeton, NJ and Oxford: Princeton University Press.
Green, Sarah (2008) "Contingencies of performativity: on relocating money, the political and the social in the Aegean". Paper presented at the Performativity as Politics: Unlocking Economic Sociology conference, 23–25 October, University of Toulouse, France.
Green, Sarah (2010) "Performing border in the Aegean: on relocating political, economic and social relations". *Journal of Cultural Economy* 3(2): 261–278.
Green, Sarah (2012) "A sense of border", in Thomas M. Wilson and Hastings Donnan (eds) *A Companion to Border Studies*. Oxford: Wiley-Blackwell, pp. 573–592.
Green, Sarah (2013) "Money frontiers: the relative location of euros, Turkish lira and gold sovereigns in the Aegean", in Penny Harvey, Eleanor Casella, Gillian Evans, Hannah Knox, Christine McLean, Elizabeth Silva, Nicholas Thoburn and Kath Woodward (eds) *Objects and Materials: A Routledge Companion*. Abingdon: Routledge, pp. 302–311.
Green, Sarah (2015) "Making grey zones at the European peripheries". In Ida Harboe Knudsen and Martin Demant Frederiksen (eds) *Ethnographies of grey zones in Eastern Europe: relations, borders and invisibilities*. London and New York: Anthem Press, pp. 173–186.
Herzfeld, Michael (1986) *Ours once more: folklore, ideology, and the making of modern Greece*. New York: Pella Publishing.
Hirschon, Renée (ed.) (2003) *Crossing the Aegean: an appraisal of the 1923 compulsory population exchange between Greece and Turkey*. New York and Oxford: Berghahn Books.
Horn, David G. (1991) "Constructing the sterile city: pronatalism and social sciences in interwar Italy". *American Ethnologist* 18(3): 581–601.
Kølvraa, Christoffer and Jan Ifversen (2011) "The European Neighbourhood Policy: geopolitics or value export?" In Federiga M. Bindi and Irina Angelescu (eds) *The frontiers of Europe: a transatlantic problem?* Rome and Washington, DC: Brookings Institution Press.
Ladas, Stephen P. (1932) *The exchange of minorities: Bulgaria, Greece and Turkey*. New York: Macmillan.
Reeves, Madeleine (2014) *Border work: spatial lives of the state in rural Central Asia*. Ithaca, NY and London: Cornell University Press.

Reeves, Madeleine (2016) "Infrastructural hope: anticipating 'independent roads' and territorial integrity in southern Kyrgyzstan". *Ethnos*, doi: 10.1080/00141844.2015.1119176.

Sassen, Saskia (1996) *Losing control? Sovereignty in an age of globalization*. New York and Chichester: Columbia University Press.

van Houtum, Henk (2012) "Remapping borders", in Thomas M. Wilson and Hastings Donnan (eds) *A Companion to Border Studies*. Oxford: Wiley-Blackwell, pp. 405–418.

Weizman, Eyal (2007) *Hollow land: Israel's architecture of occupation*. London: Verso.

21 Infrastructure as gesture

Gisa Weszkalnys

A licensing round: *March 2010. The first licensing round for petroleum exploration rights in the Exclusive Economic Zone (EEZ) of São Tomé and Príncipe is launched at APPEX, "A truly global A&D [acquisitions and divestitures] conference" held in the Business Design Centre in Islington, London. The participants include exploration firms, individual country delegations, and service companies such as PGS, which has acquired STP's seismic data and now supports the country's presence at the conference. PGS seeks to capitalize on STP's prospective oil. Products are being shown off on large-sized posters, maps, and leaflets. Pens, sweets, coffee, biscuits, and other freebies are handed out. The PGS representatives assure me that the turnout is fulfilling their expectations. At least two companies have already shown interest in visiting PGS's Surrey data room. The EEZ is virgin territory, they explain, and frontier areas attract interest. They expect bids to come in soon. Three per block would be good. On a screen in a darkened auditorium, STP's Prime Minister Rafael Branco launches the licensing round. His failure to attain a visa prevented him from being there in person. The long-awaited licensing round was repeatedly delayed by conflicting political interests, mere foot dragging, or maybe by nothing at all. Time runs slowly in Africa, PGS representatives tell me. All that counts is that "today is an auspicious day for us," as one of them proclaims. Ten years of seismic surveying and considerable investments – about $100,000 per day just to hire the research vessel – are finally coming to fruition.*

A citizens' workshop: *August 2015. About 140 Berliners gather in the Park Inn Hotel at Alexanderplatz, a public square in Berlin's eastern center. They have come to discuss with city planners, various experts, and each other Alexanderplatz's future fate. A master plan for the square's redevelopment, first conceived in 1993 but only partially implemented to date, is now considered in desperate need of revision. However, the parameters for the development will remain in place, explains Berlin Senate's building director in her opening talk. Her words are carefully chosen: the aim is to update, not to redraw, the plan. In any case, as the architect who designed the plan emphasizes – repeating his view of twenty years ago – Alexanderplatz's current socialist design is hardly worth keeping. When pressed, his prognosis is optimistic: "Two-thirds of the* *envisaged high-rise buildings will be built within the next five years." "Capital has confidence in the location," comments one of the participating experts, citing the developers' preliminary €73 million investment in infrastructures as evidence. Yet, he adds wryly, their confidence has not quite sufficed for highrise buildings. What we are doing here, says one citizen, is to help dream the new Alexanderplatz into existence – complete with appealing shops and restaurants, adequate amenities, and affordable apartments – even as the master plan seems increasingly obsolete.*

In this chapter, I consider a specific modality of infrastructures in relation to the contradictory dynamics of contemporary capitalism.[1] I call this modality "infrastructure as gesture." The infrastructures I examine include a range of practices and devices, such as the licensing round for São Tomé and Príncipe's EEZ and the citizens' workshop for Alexanderplatz. I argue that, as gestures, infrastructures are neither simply means to an end, that is, instruments in the realization of larger-scale projects. Nor are they ends, or project outcomes, in themselves. Instead, infrastructures as gestures suggest the existence of productive potential – often over extended periods of time and in situations where this potential may threaten to remain unrealized. They provide us with a clue to what sustains a notion of capitalism's propulsive force, which we often take for granted, in the face of its characteristic contradictions (Harvey 1989). Infrastructures as gestures thus differ in important ways from infrastructural projects that have blatantly failed (Green, this volume), from those that have been called into question by their users (von Schnitzler 2013), and from infrastructures that ought not to work but have nonetheless persisted (Richardson 2016). By contrast, I argue that, in their gestural form, infrastructures contribute to the postponement of failure. Specifically, they prevent the projects of which they are part from being written off or abandoned.

The gesture has been somewhat peripheral in anthropological theorizing – despite Geertz's famous invocation of the wink and the twitch in his essay on thick description, and despite its prominent place in the writings of scholars such as Mauss, Elias, and Goffman.[2] In developing the gesture's analytical purchase beyond its conventional reference to a type of bodily movement, I draw not on anthropology, however, but on the work of Giorgio Agamben, who has provided one of the most compelling discussions of the gesture as a philosophical concept. Agamben sought to formulate an ethics of encounter in which the "formless kind of life" embodied by the gesture is a critical element (ten Bos 2005: 27). Building on Varro and Aristotle, Agamben pointed to a subtle distinction between the gesture's Latin root, *gerere* meaning to carry, manage, or conduct, and related action verbs, including *facere* (making, creating) and *agere* (acting, performing). In this view, "[t]he gesture is the exhibition of mediality: it is the process of making a means visible as such" (Agamben 2000: 58). The gesture, Agamben notes, is where "nothing is being produced or acted, but rather something is being endured and supported"

(2000: 57). Similarly, though in a very different way from Agamben's philosophical project, I argue that although the infrastructure as gesture usually fails to be productive, it is rarely "just" a gesture. That is, infrastructural gestures are not simply tokens, not vacuous, even as ambiguity remains inherent.

I will develop the notion of the gesture's indeterminate yet sustaining force by comparing two quite dissimilar cases. The first is the protracted quest for what petro-industry experts call "first oil" in São Tomé and Príncipe (STP), a micro-island state located in the oil-rich Gulf of Guinea. First oil refers to the initial oil pumped from a newly commercialized exploration well. It acts on forms of speculative knowledge and engages one or more capital, technology, and knowledge-intensive investment projects that are the indispensable but inherently risky "motor[s] of capitalist wealth creation" (Røyrvik 2011: 5). The second case is an equally drawn-out effort to complete one of Berlin's most anxiously anticipated urban development projects, Alexanderplatz, a public square and transportation hub in the city's eastern center.

When I started out research in STP in 2007, few people expected that, nearly a decade on, oil would still remain but a distant prospect. Contracts for petroleum extraction in STP's offshore territory were signed in the late 1990s, followed by seismic research and exploratory drillings. However, the quest for first oil is always touch and go. Blockages and delay threaten at multiple points. Insufficient capital, labor, and expertise, political and institutional weaknesses, geological and ecological conditions, as well as burst commodities bubbles are among the factors that may halt anticipated resource booms (Dean 1987). First oil's long lead-up time and decades of dormancy are experienced as a rupture of ordinary productive processes, as they have been in STP where no significant discoveries have been made to date. The unfulfilled promise of STP's resource assets has led me to examine my earlier research on Alexanderplatz with fresh eyes (Weszkalnys 2010). Not unlike oil in STP, the implementation of a master plan for Alexanderplatz, first proposed in the early 1990s, has been encumbered by material intransigence and the seemingly inscrutable economic logic of real estate markets.

STP's oil and Berlin's Alexanderplatz each reveal a complex entanglement of the interests and desires of state actors, corporations, developers, investment funds, and citizens, which are supported in systematic but incomplete ways by infrastructural work. The technical, legal, and commercial infrastructures examined below sustain the distinctive temporality of dormancy and delay characteristic of both the Alexanderplatz development project and STP's oil exploration. Here the attainment of concrete outcomes (buildings, first oil) gets readily overtaken by the circulation of facts about them. Productivity is put on hold for a variety of reasons, resulting in what, following Marx, I will refer to as a "pause." In his analysis of the circuits of productive capital in volume 2 of *Capital*, Marx demonstrated the obstruction posed to capitalist value expansion and accumulation, for example, by labourers' need for rest, by seeds sprouting in the soil, or by a shortage of necessary tools in

Infrastructure as gesture 287

the market. Productive capital is held "in readiness" but remains fallow, although this fallowness "is a requirement for the uninterrupted flow of the process of production" (Marx 2013: 647). From one perspective, such pauses are the tacit drivers of an accelerating capitalist temporality: a problem to be avoided through managerial and technological change as well as credit systems remains in the interest of higher turnover rates and profits. However, from another perspective, pauses are partly generated by the multiple contradictions inherent in the dynamics of capitalist production (Harvey 1989: 181–3). Here capital investment in suspense – sometimes for a given period a company might spend on the waiting list for a sought-after drilling barge or for the time it takes to complete bureaucratic procedure in a planning process, and sometimes indefinitely. It is in the expansive moment of the pause that infrastructures acquire their gestural qualities. Despite their differences, the two cases discussed here show how epistemic instruments and technical devices – such as contracts, exploration zones, and test wells in STP, and a legally binding masterplan, transport infrastructures, and even some incipient constructions at Alexanderplatz – have become *gestures* of potentiality without compelling a predetermined outcome.

Infrastructures of first oil

In a chronicle of STP's nascent petroleum economy, Luís Prazeres (2008), the former head of the country's National Oil Agency, neatly sums up the infrastructural work that has been carried out to generate first oil there. Since the late 1990s, maritime boundaries have circumscribed the prospective hydrocarbon asset, expected to be located principally offshore; three licensing rounds allocated access to it[3]; mechanisms for good governance and transparency have been implemented; and a series of agreements have defined the obligations of the country's various industry partners. The National Oil Agency has been part of this effort as the body charged with managing the technical aspects of future hydrocarbon exploration (Weszkalnys 2011). More recently, the Agency organized the licensing round for the Santomean EEZ, discussed at the start of this chapter, which further buttressed a notion of Santomean oil prospects in the absence of their commercial realization.

These legal, commercial, and technical infrastructures are constitutive of a socio-material arrangement of measurement, connection, and qualification characteristic of the global oil industry (Barry 2006). Importantly, with the continued deferral of STP's first oil, these devices have acquired additional salience. First, they supply the tangible scaffolding to what is largely a speculative endeavor (Tsing 2005: 63). Second, they provide an "informational enrichment" (Barry 2014: 141) of geological matter, making it amenable to the exploitative fantasies of states and their economic partners (Braun 2000). Third, in the face of a sluggish exploration process, they have become gestural. Like measurements of a foetal heartbeat, they furnish hope by signalling dormancy not death. Together, they prevent the pause into which STP's first oil has entered from turning into a failure or loss. A closer examination of three such devices – the contract, the zone, and the well – will illustrate their sustaining or gestural force (cf. Agamben 2000).

The start of what is locally referred to as STP's "petroleum era" (*era do petróleo*) is often associated with the signing of a contract between the Santomean government and the Environment Remediation Holding Company (ERHC), a little-known US oil company, in May 1997. The contract granted ERHC some extraordinary allowances in the exploitation of STP's hydrocarbon resources. For a fee of US$5 million, it assigned the company 40 % of the revenues from future oil and preferential rights in future concessions. ERHC promised to raise the funds necessary to kick-start exploration activities. It would act as negotiator with any other company wishing to explore Santomean oil, and earn a 5 % fee from any payable bonuses. That is, rather than providing a course for action, the contract established a promissory value. Despite the company's limited expertise and financial resources, ERHC staff convinced the Santomean officials of their ability to carry the project through and to raise US$100 million in seven months. These promises were supplemented by a number of gestural moves: a maritime boundary claim was filed, a joint venture oil company was formed between ERHC and the Santomean government, and in 1998 another contract was signed with Mobil, later ExxonMobil, obliging the company to initiate seismic research in STP's offshore territory where the key prospects were expected to be located (Seibert 2006: 372).

Over the next few years, ERHC and the Santomean government broke off, revised, and entered into new agreements. Accusations of bribery and corruption flew through the air. In 2001 the company was acquired by Nigerian businessman, Emeka Offor, and subsequently battled bankruptcy and an investigation by the US Securities and Exchange Commission.[4] While imperfectly quantified oil potential has begun to produce some value for ERHC,[5] for the Santomean state ERHC's involvement is deemed responsible for a substantial loss of possible earnings and is now criticized as a liability. However, such argument benefits from hindsight, I was reminded by Afonso Varela, the National Oil Agency's former legal director. At a time when nobody was interested in STP, he argued, ERHC effectively turned the country into a petroleum frontier. It indirectly generated 2,723 km of 2D seismic data of STP's oil prospects, which were indispensable to attract additional investors (cf. Seibert 2006: 372).

A second gesture in STP's quest for first oil was the country's filing of a maritime boundary claim and the establishment of an Exclusive Economic Zone (EEZ) with the United Nations Law of the Sea Commission in New York City in 1998. Filing such claims, as a legislative act, has important consequences for the demarcation of new resource frontiers as well as the identification of owners and their legitimate partners. Dreams of sovereign substances and petroleum-based national self-sufficiency were soon challenged, however. Seismic surveys of STP's offshore hydrocarbon potential, carried out by a subsidiary of the global petroleum-services provider Schlumberger (paid for by ExxonMobil), had located the most valuable prospects in areas bordering Nigerian waters (Seibert 2006: 372–3). While Equatorial Guinea and Gabon readily accepted the suggested boundary of a Santomean EEZ based on a principle of equidistance, Nigeria proved recalcitrant. It questioned the principle's appropriateness on the basis of its much larger coastline. Three years of protracted negotiations ensued, leading to another important item of bilateral jurisdiction: a zone managed jointly but unevenly split between the two states, with Nigeria receiving 60 and STP 40 % of any revenues that may be generated from it.

The delineation of the joint development zone (JDZ), covering 34,450 km^2, was a critical gesture, sustaining a notion of exploitable potential and opening up possibilities for anticipatory gain from substances not yet extracted. Now, exploration blocks could be allocated in auctions for exploration rights. However, especially the second of these licensing rounds, held in 2004, turned farcical the conventional wisdom that auctions are foolproof instruments for establishing a fair and real price. A report by STP's attorney general alleged clandestine decision-making involving Nigerian and Santomean government figures and their advisors, and called for the annulment of the licensing round.[6] Similarly, the authority managing the zone, the JDA, which has its headquarters in Abuja, has been seen as a fitting enactment of STP's absent oil – an inflated bureaucratic apparatus with a budget of several million dollars per year, eating into STP's limited petroleum revenues.[7]

Finally, at the start of 2006, "encouraging early signs" from Obo-1, the first exploration well in Block 1 of the JDZ drilled by Chevron Texaco and the most "low-risk target" according to the company's technical expertise, made ERHC share prices shoot up. Thousands of feet of steel had been lowered to perforate the icy-cold sea floor, a drilling riser bringing up the mud, people busy operating the equipment, measuring, analyzing, and ascertaining that the technology remained stably connected in this floating environment. Wells can increase companies' stockmarket value by turning so-called possible and probable into proven reserves (cf. Mitchell et al. 2012: 30); but the geological conditions they reveal may also disrupt a project previously deemed technologically feasible and economically sound.

Speaking to the press, Chevron's expat representative, Tim Parsons, recommended caution before commercial viability was proven: "[I]t is too soon to speculate about a date for the first barrels." Data so insufficiently analyzed and confidential, it would be unethical for the company to even start guessing what they might reveal. For the moment, the reservoirs were deemed not to "justify economic development on their own." Indeed, in 2010, Chevron withdrew from the JDZ for reasons that are likely to have included a careful balancing of geological prospects, technological possibilities, assessments of future oil markets, and the company's need to satisfy both shareholder expectations and long-term crude supply for an integrated business. The disappointment was temporarily relieved by French multinational Total and its promise of a US$200 million investment to explore the JDZ's Block 1. However, this company, too, pulled out less than two years later, spelling, as some observers suggest, the end of Santomean oil hopes (Seibert 2013).

Announcements of "no oil," however, have been swiftly rephrased as "no oil yet." Official pronouncements have remained optimistic. As STP's minister of natural resources claimed in an interview with a local newspaper in October 2013: "Companies have their politics, their profit margins and other [considerations], and they act in accordance with their expectations .... [W]e have confirmed reserves [of hydrocarbons] in sufficient quantities to make [Block 1] viable." Recent efforts to open up STP's exclusive economic zone with seismic research and the licensing round discussed at the start of this chapter continue to act as gestures of the prospect of oil. Similarly, sporadic official announcements, assessments carried out by the IMF or the African Development Bank, new plans to deploy advanced exploration technology in the JDZ, and recent exploration contracts for blocks in the EEZ have not ceased to sow optimism.[8] In lieu of productive value, they continue to hold out the promise of a profitable future.

A square suspended

I now wish to trace an instance of gesturing beyond the extractive sector. A case in point comes from my earlier research on an attenuated urban development project in post-unification Berlin (Weszkalnys 2010). Between 2001 and 2002 I carried out fieldwork in Berlin – a city caught, it seemed then, in an endless cycle of demolition and rebuilding following German unification a decade earlier. My research explored this dramatic transformation. I was particularly drawn to the controversy around Alexanderplatz, an emblematic square in the city's eastern center. If oil developments in STP have been associated with expectations of economic growth, prosperity, and greater autonomy from the grip of international donors and global governance agencies, the planned development of Alexanderplatz similarly supported the projection of a specific future imaginary. In this case, it was one of bringing the city back to an assumed normality after forty years of national division. This was to be accomplished through a massive spatial reordering of the square that, till then, had been characterized by its distinctive socialist design, in public–private partnership with a disparate group of national and international real-estate and investment firms. The controversy around Alexanderplatz crystallized some important issues about the painful process of building a future out of Berlin's fragmented cityscape and the conflicting ontologies of space and people, "East" and "West," in the new Germany.

A square suspended, *ein Platz im Wartestand*, was the nickname that Thomas, a member of a civic action group I worked with at the time, attributed to Alexanderplatz back in 2001.[9] When I met Thomas again in 2015, after many years of being out of touch, the group of which he had once been a member to defend a "gentle" redevelopment of Alexanderplatz, had long

Infrastructure as gesture 291

dissolved. But, we agreed, the square still lay in anticipation of its future transformation, notwithstanding some visible changes: partially reorganized traffic routes, a new three-level underground car park, embellished street furniture and pavestones, and even a new building or two sealing Alexanderplatz's frayed seams. Yet this was still a large step removed from the radical change that had once been envisaged.

I-B4a,[10] as the master plan for Alexanderplatz is known by Berlin's planning administrators is, in some sense, a hangover of the optimistic post-unification period when Berlin was projected to become a booming capital. First conceived in 1993, this plan came into force in April 2000. Its vision is one of near complete redevelopment: five high-rise buildings of up to 150 metres will be erected around the square, plus several more in the vicinity – comprising a volume of 417,700 square metres of mixed-use functions, three times the volume available at the time when the planning process was initiated. This vision has been slow to materialize. As a result I-B4a has displayed both fragility and obduracy (Hommels 2005; Richardson 2016).

When I returned to Berlin in 2015, I attended the workshop discussed at the start of this chapter, following an earlier call by Berlin's parliament to review the plan's future fate. Years of non-implementation, as Thomas explained to me, had allowed time to reconsider, for example, the value of the GDR architecture around the square. Two of the former socialist buildings, Haus des Reisens and Haus des Berliner Verlages, have now attained "listed" status, setting unexpected constraints for the master plan's realization. What's more, an oversight by Berlin's planning administration has meant that the two newly erected buildings correspond only minimally with the high-rise vision. With an eye on short-term gain, developers have opted for a lighter, less costly construction technique than would be necessary for these buildings to be integrated into the more voluminous high-rises. Other, historical infrastructures have proven recalcitrant, too: a huge World War II bunker and underground train tunnels are obstacles to one of the planned building's foundations.

As an item of local state planning and jurisdiction, I-B4a has proven inadequate in many ways. Yet few would call for a complete abandonment of the project. First, although the investors have consistently claimed economic conditions in Berlin to be unfavorable to development on the scale envisaged, there is a clear interest in hanging on to the significant square footage inscribed in the plan. And while Berlin's planning administration might consider I-B4a a hindrance to the stated goal of urban enhancement, challenging the plan could have major political and legal repercussions. In the 2015 workshop, the Berlin Senate's Building Director raised the possibility of a revision of the existing contracts with the investors. However, in conversations with administrators following the event, it became clear that such a revision was unlikely. Not only would it risk reopening a Pandora's box of dispute and delay, it might also lead the investors to seek indemnification, not least for those €73 million already spent on infrastructures. Last, some of the citizens who participated in the workshop clearly did consider the event an opportunity to argue for a thorough overhaul of the existing plans. Comments scribbled on yellow, red, and blue cards and on writing boards distributed throughout the venue belied the apparently consensual atmosphere. They asked whether Berlin required any high-rise developments at all, demanded respect for the GDR architecture, and noted, quite simply, the master plan's obsolescence. However, there was also much worry about what the future might bring. Many residents expressed a sense of devaluation, or at least a lack of correspondence between their own aspirations and the square's ugly presence, largely associated with post-unification socio-economic changes. In this view, too, the desire for "improvement" was undiminished.

In short, I-B4a has helped to sustain a notion of great economic, aesthetic, and ethic potential in the heart of Berlin's eastern center. Alongside the urban infrastructures that the future Alexanderplatz and the incipient building works, it is part of a repertory of gestural features pointing to a modern, unified Berlin (cf. Kendon 1997: 119). Although I-B4a has functioned perhaps most effectively in structuring present relations between Berlin's government, private investors, and citizens (cf. Baxstrom 2013), its anticipation of a developed Alexanderplatz has not been completely unsubstantiated. Planning, here, has been a matter of contingency and accommodation rather than a linear progression from intentions to results (Weszkalnys 2010; see also Abram and Weszkalnys 2013). The 2015 workshop could be seen as part of an effort to fix the plan "in increments," befitting the size and complexity of this infrastructural system where "changes take time and negotiation, and adjustment with other aspects of the system are involved" (Star 1999: 382). I-B4a has thus been made to withstand the elasticity of time (Weszkalnys 2010: 113) produced by the continued out-of-step temporalities of state planning, real estate, and investment markets.

Pausing and gesturing

In this chapter I have explored the relationship between processes of pausing and gesturing – that is, the role of infrastructures in sustaining a specific temporality characteristic of capitalist development. Here infrastructures play an important role, though not necessarily that originally intended. Façade, fake, or failure – anthropologists have highlighted a number of ways in which infrastructures gain visibility without fulfilling their expected purpose (Star 1999). So-called white elephants, for example, operate in what Larkin (2013: 335) dubs a "poetic" mode and embody a politics reliant on "arbitrary symbolic acts" (Mbembe and Roitman 1995: 337). White elephants don't come to anything because, by definition, they are expressions of corrupt rule, underwritten by bribery and embezzlement (Appel 2012). In the contemporary economy of appearances, infrastructures may also provide fraudulent evidence propping up the illicit collusions between corporate and state agents and new circuits of financialization (Tsing 2005). Last, infrastructures that have proven blatantly harmful may be kept in place by political processes that aim to overrule unsustainable material realities (Richardson 2016). By contrast, the infrastructures discussed in this chapter are more indeterminate. Contracts, licensing rounds, economic zones, wells, plans, and workshops participate in dispersed socio-material arrangements designed to bring greater certainty to unwieldy, highly contingent, projects but inadvertently upend their stated goals. Instead of contributing to the realization of the potential that was envisaged they become gestures of what *might* be. Even as their effects remain contested, they hold in suspense the possibility that, eventually, they will lead to something.

At first glance, the two projects explored in this chapter might seem to have little in common: they take place on different continents, involving different sets of actors and technologies in the pursuit of different outcomes. However, they find themselves in a similar temporal moment, which I referred to as an extended pause. The time of the pause is not empty, not devoid of labour *per se*, even if the material transformations this labour generates can remain somewhat invisible. It is about ascertaining potentialities, and thus constituting, for example, geologic substances as a resource and plots of inner-city land as real estate. In the pause, the realization of economic potential is suspended but nevertheless maintained by a variety of infrastructural gestures, displaying a specific temporal ethics that attenuates or postpones failure.

Potentiality, in the ethnographies that this chapter explored, presents itself both as "futures fold[ed] into presents" (Fortun 2008: 285) and as stymied, marked by blockages and setbacks (Røyrvik 2011). The speculative practices of oil corporations and investment firms inscribe value of a sort that remains unsubstantiated. Contracts are divested of their legal force by reference to economic pragmatism. Wells reveal not resources but a lack of viability. And supposedly real constructions are but proxies of the original. The outcome, however, is not the collapse of the projects in question but their continued suspension, in other words, a sustained pause. In lieu of productive value, the infrastructure as gesture thus holds out the promise of a profitable future. Potentiality is continually reaffirmed. These gestures invite us to critically re-examine contemporary capitalism's persistent claims to boundless creativity. Instead, they highlight a multiplicity of speculative forms and temporal-material realignments that emerge when things slow down while everything else keeps moving.

Notes

1 Portions of this chapter are reproduced by permission from my article "Geology, Potentiality, Speculation: On the Indeterminacy of 'First Oil'," *Cultural Anthropology* 30(4).
2 Linguistic anthropologists have noted the gesture's important supportive role in communication, its ability to render speech more precise, to furnish additional meanings, or to substitute for it altogether (Kendon 1997). French anthropologist Marcel Jousse, for example, considered the gesture a predecessor to spoken language, underpinning our ability to imitate others and thus to be in the world. For

Jousse, the gesture was part of what makes us uniquely human (Sienaert 1990). At the same time, enormous variety in gesture use has been observed across space and time as well as variety in the ontology of the gesture, for example, as an expression of "inner" or "unconscious" feelings or as an embodiment of ethics (Braddick 2009; Jackson 2013; Kendon 1997).
3 The first two licensing rounds in 2003 and 2004 pertained to the JDZ with Nigeria; a third round was held in 2010 for STP's EEZ.
4 Any proceedings regarding ERHC were formally closed in April 2012.
5 Though overall a loss-making operation, ERHC sold some of its participating interests in Santomean oil blocks in 2006, making US$45,900,000. It also received US$51,800,000 from JDZ signature bonuses.
6 Still, several PSCs regarding blocks 2, 3, and 4 were signed in 2005.
7 Signature bonuses from the JDZ licensing rounds have amounted to US $324,000,000 of which STP received approximately 40%. The JDA's total budget 2004–2013 has been US$92,464,297, of which STP's nominal contribution has been a little more than a third. However, US$22 million of this amount has been loaned to STP by Nigeria (see https://eiti.org/sao-tome-and-principe).
8 *Exploração conjunta de petróleo com a Nigéria dentre de 18 meses*, RFI Português, April 4, 2014; *Galp, Kosmos awarded Sao Tome block*, Rigzone, October 27, 2015.
9 Until the mid-twentieth century, the expression "*im Wartestand*" connoted a specific status of non-active service for civil servants whose position had been dissolved or made redundant.
10 More precisely, there are several partial construction plans in the Alexanderplatz area (I-B4a, I-B4a-3, I-B4ba and I-B4bb, I-B4ca and I-B4cb, I-B4d, I-43a and I-43b, I-70a and I-70b). I use I-B4a as shorthand, also because it is the one most frequently discussed, comprising the most central area of Alexanderplatz.

References

Abram, S. and G. Weszkalnys (2013) "Elusive Promises: Planning in the Contemporary World. An Introduction," in S. Abram and G. Weszkalnys (eds) *Elusive Promises: Planning in the Contemporary World*. New York: Berghahn, pp. 1–33.
Agamben, G. (2000) *Means Without End: Notes on Politics*. Minneapolis: University of Minnesota.
Appel, H. (2012) "Walls and white elephants: Oil extraction, responsibility, and infrastructural violence in Equatorial Guinea". *Ethnography* 13(4): 439–465.
Barry, A. (2006) "Technological zones". *European Journal of Social Theory* 9(2): 239–253.
Barry, A. (2014) *Material Politics: Disputes along the Pipeline*. Malden and Oxford: Wiley Blackwell.
Baxstrom, Richard (2013) "Even Governmentality Begins as an Image: Institutional Planning in Kuala Lumpur," in Simone Abram and Gisa Weszkalnys (eds) *Elusive Promises: Planning in the Contemporary World*. Oxford: Berghahn, pp. 137–154.
Bowker, G. C. (1994) *Science on the Run: Information Management and Industrial Geophysics at Schlumberger, 1920–1940*. Cambridge, MA and London: MIT Press.
Braddick, M. J. (ed.) 2009) *The Politics of Gesture: Historical Perspectives*. Oxford: Oxford University Press.
Braun, B. (2000) "Producing vertical territory: Geology and governmentality in late Victorian Canada". *Cultural Geographies* 7(1): 7–46.
Dean, W. (1987) *Brazil and the Struggle for Rubber: A Study in Environmental History*. Cambridge: Cambridge University Press.

Harvey, D. (1989) *The Condition of Postmodernity: An Enquiry into the Origins of Cultural Change*. Oxford: Basil Blackwell.
Hommels, A. (2005) "Studying obduracy in the city: Toward a productive fusion between technology studies and urban studies". *Science, Technology & Human Values* 30(3), 323–351.
Jackson, M. (2013) *Lifeworlds: Essays in Existential Anthropology*. Chicago, IL and London: University of Chicago Press.
Kendon, A. (1997) "Gesture". *Annual Review of Anthropology* 26: 109–128.
Larkin, B. (2013) "The politics and poetics of infrastructure". *Annual Review of Anthropology* 42: 327–343.
Marx, K. (2013) *Capital: A Critical Analysis of Capitalist Production*. Ware: Wordsworth Editions.
Mbembe, A. and J. Roitman (1995) "Figures of the subject in times of crisis". *Public Culture* 7(2): 323–352.
Mitchell, J., with V. Marcel and B. Mitchell (2012) *What Next for the Oil and Gas Industry?* London: Chatham House.
Nolan, P. A. and M. C. Thurber (2010) "On the state's choice of oil company: Risk management and the frontier of the petroleum industry, Working paper no. 99. PESD, Stanford University.
Pálsson, G. (1998) "The Birth of the Aquarium: The Political Ecology of Icelandic Fishing. in T. S. Gray (ed.) *The Politics of Fishing*. New York: Palgrave Macmillan, pp. 209–227.
Prazeres, L. dos (2008) *Dossier Petróleo: Cronologia Histórica 1876–2004*. São Tomé: Banco Internacional de São Tomé e Príncipe.
Richardson, T. (2016) "Objecting (to) infrastructure: Ecopolitics at the Ukrainian ends of the Danube". *Science as Culture* 25(1): 69–95.
Røyrvik, E. A. (2011) *The Allure of Capitalism: An Ethnography of Management and the Global Economy in Crisis*. New York and Oxford: Berghahn.
Seibert, G. (2006) *Comrades, Clients and Cousins: Colonialism, Socialism and Democratization in São Tomé e Príncipe*. Leiden and Boston: Brill.
Seibert, G. (2013) "São Tomé and Príncipe: The end of the oil dream? *IPRIS Viewpoints*, no. 134, September.
Sienaert, E. R. (1990) "Marcel Jousse: The oral style and the anthropology of gesture". *Oral Tradition* 5(1): 91–106.
Star, S. L. (1999) "The ethnography of infrastructure". *American Behavioral Scientist* 43(3): 377–391.
ten Bos, R. (2005) "On the possibility of formless life: Agamben's politics of the gesture". *Ephemera* 5: 26–44.
Tsing, A.L. (2005) *Friction: An Ethnography of Global Connection*. Princeton, NJ: Princeton University Press.
von Schnitzler, A. (2013) "Traveling technologies: Infrastructure, ethical regimes, and the materiality of politics in South Africa". *Cultural Anthropology* 28(4): 670–693.
Weszkalnys, G. (2010) *Berlin, Alexanderplatz: Transforming Place in a Unified Germany*. Oxford and New York: Berghahn.
Weszkalnys, G. (2011) "Cursed resources, or articulations of economic theory in the Gulf of Guinea". *Economy and Society* 40(3): 345–372.
Weszkalnys, G. (2013) "Oil's Magic: Contestation and Materiality," in S. Strauss, S. Rupp and T. Love (eds) *Cultures of Energy: Anthropological Perspectives on Powering the Planet*. Walnut Creek, CA: Left Coast Press, pp. 267–283.

22 The black list

On infrastructural indeterminacy and its reverberations

Madeleine Reeves

Deportation – the practice of removal of unwanted non-citizens from the territory of the state – has increasingly come to figure in countries of the Global North a tool of migration management (Bloch and Schuster 2005; Coutin 2015; Drotbohm 2011), a tendency that Gibney (2008) describes as a "deportation turn" in Western states' treatment of unwanted non-citizens. Accompanying this qualitative increase in forcible removal has been a new concern among anthropologists of migration to explore how emergent logics of expulsion from the nation-state subtend contemporary projects of sovereignty. Peutz and de Genova (2010: 2) write, for instance, of a "global deportation regime": that is, an:

> increasingly unified, effectively *global* response to a world that is being actively remade by transnational human mobility, in which state power can only perceive the freedom of movement as the index of a planetary social order that is ever more woefully "out of control" and "insecure."

De Genova writes elsewhere of the "caprices of the global deportation regime's Rule of Law and its endless interstate matrix of barbed-wire borders" (2010: 58); van Houtum (2010), of a "global apartheid" of the EU's external border regime, sustained through threat of forcible removal.

This literature alludes at several points to new practices, architectures, and technologies of removal. Comparatively little studied, however, are the human-technical systems of determination that lie behind such instances of detention and deportation: the contingent material, technical, administrative, and informational configurations through which "deportability" emerges as a social fact and lived condition. When infrastructure is addressed in the literature on deportation, it is often through the idiom (and often, indeed, through the material form) of border fences and removal centers, handcuffs, and airplanes. The "endless interstate matrix of barbed-wire borders" appears, in this reading, as bounded, finite, determinate and self-contained: unambiguous in its material intransigence and transparent in its political rationalities.

In so doing, I suggest, it leaves out of view precisely the *infrastructural* dimensions of deportability. By this I refer to the contingent legal and administrative configurations, the socio-technical arrangement of paper files, computer databases, and algorithms that would determine whether a particular individual has "overstayed," whether her illness presents an "epidemiological risk," thus prohibiting entry, or whether a traffic offence is recorded as a datum by a traffic policeman or effaced through informal payment.

I argue in this chapter that to understand the affective force of deportability we need to explore these socio-technical configurations and their *non*-coherences; or put differently, the way that chance figures in infrastructural systems (Dunn and Cons 2013; cf. Fisch this volume), and the way that such indeterminacy comes to be internalized and embodied, becoming not merely an afterthought or consequence of any given infrastructural intervention, but intrinsic to how an apparatus comes to operate infrastructurally. Just as the passports, visas, residence registrations, work permits, and border stamps that regulate one's right of entry are integral to the legal production of personhood – and, prospectively, of one's subjective experience of (im)mobility, fear or entrapment (Navaro-Yashin 2007; Kelly 2006; Jansen 2009) – so, too, data-management systems and algorithms come to embody the uncertainties that are intrinsic to the bureaucratic form itself.

To develop this argument I focus upon one emergent apparatus of determination in contemporary Russia and consider its reverberations in rural Kyrgyzstan: the database of foreign citizens and stateless persons who are to be denied entry to Russia, known colloquially as the "black list" (*chernyi spisok* in Russian; *kara tezme* in Kyrgyz). The black list is materially extensive, socially embedded, technically complex, and politically consequential. Compiled by the Federal Migration Service (FMS) of the Russian Federation, the black list integrates a variety of previously disparate sources of digital data into a single searchable repository concerning each non-citizen's migration and residency status, work and tax status, criminal record, administrative offences, and traffic violations.

I consider this apparatus of determination as *emergent* because of its novelty and its intrinsic unboundedness. The database is vast and expanding, combining data from 11 government ministries and agencies. Indeed, it is often cited in official pronouncements as outstripping other global experiments in data integration (Fergana.ru 2015a). Some of the contributing agencies, such as the ministries of Internal and Foreign Affairs, the state security services (FSB), the Ministry of Defence, the Foreign Intelligence Service, the Ministry of Justice and the Federal Migration Service are directly concerned with issues of state security and legal protection. But the database also includes information from a variety of other agencies concerned with consumer protection (Rospotrebnadzor), epidemiological control, drug control, and financial regulation (Rosfinmonitoring). As a Kyrgyzstani Foreign Ministry official noted in 2013, this recording of epidemiological and other data meant that people could effectively find themselves "falling" into the list simply because they were admitted to hospital with an infectious disease (Asanov 2013).

I consider this an apparatus of *determination* since the database is used to make critical, and life-changing decisions concerning a non-citizen's right to remain in the Russian Federation. Following changes to Russian immigration law that came into force in 2012–13 (Zakon RF 321-FZ 2012), any non-citizen who has committed two or more criminal or administrative offences in the preceding three-year period – such as speeding or parking offences – will be liable to deportation and subject retroactively to an entry ban (*zapret na v'ezd*) to Russia for between three and ten years (Gannushkina 2014; Zakon RF 321-FZ 2012). As of mid-2015, the black list included the names of over 1,300,000 foreign citizens who are to be refused re-entry, or around 12 % of the country's total migrant population of 11 million (Fergana.ru 2015b, quoting the head of the FMS).

Infrastructuring deportability

How should we conceive of this vast digital thing? In a recent discussion of migration dynamics, Biao Xiang and Johan Lindquist (2014) stress the importance of analyzing migration through its modes of infrastructural mediation. They consider the multiple state and non-state agencies, administrative technologies, commercial interests, and social relations that have increasingly come to regulate international migration, making migratory futures simultaneously more accessible and more suffused with risk. Rather than foregrounding apparatuses, networks, systems, or regimes, their attention to infrastructure stresses the "internal constitution and modular components of migration": components that include both quotidian practices associated with transnational mobility (form-filling and queuing, for instance), and a set of diffuse and expansive techniques, materials, and regulations that mediate migrant experience. They develop an analogy with Latour's (1999: 182) argument for the complex human and non-human assemblages that enable an airplane to fly: "Flying is a property of the whole association of entities that includes airports and planes, launch pads and ticket counters. B-52s do not fly, the US Air Force flies." Analogously, Xiang and Lindquist argue, it is not so much migrants who migrate, but rather "constellations consisting of migrants and non-migrants, of human and non-human actors" (Xiang and Lindquist 2014: S124; cf. Chu 2010: 109).

Xiang and Lindquist's approach directs attention to the multiplicity of disparate relations and mediating technologies through which a migration regime comes to materialize. The black list, I suggest, can be explored analogously in terms of its infrastructural capacity: that is, in terms of the complex, recombinant human and non-human systems through which human movement is systematically channeled, filtered, and denied. But there is a twist here, which has to do with the political and experiential implications of infrastructural *in*determinacy: the fact that the black list is typically encountered as arbitrary in its pronouncements and impenetrable in its logics of operation. While ideationally at least, the FMS's new database is efficient, conclusive, and incorruptible (as the head of Russia's migration service put it: "the computer doesn't take bribes" [*mashina vziatok ne beret*] (Valaleev 2013)), migrant workers and their families typically speak simply of "falling into the list" (*popast' v spisok* or *spisokko tüshöö*): expressions that allude to the experiential arbitrariness of inclusion and the sense of entrapment that can result. To Kyrgyz migrant workers and their families living in and between rural Batken district and Moscow, the database seemed at once arbitrary and deadly serious: no one could be entirely sure that they, too, hadn't already fallen into the list. Indeed, Agnieszka Kubal (forthcoming) has described the entry ban as a form of "surreptitious deportation," since the retroactive application of the law renders deportable those migrants who "were charged with offences that, at the time of conviction, would not have any immigration law related consequences."

From this follows the central question that animates this chapter. If infrastructures should be considered less as determinate material and technical formations than as unstable and experimental interventions in social life (Jensen and Morita 2016), how might we attend, analytically and ethnographically, to the consequences of their indeterminacy? To develop a response to this question, I proceed by first introducing the black list as I encountered it – as a circulating object of dense commentary and speculation in rural Kyrgyzstan.

Falling into the list

In the mountainous Kyrgyz border town of Batken, with a population of 13,000, airline ticket kiosks surrounding the town's central market began to advertise a new service in 2013. A simple A4 sign posted in the window would announce, in a locally familiar Kyrgyz-Russian idiom that "we check the black list" (*chernyi spisok teksherebiz*). In this remittance-dependent town, where livelihoods and aspirations for a materially secure future are pinned to precarious labor in the Russian metropolis, no further elaboration was required. The "black list" refers to the reviled FMS database. For a fee of around ten dollars, the sales clerk will enter the prospective passenger's passport details into an online web form, which will reveal their fate: the individual either is, or is not, issued a refusal of entry to the Russian Federation.

Though couched with warnings that they have merely an "advisory" quality, this information allows the prospective passenger to avoid buying an unusable ticket; or worse, flying to Russia only to be denied entry and having to purchase an immediate return ticket. Out of the complex lived reality of migrant existence the algorithm determines a binary response: the individual migrant is either legal or illegal, to be granted entry into the country or denied it. Through its abstraction of a result from the multiplicity of data that produced it, however, the black list also magnifies the space of speculation: How did one "fall into" the list? Is it possible that it could be in error? How might one remove oneself from the list? What kinds of documents would one need to source and relations would one need to mobilisze to produce a new passport under a new name? Or, might one find oneself later "on the list" because of a not-yet-recorded offence? Moreover, for all the finitude of the decision, the length of the ban, the state agency that issued it, and the reasons for refusal of entry are not provided by the online checks on which most migrants rely: for that one needs to travel to the branch office of the migration service in the capital, Bishkek.

The reasons for the proliferation of uncertainty around the black list lie in its logics of operation. The database is not a finite record but is constantly updated with newly inputted data. Stories abound of wrongly inputted information; or of finding oneself punished because someone else was operating with a counterfeit version of their residence registration or work permit. More generally, the nature of life and work in Russia for seasonal workers from Kyrgyzstan – the political economy of temporary housing, the presence of restrictive work quotas, the unwillingness of employers to hire according to written contracts; the pervasive employment of "fictive citizens," the borrowing and lending of documents, and the widespread resort to informal payments to bypass official fines – mean that virtually all migrant workers are at risk of some form of prior administrative violation (FIDH-ADC Memorial 2014; Kluczewska 2014; Reeves 2013; Malakhov 2014). As one lawyer commented in June 2015, the question isn't whether or not someone has violated the law, but whether *that* violation, at *that* moment, leaves a digital trace. Indeed, when the International Organization for Migration conducted research among Tajik men who had fallen foul of the entry ban in 2014, they found that 80 % of those refused re-entry had no idea for *which* offense this had occurred (IOM 2014: 2).

When I met with 33-year-old Takhmina in Batken town in the summer of 2014, she was anxiously trying to renew her passport under a new name. I had last seen Takhmina six years earlier in Moscow. She had lived for most of the intervening years in a variety of dormitory apartments, returning annually to visit her elderly parents and in-laws in Batken. It was on the last such return visit – for what she anticipated would be only a brief absence from her cleaning job – that she found herself blacklisted. Her husband and older son were still in Moscow. When we met at her parents' home in 2014, Takhmina was on her way to Bishkek, to try to understand how she had violated the migration legislation and to see whether she could change her passport to a new identity. "The first time I checked I wasn't on the list," she explained, "but then a few weeks later when I looked again, it turned out I was [*kaira bar bolup kaldy*]. I couldn't believe it so I decided to go there to check."

Checking was not straightforward, however, since Bishkek was an 18-hour drive from Batken. And replacing the passport was fraught with obstacles if one didn't have the right contacts (*taanysh*). Documenting a change in name would require mobilizing a host of prior paper identities, including a changed birth certificate, and Takhmina was anxious that although she had a *bona fide* Kyrgyz passport, the fact that she had only recently obtained Kyrgyz citizenship (like many women who married into Batken's border villages she was born in Tajikistan) would raise even more questions about her motivations. The process was costly and risky too: a changed name would no longer correspond with the name on her marriage certificate, or the high school diploma that she relied upon to certify her right to work as a cleaning lady for a secondary school in Moscow. Once the passport was changed, she would have to change these documents too and that meant more queuing, more payments, more unwanted questions.

Takhmina was also concerned about what kinds of data would travel: she had heard of other people from Batken whose new biometric passports allowed their (original) identity to be tracked, even as they traveled under a new name. In the case of one of her school friends this had led to a three-year entry ban being extended to ten years. While three years was an "imaginable" absence, Takhmina explained, ten years felt like a profound interruption to her future life plans: earning enough money with her husband to build a home in Batken and to send their son and daughter to University. Was it, she pondered, worth the risk?

Takhmina's bewilderment was far from unique, as evidenced by the multiplicity of online Kyrgyz-language forums that have emerged under the headings "deportation" and "black list." One young woman, who had arrived in Moscow's Domodedovo airport from Bishkek, was put on a return flight. "I don't understand," she wrote on one Kyrgyz-language forum, "was I deported, or wasn't I?" Another, having managed to change her passport to re-enter the country under another name, asked the forum: "Hey, those of you who have fallen onto the black list and then returned after changing your name, can you tell me: is it enough to change your s[urname].n[ame].p[atronymic] or do you also need to change your CMI [compulsory medical insurance]?" Another contributor asked whether members had had any luck lodging complaints to the FMS about incorrect entry to the black list. A fourth wondered about the possibility of remaining in the country incognito:

> Hello all. My friend was arrested by the police, they took his fingerprints, wrote a protocol, took him to court. They said that he had to leave the country within 15 days. He gathered up the 5,000 [rouble] fine, and has paid off the fine so I'm wondering, is it OK if he just stays without leaving [the country]? [...] When the same thing happened to my brother, I bought him a ticket to send him home, so that he wasn't taken to court. But now he's back in Kyrgyzstan and he's got no work, just sits around drinking. So I'm debating now whether it isn't better for [my friend] to risk just stay here. What do you think?
> (Comments to the forum thread "deportation" [*deportatsiia*], January–March 2015, www.super.kg; author's translation from Kyrgyz).

Such questions point not just to the practical concerns relating to deportation but to a broader sense of indeterminacy surrounding the possibility of future planning in a context where conditions for staying are fundamentally revocable. If deportation draws attention to a legal act, *deportability* directs attention to a lived condition of uncertainty: a state in which one might be forcibly returned, refused entry, or even imprisoned – or one might not (Reeves 2015).

The indeterminacy of infrastructure

I suggest that we should approach this indeterminacy as intrinsic to the infrastructural form itself. In contrast to approaches that have taken the finished form of the infrastructural "thing" as the focus of ethnographic attention, recent scholarship on the political lives of infrastructure has drawn attention to their open-endedness and their unpredictable political effects (Anand 2012; Harvey and Knox 2015; Jensen 2010). In her study of infrastructural disrepair in China, for instance, Julie Chu notes that infrastructures can be thought of as "relations of relations." Rather than bounded systems, they are better conceived as "partial objects" that are "always gesturing to other flows and transactions for their completion as meaningful social forms" (2014: 353; see also Reeves 2016; Weszkalnys 2015). In research on engineering in Peru, Penny Harvey (2012: 88) demonstrates how the perceived "gaps" that infrastructures such as new roads are meant to overcome can "more productively be approached as intervals, a space-time that marks difference rather than absence." Harvey argues that this requires a "topological" shift in perspective, such that "the plugging of a gap does not bring closure but opens up other relational possibilities" (2012: 85).

Such attentiveness to the absences and uncertainties opened up by new experiments in engineering the social can afford a critical perspective upon systems of migration "management." These systems are premised upon overcoming absences – in knowledge, in data management, in the human capacity to check documents, or in the military capacity to "close" borders (Amoore 2011; Broeders 2007; Feldman 2012). Indeed, Russia's black list would appear as a paradigmatic attempt to *overcome* indeterminacy, to, quite literally, close a "gap." Developed in response to a perceived threat from irregular migrants, this technology of control, in official pronouncements at least, operates by rendering legible and punishable the transgressors of Russia's laws of entry and legal residence. Underlying the assertion that the "computer doesn't take bribes," for instance, is a faith in the categorical determinations of the FMS algorithms to pronounce rightful legal presence in the nation-state. In this reading, there is no space for human error, nor for the all-too human tendency for administrative orders to be overruled through informal payments. The database doesn't cheat or lie; it merely records and reveals a right (or not) to remain. Speaking in March 2015, Romodanovskii highlighted the punitive and pedagogic potential of this digital determinacy: "Each foreigner who comes to us automatically leaves a trace [*sled*] about themselves," he explained.

By analysing those traces, the computer is able to send a signal about violations, on the basis of which our employees make decisions [concerning removal]. Previously, decisions about deportations [*vydvorenii*] and five-year prohibition of reentry of foreigners had to be taken by the courts and they could deal only with tens of thousands of foreign citizens. Today [by contrast] we have prohibited entry for 1,240,000 people. [Now that] we have an automated system for controlling the length of stay of foreigners it has been possible to realise a most important principle: the inevitability of punishment [*neotvratimosti nakazaniia*]. Such a system does not exist even in the countries of Europe.

(Fergana.ru 2015a)

Critical scholarship on state surveillance has drawn attention to the unexpected consequences of such logics of surveillance, just as it has critiqued the "techno-credulity" that underlie assertions such as Romodanovskii's (Zedner 2009: 257). Lyon (2009: 44), for instance, has shown how new forms of biometric data-gathering give rise to logics of categorization and classification based on the creation of "risk profiles," with pernicious effects. In her study of ethnic Korean return migration from China, Kim shows how the "strict evidentiary requirement imposed in the name of fraud *prevention* actually made for its *proliferation*" (2011: 770, original emphasis). Likewise, van Houtum (2010: 957) has argued that the creation of the EU's "risk analysis" model for allocation of Schengen visas has served to "create a border industry that constructs more, not less 'illegality', xenophobia, and fear."

The black list, too, has resulted in no shortage of false calls. Critiques have been voiced not just by those shocked or indignant to have inadvertently "fallen into" the list but also by software engineers who have questioned the algorithmic basis of the system. What is distinctive here, however, is the degree to which the "false call" seems to be recognized by those subject to it not simply as a by-product of insufficient accuracy but as intrinsic to its mode of operation. Rather than a case of governing mobilities through biometrics (Amoore 2006), we could conceive of the black list as a kind of governance through *indeterminacy:* that is, through the proliferation of legal, practical, and existential uncertainties via the proliferation of digital data and the invisibility of its multiple appropriations.

For what is striking from interviews and conversation is an awareness of how the contingency and arbitrariness of deportability suffused everyday domains of life, shaped routines and modes of dress and comportment, and regulated movement to avoid the likelihood of contact with street-level bureaucrats. Such practices were often coupled with ironic commentary about the effects of this unpredictability. As one of my long-term interlocutors in Moscow, Kairat, put it: "Here we are quieter than the lamb (*biz bul jakta koidon joosh*), Madeleine, that's why Russians love us."

In two very different domains – those of refugee camps, on the one hand, and unrecognized border enclaves, on the other – Dunn and Cons (2013) have developed an argument about "aleatory sovereignty" or "rule by contingency." Critiquing contemporary accounts of sovereignty as premised upon a finite "state of exception," they argue that "the notion of state of exception is grounded in an absolute certainty that belies the anxiety and confusion that often characterizes borders and refugee camps" (2013: 94). Uncertainty, in their reading, is intrinsic to the very modality of governing that characterizes such sites. Rather than "exceptional," such spaces are better considered "sensitive"; for in a context of plural regulatory authorities, one never quite knows whose rules rule. This argument can fruitfully be applied to the mode of governance instantiated by the "black list." Not only is the migrant confronted with multiple "petty sovereigns" (Butler 2011) (from road police and migration officers to medical personnel), they are also confronted with the intrinsic uncertainty as to whether a given action will constitute a fall from grace that may land themselves on the list. The ban is both violent *and* experientially arbitrary.

Quite how arbitrary this process is became evident in 2015 following Kyrgyzstan's accession to the Eurasian Customs Union. Following a meeting between President Putin and Kyrgyzstan's president Atambaev, Russia removed the names of 49,540 Kyrgyzstani citizens from the black list (of a total of around 250,000), allowing them re-entry to the Russian Federation. This decision, celebrated in Kyrgyzstan, was an explicitly political act. In Russia it was presented as a magnanimous gesture towards a smaller neighbor that had asserted its political and economic alignment.

Yet, the very unexpectedness of the decision added to its sovereign mystique. There was no elaboration of how the figure of 49,540 pardoned non-citizens was arrived at or how the decision would be executed (were the offending migrants' names conclusively removed from the black list or were their putative offenses merely ignored?) This, I would suggest, is precisely the point: rather than disrupting the black list's logic of operation, its temporary suspension at a moment of political rapprochement served to confirm its intrinsic impenetrability and the arbitrariness of its exclusions.

Conclusion

The FMS database is paradigmatic of emergent new infrastructures of border security and migration management that rely on alphanumeric and biometric data to monitor citizens' and non-citizens' movements into and within the nation-state. Such infrastructures uncouple the work of bordering from the state's territorial limits, with regulation shifting simultaneously "outwards" and "inwards." These databases are geographically dispersed, individualizing in their determinations, and draconian in their effects. As such the black list can be read as one of the proliferating technologies of risk management in the global governance of mobility that illuminates what Bigo (2001: 112) calls the "Möbius ribbon" of internal/external security.

In the context of Russian migration policy, the introduction of entry bans as a form of retroactive punishment for administrative offences articulates with broader biopolitical and geopolitical logics shaped by Russia's changing relations with its "near abroad," by growing anxieties about shifting demographics, and by concerns that the presence of large numbers of irregular migrants from the former Soviet space is prohibiting the EU's easing of visa regulations for Russian citizens. Yet rather than approaching the black list simply as a governmental technology in which new domains of life come under biopolitical control, I have considered it rather as an apparatus that multiplies spaces and relations of indeterminacy, with significant political effects.

For the apparatus to work infrastructurally – as part of an unremarkable system of integrated data management – depends upon other systems and objects of control and regulation operating at other scales, from courts and police stations to visas and entry stamps, airport holding centers, webforms and electric currents. Seen from this angle, we can see how the black list acts infrastructurally to a greater or lesser degree depending on context: in an airport, the database connects with these other systems of border security more or less efficiently; at a rural land crossing between Kyrgyzstan and Kazakhstan, where paper ledgers are used to record passing traffic and human border crossings, much less so. It is precisely an awareness of these differential infrastructural capacities that has allowed for a flourishing informal market in costly "detour transport" across unregulated land borders for those who have been blacklisted but who still need to enter Russia to work.

Indeterminacy, however, relates not just to the degree of integration internal to a system. It is at once deeply material (cf. Hull 2013) and intrinsic to the modes of political subjectivity that it elicits. One pressing question for an anthropology of infrastructure, then, is how we are to account for this indeterminacy, ethnographically and analytically. Ethnographically, it challenges us to explore infrastructure in ways that are attentive to its unboundedness, recognizing the intrinsic uncertainty over where a given infrastructure begins and ends; and who or what it enfolds. Conceptually, it demands attentiveness to the social and political consequences of this unboundedness. My contention is that while the "infrastructural turn" within anthropology has generally stressed the open-endedness and contingency of infrastructural formations in theoretical terms, *ethnographically*, studies of infrastructure have tended to proceed from material-technical formations that are encountered as finite, bounded, and determinate in their effects.

If we approach infrastructures less as complete technical or material forms, however, what comes into focus are precisely the improvisations and gaps that are intrinsic to infrastructural modes of operation. Such "gaps" are not necessarily signs of failure or lack; they can be essential to enable the kinds of improvisations that allow a complex technical system to function (Fisch this volume). But the proliferation of gaps can also have other kinds of effects – such as the opportunity for new exertions of sovereign violence. In the case of the black list, the attempt to "overcome a gap" in knowledge about immigrants' ir/regular status replicates spaces of uncertainty in ways that enable new exertions of sovereign power and facilitate new forms of subordination. In this context, I suggest, the widely shared uncertainty about having "fallen into the list" should not be seen merely as an epiphenomenon resulting from insufficient knowledge about the law or inaccuracies in modes of data gathering but as intrinsic to the way that the black list operates *infrastructurally*: as an unbounded socio-material form that depends upon other infrastructures, other systems, and other social relations for its completion.

Bibliography

Amoore, Louise (2006) "Biometric Borders: Governing Mobilities in the War on Terror." *Political Geography* 25(3): 336–351.
Amoore, Louise (2011) "Data Derivatives: on the Emergence of Security Risk Calculus for Our Times." *Theory, Culture and Society* 28(6): 24–43.
Anand, Nikhil (2012) "Leaky States: Water Audits, Ignorance and the Politics of Infrastructure." *Public Culture* 7(2): 305–330.
Asanov, Bakyt (2013) "Diagnoz: 'Chernyi spisok'." *Radio Azattyk*, December 24. http://rus.azattyk.org/content/article/25210619.html.
Bigo, Didier (2001) "The Möbius Ribbon of Internal and External Security(ies)," in M. Albert, D. Jacobson and Y. Lapid (eds) *Identities, Borders, Orders: Rethinking International Relations Theory*, vol. 18. Minneapolis: University of Minnesota Press, pp. 91–116.
Bloch, Alice and Liza Schuster (2005) "At the Extremes of Exclusion: Deportation, Detention and Dispersal." *Ethnic and Racial Studies* 28(3): 491–512.
Broeders, Dennis (2007) "The New Digital Borders of the EU: EU Databases and the Surveillance of Irregular Migrants." *International Sociology* 22(1): 71–92.
Butler, Judith (2011) *Precarious Life: The Powers of Mourning and Violence*. London: Verso.
Chu, Julie (2010) *Cosmologies of Credit: Transnational Mobility and the Politics of Destination in China*. Durham, NC: Duke University Press.
Chu, Julie (2014) "When Infrastructures Attack: The Workings of Disrepair in China." *American Ethnologist* 41(2): 351–367.
Coutin, Susan (2015) "Deportation Studies: Origins, Themes and Directions." *Ethnic and Migration Studies* 41(4): 671–681.
De Genova, Nicholas and Nathalie Peutz (2010) *The Deportation Regime: Sovereignty, Space, and the Freedom of Movement*. Durham, NC: Duke University Press.
Drotbohm, Heike (2011) "On the Durability and the Decomposition of Citizenship: The Social Logics of Forced Return Migration in Cape Verde." *Citizenship Studies* 15(3/4): 381–396.
Dunn, Elizabeth and Jason Cons (2013) "Aleatory Sovereignty and the Rule of Sensitive Spaces." *Antipode* 46(1): 92–109.
Feldman, Gregory (2012) *The Migration Apparatus: Security, Labor and Policymaking in the European Union*. Palo Alto, CA: Stanford University Press.
Fergana.ru. 2015a. "Konstantin Romodanovskii: FMS zakryla v'ezd v Rossiiu bolee 1,2 mln inostrantsev." *Fergana.ru*, March 18.
Fergana.ru. 2015b. "FMS Rossii otkazalas' ot idei migratsionnoi amnistii. V'ezd zapreshchen bolee 1,3 mln inostrantsam." *Fergana.ru*, April 15.

FIDH-ADC Memorial. 2014) *From Tajikistan to Russia: Vulnerability and Abuse of Migrant Workers and Their Families.* Paris: International Federation for Human Rights.
Fisch, Michael. n.d. "Remediating Infrastructure: Tokyo's Commuter Train Network and the Margin of Indeterminacy," this volume.
Gannushkina, Svetlana (2014) "Naibolee sushchestvennom izmenenii v migratsionnom zakonodatel'stve za 2013 god." Workshop on Migratsiia i Pravo [Migration and Law], Moscow, May 22.
Gibney, Matthew J. (2008) "Asylum and the Expansion of Deportation in the UK," *Government and Opposition* 43(2): 146–167.
Harvey, Penny (2012) "The Topological Quality of Infrastructural Relation: An Ethnographic Approach." *Theory, Culture and Society* 29(4/5): 76–92.
Harvey, Penny and Hannah Knox (2015) *Roads: An Anthropology of Infrastructure and Expertise.* Ithaca, NY: Cornell University Press.
Hull, Matthew (2013) "The Materiality of Indeterminacy ... On Paper, At Least." *HAU: Journal of Ethnographic Theory* 3(3): 441–447.
IOM (International Organization for Migration) (2014) *Tajik Migrants With Re-Entry Bans to the Russian Federation.* Dushanbe: International Organization for Migration. http://publications.iom.int/system/files/pdf/tajik_migrants_report_15jan.pdf.
Jansen, Stef (2009) "After the Red Passport: Towards an Anthropology of the Everyday Geopolitics of Entrapment in the EU's 'Immediate Outside'." *Journal of the Royal Anthropological Institute* 15(4): 815–832.
Jensen, Casper Bruun (2010) "Researching Partially Existing Objects: Ontologies for Developing Things," in *Ontologies for Developing Things: Making Healthcare Futures Through Technology.* Rotterdam: Sense Publishers, pp. 19–31.
Jensen, Casper Bruun and Atsuro Morita (2016) "Infrastructures as ontological experiments." *Ethnos* (special issue: Infrastructures as Ontological Experiments). Online First: DOI: 10.1080/00141844.2015.1107607.
Kelly, Tobias (2006) "Documented Lives: Fear and the Uncertainties of Law During the Second Palestinian intifada." *Journal of the Royal Anthropological Institute* 12(1): 89–107.
Kim, Jaeeun (2011) "Establishing Identity: Documents, Performance, and Biometric Information in Immigration Proceedings." *Law and Social Inquiry* 36(3): 760–786.
Kluczewska, Karolina (2014) *Migrants' Re-Entry Bans to the Russian Federation: The Tajik Story.* Bishkek: OSCE Academy. www.osce-academy.net/upload/file/Policy_Brief_16.pdf.
Kubal, Agniezska. Forthcoming. "Entry Ban as Surreptitious deportation? Situating zapret na vezd in Russian immigration law and practice in a comparative perspective." *Law and Social Inquiry.*
Latour, Bruno (1999) *Pandora's Hope: Essays on the Reality of Science Studies.* Cambridge, MA: Harvard University Press.
Lyon, David (2009) "Biometric, Identification and Surveillance." *Bioethics* 22(9): 499–508.
Malakhov, Vladimir (2014) "Russia as a New Immigration Country: Policy Responses and Public Debate." *Europe-Asia Studies* 66(7): 1062–1079.
Navaro-Yashin, Yael (2007) "Make-believe Papers, Legal Forms and the Counterfeit: Affective interactions between Documents and People in Britain and Cyprus." *Anthropological Theory* 7(1): 79–98.

Peutz, Nathalie and Nicholas de Genova (2010) "Introduction," in Nicholas de Genova and Nathalie Peutz (eds) *The Deportation Regime: Sovereignty, Space, and the Freedom of Movement*. Durham, NC: Duke University Press, pp. 1–32.

Reeves, Madeleine (2013) "Clean Fake: Authenticating Documents and Persons in Migrant Moscow." *American Ethnologist* 40(3): 508–524.

Reeves, Madeleine (2015) "Living from the Nerves: Deportability, Fear and Thrill in Migrant Moscow." *Social Analysis* 59(4): 119–136.

Reeves, Madeleine (2016) "Infrastructural Hope: Anticipating 'Independent Roads' and Territorial Integrity in Southern Kyrgyzstan." *Ethnos*. Online First: DOI: 10.1080/00141844.2015.1119176.

Valaleev, Mikhail (2013) "Mashina vziatok ne beret." *Rossiiskaia gazeta-federal'nyi vypusk*, June 14. http://www.rg.ru/2013/06/14/romodanovski.html.

van Houtum, Henk (2010) "Human Blacklisting: The Global Apartheid of the EU's External Border Regime." *Environment and Planning D: Society and Space* 28: 957–976.

Weszkalnys, Gisa (2015) "Geology, Potentiality, Speculation: On the Indeterminacy of 'First Oil'." *Cultural Anthropology* 30(4): 611–639.

Xiang, Biao and Johan Lindquist (2014) "Migration Infrastructure." *International Migration Review* 48(S1): S122–S148.

Zakon RF 321-FZ. 2012. Federal'nyi zakon "O vnesenii izmeneniia v stati'iu 26 Federal'nogo zakona 'Iz poriadki vyezda iz RF i v'ezda v RF'."

Zedner, Lucia (2009) "Epilogue: The Inescapable Insecurity of Security Technologies?" In Katja Franko Aas, Helene Oppen and Heidi Mork Lomell (eds) *Technologies of InSecurity: The Surveillance of Everyday Life*. London: Routledge, pp. 257–270.

23 Infrastructural inversion and reflexivity
A "postcolonial" biodiversity databasing project in India

Moe Nakazora

Infrastructural inversion in biodiversity?

Within social studies of science it is now commonplace to note that, because infrastructures are embedded within or sunk inside other social and technical arrangements, they tend to be taken for granted, forgotten, and remain invisible (Bowker and Star 1999). Despite its centrality for the progress of science, infrastructural work has not been well recognized by relevant communities of practitioners such as biodiversity scientists, for whom issues of digital data-handling techniques tend to be seen as mundane, unexciting and low status (Star 1999: 385f). Studying infrastructures, therefore, has required methods for surfacing and foregrounding such hidden work, which Geoffrey Bowker (1995) described with the apt metaphor of "infrastructural inversion." What this means is that we need to learn "to look closely at technologies and arrangements that, by design and by habit, tend to fade into the woodwork" (Bowker and Star 1999: 34).

Remarkably, the last decade has seen "reflexive" infrastructural inversion in new kinds of science. Exemplified by the Human Genome Initiative and other molecular biological projects, databases that used to be "hidden" infrastructure in support of scientific practice have increasingly come to be viewed as an end and topic of new scientific enterprises in their own right (Bowker 2000: 643). Furthermore, as some scholars of social studies of science have noted, this "informational turn" in science has increased the possibility of social theory (as one form of information) being incorporated into the science that it tries to grasp. An extreme version is situations in which some aspect or design of infrastructure is explicitly articulated as an "experimental" site of new democratic archive (Waterton 2010). Along these lines, the science and technology studies (STS) scholar, David Turnbull (2007), advocated for a type of "a database that does not reduce cultural and biological diversity by submitting different knowledge traditions to a one size fits all, lowest common denominator regime." According to him, such databases can be created by adopting insights from contemporary biologists and philosophers who view species not as taken-for-granted units but rather as a temporary achievement of sameness within a flow of difference.

This paper will examine a reflexive convergence between social theory and archive[1] construction in the field of biodiversity, a data-intense science. Here, I focus on a "bureaucratic" project in a rural state of India to reconsider the common assumption that "those developments taking place in a social theoretical domain have occurred largely isolated from, and unnoticed by, the majority of agencies, government departments, individuals and scientific groups" (Waterton 2010: 669).

The People's Biodiversity Register project in India is an attempt to database biodiversity and scientifically codify the environmental knowledge of local people. Based on the National Biodiversity Act (NBA), it aims at preventing misappropriation of "Indian" natural resources and traditional knowledge, and further to support their preservation and development. Although the initiative to database "Indian" biodiversity and related traditional wisdom may appear as a "new imperial project" (Richards 1993), in fact it also includes an interest in "an identity switch" of the Indian archive; that is, it entails an effort to go beyond colonialism by new database construction (see Krishna 1997). In the following, we will see how the project team, consisting of local plant taxonomists, phytochemists, and an anthropologist as a specialist in local "culture," tried to form the new "postcolonial" database. I proceed to consider what a critical method for anthropology of science to study infrastructure might look like at this juncture of "reflexive" infrastructural inversion.

Bioprospecting and emergent nature/culture

In the late 1980s, many life-science corporations showed interest in natural resources and indigenous knowledge in the hope of finding leads for developing new drugs. Since then, there has been greater interest in the intellectual property rights of indigenous people and farmers. The 1992 UN Convention of Biological Diversity (CBD) mandated that drug companies accessing indigenous resources and knowledge must share any economic benefits with the source nations and communities. Although this is in many ways a fragile mandate, the CBD's idiom and institutional framework have had noteworthy effects on the practice of the parties involved. In line with the tenets of the CBD, approval of bioprospecting by scientists has required benefit-sharing agreements with the resource owners and, as a consequence, numerous nongovernmental organizations (NGOs) and indigenous activists aiming to prevent illegitimate exchange have emerged.

In relation to these developments, several anthropological studies have criticized the assumption that discrete and identifiable subjects exist, which would have "rights" to knowledge – the latter itself regarded as a fixed and corporeal object (Brown 1998; Brush 1999). According to such critical scholarship, indigenous knowledge is informed by general knowledge, lacking defined spatial and temporal boundaries, and thus not easily accommodated into the Western logic of intellectual property right.

Cori Hayden (2003) went beyond this "relativist" anthropological discourse. Demonstrating that indigenous knowledge is not self-evidently a property of discrete communities but rather an effect that must be generated, she posed the following important question: "how are subjects (property holders) and objects (indigenous knowledge) considered within the framework of benefit-sharing agreement between bioprospecting scientists and their local interlocutors?" Thus, she showed scientists' creative re-engineering of benefit-sharing strategies based on IPR, which required them to provide benefits to the communities that had shared their knowledge. In fact, scientists bought plants in urban markets instead of in the communities and they negotiated benefit-sharing relations *parallel* to the process of the plant collection, for example with a group of traditional healers. Describing these events, Cori Hayden queried how subjects and objects *temporally* emerge in the bioprospecting process. In other words, her approach recognized "indigenous knowledge" and "property holders" not as *representations* of nature or human interests but as *emergent entities* within various practices.

Performativity and emergence as integral to the database

More than ten years after Cori Hayden did fieldwork in Mexico, a new movement has emerged, which has led anthropological discourse back to the relativist critiques. Lately, state actors and NGOs of "resource nations" have launched documentation and digitalization projects of "valuable" indigenous knowledge for multiple purposes, including the prevention of the misappropriation of indigenous knowledge. As databasing attempts include the "stabilization" of indigenous knowledge to a higher degree than bioprospecting practices, critiques of the "incommensurability" between indigenous and scientific knowledge have returned (Agrawal 2002; Harmwarth 1998).

Arun Agrawal, for example, criticizes recent initiatives by anthropologists or developmental agencies to database "valuable" indigenous knowledge for its preservation and inclusion in developmental projects ("participatory development"). According to him, databasing might transform indigenous knowledge by severing it from the practices that has sustained it. Furthermore, he argues, poor farmers, who are supposed to be in direct need of knowledge, would not be able to access a written archive located in a large city (Agrawal 2002). His criticism highlights the extent to which political relationships are involved in procedures of gathering and classifying information into archive that at first glance appear neutral (Star 1999).

As alternatives to such critique, however, several "experimental" projects suggest the possibility of flexibility even within the confines of the "database." Such flexibility is based on a close convergence between social theory and archive construction. In fact, some researchers are attempting to revolutionize the basic design of the archive. They are trying, that is, to alter the basic architecture of databases in order to open up the possibility of a dynamic archive that captures knowledge in motion as performance. They are also trying to make the metadata——the categories of classification——amenable to rewriting by users (Waterton 2010). This is the case, for example, of the Australian STS researcher Helen Verran who has worked with information technology engineers and Yolngu people to archive the indigenous knowledge of the latter in a format similar to their original oral tradition, using video and interactive media (Verran et al. 2007).

Here, we see a situation in which the STS analytical concept of (temporal) emergence, which Hayden relied on for her analysis, is becoming experimentally and reflexively integrated *in* databases. It is becoming part and parcel of postcolonial attempts to make databases more "democratic" and flexible.

Infrastructural inversion and colonialism/postcolonialism in Indian biodiversity and traditional knowledge

To examine the reflexive nature of recent efforts in postcolonial databasing, I explore a "bureaucratic" project in India, in which the theory of "postcolonialism" was incorporated into argument in the contemporary biodiversity issue. As noted, Waterton argued that "experimental" databasing projects have occurred largely isolated from, and unnoticed by, bureaucratic agencies. Furthermore, Turnbull has directly criticized the recent attempts of the Indian government to database biodiversity for their "bureaucratic" and "colonial" nature: "they all suffer from trying to impose a single unifying ontology on Indigenous diversity" (Turnbull 2007: 141). However, a closer examination of these projects reveals different forms of "reflexive infrastructural inversion" and alternative forms of politics embedded within them.

In India, the initiative to database biodiversity and related traditional wisdom is located in particular colonial/postcolonial political contexts. First of all, such databasing projects were largely a response to nationalist indignation over "neocolonial" expropriation. Specifically, they were triggered by the success of the Indian government and NGOs in overturning several patents granted by the European Union (EU) and the United States (US) patent offices for neem, turmeric, and basmati rice, which were recognized as having originated in India.[2]

Moreover, the intense interest of the Indian government in new global "information" sciences included an ethical and political drive to go beyond colonialism. As V. V. Krishna notes, colonial science in India was a "planned activity from the metropolis," where "the colonies were assigned the subordinate tasks of 'data exploration' and application of existing technical knowledge, while the theoretical synthesis took place in the metropolis" (Krishna 1997: 238). For the Indian government, the contemporary global attention to data science thus provided a possibility for an identity switch, changing national science from a subordinate science to a new global science in which India has a leading role.

At the same time, however, this databasing attempt relied heavily on colonial institutions and infrastructures. Thus, the central government is responsible for the creation of databases for codified traditional knowledge (such as Ayurveda), while the state governments are responsible for documenting uncodified (orally transmitted) information.

As medical anthropologists and historians have argued, this division of codified/uncodified traditional medicine is a colonial invention (see Brass 1972; Leslie 1992). Around the turn of the twentieth century, prominent Ayurvedic practitioners established professional associations, colleges, and pharmaceutical firms and wrote textbooks organized according to a modern medical division of subjects. Inspired by the thinking of British Orientalists, they deployed a revivalist ideology, calling for "a return to the 'scientific' Ayurveda of the classical age" through the adoption of institutional practices of biomedicine, while lamenting the descent of Ayurveda into magical practices during the colonial era. Over time, the gap between "professional" Ayurveda and a host of indigenous practices with which it had once been closely associated has widened and been essentialized as a gap between the professional and folk sectors (a newly separated category) of Indian medicine (Nakazora 2015b).

In this way, the project in India contained contradictory elements and impulses; though its very purpose was to go beyond colonialism, it was built on colonial infrastructures. The latter aspect of the project led to the criticisms of "postcolonialism," among Indian leftist intellectuals.

Postcolonialism and democracy in databasing projects

In India, the "relativist" critique of indigenous databasing projects, pointing to the incommensurability between scientific and indigenous knowledge, was made in part by citing the literature on "postcolonialism" (see Chatterjee 1993). In the *Economic and Political Weekly,* a left-wing journal, the project was mainly in terms such as an "unsolvable postcolonial piracy by the nation of 21st century" (Sharma 2002: 3129). The journal saw these projects as exemplifying the durability "of power relation(s) between the ruling and the ruled," and as an attempt to objectify and classify people's knowledge and open it up for use by strangers (including potential robbers of the knowledge). In this way, databasing projects were seen to perpetuate colonial project like caste censuses (Sahai 2005). These criticisms, though almost completely ignored by the central government, were seriously considered at the state government's project in Uttarakhand, where I did my fieldwork (Nakazora 2012, 2015a).

It should be noted that unlike the central government's project, the purposes of state government projects, collectively called the People's Biodiversity Register, are not limited to prevention of misappropriation of "Indian" knowledge. Originally they began by incorporating the project templates of one local NGO in Karnataka, which aimed at a participatory documentation process in the local language and the recording of people's traditional resource rights, including their options for sustainable use. The main focus of this template was the "inclusion of people." In the project in Uttarakhand this inclusive aspect is further emphasized.

Uttarakhand is the 27th state of India. It came into existence as recently as November 9, 2000. Numerous social science studies have argued that the process of subjectivizing the "environment" in Uttarakhand is linked to the evolution of a political consciousness, inclusion, and solidarity of local people. For instance, Linkenbach (2005) argued that the *Chipko* movement of the 1970s, a key event in the environmental history of the region was largely responsible for a more general political awakening of local inhabitants, eventually leading to the successful struggle for a separate state. In view of the fact that Uttarakhand is a part of the northwestern Himalayas, an environment rich in medicinal and aromatic plants and related traditional medicinal wisdom, the state government took steps to develop a "Herbal State [*jaḍi-būṭī pra-deś*]." What this meant was that economic and social development through the commercialization of medicinal plants became significant in Uttarakhand. The People's Biodiversity Register is regarded as a part of this "Herbal State" policy.

Against the criticism of "postcolonialism," the chief director of Uttarakhand State Biodiversity Board, Dr Burful, insisted on the need to have technical solutions for going beyond colonialism *within* the project. We will now see how social theory permeates into the very planning of database.[3]

Herbarium work: "Uttarakhand is botanized"

The first task for the People's Biodiversity Register was to formalize orally transmitted people's environmental knowledge. In Uttarakhand state, this centered especially on the knowledge of traditional medical practitioners (*vaidya*). This task was allocated to Forest Research Institute (FRI) and other local NGOs.

Rather than fieldwork, the initial activities conducted by scientists at the FRI took place in a herbarium. Uttarakhand has been explored by a number of famous botanists since colonial times, as illustrated by the English army officer, Major General Thomas Hardwicke, who made the first attempt to collect plants from the region in 1796. As a result, FRI herbarium, the second-largest herbarium in India, now preserves 330,000 specimens.

Importantly, most of these specimens were collected by the assistance of *vaidya*s. (As a legacy of this, descendants of some *vaidya*s have kept their "appreciation letter" for research cooperation from British botanists, and they are familiar with botanical names for famous medicinal plants in the region.) So it can be said that the colonial knowledge in the herbarium was already entangled with local contributions.

Nevertheless, plant collection in colonial times, as remembered by contemporary Indian scientists, was both imperialist in motive and technically amateur. Although the main work of plant taxonomists in FRI is to collect "recursive" data of type specimens collected in the past, they emphasize that in most cases the details are vague and fragmentary. Thus, it requires "brain storming" to trace the original locality. What the scientists involved in the new databasing project first of all did in the herbarium, therefore, was to carefully examine the labels of specimens, especially the descriptive part. There, information invisible from the specimen themselves, such as the location of collection, the local use of plants, and the parts, can be found. In this way, scientists tried to find "original Uttarakhand" plants.

As I discuss later, this identification process was followed by efforts to correct mistakes in colonial identification (plant name) and in descriptions of local use. Scientists tried to remove such mistakes by conducting interviews with present *vaidya*s. Finally, by "moving these specimens from herbarium to digital herbarium," they aimed to sever the colonial connections between British colonizers and Uttarakhand "economic" plants.

Postcolonialism in play: inclusion of people

The "herbarium specimen-based" databasing methodology was first of all proposed for scientific and bureaucratic reasons. It was much easier than "fieldwork," since the scientific identification of specimens was already given and the problem of translation could be avoided. In Uttarakhand, *vaidya*s mainly use and preserve underground plant parts (i.e. roots, rhizomes and tubers). This contrasted with the usual practices of plant taxonomists, who depend on flowers, fruits, and leaves for identification and naming. As Dr Burful explained, if you start with locally used plants and attempt to identify their scientific names, you need to go up to the Himalayas in the flowering seasons, which means the rainy seasons, where there is a risk of flood. Also, there is a strict policy restriction on plant collecting after the *Chipko* movement, especially near Badrinath, where most of the *vaidya*s collect plants (illegally now).

At the same time, however, Veena Chandra, the head of FRI who had promoted the digitalization of herbarium specimens even before the People's Biodiversity Register project started, explained the methodology as follows: "We, as postcolonial Indians, and also as post-independent Uttarakhand residents, should have more open, lively, and interactive knowledge, rather than closed knowledge kept in the archive and allowed to be seen only by plant taxonomists." She further emphasized the importance of "returning the knowledge to original owner, *vaidya*s." Thus the methodology was also entangled with the ideology of "postcolonialism." It aimed to make accessible hitherto hidden information.

This reference to postcolonial infrastructure-making reminds us of the case of the Darwin Centre, National History Museum in London, discussed by Claire Waterton (2010). At the Darwin Centre, scientists attempted to reinvent the border between research and the public by transforming the architecture of the building "so that the museum no longer serves a colonial polity" (Waterton 2010: 657). Yet, in the biodiversity databasing project in

Uttarakhand, "postcoloniality" refers not only to the ideological claim of opening specialists' (scientific) knowledge to "lay people." It is also embedded in, and entangled with, a peculiar historical connection between local science and *vaidyas*' regional knowledge, and with the political and technical details of the present project. We will now see how the term "postcolonial" gained new meanings in the next technical stage of the project, reflecting the emergent power dynamics in the politics of classification.

What is a universal name? Inclusion of nature

In October and December 2010, members of *Sambandh,* the local NGO, organized a consultation with *vaidyas*, in order to confirm the local names of the plants in specimen and explore present uses of plants by *vaidyas*. In Pipalkoti, Chamoli district, interviews were conducted with 21 *vaidyas*. What these interviews made clear was that an exact correlation between names of medicinal plants in the *garwali* local name and their scientific identification has not been fully established. Thus, several plants have one "vernacular" name with different botanical identifications, while in the other cases a botanical identification has many "vernacular" names. Against this problem, scientists first tried to pick only local plants that had been scientifically identified and arrange them taxonomically. This was based on the assumption among plant taxonomists that, in contrast with scientific knowledge, *vaidya*'s knowledge does not have an established system of classification. Yet, because the People's Biodiversity Register project aimed to include people in the documentation process, the use of "parataxonomy," generally meaning "simplified taxonomic units that are made accessible to the layperson" (Krell 2004), was also proposed.

However, in the process of comparing their herbarium specimens with the fieldwork, scientists discovered that local names were relatively stable *compared with* scientific names. While most of the local names (84 out of 86) remained the same between the time when specimens were originally collected and the present, the scientific names had changed many times due to new methods of classification – from morphological to reproductive characteristics to generics and back – over the last century. Based on the realization of the variability of scientific names, researchers in the project began asking themselves questions like "What is scientific 'truth'?" and "Is species a universal category?"

According to Dr Naithani, making the databasing project truly "postcolonial" would not simply entail an explosion of plants and indigenous knowledge through the "universal" and "robust" methodology of science, but rather a mutual enhancement of the different systems, brought about by juxtaposition. Thus, he gave "parataxonomy" a new meaning as the setting of scientific and traditional taxonomies alongside one another, sometimes allowing for translation of one into the other (Helmreich 2005). With the introduction of this concept of "parataxonomy," the meaning of the "postcolonial" database was transformed from an issue of availing of *vaidyas*' knowledge of specimens for informational inclusion to an issue of using it to re-organize scientific knowledge.

Parataxonomy and the politics of classification

In reality, recognition of the uncertainty of scientific names is not a new "finding" but a well-known fact among plant taxonomists. In *An Introduction to Plant Taxonomy* (Jeffrey 1982), which is used as an undergraduate textbook in FRI, the third chapter is entitled "The Process of Classification." The chapter begins by asserting that "first of all, we notice that it (classification) involves the making of a decision":

> This is obviously a source of possible disagreement. Different people think differently, so the decisions made are bound to be subjective, and to vary from person to person. Less obvious, but equally true, is the fact that different people may differ in what they mean by 'the same.'... In other words, in identification, what we decide are 'the same' depends upon the criteria which we decide to use for determining sameness.
> (Jeffrey 1982: 13–14)

Here, Jeffrey implies that each species is not a representation of universal nature but rather of a temporal agreement of sameness among a community of plant taxonomists. Moreover, as Geoff Bowker notes: "the junior scientist ... will be told (be it in lectures or in 'war stories' in the lab) about where the uncertainties in a particular kind of classification or measurement lie" (Bowker 2000: 655). Thus, first year students at the FRI learn the history of Linnaean classifications, including that "taxonomies are invented, not discovered." At one lecture I attended, the lecturer explained how Stuart Max Walter's classic study (1986) demonstrated that Linnaeus used the folk classifications available to him at the time. Then, she cited an Indian case: it is a well-known fact that Van Rheede's *Hortus Malabaricus*, the main source of Carl Linnaeus's knowledge of Asian tropical flora, relied almost entirely on Indian indigenous collaborators. Those collaborators included three Konkani Brahmin scholars, who provided textual references, but more importantly, Ayurvedic physicians from the Exhava or low-caste toddy tappers, who provided the functional taxomonies of classification. Thus there is an inherent tension and uncertainty in the discipline of plant taxonomy: while it relies heavily on the concept of species, everyone also doubts its existence and universality. Although these uncertainties regarding the species concept are recognized even among junior scientists, they seemed often to be forgotten in mundane practices of the FRI scientists. However, the contemporary context of "biodiversity" discourses has turned these classificatory problems into "topics" in a new way.

Biodiversity provides FRI scientists with economic and symbolic rewards. One junior scientist told me that after the Convention of Biological Diversity

(CBD) they could suddenly attract funds, projects, and attention, even though they were "old-fashioned scientists." However this required difficult collaborations between plant taxonomy (temporally organized) and ecology (spatially organized) (Bowker 2000). Thus, it could be observed how the spatial view of an interlinked nature affected the thinking of the FRI scientists. For instance, Dr Sas Biswas, in a presentation entitled "Collecting Herbarium Specimens: Traditional versus Newer Approaches," made the following observations:

> For long, botanists have been concerned with the collection of herbarium specimens with taxonomically characterized details based on mature individuals of populations. It is now an acknowledged fact that many plant species are interdependent with the animals for their regeneration through the means of pollination, dispersal, distribution of floral entities directly or indirectly. Therefore, a species of plant which is interdependent with fauna needs to be studied and collected with field data for the herbaria.

Here, he reconsiders the concept of species from the viewpoint of interdependence with animals or other environments in a way that is clearly influenced by an ecological point of view. It can thus be inferred that the recent encounter with "ecology," and the incorporation of the view of "spatially and relationally existing plants," created a space for the FRI scientists to reflexively consider the concept of species as a topic and even to recognize the "superiority" of local nomenclature. It was this recognition that led to the proposal of "parataxonomy" in the People's Biodiversity Register project. As one junior scientist in Uttarakhand wrote with approval, not only are local taxonomies stable, they also reflect a broad spectrum of information on local uses, ecology, physiology, anatomy, pharmacognosy, chemistry, and other aspects (Singh 2008).

Infrastructural inversion and reflexivity in biodiversity databasing projects

Since Bowker and Star proposed "infrastructural inversion" as a methodology for studying infrastructure, "making the hidden work of infrastructure visible" (Bowker and Star 1999: 34), several new kinds of science have seen a "reflexive infrastructural inversion," in which databases have become a topic and an end of scientific enterprise in themselves. This movement has led to social scientific "experimental" endeavors – that is, efforts to make democratic and flexible archives by incorporating social theory (as one form of information) into infrastructure.

In India, attempts to make databases of biodiversity and traditional wisdom were triggered by neocolonial anger against the recent "piracy" of "Indian" bio-information, as well as by the hope of changing the identity of

Indian science from a subordinate to a leading role. At the level of state government, "new" biodiversity databases were further expected to be "inclusive," reflecting the wider democratization process since the 1990s. As we have seen, these projects were criticized by Indian postcolonial and left-wing intellectuals.

Here I have discussed how the Uttarakhand People's Biodiversity Register project engaged reflexively with postcolonialism, by seeking technical solutions for moving beyond colonialism. The trajectory shows that "postcolonialism" actually played various roles. It changed from an initial emphasis on opening the so far hidden information of the herbarium and giving back information to *vaidyas*, to realizing the "parataxonomic" potential of scientific and traditional classification. In other words, postcolonialism changed properties as it became entangled with the technical details of the project, with peculiar historical relations between scientific and indigenous knowledge, with the geo-political landscape of the region, and with the emergent power dynamics surrounding the biodiversity sciences.

Waterton (2010) has argued for a new critical method to study infrastructure in the era of reflexive science. In her view, while scholars of social studies of science should get involved in the new, reflexive infrastructure projects currently being undertaken, they should also continue "to make the effort to understand the implicit performative and generative aspects, even of seemingly 'dead' archives" (669). The latter are:

> the kinds of environmental databases that policy makers create and use; the static-looking species databases that may actually be generative of new meanings; the 'boring' infrastructure of existing classifications; and of course, the ex-colonial edifices and archives that maintain extractive relationships to the world's bio and cultural diversity.
>
> (2010: 669)

Based on the present study, however, I am not convinced of the need to contrast "old", "boring" infrastructure that is invisibly performative versus new, reflexive infrastructures made by, or informed by, social scientists.

For one thing, the "bureaucratic" Indian case shows a process in which the database became a topic or end product in a manner that "involuntarily" created a space for reflexivity. Indeed, in interdisciplinary fields like biodiversity science, it is not unusual for scientists to encounter "other" knowledges – disciplinary, or epistemologically variable, like those of local *vaidyas*' —requiring them to rethink the uncertainties of their own field. Conversely, however, even when social scientific ideas *are* reflexively incorporated in infrastructure design, they become entangled with technical details and prior histories. Even for new experimental projects, it is thus incumbent to examine their embedded politics. This is so, not least, in order to figure out why most of these projects have such difficulties getting off the ground, tending to "remain at a conceptual level yet" (Waterton 2010: 660).

In an era of newly reflexive sciences, critiques against indigenous databasing attempts that work by pointing to the supposed incommensurability between scientific and local knowledge no longer work, since these kinds of criticism are already *premises* of the projects. What is needed is rather careful examination of the technical and political processes through which social theory and practical ideologies are actually, performatively, and partially incorporated within projects and what they include and exclude. This, I venture, offers a way forward for more "morally responsible critiques" (Verran 2001) of, and participations in, of postcolonial databasing.

Notes

1 This article uses the term "archive" as an overarching category to include a diversity of technologies used to inventory objects and knowledge, and to commit them to memory and for future use (Waterton 2010).
2 This occurs at a moment in Indian history when nationalism as necessarily a secular anti-imperialist gesture has been seriously called into question by Hindu nationalist postures that script a much more aggressive and exclusionary cultural nationalism (Rajan 2006: 70).
3 As is clear by now, the aim of the database development in the People's Biodiversity Register is to create broader infrastructural systems that link Indian bureaucracies, international patent systems, policies regarding biodiversity, different kinds of sciences such as plant taxonomy and ecology, and local knowledge. However, when I did my field research in 2010 and 2011, the project was in an initial stage in Uttarakhand and such infrastructural network remained as a "possibility" for the future. Accordingly, I focus on the making of the database in the hope of realizing such an infrastructure network.

References

Agrawal, A. (2002) "Indigenous knowledge and the politics of classification." *International Social Science Journal* 54(173): 277–281.
Bowker, G. C. (1995) "Second nature once removed: Time, space and representations." *Time and Society* 4(1): 47–66.
Bowker, G. C. (2000) "Biodiversity datadiversity." *Social Studies of Science* 30(5): 643–683.
Bowker, G. C. and Star, S. L. (1999) *Sorting Things Out: Classification and Its Consequences*. Cambridge, MA: MIT Press.
Brass, P. (1972) "The Politics of Ayurvedic Education: A Case Study of Revivalism and Modernization in India," in S. H. Rudolph and L. I. Rudolph (eds) *Education and Politics in India: Studies in Organization, Society, and Policy*. New York: Harvard University Press, pp. 342–371.
Brown, M. (1998) "Can culture be copyrighted?" *Current Anthropology* 39(2): 193–222.
Brush, S. (1999) "Bioprospecting the public domain." *Cultural Anthropology* 14(4): 535–555.
Chatterjee, P. (1993) *The Nation and Its Fragments: Colonial and Postcolonial Histories*. Princeton, NJ: Princeton University Press.
Harmsworth, G. (1998) "Indigenous values and GIS: A method and a framework." *Indigenous Knowledge and Development Monitor* 6(3): 1–7.

Hayden, C. (2003) *When Nature Goes Public: the Making and Unmaking of Bioprospecting in Mexico.* Princeton, NJ: Princeton University Press.
Helmreich, S. (2001) "After culture: Reflections on the apparition of anthropology in artificial life, a science of simulation." *Cultural Anthropology* 16(4): 613–628.
Jeffrey, C. (1982) *An Introduction to Plant Taxonomy.* Cambridge: Cambridge University Press.
Kalyan, V. (2009) "Open the Traditional Knowledge Digital Library." Available via: www.sinapseblog.com/ (accessed June 15, 2016)
Krell, F. T. (2004) "Parataxonomy vs. taxonomy in biodiversity studies." *Biodiversity and Conservation* 13(4): 795–812.
Krishna, V. V. (1997) "A Portrait of the Scientific Community in India: Historical Growth and Contemporary Problems," in J. Gaillard, V. V. Krishna and R. Waast (eds) *Scientific Communities in the Developing World.* New York: Sage Publications, pp. 236–280.
Leslie, C. (1992) "Interpretations of Illness: Syncretism in Modern Ayurveda," in C. Leslie and A. Young (eds) *Paths to Asian Medical Knowledge.* Berkeley, CA: University of California Press, pp. 177–208.
Linkenbach, A. (2005) "Nature and Politics: The Case of Uttarakhand (North India)," in G. Cederlöf and K. Sivaramakrishnan (eds) *Ecological Nationalisms: Nature Livelihoods and Identities in South Asia.* Delhi: Permanent Black.
Nakazora, M. (2012) "The scientists adopting postcolonialism: Case study of a medicinal plant databasing project in Uttarakhand, India [Posutokoloniarizumu o torikomu kagakushatachi: Indo Uttarakando shu ni okeru yakusōshu databaseka project o jirei to shite]." *Shakaijinruigaku-nenpō* [Annual Review of Social Anthropology] 38: 129–149.
Nakazora, M. (2015a) "Pure gifts for future benefit? Giving form to the subject in a biodiversity databasing project in India." *NatureCulture* 3: 106–121.
Nakazora, M. (2015b) "Between commensurability and incommensurability: Emergence of Ayurveda in the contact zones with biomedicine, alternative medicine, and intellectual property right regime [Honyakukanousei to fukanousei no aida: seibutsuiryou, daitaiiryou, chitekishoyuukenseido tono settushokuryouiki ni okeru ayuruveda no seisei]." *Jinbungakuhou* 107: 111–142.
Rajan, K. S. (2006) *Biocapital: The Constitution of Postgenomic Life.* Durham, NC: Duke University Press.
Richards, T. (1993) *The Imperial Archive: Knowledge and the Fantasy of Empire.* New York: Verso.
Sahai, S. (2005) "A review of the documentation of the indigenous knowledge (IK) associated with biodiversity in South Asia." Draft by Gene Campaign for Discussion for IK Documentation in South Asia.
Sharma, D. (2002 "Biopiracy fears cloud Indian database." *Economic and Political Weekly* 37(5): 3122–3125.
Singh, H. (2008) "Importance of local names of some useful plants in ethnobotanical study." *Indian Journal of Traditional Knowledge* 7(2): 365–370.
Star, S. L. (1999) "The ethnography of infrastructure." *American Behavioral Scientist* 43(3): 377–391.
Turnbull, D. (2007) "Maps narratives and trails: Performativity, hodology and distributed knowledge in complex adaptive systems: An approach to emergent mapping." *Geographical Research* 45(2): 140–149.

Verran, H. (2001) *Science and an African Logic*. Chicago, IL: University of Chicago Press.

Verran, H., Christie, M., Anbins-King, B., van Weeren, T., and Yunupingu, W. (2007) "Designing digital knowledge management tools with Aboriginal Australians." *Digital Creativity* 18(3): 129–142.

Walter, S. M. (1986) "The name of the rose: A review of ideas on the European bias in angiosperm classification." *New Phytologist* 104: 527–546.

Waterton, C. (2010) "Experimenting with the archive: STS-ers as analysts and co-constructors of databases and other archival forms." *Science Technology & Human Values* 35(5): 645–676.

24 Survivals as infrastructure

Twenty-first-century struggles with household and family in formal computations

Jane I. Guyer

Introduction

In recent analyses of infrastructure, the rise to prominence of the coordination of information and energy flows, beyond the time–space coordination of materials and people, is a profound shift in focus that introduces new participants, with emergent qualities of agency. Jensen writes, 'infrastructures are increasingly used for the production, distribution, and sharing of information' (2013: 1). It is clear that systemic terms and metaphors, such as flow, production, distribution and others, can be transferred from one domain to the other – the material to the immaterial, then to the immaterial in material forms such as documents – thus opening up novel fields to well-worked theoretical approaches and analytical terms based on an expectation of systemic properties of some kind.

There is also, however, the actors' own transfer of specific terms from one infrastructure, or domain, to another, and from one era to another, within changing configurations of other elements, as indicated in the focus of actor network theory on *agencements* (also termed assemblages or devices) (Callon 2008). This particular process necessarily raises the question of the historical provenance and course of change of the components of new infrastructures, their relational composition, and the criteria for designating those considered as the 'actors' who shape the assemblage, in emergent as well as established practice. Compositions can arise both from deliberate crafting and also from elements falling into place by situational logics. My focus on a very old, persistent concept such as the 'household' is chosen both because it is intrinsically of interest to me, as an economic anthropologist, and because the quite voluminous documentation of its deployment over time and place can offer domains in which the processes of relational 'emergence' in novel infrastructures can be examined in detail, as Rabinow (2008) advocated.

Understanding how certain, apparently stabilized, elements are revised and recontextualized over time becomes, then, one challenge of infrastructure studies. Modern governance tracks and coordinates many domains, so, necessarily, some components endure, either for convenience, by protection, or through their importance to *multiple* administrative infrastructures, from taxation to public welfare. To establish 'trends' and comparing under national or international rubrics, the names and the definitions of such elements must be stabilized. The detailed technical, social and political artisanship through which 'elements' are recognized and combined with each other is a central theme in my essay collection (Guyer 2016). The concept of the household would qualify as what I term there a 'legacy': an element preserved and morphed in meaning, combination and application over very long periods of time. Such legacies offer an important focus for research that combines historical, political economic and ethnographic theory and method.

Examining these enduring elements from the artisanal perspective, or the pattern-emergent perspective, one can search in detail for what would qualify as 'tinkering': making small expert adjustments. For example, as property law and personal relationships shift in the twenty-first century, who is 'tinkering' with 'the household' as a unit, and how? The newspapers report wealthy families incorporating legally, not to produce or trade anything as in family businesses of the past, but solely for the purpose of property ownership and the tax advantages it brings (Guyer 2015). What, then, is a 'household' in this case, where financial flows become crucial? Does it consist of the owners alone, if the property is lying empty much of the time? Probably not, but the official dispensations are worth tracing out. Does it have to meet public health standards, as if it were being occupied by a group of actual people? How is all this being done, in legal terms? And does the eventual compilation of the information under *all* the relevant definitions facilitate either a vast cumulative archive of classified information that forms a single large pool for public purposes? And/or is an old concept, such as 'household', more like a sluice gate in a vast irrigation network or a lock in a canal system when worked by specific operators? Both the named pooled archives and the localized devices that go under old names are components within the new infrastructures of the information age and the global economy.

The household serves as an example. It has become what may well be amongst the oldest components of administrative infrastructure, sometimes implicitly naturalized to 'the family', which comes forward from the Roman *familia* and Greek *oikos*, from whence 'economics'. Under the Roman Empire it was a unit for taxation and conscription into military service. Over two thousand years later, it is now required by the international financial institutions as an economic administrative category, in places with highly varied kinship systems, for collecting data on the cost of living, to be used for the comparative purpose of calculating the consumer price index (CPI), measuring inflation and, thereby, judging the rate of growth of the gross domestic product (GDP), to apply to categories of action at a level above the classic modernist model of the nation-state. At the same time, personal relations may also be changing, at the intimate level of co-residence and shared interests.

Household as element

In the following, I use the household as an example of a repeatedly recrafted enduring device, some of whose moments of recrafting are accessible from records and would still be accessible through ethnography. I end with questions that could be posed of other long-lasting devices with respect to emergent futures in the increasingly mobile, non-sedimentary, world that infrastructure studies is bringing to the fore. I trace out briefly, in advance, the steps through which this concept has moved.

In classical times, the *familia* was a legal unit, defined by the law on property and status and their transmission across generations, within civic organization and culture. In that era, the *familia* included slaves and other dependents, as well as livestock and inanimate property. In medieval times a noble 'household' would include resident servants and tradespeople, as well as property. Indeed the cost of the British royal household was a justification for a new tax on the citizenry, the Hearth Tax, imposed after the restoration of the monarchy in 1660. From the reform movements of the late eighteenth century, the variables in household documentation expanded to examine the dependencies more closely, including rent-paying lodgers and other unrelated residents. In the twentieth century, the household became a formalized unit of economic measurement, particularly with respect to the standard of living. In the twenty-first century, the asset value of the house itself has become more prominently documented, more with respect to market value and local property tax regimes than to personal status law.

Many large and small shifts comprise this history. With the secularization of vital registration and the individuation of personal records, the household focus of information on those eligible for military conscription surely dropped out. Other functions may also have been excised from this particular 'pool' of information. Under colonial rule and the economic supervision of international financial institutions, the household has been transported to parts of the world where, although familial and residential histories differ, the concept is imposed as a stable anchor to the database. The use of a concept such as 'household' can thus sharpen attentiveness to those moments and places where recrafting has taken place, that both preserves and changes its implications: for the pools and sluice gates in the network of flows, and for the people who inhabit the ecologies affected by all the assemblages that compose infrastructures. Its 'entanglement' (Callon 2008) with other elements, has shifted. We can track two different internal emphases, and their varied combination, by identifying the two halves of the word itself: the 'house' as a material good and a container, and the 'hold' as the relations of interdependency amongst people (from the feudal concept of a 'holding').

The household as a formal administrative unit

A brief review of British history can set the stage. The Domesday Book census of property, collected in 1086 after the Norman Conquest, was crafted to identify people with property for purposes of taxation, control and conscription of the subordinates resident on the property. The holding was the central unit. Subsequent inventories shifted towards the house itself and its inhabitants. The Hearth Tax of 1662 was a moment when the criteria of 'the household' were recrafted to prioritize the physical building and its owner over the inhabitants as a group. In the late nineteenth and early twentieth centuries, government concern with the welfare of workers and children prioritized relationships, although the property tax element was not eliminated. A key moment was the creation of the regular national census in 1801, collected by household: not as enduring units but as the 'roof over the head' of whichever individuals were there overnight on a specific date. The first national census did refer back to military conscription as a purpose.

The interdependence of 'house' and 'holding', real property and responsibility for others, shifts as the regimes shift. For example, especially among the poorer classes the equation of 'house' and 'hold' becomes more tenuous as the real property component changes. The *legal* prioritization applies to assets and to dependency in its formal-genealogical-provable sense, while the daily prioritization of *consumption* implicates a co-residence unit; whoever is living there, in whatever numbers and relationships, for however long. We may now be seeing that, with the rise in mobility and housing rental, following the era of post-war aspiration to owner-occupancy and the provision of housing to the poor by the state, the 'house' and the 'hold' are becoming more and more tenuously mutually implicated. The deeper question then becomes: what does such co-residence entail for mutual responsibility in the domain of consumption and interpersonal claims and asset-management? The flow of resources amongst people, moderated and documented by the state through its increasingly complex infrastructures of information and distribution, would depend on the model and the breadth of its applicability.

Doubtless any cracks in the system would provoke people to improvise resolutions of various legal, and possibly extra-legal, kinds, in *specific* contexts. So this would fall under the rubric of tinkering-artisanship, from within and below. As a complementary focus, we could identify *all* the places where the household figures as an operative element in particular formal systems, and then trace out the work it does, on the larger-scale, emergent, pattern-creation level, since not all macro-dynamics can be crafted in a completely controlled fashion.

The household under the family-household model

1 A taxation unit

'The family' of a married couple and their children, as a social form coincident with the household, was articulated first (in Europe) under the power of the church and feudal law, which defined personal identity and the nature of the tribute-taxation unit. In England, the parish authorities were the final authority on status by virtue of mediating rituals of status change and archiving the registries of births, marriages and deaths.

In England in 1662, the Hearth Tax transferred one of these tax obligations to the sovereign state. At one shilling per hearth, paid twice per year (Michaelmas and Lady Day), it contributed to the support of the royal household. It was payable by the occupier, not the owner. Pragmatically, the hearths simply had to be counted, not measured and classified, as would be the case with land. There were precedents, in the Ottoman Empire and in France, since while the hearth is immovable, people can abscond. The measure was deeply resented in Britain, in part because of the house inspection that it involved, and it led to dangerous measures for tax evasion, like stopping up chimneys and even connecting more than one fire to a single chimney. Possibly it gave a great boost to what became 'pub culture', because it encouraged people to go somewhere else to eat and keep warm. The tax was abolished in 1698.

With regard to official definitions of residential organizations, we have another historical example of the distinction between house and holding. Under the Poor Laws, as instituted in 1601, there were provisions for parishes to collect 'rates' on houses, as property, to pay for the poor house, which would be seen entirely as a consumption unit, supported by the community as a whole. By now, institutions such as prisons, shelters and residential religious communities are explicitly included in the designation of the 'household' as a consumption unit, while rates have become local taxes to support many other collective projects in local governance. In 1990, in Britain, they were replaced by a poll tax, and then back to a 'council tax', 'based on the estimated market value of property ... with a discount for people living alone'.[1] So this particular tax went from house, to person, and back to property value, first of all over centuries, but then recuperated for re-application over a very short period of time in the late twentieth century.

2 Dependency within the household

In the eighteenth century, with the development of friendly societies, a public interest in the monetary aspects of household dependency became more explicit. As social infrastructures, the societies usually made provision for support of members during illness, widowhood, seasonal unemployment, and other stresses, and for the disabled, orphans, the mentally impaired, the aged, etc. This was partly to mitigate the effects of the Poor Laws, which put the destitute into institutions. In *The State of the Poor* from 1797, Frederick Morton Eden (1797) culled the sources from both the parish and friendly societies, and analysed the data in terms of dependency and need. He offers cases where the 'family' is clearly a 'household' in the sense that its members occupy a house and eat from a common hearth, and yet (see vol. III, p. 904, for November 1795) income both in cash and in kind is unstable for both the man of the house and his wife.

The nineteenth-century era's focus became more precisely trained on the quality of the house and welfare of the children. Cole and Postgate (1961 [1938]:

328   *Jane I. Guyer*

361) report on the Society for the Improvement of the Condition of the Dwellings of the Labouring Classes, organized in the mid-century by the Labourers' Friend Society (founded in 1830). The Housing Act of 1890 gave local authorities the power to clear unsanitary dwellings and provide houses (1961: 413).

Charles Booth's survey of the *Life and Labour of the People in London*, undertaken in the 1880s, focused close attention on 'Poverty (tested by Crowding) Compared with Earnings': 'we reckon as living in crowded conditions those whose house accommodation is limited to one room for each two or more persons', and he finds that this corresponds closely to 'those whose earnings were supposed not to exceed 21s a week for a "small" family' (Booth 1891: 44). A footnote adds that a small family is considered to consist of about four members, and provides the best basis of comparison with the earnings of the head of the family only (14). Booth was attempting to 'make a comparison between earnings and style of life for the whole population', and compiled a table of wages in 43 trades and the rates of overcrowding for each. On household composition, he wrote:

> it must be remembered that no special blood relationship exists between the members of the census family. Boarders, lodgers, visitors and domestic servants are included. The bond is merely that of the household. Those who live under the same roof, or in the same apartments, probably using the same kitchen fire, are accounted as members of one family.
> (36)

We should note, however, that Booth correlates all this with individual earnings in the trades and, accepting the concept of 'head of the household', presumes that all members of the household are dependent on that person's income. The mean family size is similar to the findings of Gregory King for the seventeenth century (Glass 2008 [1965]), between four and five, but then Booth noted (40) that probably children go out to work very young. Where they live is not then probed, although he does note that some workers live within, or above, their place of work.

We can note here the focus on the family – and its internal structure, earnings base and condition of comfort – rather than the house in its other aspects. Rent is a consumption cost, since the poor would not own their own houses. It is this framing that comes forward into the CPI, created in 1913 and first implemented during the Great War, when the provision of consumption items was the subject of a massive national project of rationing (Guyer 1993). This concern with general welfare, and particularly the care and education of children, comes forward through the Great Depression, then World War II, and then the era of the welfare state. The cost of taxation and the financing of purchases, as well as upkeep and renovation, get assimilated into rent, which rises sharply in recent decades.

3 The Consumer Price Index: 'shared resources'

Living under the same roof and using the same hearth (i.e. the implication of 'sharing', see UN below) are still definitional of a household. A standard 'basket of goods' that is defined and tracked over time through household surveys, to equate with income (at the household level), produces various indices: the quality of life in different population quintiles, the purchasing power of the money (at the systemic level, as a measure of inflation) and, in the last decades of the twentieth century, for international comparison of economic indicators (monitored by the IMF). Since a holistic profile of the population's consumption is at stake, residential institutions are included, although the household remains the basic unit of the survey.

It may be important, as well, to examine the inclusion (or not) of all the *people*, the lodgers and visitors of Booth's definition of a family for economic purposes. What counts as a 'member' may become more precisely defined in kinship terms in the twentieth century, or residence patterns themselves may simply change. The post-war culture of the mid-century certainly promoted (or enabled) a coincidence of the nuclear family and the household. Policy promoted the 'owner-occupier', with a growing emphasis on 'family values' and the growth of financial supports for the economic life cycle (as envisaged by Modigliani 1986). It becomes clear, then, that it is the family as narrowly defined, and consumption under a single, common (real or institutional) roof, in varying sorts of convergent manner with respect to 'resources', which defined the unit for the CPI. It was the spending patterns, by income quintile, that were at stake: with respect to informing inflation calculators, judging the relative prices of goods, and classifying households into categories relative to welfare indicators and thereby qualification for social services.

Since much in government and corporate planning is inflation-adjusted, it is possible that the annually calculated CPI, based on household studies, is among the most crucial of the components of governance infrastructures. In an era of rapid demographic and financial change, though, certain aspects of the 'family=household' model became awkward, especially in configuring the 'house' and 'holding' aspects with respect to the newly developing infrastructures of financial and asset management.

4 Findings on the 'house=asset' aspect of the 'household'

Once rental and other costs of the roof and the shared accommodations of a house are folded into the CPI as consumption, they become possible to track. It is clear that these costs have risen very markedly, particularly in the decades since 1980. The proportional weight of housing costs has gone from 13.4 per cent (1917–1919), to 18.1 per cent (1934–1936) (Stapleford 2009: 162). By 2006 it was reported at 32.76 per cent,[2] and for 2012, 41 per cent (Guyer 2014). Rising rapidly, but how and why?

To do justice to these questions, we can parallel them to census changes (Guyer 2014). *In situ* examination of their categories and forms of application could be a way into the dynamics of the emergence of nodes within infrastructures in the process of creation or recrafting. What the particular tables for the United States in 2012 show (Guyer 2014: 14) is two striking implications for the concept of the household: first, that in the younger (20 to 29 years) and older (65+ years) age brackets, at least one third of the households are 'non-family' households. And secondly, that 61 per cent of all households have only one or two members, which accounts for 45 per cent of the population. If this really captures the bases we now have for 'sharing resources' (as per the UN), then it is no wonder that the 'sharing economy' has taken off between non-related people.

In the 1980s and onward, under the conditions of the 'neoliberal economy', the CPI experts tried to identify the 'consumption' aspects of housing to separate them from the 'investment' aspects. This has proved a very difficult nut to crack.

As real estate prices rose in the 1980s, the American CPI separated out what it called 'shelter services', and equated this cost for owner-occupiers with the rental income forgone by living in the house. But of course the rental cost would have to cover all the financial and transaction costs as well, so very substantially over and above what Thomas Piketty referred to as the value of housing as 'rental value of dwellings, defined as the increment of well-being due to sleeping and living under a roof rather than outside' (2014: 213). Here is Randal Verbrugge (2006) on the 'Puzzling Divergence of Rents and User Costs, 1980–2004', with respect to volatility as well as level:

> (T)he data suggest that despite the large persistent divergences, these did not imply the presence of unexploited profit opportunities: though detached housing is readily moved between owner and renter markets, and the detached-unit rental market is surprisingly thick, transactions costs would have prevented risk-neutral investors from earning expected profits by buying a property to rent out for a year, and would have prevented risk-neutral homeowners from earning expected profits by selling their homes and becoming renters for a year.
>
> (Verbrugge 2006:1)

Journalists write about the financialization of housing and other related practices, where a substantial part of the price premium can be attributed to location and not 'shelter services': the major cities, the coastal and mountain vistas, and safe countries where money capital can be stored in a material form that will be protected by the law and general civility. Likewise, derivatives have been developed with respect to the incomes from residential property, and financial companies moved very rapidly into valuable housing markets. Here we glimpse the interaction of the recrafting of infrastructural devices already in existence, that have historical gravitas as well as the emergent qualities of the very large flows, for the crafting of which the element of

Survivals as infrastructure 331

'power' is not irrelevant. However, the macro-analysis of 'emergent' dynamics would need to be examined closely to identify the moments where emergence gains its own momentum. The conceptually stable elements, and especially those that reflect and affect the condition of the people, such as 'the household', may well offer entry points for the study of the relationship between recrafting and emergence.

Traditional indices, and their reinterpretation for what used to be called 'quality of life', may well be in flux at the present moment when a key element of the household, namely the house itself, is far more valuable as a material structure than as a holding for relationships. We even witness confusion in the newspapers (in England, March 2015) over various new government measures and claims that 'Households are better off than five years ago' (*The Independent*, 20 March 2015: 1). It is unclear what this might mean and how to account for it, especially since it constituted a 'main battleground' of the, then upcoming, general election. The question of 'what is a household?' is there between the lines, as the article veers back and forth from taxpayers to age groups to income quintiles. And we can wonder which 'young people' (immigrants?) are indicated in the following: 'Average incomes of pensioners had risen, but those of working-age people had fallen, especially among people in their twenties.'

My summary thought is that the property component of the house is now the focus of far more concerted attention in the formal sector, both government and business, than the dependencies. Indeed, we seem to have expanded the application of the word 'vulnerable' to people who would have been in those dependency relationships by virtue of age, disability or some other factor of life. From 'house' to 'house' in the use of the family-household concept, with the 'holding', in human terms, rising and then falling in prominence. But who are these people to each other, then, who co-inhabit the census-CPI household? And what extra-household transactions are becoming increasingly important to the 'holding' of interdependency?

International application

If the salient features of 'household' are shifting awkwardly within Western contexts, then we can surmise even greater complexity in its application in contexts where the composition of kinship and dependence, the formulation of incomes streams and mutual responsibilities, and the definition of assets have all differed widely, especially in the relative importance of transactions of mutuality across the boundaries of the residential unit (see Guyer 1981; Guyer and Peters 1987, on Africa). Nevertheless, the IFI requirements for global monitoring do impose a general definition:

> Households comprise one or more individuals living together and sharing resources. The official UN definition also includes people living in military accommodation, convalescent homes, and boarding schools. Such people are treated as belonging to private households. But for the purpose

of CPI construction, consideration must also be given to the inclusion of other institutional households such as those living in religious institutes, hospitals, prisons, retirement homes etc. Temporary foreign workers may live together in special housing blocks, which may be treated as institutional households in the census

(UN 2009, section 2.17: 10)

This clearly includes newly insurgent social forms: from the individual living alone to teams of migrant workers and militias. The widening encompassment of residential groups as 'households' that neither own nor occupy a house, nor depend on each other in the familial sense, illustrates the way in which an essential administrative term can be repositioned in infrastructures over time: protected from elimination, morphed in meaning and rendered quite blurred in applicability. Tracking exactly how such concepts and instructions on how to realize them work out in different governmental and cultural contexts would further illuminate the dynamics of the assemblage of legacy elements into new infrastructures.

Final comparative questions

Some social aspects of the variety of households, such as the new mobility and complexity of inter-household transactions, are familiar to anthropologists. But the United Nations 'Practical Guide', and the census, could also be followed up ethnographically, especially with respect to those 'single person' households that are emerging in large numbers in these times of rapid transition in labour structures alongside the financialization of houses as assets. At the other end of the demographic spectrum, one might also wish to look more closely at the large households of non-familial members and the legacies of non-resident 'next-of-kin' in property law. Which part of the contribution to the patchwork value of a house belongs to whom and is heritable by whom? The literature on co-residence, households and inter-household transactions, in contexts where the family-household was not so early defined and regulated as it was in Europe, would be very relevant to consider here.

We could go much further, also, by bringing to bear cases where a transition in the property and finance law is in full swing, such as Deborah James (2015) describes for the African population of South Africa. In comparative cases, we might see how indigenous concepts for material infrastructures, land, location, relationship units, dependencies, co-residence and inheritance are now made to work in people's own discourses and practices. How do such definitions and dynamics confront the formal instruments at the UN-CPI guide?

I am convinced, in any case, that anthropology has a great deal to offer in examining, in the West and elsewhere, how the 'house' and the 'holding' are being brought together by multiple parties, as well as the tensions and struggles entailed by these accommodations. Theoretically, we need to consider power in their composition as well as the ethnography of emergent practice, but we are still strongest with respect to anthropology's capacity to bring detailed ethnographic approaches to specific recrafting of devices, and tinkering with components. Simply by virtue of lasting through time, infrastructures carry the legacies of their multiple components forward from past configurations. The interaction of the deliberate, precise and situational artisanal interventions, through particular constructs and destructs, with the emergent dynamics of patterns and flows, can be examined closely through the study of classic elements such as the household.

Notes

1 Wikipedia entry, http://en.wikipedia.org/wiki/Rates_in_the_United_Kingdom. Consulted 22 March 2015.
2 www.bls.gov/cpi/cpifact6.htm.

References

Booth, Charles (1891) *Life and Labour of the People in London*. Second series: Industry. Comparisons, Survey and Conclusions. Reprinted 1970 from 1902/1904 edition, New York: AMS Press.
Callon, Michel (2008) "An Essay on Framing and Overflowing: Economic Externalities Revisited by Sociology," in Michel Callon (ed.) *The Laws of the Markets*. Oxford: Blackwell, pp. 244–269.
Cole, G. D. H. and Raymond Postgate (1961 [1938]) *The Common People. 1746–1946*. London: Methuen.
Eden, Frederick Morton (1797) *The State of the Poor*. London: J. David.
Glass, D. V. (2008 [1965]) Two Papers on Gregory King," in D. V. Glass and D. E. C. Eversley (eds) *Population in History: Essays in Historical Demography*, vol. 1, *General and Great Britain*. New Brunswick, NJ: Transaction Publishers, pp. 159–180.
Guyer, Jane I. (1981) "Household and Community in African Studies". *African Studies Review* 24(3/4): 87–137.
Guyer, Jane I. (1993) "Toiling Ingenuity': Food Regulation in Britain and Nigeria". *American Ethnologist* 20, 4: 797–817.
Guyer, Jane I. (2014) "Gross Domestic Person? *Anthropology Today* 30(2): 11–15.
Guyer, Jane I. (2015) "Housing as 'Capital'". *Hau: Journal of Ethnographic Theory* 5(1): 495–500.
Guyer, Jane I. (2016) *Legacies, Logics, Logistics: Essays in the Anthropology of the Platform Economy*. Chicago, IL: University of Chicago Press.
Guyer, Jane I. and Pauline Peters (1987) "Introduction. Conceptualizing the Household: Issue of Theory and Policy in Africa". *Development and Change* (special issue) 18(2): 197–214.
James, Deborah (2015) *Money from Nothing: Indebtedness and Aspiration in South Africa*. Stanford, CA: Stanford University Press.
Jensen, Casper Bruun (2013) "Infrastructures and Development Aid: Fields, Fractals, and Frictions," in Casper Bruun Jensen and Brit Ross Winthereik (eds) *Monitoring Movements in Development Aid: Recursive Partnerships and Infrastructures*. Cambridge, MA: MIT Press, pp. 1–30.

Modigliani, Franco (1986) "Life Cycle, Individual Thrift and the Wealth of Nations". *American Economic Review* 76(3): 297–313.

Piketty, Thomas (2014) *Capital in the Twenty-First Century.* Cambridge, MA: Harvard University Press.

Rabinow, Paul (2008) *Marking Time: On the Anthropology of the Contemporary.* Princeton, NJ: Princeton University Press.

Stapleford, Thomas A. (2009) *The Cost of Living in America: A Political History of Economic Statistics, 1880–2000.* Cambridge: Cambridge University Press.

United Nations (2009) *Practical Guide to Producing Consumer Price Indices.* Geneva: UN.

Verbrugge, Randal (2006) "The Puzzling Divergence of Rents and User Costs, 1980 to 2004". Paper presented at the OECD-IMF Workshop on Real Estate Price Indexes, Paris, 6–7 November. Available at https://editorialexpress.com/cgi-bin/conference/download.cgi?db_name=NASM2007&paper_id=104.

Part VI
Digital infrastructures

The chapters in this section consider how digital infrastructures are reshaping approaches to, and understandings of data, information and infrastructures themselves. Information and data infrastructures have become more visible to social analysts in recent years as developments in digital technologies increasingly blur the distinctions between informational systems. Smart motorways, computer-controlled air and rail systems, and the myriad devices that track, map and monitor environments, movements, and bodies shape how we interact with each other and with the world. They also generate and circulate huge amounts of data. The velocity, volume, and variety of digital information that characterizes "big data" mark a qualitative shift in how and what we can know.

By looking at how understandings of climate change are related to changes in data infrastructures, the chapter by Paul Edwards offers a historian's account of these changes. He argues that from the 1970s, climate change, which had previously been addressed as a purely scientific issue, became a matter of political and social concern. The emergence of a new form of climate data – simulations of both past and future states, derived from global climate models – was central to this transformation.

More recently, infrastructural changes related to computing and the Internet, in tandem with new sociopolitical norms of transparency and open access, have opened climate data to a myriad of new uses. City planners, health officials, water managers, military services, and disaster response agencies all began to use climate data as part of their planning processes. But amid this surfeit of information, a new and problematic gap appeared between the scientific data infrastructure and the knowledge systems most commonly used by policy-oriented planners.

Even user communities with considerable climate-related expertise, such as water managers, differ from climate scientists in their understanding of what climate data are, how they can credibly be used, and how the inevitable uncertainties can be managed and communicated. Edwards argues that the rapidly increasing availability of climate data has not been matched by a concomitant increase in translational information, nor by software or social systems capable of choosing and processing climate data for the vast variety of potential users and uses of this data.

The problem of reconfiguring data as actionable knowledge is the starting point for Hannah Knox's chapter. Knox is also concerned with climate change data, but her focus is on the concerns of local government workers with responsibilities for creating informational infrastructures for climate action. Their problem is how to arrive at action amid the plans, strategies, and discussions that fill their working lives. At some level, plans involve the formulation of a project that Knox refers to as "a subjunctive engagement with an as-yet-unrealised future." Action is what is done to bring some version of that future into being. But in climate change politics the plans often appear to defer action. She notes that this issue is commonly addressed by treating climate change as an inherently "informational" problem. The desire to compile and share information becomes a priority, and projects for climate change mitigation become focused on developing information infrastructures – common frameworks, regulations, standards, and platforms to enable the sharing and storing of information.

Knox argues that this infrastructural response has a double orientation. On the one hand it takes the form of a modernist infrastructural intervention assuming a bounded and linear connection between infrastructure and social effect. At the same time, government workers recognize the un-boundedness both of the problem of climate change and of the informational response, and they are thus interested in more eco-systemic approaches. Such approaches, however, have difficulty configuring climate change as a stable problem of governance. Instead they generate ongoing relationships and processes that undermine the capacity to trace causality and know whether any particular action has had the appropriate effect. In this setting, experiments, pilot projects, and tests abound, actions appropriate to the condition of acting without the conventional parameters of a plan.

Focusing on the digital infrastructures of the UK's National Health Service, Andrew Goffey is also interested in new techniques of governance. Heralded as revolutionary, the transformational potential of this system did not take the straightforward course of joined-up personalized health care that some had hoped for. On the contrary, it seemed to generate an increasingly impersonal system. The problem, as Edwards and Knox pointed out in relation to climate change data, related to the difficulty of translating between infrastructural ontologies, and especially between the centralized control of established information systems and the expansive generative potential of digital connectivity. Furthermore, the problem of the different uses to which data is put is compounded by the different informational forms that the system has to render compatible. These are problems of machinic translation.

Goffey alerts us to the importance of addressing the discontinuities in information and data forms. The drawing together or integration of different forms involves processes of technical mediation. It is the form, rather than the content, that is crucial here. Data and informational forms have to be compatible if they are to "join up." Hence the work of writing, listing, numbering, and computing required for the production of the data set. However sophisticated the coding systems, they require a syntax and a semantics to enable the extraction of meaningful patterns of information. In practice, the possibilities for disambiguation are limited. Digital connectivity thus generates a new problem for practitioners seeking a more immediate and comprehensive insight into patient needs. In Knox's terms, the new infrastructure has facilitated bureaucratic action but not practices of care.

The informational form is also the subject of Adrian Mackenzie's chapter. In his discussion of the nominalization of infrastructure, he takes us to what he refers to as the delirium of continuous coding. His chapter starts from the observation that one of the problems we encounter when trying to make sense of contemporary communication infrastructures is the sheer variety of channels, modalities, platforms, scales of operation, and levels of infrastructural interdependency. As in other chapters, this diversity lies behind the complications that arise when software is deployed as a system of control and ordering.

Moving away from the bureaucratic need for causal narratives, however, Mackenzie explores combinatorial exuberance as it emerges at the interface between the fictional and the factual. The question that Mackenzie poses returns us to the issue of infrastructural ontology, as he asks about the social form of the software itself. Digital infrastructures are social, but not only in the senses that social scientists are used to dealing with. Rather, the sociality explored by Mackenzie is indifferent to differences between people and infrastructures or design and deployment. Digital infrastructures nevertheless emerge from particular coding practices, and it is these that Mackenzie is drawn to as he takes us to Github, a platform "where software is built." Github is a site of collaborative software development. The site serves as a forum for discussion and for the management and creation of software repositories. Here, programmers can contribute to others' repositories, and access the processes by which others change and manage code. Yet this relatively familiar mode of sociality is complemented by an altogether different kind once we turn to the assemblage of repositories on the Github platform. Mackenzie introduces us to the naming practices that underpin the activities of the Github platform, and the nominalization of infrastructure. Doing so, he offers methodological guidance for the social scientists interested in the imitative and combinatorial fluxes that comprise our digital infrastructures.

The possibilities outlined by Mackenzie resonate with the chapter by Geoffrey C. Bowker. Bowker insists that infrastructure is ontology and as such carries revolutionary possibilities. His particular concern is with the knowledge infrastructures of universities and academic production. He argues that we are living in a transitional period, a moment when we can make conscious decisions about which qualities to embed into technical systems that will soon (if they have not already) become infrastructural, opaque and resistant to interrogation and change. Bowker suggests that we need to attend to the algorithms underpinning the rhythms of academic productivity, as we move between websites, Wikis and all manner of online materials; cutting and pasting, connecting and layering the thoughts of others onto our own. Knowledge circulation speeds up, but so too do hoaxes and cases of plagiarism, and systems that seek to catch or curtail the fakes. Similar to Knox's description, digital infrastructures can also undermine the capacity to know and to learn. Bowker's radical suggestion is that, rather than continually trying to fight against or to keep up with the connective exuberance of digital infrastructure, we need a new cognitive division of labor that aligns with its contemporary forms.

In this new knowledge landscape, universities would no longer patrol the borders between validated and unvalidated knowledge but would rather play a central coordinating role. Public laboratories, crowd sourcing, Github style enterprises might thus, perhaps, extend and democratize knowledge infrastructures, enabling new alignments, and new forms of social understanding. Here contingency rather than control becomes fundamental to emergent knowledges. As with Github, it is the database rather than the text that stands to emerge as the new academic product. This is not a naïve call, for Bowker is well aware of the pitfalls and complications described elsewhere in this volume. However, it is an impassioned call for continued experimentation, and for play in and around emergent digital infrastructural possibilities.

25 Downscaling

From global to local in the climate knowledge infrastructure

Paul N. Edwards

The climate knowledge infrastructure was built to generate understanding of the global climate system. Its deep history, as well as its more recent role in climate politics, coupled it to national governments in both scientific and political terms. This infrastructure is currently challenged to "downscale" climate knowledge to meet the demands of city, county, and state agencies, as well as a wide variety of non-governmental organizations.

Downscaling means much more than producing higher-resolution climate data. It requires building technical, social, and institutional gateways that permit the transfer of knowledge – forecasts, causal theories, data, and interpretive or translational information – both to and from other knowledge infrastructures. This chapter argues that although the focus on a planetary scale matched the character of the problem as initially conceived, the same features that made it effective at the planetary scale are now inhibiting use of climate knowledge for local, state, and regional planning. Processes now in play are likely to resolve these infrastructural mismatches, at least in part, but the legacy of knowledge built to serve global and national needs will remain a stumbling block for years to come.

What is a "knowledge infrastructure"?

Why should we think about knowledge in terms of "infrastructure," a term that normally conjures up roads, bridges, and sewer systems? Precisely by drawing the analogy between material constructions and well-grounded (note the metaphor) understandings of the world, the phrase helps to destabilize the sense of abstraction and disembodiment that too often cloud thinking about what "knowledge" is. No fact long survives without people, equipment, instruments, standards, networks, and/or organizations that supply evidence, theories, and connections to other facts and other infrastructures or actor-networks. In short, the phrase "knowledge infrastructures" captures the stabilizing effects of historical and material commitments.

From its origins in the 1980s with scholarship on "large technical systems" and blossoming in the 2000s following the seminal work of Susan Leigh Star and Geoffrey Bowker, infrastructure studies has articulated a well-developed theory of how infrastructures develop and change (Edwards et al. 2007). In a nutshell, the theory goes something like this: infrastructures are enduring sociotechnical assets that support basic human needs or goals such as transportation, communication, and energy. They often originate as sociotechnical *systems*. "Systems," in this conception, are centrally designed and controlled, typically in the invention and development phases of new techniques and technologies. At that point, they remain the province of their developer, whether a single individual, a team, or an organization. Once these systems begin to travel, they also begin to vary. Both users and other developers modify or extend them, and competing or alternative technologies and enterprises arise.

This variation is the norm rather than the exception: consider the many similar, but incompatible devices and techniques built during the early days of railroads, electric power, or computers. Consequently, when a need arises to link heterogeneous systems into *networks*, devices and/or social apparatus known as *gateways* must be developed to connect systems' varying social, technical, legal and other elements (Egyedi and Spirco, 2011; Egyedi 1996). Gateways such as AC/DC converters are technical, but many – perhaps most – gateways consist of codified, embedded social agreements such as standards, laws, or published APIs (application program interfaces). Individuals, groups, and institutions, as well, can play gateway roles. The network phase of development involves many actors, and it signals that a growing community is increasingly committed to particular functions and norms of interaction.

In later phases, *webs* or *internetworks* – networks of heterogeneous networks – may develop. For example, shipping, rail, and trucking networks developed symbiotically yet independently, but starting in the 1960s these networks gradually became integrated into a global internetwork. A tipping point in this integration was the rise of the ISO standard shipping container, a classic example of a gateway – all the more so because the container is not so much a device or invention as a standard, i.e. a social agreement, specifying allowable shapes, sizes, and structures (Busch 2011; Egyedi 2001; Klose 2015). Networks and internetworks exhibit more decentralized control. Because they are made up of many independent systems and networks, they can only rarely (if ever) be designed, controlled, or standardized from above (Bowker and Star, 1999; Edwards et al., 2007). Instead, infrastructures are complex ecologies whose component systems must continually evolve to match the changing characteristics of the related systems around them. In a final phase, infrastructures can splinter into more specialized elements, or die altogether (Graham and Marvin 2001). As a rule, then (though with exceptions), infrastructures are not systems, but networks, webs, or assemblages.

Knowledge infrastructures follow a similar pattern. They are "robust networks of people, artifacts, and institutions that generate, share, and maintain specific knowledge about the human and natural worlds" (Edwards et al. 2013; Edwards 2010). They, too, evolve from systems to networks to webs. Like "hard" infrastructures, their stability, reliability, and transparency stem from historical and material commitments made over long periods of time.

Like other infrastructures, knowledge infrastructures shift and change over time. Rarely is anything we call "knowledge" perfectly certain or stable; instead, knowledge consists of coherent claims – today, often expressed as probabilities – warranted by established evidentiary systems. Probabilistic knowledge can be both useful and actionable. Demographic and labor statistics, international disease tracking, rapid flu vaccine development, and weather forecasts are all products of knowledge infrastructures. Few weather forecasts are perfectly accurate, yet the range of error is now so small that people and industries routinely rely on them. Similarly, neither flu tracking nor flu vaccinations are perfectly reliable, yet their consistently high success rates justify social confidence.

People rely on these mature knowledge infrastructures as part of their daily routines. Precisely for this reason, over time these infrastructures (like others) become invisible to users, except when they fail. Further, while they enable and empower, knowledge infrastructures also constrain. The routines of thought and action they facilitate can obscure other potentially valuable approaches, sometimes with serious consequences.

Measurement and climate knowledge: a little history

"Climate" refers to average weather patterns on timescales from years to decades to centuries and beyond. Such patterns include the seasonal cycle, the El Niño/La Niña cycle, and the ice ages. Particular places have their own unique climates, but the physical systems that create those climates are global and interactive. Historically, scientific studies of climate examined both regional climates and the global climate system. Before the nineteenth century, however, very few investigators had access to data about the entire planet, so *detailed* climate knowledge originated as descriptive (rather than causal) accounts conceived as aspects of geography. Many local, unrelated climate knowledge practices developed, each with its own data and vocabulary. With world empires and the rise of science came increasing access to global data, and scientific climatology – seeking to understand causes as well as consequences – slowly turned in the direction of a more unified, globally oriented approach.

The historical pattern described in the previous section can be readily observed in the case of climate knowledge. Detailed understanding of global climate requires observations of the world's atmosphere, its oceans, and its ice. Records of these phenomena, built up over time, constitute the basic data of scientific climate studies. Scientists created the first formalized observing networks in the seventeenth century, sharing their data by mail. These data took both qualitative and quantitative forms; lacking a shared physical understanding, each observer recorded what seemed most relevant to him or her, often in idiosyncratic ways: the sky was "clear blew but yellowish in the NE," reported Robert Hooke in 1667 (cited in Nebeker 1995: 15).

The telegraph's arrival in the mid-nineteenth century made possible, for the first time, near-real-time mapping of weather over large areas, as well as the first efforts at weather prediction based on those maps. This spurred the formation of national weather services – wide-area observing *systems*, each with its own standards and routines for mapping and predicting weather – in Europe and the United States. Such systems joined isolated observing stations into national networks with partially standardized observing hours, instruments, and recording forms. Stations reported by telegraph to central offices, which mapped their observations and distributed weather predictions. Newspapers began publishing these weather maps daily as early as the 1870s.

National weather observing systems quickly formed international *networks* – and faced the typical problem that the national systems each had their own, sometimes incompatible standards for observing hours, units, instruments, and so on. In 1853, the American naval scientist Matthew Maury secured agreements from the world's major shipping nations to record weather observations at sea on standard recording forms. These forms were sent to the US Naval Observatory for plotting and redistribution worldwide, thus creating the oldest continuous quasi-global weather record. Several European nations participated in a telegraph-based weather data network as early as 1857. The earliest meeting of what would become the International Meteorological Organization was held in 1871. Before the end of the nineteenth century, the concept of a telegraph-based Réseau Mondial (global network) for real-time weather data collection had been floated. Technical and organizational inadequacies, not to mention two world wars, delayed the full realization of such a network until the 1960s, when the postwar World Meteorological Organization (now under United Nations auspices) initiated the World Weather Watch.

By the end of the nineteenth century, climatologists were making use of the growing number of long-term, semi-standardized records to plot monthly average temperatures and other variables at all subpolar latitudes. Emerging climatological theories now comprehended major global features such as the tropical, mid-latitude, and polar circulatory cells, and correctly assessed their causes.

As new instruments and instrument platforms appeared, and as understanding grew of the links between terrestrial, marine, polar, and upper air phenomena, international data *internetworks* emerged. By the 1970s, these webs brought information from satellites, instrumented buoys, ships, airplanes, weather balloons, and other platforms to central processing facilities. These were true internetworks – rather than merely extensions of existing networks – because some platforms and instruments functioned very differently from older devices and were managed by different institutions. For example, weather stations traditionally took periodic measurements at fixed points, but ground radars produce continuous images, while satellites measure very large volumes of air. As a result, radar stations first developed as part of the air traffic control system, and the space agencies responsible for satellites still remain largely independent of weather services or climate science (Cirac Claveras 2014; Courain 1991). Weather and climate data internetworks, such as the World Weather Watch and the Global Climate Observing System

(GCOS), constructed gateways that linked these independently constructed and managed systems and networks.

From measurement to modeling: computer simulation

Climate knowledge comes not just from the data these internetworks provide, but from theory and analysis, which lead in turn to the ability to project futures grounded in physical understanding. In the 1950s, computer modeling rapidly took root as the central tool of weather forecasting (Nebeker 1995). Simulation modeling proved so superior to all other techniques that today, virtually all weather forecasts begin with global model results, though human interpretation still plays a significant role in local forecasting (Daipha 2015).

By the 1960s, computer models became the favored tool of climate scientists (distinguished from a previous generation of "climatologists" by their focus on geophysics rather than geography). Global climate models do not use current weather observations at all. Instead, they generate their own, simulated global climates. Although equations of fluid dynamics lie at the core of these models, a great deal of empirically derived information is present in "model physics" parameters such as solar output, air chemistry, aerosol distribution, and many others. The physics of climate are extremely complex, because relevant phenomena occur on scales from the molecular (e.g. the radiative characteristics of constituent gases) to the planetary (e.g. atmospheric "long waves" with wavelengths of thousands of kilometers) and even the solar system (orbital cycles responsible for the periodic ice ages). Oceanic phenomena such as the El Niño/Southern Oscillation or the Gulf Stream current also play major roles. Modeling the smaller-scale phenomena in detail would be computationally intractable, so they are "parameterized," i.e. represented via related, but larger-scale variables that are more easily included.

As time went on, the practice of computer modeling spread throughout the sciences. Meanwhile, in the 1980s and 1990s, emerging climate politics led to increasing research budgets, as well as to scientific interest in elements of the climate system beyond the atmosphere and oceans. As a result, climate models became a point of interaction for many scientific communities, including glaciology, hydrology, ecology, atmospheric chemistry, and many others. A slow, imperfect process of infrastructural adjustment ensued, as each science revised its methods of analysis to enable interaction with the others around issues of climatic change.

The quality of climate models can be evaluated by making them simulate past climates. This is done by setting their parameters (such as greenhouse gas levels, continental position, orbital obliquity, and solar output) to those of a particular time period, then comparing the long-term trends in their simulated climates with observations from that period. Like the real climate, models exhibit a certain amount of random variation; only long-term trends, not the day-by-day or even year-by-year details of the simulations, can be compared. While many aspects of the climate system are still not fully understood, the ability of climate simulations to reproduce the twentieth-century climate, and the absence of credible alternative explanations of climate dynamics, gives reasonable confidence in their capability (Stocker et al. 2013).

These evaluations require global data. Assembling a *global* data image from the information collected by many parties – national weather services, separate climate observing networks, satellites, ocean observing systems, and others – involves much more than simply gathering the records. Early climatologists used small numbers of records (tens to hundreds), drawn from trusted weather stations with long, stable histories, to calculate trends. The cacophony of differing standards, data formats, and communication technologies around the world made it difficult to make use of more data to create more detailed time series.

Today, computers permit the aggregation of many more records to produce a much more precise picture. Computerized data analysis models use algorithms to reconcile differences in instrument characteristics, observing times, station siting, recording errors, and many other factors. In *A Vast Machine* (Edwards 2010), I called this process *"making data global,"* pointing to the central role of such models in the climate knowledge infrastructure. The largest of these to date, the Berkeley Earth Surface Temperature project, presently incorporates over 1.6 billion data records from more than 39,000 stations worldwide.

Global knowledge and the Intergovernmental Panel on Climate Change

As we have seen, climate knowledge "upscaled" over the course of the twentieth century, especially after 1950. The nature of the phenomenon justified a focus on the planetary scale. But the planetary focus was not just conceptual or theoretical. It required material and organizational commitments: institutions, instrument networks and internetworks, and discursive framing of climate problems, as well as data and models. This *infrastructural globalism*, as I have called it (Edwards 2006), produced lock-in effects with momentous consequences.

For example, global climate simulations can project future trends, and this is the role in which most people know them. Based on global models, a scientific consensus emerged in the late 1970s: a global warming of 1.5–4.5°C would ensue when carbon dioxide concentrations doubled (to 550 ppm) over those of the pre-industrial atmosphere (270 ppm). These numbers – the global average temperature anomaly[1] on carbon dioxide doubling – became major benchmarks in climate change studies. Framed in this way, scientific concern over global warming reached its first crescendo in 1990 with the first scientific assessment of the Intergovernmental Panel on Climate Change (IPCC).

Flush with the success of global accords on ozone depletion, the most successful global treaty of any kind in world history, the IPCC's founders – heavily influenced by their conception of climate as a global system and climate change as a global problem – sought to forestall dangerous climatic change by means of a global political process. They designed a knowledge assessment system that they hoped would short-circuit a protracted political debate by front-loading the integration of scientific understanding into climate policymaking. This took the form of an elaborate peer review in which draft reports are reviewed not only by scientists, but also by national governments and non-governmental organizations. IPCC authors are required to respond to every one of the tens of thousands of peer comments. Since the large majority of all research considered in IPCC reports has already been peer reviewed by scientific journals, this is certainly the most comprehensive review process in the history of science.

This process inspires confidence from the vast majority of scientists, who accept IPCC reports as highly authoritative summaries of the current state of knowledge. Yet the political aspect of the IPCC process has not functioned as originally imagined. The strategy of engaging national governments with a view toward a global climate treaty was risky to begin with. Global environmental agreements are few in number, and those which have been very successful – such as ozone accords, or the Partial Test Ban Treaty banning tests of nuclear weapons in the atmosphere – have worked mainly because they affected only a small number of nations and industrial sectors. Unlike those issues, climate change demands massive transitions in energy systems, agriculture, and many other arenas, with potentially profound effects on the livelihoods and lifestyles of billions.

Some governments and NGOs – particularly those with high stakes in fossil fuels and other interests threatened by decarbonization of the world energy economy – have used their power as peer reviewers to reduce the strength of IPCC knowledge claims, often by lobbying to weaken expressions of confidence. Others have repeatedly and disingenuously attacked the organization on both procedural and substantive grounds, attempting to cast it as a scientific conspiracy (Edwards and Schneider 2001; Hoggan and Littlemore 2009; Oreskes and Conway 2010). Following the 2009 "Climategate" incident, a major external review of IPCC procedures concluded that the organization lacked transparency (Shapiro et al. 2010).

Based in part on the first IPCC report, the United Nations Framework Convention on Climate Change was signed in 1992. The second IPCC report declared that "the balance of evidence suggests a discernible human influence on global climate" (Houghton et al. 1996). The third (2001), fourth (2007), and fifth (2013) IPCC assessments refined those conclusions, culminating in the fifth report's unequivocal statement that "it is *extremely likely* that human influence" is the principal cause of global warming since the mid-twentieth century (Stocker et al. 2013: 15).

As we have seen, climate models are necessarily global in scale, and due to the historical limits of computer power, climate model grid cells initially covered areas of around 250,000 km^2, i.e. about the size of Colorado, or the entire United Kingdom. At this very low resolution, few scientists were willing to make claims about the future of any particular place – yet this is exactly what political choices normally require. The political question is almost never "what will happen to the world?", but instead "what will happen to me and my constituents?" As ocean modeler Robert Chervin put it to me long ago, "climate models will begin to have political impact when their grid scales reach the size of a Congressional district."

Thus the globalist historical and material commitments of the climate knowledge infrastructure strongly influenced both the IPCC, a hybrid scientific-political organization, and the FCCC, a global policy process. This state of affairs produced considerable inertia when the FCCC policy process stalled after the 1997 Kyoto accords, widely acknowledged as weak, overly narrow in scope, and ineffectual. Hope springs eternal, but the evidence of the past two decades is that the greatest potentials for climate action no longer lie – if they ever did – in a comprehensive global agreement.

Yet knowledge about the *global* climate cannot easily be mobilized at the regional, national, and urban scales on which policymaking can operate effectively. Even less can global knowledge engage with the temporal and spatial scales on which policy choices are rewarded or punished by their publics. At present, we are witnessing a slow and creaky shift of the knowledge infrastructure toward these smaller scales of governance.

Downscaling the infrastructure: from useful data to usable knowledge

Infrastructures are extended when new gateways – in actor-network terms, new intermediaries – connect them to other systems or networks. Knowledge infrastructures are no exception. As we have seen, climate simulations provided one such gateway, linking many sciences between the 1970s and the 2000s. Glaciology, ecology, agriculture, soil, atmospheric chemistry, and many others "upscaled" the knowledge they produced in order to join the field now often called "Earth system sciences."

In the early twenty-first century, as the pace of warming continued unabated, attention shifted from mitigation (preventing or limiting anthropogenic climate change) to impacts and adaptation. Regions, states, and cities may potentially become agents of mitigation, but all will need to adapt. Today, city planners, health officials, water managers, military services, and disaster response agencies are beginning to use climate data in their planning processes (Bierbaum et al. 2013; Bulkeley 2010).

These trends place new demands on the climate knowledge infrastructure. While climate data are already being used to address critical planning issues, a yawning gap currently exists between the forms in which climate knowledge is typically generated by scientists and the knowledge systems most commonly used by policy-oriented planners. Knowledge of *global* trends almost never translates automatically into usable knowledge at the local, state, or even the regional scale. Planners are mainly concerned with what will happen in the geographic area for which they are responsible. Some users, such as watershed managers making contingency plans for droughts, floods, and changing precipitation patterns, or health professionals concerned with heat waves, already have considerable climate-related expertise, especially with respect to local, regional, or national climate patterns. They would like detailed information about likely future trends *for their own areas,* but global trends are unimportant to them, and they are not interested in every aspect of climate change. Heat waves, water supplies, and extreme weather events such as hurricanes and floods top the list of cities' concerns.

As a result, these user groups differ from climate scientists in their understanding of what climate data are, how they can credibly be used, and how the inevitable uncertainties can be communicated and managed. I now describe two examples of how this problem occurs "on the ground." Both examples come from a master's-level course on climate change informatics, which I co-taught with climate scientist Richard Rood at the University of Michigan (to whom I owe many of the insights in this chapter) in 2014 and 2015. In 2014, two of our student teams worked with scientists at the Centers for Disease Control who were interested in improving community readiness for health-threatening heat waves. Two other teams worked with Tampa Bay Water, responsible for managing the watershed for that part of Florida. We chose these groups partly because some of their members had attended Rood's 2013 summer workshop on "downscaling" climate data.

Downscaling is a set of techniques for increasing the resolution of climate data. Applied to historical data, downscaling can generate more detailed, synthetic data for areas that were not well instrumented. Simulated future data from climate models can also be downscaled; in one technique, a high-resolution regional model is embedded in a lower-resolution global model. Since each grid cell (essentially a single data point) in a typical modern climate model covers an area of around 2,500–10,000 km^2 – as large as the smallest US states and European countries, and far larger than most cities and counties – higher-resolution climate data are highly desirable for planning and policymaking.

None of the available downscaling techniques produces perfectly reliable data, largely because no climate model can do so either. Each of the dozens of global climate models has virtues and vices. Some underpredict polar warming, while many do poorly in coastal West Africa and western South America, where upwelling ocean currents create complex atmospheric effects. As a result, climate scientists rarely if ever take downscaled data at face value. Instead, just as with the original climate model output, they prefer to analyze carefully chosen ensembles (sets) of downscaled data. There is currently no standard "recipe" either for choosing or for analyzing such an ensemble. Instead, downscaling remains the province of expert judgment, and stirs controversy among climate scientists. In other words, downscaling has not yet been routinized, standardized, and integrated into the climate knowledge infrastructure.

These problems and controversies are of little interest to users from other domains, who would simply like to get the "best" available climate data for

348   Paul N. Edwards

their area. Both professional groups we worked with were highly sophisticated data analysts, and since both had attended the downscaling workshop, they also understood the reasons behind climate scientists' reticence to offer any single "best" dataset. Yet this was only the beginning of the litany of problems they encountered in trying to make use of climate model output. Arcane filenames such as "arrm_gfdl_2.1_min_tnxmminm_september_1971–2000" are readily comprehensible to climate scientists, but gibberish to others.[2] Data conventions and software libraries that are common in climate science, such as CIM (Common Information Model) and netCDF (Network Common Data Form), are completely unknown in many other areas. Climate models use numerous grid schemes, including not only standard latitude–longitude grids but triangular, icosahedral, and other unusual forms; very little climate data is published in the GIS (Geographic Information System) file formats now commonplace in other geographically oriented sciences as well as government and commercial mapping services. None of these hurdles are impossible to overcome, but all of them increase the friction involved in translating climate data into forms usable by other fields.

In terms of knowledge infrastructures, these are gateway problems. Data relevant to users' problems exist and can be accessed, but they lack the metadata and/or interpretive frameworks that could permit them to travel outside their original disciplinary settings. Users want to create bridges between their own knowledge infrastructures – watershed management, public health – and climate science, but they cannot find straightforward (or even convoluted) ways to make use of climate data directly. Experience in many work environments suggests that where some alternative exists to frustrating, unfamiliar forms of information, users often prefer that alternative, even if its quality is known from the outset to be lower. In this case, the easy alternative for historical information is the weather record from the local airport, the most familiar, stable, and long-term record available in many cases. Airports – wide-open, flat areas located far from city centers – are often unrepresentative of the conditions of interest downtown, or elsewhere in the region. Yet they are trusted, so they are used.

Studies of successful knowledge integration efforts routinely conclude that gateway-building across divides like these requires considerable, and ongoing, human effort. A review article summarizing some of these studies found that "climate science usability is a function both of the context of potential use and of the process of scientific knowledge production itself. ... [N]early every case of successful use of climate knowledge involved some kind of iteration between knowledge producers and users" (Dilling and Lemos 2011). A key organizational dimension of this iterativity is the need to create a sense of individual and organizational "ownership" of problems, methods, and solutions (Kirchhoff et al. 2013; Lemos et al. 2014). In other words, sometimes *people* make the best gateways.

In a media environment bedazzled by "big data," it is easy to forget that making knowledge is always work. Translating knowledge into new frames, for new purposes, is work too. Among the crucial elements of that work is building trust and authority, which is rarely if ever accomplished simply by providing information. The rapidly increasing availability of climate data has not been matched by a concomitant increase in translational materials or human translators, nor by software or social systems capable of choosing and processing climate data for the vast variety of potential users and uses.

Global CO^2 concentrations topped 400 ppm in 2015. Most observers expect the 550 ppm mark to be surpassed around the middle of this century, and there is currently little reason to expect that it will stop rising then. If climate sensitivity to greenhouse gas doubling is around the middle of the projected range, this means global warming of 2.5–3°C within a few decades. The consequences will affect every place in the world, but not in the same ways. Downscaled climate knowledge, coupled more closely to the knowledge systems of cities, states, and regions, as well as to particular knowledge needs, may help them reduce or prevent some of the worst outcomes.

Notes

1 For technical reasons, climate scientists focus on the difference (anomaly) between two average global temperatures (a baseline and some perturbed state), rather than on their absolute values.
2 Decoded, the filename refers to the Asynchronous Regional Regression Model of the Geophysical Fluid Dynamics Laboratory, version 2.1, output of the variable "minimum highest daily minimum temperature" for the month of September for each year 1971–2000.

Bibliography

Bierbaum, R. et al. (2013) "A comprehensive review of climate adaptation in the United States: more than before, but less than needed," *Public Health Resources* 18(3): 361–406.
Bowker, Geoffrey C. and Susan Leigh Star (1999) *Sorting Things Out: Classification and its Consequences.* Cambridge, MA: MIT Press.
Bulkeley, Harriet (2010) "Cities and the governing of climate change," *Annual Review of Environment and Resources,* 35: 229–253.
Busch, Lawrence (2011) *Standards: Recipes for Reality.* Cambridge, MA: MIT Press.
Cirac Claveras, Gemma (2014) "POLDER and the age of space earth sciences: A study of technological satellite data practices." Doctoral thesis, École des Hautes Études en Sciences Sociales, Paris.
Courain, Margaret E. (1991) "Technology reconciliation in the remote-sensing era of United States civilian weather forecasting: 1957–1987." Graduate Program in Communication, Information and Library Studies, Rutgers, New Brunswick, NJ.
Daipha, Phaedra (2015) *Masters of Uncertainty: Weather Forecasters and the Quest for Ground Truth.* Chicago, IL: University of Chicago Press.

Dilling, Lisa and Maria Carmen Lemos (2011) "Creating usable science: Opportunities and constraints for climate knowledge use and their implications for science policy," *Global Environmental Change* 21(2): 680–689.

Edwards, Paul N. (2006) "Meteorology as infrastructural globalism," *Osiris* 21: 229–250.

Edwards, Paul N. (2010) *A Vast Machine: Computer Models, Climate Data, and the Politics of Global Warming*. Cambridge, MA: MIT Press.

Edwards, Paul N. et al. (2007) *Understanding Infrastructure: Dynamics, Tensions, and Design*. Ann Arbor, MI: Deep Blue.

Edwards, Paul N. and Stephen H. Schneider (2001) "Self-Governance and Peer Review in Science-for-Policy: The Case of the IPCC Second Assessment Report," in Clark A. Miller and Paul N. Edwards (eds), *Changing the Atmosphere: Expert Knowledge and Environmental Governance*. Cambridge, MA: MIT Press, pp. 219–246.

Edwards, Paul N. et al. (2013) *Knowledge Infrastructures: Intellectual Frameworks and Research Challenges*. Ann Arbor, MI: Deep Blue.

Egyedi, Tineke (1996) "Shaping standardization: A study of standards processes and standards policies in the field of telematic services." Doctoral thesis, Technische Universiteit Delft, Delft.

Egyedi, Tineke (2001) "Infrastructure flexibility created by standardized gateways: The cases of XML and the ISO container," *Knowledge, Technology & Policy* 14(3): 41–54.

Egyedi, Tineke and Jaroslav Spirco (2011) "Standards in transitions: Catalyzing infrastructure change," *Futures* 43(9): 947–960.

Graham, Stephen and Simon Marvin (2001) *Splintering Urbanism: Networked Infrastructures, Technological Mobilities and the Urban Condition*. New York: Routledge.

Hoggan, James and Richard D. Littlemore (2009) *Climate Cover-up: The Crusade to Deny Global Warming*. Vancouver: Greystone Books.

Houghton, John T. et al. (eds) (1996) *Climate Change 1995 – The Science of Climate Change: Contribution of Working Group I to the Second Assessment Report of the Intergovernmental Panel on Climate Change*. Cambridge: Cambridge University Press.

Kirchhoff, Christine J., Maria Carmen Lemos, and Nathan L. Engle (2013) "What influences climate information use in water management? The role of boundary organizations and governance regimes in Brazil and the US," *Environmental Science & Policy* 26(6): 6–18.

Klose, Alexander (2015) *The Container Principle: How a Box Changes the Way We Think*. Cambridge, MA: MIT Press.

Lemos, Maria Carmen et al. (2014) "Moving climate information off the shelf: Boundary Chains and the role of RISAs as adaptive organizations," *Weather, Climate, and Society* 6(2): 273–285.

Lepore, B. J. (2014) "Climate change adaptation: DOD can improve infrastructure planning and processes to better account for potential impacts." US Government accountability Office (GAO). www.gao.gov/assets/670/663734.pdf.

Lutsey, N. and Sperling, D. (2008) "America's bottom-up climate change mitigation policy," *Energy Policy* 36(2): 673–685.

Nebeker, Frederik (1995) *Calculating the Weather: Meteorology in the 20th Century*. New York: Academic Press.

Oreskes, Naomi and Erik M. Conway (2010) *Merchants of Doubt: How a Handful of Scientists Obscured the Truth on Issues from Tobacco Smoke to Global Warming*. New York: Bloomsbury Press.

Shapiro, Harold T. et al. (2010) "Climate change assessments: Review of the processes and procedures of the IPCC." InterAcademy Council, Amsterdam.

Stocker, T. F., D. Qin, and G. K. Platner (2013) "Climate Change 2013: The Physical Science Basis – Summary for Policymakers." Working Group I Contribution to the Fifth Assessment Report of the Intergovernmental Panel on Climate Change (IPCC). www.ipcc.ch/pdf/assessment-report/ar5/wg1/WGIAR5_SPM_brochure_en.pdf.

26 The problem of action

Infrastructure, planning and the informational environment

Hannah Knox

> If you want to build a ship, don't drum up people together to collect wood and don't assign them tasks and work, but rather teach them to long for the endless immensity of the sea.
>
> Antoine de Saint-Exupéry (1992)

Introduction: 'Actions speak for themselves'

At the 2010 meeting of the 'Covenant of Mayors' held at the European Parliament in Brussels, the mayors and civil servants in attendance were treated to a rendition of a song by Danish musician and composer Søren Eppler entitled 'Me and You'. Composed for the Zealand region to 'provide optimism and energy'[1] on the issue of climate change, Eppler's song provided a performance of the desire and vision of the Covenant of Mayors: to promote energy efficiency and the development of renewable energy in the European regions. Weaving a picture of a harmonious coming together of nature, society and technology the song opened:

> I dreamt that I was living in a culture, developing on (sic) clean technology
> in co-creating climate
> with the nature
> that's giving me this higher energy.

It ended with the upbeat message:

> Finally we did do what we must do
> Living in the dream that's coming true
> Finally we did do what we must do
> We are in the Now – and in the New!
> Living in the dream that's coming true
> We are in the Now and in the New![2, 3]

The problem of action 353

Played by Eppler himself on a keyboard at the front of the banked benches of the European Parliament chamber, the song provided participants with a kitsch dream-image of a utopian future where not only were environmental problems resolved but the governmental actors were assured, importantly, that 'we did do what we must do'.

The question of 'doing', or more precisely 'action', is foundational to the politics of climate change promoted by organisations like the Covenant of Mayors. The core commitment of the 6,298 local authorities that voluntarily signed up to the Covenant of Mayors is to agree to write a sustainable energy *action* plan. The opening quote that 'actions speak for themselves' is taken from an early version of the Covenant of Mayors website, meanwhile the current website displays a montage photo superimposed with the words: Mayors in Action (Figure 26.1).[4]

Calls to Action are ubiquitous within climate change mitigation policy. In Manchester, UK, a city which has itself signed up as a member of the Covenant of Mayors and where I have been conducting an ethnography of climate change mitigation since 2011, there have been several climate change action plans, including the 2009 Call to Action, the 2009 Call to Real Action, the 2009 Manchester: A Certain Future – Our Co$_2$llective Action on Climate plan, and the Greater Manchester Climate Change Strategy, which aimed to 'set out common objectives and headline actions'[5] for the city-region of Greater Manchester.[6] Action appears as both the means and the ends of climate change policy, an ambition that is ubiquitous but also suffers from complex problems of deferral.

For while discussions about what to do about climate change invoke action, these calls for future action are also founded on an ongoing assessment and

Figure 26.1 Screen shot of image from Covenant of Mayors website

evaluation that is concerned with the paucity of past action, the difficulty of acting in the present and the necessity of finding a way to act in the future. A frequent retort during discussions among people I did fieldwork with was a frustration with how to move beyond discussion and strategy and to arrive at action itself. So, for example, at a meeting of an organisation called the North West Climate Change Partnership, during a reflection on the organisational form of the partnership several participants lamented that while the partnership was a good vehicle for networking, it never seemed to *do* anything. In other respects these are people who are busy and active in all kinds of ways. Why then, does the work that is going on fail to count as action? And why does it seem to them that action often fails in its capacity to take place in the present?

On plans and actions

In anthropology, much of the discussion about the way in which we think and write about action in an analytical sense has hinged on the relationship between planning or design on the one hand and action or implementation on the other. Many ethnographic, ethno-methodological and philosophical accounts have been at pains to demonstrate that, contrary to a dominant western conceptualisation of a separation between cognitive subjects and enacted objects, between minds and environments or between plans and actions, action needs to be resituated as a practical mode of being in the world. Ingold (2000) for example, one of the most vociferous critics of behaviourism or cognitive psychology, has produced a consistent and damning critique of the supposition that thought precedes action. Instead, Ingold demonstrates how people do not somehow create an image of the world in advance of their action within it, but produce understandings of the world through situated, embodied engagement with the environment that surrounds them (Ingold 2000).

If Ingold is interested in critiquing the plan in support of his effort to arrive at a theory of the continual processes by which humans and environments co-emerge in a process of constant becoming, Suchman, in her study of human–machine interactions, holds onto the importance of the plan as a feature of modern knowledge, but shows how it too is the outcome of situated action (Suchman 2007).

Ingold's critique of the plan is in many ways a critique of modern knowledge with its tendencies towards abstraction and reductionism. Just as James Scott (1998) illustrated, through historical and ethnographic work, how the hubris of modernist planners worked to delimit the possible definitions of action, privileging the creation of the built environment by government experts, architects and engineers with the effect of de-legitimising other ways of acting in the world, Ingold also worries about the dehumanising effects of rational modern knowledge forms.

Suchman's analysis of planning as itself situated action, on the other hand, recovers the humanity in the modern knowledge practices that Ingold aims to distance himself from. By putting emergent social practice at the heart of planning activities, Suchman opens up the possibility of an anthropology of planned technical activity itself, a project that has been taken up in recent years by many anthropologists interested in the workings of the modern state (Ferguson 1990, Riles 2000, Gupta 2010, Hull 2012).

One argument that has emerged out of this work concerns the temporal qualities of planning and the implications of the future orientation of planned action. A recent edited collection by the anthropologists Simone Abram and Gisa Weszkalnys (2011) builds on an anthropological analysis of planning and intervention as sites of situated action in order to illustrate how planning relies on the temporality of the promise. For Abram and Weszkalnys, understanding planning requires that we understand its promissory qualities and the effects that these promissory qualities bring forth. Drawing on a series of ethnographic analyses of planned social change in very different locations, they demonstrate how the planning of built environments entails a promise towards the future that is variously materialised, reformulated or abandoned, depending on the particular project and the circumstances in which it is pursued (Abram and Weszkalnys 2011).

Planning thus seems to lend itself to an ambition towards defined goals of material intervention, imbued with utopian images of how society can be transformed. Planning in these studies primarily orientates itself towards action by defining the parameters of future action in a promissory mode and then putting in place the relationships, funds, standards and agreements that enable the work of bringing new material environments into being. As Penny Harvey and I have described elsewhere (Harvey and Knox 2015), this is a process that requires first the formulation of a project, a subjunctive engagement with an as-yet-unrealised future, and then a pragmatic process of bringing some version of that future into being through practices that work to demarcate and manage clear boundaries between the project itself and the sphere into which it intervenes.

In these studies of planning, then, its success or failure derives from an assessment of the relationship between the promise and its actualisation. In the quote from Eppler's song, however, the status of the kinds of actions that he describes appears to be at odds with the temporalities invoked in the planning logics described by Abram and Weszkalnys. For Eppler does not describe a provisional future, nor does he hint at the contingencies of action in the present; rather he indexes the uncertainty of how to move between the present and the future by projecting forward into the future-perfect an imagination of a moment where we *will have done what we needed to do*. Here we do not have a plan of how to get to the future but rather an appeal to the future that requires as yet undefined action in the present.

If the quote from Eppler's song and the more generalised anxiety about action indicates a fault line in the practices of modern government planning, then the question remains where this fault line has come from, and what responses to it are being devised.

356 Hannah Knox

Green and digital

> It is all very well to have these idealistic treaties on how things should be different but it doesn't tell people: what they should do when they come into work on Monday morning.
>
> Phil, Research Participant, November 2013

Above an upmarket upholstery shop in a leafy Cheshire town are the offices of a small IT company run by a man who is no stranger to the tension between action and planning. Zeb is both a businessman and someone who has for a long time been part of governmental efforts to bring public resources to bear on the development of IT infrastructures. I am introduced to Zeb because of a collaboration he has recently become involved in to explore how digital technologies might provide solutions for climate change. Funded by the European Union FP7 programme, the collaborative project he is part of involves a partnership between the Cheshire IT company, a research institute in eastern Germany and officers working for the European Union. The aim of the project was to develop an understanding of the 'state of the art' of green-digital activities in European cities and to develop seminars, training and an 'action toolkit' that would enable the spread of best practice around Europe and beyond.

At the outset, the project was conceived very much in the framework of governance where a knowledge deficit must be filled in order to inform action. The project aims were threefold (Figure 26.2).

An early preoccupation of the project partners was how to establish the parameters upon which future action would be able to take place and this involved developing an understanding of precisely the contours of the problem in hand. What, Zeb and his colleagues asked, were the significant relationships at play between digital technologies and climate change?

On the basis of reading various research reports about the role of IT in cutting carbon emissions produced by organisations like McKinsey, the EU, the Climate Group, ARUP and Accenture, Zeb, his team and myself spent much time speculating about the multiple relationships between digital technologies and climate change that the project might want to address. These ranged from the idea that the capacity of digital technologies to collate and disseminate information could lead to the radical reorganisation of cities, to a worry about how to mitigate the carbon emissions of digital technologies themselves. One person pointed out that data was available that showed that server farms were large users of energy both because of the IT equipment they housed and the air conditioning they required to keep them cool. Was there a way to make them more energy efficient? Meanwhile the personalisation of smart phones raised the possibility that new ways of visualising energy expenditure and usage might reformulate citizen's relationship with the city, with energy and with environment. Digital technologies seemed to offer the potential for monitoring the presence of practices, substances and things, of

> **1. Develop Framework and Tools**
>
> The project will develop a common framework, tools, and information resources for classifying, measuring, reporting and supporting city actions in the context of the Covenant of Mayors.
>
> **2. City Support and Action**
>
> These framework and tools will be transferred to cities and their implementation partners through a series of targeted exchange and learning activities with experts and other signatory cities with a view to triggering implementation. A strategy for continued exploitation and support activities beyond the project's lifetime will be put in place.
>
> **3. Outreach and Engagement**
>
> Networking and visibility events will be held to increase the number of signatories and showcase cooperation opportunities with key policy and practices communities, including a special focus on engaging with Chinese cities currently developing similar initiatives.

Figure 26.2 Aims and objectives of the Green Digital Project

visualising carbon-producing effects, and of projecting and modelling future energy scenarios.

The complexity of these issues was summed up when Zeb wryly observed that the rise in carbon emissions had tracked the rise in digital technologies. Stopping short of actually positing a causal relationship between these two processes, Zeb's observation nonetheless indexed the difficulty of disentangling digital technologies as a solution for carbon emissions from digital technologies as a cause of the same problem.

If in the Cheshire offices we were speculating about the complex lines of causality between digital technologies and climate change, in the research institute in Germany an academic research team was working on a theoretical framework that could tame and reframe this complex of emergent relationships. The head of the research group, Kris, was keen to use the socio-technical systems theory of the sustainability theorist, Frank Geels, which he felt offered a way of simplifying and making actionable these complicated interlocking relationships that everyone agreed the project was going to have to deal with.

Geels is well known among those working at the interface of policy and the social science of innovation for developing 'transition' theory. Transition theory aims to establish a method of dealing with environmental problems such as climate change, biodiversity and resource depletion that 'differ in scale and complexity from the environmental problems of the 1970s and the 1980s such as water pollution, acid rain, local air pollution and waste problems' (Geels 2011: 495). It is concerned, then, with dealing with and mapping precisely the complex circular effects of the kinds of entangled relationships that Zeb's team were grappling with. Invoking what he calls a 'multi-level perspective' or MLP, Geels proposes a way of describing problems like climate change as the interlocking interplay between socio-technical systems of different orders, with a particular focus on sustainable development.

What is particularly interesting for this volume is that the socio-technical transitions and the multi-level perspective seem to both critique and extend forms of governance that would have been located within what we might call an infrastructural mode of planning. As touched on above, anthropological discussions of state planning have frequently centerd on the way in which the improvement of society is pursued through infrastructural transformations in the built environment (Rabinow 1995; Bear 2007; Anand 2011; Collier 2011; Dalakoglou and Harvey 2012; Harvey and Knox 2015). Thus, planned social change has been a matter of demarcating the kind of society that is desired by creating material systems (neighbourhoods, electricity networks, roads, waterways, railways) that might enable that society to be brought into being.

What Geels' transition theory hints at is the limit condition of this infrastructure-state (Guldi 2012). Transition theory aims to understand the relationship between what Geels terms infrastructural 'lock-in' and the potential unboundedness or 'splintering' (Graham and Marvin 2001) of contemporary infrastructural relations once they are conceived in the frame of ecological sustainability. Reframed by problems like climate change, institutional actors have to not only consider specific instances of intervention via the implementation of discrete infrastructural systems but also conceive of other ways of intervening in the complex entanglements between the social, economic, technological and natural worlds and find new means of accounting for these interventions. In transition theory this has led to the development of the idea of a multi-level perspective, or MLP, which aims to identify 'niche innovations', 'socio-technical regimes' and 'sociotechnical landscape' as three 'levels' that must be taken into account in attempts at a change towards a more sustainable future (Geels and Schot 2007). In this effort to grid ecological complexity we see an attempt to resolve a tension between an approach to planning that works on the basis of demarcating boundaries around domains of intervention and an approach to planning which acknowledges the unboundedness of the problems in hand.

The problem of action 359

The idea of the world as a system has a long history in ecological thought and indeed it might be argued that the anomaly in this story is the modern era where the idea of being able to separate out a domain of responsibility or action as a coherent or bounded technological form that we might call an 'infrastructure' was established (Callon 1998; Harvey and Knox 2015; Graham and Marvin 2008). Claudia Aradau (2010) has argued that the notion of infrastructure as a generic object of state or governmental concern is a relatively recent historical object, having emerged as recently as the 1950s (see also Carse this volume). While prior to this time, nation-states were of course concerned about what we now call infrastructural forms, things like roads, bridges, railways and energy networks, were not, prior to the 1950s, conceptually grouped together as a category 'infrastructure'.

Ecological thinking, on the other hand, has existed as a shadow to the modern, infrastructural way of thinking throughout the twentieth century. Ecological thinkers from Stuart Brand, who set up the Whole Earth Catalogue (Brand 2009), to Herman Daly, author of the idea of the steady state economy (Daly 1996), have long worked against reductive and bounded understandings of economy and nature. Similarly, Gregory Bateson's (1973) unusual brand of cybernetic anthropology and the ecological anthropology of Roy Rappaport (1968) attempted in the 1960s to bridge the divide between the social and the ecological in non-modern settings, addressing human worlds in much more extended and materially embedded ways. Meanwhile, even academics working in planning have recognised that certain 'wicked problems', of which climate change is a perfect example, were always going to challenge the epistemological foundations of infrastructure planning (Rittel and Webber 1973).

Nonetheless, as climate change has emerged as a problem of governance, we can see how an attention to eco-systemic relations works to unsettle the epistemological foundations of modernist planning practices of infrastructure development. The political struggles in the field of climate change mitigation are no longer focused on primarily on the truth-status of anthropogenic climate change but rather circle around the question of how to refashion contemporary forms of planning and intervention to deal with the social–material entanglements that climate science now evidences (Knox 2015). As we will see in the next section, this destabilises the epistemological basis of planned social change, and introduces the problem of how to act with which this chapter began.

Information (eco)systems

Returning to the EU Green Digital Project, Geels' socio-technical transition theory was seen by the German team to offer one way of understanding the complex field of relationships into which they were to going to have to intervene. The hope was that transition theory, with its regridding of complex intertwined relationships, would help them to be able to distil a set of actors and relationships through which intervention and action could be operationalised in this complex emergent field.

Nonetheless, action was to remain problematic. Even having identified the people, locations and scales where actions might be both found and distributed, the team still had to do the work of deciding what would count as action.

One form that was frequently mobilised to think through what would count as an action, and to describe how action would be marked, counted and measured was the spreadsheet. Spreadsheets provided a powerful way of gridding objects and the relationships between them. A 'refresh' of the Manchester action plan was structured around the gridded form of an extended spreadsheet running to 27 pages, which aimed to demarcate new actions in the areas of Buildings, Energy Transport, Green and Blue Infrastructure, Sustainable Consumption and Production. Similarly, the green and digital project worked with the problem of how to constitute the field of action by collecting potential actions and lining them up in the spreadsheet format.

One of the main outputs of the Green Digital Project was to arrive at a set of 'action tools' that would be able to appear on the project website as a repository of resources that the actors identified in the transition diagram could use. Before being uploaded onto the website, however, these tools first had to be defined and the spreadsheet was a vital technology to assist in this process of definition.

By gridding actions against targets, the spreadsheet offered a means of making sense of the variety of different possible actions that could be imagined. The spreadsheet grouped actions into five different sheets pertaining to the categories of: all actions, culture, knowledge, practices and structure. In each sheet the tools were given a title, a description, a type (indicating whether they functioned as stories, documents, templates or software) and a code which linked each tool back to the aims of the project document itself. There was also a column that described which 'level' of actor the tools would be relevant to (1, 2 or 3), linking the gridding of the actions directly to Geels' multi-level analysis (see Figure 26.3). Through this emergent gridding exercise, a sense of the field of actions which the project was working to achieve was iteratively produced. The 'frame' of the spreadsheet both allowed for a structuring of what would otherwise seem potentially disparate activities – from an online portal for funding opportunities, to competitions, to pieces of software, to urban planning procedures or guidelines – to be brought together as 'actions' orientated to the ambition of mobilising digital technologies to achieve carbon reductions.

In spite of agreeing that the spreadsheet was necessary, Zeb worried that it risked over-objectifying what they were trying to achieve. Although the spreadsheet was the form through which actions could be demarcated, he was hesitant about assuming that the form would have a direct causal relationship with the outcome. Those who were engaged in the work of categorising and gridding this emergent, complex, interconnected problem were not so much attempting to get to an ultimate or singular description of the way in which

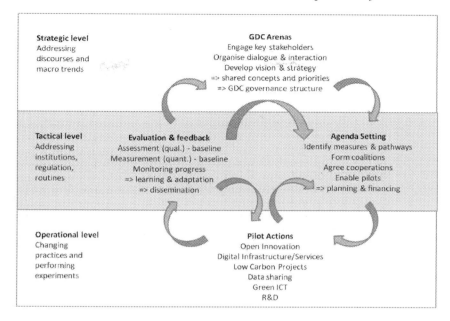

Figure 26.3 Overview of action fields for Green Digital Charter (GDC) implementation

the world is as experimenting with ways of patterning or making sense of a shifting terrain in order to provide orientation for intervention.

If in infrastructure-based planning, then, people were able to make judgements about the success or failure of a project by assessing the alignment between the promise and its materialisation in action, here the problem was the ongoing question of how to devise a new mode of formatting that acknowledged projects, processes and initiatives as already existing but not categorised as action, and to use the categorisation of these practices as forms of activity in order to stimulate further similar actions. By categorising already existing activities as climate change actions, projects were simultaneously able to map the field of 'what we will have had to do' and create the basis upon which more people might do more of this particular kind of doing.

Actions and outcomes

This identification of actions as having already occurred and yet needing to be scaled up, expanded, generalised and normalised raises the final question that I will address in this chapter: how could these already existing and future actions be re-linked to the problem of climate change? Climate change 'action' is a field replete with discrete and distributed activities, but the legacy of an ambition for centralised control means that the question remains whether these activities 'add up' to a concrete effect or whether they will in the end be wiped out by other sets of relationships and processes. The after-the-fact identification of actions raises the question of whether what people needed to do was to measure the effects of those actions to determine whether or not they really were appropriate ways of intervening in climate change and reducing carbon emissions, or whether this process of measurement was folly in itself.

One response has been to return to the route of measurement, a choice that often leads to the accusation that all that is being done is to devise indices of success which are themselves frequently revealed as flawed and meaningless (see Knox 2014; Verran 2012). A second response is to retreat from a concern with whether people are capable of knowing whether what they are doing is having a beneficial effect, and replacing a form of managerialism with a form of moral pragmatism understood as a 'faith' in the belief that they are doing the right thing. Zeb's concern that the aim of the spreadsheet might slip from a heuristic tool to a pseudo-scientific stabilisation was something he shared with others in working in climate change mitigation. Many of those involved in devising 'actions' that could reduce carbon emissions saw these actions as contributing not so much to a tangible structure of carbon emissions reductions, indexed by something like the spreadsheet, but to a more ineffable process of change in which people would begin to do and think things differently. Thus, just as Zeb worried that 'Regrouping things into a table format isn't supposed to be a scientific exercise', others worried that people were focusing on the cause–effect relationship between action and outcome rather than it being, as one environmental consultant put it when talking about putting food miles on packaging, 'as much about people gaining a political understanding rather than necessarily dictating some moral line'. Actions, then, were often seen as a means to generate energy, enthusiasm and awareness, what was called 'culture change,' rather than necessarily being expected to directly reduce carbon emissions. Thus it was that in a meeting of people trying to reduce Manchester's carbon emissions, Zeb chose to paraphrase the Antoine de Saint-Exupéry quote that opens this chapter and quipped, *'plans are nothing, planning is nothing – all we have is ships and the longing for the open sea'*.

Conclusion

It has been noted in various different discussions about urban settings that we are living in a time of experiments (Jensen 2015; Jensen and Morita 2015). Many of the 'actions' that are devised in climate change mitigation are also conceived as 'tests' or 'pilot' projects which people hope might provide a model that can be scaled up from experiment to infrastructure in the future (Bulkeley and Castán-Broto 2012; Karvonen 2014; Huse forthcoming). In Manchester there were several of these experiments, which ranged from experimental eco-houses to pilots of national government schemes, from prototype open-source energy monitors to test models that would be able to measure energy efficiency improvements in people's homes. Part of what

The problem of action 363

seems to be a broader movement of 'prototyping culture' (Corsín Jiménez 2014), the experiment here seemed to offer a form of practice that was appropriate to the condition of acting without the conventional parameters of a plan, without a clearly demarcated frame and without the potential of measurable effects. The experiment is one answer to the problem of action, offering the possibility of escaping the difficulties faced by those working in bureaucratic settings who are still in hock to the practices of framing and forms of boundary work that have dominated planning practices since the nineteenth century.

This chapter has argued that the appearance of these new techniques of governance – the experiment, the unaccounted for action, the re-description and re-imagination of already existing practices as the basis for future action – are crucial for understanding how contemporary governmental actors are imagining and formulating infrastructures of the future. As people re-evaluate the relationship between a future version of the world that emerges out of complex ecosystemic relationships and action in the present that can no longer be deterministically measured as the direct cause of particular future effects, the imaginaries of what infrastructure might be and how it might be planned is also being reassessed. In one sense infrastructure might be seen as being freed from the discipline of planning, allowing for a splintering or opening up of infrastructure as it becomes more experimental, more distributed, but also more entangled with private capital. On the other hand, there are hints of a new discipline, where other normative moral judgements about the benefits of particular forms of intervention trump rational forms of planning. Building on the work of those anthropologists who have critiqued the abstractions and framing of rational plans and the centralised infrastructural forms that these plans have enabled, I suggest that the appearance of modes of intervention that put action first also need to be critically assessed. Interventions that draw on people's 'faith' or trust in the signs of a portentous future to justify action in the present might not be analytically reductive but they nonetheless bring their own forms of closure. Moreover, attending to other people's reworking of the relationship between the plan and the action, offers an opportunity for us to revisit anthropological debates about how people proceed in the world and the role that informational models of complex and entangled eco-systemic processes play in the means by which people find ways of choosing how and when to act.

Notes

1 Region Zealand 2010 Climate Song Leaflet.
2 The rendition was filmed and is available at: www.youtube.com/watch?v=NVsVhjgh_3I.
3 The song 'Me and You' is part of a 42-song cycle by Søren Eppler, called 'un-songs'.
4 http://www.covenantofmayors.eu/index_en.html.
5 Greater Manchester Climate Change Strategy. Greater Manchester Combined Authority Report, 29 July 2011, p. 2.

6 Greater Manchester is made up of the ten local authority areas of: Altrincham, Bolton, Bury, Manchester, Rochdale, Stockport, Trafford, Tameside, Warrington and Wigan.

References

Abram, Simone and Gisa Weszkalnys (2011) "Introduction: Anthropologies of planning – temporality, imagination, and ethnography". *Focaal* 61: 3–18.

Anand, Nikhil (2011) "Pressure: the politechnics of water supply in Mumbai". *Cultural Anthropology* 26(4): 542–564.

Aradau, Claudia (2010) "Security that matters: critical infrastructure and objects of protection". *Security Dialogue* 41(5): 491–514.

Bateson, Gregory (1972) *Steps to an Ecology of Mind: Collected Essays in Anthropology, Psychiatry, Evolution, and Epistemology.* San Francisco, CA: Chandler.

Bear, Laura (2007) *Lines of the Nation: Indian Railway Workers, Bureaucracy, and the Intimate Historical Self.* New York: Columbia University Press.

Borges, Jorge Luis and Andrew Hurley (2000) *Collected Fictions.* London: Penguin.

Brand, Stewart (2009) *Whole Earth Discipline: An Ecopragmatist Manifesto.* New York: Viking.

Bulkeley, Harriet and Vanesa Castán Broto (2013) "Government by experiment? Global cities and the governing of climate change". *Transactions of the Institute of British Geographers* 38(3): 361–375.

Callon, Michel (1998) *The Laws of the Markets.* Oxford: Blackwell Publishers/Sociological Review.

Collier, Stephen J. (2011) *Post-Soviet Social: Neoliberalism, Social Modernity, Bio-politics.* Princeton, NJ: Princeton University Press.

Corsín Jiménez, Alberto (2014) "Introduction: Prototyping cultures" (special issue). *Journal of Cultural Economy* 7(4): 381–398.

Dalakoglou, Dimitris and Penny Harvey (2012) "Roads and anthropology: Ethnographic perspectives on space, time and (im) mobility". *Mobilities* 7(4): 459–465.

Daly, Herman E. (1996) *Beyond Growth: The Economics of Sustainable Development.* Boston, MA: Beacon Press.

de Saint-Exupéry, Antoine (1992) *Wind, Sand and Stars.* Orlando, FL: Houghton Mifflin Harcourt.

Ferguson, James (1990) *The Anti-politics Machine: 'Development,' Depoliticization, and Bureaucratic Power in Lesotho.* Cambridge: Cambridge University Press.

Geels, Frank (2010) "Ontologies, socio-techical transitions (to sustainability) and the multi-level perspective". *Research Policy* 29(4): 495–510.

Geels, Frank W. and Johan Schot (2007) "Typology of sociotechnical transition pathways". *Research Policy* 36(3): 399–417.

Graham, Stephen and Simon Marvin (2001) *Splintering Urbanism: Networked Infrastructures, Technological Mobilities and the Urban Condition.* London: Routledge.

Guldi, Jo (2012) *Roads to Power: Britain Invents the Infrastructure State.* Cambridge, MA: Harvard University Press.

Gupta, Akhil (2012) *Red Tape: Bureaucracy, Structural Violence, and Poverty in India.* Durham, NC: Duke University Press.

Harvey, Penny and Hannah Knox (2015) *Roads: An Anthropology of Infrastructure and Expertise.* Ithaca, NY: Cornell University Press.

Huse, Tone. Forthcoming. "Rethinking urban climate mitigation: From a politics of limitations to the opportunities of experimentation". PhD thesis, University of Tromsø.

Ingold, Tim (2000) *Perception of the Environment: Essays on Livelihood, Dwelling and Skill*. Oxford and New York: Routledge.

Jensen, Casper Bruun (2015) "Experimenting with political materials: environmental infrastructures and ontological transformations". *Distinktion: Scandinavian Journal of Social Theory* 16(1): 17–30.

Jensen, Casper Bruun and Brit Ross Winthereik (2013) *Monitoring Movements in Development Aid: Recursive Partnerships and Infrastructures*. Cambridge, MA: MIT Press.

Jensen, Casper Bruun and Atsuro Morita (2015) "Infrastructure as Ontological Experiments". *Engaging Science, Technology, and Society* 1: 81–87.

Karvonen, A. and B. van Heur (2014) "Urban laboratories: experiments in reworking cities". *International Journal of Urban and Regional Research* 38(2): 379–392.

Knox, Hannah (2014) "Footprints in the city: models, materiality, and the cultural politics of climate change". *Anthropological Quarterly* 87(2): 405–430.

Knox, Hannah (2015) "Thinking like a climate". *Distinktion: Scandinavian Journal of Social Theory* 16(1): 91–109.

McNaughton, S. J. and Michael B. Coughenour (1981) "The cybernetic nature of ecosystems". *American Naturalist* 117(6): 985–990.

Rabinow, Paul (1995) *French Modern: Norms and Forms of the Social Environment*. Chicago, IL: University of Chicago Press.

Rappaport, Roy A. (1968) *Pigs for the Ancestors: Ritual in the Ecology of a New Guinea People*. New Haven, CT: Yale University Press.

Riles, Annelise (2000) *The Network Inside Out*. Ann Arbor: University of Michigan Press.

Rittel, Horst and Melvin Webber (1973) "Dilemmas in a general theory of planning". *Policy Sciences* 4(2): 155–169.

Scott, James C. (1998) *Seeing Like a State: How Certain Schemes to Improve the Human Condition Have Failed*. New Haven, CT: Yale University Press.

Suchman, Lucy (2007) *Human-Machine Reconfigurations: Plans and Situated Actions*, 2nd edition. Cambridge: Cambridge University Press.

Verran, Helen (2012) "Number", in Celia Lury and Nina Wakeford (eds) *Inventive Methods: The Happening of the Social*. London: Routledge.

27 Machinic operations
Data structuring, healthcare and governmentality

Andrew Goffey

The National Programme for IT, or NPfIT for short, was a flagship IT project of the first Labour administration initiated by Tony Blair in 2002. Headed by Richard Grainger and costing an alleged £18.7bn, it was widely billed as the 'biggest IT project in the world', and while it would be unfair to say that it failed spectacularly, it was indeed one of the biggest and most expensive of a rapidly growing number of public sector IT fiascos. In the historical context of proclamations on information superhighways (especially in the US) and a proliferation of high-level public administration announcements about the virtues of 'interoperability', the project was billed as a comprehensive endeavour to bring the National Health Service in Britain into the present, unifying disparate local IT systems that numbered in their thousands, employing widely differing standards and practices of data gathering. NPfIT would ensure citizens could continue to have access to high standards of free healthcare without fear that a system that was already exhibiting distinct signs of creakiness might become ever more backwards and idiosyncratic in an era of rapid technological shift. NPfIT was finally dismantled in 2011 by the Conservative–Lib Dem coalition government, with widely varying estimates of the overall costs of the project to the public purse. Yet the failure of NPfIT did not prevent the Coalition administration from promising in its wake an 'Information Revolution in the NHS'. This revolution would fulfil many of the promises made by the original project, without the administrative overheads and inefficiency of the suspiciously centralised original model. Nor, indeed, did the publicly touted failure of NPfIT prevent subsequent administrations from putting to use the infrastructural changes that the project did achieve.

Subsequent events give good reason not to take the rhetoric of the information revolution at face value. Given the current situation of healthcare provision in the United Kingdom (to say nothing of the broader attacks on public healthcare provision), we are forced to consider a little more directly some of the dynamics at play – between public administration and private contractor, state health professional and citizen – and, more broadly to address the question of what we can learn from this case study about the changing forms of governmentality associated with national healthcare provision in a problematically globalising world. What can an exploration of the accelerating

Machinic operations 367

trend towards digitisation and technical mediation through *digital* infrastructures tell us about the changing organisation and deployment of power relations in contemporary societies of the Global North? More specifically, through a discussion of some aspects of the ongoing infrastructural transformation of the National Health Service in the United Kingdom, this chapter asks what light an exploration of such infrastructures casts on the shifting practices of *governmentality* in contemporary societies.

The public sector IT project: a politics of disruption?

The sheer proliferation of IT infrastructure projects in the public sector in the United Kingdom in recent decades – in the National Health Service in particular but not exclusively so – and the equal profusion of failures and problems with these projects, raises significant questions.

Efficiency is generally the explicitly, if euphemistically, stated rationale for the development of IT infrastructure projects. This framing is accepted as much in the critical public policy research addressing the failings of such projects as in the broader discourse around information technology. NPfIT was no exception to this general rule – as both the Department of Health's 1998 document *An Information Strategy for the Modern NHS 1998–2005*, which predated it, and the Coalition government's 2012 document *The Power of Information: Putting all of us in control of the health and care information we need* (which postdated it) both tended to suggest.

The longer term history of software development and broader public discourse about information technology gives plenty of reasons to doubt the sincerity of such statements. Whether one considers the 'productivity paradox' of information technology, encapsulated in Solow's pithy phrase, 'we see computers everywhere except in the productivity statistics',[1] recurrent and generally well-documented reports about the rate of failure of management information systems, or, of course, high-profile (and highly expensive) failures such as NPfIT, arguments for the 'efficiency' of digital infrastructural technologies can, at the very least, be taken with a pinch of salt.[2] Recurrent project failure, however, is not a strong argument against the idea that digital infrastructures are not a significant element in the reorganisation of power relations: the introduction of such complex actor-networks as information systems into organisations rarely results in transformations that entail *less* use of technology.

It is evident, even from a rather cursory consideration of the consonance of digital-infrastructural 'modernisation' in the public sector and broader discourses – around public healthcare provision, pensions, welfare payments and so on – that such infrastructural projects can be quite readily understood as consistent more broadly with neoliberal strategies in the transformation of practices of government.[3] Claims for the virtues of an 'information revolution' in the NHS[4] for the 'empowerment' of patient choice, for example, are readily interpreted in terms of a broader strategic shift in the organisation of

368 *Andrew Goffey*

practices of government. The transformation of public health and public health discourse, and information technology more broadly can be understood as having very close links with the kind of emphasis on individual choice and personal responsibility generally associated with neoliberalism. The specifically 'biopolitical' premises of a heavily informatised healthcare sector in the United Kingdom are writ large in government discourse – as the 2011 DOH document, 'Innovation, Health and Wealth: Accelerating Adoption and Diffusion in the NHS', suggests.[5] But the broader drift of such discourse, its links to information technologies and the desirability of infrastructural transformation has been evident in well-known policy and policy-related documents since the early 1990s at least.[6]

Given that much in the policy discourse around information technology confirms key observations of theorists of governmentality, often in a remarkably explicit way, it is hardly surprising that such academic work has elected not to problematise infrastructures and information technology more broadly.[7] Yet, this absence in work on the practices of government is regrettable. It seems to leave a very significant element of the sociotechnical networks that facilitate the 'action at a distance' characteristic of practices of government[8] unexplored (how *would* a Foucauldian interpret the myriad failures of government IT projects?). More broadly, it allows a hegemonic technoscientific account of computation, an account which emphasises its links to mathematics, to formal logic and to the achievements of science (in which the technology can be explained as an 'application' of science) to go unchallenged.

However, historically, there are as many reasons to associate the growth of computation with bureaucracy and the materiality of administrative practices as there are to link it with science.[9] Here it can be argued that numerous of the insights generated in the study of information infrastructure development, considered more generally as a process of technical mediation,[10] can help us understand more precisely some of the *material* reconfigurations without which the broadly neoliberal characteristic of certain governmental strategies would not work. What such studies show, often in quite precise detail, is the way in which processes of technical mediation, in shaking up and redistributing – de- and re-territorialising – the interests of actors involved in them, transforming the ways in which they are 'inscribed' within those infrastructures, facilitate relatively durable transformations in social relations. New technologies for mediation transform the milieus in which actors concerned at all the scales infrastructure provision operate.[11] Governments have to rethink policy initiatives to constitute new markets for data, or address growing problems of confidentiality, administrators work out how to game new sets of metrics, or reckon with the budgeting pressure of onerous new IT demands, doctors and nurses wrestle with new technologies or find workarounds that transform their daily routines, patients are subjected to new methods of resource allocation by 'rating' their doctors – they are obliged to be free – and so on.

This transformative capacity, touted as a virtue, rather imprecisely and somewhat naively, by the idea of 'disruptive' technology, and called for implicitly by management consultants, think tanks and politicians under the rubric of 'culture change', in some respects points directly to a reconfiguring of subjectivity (which the all-purpose reference to 'actors' often leaves unthematised, particularly in science and technology studies[12]).

Problematising 'information'

A widespread failure to problematise the technoscientific underpinnings of thinking about information technology and computation more generally is of course not the unique province of social scientists. It is readily evident in the more exclusively technical writings about infrastructure. There is now a quite considerable body of science and technology studies literature, much of which emerged subsequent to the first flourishing of the Internet, that has gone some way to problematizing infrastructure.[13] For the purposes of this essay, one feature in particular of this literature is worth mentioning. It concerns the manner in which certain rather crucial technoscientific terms, which are usually central in formulating the purpose of digital infrastructures, including 'data' and 'information', are often taken as more or less self-evident. In respect of this, the 'purpose' of a complex of digital infrastructural technologies such as the Internet is one of the transmission and exchange of information.

The rather partial problematisation of the notion of *information* (and its twin *data*) in discussions of digital infrastructure – as if this means more or less the same thing in different kinds of 'knowledge' work – has obvious limitations. In the first instance, while the term 'information' itself has a range of meanings, it is, evidently, a crucial element in the language of modernisation associated with infrastructure projects in contemporary Western societies. But it means very different things when associated with, say, the paperwork characteristic of 'traditional' bureaucracy or the databases of the 'post-bureaucratic' era. The methodological precaution of being sensitive to the *discontinuities* in and around infrastructures[14] is critical when considering 'information'. In this instance, the continuity readily implied by technoscientific terms such as information makes a connection between healthcare infrastructure and the collaborative, information-sharing practices around which the Internet was constituted. But this also makes it all too easy to overlook the very significant bureaucratic element of the transformations operative in public sector infrastructure projects. Administering healthcare is not a knowledge practice in the same way as, say, the work of biologists is: data collection and information sharing mean very different things that incautious references to 'information' overlook. In this respect, the purported 'empowerment' of the individual that timely access to information in the NHS was to facilitate, condenses a more complex set of transformations which policy and think tank discourse about 'information exchange' can easily, and perhaps fortuitously, render obscure.

A second, related, point is that 'information' – given its provenance in discourses around digital technologies and computation more broadly, as well as other fields such the neoclassical economics that took shape out of, for example, operations research in WWII,[15] linguistics, cognitive science and so on – is an excellent example of precisely the kind of 'universal' that information infrastructure researchers acknowledge must be questioned.[16] Indeed, if developing a more 'governmentalist' stance towards the understanding of infrastructures is to succeed, then problematising more directly the function of technoscientific terms such as that of 'information' is vital. This is a term that quite routinely enters into discussions about what infrastructural work is about – such as accounts of the development of standards typically argued to be central to the effective functioning of infrastructure – but the literature tends to convey the sense that what is problematic about endeavours to universalise specific information standards is not the informatic *form* as such but its content.

A third point, then, and this is particularly important for understanding the implication of infrastructure in power relations, is that strategically speaking what matters the most about digital infrastructural mediation is precisely effecting a change in the conditions under which and the terms on which certain kinds of discourse production may be accomplished. The technical mediation of the possibilities of discourse production in the complex networks of technical devices characteristic of an information infrastructure points towards a rather powerful form of *inscription* that transforms the processes and practices of *enunciation* through which particular kinds of subjectivity are formed and transformed. The 'technoscientific' acceptance of a term such as 'information' thus acquires a strategic value: on the one hand it seems to come from nowhere, you can't be against it, it has a sort of self-evident neutrality (in principle) and it is implictly addressed to quasi-rational actor. On the other it implies a reconfiguration of discourse production – and the social relations such production can sustain – around a different set of (political) actors, with different kinds of expertise.

Problematising information, of course, is not the same thing as denying its existence. There is a strong sense in which we may correlate the generation of putatively immaterial information (or, for that matter, 'good clean data') with the successful functioning of an infrastructure: as Ruhleder and Star point out, infrastructure in all its messy materiality can truly be said to exist when it effectively disappears into the background, when, as they put it, transparency, and hence purposive usability, is achieved.[17] But as such, this only begs a further question about how infrastructure reshapes and repositions particular kinds of subject.

Data structuring

The absence of a more critical, problematising stance towards terms such as information can make it difficult to understand important aspects of the work of *translation* involved in processes of digital infrastructure development. In the theoretical accounts of it that have been generated in computer science and allied disciplines, information tends to have a rather idealised, unsituated quality, participating in a broader conceptual erasure of *enunciation* that is nonetheless a prerequisite for the construction of information technology systems (and hence infrastructures). When they are understood as 'modelling' or 'representing' information and the steps involved in its processing, the data structures and algorithms that form the basis of all software become intermediaries rather than mediators. The active role of computational artefacts in producing what may then come to be understood *as* information disappears, allowing the immaterial properties of information to float free. In this respect, there is, indeed, a politics to digital infrastructure projects of the kind that have proliferated in recent decades, one which resides, in part at least, in the transformations entailed in the production of apparatuses for the production of information and data.

Bowker et al. note that *data* is, in many ways, at the heart of questions about infrastructural technologies:

> In the daily working world of science, infrastructural tensions and conflicts are very often resolved (or not) at the level of data. Data, and the anxieties and tensions it occasions, represents the front line of cyberinfrastructure development .... From one view at least, cyberinfrastructure is principally *about* data.[18]

This claim is borne out readily in relation to crucial work preparatory to the development of software within NPfIT and its aftermath: the production of the numerous *datasets*, standardised specifications of data to be collected referent to the many specialisms operative in contemporary secondary healthcare practice (now collectively known as the NHS Data Model) and their subsequent repurposing with a view to promoting the secondary use of clinical data. Such datasets and the data 'model' they constitute are exemplary forms of 'the particular technical devices of writing, listing, numbering and computing that render a realm into discourse as a knowable, calculable and administrable object.'[19]

Qua 'standardised', of course, datasets are in the position of having to negotiate a familiar problem for infrastructure production: the tension between the local and the global, between local variations regarding what it may be thought relevant to know about, say, the diagnosis of a breast cancer; the desirability for clinicians of making meaningful global comparisons (its link with evidence-based medicine); and the need to ease the work of systems designers and developers. Some datasets at least entailed regular and involved consultation with specific groups (e.g. the National Cancer Data Set), factoring in revisions as the process of negotiating relevant data 'items' unfold. Such tensions also become manifest within the software development process itself – consultants and other practitioners who may be involved in design, development or testing processes, for example, raising questions about the pertinence of particular data items, or – as was more broadly the case in the NHS – insisting on the specifics of local practice. Practitioner discussions over what it is meaningful and important to know about a patient in a specific context are only part of the story. In spite of NPfIT's focus, dataset production in the NHS has extended well beyond the desideratum of producing 'good, clean data' for clinical purposes. Indeed, a cursory review of the 'data dictionary' developed under the aegis of the *Information Standards Board for Health and Social Care*, which contains all the datasets utilised within the NHS – which use is glossed as being in support of 'business analysis' – includes, in addition to clinical data, commissioning data, central return data, administrative data and others.[20] This trajectory of dataset production is marked most clearly in a government consultation document from 2013 that emphasises the link between recording and use of data in hospitals (notionally: for patient care) and the 'coverage, timeliness, and quality of the data extracted centrally for secondary [i.e. non-clinical] uses',[21] a shift away from the central focus given to clinical care in the policy documents of the late 1990s and early 2000s.

This shift is also marked in related literature that emerged during and subsequent to NPfIT: a discussion of the so-called 'big-data' revolution in healthcare, produced for the US government, is telling in this regard: healthcare providers 'have a unique role not only as the primary point of care, but also as one of the primary points of data origination and capture', which shift imposes on them the task of 'ensuring consistent and comprehensive data capture, and reinforcing the culture of information sharing'.[22] Information sharing, in this, context is about the discovery of 'new opportunities'. Viewed through a governmental lens, the complex information technological infrastructures for data collection that were established through NPfIT and successor strategies effect a reorganisation of the possibilities of discourse production within healthcare. In this respect, and regardless of the more obvious and publicly perceptible political resonances around 'data', the alignment of interests in and around the work of deciding not just what data to collect but also the configuration of *how* such data was to be collected itself entailed a crucial process of the delegation of the political – and economic – restructuring of work practices (typically glossed as 'culture change') to specific technologies.[23] The public availability of clinical datasets and their further incorporation into the 'interoperability toolkit' made available to third-party software developers, who are thereby enabled to produce software that targets healthcare practices (without the need to go through the complex negotiation of access to clinical expertise within the hospital setting), underlines the tacit repositioning of the producers of the expert knowledge that generate such datasets in the first place. The production of datasets is as much about the material *form* that inscriptions are to take as it is about the referential 'content' of such inscriptions: once elements of clinical expertise are captured through the modelling or structuring of discourse *as* data, further mediation by technical devices is possible, regardless of stakeholder engagement.

The double binding of enunciation

The 1998 DOH *Information for Health* strategy document, which outlines much of the administrative thinking that was at the inception of NPfIT, took care to mark what it saw as a shift away from the use of information technology for managerial purposes and towards its use for clinical purposes.[24] It tacitly recognised the importance of securing adherence (more colloquially: 'buy-in') on the part of practitioners, given the problematic nature of the way in which the 'efficiency' of hospitals was being calculated.[25] Prior to NPfIT there had already been recognition that data collection should be accomplished 'operationally' rather than through additional, more obviously managerial means.[26] In a social media era of cookies and widespread dataveillance, the idea that (administrative, or managerial) data about what someone might be doing should be collected directly through 'operational' systems, through what they are actually doing, may seem unremarkable. But, in the healthcare context, it points to an ideal coinciding of clinical practice and audit, an ideal further confirmed by a growing emphasis on the *real time* use of such data (the view, for example, that GPs are only motivated to use systems if they can see an immediate benefit in doing so).

It is in the context of this broader acknowledgement of the inconveniences of the intrusive and time-consuming work of administrative data entry, and hence – within the organisation and development of the IT project – the ongoing task of recruiting all important allies (specifically consultants and other senior clinical staff presumed to exercise influence within hospitals) into the work of infrastructure production, that we can read the proposed – and now contractually mandated – use of SNOMED Clinical Terms.

SNOMED – the Systematic Nomenclature of Medical Terms – is a classic example of an infrastructural technology, analogous in some respects to the ICD-10 (International Classification of Diseases) coding system explored by Bowker and Star.[27] Like ICD-10 codes, SNOMED is a system designed to facilitate better recording of data through its systematic organisation as a set of alphanumeric terms. Unlike ICD, it is considerably more comprehensive as a coding system in that it not only extends its coding scope well beyond diagnosis but also possesses a syntax that effectively facilitates the generation of complete SNOMED 'sentences'. Crucially, SNOMED also accords a 'semantics' to strings of data that, computationally would otherwise be completely meaningless. This makes it possible for IT systems to more easily extract meaningful patterns of information from the data they gather. Context typically permits a human to disambiguate a term like 'blood pressure', but this is not normally an option for a machine because it can mean at least three things – an 'organism function', a 'diagnostic procedure' and a 'laboratory or test result'. SNOMED's 'semantics' is a way to address this problem.

Although it is not – yet – widely used in NHS IT, the interest of SNOMED has to do with how it addresses practitioner concerns about information infrastructures (intrusiveness, inflexibility, clinical imprecision and so on) with a more comprehensive delegating of the production and processing of data to technology.

Considered from an infrastructural point of view, SNOMED may be thought of as a rather utopian attempt to address the complex challenges of reconciling the tensions produced across the local/global and social/technical axes of information infrastructure[28]: facilitating idiosyncratic, or clinically precise, local variants in data collection through the combinatorial permutability of terminology, enabling fine-grained data to be processed technically according to computational standards shared by all, by virtue of the specific machine 'readability' of its codes, and so on. To put the matter in a slightly different way, as already suggested, SNOMED aims to reconcile key *contextual* differences implied in the infrastructural collection of data. These are the differences that pertain to what information technology experts refer to as *structured* and *unstructured* data. While the precise definition of these are not really clear, the imposition of structure on data is readily recognised in the 'forms' used to fill in, say, demographic details for entry into a database, for example. An alphanumeric string (including blank spaces) is, from the database point of view, unstructured. However, that same alphanumeric string, broken down into fields like 'house number', 'street name', 'city', 'zip', etc. has a structure that renders it susceptible to 'efficient' processing.

Unstructured data – and by implication, specific enunciative contexts – are not necessarily an obstacle to the smoother functioning of automated technological systems per se. The text contained in an email, for example, is unstructured, but that doesn't pose a significant obstacle to email use. What it does pose a problem for, however, is the *automated* processing of data, wherein structure is crucial to enable the ready 'extraction' of information. Unstructured data has been characterised and pinpointed as a key unexploited economic resource and a particular focus for data collection strategies within healthcare. This doesn't 'explain' the strategies adopted in digital infrastructure development. However, the widespread characterisation of data as 'unstructured' (when it is perfectly well structured from a human point of view) or 'unmodelled' (as it appears in some accounts) points to the more obvious point, which is that 'unstructured' data evidently forms that element of discourse production that cannot be captured in a computational formalism of some sort. When a medical diagnosis is recorded in a database, some of the details of the diagnosis may be captured using an alphanumeric code drawn from the ICD-10 taxonomy. Other details – the particular nuance of the diagnosis – may simply be entered in 'free text', a string of characters unpredictable as to composition and therefore difficult to process in technically practicable ways. The point about this difference is that unstructured data requires reference beyond the context of automated data processing to understand or clarify (in addition to the services of medical coders to facilitate automated processing). It can be understood and clarified as to meaning by humans ('what do you mean by "minor discolourations"?') because humans generally possess the capacity to repair interactions – to clarify or qualify as to meaning, for example. But such repair is not really possible in a computational device: considered as a context for making sense of data, an infrastructural device such as a database (for which data is structured) only possesses very limited and highly inflexible means for addressing semantics. To put the matter slightly differently, the difference between structured and unstructured data may be understood as an *enunciative* difference referent to the degree of contingency (and hence unpredictability) in discourse production[29]: a variable limit to the 'infrastructuring' of language.

In its attempt to further approximate natural language, then, it becomes readily apparent that a system of clinical terms such as SNOMED not only aims to tackle the problematic split between structured and unstructured data through its imposition of an approximate formal ontological structure on language, but aims to do so through a more complete mapping of natural language contexts of enunciation into the infrastructure of data production, which mapping further facilitates the logic of the ideal coincidence of operation and audit mentioned previously. In this respect the desire to capture good, clean data, accurately and for clinical purposes, once and once only (with no call for further elaboration or clarification, or repeated data entry) binds the clinician into a technological system over which he or she has little (if any) control. In this respect, a technology such as SNOMED submits its users to a variant form of the Batesonian 'double bind' that Star and Ruhleder have explored in their elaboration of 'infrastructural transcontextual syndrome': submitting to the post hoc structuring of the data that they produce as practitioners for clinical purposes entails at the same time becoming an agent in the transformation of the infrastructural conditions under which their practice takes place.[30]

Conclusion

A 2014 National Information Board document confidently sets out the UK government's 'vision' for 'personalised' care, effected through the 'wide-scale change' it believes to be 'driven' by technology and data. SNOMED figures as the last stage on this 'framework for action.' By 2020, not only will all care records be 'digital real-time and interoperable' but 'the entire health system will adopt SNOMED clinical terminology'.[31] Clinical practitioners and health IT professionals are less certain.[32]

From a governmental point of view, the existence of a significant mismatch between the discourse around digital infrastructures in a field such as healthcare and the material implementation of the various desiderata for control such discourse maps out, is hardly a surprise. Indeed, as Rose et al. put it, 'the mere existence of a diagram of government implies [n]either its generalised acceptance or implementation'.[33] The processes and practices of the (infra)structuring of data that have been addressed in this chapter are in this regard exemplary and are highly suggestive of the value of examining digital infrastucture projects of the kind considered here, through a 'governmental' lens. But as the issue of structured and unstructured data suggests, we do approach something of a limit to contemporary governmental findings about strategies for the constitution of largely autonomous individual subjectivity. The development of digital infrastructures for the collection of 'good, clean data', with all that that entails by way of the heavily 'asymmetric' inscription of actors within computational technology points towards a form of constraint *on* and transformation *of* discourse production for which individual freedom poses something of a problem. The pointing and clicking, scrolling, ticking and other gestures that are now so characteristic of the digital infrastructures of contemporary discourse production ('information' and 'data') in this respect mark a peculiarly intimate form of action at a distance that coheres around a semiotic-machinic hybrid of formal and natural language, In such a hybrid form, the heavily modelled bodily actions and tightly constrained choices that are necessitated by the inputting of data or the extraction of information inflexibilities point towards the logical and material priority of the operations of a complex technical system over the discursive assumption of an individual subject position. This is what is now being called 'joined up', 'personalised' health and care.

Notes

1. Erik Brynjolfsson (1993).
2. Indeed, a recent report (Standish Group 2014) suggests that in the USA 31.1% of IT systems development projects get cancelled before completion. I've been unable to verify the source of this data. One should be wary of claims about the state of 'chaos' in which software development finds itself, as suggested by this report. See also Parliamentary Office of Science and Technology (2003).
3. Peter Miller and Nikolas Rose (1990). Note, however, that the label 'neoliberalism' is one that must be used advisedly (Rose et al. 2006).
4. Department of Health (2012).
5. Department of Health (2011).
6. For example, the recommendations to the European Council by Bangemann et al. (1994), which reiterates claims made for the 'revolutionary' qualities of information.
7. Andrew Barry (2001), amongst others, might stand as an exception to this general rule.
8. Miller and Rose op. cit. for more on this.
9. Jon Agar (2003).
10. I.e. as an intrinsically *socio*-technical process. See Bruno Latour (1994).
11. Paul N. Edwards (2003) on these questions of scale.
12. Cf. Andrew Goffey and Lynne Pettinger (2014).
13. The growing interest in 'information infrastructures' can be dated to the US government's plan for National Information Infrastructures, itself following the *High Performance Computing* Act of 1991.
14. As studies of information infrastructure themselves suggest. See Geof Bowker et al. (2010).
15. Phillip Mirowski (2002), Chs 4 and 5.
16. Ole Hanseth and Eric Monteiro (n.d.), Ch. 8, 'Dreaming about the universal'.
17. Susan Leigh Star and Karen Ruhleder (1996).

18 Bowker et al. op. cit., 31.
19 Miller and Rose op. cit., 5.
20 See: www.datadictionary.nhs.uk/web_site_content/navigation/main_menu.asp.
21 NHS HSCIC (2013), 9.
22 Mckinsey and Co. (2013), 14, 13.
23 A resonance missing in the paper by Bowker et al. in part because of its more exclusive focus on *science*.
24 See *Information for Health* op. cit., 64. But see Thomas Haigh (2011) on the managerial origins of 'IT'.
25 Clive Smee (2005), 62–3.
26 Sean Brennan (2005), 62.
27 Geoffrey C. Bowker and Susan Leigh Star (1999).
28 Star and Ruhleder (1996) op. cit. and the further discussion in Bowker et al. (2010), 101–2.
29 The growing importance of natural language processing techniques or text analytics in this area points towards the direct targeting of discourse production. See Holzinger et al. (2013), 13–24, for a technical discussion in relationship to electronic patient records.
30 I read Star and Ruhleder here against the grain a little. Double bind problems of the kind they study can be readily characterised as a way in which technical devices overcome 'obstacles to transformation' in effecting infrastructural change.
31 National Information Board (2014), 58.
32 Anne Randorff Højen et al. (2015), 140–5; Mandi Bishop (2014).
33 Rose et al. op. cit., 99.

Bibliography

Agar, Jon (2003) *The Government Machine. A Revolutionary History of the Computer.* Cambridge, MA: MIT Press.

Bangemann, Martin et al. (1994) *Europe and the Global Information Society.* Recommendations to the European Council. Online at http://channelingreality.com/Digital_Treason/Brussels_1995/Bangemann_report.pdf (accessed 10 June 2016).

Barry, Andrew (2001) *Political Machines: Governing a Technological Society.* London: Athlone.

Bishop, Mandi (2014) "The Secret Life of the SNOMED Code: Why Patient's 'Problem List' is a Problem". Online at http://healthstandards.com/blog/2014/04/21/snomed-problems/ (accessed 10 June 2016).

Bowker, Geoffrey C. and Susan Leigh Star (1999) *Sorting Things Out: Classification and its Consequences.* Cambridge, MA: MIT Press.

Bowker, Geoffrey C., Karen Baker, Florence Millerand and David Ribes (2010) "Toward Information Infrastructure Studies: Ways of Knowing in a Networked Environment", in J. Hunsinger, L. Klastrip, and M. Allen (eds) (2010) *International Handbook of Internet Research.* Dordrecht: Springer.

Brennan, Sean (2005) *The NHS IT Project.* Oxford: Radcliffe Publishing.

Brynjolfsson, Erik (1993) "The Productivity Paradox of Information Technology: Review and Assessment", *Communications of the ACM*, December. Online at http://ccs.mit.edu/papers/CCSWP130/ccswp130.html (accessed 12 January 2016).

Department of Health (2011) "Innovation, Health and Wealth: Accelerating Adoption and Diffusion in the NHS". Online at www.institute.nhs.uk/images/documents/Innovation/Innovation%20Health%20and%20Wealth%20-%20accelerating%20adoption%20and%20diffusion%20in%20the%20NHS.pdf (accessed 11 November 2015).

Department of Health (2012) "The Power of Information: Putting All of Us in Control of the Health and Care Information We Need". Online at www.gov.uk/governm ent/publications/giving-people-control-of-the-health-and-care-information-they-need (accessed 10 June 2016).

Edwards, Paul N. (2003) "Infrastructure and Modernity: Force, Time, and Social Organization in the History of Sociotechnical Systems", in Thomas J. Misa et al. *Modernity and Technology*. Cambridge, MA: MIT Press.

Goffey, Andrew and Lynne Pettinger (2014) "Refrains and Assemblages: Exploring Market Negotiations and Green Subjectivity with Guattari", *Subjectivity* 7(4): 385–410.

Haigh, Thomas (2011) "The History of Information Technology", *Annual Review of Information Science and Technology* 45(1): 431–487.

Hanseth, Ole and Eric Monteiro (n.d.) "Understanding Information Infrastructure", unpublished manuscript. Online at http://heim.ifi.uio.no/~oleha/Publications/bok. html (accessed 10 December 2015).

Holzinger, Andreas et al. (2013) "Combining HCI, Natural Language Processing, and Knowledge Discovery: Potential of IBM Content Analytics as an Assistive Technology in the Biomedical Field", paper presented at the Third International Workshop, HCI-KDD 2013, SouthCHI 2013, Maribor, Slovenia, 1–3 July.

Højen, Anne Randorff, Kirstine Rosenbeck Gøeg and Pia Britt Elberg (2015) "Re-use of SNOMED CT Subset in Development of the Danish National Standard for Home Care Nursing Problems", in Ronald Cornet et al. (eds) *Digital Healthcare Empowering Europeans: Proceedings of MIE2015*. Amsterdam: IOS Press.

Latour, Bruno (1994) "On Technical Mediation: Philosophy, Sociology, Genealogy", *Common Knowledge* (3/2): 26–64.

Mckinsey and Company (2013) "The "Big Data" Revolution in Healthcare: Accelerating Value and Innovation". Online at www.mckinsey.com/industries/healthca re-systems-and-services/our-insights/the-big-data-revolution-in-us-health-care.

Miller, Peter and Nikolas Rose (1990) "Governing Economic Life", *Economy and Society* 19(1): 1–31.

Mirowski, Phillip (2002) *Machine Dreams: How Economics Became a Cyborg Science*. Cambridge: Cambridge University Press.

NHS England and the Health and Social Care Information Centre (2013) "National Hospital Data and Data Sets: A Consultation". Online at www.england.nhs.uk/wp -content/uploads/2013/07/hosp-data-consult.pdf (accessed 10 December 2015).

National Information Board (2014) *Personalised Health and Care 2020. Using Data and Technology to Transform Outcomes for Patients and Citizens*. Online at https:// www.gov.uk/government/uploads/system/uploads/attachment_data/file/384650/NIB_ Report.pdf (accessed 10 January 2016).

Parliamentary Office of Science and Technology (2003) "Government IT Projects", Report 200. Online at www.parliament.uk/documents/post/pr200.pdf (accessed 10. 1. 16)

Rose, Nikolas, Pat O'Malley and Marina Velverde (2006) "Governmentality", *Annual Review of Law and Social Science* 2: 83–104.

Smee, Clive (2005) *Speaking Truth to Power: Two Decades of Analysis in the Department of Health* (Oxford: Radcliffe Publishing.

Standish Group (2014) "Chaos Report 2014'". Online at www.standishgroup.com (accessed 20 December 2015)

Star, Susan Leigh and Karen Ruhleder (1996) "Steps toward an Ecology of Infrastructure: Design and Access for Large Information Spaces', *Information Systems Research* 7(1): 111–134.

28 Infrastructures in name only?
Identifying effects of depth and scale

Adrian Mackenzie

Recently released NSA documents revealed the existence of FOXSCORE, a massive database that bugs traffic from major internet exchanges. General Keith Alexander, director of the National Security Agency, assured the public that the program is rubber stamped by a secret court.

Recently released NSA documents revealed the existence of WAGONWIND, a USB hardware host tap that deanonymizes communications satellites. An anonymous administration source assured the public that the program would only be used in the event of a national emergency.

(http://divergentdave.github.io/NSA-O-Matic/)

NSA-O-Matic is a piece of software that generates *names* of fictional US NSA (National Security Agency) surveillance systems by compounding names of actually existing devices, protocols and standards. We know from the files released by Edward Snowden something of the existence of sprawling cyber-security systems such as XKEY, TREASUREMAP, SKYNET and so forth (CJFE 2015), all of which might be broadly understood as knowledge infrastructures. The Snowden revelations, in all their confusing variety, attest to a combinatorial expansion. The humour of NSA-O-Matic derives partly from the disparity between the existence of a seemingly technically far-fetched juxtaposition – USB hardware that deanonymises communications satellites? – and our still somewhat inchoate and stunned awareness of tendrils growing into every aspect of contemporary communications (wireless routers, Skype conversations, network hubs, mobile phone conversations, social media, email messages, etc.). The public assurances extracted from US government figures such as General Keith Alexander or Senator Dianne Feinstein only emphasise the threadbare democratic mandate for the existence of such systems.

The combinatorial expansion is not unique to the NSA or government intelligence agencies of a similar ilk. The sheer variety of channels, devices, standards, modalities, platforms, scales of operation and levels of interdependency challenges knowledge of infrastructure. At least in relation to networked communication and knowledge, our sense of scale and opacity owes much to names in combination. NSA-O-Matic spoofs putative infrastructures. It compounds names to evoke opacity and depth. While important efforts are being made to map the connections between NSA 'programs' named in the Snowden documents and specific communications and computing devices that many of us use daily (*Guardian News* 2015), the sheer litany of systems, platforms and elements that surface in these documents defy easy analysis. Yet this abundance imbues infrastructures with much of their structural depth, flexibility, power and fragility. If we stay close to the combinatorial play of NSA-O-Matic, we might apprehend something of the unfurling, unstable opacity of contemporary infrastructures. The names of constituent fragments may attest to their splintering (Graham and Marvin 2001), to their naturalisation (Bowker and Star 1999, 326) but also to their existence in time.

All structures, no matter how subterranean, act semiotically. Rusted bolts, cracked concrete plinths, the stanchions, bars, girders, plugs, cables, stone, steel, glass, rubber, oil, plastic, electricity, gas and springs participate in semiosis. They function as indices for infrastructural interpretants: rust suggests moisture, cloudy or black oil suggests wear, a buzzing indicates something loose, etc. On accompanying diagrams, labels name components, processes, flows and structures. At least for their interpretants, *semiosis* affects what counts as infrastructure.[1] If, like NSA-O-Matic, we apprehend infrastructures in name only, how do they appear to us? Somewhat inverse to tendencies to see depth and scale as the underpinning power dynamic, many contemporary information infrastructures proliferate names. While we might approach contemporary instances in terms of the growth of forms such as 'platforms' (Gillespie 2010) or programmed or protocol control (Beniger 1986; Galloway 2004), their aggregate consistency and variety owes much to the named entities that thread through many different media, communication, administrative and operational practices. Naming practices or *nominalisation of infrastructure,* then, might offer a viable way of navigating the dense patterns of code, protocols, standards, devices, statements and operations that thicken people's infrastructural practices.

Mapping infrastructures in names only

Where can nominalisation of infrastructure be studied? Software development, maintenance, repair and deployment entail designating and manipulating names. All code inhabits name spaces.[2] Methodologically speaking, focusing on names might seem a bit counter-productive, since attention to materiality, devices, things, non-human actors and practice in general has been one of the hallmarks of the social studies of infrastructure. In code-based settings (and code inflects almost all knowledge infrastructures today), naming is a crucial practice. Naming operationally links people and things, places and devices together in complicated associations. Nearly all code heavily relies on naming practices. Whether viewed as a series of statements, commands or functions, naming and the forms of address associated with names weave inextricably through software.

Code repositories store the source code, associated documents, files, configuration information and a variety of other materials associated with software.[3] The largest repository of code repositories, the code repository platform Github.com [http://www.github.com] with around 20 million repositories (in 2015) sprawling across many domains, epitomises nominalisation of infrastructure. Github attracts tremendous amounts of code – for instance, Google Corporation recently announced the closure of its own code repository service Google.code.com and migration of all code deposited there to Github (Google 2015); Microsoft Corporation has recently opened the source code of Windows, its main product, on Github, etc. Github is rather like NSA-O-Matic writ large, since the code repositories it hosts not only address almost any kind of digital hardware and software practice one can imagine but seem to be animated in their growth since 2007 by the same combinatorial delirium that NSA-O-Matic, itself a Github-hosted project, displays. It is difficult to characterise the heterogeneity of things, devices, conventions, platforms and organisations named in Github code repositories, and indeed, this difficulty is one of the motivations to approach what happens there in terms of names.

Github itself looks like a typical contemporary social media platform. It has many of the appurtenances of participation ('followers', 'groups', 'watchers', 'stars', etc.) and invokes the ethico-economic injunction to 'share' (John 2013). Github seeks to render coding itself 'social'. It treats coding as a social practice of participation, somehow akin to photo-sharing or chatting with friends using a social media platform. In this respect, infrastructures become the objects of social rituals and branded identifications. The trappings of social media and its imperatives – 'be social, share code' – with their focus on networks of relations between people largely occlude the tremendous combinatorial processes occurring on Github and git-like platforms more generally. The fluxes of imitation of names and their recombinant energy constantly overflow the imperative to 'be social'.

Is Github, then, a hub because it somehow has captured the nominalisation of infrastructure, or somehow made naming itself into the archive of this nominalisation? Is Github a logistical success story (say like Singapore's role in container shipping) or a tremendous organic accumulation (say like Lagos in Nigeria, with its complicated work-around flows of people, trade, oil and politics)? Neither of these alternatives are quite right. Like many platforms, services, devices and systems, the logistical success of Github (in coding and software deployment) depends on the tremendous morass of eccentric, abandoned, rarely used, ephemeral, miscellaneous and incredibly specific code and coding found there. The nominalisation of infrastructure and its subsequent containerisation in code speeds up and renders infrastructure development more flexible and variable. In this respect, Github is somewhat like a logistics hub in which moving things around somehow coincides with naming them.

The coincidence of making and naming, developing and operating perhaps challenges any sense of solidity we might have in relation to infrastructure.

The names of repositories hosted on Github display a baffling polysemy. Repository names on Github can be any combination of letters or characters. These range from the almost casually random yet still recognisable names such as 'asdf' (the first four characters on the home-row of an English keyboard) or '1234', both of which number in the thousands, through to highly recognisable names such as linux or apache. Both of the latter projects are well known as key infrastructural elements of contemporary digital networks. On the one hand, the distance between repositories called 'asdf' and 'linux' is great. The former typically represent ephemeral contacts between individuals and infrastructures (for instance, many such repositories are the traces of people trying out or learning to use Github as an online code repository) and the latter encompass information network architectonics resulting from much collective effort. The linux kernel in particular represents one of the main cases in which coding work both became more visible as a cultural and social practice (Coleman 2012; Kelty 2008; Mackenzie 2006), and practically permeated the information infrastructural *stack*. [4]

Between the two extremes of the random keypress repositories and the installed bulk of linux or apache lies a very diverse and dense population of names. If we could read them serially in their spread and diversification over time, these names would diagram infrastructures multiplying, combining and decaying in layers. Processes of repair, re-invention, appropriation, capitalisation and speculation are engrained in the distribution of names. The gamut of names of Github repositories, enough to populate a small country, is somewhat heterogeneous, pluralistic and full of transient multiplicities, but axes of organisation and centralisation that assemble infrastructural elements into something like the 'full stack' associated with the digital networks can be discerned there. Infrastructures like Github allocate all things a position in a common *namespace*. The Github platform, with its infrastructures for storage, searching, tracking and graphing of coding work, arrays all repositories on the same surface. In this respect, it renders all differences superficial, and this superficiality is perhaps a somewhat novel experience in relation to infrastructure. The relations and connections between disparate bodies of code of many different ilk have only recently started to congregate in a common namespace.

Figure 28.1 shows the most popular repositories on Github in 2014. Not all Github code repositories can be read as infrastructures, including several thousand repositories simply called test. But many of them, ranging from operating systems such as Linux to code libraries for managing cloud-based deployments (puppet, chef, etc.) present a range of different namings. Some names represent generic practices – blog, web, data, test. Others symbolise highly valued platforms – liferay-portal or edx-platform. Some index individual configurations of practice – dotfile and homebrew repositories usually store individual software developers' configuration files, a log in effect of how

Infrastructures in name only? 383

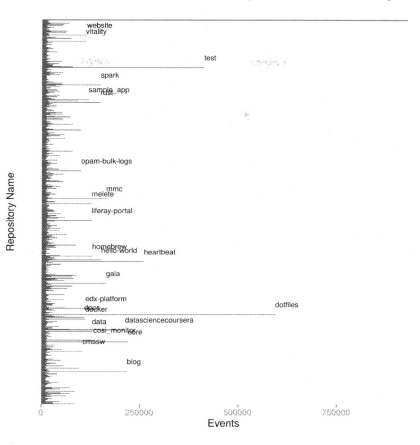

Figure 28.1 The most popular repositories on Github in 2014

they arrange an equipmental totality to work on code. Finally, another set of names, such as rust, a systems programming language, spark, an 'engine' for large-scale data processing, docker, a platform to build, ship and run distributed applications, and heartbeat, a system for monitoring web systems and services, designate current infrastructural practices as points of identification.

Names as cluster points

Every name condenses associations between people and infrastructures. For instance, on Github, the names of code repositories when fully specified have a number of components. Take the 70,000 or so repositories whose names include the term JQuery. JQuery is a software library that supplies code for the buttons, animations, dynamic menus, etc. that we associate with interactive web pages (for instance, for buying a train ticket online). JQuery's popularity amongst web developers – more than 50 per cent of all websites were making use of it in 2012 (W3Techs 2012) – arises from the way that it allows web pages written in HyperTextMarkupLanguage (HTML) to be programmatically manipulated as a set of named elements. JQuery subjects the screen as a set of named elements subject to operations. Statements written using JQuery operate to generate text and graphics that people read, scroll, click and select. This relatively banal example of how a page becomes a field of named entities exemplifies a much more general tendency. In the much more obviously infrastructural operations of Amazon Web Services Elastic Compute 2 (AWS EC2), something similar appears. The approximately 21,000 Github repositories relating to AWS EC2 delineate a great range of concerns, but nearly all offer ways of naming, addressing and configuring instances of linux services operating in Amazon's data centers. Since they use different programming languages – Haskell, Ruby, Python, Java or Javascript, many different naming conventions permeate these repositories, but all of them invoke the operation of infrastructural elements in AWS EC2: disks, clusters, nodes, databases, servers and services spin up and spin down.

How does a cluster of 70,000 JQuery repositories or 20,000 AWS EC2 repositories take shape? Many repositories differ from each other *only* in name. Some thousands of the jQuery repositories clone the primary jQuery/jQuery (or the jQuery Foundation's primary jQuery repository). Such repositories differ only through the name the person or organisation with whom they are concatenated. Despite this imitation, the fully qualified naming of things is an important preoccupation in contemporary infrastructural semiosis. In the case of Github, every repository has a unique proper name, even if it directly clones another repository. Nomination combines a person or organisation and a thing, device, system, convention, protocol or infrastructure. The base name for all the copies of JQuery is jquery/JQuery. The left-hand part of the name is a person or an organisation, in this case, the JQuery organisation or the jQuery Foundation, while the right-hand part points to a repository containing code that inevitably points to many further named elements. The full name of a repository always combines a person or organisation (BBC, Google, Twitter, WhiteHouse, torvalds, etc.) and a thing (jQuery, bootstrap, linux, dotfile, etc.). Thus the fully qualified name of repository inextricably points in more than one direction. It does not index or symbolise either people or things but always a concatenation of organisation/person and device/thing. Such concatenations are familiar in science and technology studies accounts of technologies and scientific knowledges (relations between people and things, for instance, lie at the base of actor-network theory accounts of translation and displacement (Callon et al. 1983) or human–machine configurations (Suchman 2006)). Their sheer repetition does, however, intensify and thicken contemporary infrastructures in two specific ways: by linking infrastructural operations to subject positions; in combinatorial variations.

Infrastructures in name only? 385

The very operation of the thing/device/system/framework/protocol/tool/technique and the position assigned to the subjects who make statements about the infrastructure come much closer together and indeed mingle in code. Strictly speaking, the subject position marked by the left-hand end of a Github repository name overflows the / that separates it from the body of code that addresses devices or systems on the right-hand side. The situation here is captured well in Michel Foucault's account of the constituting and generating operations of statements in *The Archaeology of Knowledge*:

> In each case the position of the subject is linked to the existence of an operation that is both determined and present; in each case, the subject of the statement is also the subject of the operation (he who establishes the definition of a straight line is also he who states it; he who posits the existence of a finite series is also, and at the same time, he who states it); and in each case, the subject links, by means of this operation and the statement in which it is embodied, his future statements and operations (as an enunciating subject, he accepts this statement as his own law).
>
> (Foucault 1972: 94–95)

Repositories comprise sequences of statements instituting the operating limits, the patterns of inscription and transcription, the regularities and usages that position subjects in infrastructures. These statements take effect, or implement something, only through the coincidence that Foucault describes here. The subject of the statement is also the subject of the operation. This is reminiscent of more recent accounts of performativity and things, but the embodiment of the operation in the statement – and effectively I am suggesting that the repository name refers to such statements – also mobilises future statements and operations. How so, in terms of what happens on Github repositories?

The combinatorial repetition and imitation of repositories also thickens infrastructures through small variations and combinations. While several thousand repositories directly clone jquery/jquery, the remainder vary from it. The vast majority of the repository names in which jquery appears also contain some other name. Composite names comprise much of the proliferating variation that combines jquery with other things. For instance, names such as:

jquery-postcode-anywhere
jquery-bingsearch
select2-json-php-mysql-bootstrap-jquery
jquery-django-formset
twitter-jquery-plugin

designate a range of compositions occurring around jquery, ranging from postal address systems (postcodes) through web search engines, layers in the Internet stack (web servers, databases, web frameworks) and social media platforms. This sample of composite names is by no means representative since much of the compositional semiosis around jquery pivots on individual elements of web page user interfaces such as forms, menus, scrollbars and so on. Whether they stick closely to the graphic display of text and image or range more widely into the linkages between infrastructural layers, the combinatorial variation that begins to appear in these repository names operates much more widely in mobilising infrastructures. Imitative and combinatorial fluxes run across the millions of repositories on Github just at this banal level of repository names and naming.

'DevOps' and continuous deployment: when operating becomes naming

Other more fine-grained imitative and combinatory fluxes run much more deeply through the elements of coding, configuring, maintaining and repair work going on in the code. The workings of deeper imitative fluxes are not easy to see in repository names. They might be discerned by selecting from amongst the millions of named repositories on Github some of those that relate not so much to the design and development of software but to its deployment, maintenance and repair. Amidst the millions of repositories on Github, disrepair and abandonment are extremely common. Many repositories contain a few items uploaded on some date. Others have not been touched for months or years. Some repositories on Github, however, show almost continuous patterns of contribution (developers adding or modifying the code). Others, perhaps fewer again, are not only often modified but constantly copied.[5] As we have seen earlier, the copying of a repository through the operation of forking or cloning is extremely common amongst developers as they diagrammatically construct services, platforms, devices and architectures. The many repositories containing names such 'dot' or 'dotfiles' or 'conf' do something similar at the level of individual developers' development configuration. That is, they ensure a common and stable development environment for software developers amidst the many different configuration options possible (in relation to editors, compilers, file systems and various elements of the infrastructure that have to be rendered locally operable so that development for larger-scale deployments can occur).

Some copying does not feed into code development. It is cloning for operational deployment. So-called 'DevOps' – development-operation – repositories expand infrastructural nominalisation beyond software development. They blur the line between making and operating. The operation of infrastructures, its day-to-day adjustments, work-arounds, contingencies and frictions, intersects with the making or development of the infrastructure. Perhaps the most straightforward example of a DevOps repository would be github/Github. The repository is not publicly visible on Github, yet its existence underpins the ongoing life and dynamism of Github as a social coding platform. github/Github names Github itself. As the several hundred developers employed by Github add, modify, or repair elements of the platform

Infrastructures in name only? 387

itself, their changes flow into the operation of Github through continuous deployment routines that draw down changes from the github/Github repository onto the operating code of the Github platform. DevOps – development operations – blurs the line between making and running, between designing and maintaining. We could also identify much more mundane versions of DevOps processes occurring in many repositories on Github.

DevOps repositories often contain specialised code focused on the deployment of devices, systems, other software, services and platforms. This specialised information is itself subject to generalisation by virtue of its nominalisation, a process that gathers a range of attributes together and provisionally freezes it or renders it more substantial. Configuration repositories abound on Github because they allow the often intricate configuration details of contemporary software systems to be replicated quickly. Given that the scale of much information infrastructure is predicated on replicating the same thing multiple times, these configuration repositories reposition the management of infrastructure much closer to software development (e.g. a data center might be understood as a collection of identical computers linked together in ways that permit their processing to be coordinated and divided in many different ways; 'identical' here, however means managed through processes of replication).

'DevOps' refashions infrastructures through continuous deployment. It does this by eliding differences between making and operating and by extending the code namespace, with all its combinatorial variations, to include deployment. This extending nominalisation is a striking feature of such infrastructures, and one that may affect the mode of existence of infrastructures more generally. Different infrastructural figures such as 'the platform', 'the stack', 'deployment' and 'build' intersect with various organisational, aesthetic, ethical and commercial regimes of engagement. A combination of different materials ranging from images, texts, cloud or distributed computing services, various database and search engines, through to code repositories with their groups of contributors comprise the loose but interwoven infrastructures typical of such platforms. They hold together in relational patterns that arise from recursive practice.

Conclusion

The compound names generated by NSA-O-Matic resonates for us today because information infrastructures expand combinatorially. I have been suggesting that the flux of names in all their combinations and variations thickens or stacks contemporary infrastructures, and accretes subject positions associated with that deepening. Whether mundane or sublime, I have been suggesting that names and naming practices help us practically engage with the full-stack complexities of contemporary infrastructures. Names in their linkages of people and devices, of 'dev' understood as a person, the software developer, 'dev' as a common abbreviation for device, and 'DevOps' as development operation flow widely and deeply in contemporary software development. They attest to different and often overlapping movements. The imitative fluxes of names point to processes of replication and copying that propagate devices, protocols, standards and things in various configurations. I suggested that in contemporary information infrastructures, the form of the stack presents one organising axis of this propagation. But this layered architecture is viscously mixed in the concatenated names of many of the repositories on Github. Both the replication of particular forms – linux, jquery – and their mutating combination can be seen in the repository names.

Names not only provide a methodological traction on the infrastructural flux associated with software and coding practices, giving us some sense of the relative centrings and the predominant infrastructural rituals of our worlds. Nominalisation operates generatively in several different senses. First of all, the very act of naming every collection of code, code that may or may not do something in the world, implies an increasing addressability of diverse bodies of code. This addressability supports and engenders what I have been calling, loosely following Peirce, nominalisation of infrastructure. Second, the expansion of what is called a code repository to include almost any aspect of the structure, configuration, documentation, and deployment work associated with contemporary infrastructures means that the same combinatorial composition that structures bodies of code can generalise to include the deployment and operation. Third, this nominalisation of infrastructure is somewhat indifferent to distinctions between making and using, between design and deployment, and indeed to differences between what people and devices do. Across all of these distinctions, naming and calling by name operate interchangeably, sometimes addressing a subject, sometimes addressing other kinds of being. This indifference or redrawn difference between people and infrastructures generates a constant unfurling deployment in time and space. It lends itself to replication and variation, to changes in scale and variations in configuration, and combinatorial expansion. DevOps epitomises one highly distilled version of the nominalisation of infrastructure.

Notes

1 In 'Pragmatism in Retrospect: A Last Formulation', C. S. Peirce writes, 'by semiosis, I mean ... an action, or influence, which is, or involves, a cooperation of *three* subjects, such as a sign, its object, and its interpretant, this tri-relative influence not being in any way resolvable into actions between pairs' (Peirce 1955: 282). He goes on to note that the interpretant, the entity affected by an encounter with a sign is not necessarily a person, although it is easier to think about semiosis in terms of people.
2 Code and coding have been widely discussed as making contemporary infrastructure what it is. The conceptual genealogies I draw on include science and technology studies accounts of information and scientific data infrastructures (Bowker 2005; Edwards et al. 2011), as well as anthropological accounts of software in terms of recursion and freedom (Kelty 2008; Coleman 2012) (although it lies quite a long way from debates about open vs closed source code, the debate that

monopolised attention to software during much of the last decade) and connections between network infrastructure and contemporary urban experience (Graham and Marvin 2001; Thrift 2014).
3 The practices of working with code repositories on Github are quite complicated, and not the focus on discussion here. The advent of the git approach to the management of code has led to a very wide-ranging set of changes in the production of code, and Github has become the 'largest code repository on the planet' (Git 2014) by centralising some of these shifts. Software engineering researchers have taken a keen interest in these repositories precisely because they seem to offer access to how software is actually built (Takhteyev and Hilts 2010; Thung et al. 2013).
4 The stack comprises a diverse range of materials that could include storage systems (disk drives), servers, network resources, hardware specificities, data models and database architectures, business and transactional logics, software frameworks that connect elements of systems and architectures together, user interfaces including how screen elements such as graphics, interactive devices and text operate together. The first four layers of this stack, for instance, would be dominated by linux kernel versions, since the Android operating system, which has the largest installed base, is a version of linux. Or, if we turned from handheld devices to supercomputers, 97% reportedly use linux. This is clearly a repository of no little significance. While apache is perhaps less well known, it has for over a decade now has served the largest share of websites (around 40% or 340 million sites in January 2015 (*Netcraft* 2015)).
5 Detecting repositories on Github that display this continuous development is not straightforward and involves some use of digital methods. In this case, I made use of the GithubArchive.org datasets as published in the Google BigQuery GithubArchive dataset. See https://bigquery.cloud.google.com/dataset/githubarchive:github.

References

Beniger, James R. (1986) *The Control Revolution: Technological and Economic Origins of the Information Society*. Cambridge, MA: Harvard University Press.
Bowker, Geoffrey C. (2005) *Memory Practices in the Sciences*. Cambridge, MA: MIT Press.
Bowker, Geoffrey C. and Susan Leigh Star (1999) *Sorting Things Out: Classification and Its Consequences*. Cambridge, MA: MIT Press.
Callon, Michel, Jean-Pierre Courtial, William A. Turner and Serge Bauin (1983) "From Translations to Problematic Networks: An Introduction to Co-Word Analysis". *Social Science Information* 22(2): 191–235.
CJFE (2015) "Snowden Digital Surveillance Archive". https://snowdenarchive.cjfe.org/greenstone/cgi-bin/library.cgi.
Coleman, Gabriella (2012) *Coding Freedom: The Ethics and Aesthetics of Hacking*. Princeton, NJ: Princeton University Press.
Edwards, P. N., M. S. Mayernik, A. L. Batcheller, G. C. Bowker and C. L. Borgman (2011) "Science Friction: Data, Metadata, and Collaboration". *Social Studies of Science* 41(5): 667–690.
Foucault, Michel (1972) *The Archaeology of Knowledge and the Discourse on Language* (trans: A. Sheridan). New York: Pantheon.
Galloway, Alexander R. (2004) *Protocol: How Control Exists After Decentralization*. Cambridge, MA: MIT Press.
Gillespie, Tarleton (2010) "The Politics of "Platforms"". *New Media & Society* 12(3): 347–364.

Git (2014) "Git". http://git-scm.com/.
Google (2015) "Bidding Farewell to Google Code". *Google Open Source Blog*. http://google-opensource.blogspot.com/2015/03/farewell-to-google-code.html.
Graham, Stephen and Simon Marvin (2001) *Splintering Urbanism: Networked Infrastructures, Technological Mobilities and the Urban Condition*. London: Routledge.
Guardian News (2015) "The NSA Files". www.theguardian.com/us-news/the-nsa-files.
John, Nicholas A. (2013) "Sharing and Web 2.0: The Emergence of a Keyword". *New Media & Society* 15(2): 167–182.
Kelty, Christopher (2008) *Two Bits: The Cultural Significance of Free Software*. Durham, NC: Duke University Press.
Mackenzie, Adrian (2006) *Cutting Code: Software and Sociality*. New York: Peter Lang.
Netcraft (2015) "January 2015 Web Server Survey". http://news.netcraft.com/archives/2015/01/15/january-2015-web-server-survey.html.
Peirce, Charles Sanders (1955) *Philosophical Writings of Peirce*. New York: Dover.
Suchman, Lucy (2006) *Human and Machine Reconfigurations: Plans and Situated Actions*, 2nd edn. Cambridge: Cambridge University Press.
Takhteyev, Yuri and Andrew Hilts (2010) "Investigating the Geography of Open Source Software Through GitHub". http://takhteyev.org/papers/Takhteyev-Hilts-2010.pdf.
Thrift, Nigel (2014) "The "Sentient" City and What It May Portend", *Big Data & Society* 1(1): 1–21.
Thung, Ferdian, Tegawendé F. Bissyandé, David Lo and Lingxiao Jiang (2013) "Network Structure of Social Coding in GitHub". Paper presented at the Software Maintenance and Reengineering (CSMR), 17th European Conference, Genova, 5–8 March. http://ieeexplore.ieee.org/xpls/abs_all.jsp?arnumber=6498480.
W3Techs (2012) "jQuery Now Runs on Every Second Website. Web Technology Surveys". http://w3techs.com/blog/entry/jquery_now_runs_on_every_second_website.

29 How knowledge infrastructures learn

Geoffrey C. Bowker

Introduction

What, or indeed when (Engeström 1990), is an infrastructure? For some, the word conjures the built world – all that is crumbling in the United States ... roads, railway systems, bridges. For others, it evokes something more shimmery – information. Of course, information infrastructures are still highly material (Dourish and Mazmanian 2013): the "cloud" takes form as massive, squat server farms built in cold climes to allow for efficient cooling, cables snaking along the ocean floor (Starosielski 2015), electronic parts assembled in dire working conditions in the global south.

This chapter is about knowledge infrastructures.[1] I define knowledge infrastructures as the network of institutions, people, buildings, and information resources which enable us to turn observation and contemplation of the world into a standardized set of knowledge objects: journal articles and monographs. At the very instauration of the scientific revolution, Francis Bacon (1952 [1620]; cf. Siskin and Warner 2010) remarked that knowledge production was much like any other form of production: "The productions of the mind and hand seem very numerous in books and manufactures. But all this variety lies in an exquisite subtlety and derivations from a few things already known, not in the number of axioms." And indeed one of the founding texts of science studies is entitled *The Manufacture of Knowledge* (Knorr-Cetina 1981). Just as factories require physical infrastructure (roads, railways, canals, plants), so do institutions of knowledge production (information infrastructures, libraries, campuses).

The central arguments I make in this paper are that we have created since the Enlightenment a vast knowledge infrastructure (KI), that it is in the process of fundamental change, and that its "learning process" is double: adapting to our new socioeconomic forms and experimenting with new cognitive divisions of labor and new forms of knowledge expression in tune with this adaptation.

When is an infrastructure?

To apply the word "knowledge" to infrastructure may seem a trifle eldritch. Concepts apply when they can do work in answering a particular question: I argue here that exploring how knowledge institutions learn is centrally about understanding infrastructure.

Star and Ruhleder's (1996) canonical definition of infrastructure is a good starting point. In the diagram below, produced in collaboration with Florence Millerand, the definition is arrayed along two axes:

The list within the circle is an array of social and technical, global and local factors in a state of dynamic tension. Crucial for understanding all infrastructure is that their design space is one of distributing qualities along these axes. Here I am interested in the moment of transition between one infrastructure and another. The x-axis depicts the central design access. Qualities necessary for an infrastructure to function can be configured differently along it. Thus to the extent that one builds on an installed base (for example, adopt the generatively entrenched (Wimsatt and Schank 2004) QWERTY keyboard for computer keyboards) there is less pressure on learning, enabling a simpler transition from typewriters to computers than adopting Dvorak (schools for teaching how to use typewriters can carry skill sets across for teaching word processors). Inversely, if one breaks with the installed base (for example, untethering a telephone from its dialing roots to make it a smart

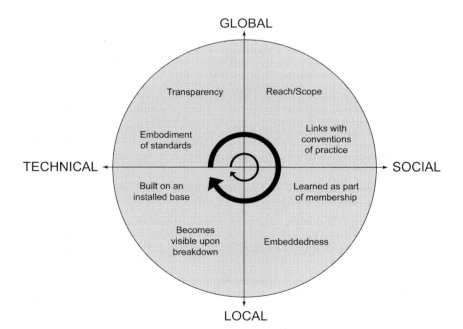

Figure 29.1 Diagram of infrastructural dimensions

phone involving new sets of skills) then more emphasis must be placed on learning it as part of membership in the emerging community, where it links to conventions of practice. Thus, the developing genre of smart phone texting involved in the first instance a proliferation of different patterns of communication as well as a whole new use for thumbs. For some groups it is now rude to call before texting; for others, one calls first and texts later. One can, as in Latour's (1988) case of the door closer choose to enforce an infrastructural standard by building it into the infrastructure (for example, auto-saving word processing documents) or, as in the early days of the personal computer, exhorting people to save their documents every five minutes.

Once the die is cast, the infrastructural choice seems inevitable: however, at the point of emergence a highly complex project of social design is going hand in hand with a similarly complex project of technical design in order to produce a seamless sociotechnical infrastructure (cf. Jensen and Winthereik 2013). To put this in actor-network terms, the old, stable product of technology/society emergent from a well-established set of mediations is being replaced by a new product, which profoundly reconfigures both. After the transitional period, the new product will again seem inevitable, natural.

This is precisely why it is so useful to consider what is happening in the academy today in terms of new knowledge infrastructures. It is not just about the vast and complex technical effort of digitizing the world's books, publishing online, creating new modes of knowledge preservation; it is a vast and complex social project of deciding which qualities to sink into the technical (by which I mean both the physical and the bureaucratic) infrastructure and which to assign to the knowledge producer, the academic. At this moment, then, we have the ability to rethink the nature of knowledge production as simultaneously, inextricably, a social and a technical enterprise. We are beyond the age of system builders (Hughes 1993) in infrastructures: this work is being done at all levels of the emergent new infrastructure by a highly heterogeneous set of actors/actants.

This does, of course, beg the question of why we should do so. There is certainly a crisis in the academy in general: transition to short-term contract work; death of the humanities (and not in the benevolent garb of the emergence of the posthuman); the turn to practical knowledge (the eternal quest for "broader impacts" so beloved of the National Science Foundation), and so forth. One can argue in a number of fields that the work of the academic is divorced both from public discourse and public utility – Dourish (2006) noted that the field of Computer Supported Cooperative Work produces "implications for design" which lie fallow as the work of design plows on regardless.

However, there is an optimistic reading of the changes we are going through. There is the possibility of imagining and instantiating a new cognitive division of labor. During the Enlightenment there were also a project to simultaneously produce new kinds of knowledge product (the Encyclopedia), new configurations of knowledge work (the development of disciplines, or the x-ologies, as Serres (1995), so beautifully designates them), and the construction of new buildings and institutions. Yet the transition between new knowledge infrastructures is as rare in human history as the transition between new information infrastructures (the list, the book, the computer). Seen thus, the current historical epoch is one where we can rethink the social and the technical through knowledge infrastructures. There is no Designer directing this from on high: the new KIs will emerge from a complex, messy process which we academics are inevitably engaged in; and an understanding of the nature of the game can render that engagement fruitful. In time with the change in the nature of the knowledge product and the organization of knowledge work, new economic models for scholarly activity (such as funding and publishing) are being developed. The Enlightenment project was never completed in its pure form. The exclusive categories of knowledge proposed by Ampère and Comte did find their ways into the architecture of the university but never fully determined the nature of academic discourse. Similarly, our new knowledge infrastructure will never achieve its *terminus ad quem*; however, some delineaments of the new forms are already discernible.

The knowledge product

On February 24, 2014, *Nature* reported: "The publishers Springer and IEEE are removing more than 120 papers from their subscription services after a French researcher discovered that the works were computer-generated nonsense." The proximate culprit was a program called SciGen, developed at MIT to prove that conferences and journals would accept gobbledegook work. Cyril Labbé, who detected the fakes (not through reading, but through an algorithm similar to Turn-it-In) had increased his own h-factor in Google scholar by seeding the academic world with his own automatic writing. On April 3, 2015, *Science* reported on the serious use of these papers – rather than demonstrating a flaw in our academic system they exploited it. The current best solution is indeed algorithmic: "SciDetect is a program to automatically detect papers created with SCIgen and similar programs. Its purpose, according to Springer, is to "ensure that unfair methods and quick cheats do not go unnoticed." For a science studies reader, this was not an unwelcome sight – after all we had been accused by Alan Sokal (2000) during the science wars of not being able to tell the difference between rubbish and insight in our assorted forms of relativism and postmodernism.

What both the *Nature* and *Science* examples together suggested was that the problem of algorithmic publication lay not with the disciplines per se, but with the current state of the work of reading. A sample piece of prose from one of the offending papers – dubbed "context free" by *Science* – asserts: "After years of compelling research into access points, we confirm the visualization of kernels. Amphibious approaches are particularly theoretical when it comes to the refinement of massive multi player online role-playing games." While it is possible to provide an interesting reading of this (Jacques Lacan studied the intricacies of automatic writing), the inevitable conclusion is that the social practice in a core part of our knowledge infrastructure, the peer review and publication process, is under severe pressure.

What is wrong with reading is that it takes time, a commodity in scarce supply for academics and publishers. This story is not an astounding fact about a particular algorithmic hoax but it says a lot about the temporality of our knowledge infrastructure. Our publication cycles are ever more rapid. Many academics piece apart their papers into LPUs (least publishable units) so that, rather than produce carefully reasoned works containing rich arguments, they publish hither and yon snippets of findings which in some notional database could be assembled into something resembling a coherent text. In many disciplines we write algorithmically. Though there are far too few studies of reading practices in academia, there are a number of fields in which methods sections are simple algorithmic productions which no one reads in depth – they at most scan to see if the references are there. The same goes for a number of literature reviews. Academic papers in this dark vision take the form of pure commodities, circulating in an ever-more rapid space and time. Put this way, it is relatively clear that our knowledge infrastructure partakes of the same complex sociotemporality as the world around them. The fakes work so well because we both write and read algorithmically.

It is easy to read these remarks as a standard *o tempora, o mores* complaint. However, that would be to miss Star and Ruhleder's (1996) point that it's infrastructures all the way down (each infrastructure is embedded and builds on an existing one). I would like to propose a more positive reading: the new knowledge infrastructure we are forging, and the new knowledge products which will result, are integrally part of our broader socioeconomic infrastructure: they both mirror and reflect on it.

To give an historical example of this integration, Alfred Sohn-Rethel (1975) in a classic article suggests that the spatiotemporal framework of Galilean absolute space and time emerges from a reflection on the state of the economy. Emergent capitalism (and I know I am risking a Sokal moment here) created the commodity form, and within that form the ideal was that capital and commodities should flow in a frictionless time and space. Sohn-Rethel's analytical move here is to show that we think with and through our socioeconomic infrastructures. Another example is afforded by David Deutsch (2013), who is one of a number who have maintained that our theories of the brain have followed the succession of the hydraulic (grand dams being written by Freud into the fabric of our brains) to the telephone switchboard (in the 1920s) to the computer (today, with our binary neurons, firing ones or zeros into the substrate of the brain). Sadly, he also follows his forebears in his argument that this time we have got it right – the brain and the universe really *are* computers. When we take the products of our academic labor as independent entities, which are removed from the complexity of socioeconomic life, we make precisely the mistake of assuming that our institutions could possibly exist as ivory towers, as if they had ever done so. The knowledge infrastructure aligns with and meditates on the set of infrastructures within which it is embedded. This is why changing a knowledge infrastructure is about a lot more than developing new digital libraries and databases to allow us to deploy the methods that we know and trust, it is fundamentally about engaging with and understanding the social and the political.

One way of understanding the shift to which we are witness is to see it as a move from a world of the spatial organization of knowledge to one of temporal organization. Manuel Lima (2014) has demonstrated vividly the spread of trees as representational forms over recent centuries – and especially since the early nineteenth century. This is the century of the triumph of what Patrick Tort (1989) has called classificatory reasoning – we used to think the world through classification systems. The grand natural history surveys and the great national censuses emerged at the same epoch and deployed the same methodologies – the tools of classification and its associated bureaucratic technologies (so beautifully described by Yates 1993) deployed the same technologies. The tools of empire were the tools of science, since the knowledge infrastructure was embedded so deeply in the sets of practices inscribed in the information and economic infrastructures of the control of nature. With the rise of algorithmic reasoning through big data, it is no surprise that we get equally from the computer evangelist (Anderson 2008) and the social theorist Latour (2002) a call for an end to theory, where theory is understood as classificatory reasoning. For Latour, the argument goes that we are moving beyond the world of Durkheim, whose sociology has reified categories such as "society," "gender," "class" and "race." Rather than seeing these as fixed categories in the world, we can examine the variable collectivities that operate at any one instance in any one place. We only needed the categories as theoretical units when we did not have access to all the data. Anderson's argument is much the same, though dressed in different garb. He was drawing on algorithmic analysis of behavior though big data as superseding categories. Marketing firms no longer need to know what "middle-class women" want, if they have access to each of us individually. The map is indeed co-extensive with the territory. Nick Seaver (2015), studying music recommender systems, has shown *in fine* that this lack of supervenient classification is how the algorithms that help shape our taste work. Natasha Dow-Schüll (2012), examining the extreme example of gambling in Las Vegas, has shown how the new form of social engineering can operate precisely as a Skinnerian black box – we really do not need to know what is going on "inside" the brain of the gambler, we only need to be able to predict individual behavior.

There are only two kinds of people who find the speed of light too slow. The first is the cosmologist, the archetypal pure scientist, who would like to be able to see further back into the putative origin of the universe. The other is the trader, who moves her offices ever closer to Wall Street to gain femtosecond advantages over her competitors, relying on electrons travellng over wires at achingly slow rates. At first blush, this is a pretty paradox: viewed infrastructurally it is of the essence of our enterprise. Algorithms inherently act in time (first do this, then that, then you get the result), without codified knowledge laid out in a table. As we move into the world of the algorithm we necessarily temporalize out knowledge in new ways.

Our emergent knowledge infrastructure, then, necessarily learns from the rich new social, organizational and economic forms that we are creating. Again, it is not the task of a system builder to make this so – rather, it is of the nature of our knowledge enterprise that it will "learn" from the network of infrastructures it is integrated into.

Interlude

There is a strong argument, then, that our deeply embedded knowledge infrastructure aligns well with our information and economic infrastructures. A corollary is that, as our epochal shift in knowledge and information infrastructures is taking place across many levels simultaneously, we are not yet locked in through generative entrenchment to some of the troubling forms discussed thus far. Academics are fully aware of the contradictions between a reading culture generated for a community of a few thousand "gentleman scientists" scattered across Europe and the dizzying proliferation of disciplines and journals we are witnessing today.

New forms of knowledge infrastructure, involving a new cognitive division of labor and new knowledge objects are proliferating in this rich space. New alignments can emerge from the complex sociotechnical spaces within which these are developed.

The division of cognitive labor

Andrew Abbott's (1988) work on the system of professions demonstrates the rise in the late nineteenth and twentieth centuries of a particular kind of social and cognitive arrangement, which is as true of our disciplines as it is of our commercial life. To be a successful profession, he argues, one needs to draw a ring around a certain "problem," develop a relatively impenetrable specialist language for describing and addressing it, and then, from within the sheltered black box of professional discourse, issue forth findings and dicta which have authority for acting in the world. A classic example is the colonization of the emergent psychiatric profession by a neuro-chemical understanding of disorders. The language developed came in the form of a classification system (the DSM), which had to be adopted if you wanted full infrastructural alignment between insurance companies (who would pay your bills), governments (who would accept your policies), and academics (many psychology departments have driven Freud from the halls of academe, such that the only acceptable language which worked across this set of resonating infrastructures was that of the triumphant sect).

The great potential of the current moment is to re-imagine the engines of knowledge production in ways which produce new forms of alignment. Jonathan Zittrain has spoken eloquently about this[2]; I shall adopt the phrase the division of cognitive labor to describe the move. A core term here is "crowdsourcing." Let us walk through the hierarchy. The simplest form is to assume that the "wider public" has little to nothing conceptual to add to our knowledge enterprise. Rather, they can do work which our underfunded public institutions do not have resources to carry out. Thus in the humanities, we have the Bentham project, which crowdsourced digital renderings of the manuscript writings of utilitarian philosopher Jeremy Bentham – so that humanist scholars in the university were presented with a machine-searchable oeuvre which they could deploy to do their cognitive work.[3] Not least of which would be the development of a form of "distant reading" (Moretti 2013): a new form of reading which did not entail laborious following of sequential text but produced new kinds of analysis freeing one from the need to read at all (and thus, in infrastructural terms, tame the massive information surplus which the computer has given us all). So a new distribution of labor and a new form of reading combine to produce potentially new knowledge forms. Slightly more cognitive distribution occurs with the GalaxyZoo[4] project in science, where the public are asked to lend in performing a work of classification: "To understand how galaxies formed we need your help to classify them according to their shapes. If you're quick, you may even be the first person to see the galaxies you're asked to classify." There is an ironic twist here, in that "when computers were women" (Light 1999) the project in hand was the Hubble sky survey of the early twentieth century. In these forms, there is deployment of an information infrastructure in order to maintain a traditional division of labor – the novelty being that what was once to be carried out within the university as institution can now be distributed much more broadly. In this picture, the university becomes a coordinating center for a much broader enterprise. The Enlightenment buildings start to crumble.

As do the walls of the university library – when complete collections are online, one no longer needs to apply for a library card to gain access to a wide literature. However, there is a significant caveat here: the publishing houses that live through copyright are firmly aligned with the old KI – information and knowledge should flow freely within the academy (a hallowed institution, where the normal rules do not apply). While it is already disruptive socially to engage a new form of information processing and knowledge production, it is as much a social and economic as a technical question whether it can succeed.

The possibilities are indeed fertile, though there are as yet few instantiations. There are a vast number of well-trained (one hopes) people with bachelor's degrees who would be delighted to do more than transcribe and count. There are an increasing number of PhDs moving out into industry or into alternate careers who are just as qualified as those in the academy to produce genuinely new knowledge: one design task is to find ways to create new kinds of knowledge engine which would allow them to deploy their cognitive skills to the fullest through continuing contributions to knowledge production.

One example is the Public Lab,[5] with the designated goal:

> The Public Laboratory for Open Technology and Science (Public Lab) ... develops and applies open-source tools to environmental exploration and investigation. By democratizing inexpensive and accessible Do-It-Yourself techniques, Public Lab creates a collaborative network of practitioners who actively re-imagine the human relationship with the environment.

The core Public Lab program is focused on "civic science in which we research open source hardware and software tools and methods to generate knowledge and share data about community environmental health." This is a genuinely new kind of knowledge production, which may feed into a university discourse, but does not assume that the universities themselves are the sole arbiters of knowledge: particularly when they do not produce knowledge of immediate local concern. Increasingly, the Quantified Self community is taking on the role of producing new kinds of medical knowledge through networks of data mavens who measure everything about their own bodies (through Fitbit and other devices) and through information pools create new ways of knowing about their own health. (One could argue, of course, that this falls into the Latour–Anderson trap of asserting that large-scale social categories are not necessary (for a passionate counter-argument, see Žižek (2000)): but it is a welcome reminder that with our emergent knowledge infrastructure we must address head on the nature and role of theory). This is the rosy-eyed version of the story. The dark side is researchers who flee academia, with its human subjects restrictions, for the open arms of industry, who have no such historical shackles: the Facebook A/B experiment is a *locus classicus*. In this, the feeds of FB users were weighted with positive or negative emotions in order to see how this affected the emotional state of the user. This truly dark project curiously endeavored to garner retrospective legitimacy through being published in the pages of *Science*.

My fundamental argument here is that the emerging new knowledge infrastructure is learning how to deploy information technology in a rich way unimaginable in the past to democratize the process of knowledge production. This is potentially quite different from the development of academic research laboratories within organizations (a feature of much science and social science over the past 150 years).

New knowledge objects

The author, it has been argued (Culler 1983), is an invention of the printing press – certainly copyright was invented (and as Johns (2009) reminds us "piracy" was invented soon after its deployment). Jerome McGann (2014) gives a magisterial analysis of the ways in which we can reinterpret classical literature – for example, the work of Edgar Allan Poe – by situating it within a much wider literary framework that decenters the lone creator. He also writes about the difficulty of instantiating these new forms of understanding: you need enormous financial resources, or perhaps a crowd, to create a new information infrastructure within which new forms of reading are possible.

The myth of the single author is the single most damaging relic of the Enlightenment knowledge infrastructure. The author is the person who produces knowledge and signs their name and affiliation at the top of the manuscript, as indeed I have done for this article. However, we need new forms of knowledge production and consumption if we are not to be buried alive in a blizzard of bits and bytes. Within management circles there is a move to go beyond the endless linearity of email, which is the bane of many of our lives, and create new kinds of sites for organizational work – for example, Slack.[6] Similarly, within the academy, we need to move beyond the paper or monograph as primary product. Again, this involves new kinds of alignment. The developers of the *Vectors* journal[7] put together graphic artists, database designers, and topic specialists to produce a new form of publication. Core here was the role of the database. In a number of fields the integration of argument, dataset, and in some cases analytic tools allows for much richer knowledge expression than papers which refer to other papers to be mined in a traditional academic library.

Indeed, one can conceptualize this new set of alignments by seeing the database and not the linear text as the core academic product; and the interface to the database as being a core site of design. If we are working together on a shared database rather than separately on producing texts, then we develop a new paradigm for knowledge dissemination. And this is precisely one of my central arguments: there is a seed here which may in the future seem inevitable, but at the present moment seems difficult because, in true Lacanian fashion, many of us are inhabiting an academia which seems "stuck." The development of new forms of knowledge expression is one form of unblocking: it depends on new forms of interaction and discourse.

Towards new knowledge infrastructures

The positive re-imagination of the university involves embracing the possibilities of new cognitive divisions of labor and new kinds of knowledge object. It is the nature of knowledge infrastructures, as with all other infrastructures, that their change involves complex sets of social alignment which must accompany the technical.

Which brings us directly to the issue of social complexity. There is no clear path that moves us from the current state of our knowledge infrastructure to some desired future state. To some extent, the solutions are, as ever always, already out there. I could proliferate examples of both of the core tendencies sketched above.

Althusser's concept (1969) of "combined and uneven development" was forged in a completely different context – the desire for a move from a knot of socioeconomic conditions (industrial capitalism) to a new set, seen as liberating – provides a good model for the ways in which our new knowledge infrastructure is learning. The motor force in his case – and I would argue for the case of knowledge – was a determination, in the last instance, of all superstructural forms (culture, arts, we would add today our relationship with the environment) by economic forces. However, he argued, a set of alignments at the level of superstructure could combine to form a conjuncture fundamental change emerged in a non-linear fashion. In this paper, I have argued for both a single motor to our changing knowledge infrastructure and for recognition of the role of contingency.

Those more accustomed to new media speak might recognize the arguments that the underdeveloped world could leapfrog the stages of infrastructural development (telegraph to telephone to cell phone) by moving directly from the mail system to cellular networks. Or again, in environmental terms, the promise of Elon Musk to allow Africa to vault directly (via batteries which capture renewable resources) into a radically new sociotechnical configuration without necessarily passing through the endless coal-fired power stations that litter the Chinese landscape. In a sense, the leapfrog is easier than the steady march, because the superstructural elements can have moved far ahead of their base and thus they pull the infrastructure and its social forms in one fell swoop. Where these historicist arguments largely fell to the ground was in another Althusserian argument: the cultural lag. Thus, Russia in 1917 vaulted, but the figure of Tsarist rule has remained unchanged – from the early days through Gorbachev and now Putin. Or again, in Chinese terms, there is the massive continuity of the empire in and out of the revolutionary period.

Which leads to the question of agency. There is a rich discourse on innovation from the edge discussing the new knowledge creation forms developing from gaming cultures such as World of Warcraft. John Seely Brown[8] sees these as the model which we must adopt in order to transform our organizational cultures. However, just because there are good exemplars out there – as I have tried to show for both the division of cognitive labor and the imagination of new knowledge objects – does not mean that we can click our heels together and hope that the world will change.

There is no one pathway forward when the tectonic plates of our knowledge infrastructure are shifting so uncertainly. Through continued experimentation, we can hope to create genuinely new forms of knowledge supported by new cognitive divisions of labor and expressed through new knowledge objects. There will surely be cultural lag. However, through play and experimentation it is possible for academics, working with non-traditional actors (be they members of the public; or, for many humanists, graphic artists and database designers) to contribute to the process through which our emergent knowledge infrastructure is learning to adapt to, express, and explore new socioeconomic forms.

Notes

1 http://knowledgeinfrastructures.org/.
2 www.youtube.com/watch?v=cnEL4aAAjgo.

3 www.ucl.ac.uk/Bentham-Project.
4 www.galaxyzoo.org/.
5 http://publiclab.org/about.
6 https://slack.com/is.
7 http://vectors.usc.edu/issues/index.php?issue=7.
8 www.youtube.com/watch?v=RZG6WTRP-6E.

References

Abbott, Andrew Delano (1988) *The System of Professions: An Essay on the Division of Expert Labor*. Chicago, IL: University of Chicago Press.

Althusser, Louis (1969) *For Marx*. New York: Pantheon Books.

Anderson, Chris (2008) "The end of theory: The data deluge makes the scientific method obsolete," *Wired Magazine* 16(7).

Bacon, Francis (1952 [1620]) *Advancement of Learning. Novum Organum. New Atlantis*. Chicago, IL: Encyclopædia Britannica.

Culler, J. (1983) *On Deconstruction*. London: Routledge and Kegan Paul.

Deutsch, David (2013) "Constructor theory," *Synthèse* 190: 4331–4359.

Dourish, P. (2006) "Implications for design," paper presented at the CHI 2006 Proceedings, Design: Creative & Historical Perspectives, Montreal, Quebec, April 22–27.

Dourish, P., and M. Mazmanian (2013) "Media as Material: Information Representations as Material Foundations for Organizational Practice," in Paul R. Carlile, Davide Nicolini, Ann Langley and Haridimos Tsouka (eds) *How Matter Matters: Objects, Artifacts, and Materiality*. Oxford: Oxford University Press, pp. 92–118.

Dow-Schüll, Natasha (2012) *Addiction by Design: Machine Gambling in Las Vegas*. Princeton, NJ: Princeton University Press.

Engeström, Yrjö (1990) "When Is a Tool? Multiple Meanings of Artifacts in Human Activity," in Yrjö Engeström, *Learning, Working and Imagining*. Helsinki: OrientaKonsultit Oy.

Hughes, T. P. (1993) *Networks of Power: Electrification in Western Society, 1880–1930*. Baltimore, MD: Johns Hopkins University Press.

Jensen, Casper Bruun and Brit Ross Winthereik (2013) *Monitoring Movements in Development Aid: Recursive Partnerships and Infrastructures*. Cambridge, MA: MIT Press.

Johns, Adrian (2009) *Piracy: The Intellectual Property Wars from Gutenberg to Gates*. Chicago, IL: University of Chicago Press.

Knorr-Cetina, K. (1981) *The Manufacture of Knowledge: An Essay on the Constructivist and Contextual Nature of Science*. Oxford: Pergamon Press.

Latour, Bruno (1988) "Mixing humans with non-humans: Sociology of a door-closer," *Social Problems* (special issue: Sociology of Science) 35(3): 298–310.

Latour, Bruno (2002) "Gabriel Tarde and the End of the Social," in Patrick Joyce (ed.) *The Social in Question: New Bearings in History and the Social Sciences*. London: Routledge, pp. 117–132.

Light, Jennifer S. (1999) "When computers were women," *Technology and Culture* 40(3): 455–483.

Lima, Manuel (2014) *The Book of Trees: Visualizing Branches of Knowledge*. New York: Princeton Architectural Press.

McGann, Jerome J. (2014) *A New Republic of Letters: Memory and Scholarship in the Age of Digital Reproduction*. Harvard, MA: Harvard University Press.

Moretti, Franco (2013) *Distant Reading*. London: Verso.
Seaver, Nick (2015) "The nice thing about context is that everyone has it," *Media, Culture, and Society* 37(7): 1101–1109.
Serres, Michel (1995) "X-Ologies," in Michel Serres and Michel Authier, *A History of Scientific Thought: Elements of a History of Science* (transl. from the French). Oxford: Blackwell.
Siskin, Cliff and William Warner (2010) *This is Enlightenment*. Chicago, IL: Chicago University Press.
Sohn-Rethel, Alfred (1975) "Science as alienated consciousness," *Radical Science Journal* 5: 65–101.
Sokal, Alan D. (2000) *The Sokal Hoax: The Sham that Shook the Academy*. Lincoln, NE: University of Nebraska Press.
Star, S. L. and K. Ruhleder (1996) "Steps toward an ecology of infrastructure: Design and access for large information spaces." *Information Systems Research* 7(1): 111–134.
Starosielski, Nicole (2015) *The Undersea Network*. Durham, NC: Duke University Press.
Tort, Patrick (1989) *La raison classificatoire: quinze études*. Paris: Aubier.
Wimsatt, W. C. and J. G. Schank (2004) "Generative Entrenchment, Modularity and Evolvability: When Genic Selection meets the Whole Organism," in G. Schlosser and G. Wagner (eds) *Modularity in Development and Evolution*. Chicago, IL: University of Chicago Press, pp. 359–394.
Yates, JoAnne (1993) *Control through Communication: The Rise of System in American Management*, vol. 6. Baltimore, MD and London: Johns Hopkins University Press.
Žižek, Slavoj (2000) *The Fragile Absolute, or, Why is the Christian Legacy Worth Fighting For?* London: Verso.

Index

Abbott, Andrew 397
Aboriginal communities, government support for campaign to shut down 69–70; *see also* Indigenous Australia, infrastructure reform in
Abram, S. and Weszkalnys, G. 61n2, 292, 355
Acer, Yücel 271
Acheson, Dean 31
action, problem of 352–64; actions and outcomes 352–4, 361–2; Calls to Action 353; past action, concerns about paucity of 353–4
activism: civic activism 108–9, 111; free culture activism 141–2; open-source activism 142, 145
actor-network theory 6, 323, 346, 367, 384, 393
Adas, Michael 32
Aegean crisis, infrastructural failure and 271–81; Aegean Sea region, characteristics of 271; arrivals on Lesvos 277; asylum-seeking 271–2; border control policies, Dublin Regulation and 280–81; boundaries 274–5; crisis, definitional variation about nature of 272; European Central Bank (ECB) 279, 280, 281n12, 281n14; European Neighbourhood Policy (ENP) 277–8; European Union (EU) 271–2, 280, 281n1; external borders, pressures on 278; Greece: financial problems of (and crisis of movements of people) 272–4; referendum in 278–80; International Monetary Fund (IMF) 279; ISIS/ISIL/Daesh 277; Lesvos (July 2015) 276–80; perfect storm on 279–80; Mediterranean trade routes 275; Middle East conflict, flight from 271–2; territory as controlled and coherent physical space 274–5; Turkey, refugee problem for 272–4
African Development Bank 290
Agamben, Giorgio 285–6, 287–8
Agar, Jon 376n9
agency: agencements, focus of actor network theory on 323; agential work of infrastructures 228; knowledge infrastructures, learning for 401; nonhuman agency, question of 256
Agrawal, Arun 311
Akrich, Madeline 36, 254
Alexander, C. and Reno, J.O. 206
Alexander, General Keith 379
Alexanderplatz, Berlin 286–7, 290–91, 292, 294n10; Berliner Verlages, Haus des 291; future transformation, anticipation of 290–91; Haus des Reisens 291; master plan for (I-B4a) 291–2; Platz im Wartestand 290–91; square suspended 290–91
algorithms, actions of 396–7
Ali, S.H. 244
Allen, Barbara L. 244
Althusser, Louis 35, 400–401
Altman, J. and Hinkson, M. 69
Altman, Jon 72n3
Amazon: data centres 384; Web Services Elastic Compute 2 (AWS EC2) 384
Amin, Ash 104
Amoore, Louise 302, 303
Ampère, André-Marie 394
Anand, Nikhil xi, 4, 9, 35, 41, 88, 91–101, 196, 205, 227, 254m 302, 358
Anderson, Chris 396
Anderson, Kevin 180
Andersson, Ruben 278
Angell, Elizabeth 190–93

Index 405

Anglican Church Missionary Society (CMS) 72n7
Anindilyakwa Land Council (ALC) 67–8, 73n10
Anthropocene 175, 178, 182–5, 242–3, 248–9, 249–50
anthropology 6, 10, 13, 35–6, 103, 115, 145, 175, 182–5, 292, 310–11, 332; cultural anthropology 157; cybernetic anthropology 359; of energy and infrastructure 203; gesture in anthropological theorizing 285–6; of infrastructures 162–3, 200, 238, 268–9, 305; development of 88; intervention and planning, anthropological analysis of 355; knowledge and "rights," studies on 310; medical anthropology 313; seismic landscapes, anthropological thinking on 162–3; without infrastructure 47–8
Anwar, Nausheen 79, 85n4
Appadurai, Arjun 175
Appel, H., Anand, N. and Gupta, A. 162, 274
Appel, Hannah 292
Aradau, Claudia 359
Arendt, Hannah 10
Arens, Richard 44
Aristotle 285
Asanov, Nakyt 297
Asdal, K. and Hobæk, B. 113n4
Ashley Madison (dating website) 16, 18n10
Association of Southeast Asian Nations (ASEAN) 78, 80; ASEAN Summit (2004) 76–7
asylum-seeking 271–2
Atambaev, Almazbek 304
Atlas project in Madrid 141–2, 143, 144, 145, 154
atomic bomb testing (and deployment) 242–3
automation 177, 180; automated data processing 374–5
Autonomous Decentralized Transport Operation System (ATOS) 116, 120, 121, 122, 123, 124–5, 125–6, 126n10
Ayto, John 28, 30, 36n2
Ayurveda 313

Bacon, Francis 391
bacteria 230–32; bacterial adaptation 248; sludge and, interactions between 232

Bainbridge, B. and Saroeun, B. 240n2
Baku-Tbilisi-Ceyhan (BTC) oil pipeline 189, 194–5
Bangemann, Martin 376n6
Bangkok: indigenous water management in 222–3; water infrastructure 223–4
Bannock, G., Baxter, R.E. and Rees, R. 34
Barad, Karen 163, 169
Barker, J., Keane, W., Redfield, P., Lins Ribeiro, G., Wiener, M. and Barker, J. 42
Barker, Joshua 4
Barnett, Colin 69
Barnhart, Robert K. 36n4
Barry, Andrew xi, 28, 158, 159, 168, 170, 174, 187–97, 275, 287, 376n7
Bastéa, Eleni 281n10
Basurama architectural collective 141, 145, 146–7, 150, 151
Bateson, Gregory 359
Batt, William H. 27, 34
Baxstrom, Richard 292
Bear, Laura 6–7, 60, 358
Beck, Ulrich 113n3
Bélanger, Pierre 244
Belbasi Nuclear Monitoring Center 189
Beniger, James R. 12, 380
Benjamin, Solly 92
Bennett, Jane 64
Bentham, Jeremy 398
Berg, Marc 12–13
Berg, Paul C. 32
Bergbäck, B. and Lohm, U. 247
Bergesen, A. 135
Berkeley Earth Surface Temperature project 344
Berlin: citizens' workshop (Park Inn, Alexanderplatz, Berlin) 284–5, 291–2; *see also* Alexanderplatz, Berlin 284–5, 291–2
Bhagavad Gita 243
Bierbaum, R. et al. 346
big data 16; knowledge infrastructures 396; machinic operations 372
Bigo, Didier 304
Bijker, W.E., Hughes, T.P. and Pinch, T.J. 253
bio-filters, marshy lakes as 233–4
biocides, dispersal of 248
biodiversity: resource depletion and 358; rewards of 317–18; UN Convention on Biological Diversity (CBD, 1992) 310, 317–18
biodiversity databasing in India 309–20; Biodiversity Register 310, 313, 314,

315, 316, 318, 319, 320n3; bioprospecting and emergent nature/culture 310–11; botanization 314–15; classification, politics of 317–18; Forest Research Institute (FRI) 314–15, 317–18; Foundation for the Revitalization of Local Health Traditions (FRLHT) in Karnataka 313–14; herbarium work 314–15; Human Genome Initiative 309; infrastructural inversion in biodiversity 309–10; National Biodiversity Act (NBA, India) 310; plant collection 314–15; scientific and local knowledge, incommensurability between 313, 320; Uttarakhand State Biodiversity Board 314, 315, 319; *vaidyas* 314–15, 316, 319
biotech labs 260–61; GM controversies and 259–62
biotechnology: bananas, beta-carotene biofortification of 260, 261, 262; genetically modified organisms (GMO) 213, 255, 259–60, 262
Bishop, Mandi 377n32
Biswas, Sas 318
black list in Russia: apparatus of determination 298; infrastructural capacity 298–9; listing 299–302, 303; speculation, space of 299–300
Blair, Tony 366
Bloch, A. and Schuster, L. 296
Blok, A. and Farías, I. 108
Blok, A. and Jensen, T.E. 102
Blok, A, and Meilvang, M.L. 102, 107, 108, 111, 112–13n1
Blok, A., Nakazora, M. and Winthereik, B.R. 9
Blok, Anders xi, 4, 89, 102–14
BMC (procedure BMC *mein bana diya*) 93, 95, 96, 97
Boellstorff, Tom 18n3
Boltanski, L. and Thévenot, L. 255, 258–9
Booth, Charles 328–9
Borjomi-Bakuriani region, water circulation in 194–5
Born, Georgina 188, 192, 196, 196n1
Borras, Jr., S.M., Kay, C., Gómez, S. and Wilkinson, J. 41
Bossen, C. and Markussen, R. 254
Bowker, G.C. and Star, S.L. 41–2, 163, 309, 318, 339–40, 377n27, 380
Bowker, G.C., Baker, K. Millerand, F. and Ribes, D. 376n14, 376n18, 377n23

Bowker, Geoffrey C. xi, 3, 4, 11, 12–13, 16, 17, 42, 48, 104, 163, 170, 227, 228, 232, 255, 256, 309, 317–18, 337–8, 388–9n2, 391–403; interactions and mediation, insights on 232
Boyer, D. and Morton, T. 184
Boyer, Dominic xii, 4, 157, 158–60, 174–86, 199
Boyle, Robert 256–7
Braddick, M.J. 293–4n2
Branco, Rafael 284
Brand, Stuart 359
Brass, Paul 313
Braun, Bruce 287
Brennan, Sean 377n26
Brenner, N. and Schmid, C. 132, 134
Broeders, Dennis 302
Broto, V.C. and Bulkeley, H. 105
Brown, John Seely 401
Brown, Michael F. 310
Brown, Wendy 275, 278
Brummelhuis, Han ten 217
Brush, Stephen 310
Brutsaert, Wilfried 219
Brynjolfsson, Erik 376n1
Bulkeley, Harriet 346
Bulkely, H. and Castan-Brotó, V. 362
bureaucracy: bureaucratic inertia, tendency towards 256; bureaucratic neologism, infrastructure's status as 32; computation, bureaucracy and 368; ecologies in beta 149
Burgett, B. and Hendler, G. 28
Burkett, P. and Foster, J.B. 176
Busch, Lawrence 340
Butler, Judith 51, 304

Calkins, Sandra xii, 213, 253–65
Callon, M. and Latour, B. 17
Callon, M., Courtial, J.-P., Turner, W.A. and Bauin, S. 384
Callon, Michel 253, 323, 325, 359
Calls to Action, climate change and 353
Campbell, Jeremy M. 3
Canadian Journalists for Free Expression (CJFE) 379
capital: automated machinery and 176–7; bourgeois capitalist order 176, 180; capitalist production, contradictions inherent in dynamics of 286–7; durability of 176–7; labor and capital in Marxian formulation 175; movement toward automated machinery 176–7; neo-capitalism, waste management as

form of 245; productive capital 286–7; propulsive force of capitalism, notion of 285; social overhead capital, synonym of 33–4
carbon democracy 178–9; *see also* energy
carbon emissions 356, 357, 362
carbon epistemics, infrastructure and revolution 178–82
Carroll, Patrick 15
Carse, Ashley xii, 5, 9, 23, 25–6, 27–39, 163, 168, 170, 233, 236, 240, 244, 359
Castells, Manuel 87
Castro, Juan José 29
catastrophes, assignment of responsibility for 10
Caucasus 188–9, 194, 195
Centralized Traffic Control (CTC) system in Tokyo 120, 126n10
CFE (Mexican para-statal power utility) 181–2
Chalfin, Brenda 9
Challenger space shuttle launch 10
Chandavarkar, Rajnarayan 95
Chandra, Veena 315, 317
Chao Phraya Delta, Thailand 215–25; Chao Phraya Dam, transformative effect of 217, 219; delta hydrology, van der Heide's report on 218; drainage basin 215–17, 218–20, 220–22, 224–5; flood-adaptive infrastructures 216–17; Greater Chao Phraya Irrigation Project 217, 218; human settlements, impossibility of 217; hydrographic patterns 222; rainfall flows 215–16, 221; rice cultivation, expansion of 218; terrestrializing the delta 217–18, 223–4; urban ecosystems 223–4; urban stream syndrome 221–2; urban watershed 222–4; water management 218, 221
Chaplin, Charlie 236
Chatterjee, Partha 98, 313
Chervin, Robert 346
Chevron Texaco 289–90
China-US geostrategic priorities 70
Chorley, Richard J. 216, 220–21
Chu, Julie 302
King Chulalongkorn 217
Churchill, Winston S. 31–2
Cirac Claveras, Gemma 342
cities: ecologies in beta 150–51; generic references 130; low-carbon and resilient cities 103; *see also* Bangkok; Berlin; Copenhagen; Jakarta; Madrid; Maputo; Tokyo, Vientiane

Ciudad Escuela 151–2
civic activism 108–9, 111
civic infrastructures 9
Clark, N. and Hird, M.J. 248
Clark, Nigel 168
classification: classification systems 396; politics of 317–18; taxonomies, invention of 317
Clifford, Nick 215–16, 220
climate change: Calls to Action and 353; digital technologies and, multiple relationships between 356–7
climate knowledge infrastructure 339–49; application program interfaces (APIs) 340; climate knowledge, production of 343; downscaling techniques 347; El Niño/La Niña cycle 341, 343; evolution of knowledge infrastructures 340–41; gateways 33–40, 348; Global Climate Observing System (GCOS) 342–3; global knowledge 344–6; global trends, knowledge of 346–7; infrastructure development and change 339–40; Intergovernmental Panel on Climate Change (IPCC) 344–6; internetworks 340, 342–3; knowledge infrastructure defined 339–41; national weather observing systems 342; Réseau Mondial 342; sociotechnical systems 340; telegraph, weather mapping and 341–2; usable knowledge, downscaling and production of 346–9; weather patterns 341–2; World Meteorological Organization 342; World Weather Watch 342–3
Clogg, Richard 275
co-operative landholdings, membership of 56–7
co-residence 324, 326, 332
code repositories 381, 382–3, 384–6; combinatorial repetition and imitation of 385–6; operational deployment 386–7
Coelho, Karen 100n8
cognitive labor, division of 397–9
Cole, G.D.H. and Postgate, R. 327
Coleman, Gabriella 382, 388–9n2
collaboration: collaborative ontic work, engagement with 152–3; strategic mobilization of collaborators 141–2
Collard, K. S., D'Antoine, H., Eggington, D., Henry, B.R., Martine, C. and Mooney, G. 73n10
Collier, S.J. and Kemoklidze, N. 255

Collier, S.J. and Lakoff, A. 28, 61n1
Collier, Stephen J. 33, 358
colonialism/postcolonialism in Indian biodiversity 312–13, 315–16
Comaroff, J. and Comaroff, J. 60
command and control, distribution of 121
Common Information Model (CIM) data 348
community involvement, by-pass of 59–60
commuters: autonomy for, loss of 117; consumer/individual and 122–4; demand, surges in 120–21
compartmentalization 115–16
compromise, achievement of 258–9
computer simulation, modeling and 343–4
computer technology, integration into urban infrastructures 115
Comte, Auguste 394
Coninck, P., Seguin, M., Chornet, E., Laramee, L., Twizeyemariya, A., Abatzoglou, N. and Racine, L. 244
Connolly, William E. 146, 188, 192, 196, 196n1
construction techniques, deficiencies in 68
Consumer Price Index 328–9
consumption, prioritization of 326
Cooper, Frederick 27, 32
Copenhagen 102–4, 106, 107, 108–9, 111–12; Climate Action Plan 102, 107–8; University of 1–2; wind turbine story, leveraging of 103–4, 110–11
copyright, piracy and 399–400
Coronil, Fernando 55
Corsín Jiménez, A., Estalella, A. and Zoohaus Collective 145
Corsín Jiménez, Alberto xii, 88–9, 104, 112, 141–56, 228, 363
cosmetic change 77–8
cosmograms 108
cosmology 396
cosmopolitics 109–10
Courain, Margaret E. 342
Coutin, Susan 296
Covenant of Mayors, European Parliament (2010) 352–3
Cowen, Deborah 28, 34, 65, 66
Crang, M. and Graham, S. 146
CRESC (Centre for Research on Socio-Cultural Change) 1–2
Cross, J. and Street, A. 201
Cross, Jamie xii, 158–9, 198–209
Crutzen, P. and Stoermer, E.F. 242

Culler, Jonathan 399
Cyprus, territorial dispute in 275

Dag Hammarskjöld Foundation 34
Daipha, Phaedra 343
Dalakoglou, D. and Harvey, P. 358
Dalakoglou, Dimitris 79
Daly Herman 359
Darwin, geostrategic position of 70–71
data: Amazon data centres 384; automated data processing 374–5; big data 16, 372, 396; biometric data-gathering, effects of 303; capture of, datasets and 371–2; computerized data analysis models 344; data capture, datasets and 371–2; data reservoirs 16; exploration of 312; global data image, assembly of 344; infrastructural technologies and 371–2; metadata 153, 312, 348; Network Common Data Form (netCDF) data 348; performativity and emergence as integral to database 311–12; smart infrastructure, analyses of 115–16, 117; structured and unstructured 370–72, 374, 376
databasing projects 313–14; see also biodiversity databasing in India
Davis, Mike 138, 243
de Boeck, Philip 4
de la Cadena, Marisol 10–11
de Soto, Hernando 48n2, 49n7
Dean, Warren 286
debate around infrastructure 253–4
decentered perspectives 228, 237–8
decentralised infrastructures 200–203
decentralization under neoliberalism 60–1
decentralized control 340
decomposition of infrastructure projects 68–9
DeLanda, M. 196
Delanty, G. and Rumford, C. 277–8
Delbourgo, J. 206
Deleuze, G. and Guattari, F. 13, 18n7, 253
Deleuze, Gilles 6, 116
deportability, deportation and: global deportation regime 296; infrastructural dimensions of deportability 296–7, 298–9; infrastructural indeterminacy and 296, 298, 301–2, 303; surreptitious deportation 299; uncertainty and 301–2
depth and scale, effects of 379–89; Amazon data centres 384; Amazon Web Services Elastic Compute 2 (AWS

Index   409

EC2) 384; Canadian Journalists for Free Expression (CJFE) 379; configuration repositories 387; continuous deployment, 'DevOps' and 386–7; Github.com 381–2, 383, 384, 385–6, 386–7, 388, 389n3, 389n5; Google 381; BigQuery GithubArchive dataset 389n5; HyperTextMarkupLanguage (HTML) 384; inscription and transcription, patterns of 385; JQuery 383–4; linking, naming and 380–81; networked communication and knowledge, scale of 379–80; nominalisation of infrastructure 380, 381–2; NSA-O-Matic 379–80, 381, 387–8; operational deployment 386–7
Derrida, Jacques 168–9, 234, 246–7
Deutsch, David 395
development economies 32–3
development projects, formulation of 52
Deville, J., Guggenheim, M. and Hrdlickova, Z. 190
Dewey, John 110, 111, 113n5
Diaz, Francisco 181–2
digital determinacy, potential of 302–3
digital infrastructures 14, 335–8, 367–8; digital technologies 357–8; infrastructures 14; technical mediation through 367; *see also* action, problem of; depth and scale; downscaling; knowledge infrastructures; machinic operations
digital technologies: climate change 357–8; smart infrastructure 115–16, 117; software development, history of 367; solutions for climate change and 356
Dilling, L. and Lemos, M.C. 348
discarded objects, pre-industrial disposal of 243–4
disciplinary society 116
disruption, politics of 367–9
distributed autonomy 120–21, 122, 123, 124, 125–6
Dittmer, J. 193, 196
DNA structure, discovery of 259
Dodd, N. 275
Dodds, L. and Hopwood, B. 244
Dombrowski, Kirk 73n11
Domesday Book 325
Donne, John 242
Donovan, Kevin P. 35, 36
Doshi, Sapana 100n6
Dossal, Mariam 95

Douglas, I. and Lawson, N. 248
Douglas, Mary 11
Douglas-Jones, Rachel 225
Dourish, P. and Mazmanian, M. 391
Dourish, Paul 393
Dow-Schull, Natasha 396
drainage basin 215–17, 218–20, 220–22, 224–5
dramaturgical resources 142–4
Drotbohm, Heike 296
drying, problem of 231–2
Dunn, E. and Cons, J. 297, 303–4
Durkheim, Emile 48, 87, 88, 120, 396

earth 187–96; earth system sciences 346; earthquakes 188, 190–92; forces of, radical uncertainty about 162; geophysical events 188; geophysical research in Georgia, infrastructure of 193–4; infrastructure 188; Kandilli Observatory in Istanbul 189, 192–3, 195; contemporary importance of 189–90; Marmara Earthquake (1999), consequences of 190–92; Marmara Sea seismic monitoring stations (MARNET) 189; North Anatolian seismic fault 189–90, 192–3, 195; seismic landscapes: eruptive capacity of 168; turbulent forces within 166; surface water run-off 194–5
earthquakes 188, 190–91; earthquake politics 191–2; responding to 164–5
Easterling, Keller 28, 135, 244, 246, 250
ecologies 61; drainage basin as ecological unit 220–22; ecological rationality, water flows and 222; ecological systems services 163
ecologies in beta 141–55; Atlas project 141–2, 143, 144, 145, 154; city liberated 145–7; *Ciudad Escuela* 151–2; collaborative work 141–2, 152–3; Community Gardens 151–2; contractual forms, authority of 148; Critical Object-Accumulation 141; dramaturgical resources 142–4; ecology in beta, notion of 145; infrastructural imagination 144–5; Madrid School of Drama Studies 141; Open Badges technology 151, 155n2; open-source (F/OS) software 145–6, 147, 151; open-source infrastructures 147–9, 151; re-sourcing, notion of 144–5, 149–50, 152; science and technology studies (STS) 153; sentient and

ambient intelligences 146; visual and iconographic systems 148; Zuloark architectural collective 141, 142, 143, 145–7, 150, 151
economics, economies and: agricultural economies, changes in 41; development economies 32–3; economic growth, infrastructural investment and 51; economic integration, European Economic Community (EEC) and 31–2; economic measurement 325; economic organization 34; economic rationality 136; European Central Bank (ECB) 279, 280, 281n12, 281n14; Exclusive Economic Zone (EEZ) of São Tomé and Príncipe 284, 285, 287, 288–9, 290, 294n3; geo-engineering, economics and 244; money flows 53–4, 58; neoliberal economics 330; Scheer, economic philosophy of 182–5; solar energy (and economy) 183–4; stock markets, weighting of 65–6; *see also* illicit economies
ecosystemic relationships 363
Eden, Frederick Morton 327
Edwards, Paul N. xii–xiii, 7, 11, 35, 42, 78, 174, 189, 253, 255, 256, 335–6, 339–51, 376n11
Edwards, P.N. and Schneider, S.H. 345
Edwards, P.N., Bowker, G.C., Jackson, S.J. and Williams, R. 162–3
Edwards, P.N. et al. 257, 340
Edwards, P.N., Jackson, S.J., Chalmers, M.K. and Calvert, S. 174, 340
Edwards, P.N., Mayernik, M.S., Batcheller, A.L., Bowker, G.C. and Borgman., C.L. 388–9n2
Egami, Setsuko 123
Egyedi, T. and Spirco, J. 340
Egyedi, Tineke 340
Einsiedel, E., Jesoe, E. and Breck, T. 244
El Niño 341; Southern Oscillation 343
Elden, Stuart 245, 274
Elias, Norbert 285
Elyachar, Julya 9, 35, 203
enclosures 116–20
Energiewende (renewable energy transition) in Germany 182
energo-metabolic substrate in Marxist theory 176, 180
energy: battery-powered LED lanterns 198; distributive politics of 204–5; electrification 178, 180–81; micro-electronic goods, fragility of 203; off-grid energy 198–208, 200, 201, 203; battery-powered LED lanterns 198; hopefulness of 207; investments in 208; Papua New Guinea, Begasin Hills in 198, 199, 203, 207; photovoltaic panels 201; role of 200; Scotland: off-grid communities in 206–7; small-scale hydro-electric system in 204; solar electricity, infrastructural architecture for 201; solar-powered systems 198–9, 202; systems in disrepair 198–9; on/off the grid 203–5; renewable energy systems 105–6, 111, 159, 181–2, 183–4, 207, 352; solar electricity, infrastructural architecture for 201; solar energy (and economy) 183–4; Yonki hydroelectric dam 198
Engels, Friedrich 176
Engestrom, Yrjö 391
engineering 7, 10, 30–31, 52
Enlightenment 242–3
enunciation 371; double binding of 373–5
Environment Remediation Holding Company (ERHC) 288
environmental infrastructures 2; degradation of, concerns over 221–2
Environmental Protection Agency (EPA) 248
Eppler, Søren 352–3, 355, 363n3
eruptive magma 164
Escobar, Arturo 32, 65
Estalella, Adolfo xiii, 88–9, 141–56
ethnography 25, 36, 40, 41, 48, 52, 60, 92, 93–8, 126n1, 128, 160, 163, 168, 170, 199, 203, 208, 228, 254, 267–70, 276–80, 293, 302–4, 305, 324–5; of climate change mitigation 353, 354–5; comparative ethnography 158–9; of emergent practice, need for 332; multi-sited ethnographic work 104–5
Eurasian Customs Union 304
Eurogroup (Troika) 278, 279–80
European Central Bank (ECB) 279, 280, 281n12, 281n14
European Economic Community (EEC) 31–2
European Neighbourhood Policy (ENP) 277–8
European Union (EU) 31, 268, 275, 303, 305, 356, 360–61; Aegean crisis, infrastructural failure and 271–2, 280, 281n1; external borders, pressures on 278; inside and outside of, blurring

distinction of 277–8; biodiversity data-basing in India 312; external border regime 296; FP7 programme 356
Evans, Grant 76, 78
evidence, infrastructures of 254–5
evidence-making 253, 257; modes of 256; testing of 261–2
Exclusive Economic Zone (EEZ) of São Tomé and Príncipe 284, 285, 287, 288–9, 290, 294n3
expectation 10–11; waves of anticipation and 146–7
experimental alignments 134
experimental method 256–7
experimental projects 309, 311–12, 319–20
experimentation, notion of 152–4
expertise 76, 77, 78, 81, 83, 84–5n3

Facebook A/B experiment 399
Farias, Ignacio 190
Federal Migration Service (FMS, Russian Federation) 297–8, 299, 301, 302, 304
Feinstein, Senator Dianne 379
Feldman, Gregory 302
Fennell, Catherine 4
Ferguson, James 33, 78, 136, 355
Ferme, Marianne 274
fetishes as infrastructure 78–80, 83
Fisch, Michael xiii, 12, 16, 88, 115–27, 297
Fleck, Ludwig 256, 257
Fleming, K.E. 275
flood-adaptive infrastructures 216–17
fluid dynamics 219
forced relocations 69–70, 296
Forest Research Institute (FRI) 314–15, 317–18
Forrest, Andrew 72n8
Foucault, Michel 6, 14, 28, 48, 110, 113n5, 116, 138, 368, 385
Frank, Andre Gunder 34
free and open-source (F/OS) software 145, 147, 151
free culture activism 141–2
Frutos, Juan Manuel 48n3
functionality, indeterminacy and 119–20
Furlong, Kathryn 35

Gad, C. and Lauritsen, P. 15
Gad, C., Jensen, C.B. and Winthereik, B.R. 115, 126n1
Gad, Christopher 18n8, 225

Gaia 171, 172n12
Galison, Peter 16
Galloway, Alexander R. 130, 139n2, 380
Gannushkina, Svetlana 298
García, Jacobo 141–2
Gates, Bill 244
Gates Foundation 260, 261
gateways 339, 340, 348
Geels, F. and Schot, J. 358
Geels, Frank 357–8
Geertz, Clifford 285
gelatinization process 176
generic cities 128–39
genetically modified organisms (GMO) 213, 255, 259–60, 262
geo-engineering, economics and 244
geomorphology 216, 220–21
geophysical events 188–9; research in Georgia, infrastructure of 193–4
geothermal extraction 164–5
geothermal metabolic processes 162
gesture, infrastructure as 284–94; Alexanderplatz, Berlin 286–7, 290–92, 294n10; Chevron Texaco 289–90; citizens' workshop (Park Inn, Alexanderplatz, Berlin) 284–5, 291–2; infrastructures in gestural form, effects of 285; pausing, gesturing and 292–3; São Tomé and Príncipe (STP) 286–7, 287–8, 289–90, 294n7; joint development zone (JDZ) 289–90, 294n3, 294n5, 294n7; sustaining force of gesture, notion of 286; unsustainable material realities 292–3; white elephants 292–3
Gibney, Matthew J. 296
Gillespie, Tarleton 380
Gilman, Nils 32
Gilpin, Alan 34
Github.com 381–2, 383, 384, 385–6, 386–7, 388, 389n3, 389n5
Glass, D.V. 328
Global Climate Observing System (GCOS) 342–3
global climate risks 104–5; see also climate knowledge infrastructure
global knowledge 344–6
globalization, fuel resources and drive towards 182–3
Goffey, A. and Pettinger, L. 376n12
Goffey, Andrew xiii, 336–7, 366–78
Goffman, Erving 285
Google 381; BigQuery GithubArchive dataset 389n5

412 Index

Gorbachev, Mikhail 401
Gordillo, G.R. 246, 247, 249, 250
governance: biopolitical systems of government 95; civic infrastructures 9; climate change as problem of 359; distributed autonomy 120–21, 122, 123, 124, 125–6; governmentality 368; shifting practices of 367; information technologies and governmentality 368; municipal administration, work of 94; municipal government rules 96; neoliberalism and 9; shifting practices of 367
GPS systems 41, 46–7, 48, 49n8
Graeber, David 72n9, 73n10, 203
Graham, S. and Marvin, S. 9, 88, 105, 137, 201, 340, 358, 359, 380, 388–9n2
Graham, S. and Thrift, N. 247
Graham, S., Desai, R. and MacFarlane, C. 196
Graham, Stephen 99
Grainger, Richard 366
Greater Chao Phraya Irrigation Project 217, 218
Greece, financial problems of (and crisis of movements of people) 272–4
Green, Sarah xiii, 267, 268, 269, 270, 271–83, 285
Greenfield, Adam 147
Griffiths, Emma 69
Groeger, Lena 179
Groote Eylandt: and Bickerton Island Enterprises (GEBIE) 67–8; Mining Company (GEMCO) 67; road development on 64–5; watery world of 66–7
Grosz, E. 128
groynes 81, 85n6
guerrilla architectural collectives 145, 149–50
Guldi, Jo 358
Gülen, L., Pinar, A., Kalafat, D. Özel, N., Horozan, G., Yilmazer, M. and Isikara, A. 190, 193
Gupta, A. and Sharma, A. 96
Gupta, Akhil 96, 98, 181, 355
Guyer, Jane I. xiv, 267–8, 270, 323–34
Guyer, J.I. and Peters, P. 331

Haffner, Jeanne 87
Haigh, Thomas 377n24
Halley Mora, Mario 43, 48n3
Hansen, T.B. and Verkaaik, O. 95, 96
Hansen, Thomas B. 99n4
Hanseth, O. and Monteiri, E. 376n16

Haraway, Donna 11, 15, 65, 163, 168–9
Hardt, M. and Negri, A. 126n6
Hardwicke, Major General Thomas 314
Harmsworth, Garth 311
Harsh, Matthew 262
Harvey, David 70, 87, 88, 138, 285, 287
Harvey, P. and Knox, H. 4, 42, 61n2, 61n3, 61n5, 61n6, 99, 100n7, 163, 174, 199, 254, 302, 355, 358, 359
Harvey, P., Conlin Casella, E., Evans, G., McLean, C., Silva, E., Thoburn, N. and Woodward, K. 2
Harvey, P., Reeves, M. and Ruppert, E. 62n10
Harvey, Penny xiv, 1–22, 25, 35, 42, 51–63, 232, 240, 250n1, 302
Hayden, Cori 311
hazardous waste, generation of 245–6
healthcare provision in globalising world 366–7
Healy, S.A. 244
Hearth Tax (1662) 326–7
Hellisheiði geothermal power plant 164
Helmreich, Stefan 100n9, 240
Hengill volcanic zone 161, 163–4, 166–7, 168, 169–71, 171n5
herbarium work 314–15
Hermant, Emile 15
Herzfeld, Michael 275
Hess, David J. 106
Hetherington, Kregg xiv, 7, 23–4, 40–50
Heynen, N.C., Kaika, M. and Swyngedouw, E. 146
Hildyard, Nicholas 61n4
Hinchliffe, S., Kearnes, M.B., Degen, M. and Whatmore, S. 147
Hird, M. J., Lougheed, S., Rowe, K. and Kuyvenhoven, C. 245
Hird, M.J. and Zahara, A. 243
Hird, Myra J. xiv, 212, 215, 242–52
Hirschman, Albert O. 85n4
Hirschon, Renée 275
Hobbes, Thomas 256–7
Hodson, M., Marvin, S. and Bulkeley, H. 105
Hoggan, J. and Littlemore, R.D. 345
Højen, A.R., Rosenbeck Gøeg, K. and Britt Elberg, P. 377n32
Holocene 178, 242, 249
Holt, Hallett S. 29, 36n6
Holzinger, A. et al. 377n29
Hommels, Anique 291
Hooke, Robert 341
Hordijk, M.A. 62n11

Horn, David G. 281n10
Houghton, J.T. et al. 345
household 323–33; co-residence 324, 326, 332; Consumer Price Index 328–9; dependency within household 327–8; family-household model 326–31; financialization of housing 330, 332; formal administrative unit, household as 325–6; 'house=asset' aspect of 'household' 329–31; household as element 324–5; household as focus 323, 324; inter-household transactions 332; owner-occupancy, aspiration to 326; poll tax 327; rates and local taxes 327; rent 328, 330; secularization of registration 325; social aspects of households 332; taxation unit, household as 326–7
Houston Ship Channel 178
Howe, C. et al. 200
Howe, Cymene 4, 181, 199
Hubble sky survey 398
Huber, Matthew T. 179
Hughes, Thomas P. 14, 178, 253, 393
Hull, Matthew 97, 305, 355
Hulme, M. 205–6
human-centered analyses, limitations of 237–8
Human Genome Initiative 309
Humphrey, Caroline 33
Huse, Tone 362
hydraulic fracturing 248
hydrogeology 188–9, 193–5, 222
HyperTextMarkupLanguage (HTML) 384
Hyslop, John 7

illicit economies of infrastructural investment 51–62
indeterminacy 296–306; administrative violation, risk of 300; aleatory sovereignty 304; biometric data-gathering, effects of 303; biometric passports, identity tracking and 301; black list 297, 298–9, 299–300, 299–302, 300, 303; border enclaves 303–4; deportability 301–2, 303; deportation 296, 298, 301–2, 303; surreptitious deportation 299; digital determinacy, potential of 302–3; epidemiological control 297; Eurasian Customs Union 304; Federal Migration Service (FMS, Russian Federation) 297–8, 299, 301, 302, 304; forcible removal 296; functionality and 119–20; global deportation regime 296; indeterminate infrastructures 293; infrastructural dimensions of deportability 296–7, 298–9; of infrastructure 302–4, 305–6; margin of 119; migrant existence, lived reality of 299–300; migration regime, materialization of 296, 298–9; over-stayers 297; passport replacement, obstacles about 300–301; refugee camps 303–4; remittance-dependence 299; Russian migration policy 304–5; seasonal work, nature of living with 300–301; state surveillance 303
Indigenous Australia, infrastructure reform in 64–73; Anindilyakwa Land Council (ALC) 67–8; Indigenous disadvantage, reproduction of 65–6; indigenous dispossession, mining and 65–6; Northern Territory National Emergency Response Act (2007) 69–70; *see also* Groote Eylandt
information (eco)systems 359–61
information infrastructure development, study of 368, 369–70
Information Standards Board for Health and Social Care 372
An Information Strategy for the Modern NHS 1998–2005 (UK, 1998) 367, 373
informational accessibility 16–17
informatised healthcare 368
infrastructural engineering 227–8
infrastructural figures 267–70
infrastructural imagination 144–5
infrastructural inversion, idea of 3–5
infrastructural investment 53–6; continued resonance for 60–61
infrastructural orders 11–14
infrastructure concept, emergence of 28, 29–31
infrastructure of evidence 255, 256, 257, 258
infrastructures of first oil 287–90
Ingold, Tim 354
inhabitable ground, Butler's concept of 51
Innovation, Health and Wealth: Accelerating Adoption and Diffusion in the NHS (UK DOH, 2011) 368
Institute for Rural Welfare (IBR) 43, 44, 46–7, 48n3
Inter-American Development Bank: development, infrastructural intervention and 47; illicit economies of infrastructural investment 52

414 Index

interdependence 275, 318, 325–6, 331, 337, 379–80
Intergovernmental Panel on Climate Change (IPCC) 344–6
International Atomic Energy Agency (IAEA) 195
International Classification of Diseases (ICD-10) 373, 374
International Congress of Navigation (1931) 30
International Energy Agency 199
International Geosphere-Biosphere Programme 242
International Information Board (UK, 2014) 375–6, 377n31
International Maritime Organization (IMO) 72n2
International Meteorological Organization 342
International Monetary Fund (IMF): Aegean crisis, infrastructural failure and 279; gesture, infrastructure as 290; seismic landscapes 164
International Organization for Migration (IOM) 300
internetworks 340, 342–3
irrigation: inundation irrigation 218; irrigation infrastructures 216–17, 217–18; perennial irrigation design and concept of 220
Irvine, Kim N. 240n9
Ishii, Miho 79–80
Ismay, Hastings Lionel 31
Ito, M. and Hideo, Y. 120–21
Izmir, movements of people through 272

Jackson, Michael 293–4n2
Jakarta, Indonesia 128, 129, 130–33, 134; concept, cause and case, equilibration of 132; detaching the city 130–33; experimentation 132–3; hibernation of land 131–2; infrastructural projects, twists and turns in 131; infrastructure, enactment of 131; Kali Baru 133; land, uses of 131–2; land banks 132; mega redevelopment, threat of 133; neighborhood improvement projects 131; neoliberal development 131; planning and budgetary decisions 132; plurality of business possibilities 133; political chess, land in games of 132; *rakyat,* generic notion of the people 131; urbanization, processes of 132
James, Deborah 332

Jansen, Stef 297
Japan International Cooperation Agency (JICA) 81, 227, 229, 231–2, 234, 235–6, 240n3, 240n4, 240n10
Japanese National Railways 120
Japanese Society for the Promotion of Science (JSPS): Chao Phraya Delta, Thailand 225; multinatural infrastructure 240; Vientiane, urban development in 84, 225, 240
Jasanoff, Sheila 260
Jeffrey, Charles 317
Jensen, Casper Bruun xiv–xv, 1–22, 67, 80, 93, 107, 112, 163, 168, 170, 188, 212, 215, 225, 227–41, 302, 323, 362
Jensen, C.B. and Morita, A. 2, 10, 152, 170, 175, 238, 254, 299, 362
Jensen, C.B. and Winthereik, B.R. 4, 12, 14, 28, 49n9, 163, 227, 254, 393
Joerges, B. and Shinn, T. 256
Joerges, Bernward 253
Johansson, Nils 247, 248
John, Nicholas A. 381
Johns, Adrian 399
Jones, Christopher 36
Jousse, Marcel 293–4n2
Joyce, Patrick 100n6
JQuery 383–4
JR East in Tokyo 116, 120, 122–3

Kahrilas, G. A., Blotevogel, J., Stewart, P. S. and Borch, T. 248
Kandilli Earthquake Observatory in Istanbul 189, 192–3, 195; contemporary importance of 189–90
Kankanala, Kalyan C. 313
Kant, Immanuel 119–20, 124
Karaman, O. 191
Karvonen, A. and van Heur, B. 362
Kawakami, Takashi 123
Kelly, Tobias 297
Kelty, Christopher M. 147, 382, 388–9n2
Kendon, Adam 292, 293–4n2
Keynes, John M. (Keynesianism, neo-Keynesianism and) 179, 191
keyword - infrastructure 27–36; infrastructure as keyword 28–9; keywords 29; World Bank 32, 33, 34
Khampiene Inthaluxa 77
Khan, Naveeda 79
Kim, Jaeeun 303
Kim, K. and Owens, G. 248
Kinchy, Abby 260
King, Gregory 328

Index 415

Kirchhoff, C.J., Lemos, M.C. and Engle, N.L. 348
Kirksey, E. and Helmreich, S. 65
Klare, Michael T. 66, 71–2n1
Kleinpenning, J.M.G. 43
Klose, Alexander 340
Kluczewska, Karolina 300
Knorr-Cetina, Karin 391
knowledge: knowledge product 394–7; production of new kinds of 393–4; modern knowledge, critique of 354; preservation of 393; production of 391, 393–4; "rights" and 310; traditional knowledge, infrastructural inversion and 312–13; traditions of, accommodation to 309
knowledge infrastructures 253; adaptation 391; agency 401; cognitive labor, division of 397–9; cultural lag 401; environmental concerns 401; evidence and 255–7; experimentation, need for innovation and 401; Facebook A/B experiment 399; GalaxyZoo project 398; infrastructural dimensions 392–3; Institute of Electrical and Electronics Engineers (IEEE) 394; interlacing of 255–6; learning for 391–402; least publishable units (LPUs) 395; positive re-imagination of 400–401; socioeconomic infrastructures, knowledge infrastructures and 395–6; spatial organization of knowledge 395–6; superstructural forms, determination of 401; temporal organization of knowledge 396
Knox, Hannah xv, 336, 337, 338, 352–65
Kobayashi, Rokuro 81
Kockelman, Paul 13
Kølvraa, C. and Ifversen, J. 278
Koselleck, Reinhart 40, 42
Kowal, emma 65
Krauss, Werner 106
Krell, F.-T. 316
Krishna, V.V. 310, 312
Kristeva, Julia 11
Krock, Arthur 31
Kubal, Agnieszka 299
Kyrgyzstan State Security Service (FSB) 297

Labban, Mazen 249
Labbé, Cyril 394
laboratory regulations, protocols and 253
Lacan, Jacques 394
Ladas, Stephen P. 275

Lakoff, A. and Collier, S.J. 42
Lampland, M. and Star, S.L. 11, 259
Land Reform Act (1969) 56
Landecker, Hannah 253
landfills 243, 245–6; leachate toxicity of 245; mining of 248
Langworth, Richard 32
Lao International Trade Exhibition and Convention Center (ITECC) 77, 82–3
Lao People's Revolutionary Party (LPRP) 76
Larkin, Brian 4, 41, 42, 64, 78, 79, 102, 105, 106, 112, 113n5, 115, 152, 167, 175, 201, 227, 254, 292
Larson, John Lauritz 30
Laruelle, François 130, 134, 137, 139n2
Latham, Michael E. 43
Latour, B. and Woolgar, S. 257
Latour, Bruno 7–8, 10, 11, 15, 102, 104, 108, 109–10, 111–12, 113n5, 119, 126n9, 157, 257, 298, 376n10, 393, 396
Lea, T. and Pholeros, P. 79, 80
Lea, T. and Rollo, S. 70
Lea, Tess xv, 4, 9, 11, 17, 24–5, 64–75
Leavitt, Marisa 225
Lefebvre, Henri 87
LeMenager, Stephanie 179
Lemos, M.C. et al. 348
Lenin, Vladimir Ilich 180–81, 183
Leslie, Charles M. 313
Lessig, Lawrence 145
Lesvos (July 2015) 276–80; arrivals on 277; perfect storm on 279–80; systems failures on 280
Levi-Strauss, Claude 35
Levitus, Robert 68
Li, Tania 41, 47, 48n2
Light, Jennifer S. 398
Lima, Manuel 396
Lindquist, Johan 298–9
Linkenbach, Antje 314
linking, naming and 380–81
Linnaeus, Carl 317
living labs 205–8
local solutions, rationalization of 58–9
logistics revolution 34
Lougheed, S., Hird, M.J. and Rowe, R.K. 245
low-carbon 103, 105, 106, 109, 111–12, 204–5
Luhmann, Niklas 259
Lutheran Development Service 198
Lynch Cisneros, Jimena 61n7
Lyon, David 303

Index

MacBride, Samantha 245
McFarlane, Colin 100n5
Macfarlane, Colin 190
McGann, Jerome 399–400
McGrath, B. and Thaitakoo, D. 223
McGrath, Brian 222
machinic operations 366–77; automated data processing 374–5; big data 372; computation, bureaucracy and 368; enunciation 371; double binding of 373–5; healthcare provision in globalising world 366–7; information infrastructure development, study of 368, 369–70; information revolution, rhetoric of 366; interoperability, virtues of 366; National Programme for IT (NPfIT) 366, 367, 371, 372, 373; patient choice 367–8; problematisation of 'information' 369–70; public-private dynamics 366–7; public sector IT project 367–9; social relations, transformations in 368–9; software development, history of 367; Systematic Nomenclature of Medical Terms (SNOMED) 373–4, 375; technoscientific terms, function of 369; translation 369–70
Mackenzie, Adrian xv, 119, 126n8, 337, 379–90
MacKenzie, E. 138
Mckinsey & Co. 356, 377n22
McNeil, J.R. 33
Madrid: Atlas project in 141–2, 143, 144, 145, 154; Community Gardens, Madrid Network of 151–2; School of Drama Studies 141
magmatic heat 162
Maguire, James xv, 11, 158, 159, 161–73
Malakhov, Vladimir 300
mapping infrastructures 380–83
Maputo, Mozambique 128–9, 130, 133–8; bifurcated urban infrastructure, re-imagination of city within 136–7; causality, forms of 134; exchange, forms of 134; genericity 134, 135; KaTembe Peninsula 136, 137; parallel growth 135; "surgical" development in 135–6; twinning the city 133–8; urban twinning 134–5, 137–8
Marine Air Ground Task Force (MAGTF) 70
Marmara Earthquake (1999), consequences of 190–92

Marmara Sea seismic monitoring stations (MARNET) 189
Marres, N. and Lezaun, J. 105, 113n3
Marres, Noortje 104, 105–6, 107, 109, 111–12, 153–4, 206, 244
Martin, R. and Sunley, P. 42
Martin, Reinhold 116
Marx, Karl 6, 48, 286–7; revolutionary infrastructure 175–8, 180–81, 183
Marxism 6, 87; infrastructure and 35; Marxist materialism 87; metabolic reinterpretations of Marxian theory 174–5, 175–8
materials 2, 6, 7, 14, 35–6, 53, 54, 55, 132, 134, 149–50, 196, 201, 212, 255, 259, 298; cheap materials 82–3; construction materials 65; documentary materials 151–2; environments and 68, 92, 98; of informational ifrastructural stacks 389n4; in landfill 243, 249; material infrastructures 255–6; materials science 178; movement of 204; objects and, relationships among 131; online materials 338, 387; people and, time-space coordination of 323; political materials 112; poor-quality materials 227; recycled materials 147, 178, 246–8, 249; reinforcement of materials 236; reprocessing materials 245; translational materials 349
Matsuki, Hirotada 81
Mattelart, Armand 78
Matthews, Andrew 100n7
Maurer, Bill 35–6, 267
Maury, Matthew 342
Mauss, M. and Beuchat, H. 87–8
Mauss, Marcel 87, 88, 120, 285
Mayer, Enrique 56
Mbembe, A. and Roitman, J. 292
meaning of infrastructure, elusive nature of 5–7
measurement 41, 45, 57, 188, 256, 287–8; climate knowledge and 341–3, 362; economic measurement 325; hydrochemical measurement 195; measurement lie 317; measurement networks 213; methods 216; of poverty 206
media speak 401
mediation: infrastructure in terms of 175; water infrastructure, politics of 96–7
Mediterranean trade routes 275
Melikadze, George 194–5
Merkel, Angela 280
metadata 153, 312, 348

Mezzadra, S. and Neilson, B. 66
Middle East oil resources 179
Mignolo, W.D. and Escobar, A. 73n11
military-industrial interests 65
Miller, P. and Rose, N. 376n3, 376n8, 377n19
mining: Aboriginal lands and militarisation 70–71; urban mining, metals extraction in 247; waste, infrastructures of 243
Mitchell, J., with Marcel, V. and Mitchell, B. 289
Mitchell, Timothy 12, 17, 28, 33, 178–80
Mitchell, William J. 126n2, 126n6
Mito Yuko 117, 126n7
Mizoguchi Masahito 117
modeling, computer simulation and 343–4
modernity: brittle nature of forms of 82–3; impacts of 174; infrastructures as symbols of 79; logic of compartmentalization, displacement of 115–16; modern knowledge, critique of 354; modernist urban planning initiatives 106
modernization theory 34
Modigliani, Franco 329
Mol, Annemaria 11
molecules, motion of 167
Monastersky, Richard 242
money flows 53–4, 58
monitoring infrastructures 187, 188, 196
Monstadt, Jochen 247
Moretti, Franco 398
Mori, Noriyuki 82
Mori Kinji 122
Morita, A. and Jensen, C. 163, 217
Morita, Atsuro xv, 1–22, 35, 84–5n3, 163, 167–8, 170, 211, 212–13, 215–26, 240
Morowski, Phillip 376n15
Morton, Timothy 146, 184
Mrázek, Rudolf 40, 48n4, 79
Mudurnu Valley 190
multi-level perspective (MLP) 358
multinational waste management corporations 244–5
multinatural infrastructure 227–40
Mumbai water supply department 91, 92; origins of 94–5; water infrastructure, politics of 91, 92
Murray, M.J. 136
music recommender systems 396
Musk, Elon 401

Nakazora, Moe xv–xvi, 4, 16, 267, 268, 269, 309–22
Namba, Miki xvi, 25, 76–86, 269
names: cluster points, names as 383–6; mapping infrastructures in names only 380–83; namespaces 382
national census, establishment of 326
National Health Service (NHS, UK) 366, 367, 368, 369–70, 371–2, 373–4
National Programme for IT (NPfIT) 366, 367, 371, 372, 373
national weather observing systems 342
natural gas and oil pipelines in US 179
natural resource management in Thailand 216
Nature 394
Navaro-Yashin, Yael 297
Nebeker, Frederik 341, 343
neoliberalism 9, 60–61, 330
Netcraft 389n4
Network Common Data Form (netCDF) data 348
networks 1, 2, 7, 8–9, 23, 27–8, 30, 32, 43, 51; actor-network theory 6, 346, 367, 384, 393; communication networks, knowledge and 379–80; Community Gardens, Madrid Network of 151–2; commuter train network 116, 120, 122–3; computer networks 187–8; global networks 71–2n1; internetworks 340, 342–3; linking systems into 340; logistical networks 66; networked infrastructural politics 8; of power and knowledge 204; terminal irrigation channels, networks of 219
Newson, Malcolm David 216, 224
Nielsen, Morten xvi, 49n6, 89–90, 128–40
Niewöhner, Jörg 254
Nimmo, Richie 18n4
Niroth treatment plant 232
Nöbauer, Herta 18n5
Nodia Institute for Geophysics in Tbilisi 189, 193–5
nominalisation of infrastructure 380, 381–2
non-humans, infrastructures and 162–3
non-linear change 10–11, 401
Nordhavn (North Harbor), turbines projected for 102, 107, 108
North Anatolian seismic fault 189–90, 192–3, 195

418　*Index*

North Atlantic Treaty Organization (NATO): Common Infrastructure Programme (1949) 31, 32; earth 193–4; earth, infrastructure and 193–4
Northern Territory National Emergency Response Act (2007) 69–70
nutrition, loops of 233–4
Nuttall, S. and Mbembe, A. 61n6, 62n12

off-grid energy infrastructures: decentralised infrastructures 200–203; electrification 198, 206–7; energo-politics 199; energy consumption, global patterns of 200; physical networks of transmission, creation and expansion of 204; social and material politics of decentralised infrastructures 201; un-electrified world, politics of 208
oil infrastructures 12, 17, 268, 277–8; contracts, petroleum extraction and 286; *see also* energy
oligopticon 15–16
online libraries 398
ontologies: ecologies in beta 145, 146, 147, 148–9, 150–52, 152–4; openness as ontology 148–9; thinking and ontology, relation between 115–16
Open Badges technology 151, 155n2
open-source activism 142, 145
open-source (F/OS) software 145–6, 147, 151
open-source infrastructures 147–9, 151
open-source urbanism 146–7, 151
open systems, metaphysics of 192
Oppenheimer, J. Robert 242–3
order and disorder, co-existence of 167
Oreskes, N. and Conway, E.M. 345
Orwell, George 14
Osaka University 1–2
Otis, Daniel 240n5
Oxford English Dictionary 27, 28, 29, 33, 36n3

Papua New Guinea, Begasin Hills in 198, 199, 203, 207
Paraguay: campesinos of 40, 43–5, 46, 47; infrastructure of rural property in 40; land reform in 43–5
parataxonomy 316–17, 317–18
Park, R.E., McKenzie, R.D. and Burgess, E. 87
Park, Robert E. 87
Peirce, C.S. 388n1
people, large movements of 271–2

people as infrastructure 203, 234, 237, 254
People's Biodiversity Register 310, 313, 314, 315, 316, 318, 319, 320n3
perennial irrigation 218–19, 220, 224
performativity, emergence and 311–12
Perrow, Charles 254
personal records, individuation of 325
Peru: fiscal and legislative power in 52–3; Sanitation Committees (JASS) in 58, 59; Sistema Nacional De Inversión Pública (SNIP) in 53, 54–5, 57, 58, 62n13
Petts, Judith 244
Petty, William 15
Peutz, N. and de Genova, N. 296
pharmakon (poison and cure) 234
Phnom Penh Water Supply Authority 235
Pholeros, Paul 4
photo-voltaic panels 201
Pickering, Andrew 124, 256, 257
Pickett, S.T., Cadenasso, M.L. and McGrath, B. 223
Pietz, William 79, 83
Pignarre, P. and Stengers, I. 152, 154
Piketty, Thomas 330
Pinch, Trevor 254, 255
Pinker, Annabel 61n7
pipelines: Baku-Tbilisi-Ceyhan (BTC) oil pipeline 189, 194–5; boundaries and 274–5; destabilizing effects of piping system 237; grids and, inefficiencies of 183; pipeline development (and leaks) 194–5
planning: eco-urban planning interventions 103–4; infrastructural mode of 358, 361; local state planning and jurisdiction 291–2; Suchman's analysis of 354–5; temporal qualities of 355
plant collection 314–15
plasticity 28, 33–4
Poe, Edgar Allan 399–400
Poerksen, Uwe 28
politics: biopolitical systems of government 95; disruption, politics of 367–9; earthquake politics 191–2; electoral politics, mobilization of 92; energy, distributive politics of 204–5; green and digital 356–9; human politics and values in infrastructures 236–7; of infrastructures 10, 11–14; minimalist bio-politics 201; networked infrastructural politics 8; political relations

in water infrastructures 92; political sedimentation of waste management 249–50; political technologies 93–8; political unruliness of infrastructures 111–12; political will 55, 57–60; popular voting 97; pragmatist material politics of urban infrastructuring 109–11; urban democratic politics, public settings of 106; water infrastructure, politics of 91–100
Pollack, M.A. and Shaffer, G.C. 259, 260
Pollock, N. and Williams, R. 227
polysemy 29; of names on Github 382
Poole, Deborah 61n7
populations 9, 15, 60, 95, 98, 183, 190, 204, 232, 234–5, 318; aggregation of 54; Indigenous populations 66
Povinelli, Elizabeth A. 42, 163, 167, 170
power relations 1, 367; infrastructure in 370; scale and power, relationship between 11
practice theory, pragmatism and 254
Prazeres, Luís 287
pressure: analytic of 92–3; mobilization of 97–8
prior relations, disruptive force of 56–7
privacy and security, balance between 14–15
productive capital 286–7
prototypes: antidotes and 182–5; prototyping culture 363
protozoan infections 234
public goods, investments as 51, 52
public-private dynamics 366–7
public work, 'public' dimension of 55–6, 61
publicization of infrastructures 102–4, 106
Puig de la Bellacasa, Maria 254
Putin, Vladimir 304, 401

Quantified Self community 399
Quaternary Stratigraphy Working Group 242
Queensland University of Technology 260
QWERTY keyboard 392

Rabinow, Paul 323, 358
radioactive waste storage 243
Raffles, Hugh 237, 240
rainfall flows 215–16, 221
Rajan, K.S. 320n2

Index 419

Rappaport, Roy 359
re-sourcing, notion of 144–5, 149–50, 152
Reagan, Ronald 34
reciprocity, forms of 134
recycling 149, 245, 247–8
Redfield, P. 201
reductionism 354
Reeves, Madeleine xvi, 11, 16, 267, 268, 269, 274, 281n6, 296–308
reflexivity 310, 318–20
refugee camps 303–4
regulatory conditions, accommodation to 54–5
Reihbein, Boike 76, 78
reinjection wells 165–6, 166–7, 172n7
remittance-dependence 299
Remy, M.I. 62n9
renewable energy systems 105–6, 111, 159, 181–2, 183–4, 207, 352
Reno, J.O. 206
Réseau Mondial 342
responsibility 10; engaged responsibility 169–70; responsibility (response-ability), notion of 11, 168–9
resurrection 246–8
Reuleaux, Franz 126n5
revolutionary infrastructure 174–85
Reykjavik Energy 161–2, 164, 165, 169, 172n8
Rheinberger, Hans-Jörg 163, 253
rice cultivation 218
Richards, Thomas 310
Richardson, T. and Weszkalnys, G. 66
Richardson, Tanya 285, 291, 292
Riles, Annelise 12, 355
Rist, Gilbert 27
Rittel, H. and Webber, M. 359
river basin infrastructure *see* Chao Phraya Delta, Thailand
river hydrology, landform development and 216
Romodanovskii, Konstantin 302–3
Rood, Richard 347
Rosas, L., Báez, A. and Coutino, M. 240n8
Rose, D.B. 71
Rose, N., O'Malley, P. and Velverde, M. 375–6, 377n33
Rostow, Walter W. 32
Rottenburg, Richard xvi, 13, 42, 213, 253–65
Røyrvik, E.A. 286, 293
Rubio, F.D. and Fogué, U. 104, 106
Ruhleder, Karen 3

Ruppert, E., Harvey, P., Lury, C., Mackenzie, A., McNally, R., Baker, S. A., Kallianos, Y. and Lewis, C. 16
Russian migration policy 304–5
Rutherford, J. and Coutard, O. 113n2
Rygg, Bente Johnsen 107

Sager, Josh 248
Sahai, Suman 313
Saint-Exupery, Antoine de 352, 362
Sánchez González, Bartolomé 43
sanitation 25, 51, 58–9, 61, 129, 137; Sanitation Committees (JASS) in Peru 58, 59; Vilcanota Valley, system in 52–3, 53–6
São Tomé and Príncipe (STP) 286–7, 287–8, 289–90, 294n7; joint development zone (JDZ) 289–90, 294n3, 294n5, 294n7; maritime boundary claim 288–9; National Oil Agency 287; official pronouncements, optimism of 290; petroleum era in, start of 288; seismic surveys of offshore hydrocarbon potential 288–9
Sassen, Saskia 275
Saussure, Ferdinand de 35
Scheer, Hermann 159; economic philosophy of 182–5
Schick, L. and Winthereik, B.R. 111
Schivelbusch, Wolfgang 12, 126n5
Schmitt, Carl 110
Schneider, Daniel 230, 232
Schultz, Julia 30
Schweizer, Harold 51
Schwenkel, Christina 33
science: as distinct order of worth 259, 262–3; drainage basin, scientific concept of 224–5; geophysics 188–9; hydrogeology 188–9, 193–5; infrastructure and, movements between 216; naming with reference to, local naming and 316; scientific and local knowledge, incommensurability between 313, 320; scientific facticity 259; scientific proofs 258; seismology 188–9, 189–93; *see also* technoscience
Science 394, 399
science and technology studies (STS) 2, 6, 10, 12–13, 30, 32, 103–4, 105–6, 109–10, 111, 115, 153, 162–3, 201, 227, 229, 238, 256, 257, 258, 262–3, 309, 312, 369, 384, 388–9n2
Scotland: off-grid communities in 206–7; small-scale hydro-electric system in 204

Scott, Heidi 243
Scott, James C. 15, 33, 92, 354
Seasonal Variation of the Eskimo (Mauss, M. and Beuchat, H.) 87–8
Seaver, Nick 396
Seeing Like a State (Scott, J.) 15
Seibert, Gerhard 288–9, 289–90
seismic landscapes 161–72
Serres, Michel 11, 12, 163, 167, 268, 393
sewage systems 3, 5, 8–9, 53–5, 57, 59, 97, 212, 222, 228–30, 275; urban lives and 235–6; Vilcanota Valley, system in 52–3, 53–6; *see also* multinatural infrastructure
Shannon. Kelly 222, 224
Shapin, S. and Schaffer, S. 256–7, 259
Shapiro, H.T. et al. 345
Sharma, Devinder 313
Shepard, Mark 126n2, 147
Shevardnadze, Eduard A. 194
Sider, Gerald 73n11
Sigmundsson, F. et al. 171n5
Simondon, Gilbert 119, 126n8
Simone, Abdou Maliq xvi, 3, 9, 18n1, 35, 42, 89–90, 128–40, 203, 233, 234, 237, 254
Simpson, Edward 18n6
Sinaert, E.R. 293–4n2
Singh, Harish 318
Singh, V.P. and Woolhiser, D.A. 216
sinkholes 227, 228
Siskin, C. and Warner, W. 391
Sistema Nacional De Inversión Pública (SNIP) in Peru 53, 54–5, 57, 58, 62n13
Skinner, B.F. 396
sludge and bacteria, interactions between 232
smart infrastructure 115–16, 117
smart phones: personalisation of 356–7; texting with 393
Smee, Clive 377n25
Sneath, D., Holbraad, M. and Pedersen, M.A. 42
Sneath, David 4, 227, 235
Sneddon, Chris 33
Snowden, Edward 14, 379
social media 379, 381, 385–6; depth and scale, effects of 379, 381, 385–6; Facebook A/B experiment 399; smart phones: personalisation of 356–7; texting with 393
social mobilization 97
social order, construction of 7–8
social overhead capital, synonym of 33–4

Index   421

social relations, transformations in 368–9
social science: of innovation, interface of policy and 358; in normative mode 48
social theory, infrastructure in 35–6
socio-material systems 104, 192
socio-technical systems 104; infrastructures as 163, 340; interlocking interplay between 358
sociology of scientific knowledge (SSK) 256
sociotemporality 395
Sohn-Rethel, Alfred 395
Soja, E. 136
Sokal, Alan 394
solar electricity, infrastructural architecture for 201
solar energy (and economy) 183–4
South Africa, property and tax law in 332
South Iceland Seismic Zone (SISZ) 165–6
sovereignty: aleatory sovereignty 304; legal sovereignty, show of 103; territorial control 275–6
soy boom 47, 48
Spatari, S., Bertram, B., Gordon, R. and Graedel, T.E. 247
spatial layouts, reshaping of 128
spatial organization of knowledge 395–6
spatiality of infrastructures 188, 196
speculative knowledge 286
spreadsheets 360–61
Srnick, N. 134
stability, idea of 166–7
standards, procedures, and metacodes 259
Stapleford, Thomas A. 329
Star, S.L. and Ruhleder, K. 35, 174, 187, 253, 255, 256, 376n17, 377n28, 377n30, 392, 395
Star, Susan Leigh 3, 10, 11, 12–13, 42, 105, 112, 163, 170, 208, 211, 253, 254, 255, 292, 309, 311
Starosielski, Nicole 391
state: aleatory sovereignty 304; infrastructure and 275–6; state failure, infrastructural failure and 274, 275; state surveillance 303
steel manufacture, infrastructure for 66
Stein, Howard 33
Steiner, Hadas 115
Stengers, Isabelle 42, 48n1, 109, 171
stock markets, weighting of 65–6
Stocker, T.F., Qin, D. and Platner, G.K. 344, 345
Stoler, Anne L. 250

Strathern, Marilyn 13, 61n6, 175, 211, 237
Strauss, S., Rupp, S. and Love, T. 158
Street, Alice 199, 201
Stroessner, General Alfredo 40
Strum, Shirley 7–8
Suchman, Lucy 354–5, 384
Sundaram, Ravi 92
Super Urban Intelligent Card (SUICA) 123–4
superstructural forms, determination of 401
surface water run-off 194–5
surveillance infrastructures 14–16
sushi restaurant 124–5
sustainability: Centre for Sustainability 245; cohabitation, sustainable forms of 216; generation of 174; gesture, notion of sustaining force of 286; initiatives on, proliferation of 106
Sutherland, Keston 176
Systematic Nomenclature of Medical Terms (SNOMED) 373–4, 375

Taguchi, Yoko 62n14
Takaya Yoshikazu 216, 217
Takhteyev, Y. and Hilts, A. 389n3
Taussig, Michael T. 100n7
taxonomies, invention of 317
techne, philosophy of 119
technical solutions 57–60
techno-political spectacles 107
technological shift 366
technopolitical knowledge 94
technoscience 224–5; function of technoscientific terms 369
telegraph, weather mapping and 341–2
temporality of infrastructures 188, 192, 196; future perfect and 23–5, 40–48, 355; past and 24, 25, 68; zones and temporalities, decoupling of 83–4
ten Bos, René 285
Thaitakoo, D. and McGrath, B. 216, 222, 223, 224
thermoelectric support 181–2
Thévenot, Laurent 61n5, 104, 110–11, 112
Thrift, Nigel 115, 146, 147, 148, 388–9n2
Thung, F., Bissyandé, T.F., Lo, D. and Jiang, L. 389n3
Timmermans, Stefan 12–13
Todini, E, 220
Tokyo, commuter train network in 115–26

Tolkien, J.R.R. 14
Tomii, Norio 118
Tonkiss, Fran 201
Tonle Sap River 235
Tort, Patrick 396
traditional knowledge, infrastructural inversion and 312–13
traffic flows, road problems and 235
train traffic diagrams, use of 118–19
transformative technology and 124–5
transition theory 358
transnational mobility 298
transparency 52, 57, 60, 191, 287, 335, 340, 345, 370; illicit economies of infrastructural investment 55–6
transportation infrastructure 10, 33, 35, 115, 123, 204, 217, 218, 220, 244–5, 286, 340; transportation projects 30
trees 234–7
Truman, Harry S. 32
Tsereteli, N., Tanircan, G., Safak, E., Varanzanashvili, O., Chelidze, T., Gvencadze, A. and Goguadze, N. 194
Tsing, Anna 58, 175, 287, 292
Tsipras, Alexis 276, 278–9
Tupayachi Mar, Teresa 61n7
Turkey, refugee problem for 272–4
Turnbull, David 309, 312

uncertainty: deportability, deportation and 301–2; earth forces, radical uncertainty of 162; management of 347
United Nations (UN): Convention on Biological Diversity (CBD, 1992) 310, 317–18; Development Programme (UNDP) 78; Environment Programme (UNEP) 247; High Commissioner for Refugees (UNHCR) 277; household in infrastructural computations 328–9, 330, 331, 332; UN-HABITAT 248
universalism 316–17
Urban Charisma 96
urban design, temporal and spatial scales in 222–3
urban development in post-unification Berlin 290–92
urban ecological design, emerging movements of 224
urban ecosystems in Thailand 223
urban forms of capitals of socialist states 76
urban infrastructures 87–90; in/visibilizing of 106, 107; infrastructural transitions 104–6; pragmatist material politics and 109–11; *see also* cities; ecologies in beta; energy; politics; transportation; water
urban mining, metals extraction in 247
Urban Parliament 143
urban redesign, material politics of 104
urban spaces as functional destinations 237
urban specialists, charismatic figures of 96
urban stream syndrome 221–2
urban topography of absolute detachment 138
urban waste infrastructures 246–7
urban water system 92
urban watershed, ecology of urban patchworks and 222–4
urks (discards of urban infrastructures), resurrection of 246–7
US Naval Observatory 342
usable knowledge, downscaling and production of 346–9
utopian urbanity 128
Uttarakhand State Biodiversity Board 314, 315, 319

Valaleev, Mikhail 299
van de Poel, Ibo 244
van der Heide, Homan 217, 218–19
van Houtum, Henk 281n11, 296, 303
Van Rheede, Hendrik 317
van Wyck, P. and Hird, M.J. 242
van Wyck, Peter C. 246
Vannini, P. and Taggart, J. 206
Varoufakis, Yiannis 278, 279–80
Varro, Marcus Terentius 285
Vaughan, Diana 10
Verbrugge, Randal 330
Verran, H. and Christie, M. 152–3, 154
Verran, Helen 9, 312, 320, 362
vibrancy of matter 64–5
Vidot, Anna 69
Vientiane, urban development in 76–85; ASEAN Summit (2004) 76–7; Association of Southeast Asian Nations (ASEAN) 76–7, 78, 80; concrete embankment project 81; cosmetic change 77–8; fetishes 78–80, 83; groynes 81, 85n6; Lao International Trade Exhibition and Convention Center (ITECC) 77, 82–3; modernity: brittle nature of forms of 82–3; infrastructures as symbols of 79; public works, construction of 81–2; riverbank management 76, 80–82; scattering effect 84; time, infrastructures

suspended in 84; Vientiane Urban Development and Administration Authority (VUDAA) 77
Viganò, Paola 222
Vilcanota Valley, sanitation system in 52–3, 53–6
Vincent, S. 62n11
Vine, David 73n12
Viveiros de Castro, Eduardo 237
von Schnitzler, Antina 4, 14, 254, 285

Wagner, Roy 211
Walford, A. and Knox, H. 204
Wall Street trading 396–7
Wallsten, Björn 247
Walsh, C.J., Roy, A.H., Feminella, J.W., Cottingham, P.D., Groffman, P.M. and Morgan, R.P. 222
Walter, Max 317
Warner, Michael 55
Wassermann syphilis test 256
waste, infrastructures of 242–50; abandoned infrastructure 247; bacterial adaptation 248; biocides, dispersal of 248; burial 243–6; extraction and reburial resembles 243; frozen block method of burial 243; geological repositories 243; hazardous waste, generation of 245–6; incineration industry 243; landfills 243, 245–6; leachate toxicity of 245; mining of 248; metals extraction, experimental employment of microorganisms in 249; middens 243; radioactive waste storage 243; recycling 245, 247–8; strata recomposition 249; urban waste infrastructures 246–7
water infrastructures 91–100; basin model 218–20; BMC (procedure BMC *mein bana diya*) 93, 95, 96, 97; councilors, work of 94, 96–7; hydraulic citizenship 92; legal water services, eligibility for 94; legitimacy in accessing water, circumscription of 91–2; Mumbai water supply department: origins of 94–5; standpost water connections 94, 95; thin pipes, legal availability of only 95
Waterton, Claire 309, 310, 312, 315–16, 319, 320n1
Webb, Sam 240n1

Weber, Max 117
Weinstein, Liza 100n6
Weizman, Eyal 281n10
wellhead awakening 161–2
Weszkalnys, Gisa xvii, 23, 61n2, 267, 268–9, 284–95, 302
White, Leslie 157
Williams, Raymond 23, 27, 28–9, 35
Williams, Rosalind 28
Wimsatt, W.C. and Schank, J.G. 392
wind turbines, politics of 102–13
Winickoff, D., Jasanoff, S., Busch, L., Grove-White, R. and Wynne, B. 260
Winner, Langdon 14, 105, 157, 253, 254
Winthereik, Brit Ross xvii, 11, 158, 159, 161–73, 225
Wittfogel, Karl 99, 99n3
Wolfe, Patrick 65
Wolford, W., Borras, S.M., Hall, R., Scoones, I. and White, B. 41, 47
Woolgar, S. and Lezaun, J. 153
World Bank 48n2; development, infrastructural intervention and 48n2; energy beyond grids, infrastructure and 199, 207; illicit economies of infrastructural investment 52; keyword - infrastructure 32, 33, 34; Vientiane, urban development in 78
World Health Organization (WHO) 234
World Meteorological Organization 342
World Weather Watch 342–3
worth, evidence, infrastructure and 253–63
worth, orders of 257–9, 262

Xiang Biao 298–9

Yamamoto Masahito 121, 124–5, 125–6
Yates, JoAnne 396
Yildirim, U. and Navaro-Yashin, Y. 191
Yusoff, Kathryn 163, 168, 169

Zalasiewicz, Jan 242
Zedner, Lucia 303
Zérah, Marie 100n5
Zittrain, Jonathan 397–8
Žižek, Slavoj 399
zones and temporalities, decoupling of 83–4
Zuloark architectural collective 141, 142, 143, 145–7, 150, 151

eBooks
from Taylor & Francis
Helping you to choose the right eBooks for your Library

Add to your library's digital collection today with Taylor & Francis eBooks. We have over 50,000 eBooks in the Humanities, Social Sciences, Behavioural Sciences, Built Environment and Law, from leading imprints, including Routledge, Focal Press and Psychology Press.

Choose from a range of subject packages or create your own!

Benefits for you
- Free MARC records
- COUNTER-compliant usage statistics
- Flexible purchase and pricing options
- 70% approx of our eBooks are now DRM-free.

Benefits for your user
- Off-site, anytime access via Athens or referring URL
- Print or copy pages or chapters
- Full content search
- Bookmark, highlight and annotate text
- Access to thousands of pages of quality research at the click of a button.

Free Trials Available

We offer free trials to qualifying academic, corporate and government customers.

eCollections
Choose from 20 different subject eCollections, including:
- Asian Studies
- Economics
- Health Studies
- Law
- Middle East Studies

eFocus
We have 16 cutting-edge interdisciplinary collections, including:
- Development Studies
- The Environment
- Islam
- Korea
- Urban Studies

For more information, pricing enquiries or to order a free trial, please contact your local sales team:

UK/Rest of World: **online.sales@tandf.co.uk**
USA/Canada/Latin America: **e-reference@taylorandfrancis.com**
East/Southeast Asia: **martin.jack@tandf.com.sg**
India: **journalsales@tandfindia.com**

www.tandfebooks.com

Printed in the United States
By Bookmasters